INFORMATION LITERACIES
FOR THE
TWENTY-FIRST CENTURY

INFORMATION LITERACIES
FOR THE
TWENTY-FIRST CENTURY

edited by
Virgil L.P. Blake
and
Renee Tjoumas

G.K. HALL & CO. • BOSTON, MASS.

INFORMATION LITERACIES FOR THE
TWENTY-FIRST CENTURY

EDITED BY VIRGIL L.P. BLAKE AND RENEE TJOUMAS

Copyright 1990
by G.K. Hall & Co.
70 Lincoln Street
Boston, Massachusetts 02111

10 9 8 7 6 5 4 3 2 1

Library of Congress Cataloging-in-Publication Data

Information literacies for the twenty-first century / edited by Virgil
  L.P. Blake and Renee Tjoumas.
        p. cm. – (Professional librarian series)
      ISBN 0-8161-1921-X
      1. Library science – Technological innovations. 2. Information
  technology – Forecasting. 3. Library science – Forecasting
  4. Libraries and readers. 5. Libraries – Automation. 6. Computer
  literacy. I. Blake, Virgil L.P. II. Tjoumas, Renee.
  III. Series.
  Z678.9.I526 1990
  025.3'0285 – dc20   89-29920
                                                             CIP

The paper used in this publication meets the minimum requirements of
American National Standard for Information Sciences – Permanence of
Paper for Printed Library Materials, ANSI Z39.48-1984.   ∞™

MANUFACTURED IN THE UNITED STATES OF AMERICA

To our families, friends, colleagues . . .
and the good Lord, without whose help and patience
this work would never have been produced

Contents

Contents

Contents

Contents

Contents

Introduction

Illiteracy is an issue as critical to the nation's future as the federal budget deficit, the U.S. trade imbalance, and the preparedness of our armed forces. But illiteracy, like high blood pressure, could be the silent killer simply because the price of negligence may not be understood until it is too late. This problem is not new, nor is it one that has remained unnoticed by observers of the national scene. Some social scientists point to the decline of Scholastic Aptitude Test (SAT) scores since the early 1960s and conclude that the literacy crisis has roots firmly implanted in two generations of students who have passed through the American school system.

Reports over the last two decades have consistently indicated that the problem of literacy is far broader than the reading, writing, and computational skills of those students electing to take the SATs. In a 1975 study of adult performance levels by the University of Texas at Austin, investigators found that 13 percent of the subjects could not correctly address an envelope and that 24 percent failed to include a return address.[1] Those adults less likely to complete these relatively simple tasks were poor, Hispanic, or Mexican. Forty-four percent of the black participants and 55 percent of the Hispanics in this study could not fulfill these basic requirements. The U.S. Department of Education, using the findings of this study, estimated that 57 million U.S. citizens could be considered functionally illiterate. The profile of these Americans, poor white, Hispanic, or black, located in declining urban centers, is strikingly similar to the portrait sketched by Thomas Childers and Joyce Post in their study of the information-poor.[2]

By 1980, it was estimated that 20 million Americans could not read, write, or complete basic mathematical operations.[3] Another 30 to 40 million individuals, it was calculated, could not read the instructions on medicine bottles, operations manuals for equipment, or the fire warnings posted in buildings. A 1982 study of 3,400 adults by the U.S. Census Bureau found that

1

13 percent of these subjects were illiterate, that is, they failed to answer correctly twenty of twenty-six questions based upon reading.[4] In the same year, a *U.S. News and World Report* article estimated that 23 million Americans, representing 20 percent of the adult population, were functionally illiterate, that is, unable to read, write, and compute well enough to read a newspaper and balance a checkbook.[5]

More dramatic, and more difficult to ignore, were the findings of the National Commission on Excellence in Education published in its report, *A Nation at Risk*.[6] The commission reported that 23 million citizens were functionally illiterate and that this number was increasing at the rate of 2.3 million each year. Thirteen percent of all seventeen-year-olds and 40 percent of all minorities were characterized as functionally illiterate. These findings placed the public school systems, from which these citizens had either graduated or dropped out, under closer scrutiny. Will Manley, in a *Wilson Library Bulletin* article, contended that the public schools in the 1970s and early 1980s had spent too little time on the basic skill of reading.[7] Schools had not only failed the current generation of students; an estimated 23 million adults, 20 percent of the adult population, could not complete job applications, pass written driver's tests, or read prescriptions on medicine dispensed by pharmacies.

More recently, in 1985, Jonathan Kozol reported that 15 percent of all high school students graduating from secondary schools located in urban centers were not reading beyond the sixth-grade level.[8] Reflecting similar dismal statistics, Patricia Cunningham found that 95 percent of 3,600 young adults who participated in a national survey, ranging in age from twenty-one to twenty-five, could read only at the fourth-grade level.[9] If the criteria for literacy were calibrated at the eighth-grade level, 80 percent could be considered literate. She concluded that in the strictest sense of the term, most young adults could not be considered illiterate. Nevertheless, they "may not be literate enough to be fully functional in a technically advanced society."[10] As recently as 1988, it was reported that between 20 and 35 percent of American adults were "not able to read, write, and compute well enough to function effectively in today's society."[11] Literacy has taken on a new dimension. It no longer means the ability to read, write, and complete basic mathematical operations. The demands of an information- and service-based economy require that these skills be at a more advanced level than those necessitated in the previous period characterized by heavy manufacturing industries.

Library professionals have long been interested in the topic of reading. Louis R. Wilson investigated *The Geography of Reading* in the mid-1930s.[12] Public libraries, in formulating outreach services funded by federal grants in the 1960s, often initiated special reading programs to train librarians for service in the inner city. Out of this experience, librarians began to focus on the issue of literacy itself. *Alliance for Excellence: Librarians Respond to "A Nation at Risk"* is the most recent indicator of this continuing interest.[13] This report further recommends: (1) the school library media centers' role in the teaching information skills should be magnified; (2) libraries of all types should become more directly and actively involved with literacy programs; and (3) more research should be conducted on both current information-seeking skills and behaviors of adults and literacy for adults.

The price for permitting these basic skills to deteriorate is already too high. The functionally illiterate are more likely to be on welfare with few options for employment in the emerging post-industrial society. In its investigation of illiteracy in New Jersey, the *Newark Star-Ledger* found that 75 percent of the hard-core unemployed were illiterate. Carmen St. John-Hunter and David Harman estimated, based upon 1979 statistics, that chronic unemployment directly costs the United States $6 billion in welfare support and an estimated $237 billion in lost wages.[14] In 1988, the U.S. Department of Labor calculated that the chronically unemployed represented an estimated $225 billion in unpaid taxes as well as lost productivity.[15]

Emerging trends in the workplace indicate that this deplorable situation is not likely to be reversed in the near future. The United States is reshaping its commercial base to service and information occupations. Such an economy requires a literate work force. For the United States, this need is emerging at a time when the size of the labor pool is actually declining. A recent survey indicates that 90 percent of all current occupations require reading on an average of two to three hours a day.[16] Not only is reading more likely to be a regular feature of most jobs, but the literacy level required surpasses that attained by most current high school graduates. A study conducted at Frostburg (Maryland) State College in 1985 indicated that the twelfth-grade reading level, as measured by the Nelson-Denny Reading Test, was equivalent to a score of 370 on the verbal test of the SAT.[17] Since the average score on the verbal SAT is 500, a student could have difficulty in compiling a total SAT score sufficient for admission to most colleges. Texts for both academic and vocational subjects were found to be written at the 14.5-grade level. Only 4.9 percent of the seventeen-year-olds in the study were found to be reading at an advanced level sufficient to comprehend scientific materials, literary essays, or historical documents encountered in professional and technical working environments. Only 39 percent of these high school seniors could comprehend materials specifically designed for school curriculum.

The implication of this situation is already apparent to some employers. New Jersey Bell expects to create 600,000 entry-level service positions by 1995. It is anticipated that they will be unable to find qualified persons for 100,000 of these positions, based on their recent experiences in recruiting. In

1988, 9,621 persons applied for entry-level positions, but only 1,013 were able to pass the entrance examination.[18]

There are other indicators of the price of illiteracy. The American social system is increasingly burdened by individuals who have been ignored by both school and adult literacy programs. The U.S. prison system in 1980 had an estimated 750,000 inmates. Sixty percent of the total prison population was illiterate.[19] The cost for housing these individuals was $6.6 billion. To make matters worse, the proportion of prison inmates thought to be illiterate has risen to 75 percent in 1988. Even more disturbing is the estimate that 85 percent of all incarcerated juvenile offenders are illiterate.[20]

It is ironic that literacy should become a major concern at the precise time that the United States has entered the information age. The old monopoly of print media, in both book and serial formats, has now been broken. There is now a great variety of information formats available that have been integrated into the American lifestyle. Television viewing, Neil Postman estimated in 1979, took up more time in a high school student's years in school (15,000 hours) than contact time in the classroom (11,500 hours). Film and sound recordings accounted for an additional 5,000 hours.[21] These estimates do not take into account the great changes in communication systems in the last few years. Cable television has broadened access to programming. The sale or rental income generated by videocassettes has now exceeded income derived from theater ticket sales. The microcomputer with its software packages and computer games has intruded upon the time set aside for recreation and study. Even books have proliferated, current output surpasses 50,000 titles per year. Serial titles continue to increase in number to satisfy the information needs of both the academic community and the general public. The information environment is quite vibrant. With such a wide range of information resources available, the concept of literacy has to be enlarged to include all information formats. Being literate in today's world means being able to "read" a diversity of media and encompasses a wide range of abilities. At the time this essay was being written, two news stories exemplified this state of affairs. On the same day that Leon Lederman of the Fermi National Laboratory spoke to students of the need to overcome illiteracy in the sciences and mathematics, Washington Redskins defensive end Dexter Manley testified before a congressional committee on his struggle to learn to read at the age of twenty-seven, after graduation from Oklahoma State University.

Failure to address the implications of the literacy crisis as the information age continues to evolve will forever alter American society. Literacy has been regarded as one of the keys to social mobility. Without a determined effort to foster literacy in its broadest sense, there may well develop two Americas. The information-rich populating one America will be able to use many of these information tools for their own purposes and the further consolidation of personal power. The functionally illiterate inhabiting the other America may become a permanent underclass. At best, the information-rich would exercise a benevolent despotism wherein their rights and properties would be fully protected and the information-poor would be left to their own devices. At worst, the information-rich could assume that they had an inherent perogative to watch over the rest of America and rule the land tyrannically. Either scenario is vastly different from the vision created by Jefferson, Madison, and Monroe and refined by Roosevelt, Truman, Kennedy, and Johnson.

America is now just one decade from the next century. The United States of our children and grandchildren will be very different from the country we and our grandfathers have known. The economy will have a different commercial base, and it will be challenged by many new competitors. It is unlikely that future generations can expect a constantly rising standard of living as we have experienced in the past. The cold war may or may not be over, but terrorism and regional conflicts abound requiring an informed citizenry and vigilant public officials. America needs to regain its former predominance in intellectual, technological, and commercial innovation in order to rejuvenate an economic growth rate that is capable of sustaining the American dream. What is not certain is how this goal can be achieved. Sharing diverse points of view can be the catalyst for the development of new ideas and innovative planning. The essays collected in this volume have been composed by scholars in such disparate disciplines as communication, computer science, instructional technology/media, economics, English, education, and library/information science education. They provide the reader with some guideposts for both reflection about the future and action. The papers address the impacts, implications, and possible outcomes in aural, visual, and print communication and the effects of computer technology on the American information environment, culture, and society. Literacy is the focus and thematic thread of these papers because it is a major issue that will determine the kind of America future generations will inherit. The editors hope that this dialogue will be joined with other efforts to devise an effective means to attain a renewed and revitalized America in the twenty-first century.

Virgil L.P. Blake and Renee Tjoumas
Queens College of the
 City University of New York
 Graduate School of Library and
 Information Studies

Notes

1. Carmen St. John-Hunter and David Harman, *Adult Illiteracy in the United States: A Report to the Ford Foundation*, paperback ed. (New York: McGraw-Hill, 1985), 17.

2. Thomas Childers and Joyce Post, *The Information Poor in America* (Metuchen, N.J.: Scarecrow Press, 1975).

3. Jonathan Kozol, "A Place to Reach and Teach Twenty-five Million Illiterate Adults," *Wilson Library Bulletin* 54, no. 10 (June 1980): 640.

4. "It's 13 Percent – Or Even Worse Than That," *New York Newsday*, 26 April 1986, 56.

5. Stanley N. Wellborn, "Ahead: A Nation of Illiterates," *U.S. News and World Report*, 17 May 1982, 53.

6. National Commission on Excellence in Education, *A Nation at Risk* (Washington, D.C.: U.S. Government Printing Office, 1983).

7. Will Manley, "Facing the Public," *Wilson Library Bulletin* 62, no. 6 (February 1988): 64.

8. Jonathan Kozol, *Illiterate America* (Garden City, N.Y.: Doubleday, 1985).

9. Patricia Cunningham, "Are We a Nation of Illiterates?" *Educational Leadership* 44, no. 8 (May 1987): 83.

10. Ibid.

11. Rudy Larini, "Illiteracy's Toll," *Newark Star-Ledger*, 23 April 1989, 1.

12. Louis R. Wilson, *The Geography of Reading* (Chicago: American Library Association and University of Chicago Press, 1938).

13. U.S. Department of Education. *Alliance for Excellence: Librarians Respond to a Nation at Risk* (Washington, D.C.: U.S. Government Printing Office, 1984), 31, 32, 33.

14. St. John-Hunter and Harman, *Adult Illiteracy*, 43.

15. Larini, "Illiteracy's Toll," 1.

16. Driek Zirinsky, "Facing Our Own Literacy Crisis," *English Journal* 76, no. 8 (December 1987): 61.

17. Arthur Whimbey, "A 15th Grade Level Reading Level for High School Seniors?" *Phi Delta Kappan* 69, no. 9 (May 1988): 43.

18. Larini, "Illiteracy's Toll," 1.

19. Wellborn, "Nation of Illiterates," 53.

20. Larini, "Illiteracy's Toll," 1.

21. Neil Postman, *Teaching as a Conserving Activity* (New York: Delta, 1979), 50.

KEYNOTE

Twenty-First-Century Information Literacies and Libraries

EARL C. JOSEPH

INTRODUCTION

There is little doubt remaining that libraries are beginning their transformation into the library of the future (LOTF). What is being created definitely involves computers and a growing list of hardware and software electronic information technology.

This paper is about future libraries – the future forced by advancing new technology. It will highlight some developing electronic information technology (EIT) trends, forces of change, emerging issues, possible breakthroughs, and forecasts for the short-range and long-range future of the library.

Current and forecasted advances in technology will continue to offer libraries new opportunities and challenges as we penetrate deeper into the high-tech information age. Changing world conditions in the new global economic era that society has entered are forecasted to continue their impact on the United States, compelling libraries to also change to meet the world competitive challenges posed. Both of these developments are accelerating and will force major changes for libraries and alter the way in which information is delivered in the future.

Is there a point of time in the twenty-first century when the balance of information that society uses for its functioning and libraries provide for their

7

publics will tilt away from paper media in favor of electronic media? Are we close to that time?

The emergence of artificial intelligence (AI) expert systems technology, artificial reality technology (next-wave, user-friendly, human-machine interfaces), the integrated services digital network, neurocomputing, and cheap and multi-terabit electronic memory, will radically change what we mean by libraries. Entirely new modes of storage and dissemination of information will emerge. These newly developing computer technologies will alter the character of the LOTF far more than was thought in the past.

Although it is doubtful that books of the future will be entirely paperless, new electronic information technology is currently making automated electronic information access systems more and more available to libraries. There is no function in the library that cannot be enhanced profoundly through advanced EIT. Already, in most college and university libraries, everything is being (or soon will be) cataloged electronically and may soon be acquired, accessed, and circulated electronically. Currently, a major part of library budgets, in some cases more than 50 percent, goes to technology or technology-related functions. Many libraries have created electronic satellites to allow remote electronic access to library information.

Instead of storing books and providing manual mechanisms for their access, LOTFs will act as networks for accessing scholarly information and providing for its storage and access through electronic means in networks – often not even storing the information but rather, providing electronic network access to its primary storage location, which may not even be associated with any library. Some libraries have already gone into electronic publishing: providing the service of compiling an "electronic" book that is "published" on paper and/or paperless. Many have become "educators": providing learning experiences for using/accessing electronic information, electronic publishing, and word processing for electronic information age needs. Others are approaching "world library" status by providing global electronic information access networks.

Information Age Library Futures

Today's EITs are based on mainframe computers, PCs, application and support software, telecommunications, computer communications networks (LANS and WANS), office automation, databases, expert systems, knowledge bases, computer-assisted design, computer-assisted manufacturing (CAB-CAM), computer-integrated manufacturing, computer-assisted engineering, materials requirements planning, flexible manufacturing systems, just-in-time systems, computerized numerical control, word processing and text editing, integrated software, spread sheets, and many others. These technologies are transforming libraries, schools, jobs,

8

businesses, financial institutions, factories, offices, government, engineering, and science. Their impact on education is just beginning. They have entered the classroom and are forecasted to alter the way education will be delivered. They are powerful tools for amplifying students' learning, teachers' teaching, and the work of school administrators and staff throughout the educational institution.

Since information and knowledge are the "electronic engines of growth" for the information age, it is cogent to ask, what is the rate of information and knowledge growth? Back at the turn of the century, in the year 1900, the production rate for new knowledge creation was doubling the amount of new knowledge worldwide about every fifty years. This number was cited in a *Science* article a number of years ago, and it was derived by counting the number of patents governments issued per year. For the 1980s, using a similar measure, the rate is now roughly every five years for the doubling of new knowledge creation – and we almost double the amount of information used in society yearly.

Now this is a lot of new knowledge creation. It means that in the next five years society could match the total amount of knowledge that society has produced from its beginning! Some basic things happen when this knowledge is applied. First, it causes change. Since we are accelerating the rate of knowledge production, we are also accelerating change. Second, the application of new knowledge allows us to do what we have been doing and still need to do, but to do it more efficiently. This means for the future we will be able to use new knowledge with less input of capital, energy, materials, and labor; thus, there is no doubt that when we apply new knowledge, one major result is displacing people from jobs. Third, new knowledge provides society with the means to do some new things that were impossible to do in the past because we did not know how; when we apply new knowledge for this purpose we create new jobs. At the rate we are producing new knowledge, there should be no lack of jobs for the future – if we apply created new knowledge to doing new things.

The information age is also transforming society into a "high-wage economy," requiring more rather than less education and use/access to information, and especially more information access and education for adults. This means educational systems/institutions need to raise their sights from preparing students for a low-wage economy towards preparing students to enter this new high-wage economic age – and libraries must be expanded to provide additional access and new information services.

We now have in use in the United States more computers than there are people. A number of corporations have already reached this stage; Unisys, for example, has in use over 100,000 computers, PCs, or terminals supporting fewer than 100,000 employees.

The computer has gone through many advances and changes since the early 1950s. We are now deep within the fourth generation of user-friendly computers. It is an era in which software and PCs are at the leading edge of technology. The fifth generation has been announced, and the software embodiment of it is here. Its hardware embodiment is expected in the 1990s. This transition is multidimensional. The computer has evolved from occupying entire rooms to taking up a desktop, to being portable. The cost has decreased from about a million dollars a box to several thousand dollars, and soon computers will cost even less than that and be able to do more. In the past, computer interface access was made only through the intervention of a human programmer or operator; now computers have become end-user-friendly, and soon intelligent systems will be the norm. Software used to be limited. Now there are many alternatives for a growing list of application areas, with many AI expert systems beginning to emerge. Hardware is no longer centralized in computer rooms; now it is being distributed, with much of it being networked through communication systems providing easy access memory at low cost. It is expected that with orders of magnitude more will be available soon at very inexpensive prices. Computers were unintelligent in the past; now they are not. Impossible-to-read, manually manipulated tapes and cards were once used to access computers; now we have user-friendly screens and keyboards. Soon we will have speech discourse systems and source data automated capture systems. In the past computers were prohibitively expensive for most people; only wealthy institutions could afford them. Now they are common in libraries, small businesses, and a growing number of schools. Soon almost everyone will be able to afford them.

Electronic Information Age Futures

Videoconferencing, computer conferencing, electronic computer bulletin boards, computer electronic mail, information utilities, compact discs (CDs), videodisk and videocassette libraries, "smart" telephones, fiber-optic communication highways, desktop publishing, portable computers and TVs, knowledge-based systems, and discoursing hardware are all on the cutting edge of electronic information technology. Each in its own unique way presents new opportunities for libraries. In a recent EIT and systems forecast and assessment study that I conducted for the Office of Technology Assessment, over 2,000 EITs were identified. Most are on an explosive growth path that will make obsolete most traditional modes of information handling and information transmission processes – especially for libraries and education.

TECHNOLOGY TRENDS AND FUTURE IMPACT

Trends

The basic, cutting-edge technology "engine of change" is the "more-for-less" technological-economic equation. For each technology, as it advances, this equation allows or forces a trend curve path for both evolutionary and revolutionary technological developments in creating *more* for *less*. That is, *more* functionality, capability, user-friendliness, speed, capacity, reliability, accessibility, quality, physical smallness, hardware and software integration – that is, more intelligent and capable systems – are created for *less* cost, capital investment, materials and energy input, pollution output, learning required to use, and so forth. For the future this means more accessibility of information by the public if institutions like libraries set up the means for increased information dissemination.

Forces of Change

The more-for-less technological-economic equation spawns more competition – clones, plug compatibles, leapfrogging, rapid introductions of next or new generations of competing systems, and higher levels of integration. Competition in turn forces the industry to respond faster with advanced changes to their systems to meet the competition. As a result, wave after wave of new and better products and services come faster and faster.

EITs will be forced to continue to change as the future brings (1) drastic cost reductions, but on a roller-coaster pricing path; (2) dramatic performance improvements; (3) an explosive functionality growth; (4) higher efficiency and quality; (5) rapid public acceptance and attendant deep levels of library, educational, social, and economic impacts; (6) fantastic developments in tools to make users more sophisticated and retrain professionals; and (7) a rapid growth in new library and business opportunities.

Emerging Issues

For libraries and education these technological forces of change provide both future opportunities and challenging problems. How will the college libraries ever keep up-to-date books and EIT hardware in their "reading" rooms, classrooms, labs, and offices if EIT changes and advances yearly and even monthly? How can librarians and teachers be kept up to date? They can only through the use of newer and newer user-friendly EIT. Where will they find the funds? They will have to use these modern technologies to raise productivity.

11

Of course, there are many other emerging issues and forces of change that libraries and education will need to face in the future. What part of education should be performed in the classroom and what part in libraries or outside the classroom? What is the basic curriculum for the information age? What must a student learn to be considered educated in the information age? What is the future role of education? Is it different for different regions?

POSSIBLE TECHNOLOGY BREAKTHROUGHS

There are many possible breakthroughs, "trump cards" that, once the technology becomes technically and economically feasible, will become the norm. Examples and forecasts of technologies that will radically change libraries are as follows.

"Current Awareness" Library Systems

For one type of "trump card" cutting-edge technology, assume a future with a very user-friendly, portable, expert system PC with several compact discs. It is also capable of speech discourse (speech recognition and speech output backed up with "intelligence"), image, and other types of sensors and has access to a wide variety of knowledge bases (access to almost all of society's amassed knowledge). Let's call it a "current awareness system." Assume further that it takes the initiative (without waiting for the user to call it into action) by sensing the user's needs (and if it does not understand the sensory information it gets, it asks questions about user needs). Additionally, when it understands the way it can be of assistance to its user, it dips into its knowledge base, or accesses a future library of the future network knowledge utility service, to obtain the knowledge needed by its user in the real time of the user's need. Then it makes the user aware of the knowledge by offering advice. Of course, the design of such a system is critical; otherwise, it will end up being a nag and lapse into disuse.

Such a system is now feasible for future development. When it is in common use, what then will be the role of the library and school? There is little doubt that there will be a role; however, one thing is sure, it will be very different from the role of today's computers.

Assuming either expert systems or the highly technology-integrated current awareness system for the future, the more basic question becomes, what is the role of humans in such a future? If we further assume that these systems are designed and used as tools to amplify human capacities, then the answer to this question is straightforward–there is a definite and growing role involving the use of considerably more information.

Why? When such a system is used as an advice-giving consulting tool, then the human has access to all of the knowledge that the tool has and the additional knowledge in his or her head. The combination gives a synergy factor allowing the human *always* to have access to more knowledge (to be more knowledgeable) than the machine. This means humans will always be needed over and above a machine and that we will always be more capable than it. For some jobs, however, the machine will be sufficient. Therefore, in such a future there is only one answer for humans – to stay ahead of machine knowledge. This means the answer is twofold: education and increased access to library information. We will need libraries and an educational system specifically designed for such an age – with new and additional roles.

Artificial Realities

The evolutionary path into the future for artificial reality systems includes:

- Next-generation user-friendly systems

- Computer-orchestrated imaging/graphics

- Computer-generated real-time dynamic image simulations of reality

- Computer-processed real-time dynamic images of reality

- 3-D imaging of reality and beyond reality

- Sensor-embedded gloves and bodysuits to allow human interaction with computer-generated and/or -processed images – to allow image interactions via pointing, gesturing, control, intervention, and so forth – to put humans into computer-generated scenes (that is, imagine 3-D TV with viewers interacting with the program as if they were in it).

- Feedback pads on sensor gloves and suits for the computer to feedback information so that viewer/interacting person can "feel" the imaged scenes

Future EIT – Neurocomputers

Neurocomputers consist of hardware that imitates the design and operation of human neural networks like those in our brains. These systems will make pattern recognition much simpler and more practical. They can learn and could create new knowledge beyond what humans have accomplished today.

Future artificial reality and neurocomputer technology for libraries and for use throughout society will cause our society to become more image-based than word-based in most everything we do.

Future EIT – Nanotechnology

Nanotechnology is hardware biomolecular computer systems capable of constructing or assembling anything so that the resulting systems are self-recreated. Eric Drexler outlines these systems in his book, *Engines of Creation*.

IMPLIED ALTERNATIVE FUTURES

The cutting edge of PC computers and networks has put society into a world of distributed systems. They are forcing libraries, schools, businesses, and government to decentralize. Couple these technology trends with political realities of global competition and you can safely forecast that society will continue to decentralize. When you add to that the fact that adults are being displaced ever more rapidly from their jobs, many times in their lives, you can see the growing need for more libraries, community colleges, and nontraditional adult educational institutions. These institutions must be more than educational centers for career preparation; their role must also be to retrain.

As computer networks are increasingly used, with very low-cost PCs, TV graphics, CD memory, and lots of educational software, an alternative will exist for students – especially older students. They will be able to use their portable networked PCs as a real-time "educators" (accessing them in the real time of their need – on the job, during a leisure-time activity, anywhere), instead of having to go to a physical, rooted school building. Will this happen? You can bet on it; in fact, it is starting. It could become the largest role for the library of the future.

LONGER RANGE FUTURES FOR LIBRARIES

There is a great need for each of us to have more access to information and education than we have now. Someday, perhaps sooner than later, our society will recognize that a high school education is not nearly enough education and will make it mandatory for everyone to continue their formal education many times throughout their lives. When this happens, schools and libraries will need to rapidly expand their systems, roles, curricula, and accessibility.

On the other side of the cutting edge of technology advance are the strides now being made with expert systems. There is little doubt about their ability to raise the productivity of human experts and professionals. This means that professionals will be unskilled when society massively applies expert systems. If there is X amount of work to be done that today would take Y professionals to complete, with future expert systems it will take considerably fewer than Y professionals. Fortunately, as new knowledge advances – and knowledge is growing at a rapid rate – there is created a long list of new jobs that require many more professionals.

This lack of professionals with up-to-date skills trend creates a number of problems. First is the problem of job displacement, which requires that the professionals displaced find new careers. This puts the pressure on libraries and education to provide information and curricula to meet this challenge. The second problem created is the one of new jobs. Society is speeding up its production of new knowledge fast enough so that enough new jobs could be made to keep well ahead of the displacement problem if our institutions (public or private, business, education, government, libraries, etc.) change fast enough to allow the new jobs a place in their ranks. If they do not, then most of our new knowledge will go into doing things more efficiently, causing job displacement – as in the past few decades when our unemployment rate went from about 4 percent to nearly 8 percent. Since we are in a global economic competitive race – today largely with Japan – there are signs that in order to compete we will need to change our institutions faster. In order to stay in the race, we will be forced to create new jobs in AI, expert systems, genetic engineering technology, and many other areas – which in turn will force libraries and educational institutions to meet the challenges posed at a faster rate.

If we do not, the United States will slide down the ranks of the developed nations and become, even before the year 2000, a third-rate nation.

THE LIBRARY OF THE FUTURE

The library of the future will continue to develop along a linear growth and advance path with many milestones or "LOTF ages," such as:

- First LOTF age: EIT desktop and user-friendly PC or terminal access to electronically computerized library catalogs

- Second LOTF age: remote EIT access to library information via networks

- Third LOTF age: most new library information stored in electronic form rather than on paper or in books on low-cost, high-capacity computer memory systems (for example, CDs and later technology)

- Fourth LOTF age: the library becomes a primary electronic publisher of user-tailored "books" and an on-line E Mail-like library transaction processing system for library information

- Fifth LOTF age: library AI expert systems primarily provide expert advice for most fields

15

- Sixth LOTF age: library "artificial reality" systems become the primary mode of access to information

- Seventh LOTF age: neurocomputing EIT is used in libraries to produce requested new knowledge and its dissemination

- Eighth LOTF age: nanotechnological EIT is used to replicate and generate knowledge for users

Forecasting is a discipline that considers fundamental questions about possible futures in such a way that no matter what alternative futures are forecasted, one can give compelling reasons for the likely occurrence of what *could* happen–not predictions for what *will* happen. The fundamental philosophical questions of what library futures are possible are linked in the minds of librarians and technologists to such questions as: What futures should we design and implement? What technologies should we use to deliver information in the future? But before we can answer these questions, we must first ask and answer this one: What new or modern technologies should we design and use in libraries? In this short essay on library futures, these questions were largely ignored. Some future directions for technology and their expected impact on libraries were covered–as needed background information for answering these larger questions.

The idea that there is a single, firm, unchanging, and absolute future possible is alien to futurists. There are many alternative futures possible; our problem is to choose and design the "best" ones. The basic method for predicting what the library of the future will be like is to not make isolated forecasts but to have cooperative research and development programs for designing alternative predictions for the library of the future, an idea that librarians have not been enthusiastic about in the past.

There is only one answer for a brighter tomorrow: greater access to the societal information base and education for application.

Section One

PHILOSOPHIC AND PUBLIC POLICY ASPECTS

Many of the themes of the keynote address are expanded and refined in this first group of papers. The major concern of these authors is the nature of America's society in the new information age. Raymond Taylor, in his "Comments on the History and Maturing of Information Science," reviews the history of information science and concludes that scholars interested in information use should first become familiar with the past. Human communication behavior and information processing technology, Donald E. Phillips writes, are intertwined. Determining how technology affects human information-seeking patterns, adds Phillips, is critical to the study of the proper role of technology in our culture. Planning the implementation of information technologies in our society mandates the formulation of an information policy. "The Unique Characteristics of Information Policy and Their U.S. Characteristics" is the concern of Sandra Braman. On the human microcosmic level, Jere W. Clark and Juanita Stone Clark, in "Economy of Thought in the Age of Information Overload," and Mary Haban, in her "Information Filtering," examine how individuals can avoid being overwhelmed by the amount of information now being generated on a daily basis. An equally important issue is denial of information access. Michael S. Ameigh discusses the consequences of restricted access to electronic databases in "Information: Who Will Corner the Market?" Ameigh is especially concerned by the increasing restrictions on government information implicit in electronic storage. Robert Jacobson's "Beyond 'The Chicken and the Egg' Dilemma: Designing a Hospitable Universal Information Utility" is also about measures to preserve free access to information in the twenty-first century.

The implicit changes in the information environment dictate a new information literacy, according to Barbara Kwasnik in "Information Literacy: Concepts of Literacy in a Computer Age." James V. Biundo, in "Humans

17

10 – Computers 6," warns that the emphasis currently being placed on computer literacy may be excessive. Biundo advocates familiarity with information technology in order to use it solely for the betterment of society. One means to ensure Biundo's goal and enhance decision-making, suggests Bill H. Washburn in "Numeracy: An Imperative for the Information Age," is to become as facile with numbers as we are with words in print.

Only through consideration of the issues raised in these papers can we begin to determine the nature of society in the twenty-first century.

Comments on the History and Maturing of Information Science

RAYMOND G. TAYLOR, JR.

I would like to begin by answering the unasked question, "Why comment on history as part of a futuristic conference on information science?" Of course, there are the obvious answers that touch on appreciating a heritage and avoiding past errors. But I believe there is a far more important, and a somewhat more subtle, reason. I would assume that many of the persons attending this conference are concerned with leadership and planning. I make this assumption because I know that we try to surmise a future – "Information Literacies for the Twenty-first Century" – at least in part to be prepared, and to prepare others, for that future. But leadership is largely a matter of perspective; certainly it requires skillful practice and a firm knowledge base, but it is quickly distinguished from management by the perspective it requires.

Now, there is an understandable and comfortable tendency to become totally absorbed in the technology of information systems and library science. It is a discipline that lends itself to high degrees of specialization. Many of you have your own versions of my personal dilemma: a desire to escape to a private place, alone with that ubiquitous tool of the trade, a microcomputer, to spend hours, days, perhaps an entire career, dealing with ever increasingly more finite aspects of the science. But to allow this to happen is to deny ourselves a perspective – it denies a full perspective of today, let alone of the twenty-first century. So if we are to be leaders, planners, educators, if we are to be certain that our own specializations are to be relevant tomorrow, we must look up from the keyboard and try to understand the historical and social context in which our sciences are emerging.

I recall from my freshman days in college the tortuous process of reading the pre-Socratic philosophers; they argued endlessly over whether the world was composed of atoms (a discrete number of small parts) or was, in some respect, singular. For many, the answer was given by Plato: the world was, in fact, an all-encompassing unity, and we could know and understand that unity if we could but reason abstractly and broadly enough. This notion fitted well with the beliefs of the Hebrew prophets and the later Western theologians. Many liberally educated persons who would not by any means fancy themselves "theologians" have also come to believe this notion as well, for there seems to be no end to the intellectual connections that can be made within and between the realms of things and ideas.

A PERSPECTIVE ON SCIENCE IN GENERAL

It would be quite a disservice for me to leave you with the impression that the pre-Socratic debate between the atomists and the unitarians (if you will) has been resolved. To find a latter-day version of this same debate we only have to look within the bastion of empirical reasoning–modern science itself. Here one would expect to find a highly unitarian perspective, a perspective that values unifying principles, replete with a vocabulary that supports those principles: the law, the theorem, the lemma. But, alas, that is not what we find.

There exists, even to this day, a rather atomistic view of science–a view that is apparently embraced by many individuals who practice science–wherein science is regarded as a means of extracting knowledge and of contributing it to the world. The task, according to this view, is to discover new facts and to add them to an existing body of information (Kerlinger 1986). Persons who hold such a view, or who engage in research for such a purpose, should find satisfaction in every properly conducted study and in its results, no matter how finite or disconnected the results may be. This historically popular and atomistic approach to inquiry has contributed greatly to our store of knowledge, as well as to our health, wealth, and lifestyle. However, such a static view of science becomes increasingly inadequate as we struggle with a plethora of data and a paucity of unifying theory and explanation.

Polanyi (1962) and others have made a case for a dynamic and unified view of science, one that accepts the importance of the present state of knowledge but sees it as a springboard to further theory and research. The unified view emphasizes the heuristic, self-adjusting, and self-referential aspect of science. It holds that every discovery interacts with every other; the first informs the second, and the second causes a reinterpretation or a new appreciation of the first. Schwartz, as editor of a collection of Polanyi essays, notes that the scientist does not build theory by adding up facts, but that he constantly seeks to construct a new view of reality (1974).

When scientists embrace a unified sense of their activities, they will constantly seek intellectual relationships, not just within their studies but also between them, and between their work and that of others. New, suspected, and untested connections are constantly being hypothesized. Scientists risk a substantial share of their lifetimes as they formulate, and often abandon, these hypotheses. But, in Polanyi's words, "it is the plunge by which we gain a foothold at another shore of reality. On such plunges the scientist has to stake bit by bit his entire professional life" (1962, 123).

More precisely, Braithwaite describes the function of science as an effort "to establish general laws covering the behaviors of . . . empirical events or objects . . . and thereby to enable us to connect together our knowledge of the separately known events" (1955, 1). Single and isolated practices, even when brilliantly conceived, properly executed, or thoughtfully interpreted, are not as likely to contribute to perspective as are unified and cooperative approaches.

INFORMATION SCIENCE IN PARTICULAR

Now let me add a word regarding the need for perspective within the field of library and information science in particular. As one information scientist recently commented, "What most of us . . . need . . . are the conceptual and linguistic tools for analyzing our experiences . . . in order to see the patterns from which we can draw general principles" (Antill 1985, 207).

Much of what is titled "information science" concerns itself with the fine points and the technology of acquisition, storage, retrieval, and transmission of data. However, in a self-conscious way, the field is also reaching beyond its early and narrow atomistic practices and is seeking perspective, unity, and a philosophical foundation in the study of communications theory and languages. It is undergoing a metamorphosis from a practical to a theoretical science. All this is not to suggest that "classical librarians" are purveyors of static information, but rather to claim that the old definitions of information are giving way to dynamic definitions.

There is a very conspicuous parallel between the history and maturing of information science and that of science in general. Those who practice or who identify themselves with the emerging field of information science are becoming increasingly aware of the importance of meaning and interpretation as opposed to the mere collection and transmission of data. In contrasting a "positive science" (i.e., an atomistic and static view) with a more phenomenological approach, Boland writes: "Positive science imagines an information system as a camera that merely takes pictures of what is simply there. . . . Phenomenology in contrast treats the information system as a communicative act that [is a] ... fragile social construction that constitutes rather than reflects social reality" (Boland 1985, 196). Again, it treats the information system as a social construction that constitutes, rather than reflects, the social reality. What a shift! What a burden and responsibility for scholars and students of information systems!

KNOWLEDGE IS A MOVING TARGET

Knowledge is not something that can be captured, recorded, and interpreted for all time. The hermeneutic problem, that is, the problem of meaning, is universal and abiding. Gadamer writes: "There would be no speaker and no art of speaking if understanding and consent were not [constantly] in question. ... There would be no hermeneutical task if there were no mutual understanding that has been disturbed and [must be found again]. It is a symptom of our failure to realize this ... [that] we think in terms of organizing a perfect and a perfectly manipulated information" (1976, 25).

Again, knowledge is a moving target. Information modifies its own physical and intellectual environment, or, more precisely, it modifies the most universal environment to which it is applied. The intermediaries of this modification consist of all the persons who use information, whether that information is understood or misunderstood, "properly" or "improperly" applied. That is to say, like a multidimensional ripple, information, and the process of obtaining information, alters the human condition. It changes our interaction with and our understanding of the environment, and thereby the environment itself is forever changed. A new intellectual milieu is generated; a new universe of discourse is opened. Previous perspectives are disturbed. Established practices are thereupon subject to reinterpretation and possibly to reformulation.

A "knowledge equilibrium" is never reached, but this is not to say that unifying principles cannot be discovered. As we examine the nature of a dynamic epistemology, it would do us well, I believe, to hypothesize that this continuous unrest occurs primarily at the level of observing and interpreting details, and that a greater stability occurs at the level of derived generalizations. Ah, perhaps there we have the fundamental required literacy for the leaders, planners, and educators associated with the emerging new information sciences of the twenty-first century: to be able to obtain and sustain a perspective; to make certain that the practices of the science do not become so finite, so separate, so specialized, that they take on a life of their very own and are no longer informed by the unifying social theories and systems to which they belong; and to understand and fully appreciate the fluid and mutually interdependent nature of the close relationship between information science and the new world in which we shall live.

Will information science content itself with becoming just another highly specialized discipline? Or will it mature to become the "master science," the science on which all unified endeavors depend?

Acknowledgment

Portions of this paper appeared in an article by Raymond Taylor and Olga Skorapa, "The Case for Organized and Thematic Research," *College Student Journal* 22, no. 4 (Winter 1988): 386-89.

References

Antill, L. "Selection of a Research Method." In *Research Methods in Information Science*, ed. E. Mumford. Proceedings of the International Federation of Information Processing. New York: Elsevier, 1985.

Boland, R. J. "Phenomenology: A Preferred Approach to Research on Information Science." In Mumford, *Research Methods,* 1985.

Braithwaite, R. B. *Scientific Explanation.* Cambridge: Cambridge University Press, 1955.

Gadamer, H. G. *Philosophical Hermeneutics.* Berkeley: University of California Press, 1976.

Kerlinger, F. *Foundations of Behavioral Research.* N.Y.: Holt, Rinehart, and Winston, 1986.

Polanyi, M. *Personal Knowledge: Towards a Post-Critical Philosophy.* Chicago: University of Chicago Press, 1962.

Schwartz, F., Ed. *Scientific Thought and Social Reality: Essays by Michael Polanyi.* New York: International University Press, 1974.

Human Communication Behavior and Information Processing Technology: Elements of a Cultural Model and Paradigm

DONALD E. PHILLIPS

Interpreting the symbolic in culture requires interdisciplinary approaches combining analytic and synthetic perspectives.[1] This paper holds that human communication behavior and information processing technology, cultural processes and phenomena that have implications in many areas of the arts and sciences and in global society, provide, when placed in interdisciplinary social and cultural science perspective, elements of a cultural model and paradigm.

Drawing upon multiple interdisciplinary philosophical and theoretical sources relevant to the study of culture and communication, including Alain Touraine (sociology), Paul Tillich (philosophy), Alvin Gouldner and Orrin Klapp (sociology), Thomas Kuhn (history and philosophy of science), Frederick Williams (communication), and other contemporary theorists, this paper develops concepts and principles that contribute to a cultural hermeneutic.

After establishing an interdisciplinary basis for analyzing elements of human communication behavior and information processing technology drawn from the foregoing sources, the paper then outlines and projects a number of issues, prospects, and applications in information creation, transmission, and management, including artificial intelligence, computers, robotics, and mass media technology use, that provide insights for an interdisciplinary and communication-oriented cultural model and paradigm for a humanistic understanding of the global information society.

Winston Churchill is reputed to have said concerning the British House of Commons, a unique structure and channel for communication, "We shape

25

our buildings and afterward they shape us."[2] The idea that the communicative environment and media of expression influence the nature and type of communication we engage in has long been recognized. While Churchill was talking about building architecture, the same point applies to computer architecture and the design of information technologies. As generations of speakers were influenced in their interactional styles by the narrow confines of the Commons, so generations of contemporary and future communicators are being shaped and will be shaped by the architecture or design of their communication media. As building architecture and design frames and shapes our experiences communicatively, so the forms of our communication help mold and channel our interactions.

The concern of this paper is to assess and develop a context for understanding the influence of human communication behavior, mediated through and related to information processing technology, as both are transforming our culture, history, educational systems, concepts of literacy, and economic and personal transactions.

ANALYZING COMMUNICATION BEHAVIOR AND INFORMATION PROCESSING TECHNOLOGY: ELEMENTS OF AN INTERDISCIPLINARY CULTURAL MODEL AND PARADIGM

Raymond Williams defines theory of culture as "the study of relationships between *elements* in a whole way of life."[3] Cultural theory, as developed by Williams, is concerned with matters of meaning, value, relationships, and how we produce history. This paper develops similar concerns building from the primary thesis and position that culture exists (is shaped) in symbolic action. It argues that, as distinctive forms of cultural and symbolic action, human communication behavior and information processing through technology are integral to the formulation of the cultural models of our information-based society and of its scientific-technical paradigms. These elements involved in our cultural and communicative situation often exist in dialectical tension, including tensions between paradigms and disciplines, which Kuhn refers to as "the essential tension."[4]

In establishing an interdisciplinary basis for analyzing elements of human communication behavior and information processing technology in a cultural context, this paper posits seven propositions or subtheses:

1. Information is the basis for symbolic action.

2. Symbolic action is the basic unit of cultural production (cf. Tillich).

26

3. Symbolic action generates social cooperation and/or conflict and is instrumental in the struggle to develop cultural models and for the control of historicity (cf. Touraine).

4. This action includes a dialectical conflict between ideology and technology (cf. Gouldner).

5. This dialectic also involves an alternation and conflict between opening and closing and requires strategies of information adaptation (cf. Klapp).

6. This dialectic manifests an "essential tension" between various disciplines of the arts and sciences, between old paradigms of inquiry and new ones, a tension that can lead to revolutionary changes in ways we view our world, communicate with each other, research, and instruct (cf. Kuhn).

7. Human communication behavior and information processing technology, termed "the new communications," reflect a converging of scientific and technical revolutions, an interaction of media forms and influences, that calls for a well-considered balancing of individual (existential), social, and technological needs and potentials, including new and revitalized information literacies.

In addition to these propositions, while various terms are detailed contextually in this paper, several key terms are identified initially:

Human communication is defined from a behavioral interaction perspective as any discriminatory response to a stimulus; that is, whenever we perceptively respond to visual, auditory, or other sensory data in our environment, a communication occurs. Everything in our environment, technological or nontechnological, animate or inanimate, can potentially communicate with us.[5]

Information is a multifaceted term that representatively includes the following dimensions: (1) *environmental interaction messages* – "the content of what is exchanged with the outer world as we adjust to it" (Wiener); (2) *data processing comprehensively considered* – "the storage, retrieval, and processing of data" in contrast to *knowledge*, which implies "an organized statement of facts or ideas" and involves communicating the results of logic or discovery (Bell); (3) *communication transmission capacity* – "a potential of signals" relative to a channel of communication (Cherry); (4) *messages that influence our images of reality* – or "that which reduces uncertainty" (Boulding); (5) synoptically, information is a symbolic resource derived through processing data in interactions with persons or the environment, by utilizing the capacities of communication channels, including *information processing technology* (i.e., symbol and signal-transacting devices such as computers or other interactive media) and by exchanging messages that reduce uncertainty and influence our images of reality.[6]

Another key term, *cultural model and paradigm*, is defined later in context.

INFORMATION AS THE BASIS FOR SYMBOLIC ACTION

Peter Bishop, author of *Fifth Generation Computers,* in evaluating artificial intelligence, places information at the base of a hierarchy of intelligence. *Information,* he argues, is easily represented as words, numbers, symbols, and facts and constitutes raw data for higher epistemological levels. *Knowledge,* expressed, for example, in linguistic or mathematical form, concerns associations between facts; its representation "is one of the greatest challenges for the developers of fifth generation computers." *Intelligence* is a level higher, "at the upper limit of language," and operates on information and knowledge. Intelligent reasoning patterns can be encoded, "but the creative 'spark' of intelligence" exceeds linguistic expression. At the hierarchy's top is *wisdom,* which is almost beyond language and involves philosophical insight. In evaluating Turing's influence on computers, Bishop adds that computer data is viewed "as sequences of symbols which are manipulated by the machine, but require interpretation by a user before they provide information."[7] *Information, then, is seen here as the basis for symbolic action, and information processing as a symbolic process requiring a communicative, behavioral transaction and interpretation by information users.*

SYMBOLIC ACTION AS THE BASIC UNIT OF CULTURAL PRODUCTION

In *Information Technology and Civilization,* Hiroshi Inose and John R. Pierce acknowledge language, identified as a code system of symbols and/or signs, as "central to human civilization, thought, and technologies." They observe that among many social influences of information technology, "the most vital are those that affect human identity." Noteworthy examples include "the impacts on the languages and means of learning on which human identity and culture depend."[8] Many scholars from different disciplines concur regarding the central cultural role of language, recognizing in various ways symbolic action as the basic unit of cultural production. Clifford Geertz contends that we create our cultural system through symbols. Geertz's cultural sociology develops a hermeneutic perspective from which he argues that thinking is "the matching of the states and processes of symbolic models against the states and processes of the wider world." In his noted essay, "Ideology as a Cultural System," Geertz contends we know the world "only through 'models' of experience not . . . simply through making sense of experience in itself." In perception we pair objects against symbolic models; we apply our models to our data and perceive experience through those models. For Geertz, culture is like a map produced by symbolic interaction and representation. Hermeneutics, for him, is the study of symbols, of symbolic maps, maps that, as for Tillich, enable us to have a world, to internalize the external. "Hermeneutical analysis," for Geertz, "is the study of symbols, for these symbolic maps provide the 'extrinsic sources of information in terms of which human life can be patterned – extrapersonal mechanisms for the perception, understanding, judgment, and manipulation of the world.'"[9] For Geertz and Tillich, symbolic action produces culture. Symbolic acts and cultural acts are correlated. Cultural acts – self-creative and defining acts – occur through symbolization. Our symbolizations produce and bear meanings, and culture exists in such meanings. Collectively, in their various systems and subsystems, in education, religion, technology, economics, politics, and so forth, *our symbol systems create our cultural systems.* For Tillich and Geertz, personality (existential concerns), society, and culture are produced and unified symbolically.[10] As living (biological and psychological) systems are constituted by codes and exist by processing information in interaction with their environments,[11] so sociocultural, including scientific-technical, systems are a product of coding and interaction with symbolic codes.

Technological innovations represent a kind of language; they are communicative extensions and expressions of ourselves – they are part of our culture's objectified symbolic modeling. Computers, computer programming and use, and the various mass and interactive media are, as McLuhan and others have argued, extensions of our primary being. Sherry Turkle's investigations of computer culture reflect on such extensions, as does her book title, *The Second Self: Computers and the Human Spirit.*[12] Ernst Kapp, over a century ago in Germany, in his *Outlines of a Philosophy of Technology,* said to be the first work to articulate and develop the hypothesis that technology functions as an extension of ourselves, and in other works, recognized that scientific and technical "inventions are a very distinct language; in them culminates mankind's striving to make of the planet a realm of beauty and the spirit."[13]

What is culture? Philosopher-theologian Paul Tillich and anthropologist Leslie White provide in their assessment of the question a basis for the view that, as I have argued elsewhere, "culture may be identified with human self-creativity and self-interpretation expressed through language, regarded as basic to culture, and with symbolically-attested ideas, behaviors, and objects."[14] Tillich views culture as produced in interaction, "as the whole of creative, receiving, or transforming acts." Culture exists in symbolic action because it is through language that we shape our environments, whether existentially, socially, aesthetically, or technologically, whether through personal creativity, social-political structuring and action, creative or scientific productions. Symbolic action enables us to produce "a universe of meaning," hence, to experience culture.[15]

PRODUCING CULTURE IN PROGRAMMED SOCIETY: CONFLICT, CULTURAL MODELS AND THE CONTROL OF HISTORICITY

Sociologists Alain Touraine and Daniel Bell, from separate continents, "almost simultaneously published books on what they called 'postindustrial society.'" While concurring about fundamental changes in international socioeconomic processes with an increased role for information processing technologies, both operate from different social paradigms. Bell interprets "these changes essentially in an 'end of ideology' direction," while "Touraine's model" predicts movement into a new era of social relations requiring understanding of "the new social classes, conflicts, and ideologies that will be developing."[16] Touraine's sociology contains elements especially relevant for a cultural model and paradigm attempting to comprehend the production of culture in programmed society.

"Touraine's action-oriented sociology envisions a new type of society emerging from the sixties, programmed society, relating it to 'the new conflicts and social movements.'" Touraine holds that society produces itself and determines its own history "by cultural achievements and social conflicts, and at the heart of society burns the fire of social movements." While industrial society, according to Touraine, was characterized by the domination of "the masters of industry" over workers and by the control of "production rates and methods," now "the characteristic feature of post-industrial society," which Touraine refers to more precisely as "programmed society," "is that the central investments are now made at the level of production management and not that of work organization."

Touraine writes:

> By contrast, in programmed society class domination consists less in organizing work than in managing the production and data-processing apparatus, i.e. ensuring the often monopolistic control of the supply and processing of a certain type of data, and hence of a way of organizing social life. This is the definition of the technocracy controlling the running of management apparatus.[17]

In a study of social protest movements of the sixties, the present writer, in partial harmony with Touraine (who stresses the redefining role of social movements), defined "sociocultural movements . . . as collective cultural and symbolic actions manifesting protest behavior and symbolizing in distinctive ways human self-interpretations and definitions or redefinitions of sociocultural situations."[18] While the "micro revolution" or "cognitive revolution" or "control revolution" in information processing technology may initially appear different from social revolutions, it is potentially as revolutionary as any historic social, political, or technological movement.[19] The tremendous acceleration of contemporary change, heightened by communication technology, promises consequences equaling or perhaps surpassing those of previous social movements or the industrial revolution. A key element in analyzing technological revolutions is to view them also from a sociocultural movement perspective, which observes that different social groups are struggling "for the control of social development" and the power to define the cultural models by which society produces its "historicity, i.e., control of the great cultural orientations by which a society's environmental relationships are normatively organized."[20]

For Touraine, a cultural model is an "image a society forms for itself of its creative capacity" in a manner that "defines the field of social relations . . . and the system of historical action." Such models of social structure are an "essential aspect of historicity," an overall vision of social structure and action.[21] Particular models and paradigms collectively contribute to the achievement of or failure to achieve historicity – fulfillment or nonfulfillment of a society's creative capacity.

Touraine acknowledges tensions in historical, scientific, and cultural action, including a "tension that simultaneously unites and separates a society's functioning and its historicity." These tensions exist in an ongoing "system of debates" and as part of a "realm of discourse" or public discursive space that must be constituted and "reconstituted on the basis of common consciousness" or public opinion. Sociocultural structure and cultural models are not givens; they exist in a "system of relations" conditioned by public debate. Programmed society is constituted and moves forward by management of the system of communication. Cultural models are determined in communicative if not actual conflict. Social structure is a dynamic creation, a product of social conflicts, relations, discourse, and debates. A society is defined by its communications, and the greater its power of communication, the greater its capacity to shape itself and the greater its historicity.[22] In programmed society we produce by our communications not only information, knowledge, and wisdom, but new sociocultural models leading toward or away from the fulfillment of our historicity.

SYMBOLIC ACTION AND THE DIALECTICAL CONFLICT BETWEEN IDEOLOGY AND TECHNOLOGY

Alvin Gouldner, in *The Dialectic of Ideology and Technology,* raises the question "as to how or on what, in a transitional era, public discourse will ground itself?" In the face of profound sociocultural changes, the "old culture of discourse" is called into question by new means of communication. The authority of previous models of society, "all formerly authoritative definitions of social reality–the conventional, the sacred, or the privileged– come into tension with the new modes of discourse, with its new mode of justification."[23] Gouldner, like Touraine, recognizes that culture is defined in public "cultures of discourse," and in the modes or media through which discourse is communicated, and by the underlying technologies that attempt to legitimate or delegitimate the methods and content of public communication. Technology does not exist without ideological justification and implications, and these involve dialectical conflicts between ideology and technology.

J. David Bolter, in his interdisciplinary historical and contemporary analysis, *Turing's Man: Western Culture in the Computer Age,* in arguments consonant with Gouldner, Touraine, and this paper's interpretation of sociocultural movements, writes of "the computer as a defining technology." Bolter notes that, while the computer "leaves intact many older technologies," nevertheless, as "a machine that controls machines," it occupies a unique place in our culture as the central technology that more than any other defines our era. Bolter observes: "For us today, the computer constantly threatens to break out of the tiny corner of human affairs (scientific measurement and business accounting) that it was built to occupy, to contribute instead to a general redefinition of certain basic relationships: the relationship of science to technology, of knowledge to technical power, and, in the broadest sense, of mankind to the world of nature."[24]

This "process of redefinition" through technology "has always served both as a bridge and a barrier" between humans and their environment, adding to their comfort but producing a sense of alienation from nature. Defining technologies also function as representational and literal ways of viewing "a culture's science, philosophy, or literature" and can "serve as a metaphor, example, model, or symbol."[25] This dialectical interaction of ideology and technology is profound; it defines and redefines our situation and ourselves. Bolter says that "by promising (or threatening) to replace" humans, the computer is providing a new definition of humanity as an "information processor," and of nature as "information to be processed."[26]

"Turing's men" (and we should add women)–a phrase based on the influential work of mathematician and logician A. M. Turing and his paper "On Computable Numbers" (1936), which Bolter calls "the manifesto of the new electronic order of things," and his paper "Computing Machinery and Intelligence" (1950)–is the term Bolter gives to those who share such a view of human-computer interaction. Bolter argues that "we are all liable to become Turing's men, if our work with the computer is intimate and prolonged and we come to think and speak in terms suggested by the machine." For Bolter, computer users become part of the cognitive model that governs their technology.[27] *In what could be considered a kind of reversal of McLuhan's "media as extensions of ourselves" concept, Bolter gives us another side of the human-information-processing dialectic, saying in effect that we also become extensions of our technology.* This phenomenon is comparable to Churchill's architectural observation that "we shape our buildings and afterward they shape us." Bolter says that "Turing's man is the most complete integration of humanity and technology, of artificer and artifact, in the history of Western culture." For Turing, the computer models our humanity, especially our capacity for rational thought, a view essential to Turing's confidence in artificial intelligence. In creating such intelligent machinery we produce and to various degrees define and redefine ourselves technologically.[28]

Ultimately, for Bolter, the computer is not a creator itself but a creative tool. Consequently, he argues for "a synthesis of man and computer," not a replacement of humans by machines. In his view, "'synthetic intelligence' would be a happier name and a better goal than 'artificial intelligence.'"[29] From this paper's perspective, similar to Bolter's view, human communication behavior and information processing technology exist in dialectical tension and interrelatedness: we define our machines and they define us.

For Gouldner, ideologies are "social theories" that have both rational and empirical substantiation and are mediated through language. They are also belief systems and provide a ground, sometimes in a specific type of media technology, for "cultures of discourse." They depend upon information literacies. Rational discourse, for example, is grounded in print media, according to Gouldner. Ideologies are at least partly grounded in technological orientations. Technologies are not neutral; they impose, partly through the type of languages they require, a way of viewing reality, and through languages they are partly constitutive of our personhood. The dialectic of ideology and technology includes the fact that as we speak new languages, or utilize new communication systems, we construct and reconstruct ourselves. Ideological change (which comes in part through technological change) "is a linguistic conversion that carries with it a reorganization of the self."[30] As we change our use of symbol-using processes, we change ourselves. Technological change becomes personal and social change.

Information literacies provide a bridge and a channel between ideology and technology. Information, for Gouldner, like Geertz, does not give us meanings independently. Meaning is "not dictated by the number of documents, by the facts or bits of information," but depends in part "on prior commitments to conceptual schemes, theories, and perspectives."[31] Expanded literacies are needed in order not only to use but to evaluate information in our changing symbolic environment. *Part of the acquisition of literacies should be the development of frames of reference or contexts for evaluating information, as well as developing skills in data manipulation.*

The dialectic of ideology and technology, with the intervening issue of information literacies, has important social implications. Gouldner argues:

> The goals of even the most computerized bureaucracy still require the justification of ideology to the degree that they require the willing cooperation of persons in and out of the organization. The most significant evidence of this in recent times was the failure of American intervention in Viet Nam, an effort that broke down domestically as well as within the army itself. All the technological prowess of the civilian and military bureaucracies failed to achieve the goals assigned them primarily because they had no ideological justification for the war. If the "end of ideology" thesis was taken seriously by political managers – and there is no doubt it was – the American failure in Viet Nam should have disabused them. Fundamentally, the American catastrophe in Viet Nam was not at the level of bureaucratic expertise, for there the technological instruments were more advanced than anywhere, but, rather, the failure was at the executive level. The war in Viet Nam made plain a fundamental error of the "end of ideology" thesis, as of any view implying that science and technology in industrial societies now have a self-sufficient and self-justifying hegemony; it revealed the fundamental weakness of the technocratic consciousness.[32]

Technology needs critical evaluation and the critical discourse of ideology to safeguard its cultural role. Technology and ideology exist in a needed dialectical tension in which each helps to define the other and in which some types of syntheses are inevitably required.

THE DIALECTIC OF OPENING, CLOSING, AND INFORMATION ADAPTATION

Sociologist Orrin Klapp has developed a model of social order based on human communication behavior and adaptive responses to our information-filled environment and information-processing challenges. After evaluating major historical models and recent models of social order, including philosophical, religious, scientific, and political models, and while valuing contributions from these multidisciplinary sources, Klapp presents an information-processing-based systems model of social order. Some key contributing elements in Klapp's theory are outlined below.

Life itself is a process of communication behavior and information processing. All environmental and cultural systems, biological, psychological, sociological, and technological, are life processes or extensions of life processes playing the same game. Life is built on and functions by information. Klapp says that, in broad terms, he would "define the game of life as the effort of living things, from the cell to the society, to win information from the environment and to build their own order – whether or not at the expense of others." Survival of species is based on "the game against entropy," which "is played by taking and using information, whether as organic molecules and genes . . . or as codes, habits, memories, knowledge, and culture." Klapp notes Quastler's biological calculation "that a bacterium contains one thousand bits of information–a particular pattern as unlikely as a coin toss turning up 'heads' one thousand times in a row.'"[33] Life feeds on and is organized by information from the cell to the cultural system.

Information processing as the basis of the cultural system requires the proper quantities of information, including avoidance of information overload; hence, it necessitates a rhythm or dialectic of opening and closing and strategies of information adaptation. Klapp documents information overload problems, which are compared to a "gigantic traffic jam" and consist of too much noise, auditorially and metaphorically, too many messages via television, advertising, office mail (electronic or other), or via too many books, journals, periodicals, and so forth, to monitor.[34] Daniel Bell reinforces Klapp's concern when he discusses "the end of the alexandrian library":

> Clearly, if the explosion in information continues, it cannot be handled by present means. If by 1985 the volume of information is four (low estimate) or seven times (high estimate) that of 1970, then some other ways must be found to organize this onslaught of babel. In one of these pleasant exercises that statisticians like to undertake, it is estimated that under present projections, the Yale University Library would need a permanent staff of 6,000 persons by the year 2040 to cope with the books and research reports that would be coming annually into the library.[35]

Bell observes that "automated information systems," including computerized indexing and abstracting services, on-line searching of databases, networking, and on-demand production of documents utilizing a framework of "specialized centers" and "large-scale networks" with a "national system," will do much to address such needs.[36]

Klapp observes that along with the rights of access to information and rights to communicate, we need rights of protection of privacy, freedom of information choice, and freedom from information overload. Excessive information becomes noise in our communication channels. Noise is "the chaos from which we try to construct meaning." While much noise is inevitable, noise based on information overload is entropic or anti-informational.[37]

A "crisis of social noise" is problematic for society as a whole and for information-rich elites who often in their specializations encounter too much of a good thing–too much information to process and use creatively. Some social movements, including environmentalism and perhaps antinuclear protest, and some consciousness and religious movements may be seen in part as reactions to too much or too intrusive information. Part of the protests of the sixties and early seventies, including parts of the student protest movement, involved challenges to technocratic and bureaucratic manipulations of individuals, where individuals were processed much like information and where the university, and especially the multiversity, became a type of knowledge industry, producing students according to preprogrammed specifications with possible loss of creativity, personhood, and existential freedom.[38]

How can the "crisis of social noise" and information overload be addressed? Klapp outlined a number of solutions built around a dialectic of opening and closing. Opening is a scanning for needed and desired information, an expansion and experimentation. Closing is a response to too much information, social noise, entropic communication, sometimes manifested by protest, withdrawal, alienation, or desire for selectivity and consolidation. Opening and closing occur as a natural rhythm in healthy individual and social systems. Each part of the dialectic is essential for adequate adaptation to information. The dialectic is a necessary strategy. Klapp observes:

> So we may think of opening and closing as part of a shifting strategy to get the most of the best information and the least of the worst noise, depending on a tradeoff in the signal-to-noise ratio. When the environment becomes adverse, from noise or information overload, more closing is needed. A society or person who tried to take in everything would be like a clam who tried to siphon all the sludge at the bottom of a bay. In strict accounting, every bit of information and noise, beauty, and ugliness enters the human reckoning. Oscillation between opening and closing is the normal way to play the game.[39]

"THE ESSENTIAL TENSION":
PRODUCTIVE INTERDISCIPLINARY AND INTERPARADIGMATIC CONFLICTS

Cultural model and paradigm refers to a society's creative self-interpretation, self-representation, and self-production, as structured processively in symbolic action, dialectical tensions, public debates and discourse, and sociocultural and scientific-technical movements (cf. Tillich, Touraine, Gouldner, Klapp, and Kuhn). *Cultural model* is the broader term. It refers to the linkage of interdisciplinary elements important in structuring social systems and is characterized as interparadigmatic, linking various paradigms or normative conceptualizations and ways of practicing various arts and sciences, all existing through human communication behavior, increasingly mediated through information processing technologies with various paradigms requiring diverse information literacies. Several elements in Thomas Kuhn's work, particularly *The Essential Tension,* which updates and revises parts of his earlier *The Structure of Scientific Revolutions,* are observed as contributory to a broader cultural model and paradigm related to human communication behavior and information processing technology.[40]

Hermeneutic discovery was for Kuhn a discovery of his first scientific revolution. Noting that Galileo and Descartes created a way of reading texts, Kuhn says that reading Aristotle (observe the value of this literacy in scientific interpretation) revealed to him a universal change in the way humans perceived nature and related language to it.[41] Scientific revolutions produce and are produced by new ways of reading or interpreting and symbolizing reality. Part of a cultural model and paradigm concerns how scientific-technical revolutions are caused by changes and reflect changes in the ways we read, conceptualize, and communicate particular ways of seeing the world. Turing's man, for example, represents a type of technologically based worldview. We need to understand the underlying assumptions and implications of each of our technologies.

Sociological and persuasive factors also shape scientific communities and revolutions. Kuhn regards symbolically induced and "professionally shared imperatives" as vital to scientific progress. He argues that theories are not determined by apodictic proof but utilize "techniques of persuasion" and "argument and counterargument in a situation in which there can be no proof." Theory selection depends upon a combination of subjective and objective factors: "Empirical facts are not simply given; they must be contended for, brought into conformity with theory and experience, and established as more viable than their theoretic competitors."[42]

Paradigms (Kuhn also uses the term *disciplinary matrix*)[43] are a product of debates even in the history of science. Scientific revolutions stemming from and producing paradigm changes are based not only on manipulation of objective phenomena but on how these phenomena are symbolized and interpreted. Translation, persuasion, consensus, and even conversions (of scientific conviction) are involved. Paradigm changes are changes in the way a community or communities view nature and apply symbolic codes to it. As humans produce history through social conflicts and public debate and discourse, so in scientific change, not always as visibly to the public, new paradigms and ways of communicating are produced; science, technology, and history are human, cultural creations.

Kuhn's distinction between consensual and divergent thinking is significant for the tension between disciplinary and interdisciplinary approaches to cultural models and paradigms. The most productive theory and research require adaptive responses to inevitable conflicts between these basic modes of thought:

> Scientific revolution and progress, he believes, comes through consensual attention to central problems with commonly shared assumptions and methodologies. While divergent thinking, the liberty to explore many areas and use varied approaches, is important, convergent thinking is equally

essential to scientific advance. The essential tension is between these two necessary modes of thought. Since these patterns are inevitably in conflict, it follows that "the ability to support a tension that can occasionally become almost unbearable is one of the prime requisites for the very best sort of scientific research."[44]

While consensus and rule-governed research grounded in scientific tradition seems most likely to produce revolutionary changes in science, there is still an important role in science (and in the other arts, social sciences, and humanities) for divergent thinking. The "essential tension" is an inevitable but productive area of interdisciplinary and interparadigmatic conflict and consensus. This dialectical conflict, both ideologically and scientifically, is productive, creative, and sometimes revolutionary.

The "essential tension" in scientific investigation appears in researchers' "needs to adopt a network of intellectual and procedural commitments and in their capacity for relinquishing this network for a new framework created by themselves."[45] As theorists and researchers develop interdisciplinary approaches to new information processing technologies and related literacies and consider impacts and relevant modes of analysis, recognizing the "essential tension" as productive of the best scientific research offers an encouragement and a challenge.

"THE NEW COMMUNICATIONS":
CONVERGING SCIENTIFIC AND TECHNICAL REVOLUTIONS, INTERMEDIA INFLUENCES, INDIVIDUAL/SOCIAL NEEDS, AND INFORMATION LITERACIES

Human communication behavior and information processing technology, termed the "new communications," reflect a converging of scientific and technical revolutions, an interaction of media forms and influences, that call for a well-considered balancing of individual (existential), social, and technological needs and potentials, including new and revitalized information literacies. Before proceeding to a final section outlining some further important issues, prospects, and applications in information creation, transmission, and management, this section offers some perspectives on the "new communications," drawing from communication theorist Frederick Williams.

An effective cultural model and paradigm requires synthesis of historical, theoretical, and professional concerns related to the various contexts of communication, especially intermedia variables. It is useful to compare and understand the development of traditional media and new technologies. Continued research, theorizing, and critical evaluation are needed as to how historical and contemporary communications media and associated information literacies interact and how they shaped and are shaping our sociocultural situation. Historical and theoretical perspectives are needed regarding interactions of print media, photography, radio and television broadcasting (including their educational use and impact), audiovisual recording devices, cable, satellite, and computer communication systems.

Williams takes a position important for those encouraged by recognizing significant continuity and somewhat less discontinuity in the converging technological revolutions, particularly merging developments in computing and telecommunications. While holding that motives for human communication are essentially constant and new communication technologies inherently extend earlier media, Williams contends that contemporary use of the spectrum of available media manifests three broad changes: *specialized* use of new media, use of *"combined capabilities* for voice, image, and text in the same communication systems," and use of "computers and digital encoding to *automate* many aspects of the transmission and formalities of messages [emphasis added]."[46]

In the new communication technologies we are still, although in some significant alternative ways, encoding, storing, and transmitting "texts and/or images"; there is considerable continuity between traditional and contemporary communication purposes of informing, instructing, entertaining, and persuading. Most information processing technologies extend earlier developments, often reflecting the interrelatedness of communication contexts and activities, although their effects are sometimes revolutionary.[47]

ISSUES, PROSPECTS, AND APPLICATIONS IN INFORMATION CREATION, TRANSMISSION, AND MANAGEMENT

In the preceding sections of this paper, seven propositions or subtheses were outlined relative to the central thesis that culture exists in symbolic action. Information was seen as the basis for symbolic action, and symbolic action as the basic unit of cultural production. Symbolic action was seen as generating both social cooperation and/or conflict and as instrumental in the struggle to develop cultural models, as well as the struggle for the control of a society's historicity. This symbolic action as the basic unit of cultural production includes a dialectical conflict between ideology and technology and involves an alternation and conflict between opening and closing, requiring information adaptation strategies. An "essential tension" was seen as related to productive interdisciplinary and interparadigmatic conflicts, which can lead to scientific revolutions. The "new communications" were seen as reflecting a convergence of scientific and technical revolutions and as exhibiting intermedia influences that call for a balancing of social needs, including new and revitalized information literacies. The final sections of this paper outline some issues, prospects, and applications, with related observations and contentions, that extend this paper's perspectives. These draw further upon interdisciplinary theory and research sources. These observations are necessarily selective but are intended to provide a further framework for consideration of needs, concerns, and potentials.

ISSUES

1. *What are information literacies? My position is that the issue of information literacies expresses a concern for total symbolic development. Literacy involves the ability to use the appropriate symbol system in the appropriate context.*[48] Literacy is contextual. One can be literate in one context and semiliterate or illiterate in another. *Illiteracy exists where symbol-using skills are inadequate to a relevant situation.* Within a concern for total symbolic development, literacy is a communications ability, an information processing ability, an ability to encode, transmit, and decode messages – translatable symbols and signs – in a relevant context.

2. *What information literacies may be necessary as we move into the twenty-first century?* Perhaps to answer this, a prophetic or predictive literacy may be required. Projecting from current needs and developments, it appears a variety of electronic-oriented technological and also traditional (but rather differently expressed) literacies will be required. As Chandler points out, even voice-controlled computers of the future will still express the basic nature of all literacy-requiring technologies as "systems for manipulating symbols."[49] My position is that comprehensive but selectively developed literacies for particular contexts will be required, including, for example, reading, writing, visual, auditory (listening), computer, and media use literacies. In my view, interdisciplinary literacies are necessary. While specialization is understandable and necessary in complex societies, it is and would be tragic and threatening to produce students who are computer-literate and technologically literate but semiliterate or illiterate in history, art, music, literature, and other social and cultural studies and skills. Likewise, it may be equally tragic and dangerous to produce students in the social sciences and humanities who are semiliterate or illiterate in at least basic information processing technology skills.

3. *How can the power of information literacies as agents of sociocultural reform be recognized?* Kozol and others recognize the power of literacies as historical and cultural forces.[50] The transmission of social values, maintenance of basic human rights, and development of human resource potentials – economic, political, religious, social, scientific, and so forth – all depend in significant ways upon information literacies. Similarly, crime, urban decay, unemployment, social strife, and wasted human resources are often substantially attributable to literacy deficiencies. Information literacies

should be given top priority in our national and education agendas, and programs for literacy development need continued attention.

4. Numerous *particular issues* stem from the functioning of human communication behavior and information processing technology and from the question of related literacies. Some additional issues, cited representatively here, include those of information access, management, and control; standardization and regulation; effects upon users (including ergonomics); the marketing and transfer of high technology; military, industrial, and educational uses and implications; questions of security, privacy, accuracy, computer crime, and ethics; and the development of national and international communication networks.[51]

PROSPECTS AND APPLICATIONS

The prospects and applications in the interaction of human communication behavior and information processing technology are revolutionary in potential. In concluding this paper, three areas of such potential are briefly considered.

1. *What are the limits of miniaturization in encoding information and knowledge? How far may the "micro revolution" extend?* Future historians of science, technology, and culture will be required to map the extent of the movements and revolutionary developments now in process. A few examples may suggest some of the remarkable potentials involved.

Micro storage potentials are increasingly impressive. Laurie points out that "a digitally recorded TV medium like the Philips laser-read disc will hold about 4,000 books."[52] Large, in discussing the revolutionary potentials of silicon chips, points out:

> Today's chips are so intricate that the latest designs put the equivalent of a street map of greater London, back alleys and all, into each of those quarter-inch fragments. One of the more expensive desktop computers of 1982 contained chips which each held 600,000 components—more than the number of parts in a jumbo jet. Those components were packed so tightly that 25,000 would sit on a pinhead, and the lines carrying the messages around were no thicker than one 60-millionth of an inch. A team of five such chips, providing the computer's calculating heart, could transfer information eighteen million times a second. That computer worked a hundred times faster than its 1972 equivalent, was more than a hundred times smaller, and was about ten times cheaper in real terms.[53]

Extending the concept of these potentials, Large cites corporate futurist Earl Joseph of Sperry Computers (now Unisys), who predicts, perhaps hazardously but intriguingly,

> that the pocket office will arrive in the 1990s, to be quickly followed by the "information centre" worn as an ornament—the equivalent of the Library of

Congress tappable from your wrist. The 1990s will also see the first miniaturised factories, run by "intelligent" robots directing other robots. [Joseph] forecasts 2010 as the year of the ultimate victory of miniaturisation – the capacity of the human brain within one tiny chip.[54]

If the projected timetable is possibly too optimistic, perhaps the important conclusion is rendered by Large when he says, "We are not yet touching the limits of miniaturization."[55] How will such potentials affect our universities, libraries, learning centers, and means of educating? Much will depend on the dialectic of ideology and technology, and upon what models we create and how we choose through public debate as well as corporate and personal policy (including the dialectic of opening and closing) to shape our historicity in the face of such possibilities. The prospects are comparable to those of our space program: we don't have to be there, but we can be if we make the commitment.

2. *How do we respond when "'intelligence' no longer means, uniquely, human intelligence?"* This question is posed by computer artist Harold Cohen, cited in Bishop's *Fifth Generation Computers:* "We may be living on the wave-front of the most far-reaching cultural revolution in human history, but beliefs change slowly, and we have yet to come to terms with the fact that 'intelligence' no longer means, uniquely, human intelligence."[56]

How will developments in artificial intelligence ("the science of making machines do things that would require intelligence if done by people")[57] affect our learning situations and processes? Again, historical action and debate will help answer this question, but in an era of expert systems playing chess, making medical diagnoses, interviewing people, "seeing," "acting," "speaking" (electronically, synthetically), and performing numerous other functions, it is obvious that prospects are exhaustive. If these functions are occurring in an era of fifth-generation computers and their robotic subsystems, what will sixth- and seventh-generation computer systems and beyond bring? While philosophically and pragmatically distinctions can be made fairly clearly between human and artificial or synthetic intelligence, the functions of these kinds of machine intelligence are still impressive. Already, expert systems can outstore, and in some cases outperform and outthink, human counterparts. Creative computer functioning – computers that can learn, teach, create – appear increasingly in prospect as we move toward the twenty-first century. Forsyth, in discussing machine learning, says, "The exciting thing about machine learning is that it represents one more step away from programming," which is prescribing how to do something, "towards instructing (specifying what goals we want achieved)." As Forsyth says, "The age of the creative computer is about to begin."[58]

As we move partly beyond programming to increased artificial intelligence, there are exciting possibilities. Scientific and technological development appears closer to passing Turing's test for the substitution of a human interactant with a computer.[59] In evaluating the field, Yazdani says, "Artificial intelligence (AI) is concerned with constructing computer programs which exhibit abilities associated with human beings, such as understanding natural language, solving problems, playing games, as well as learning for itself."[60]

The prospects for and applications of artificial intelligence are dramatic. Sherry Turkle observes that mathematician and cybernetics founder Norbert Wiener, impressed by the computer program that defeated at chess its creator, Arthur Samuel, "suggested that the implications bordered on the theological: 'Can God play a significant game with his own creature? Can any creator, even a limited one, play a significant game with his own creature?'"[61]

The development of such potentials, including the use of interactive and mass media in educational, social, and corporate environments, constitutes a continuing revolution.

3. *What kinds of models and paradigms are desirable as we address the revolutionary impacts of information processing technology?* A case has been made for an interdisciplinary, interparadigmatic approach that involves recognizing information as the basis for symbolic action, and symbolic action as the basic unit of cultural production. Information processing technology enhances our ability to act symbolically. The dialectic of this action is expressed in information adaptation strategies, in tensions between paradigms and modes of thinking, and it calls for a balancing of existential, social, and technological needs, including new and revitalized information literacies. In order to achieve such a balancing, interdisciplinary approaches incorporating elements of various arts and sciences, including communicative, historical, social, scientific, and technological concerns, will be required. If culture exists in symbolic action, then the shaping of its symbolic maps, based on the models for which we contend, is ours to determine. We shape our technology and afterwards it shapes us.

Notes

1. This study partly extends and applies, drawing upon new sources and subject matter, selected philosophical and theoretical perspectives inceptively developed in Donald E. Phillips, "Communication and Conflict: Social Movement Studies as Interdisciplinary Social and Cultural Science Synthesis," paper presented at the annual meeting of the Popular Culture/American Culture Association, Montreal, Canada, March 28, 1987.

2. Attributed to Churchill in Dr. Paul Barefield's course in British Public Address, University of Oklahoma, summer 1971.

3. Raymond Williams, "The Analysis of Culture," in *Culture, Ideology, and Social Process*, eds. Tony Bennett, Graham Martin, Colin Mercer, and

Janet Woollacott (London: Set-Batsford Academic and Educational/Open University Press, 1981), 47.

4. Thomas S. Kuhn, *The Essential Tension: Selected Studies in Scientific Tradition and Change* (Chicago: University of Chicago Press, 1977).

5. Cf. Franklin H. Knower, "What Do You Mean–Communication?" *Central States Speech Journal* 21 (1970): 18-23, for an identification of dimensions of the term *communication*, including the concept of "stimulus response behavior."

6. Norbert Wiener, *The Human Use of Human Beings: Cybernetics and Society* (Garden City, N.Y.: Anchor-Doubleday, 1954), 17; Daniel Bell, "The Social Framework of the Information Society," in *The Computer Age: A Twenty-Year View*, eds. Michael L. Dertouzos and Joel Moses (Cambridge, Mass.: MIT Press, 1979), 168; for references to Wiener, Cherry, and Boulding, cf. Hamid Mowlana, *Global Information and World Communication* (New York: Longman, 1986), 167.

7. Peter Bishop, *Fifth Generation Computers: Concepts, Implementations, and Uses* (Chichester, Eng.: Ellis Horwood; New York: Halsted-John Wiley, 1986), 17, 27-28.

8. Hiroshi Inose and John R. Pierce, *Information Technology and Civilization* (New York: W. H. Freeman, 1984), 122, 125.

9. Quoted in Jeffrey C. Alexander, *Twenty Lectures: Sociological Theory since World War II* (New York: Columbia University Press, 1987), 289, 304-7.

10. Alexander, *Twenty Lectures,* 289, 304-7; Paul Tillich, *Systematic Theology* (Chicago: University of Chicago Press, 1967), III, 66-69; Paul Tillich, *Theology of Culture*, ed. Robert C. Kimball (New York: Galaxy-Oxford University Press, 1964), 46-47.

11. Cf. James G. Miller, "Living Systems: Structure and Process," *Behavioral Science* 10 (1965): 337-79.

12. Sherry Turkle, *The Second Self: Computers and the Human Spirit* (New York: Simon and Schuster, 1984).

13. James M. Curtis, *Culture as Polyphony: An Essay on the Nature of Paradigms* (Columbia, Mo.: University of Missouri Press, 1978) 62, citing Ernst Kapp, *Grunlinien einer Philosophie der Technik* (Braunschweig: George Westermann, 1877).

14. Donald E. Phillips, *Student Protest, 1960-1970: An Analysis of the Issues and Speeches,* revised ed., with a comprehensive bibliography (Lanham, Md.: University Press of America, 1985), 64.

15. Tillich, *Systematic Theology*, III, 68-69.

16. J. W. Freiburg, foreword, in Alain Touraine, *The Self-Production of Society*, trans. Derek Coltman (Chicago: University of Chicago Press, 1977), xiii-xiv.

17. Alain Touraine, *The Voice and the Eye: An Analysis of Social Movements*, trans. Alan Duff (Cambridge, Eng.: Cambridge University Press; Paris: Editions de La Maison des Sciences de L'Homme, 1981), 6.

18. Phillips, "Communication and Conflict," 8.

19. Cf. Peter Laurie, *The Micro Revolution: Living with Computers* (New York: Universe, 1981); Peter Large, *The Micro Revolution Revisited* (Rowman and Allanheld, N.J.: Francis Pinter, 1984); Howard Gardner, *The Mind's New Science: A History of the Cognitive Revolution* (New York: Basic Books, 1985); James R. Beniger, *The Control Revolution: Technological and Economic Origins of the Information Society* (Cambridge, Mass.: Harvard University Press, 1986).

20. Touraine, *Voice and Eye*, 14-15.

21. Touraine, *Self-Production*, 19.

22. Ibid., 74-75, 95, 298, 378-79.

23. Alvin W. Gouldner, *The Dialectic of Ideology and Technology: The Origins, Grammar, and Future of Ideology* (New York: Continuum-Seabury, 1976), 17.

24. J. David Bolter, *Turing's Man: Western Culture in the Computer Age* (Chapel Hill: University of North Carolina Press, 1984), 9.

25. Ibid., 11.

26. Ibid., 13.

27. Ibid.

28. Ibid.

29. Ibid., 238.

30. Gouldner, *Ideology and Technology*, 31-33, 39, 53, 68, 84.

31. Ibid., 93, 18-30, 105.

32. Ibid., 243.

33. Orrin E. Klapp, *Models of Social Order* (Palo Alto, Calif.: National Press Books, 1973); Klapp, *Opening and Closing: Strategies of Information Adaptation in Society* (Cambridge, Eng.: Cambridge University Press, 1978), 154-55.

34. Klapp, *Opening and Closing*, 47-48.

35. Bell, "The Social Framework of the Information Society," 191.

36. Ibid., 191-92.

37. Klapp, *Opening and Closing*, 1, 5, 44.

38. Ibid., 10, 18; Phillips, *Student Protest*, 6, 7, 248-49.

39. Klapp, *Opening and Closing*, 20.

40. Cf. Kuhn, *Essential Tension*, and Thomas S. Kuhn, *The Structure of Scientific Revolutions*, 2d ed. (Chicago: University of Chicago Press, 1970).

41. Kuhn, *Structure of Scientific Revolutions*, x-xiii.

42. Ibid., 320; Donald E. Phillips, "Inevitable Conflict" (review of *The Essential Tension* by Thomas S. Kuhn), *Journal of Communication* (Spring 1980): 206.

43. Kuhn, *Essential Tension*, 307-19.

44. Ibid., 226; Phillips, "Inevitable Conflict," 206.

45. Kuhn, *Essential Tension*, 237; Phillips, "Inevitable Conflict," 206.

46. Frederick Williams, *The New Communications* (Belmont, Calif. : Wadsworth, 1984), 172; Donald E. Phillips, "The New Communications" (review of *The New Communications* by Frederick Williams), *Kansas Speech Journal* (Spring/Summer 1987): 23-24.

47. Williams, *New Communications*, 174.

48. Cf. Merald W. Wrolstad and Dennis F. Fisher, eds., *Toward a New Understanding of Literacy* (New York: Praeger, 1986), x, 3, 39; Richard Sinatra, *Visual Literacy Connection to Thinking, Reading, and Writing* (Springfield, Ill.: Charles C. Thomas, 1986), 4, 33; David Harman, *Illiteracy: A National Dilemma* (New York: Cambridge Adult Education, 1987), 2-4.

49. Daniel Chandler and Stephen Marcus, eds., *Computers and Literacy* (Milton Keynes, Eng.: Open University Press, 1985), 4.

50. Johnathan Kozol, *Illiterate America* (Garden City, N.Y.: Anchor-Doubleday, 1985).

51. Cf. Hamid Mowlana, George Gerbner, and Marsha Siefert, eds., *World Communications: A Handbook* (New York: Longman, 1984); B. G. Pearce, ed., *Health Hazards of VDTs?* (New York: John Wiley, 1984); Herbert S. Dordick, Helen G. Bradley, and Burt Nanus, *The Emerging Network Marketplace* (Norwood, N.J.: Albex, 1981).

52. Laurie, *Micro Revolution*, 41.

53. Large, *Micro Revolution Revisited*, 2-3.

54. Ibid., 17.

55. Ibid., 26.

56. Bishop, *Fifth Generation Computers,* 25.

57. Ibid., 30; cf. Masoud Yazdani, ed., *Artificial Intelligence: Principles and Applications* (London: Chapman and Hall, 1986), 31.

58. Richard Forsyth, "Machine Learning," in Yazdani, *Artificial Intelligence*, 206, 223.

59. Cf. Bishop, *Fifth Generation Computers*, 30; John Haugeland, *Artificial Intelligence: The Very Idea* (Cambridge, Mass.: Bradford-MIT Press, 1985), 133.

60. Yazdani, *Artificial Intelligence*, 33.

61. Turkle, *Second Self,* 279, citing Norbert Wiener, *God and Golem, Inc.* (Cambridge, Mass.: MIT Press, 1964), 17.

The Unique Characteristics of Information Policy and Their U.S. Consequences

SANDRA BRAMAN

In most areas in which policy is made, such as defense and agriculture, decision-makers and analysts have the use of tools and experience developed over hundreds of years. In contrast, (1) information has only recently come to be an area of explicit policymaking focus in nations around the globe. This fact contributes to other unique characteristics of information policymaking in every nation-state and internationally: (2) Information is atypical among issue areas in the unusually large number and diversity of players and decision-making arenas. (3) Decisions made about information have an enormous impact on events and policy made in other issue areas, while the reverse is true to a far lesser degree. (4) Information does not fit into categories used by traditional policy analysis tools. (5) Information policy made at different levels of the political and social structure, from the local to the global, is remarkably interdependent.

These general characteristics combine with an additional source of complexity in the United States, a multiplicity of conflicting but contemporaneously applicable regulatory systems, resulting in four types of problems for information policymaking: conceptual, informational, structural, and orientational.

CHARACTERISTICS OF INFORMATION POLICY

Political scientists group together issues that are related to the same subject into what they term "issue areas" (Potter 1980; Rosati 1981; Sampson 1982; Underdal 1981; Zimmerman 1973). Information is a newcomer as an issue area, only recently receiving specific attention.

Consensual approaches to thinking about particular policy issue areas in ways that provide a basis for decision-making are called "regimes." A regime may be conceptualized as a normative and regulatory international framework or "meta-agreement" (Keohane and Nye 1977) that is less rigid and formal than a legal system but nonetheless serves to bind all parties involved. A regime sets operational definitions, establishes a hierarchy of values, and sets negotiating rules and procedures; an information policy analyst has called a regime "an organizing device which focuses on converging expectations regarding principles, norms, rules and procedures in particular issue areas" (McDowell 1987, 5). Regimes vary in degree of formality, with the General Agreement on Tariffs and Trade (GATT) often cited as the classic model (Holsti 1978; Kegley 1985; Keohane 1980, 1982; Krasner 1982a, 1982b, 1983; Rosenau 1984).

Because of the recency of the emergence of information as an issue area, an information policy regime is just now evolving. Porat (1977) claims that building a coherent national policy in this area is not possible until the nature of the regime becomes clear. Others acknowledge that the recency of efforts in this field further complicates an already difficult decision-making process (Dunn 1982; Nora and Minc 1980; Woolcock 1984). Noll and Owen (1983) point out that not only are regimes the creation of special interests, their emergence will create and destroy groups with special economic concerns. All parties involved in the battle over the shape of the emerging information policy regime have high stakes.

This characteristic of recency is one of several that make information atypical among issue areas. It certainly distinguishes information from relatively ancient issue areas, such as defense and agriculture. Only a decade ago, some U.S. policymakers viewed information only as that aspect of policy that had to do with selling its goals (Deibel and Roberts 1976). In the evolutionary information policy review process described by Rowland (1982), the United States is still at an early stage.

Today, however, information is central among U.S. concerns. As Porat predicted in 1978, with recognition of the growing role of information in the economy, information matters have come to the center of the policy agenda. Diana Lady Dougan, the lead information policymaker for the State Department under the Reagan administration, makes clear why: "We know that the manipulation and control of information are among the greatest weapons of conquest in the modern world. We know, above all, that information is power – more valuable than oil and more precious than gold" (1983, 1).

A second way in which information policy is atypical among issue areas is that an unusually large number of players and types of players have traditionally been involved with it. In contrast to an issue area like tuna, in which a fairly restricted group of players has a tradition of involvement and there are few ambiguities regarding appropriate or necessary participants, literally dozens of entities – governmental, quasi-nongovernmental, and private – have a history of interest in matters related to information policy. Bortnick (1983), Bushkin and Yurow (1980), Dizard (1982), Leeson (1984), Oettinger (1977), and others have provided exhaustive catalogings of players active in the United States. They include states, municipalities, and each branch of the federal government. Within any single branch of government several different agencies can be involved, often in direct conflict with each other; the State Department, for example, has long been battling the Commerce Department for control in this area, and both are at loggerheads with the White House. In one example described by Smythe (1981), the single issue of electronic funds transfer systems has been explored by at least four different committees of the House of Representatives, none of which has enough authority to deal with all the technological, financial, and regulatory questions raised by the possibility of such a system.

In addition to making laws, a number of policy tools are available to elements of the government. Procurement, particularly at the federal level, shapes private-sector development of products and services by defining the most influential market. The federal government also has privileged access to information, including property rights in all information produced under its aegis (Greenstein 1984) and the right to demark certain categories of information (about cryptography, or nuclear energy, for example) as off-limits for anyone outside of government (Cheh 1982). The government's self-governing activities offer another means through which information policy can be made (OTA 1981). The most vivid current example of this is the implementation of Office of Management and Budget (OMB) Circular A-130, dictating rules for the collection, processing, and distribution of information by federal agencies (Sprehe 1987). Other tools available at any level of government include institution building, the appointment power, establishment of special commissions, and support for research and development. Oversight activities and the "raised eyebrow" also have their utility.

The most important players in the United States in information policymaking, however, are those outside of government, in the private sector. There are three routes of private-sector influence on the government. The private sector often fills a policymaking vacuum left by inaction or confused action on the part of governmental entities, as in corporate representation of U.S. interests in international policymaking bodies such as the International Telecommunications Union (ITU). The private sector also heavily influences governmental policymaking processes, as in corporate "capture" of the regulatory agencies governing their activities so that corporate interests weigh heavily in the decision-making calculus (Krasnow, Longley, and Terry 1984). Control over the information upon which government decision-makers base their policy is another key form of power. Last, the private sector and its decision-making procedures (Chandler 1977) are structural forces that in and of themselves bias the decision-making process. This centrality of nongovernmental decision-makers multiplies the problems of attaining consistency across the policy range and consensus among policymakers.

Third, information policy decisions affect other issue areas to a unique extent. Discussions of the wide social and political impact of information policy, such as that by Halloran (1986), implicitly make this point. The ways in which other issue areas have an information policy component occur on many levels. Since production and trade of goods inextricably involve information flow (and increasingly so as these activities are computerized), policies that deal with information inevitably affect goods as well. More profoundly, the importance of information as a constitutive force in society means that decisions about information affect large portions of society and therefore influence the making and implementation of policy in other issue areas. Because information creation, flows, and use play such a heavy role in determining how society itself will be shaped, the sphere of impact in information policy provides the context in which policymaking for other issue areas is carried out.

Fourth, information does not fit easily into traditional typifications of issue areas as "high" (defense, for example) or "low" (tuna). As Stoil notes, information is atypical because it "is both 'low' policy in the sense that it deals with fairly arcane subjects outside the usual realm of State Department expertise; it is 'high' policy in the sense that its impacts in the 1980s provides big pay-offs for a large number of powerful domestic actors" (1983, 106). The rising salience of information is thus contributing to a global shifting of policymaking priorities (Cruise O'Brien 1980; Oettinger 1977).

Fifth, information policy made at different levels of the social structure is highly interdependent, reflecting the contribution of new modes of information processing, distribution, and use to expanding and deepening global technological, economic, social, political, and cultural interdependence (Boettinger 1984; Cerni 1982; Cerni and Gray 1983; Dewandre 1986; Halloran 1986; Hamelink 1984; Pipe 1984; Rutkowski 1981, 1983). Thus, there is a need for harmonization of regulatory systems from different decision-making arenas, both public and private and both within and across the boundaries of nation-states. Any single domestic regulatory system has import both for the international arena and for other domestic systems. Wall (1984) points out that it is in the area of information policy that the European Economic Commission (EEC) for the first time explicitly applied commission law to member states. Of course, not all domestic regulatory systems have the same degree of impact internationally; the U.S. system clearly is the most significant, to the degree that it has been accused of deliberately attempting to exercise its regulatory powers extraterritorially – that is, to apply domestic law outside the boundaries of the United States (Bruce 1981, 1985; Goldberg 1985; Marchand 1981). Pragmatically, global coordination can enhance the possibilities for worldwide acceptance of U.S. policy (Leeson 1984). Renaud (1987) argues that this interdependence is a positive good, forcing developed countries to take the needs and concerns of developing countries into account. Spero, a less sanguine commentator, feels only that, "with interdependence, greater and more constant consultation, cooperation, and even policy coordination are necessary to avoid intolerable disruptions of national and international economies" (1981, 83).

Interdependence also characterizes information policy within a single nation-state. In the United States, the federal government, the states, and the municipalities are all involved, with international problems played over again at the interstate level. As a result, federalism is a key information policy issue (Hanks and Coran 1986; Noam 1983). Lee and Sloan (1987), for example, describe how decisions at the level of the local exchange influence policymaking at other levels. Meanwhile, governmental policy also interacts with decisions made by private decision-makers. This interdependence of regulation at different levels of the social structure is seen both as necessary (Soma et al. 1983) and as a potential "policy trap" (Pepper and Brotman 1987). It is an old habit – the 1934 Communications Act intermingled municipal, national, and foreign policy at the same time in Section 222 by demarking an international telecommunications arena distinct from the domestic and designating five cities as gateways for information flows across the border.

In sum, the policy issue area of information is distinguished internationally from other issue areas by five characteristics: recency of recognition, number of players and types of players, extent of effect upon other issue areas, lack of fit with traditional ways of categorizing policy issues, and degree of interdependence among information policies of different levels of the social structure. A policymaking regime for information is only now evolving, with its final shape still unclear.

DEFINING THE INFORMATION POLICY DOMAIN

In an emergent policy area, the domain must be defined so as to include not only policy that is manifest, or visibly pertinent, to the issue area; policy that is latent, existing but not visible, must be included as well.

This notion of latent policy has gained currency in a variety of fields (Cardozo 1921; Lambright 1976; Skocpol 1985; Trauth 1986). Policy can develop in a latent form in several ways. It can be policy that pertains to one subject area but is created as a side effect of decisions aimed at other subject areas altogether. Regulation developed by the Securities and Exchange Commission (SEC), for example, is directed toward management of financial markets and consumer protection but affects information policy as particular modes of information creation and flows by specific classes of people and organizations are developed. Ploman (1982b), Middleton and Chamberlin (1988), and Branscomb (1986) all point to sources of this type of latent information policy in their law texts. Latent policy can also develop when its subject matter is categorized under other names–what has traditionally been considered communication law, for example, is certainly information policy as well. Latent policy can develop synergistically when bits of policy from a variety of decision-making arenas interact to produce something quite different in combination. Because the whole can be more than the sum of its parts, interactions among policies that made sense on their own can produce totally unexpected results. Aines (1986) points to an additional way latent policy can develop–through collisions and frictions between groups within the government, between government and the private sector, and among factions in the private sector.

The combination of latent and manifest information policy produces a field that has been variously defined. A common approach has been to simply list subjects that should be included. Pool (1983), for example, does this when he defines the domain to include availability of resources (raw materials, money, and labor), organization of access to resources (by market, rationing, taxation, and so forth), and regulation and probems encountered at system boundaries (such as transborder data flow [TBDF] and censorship). Dunn (1982) lists four types of applications to be addressed by information policy–creation, distribution/communication, storage and retrieval, and use/application. Leeson (1984) lists five areas of information policy: technical knowledge and its diffusion, physical components, structure of facilities and networks, services offered and terms and conditions of use of facilities and networks, and treatment of communicated information itself. For the British Tunstall (1986b), aerospace defense research and development and industrial planning should be included as well.

Other writers consider information policy within the context of economic policy in general (Halloran 1981; Neu, Neumann, and Schnoring 1987; Picard 1985). For Vizas (in Straus 1982, 75), information policy is that which has an impact on contractual obligations and relationships. For the National Telecommunications and Information Administration (NTIA), information policies are "policies about the conditions of information availability" (Bushkin and Yurow 1980, 2). Porat (1977) fits information policy issues within a framework built around the notions of infrastructure and superstructure.

Two problems with approaches that simply list items to be included are the danger that they leave something out and their inability to provide a guide to formation of coherent, overarching policy. The more abstract approaches provided by writers such as Halloran (1981) and Porat (1977) are more all-encompassing and intellectually consistent but do not provide a good match with the realities of the information marketplace. These are problems because, as Hedge and Mok (1987) note, at a minimum, policy study must be systematic and relevant to the needs of decision-makers.

A third type of approach, therefore, is used here: information policy is that which applies to every stage of the information production chain. The information production chain, in a formulation adapted from Machlup (1980) and Boulding (1966), includes information creation (creation, generation, and collection), processing (cognitive and algorithmic), transportation, distribution, storage, destruction, and seeking. This approach to defining the domain of information policy is all-inclusive, has heuristic and organizational value, provides a match between theory and real-world activities and modes of thinking, and is sensitive to both latent and manifest policy. It is among the advantages of this approach that it permits the exclusion of types of information, actors, or modes of processing from either specific or all stages of the chain, thus incorporating the sensitivities of those who resist the commoditization of information (or at least certain types of it), as well as the concerns of those eager to profit from the commoditization process.

CONFLICTING REGULATORY APPROACHES IN THE UNITED STATES

These general characteristics combine with an additional source of complexity in the United States: a multiplicity of conflicting but contemporaneously applicable regulatory systems. Pool (1983), in his deservedly influential *Technologies of Freedom*, describes sources of conflict among the print, broadcast, and common carriage regulatory systems in the United States. Branscomb (1983a) makes the further distinction between the print (mail) and electronic (telephone) common carriage systems (since they are governed by different sets of regulations), and between items treated distinctly within a single regulatory system, as broadcast and cable TV have been. There are various international regulatory systems (technical, political, economic, and so forth), as well as systems within each country with which bi- or multilateral agreements on information matters are sought (Feller and Jacobsen [1986] describe dozens of such agreements, which often conflict among themselves [OECD 1983].)

Other regulatory systems, developed in other bodies of law, also contribute to information policy. Intellectual property law (copyrights, patents, and trade secrets), for example, invests property rights in information production. SEC rules mandate specific types of information collection, storage, and transmission. Other types of forced information flow are required for compliance with the requirements of administrative agencies, from the Office of Safety and Health Administration (OSHA) to the Food and Drug Administration (FDA) and on. The Internal Revenue Service (IRS) generates its own type of forced information flow. Information industry questions appear throughout the history of antitrust law. In all of these areas, information policy is that which governs informational relationships among individuals, corporations, and the government.

Depending on how one counts, ultimately dozens of regulatory systems must be taken into account when trying to picture the whole of U.S. information policy. Not only does this make it difficult to conduct policy analysis, but many problems arise just because there is such a multiplicity of regulatory systems. Most information transmission or processing events are potentially governed by several conflicting regulatory systems at the same time. When the *Wall Street Journal,* for example, uses satellites to transmit its copy to printing plants around the country, with telephone lines carrying the information from the satellite receiving station to the printing plant, resulting in a printed newspaper delivered to the door by the traditional medium, a child, common carriage, broadcast, print, and child labor laws all apply. Examples of this problem proliferate as technological development continues to outpace societal responses.

In addition, the utility of specific regulatory tools is currently under attack. There is broad disagreement over the salience of behavioral, structural, and content regulation in the present environment. The many varieties of deregulation, unregulation, reregulation, and forbearance from regulation currently in use demonstrate the range of experimentation the country is going through.

Not only is there disagreement over the utility of these various types of regulatory tools, there is no consensus on an appropriate regulatory model. While the basic understanding of the nature and purpose of regulation have not changed–

> American regulation is a reflection of the democratic and egalitarian principles held by the Founding Fathers, especially their fear of centralized government power. Its organizing principle is that decisions should be based upon objective analysis in a process that allows people who are likely to be affected by the decision to have their views heard and considered. Elaborate rules regarding the rights of participation, the evidence pertaining to a decision, and the statutory basis for a policy action have developed to serve this principle. (Noll and Owen 1983, 13)

–there is growing disagreement over just what is meant by terms like *objective,* and over how to determine which parties are legitimate participants in the process. A number of regulatory models are contending, in a shifting legal environment (Grant 1985; Kling 1983; Panitch 1980; Schmitter 1985;

von Weizsacker 1986). Many commentators believe that developments in administrative law are the key to the future (Davis 1977; Geller 1983; Gellhorn and Byse 1970; Owen 1970; Pond 1983; Schwartz 1977), but exactly what those developments will be is not yet known. Uncertainty over the regulatory structure and the effectiveness and desirability of both traditional and new regulatory tools increases the difficulty of information policymaking.

PROBLEMS WITH THE U.S.
INFORMATION POLICYMAKING PROCESS

The effect of the general characteristics of information policy combined with the multiplicity of regulatory systems in place yields several problems with the decision-making process for information policy in the United States. Conceptual problems are those that derive from difficulties in perceiving, defining, and understanding particular issues. Informational problems are those that emerge from the ways in which information is provided to and used in the policymaking process. Structural problems are those difficulties that arise from conflicts or contradictions in the structure of the policymaking process. Orientational problems result from confusion over the goals of the policy process; these are the political, constitutive questions. While all of these types of problems are endemic to the policymaking process, they are exacerbated in this field by the rapidity of today's technological change.

CONCEPTUAL PROBLEMS

A myriad of conceptual problems has arisen in this area as a consequence of the outrunning of theoretical developments by technological change. As MacBride notes, "New technologies, advancing by their own momentum, often urged on by political pressure and economic requirements, impose themselves before they can be properly assessed or assimilated" (1986, vii).

Many conceptual problems arise from the clashes among conflicting regulatory structures (Goldberg 1985; Johnson 1986; NTIA 1985; Rowland 1982). Basic concepts like access and fairness mean different things within different regulatory systems. Other basic concepts, like diversity, and free flow, have received no adequate definition. There is even confusion over the nature of the thing to be regulated – is it a medium (Le Duc 1982), a message (Trauth, Trauth, and Huffman 1983), a stream of electrons (Noam 1987), or an enterprise or a market (Smythe 1981)? With such conceptual difficulties, policymakers may easily look at the wrong facts, arguments, or issues (Cornell, Pelcovits, and Brenner 1983).

Some problems stem from disagreements over regulatory philosophy. The meaning of a notion like "the public interest" is only clear if there is a consensus over the way the state should relate to the public. As Aufderheide notes, "Questions of public interest have been perhaps the most invoked but least engaged part of the recent debate" (1987, 81). She defines the term to mean universal access to and use of telecommunications; others would equate it with serving the needs of users (meaning primarily large corporate users) (NTIA 1985), or would support the FCC in equating it, today, with the marketplace (Frieden 1981, 1983; Haight 1979). Perhaps most realistically, Krugman and Reid define the public interest as "what the majority of Commissioners decide it is on any given day" (1980, 312), presumably just what President Truman feared when he opposed the inclusion of this criterion because he felt it would be used by special interests. They describe the public interest as fluid and changing from issue to issue. Krasnow, Longley, and Terry (1984) believe the attempt to fulfill the statutory mandate to heed the public interest has actually hampered the development of coherent policy, while Dougan (1983) points out that serving the public interest in some areas may have unintended effects–what is called here "latent policy"–in others. Stern, Krasnow, and Sunkowski (1983) believe that the requirement to serve the public interest may preclude the use of certain regulatory tools, such as forbearance, because these tools do not require specific cases to be examined individually, nor do they mandate governmental responses to public problems, needs, and/or interests.

A last cluster of conceptual problems comes from the four types of contradictory assumptions that underlie much of the debate over information policy matters. It is a contradiction to treat information as if it were a physical good; to treat information technologies as if they were separate and distinct; to treat technical issues as if they had no social, political, economic, or cultural consequences; and to act as if a free marketplace exists. These assumptions result in the building of legal fictions into the information regulatory environment, in which rules are made to govern an environment that does not actually exist.

The contradiction of treating information as if it were a good is embedded within several bodies of law. Irwin (1984) identifies additional incorrect regulatory assumptions that flow from this contradiction. As examples, he notes the assumptions that technological change is endogenous in origin and subject to corporate control, whereas it is also exogenous and subject to factors beyond the ability of any type of organization to govern; that technologies for provision of services are not fungible, when in fact in many instances they are; that economies of scale inevitably apply to the information industries, when that is not invariably the case; and that the various information services and industries are rigidly defined, when in fact they are shifting constantly.

A second contradiction that appears is treating information technologies as if they were separate and distinct. Despite technological convergence, technological distinctions that no longer exist continue to shape policy. Today's regulatory systems were designed around technologies that in the past seemed clearly distinct but are no longer so. While in the past one did not confuse a newspaper with a telephone call, today both might be received over a TV screen. Occasional lone voices, such as Bollinger's (1977), can be heard recommending the continued use of technological lines as bases for distinct regulatory systems, but these are certainly in the minority. The more common view is that it is illogical, pointless, and generally problematic to continue this way. According to Stern, Krasnow, and Sunkowski (1983), the FCC is turning to a functional approach as a way out. Trauth (1986) similarly suggests that information systems rather than technologies be used as an organizing approach.

A third contradiction is treating technical issues as if they have no social, economic, cultural, or political dimensions. The consequence of this assumption is that many critical decisions, such as choice of providers, transmission links, storage and processing facilities, software, and databases, have rarely been discussed in political arenas, remaining hidden under "the veil of technical options" (Rutkowski 1983, 20). In Skolnikoff's (1967) analysis, the cost of ignoring technological decisions is very high in the area of foreign policy goal attainment. Granger (1979) attributes much of the general failure of technology policy to the inability to cope with the social impacts of new technologies. Horwitz calls treating technical issues as if they had no other impacts a "smokecreen" (1986, 133) raised to protect control over other matters. To Noam, this problem can lead to an abdication, to shifting or hiding policymaking responsibilities:

> Hundreds of papers on ISDN have been published, virtually all of them from a technical perspective and with a near-total absence of acknowledgment of the economic and political issues involved. Virtually no public discussion of the ISDN concept and its investment needs has taken place. Instead, decisions in favor of ISDN have been made outside of public view by engineering bureaucracies in government and equipment firms. (1987, 44)

Matellart (1978) and Garnham (1983) offer an ideological critique of the conflation of the social, political, economic, and cultural with the technical. For Matellart, this phenomenon is inevitable, serving as an apolitical technocratic mask for the actual capitalist project. Garnham similarly sees ahistorical and asocial views of information as ideological support for the commoditization process. If the EEC rejection of an IBM communication protocol in favor of X.25 – a technological decision made for political, social, economic, and cultural reasons – is any indication, the Europeans are more sophisticated than the Americans in this regard.

A fourth contradiction that appears, acting as if a free marketplace exists, is described by Porat:

The impulse to place our faith in the market contravenes an unyielding empirical reality: the invisible hand has been preempted by a few million very visible bureaucrats. We have already acquiesced to a form of corporate socialism for our largest enterprises; those firms which are not directly regulated by the government are regulated by their managers. (1977, 330)

Chandler persuasively describes the replacement of the invisible hand with one that is visible and largely private-sector, rather than resting in government bureaucracies:

Modern business enterprises took the place of market mechanisms in coordinating the activities of the economy and allocating its resources. . . . The market remained the generator of demand for goods and services, but modern business enterprise took over the functions of coordinating flows of goods through existing processes of production and distribution, and of allocating funds and personnel for future production and distribution. As modern business enterprise acquired functions hitherto carried out by the market, it became the most powerful institution in the American economy and its managers the most influential group of economic decision makers. (1977, 1)

The constitutional problems that arise with the removal of key decisions from the public sector to the private, with management principles replacing political judgment in organizing society, were briefly discussed above. Additional problems arise from the conceptual slippage between the image of the marketplace and reality.

INFORMATIONAL PROBLEMS

There are two types of problems that emerge from the roles information itself plays in the policymaking process: those that stem from lack of information, and those that stem from the effects of the skewing of information.

There are many complaints that the information needed in order to make information policy decisions based on knowledge is not available. Snow (1985) notes that most current and past policy decisions have depended for validity on empirical support for assumptions that has not been available. Specific examples are rife. The GAO (1986) is upset over the inadequacy of FCC monitoring of telephone use. Horwitz (1986) criticizes the lack of information used in the rate-setting process, and AT&T dominance of what information there is. Levin (1986) claims that the entire body of FCC deregulatory decisions is based on bad, outdated, nonacademic, unscientific studies. Lee and Sloan (1987) note that the critical elements of local exchange policy decisions are being made in an informational vacuum. Bruce (1985) claims we lack critical information about the impacts of policy decisions and about the policies and service concepts of other countries.

Patterson (1985) points out that we do not know how different information systems interact with different types of democracy. Leeson (1984) felt crippled by a lack of information about the impact of trade barriers and about the likelihood of changes in the policies of other countries. The UN Conference on Trade and Development (1984) has complained about the lack of information on the impact of service industries on the economy. Parkman (1981) would like to know more about the market before license allocation decisions are made. Aines (1985) is concerned that the United States is not collecting the kind of information about other countries that they are collecting about us. Commissioner Fogarty, dissenting from the Computer II (1984) decision, bases much of his reasoning on the lack of knowledge of the "real-world consequences" of that policy. Even FCC chair Patrick is suspicious of the government's ability to regulate because government generally does not have – and the FCC generally does not have – access to all of the information that is needed to make effective, consistent decisions that actually maximize the public interest (quoted in Halonen 1987b, 39). Similarly, the Supreme Court often declines to make decisions in the information policy area because of lack of information (Braman 1988).

The difficulty of acquiring sufficient and appropriate information for policymaking purposes is enhanced by the technical nature of the information involved. U.S. decision-makers have repeatedly claimed themselves incapable of understanding technological development well enough to regulate it (e.g., Berman 1974; Burch 1985; Fowler and Brenner 1982; Rutkowski 1983; Siff 1984).

This lack of information contributes to the lack of attention paid to ethnic, geographic, and ideological minority concerns (see, e.g., Branscomb 1983b; Dizard 1982; Fejes 1980; Langdale 1982; Loo and Slaa 1982; Schiller 1982). Rowland (1982) emphasizes the way in which reliance upon the private sector, with its own interests, contributes to this informational skewing. In his view, private sector-supplied information serves a narrow range of purposes and expresses a shallow level of cultural and political experience. Individual concerns are also left out of a process that tends to define *user* as a transnational corporation rather than as a human being (Levine 1986; Neumann and Wieland 1986; Rutkowski 1983). Further, government reliance upon private sector information has repeatedly delayed critical developments; in one notable example, launching of the geosynchronous satellites so critical to global communications was delayed for years until the FCC stopped believing AT&T's insistence that it could not be done and started believing Boeing's claim that it could. The heavy role of the private sector in providing information to decision-makers is one of its key forms of power (Noll 1986). In addition, this encourages policymaking reliance on economic analysis in lieu of, rather than in addition to, social and political analyses of policy decisions (Snow 1986; Webster and Robins 1986).

Rutkowski's (1981) response to these informational deficits is to recommend incorporating real representation of a broader range of groups into the decision-making process, rather than resting with the FCC's assumption that "interested parties . . . can be relied upon to bring serious questions to our attention" (quoted in Committee on Government Operations 1982, 7). Kling (1980, 1984) suggests a type of social impact analysis that could systematically provide information to governmental organizations seeking to use new information technologies.

STRUCTURAL PROBLEMS

Structural problems are those problems that arise from conflicts or contradictions among the elements of the structure of the policymaking process. They are rife in the United States because of the complexities of the process, resulting in a reduction of the capability of the state to make policy coherently and effectively. The multiple regulatory systems, variety of types of regulatory tools, and number of decision-makers and arenas in U.S. information policy, as well as the general characteristics of information policymaking, have been discussed. The fact that so much U.S. information policy is latent rather than manifest also increases the number of structural problems, for latent policy is both pluralist and incremental (Lambright 1976).

Among the many specific problems that result are ineffectiveness (Bruce 1985; Geller 1983; Sullivan 1985) and inefficiency (Fogarty dissent in Computer II 1984; Fredell 1986; Noll and Owen 1983; NTIA 1985; Rutkowski 1981), yielding what Horwitz claims is "anarchy for the system as a whole" (1986, 146). There is no comprehensive policy review (Dube 1967; Rowland 1982; Tunstall 1986), which makes it possible for the conditions that permit the commitment of insufficient resources to information policy to continue (AT&T 1971; GAO 1982, 1986; Hager 1986; Krasnow, Longley, and Terry 1984; Leeson 1984). Structural problems are blamed for the U.S. failure to provide leadership in information policy internationally and domestically (Branscomb 1983; Bruce in Schiller 1982, 183; McDowell 1987; NTIA 1985; "OECD Data Declaration . . ." 1982; Rutkowski 1981; Spero 1982). National credibility is undermined (Levin 1982; Leeson 1984; Schiller 1986). Litigation costs are increased (Crofts and Mead 1980; Ploman 1982b). In sum, there is a sense that the making of information policy requires great subtlety and sophistication, and that "the United States is still neither institutionally nor psychologically prepared for such implementation" (Ganley and Ganley 1982, 82). One of the most significant consequences of the dispersion of U.S. information policymaking power is that it makes the bypass of normal decision-making channels possible. In one recent example, the decision to place all government databases, civilian as well as military, under the control of the National Security Agency has been criticized not just because it indicates a militarization of U.S. information resources, but also because it arose outside of normal decision-making channels. Congress, in whose bailiwick responsibility for such a matter should fall, was excluded, and it is not clear just how the decision came about and who was responsible (Fredell 1985; Levine 1985). This kind of sidestepping of public decision-making procedures is particularly troublesome from the constitutional point of view.

Some argue that the structural problems in the U.S. information policymaking process will themselves yield a particular form of decision-making by default. Aines predicts that "failure to create an improved federal policy-making capability may propel us toward the information czar approach, like it or not" (1986, 25). Others see such a result not as inevitable but as desirable. In Chiron and Rehberg's words, centralizing and unifying the process makes particular sense because "it seems artificial and inefficient to try to divide regulatory and policy making functions" (1986, 55). For Leeson (1984), it simply makes more sense than not to base policy on a unified view.

Others see the dispersal of functions as an advantage. Rutkowski claims that demands for a single, high-level policymaking body are naive because the issues are so complex and rapidly changing, diverse values are involved, effects of policy decisions are unclear, and the threshold questions for the U.S. government have gone unanswered. In describing today's decision-making environment, he offers a relatively rare positive voice and suggests a marketplace model for political decision-making: "The existing scheme may not produce nicely organized policy, but it does allow considerable freedom for individual participants to exercise their initiative to shape a collective result through diverse actions" (1981, 37).

Distributed policymaking has the advantages of involving more people and allowing for substantial innovation; still, Rutkowski admits, centralization of decision-making functions carries the alternative advantages of efficiency and orthodoxy. It is just those characteristics that concern those who fear the centralization of information policy because they distrust all centralized development. Siff (1984) believes those dangers are exacerbated in the ISDN environment. Noam (1987) believes decentralized decision-making is a central characteristic of the new type of open network that is developing, for which unified planning would be impossible.

ORIENTATIONAL PROBLEMS

If conceptual problems involve knowing what you're doing, informational problems involve knowing where you are and understanding the consequences of your actions, and structural problems involve capability, then orientational problems center on knowing where it is you are going. No meaningful policy emerges if the goals of that policy have not been clearly set. These are the political questions – those a community as a whole answers when it constitutes itself.

There are three fundamental orientational problems, all normative. They should be considered sequentially: What kind of social organization do we want? What kind of informational organization best serves that kind of society? What kind of regulatory system best builds and sustains that kind of informational organization?

The orientational confusion of U.S. policymakers is clear from the variety of principles offered as justification for policy. There are differences over which principles should be included in the decision-making calculus and over their order of priority, as well as tensions between conflicting principles and between the application of principles at different levels of the social structure.

The desire to use information systems to promote national unity goes back to the inclusion of the postal provision in the Constitution. At its inception, AT&T promoted the same principle, proclaiming, "Some day, all the people of the United States will sing the Star Spangled Banner in unison by means of the telephone" (quoted in Pound 1926, 5).

There is some desire to ensure that benefits of the new technologies will be available to all. The principle of serving the public interest, clearly related, has the difficulties discussed above. Ensuring access, common carriage, and universal service are related goals. Noam (1987) points out that these terms gain new meaning as the network evolves. Access today, for example, refers not just to individual human users but to other networks as well. No one has ever summarized the notion of universal service more eloquently than Vail, first president of AT&T, who saw universal service as the central element of a "grand system":

> To connect one or more points in each and every city, town or place in the State of New York, with one or more points in each and every city, town, or place in said State, and in each and every other of the United States, and in Canada, and Mexico; and each and every of said cities, towns, and places is to be connected with each and every other city, town, or place in said State and countries, and also by cable and other appropriate means with the rest of the known world. (quoted in Casson 1910, 174-75)

The NTIA (1985) agrees that universal service remains the cornerstone of U.S. policy and should be inclusively defined. Despite the introduction of numerous bills into Congress proposing universal service, however, as an object of serious discussion it has barely made it to the policy table. There are disputes over what universal service would include (broadband or narrowband, computer services or plain old telephone service [called POTS]?) and over who should be responsible (service providers? national regulatory system? state regulatory units?). Aufderheide argues that "neglect of meaningful standards for universal service puts at risk the social underpinnings of a democratic, information-reliant society" (1987, 95).

Placing information policy in the service of other goals, such as trade, foreign policy, or economic goals, is frequently done (Bruce 1985; GAO 1982). The strategic use of information policy for foreign relations purposes goes back at least to the 1920s, when the United States considered predominance in radio communication to be on a par with leadership in oil and shipping as bases for expansion efforts (Smythe 1981). Support for national security strategy is another goal served by information policy (National Research Council 1986; Oettinger 1977). The NTIA (1985) focuses on the importance of information policy for the economy.

Another goal is to shape a particular kind of order. Thus, the former head of INTELSAT, an American, could describe that organization's goals as "consistent with the continuing search for an 'enlightened' world order" (Colino 1986, 198). That world order should include a single, integrated global system (Goldberg 1985) that can, incidentally, serve commercial goals (Ahern and Greenberg 1981).

Serving the marketplace has been a guiding principle for information policy, and a dominant theme since the late 1960s. Sterling (1982) analyzes the FCC's shift to the marketplace as a regulatory technique chosen in the search for a system that could adapt efficiently to change, what Noll and Owen (1983) call the identifying element in today's environment. FCC chair Patrick (1987) explicitly stresses cost-effective efficiency as the reason for letting the marketplace rule.

Economic efficiency is another principle that is often used as a guide for the shaping of U.S. information policy (Colino 1986). For Wenders and Egan (1986), debate over the AT&T divestiture boils down to a discussion over the degree to which economic efficiency should influence information policy. The Reagan administration made the cost of implementation of policy decisions central to decision-making on information matters; one result of this concern has been an attack upon the Freedom of Information Act (FOIA), which is now deemed to be costing too much (Ullmann and List 1985). The NTIA (1985) has noted the cost of implementing Computer II. A goal of the Electronic Communications Privacy Act of 1986 was to provide the business community with the certainty necessary to stimulate greater investment in information technologies and services (Wiley and Leibowitz 1987). One difficulty with using economic efficiency as a decision-making principle, however, is that there is no agreement on which regulatory tools actually best serve the purpose (Snow 1985).

Sheer competitiveness also drives policy. The Rostow Report presented to President Johnson stressed it: "An accepted goal of national policy [is] that the United States remain a leader among the nations in communications science and technology, and telecommunications service" (quoted in Haight 1979, 245). Innovation can serve the same role. The NTIA, for example, says, "It is clear that technology will continue to develop and we must encourage it" (1985, vii). A 1983 addendum to the Federal Communications Act states as a policy of the United States the encouragement and provision of new technologies and services.

The policy recommendations of the many presidential studies and commissions are diffuse, but they do concur in advocating a deepening of regulatory involvement in information activities. As Myerson comments, speaking of the French parallel, "The history of French telecommunications law demonstrates unmistakably that the government, however well-intentioned, simply cannot resist the temptation to control communications if given the opportunity" (1985, 144).

It is a tacit principle that information policy should serve the needs of the government itself, though there are concerns over matters such as security and privacy. Carter's reorganization plans are an example of information policy developed as an offshoot of the desire for greater efficiency in government, as are current OMB regulations concerning information gathering and dissemination as a matter of agency efficiency and cost-effectiveness.

Techniques themselves sometimes appear to become operating principles. Thus, Horwitz (1986) warns against permitting deregulation to become the end instead of the means. Trauth, Trauth, and Huffman (1983) make the same comment about competition, noting that if it becomes an end in itself, the consequence may be less, rather than more, diversity.

A number of other goals, each with definitional problems and often so diffuse as to be inoperable, are offered. The free flow of information, international cooperation, and peace are among the driving principles that have been offered to justify information policy.

Not only is it difficult to agree on what each of these principles would concretely mean in developing implementable and effective information policy, but they often conflict with each other. Desires to protect national security run counter to the free flow of information, increasing efficiency can reduce access, and so on. Some tensions arise from the attempt to apply the same principle at different levels of the social structure—there cannot, for example, be self-determination on the same issues at both the national and local levels.

Prioritization among these many competing principles seems to change over time. Following Watergate, questions about the erosion of individual rights and freedoms in the new information age dominated congressional concerns, but by the late 1970s attention had turned to security protections for federal databases (Spero 1982). In the 1930s the FCC was concerned about a fiduciary responsibility of all broadcast licensees to represent all U.S. voices; today the goal is to protect the speech rights of those broadcasters themselves. The divestiture and recent deregulatory decisions have undermined many traditional principles, according to Horwitz (1986).

U.S. information policymakers are often criticized for applying principles inconsistently. Chiron and Rehberg (1986) note that INTELSAT reserves the right to choose principles case by case, as long as the ultimate goal of serving U.S. interests is furthered. There are increasing complaints about principles being applied differently in the domestic and international environments in areas such as choice of planning approach (Levin 1982) and stance toward protectionism (Leaf 1985), though Burch (1985), former chair of the FCC and current director general of INTELSAT, defends such usage because the United States is unique.

The multiplicity of principles offered and the tensions among them when they need to be balanced are indicative of a lack of orientation when it comes to setting information policy in the United States. Because policymakers are unsure about exactly where they are going, there are disagreements about the path that should be taken. These principles need not, however, be seen as mutually exclusive. Michael (1986) identifies the bringing together of these diverse goals as the task of information policy.

CONCLUSION

The unique characteristics of information policy, combined with the multiplicity of applicable regulatory systems in the United States, yield conceptual, informational, structural, and orientational problems for the U.S. information policymaking process. Exploration of these problems leads to suggestions for working policymakers, for researchers, and for higher education.

While working policymakers cannot put aside immediate problems until larger theoretical issues have been resolved, it is possible to approach problems that range from regulation of the telephone network to rules for access to government information with awareness of their theoretical context and large-scale socioeconomic, political, and cultural impact. This discussion outlines an agenda for researchers, detailing both theoretical and empirical problems. And for those involved in higher education, it illustrates the fact that to be "information-literate" in the twenty-first century will be to understand information technologies, messages, institutions, and effects within the context of ongoing explorations in both epistemology and the sociology of knowledge.

References

Ahern, V. M., and Greenberg, E. M. (1981). "Communications Satellites." In L. Lewin, ed., *Telecommunications in the United States: Trends and Policies,* 85-100. Dedham, Mass.: Artech House.

Aines, A. A. (1986). "Principles to Guide Forming of Info Policy." *Government Computer News* 5, no. 15 (August 1): 25ff.

_____. (1985). "U.S. Know-how Leaks Out, but Little Is Gathered Back." *Government Computer News* 4, no. 16 (August 30): 33ff.

AT&T Co., 32 FCC2d 691 (1971).

Aufderheide, P. (1987). "Universal Service: Telephone Policy in the Public Interest." *Journal of Communication* 37, no. 1: 81-96.

Berman, P. J. (1974). "Computer or Communications? Allocation of Functions and the Role of the Federal Communications Commission." *Federal Communications Bar Journal* 27, no. 2: 161-230.

Boettinger, H. M. (1984). "Doctrine, Decision and Development in International Telecommunications." *Telecommunications Policy* 8, no. 22: 89-92.

Bollinger, L. (1977). "Freedom of the Press and Public Access: Toward a Theory of Partial Regulation of the Mass Media." *Michigan Law Review* 75: 1-42.

Bortnick, J. (1983). *International Telecommunications and Information Policy: Selected Issues for the 1980's.* Washington, D.C.: Government Printing Office.

Boulding, K. (1966). "The Economics of Knowledge and the Knowledge of Economics." *American Economic Review* 56, no. 2: 1-13.

Braman, S. (1988). "Information Policy and the United States Supreme Court." Unpublished Ph.D. dissertation, University of Minnesota.

Branscomb, A. W. (1986). *Toward a Law of Global Communication Networks.* New York: Longman.

_____. (1983a). "Communication Policy in the United States: Diversity and Pluralism in a Competitive Marketplace." In P. Edgar and S. A. Rahim, eds., *Communication Policy in Developed Countries,* 15-56. London: Kegan Paul International.

_____. (1983b). "Global Governance of Global Networks: A Survey of Transborder Data Flow in Transition. *Vanderbilt Law Review,* 36, 985-1043.

Bruce, R. R. (1985). *Definitions of Services: Line Drawing, Industry Structure, and Institutional Arrangements*. Committee for Information, Computer, and Communications Policy, DSTI/ICCP/85.31. Paris: Organization for Economic Cooperation and Development.

_____. (1981). "U.S. Regulatory Changes Will Affect All Countries." *InterMedia* 9, no. 6: 16-18.

Burch, D. (1985). "Common Carrier Communications by Wire and Radio: A Retrospective." *Federal Communications Law Journal* 37: 85-105.

Bushkin, A. A., and Yurow, J. H. (1980). *The Foundations of U. S. Information Policy*. NTIA SP=80=8 (June). Washington, D.C.: Dept. of Commerce.

Cardozo, B. N. (1921). *The Nature of the Judicial Process*. New Haven, Conn.: Yale University Press.

Casson, H. N. (1910). *The History of the Telephone*. Chicago: A. C. McClung & Co.

Cerni, D. M. (1982). *The CCITT: Organization, U.S. Participation, and Studies toward the ISDN*. Boulder, Colo.: National Telecommunications and Information Administration.

_____, and Gray, E. M. (1983). *International Telecommunication Standards: Issues and Implications for the 1980s*. Boulder, Colo.: National Telecommunications and Information Administration.

Chandler, A. D., Jr. (1977). *The Visible Hand: The Managerial Revolution in American Business*. Cambridge, Mass.: Belknap Press of Harvard University Press.

Cheh, M. M. (1982). "Government Control of Private Ideas – Striking a Balance between Scientific Freedom and National Security." *Jurimetrics Journal* 23, no. 1: 1-32.

Chiron, S. Z., and Rehberg, L. A. (1986). "Fostering Competition in International Telecommunications." *Federal Communications Law Journal* 38: 1-57.

Colino, R. R. (1986). "Global Politics and INTELSAT: The Conduct of Foreign Relations in an Electronically Interconnected World." *Telecommunications Policy* 10, no. 1: 195-208.

Computer II, 77 FCC2d 384 (1984).

Cornell, N. W.; Pelcovits, M. D.; and Brenner, S. R. (1983). "A Legacy of Regulatory Failure." *Regulation* 7, no. 4: 37-42.

Crofts, G. G., and Mead, L. M. (1980). *"The FCC as an Institution."* In L. Lewin, ed., *Telecommunications: An Interdisciplinary Survey.* 2d ed., 40-120. Dedham, Mass.: Artech House.

Cruise O'Brien, R. (1980). "Specialized Information and Interdependence: Problems of Concentration and Access." *Telecommunications Policy* 4, no. 1: 42-48.

Davis, K. C. (1977). *Administrative Law,* 4th ed. St. Paul, Minn.: West.

Deibel, T. L., and Roberts, W. R. (1976). *Culture and Information: Two Foreign Policy Functions.* Beverly Hills, Calif.: Sage Publications.

Dewandre, N. (1986). "Europe and New Communication Technologies." In M. Ferguson, ed., *New Communication Technologies and the Public Interest: Comparative Perspectives on Policy and Research,* 137-49. Beverly Hills, Calif.: Sage Publications.

Dizard, W. P. (1982). *The Coming Information Age.* New York: Longman.

Dougan, D. L. (1983). *Promoting the Free Flow of Information.* Current Policy #531. Washington, D.C.: Department of State (November 30).

Dube, S. C. (1967). "A Note on Communication in Economic Development." In D. Lerner and W. Schramm, eds., *Communication and Change in the Developing Countries,* 92-97. Honolulu: East-West Center Press.

Dunn, D. A. (1982). "Developing Information Policy." *Telecommunications Policy* 6, no. 1: 21-38.

Fejes, F. (1980). "The Growth of Multinational Advertising Agencies in Latin America." *Journal of Communication* 30, no. 4: 36-49.

Feller, H. H., and Jacobsen, C. (1986). *Treaties and Other International Agreements for Telecommunications,* FCC report no. 66. Washington, D.C.: Office of Engineering and Technology.

Fowler, M. S., and Brenner, D. L. (1982). "A Marketplace Approach to Broadcast Regulation." *Texas Law Review* 60: 207-57.

Fredell, E. (1986). "OTA Diagnoses Ills of federal Info Policies." *Government Computer News* 5, no. 15 (March 14): 1ff.

_____. (1985). "Agencies Balk at Control Given NSA." *Government Computer News* 4, no. 18 (September 27): 19ff.

Frieden, R. M. (1983). "International Telecommunications and the Federal Communications Commission." *Columbia Journal of Transnational Law* 21: 423-85.

_____. (1981). "The Computer Inquiries: Mapping the Communications/Information Processing Terrain." *Federal Communications Law Journal* 33: 55-115.

Ganley, O. H., and Ganley, G. D. (1982). *To Inform or to Control? The New Communications Networks.* New York: McGraw-Hill.

Garnham, N. (1983). "Toward a Theory of Cultural Materialism." *Journal of Communication* 33, no. 3: 314-29.

Geller, H. (1983). "Talk vs. Action at the FCC." *Regulation* 7, no. 4: 15-18.

Gellhorn, E., and Byse, C. (1970). *Administrative Law*, 5th ed. Mineola, N.Y.: Foundation Press.

Goldberg, H. (1985). "One Hundred and Twenty Years of International Communications." *Federal Communications Law Journal* 37, no. 1: 131-54.

Granger, J. V. (1979). *Technology and International Relations.* San Francisco: W. H. Freeman & Co.

Grant, W., ed. (1985). *The Political Economy of Corporatism.* New York: St. Martin's Press.

Greenstein, R. L. (1984). "Federal Contractors and Grantees: What Are Your First Amendment Rights?" *Jurimetrics Journal* 24, no. 3: 197-209.

Hager, P. (1986). "Lack of Leadership, Money Hampering Info Policy." *Government Computer News* 5, no. 3 (February 14): 9.

Haight, T. R., ed. (1979). *Telecommunications Policy and the Citizen.* New York: Praeger Special Studies.

Halloran, J. D. (1986). "The Social Implications of Technological Innovations in Communication." In M. Traber, ed., *The Myth of the Information Revolution: Social and Ethical Implications of Communication Technology*, 46-63. Beverly Hills, Calif.: Sage Publications.

_____. (1981). "The Context of Mass Communications Research." In E. O. McAnany, J. Schnitman, and N. Janus, eds., *Communication and Social Change*, 21-57. New York: Praeger.

Halonen, D. (1987). "Patrick Picks up the Reins at the FCC." *Broadcasting* (April 20): 36-40.

Hamelink, C. (1984). *Transnational Data Flows in the Information Age.* Lund, Sweden: Studentliterratur AB.

Hanks, W. E., and Coran, S. E. (1986). "Federal Preemption of Obscenity Law Applied to Cable Television." *Journalism Quarterly* 63, no. 1: 43-47.

Hedge, D. M., and Mok, J. W. (1987). "The Nature of Policy Studies: A Content Analysis of Policy Journal Articles." *Policy Studies Journal* 16, no. 1: 49-62.

Holsti, K. J. (1978). "A New International Politics? Diplomacy in Complex Interdependence." *International Organization* 32, no. 2: 513-30.

Horwitz, R. B. (1986). "For Whom the Bell Tolls: Causes and Consequences of the AT&T Divestiture." *Critical Studies in Mass Communication* 3, no. 2: 119-54.

Irwin, M. R. (1984). *Telecommunications America: Markets without Boundaries*. Westport, Conn.: Quorum Books.

Johnson, E. (1986). "Telecommunications Market Structure in the United States: The Effects of Deregulation and Divestiture." *Telecommunications Policy* 10, no. 1: 57-67.

Kegley, C. W., Jr. (1985). "Decision Regimes and Foreign Policy Behavior." Paper presented to the Conference on New Directions in the Comparative Study of Foreign Policy, Ohio State University, Columbus, Ohio, May 9-11.

Keohane, R. O. (1982). "The Demand for International Regimes." *International Organization* 36, no. 2: 325-55.

_____. (1980). "The Theory of Hegemonic Stability and Changes in International Economic Regimes, 1967-1977." In O. Holsti, R. Siverson, and A. George, eds., *Change in the International System*, 131-62. Boulder, Colo.: Westview Press.

_____, and Nye, J. (1977). *Power and Interdependence: World Politics in Transition*. Boston: Little, Brown.

Kling, R. (1984). "Assimilating Social Values in Computer-based Technologies." *Telecommunications Policy* 8, no. 2: 127-47.

_____. (1983). "Value Conflicts in Computing Developments: Developed and Developing Countries." *Telecommunications Policy* 7, no. 1: 12-34.

_____. (1980). "Social Analyses of Computing: Theoretical Perspectives in Recent Empirical Research." *Computing Surveys* 12, no. 1: 61-110.

Krasner, S. D., ed. (1983). *International Regimes*. Ithaca, N.Y.: Cornell University Press.

____. (1982a). "Regimes and the Limits of Realism: Regimes as Autonomous Variables." *International Organization* 36, no. 2: 497-510.

____. (1982b). "Structural Causes and Regime Consequences: Regimes as Intervening Variables." *International Organization* 36, no. 2: 185-205.

Krasnow, E. G.; Longley, L. D.; and Terry, H. A. (1984). *The Politics of Broadcast Regulation*, 4th ed. New York: St. Martin's Press.

Krugman, D. M., and Reid, L. N. (1980). "The Public Interest as Defined by FCC Policymakers." *Journal of Broadcasting* 24, no. 3: 311-25.

Lambright, W. H. (1976). *Governing Science and Technology.* New York: Oxford University Press.

Langdale, J. (1982). "Competition in Telecommunications." *Telecommunications Policy* 6, no. 4: 283-99.

Leaf, J. J. (1985). "'America First' Rules in United States, Say Foreign Exporters." *Electronics* 58, no. 36: 28-29.

Le Duc, D. R. (1982). "Deregulation and the Dream of Diversity." *Journal of Communication* 32, no. 4: 164-78.

Lee, A., and Sloan, T. (1987). *Competition in the Local Exchange Telephone Service Market.* NTIA 87-210. Washington, D.C.: Government Printing Office.

Leeson, K. W. (1984). *International Communications: Blueprint for Policy.* Amsterdam: North-Holland.

Levin, H. J. (1986). "U.S. Broadcast Deregulation: A Case of Dubious Evidence." *Journal of Communication* 36, no. 1: 25-40.

____. (1982). "Foreign and Domestic U.S. Policies: Spectrum Reservations and Media Balance." *Telecommunications Policy* 6, no. 2: 123-35.

Levine, A. S. (1986). "Officials on Panel Examine Impact of Circular A-130." *Government Computer News* 5, no. 14 (July 18):12.

____. (1985). "Central Agency Watch." *Government Computer News* 4, no. 9 (May 24): 58.

Loo, H., and Slaa, P. (1982). "Information Technology: Public Debate in the Netherlands." *Telecommunications Policy* 6, no. 2: 100-110.

MacBride, S. (1986). Foreword to M. Traber, ed., *The Myth of the Information Revolution: Social and Ethical Implications of Communication Technology,* vii-viii. Beverly Hills, Calif.: Sage.

Machlup, F. (1980). *Knowledge and Knowledge Production.* Princeton, N.J.: Princeton University Press.

Marchand, D. M. (1981). "The Impact of Information Technology on International Relations." *InterMedia* 9, no. 6: 12-15.

Matellart, A. (1978). "The Nature of Communication Practice in a Dependent Society." *Latin American Perspectives* 5, no. 1: 13-34.

McDowell, S. (1987). "Building Consensus in the OECD: The Case of Transborder Data Flows." Presented to the Canadian Political Science Association, Hamilton, Ontario, Canada, June 6-8.

Michael, J. (1986). "Information Law, Policy, and the Public Interest." In M. Ferguson, ed., *New Communication Technologies and the Public Interest: Comparative Perspectives on Policy and Research,* 102-21. Beverly Hills, Calif.: Sage.

Middleton, K. R., and Chamberlin, B. S. (1988). *Law of Public Communication.* New York: Longman.

Myerson, M. (1985). "The Pursuit of Pluralism: Lessons from French Communications Law." *Stanford Journal of International Law* 21: 95-155.

Neu, W., Neumann, K., and Schnoring, T. (1987). "Trade Patterns, Industry Structure, and Industrial Policy in Telecommunications." *Telecommunications Policy* 11, no. 1: 31-44.

Neumann, K., and Wieland, B. (1986). "Competition and Social Objectives: The Case of West German Telecommunications." *Telecommunications Policy* 10, no. 1: 121-31.

Noam, E. M. (1987). "The Public Telecommunications Network: A Concept in Transition." *Journal of Communication* 37, no. 1: 30-48.

_____. (1983). "Federal and State Roles in Telecommunications: The Effects of Deregulation." *Vanderbilt Law Review* 36, no. 4: 949-83.

Noll, R. G. (1986). "The Political and Institutional Context of Communications Policy." In M. S. Snow, ed., *Marketplace for Telecommunications: Regulation and Deregulation in Industrialized Democracies,* 42-65. New York: Longman.

_____, and Owen, B. M. (1983). *The Political Economy of Deregulation: Interest Groups in the Regulatory Process.* Washington, D.C.: American Enterprise Institute.

Nora, S., and Minc, A. (1980). *The Computerization of Society.* Cambridge, Mass.: MIT Press.

Organization for Economic Development and Cooperation. (1983). *Transborder Data Flows: An Overview of Issues,* DSTI report no. ILLP8239. Paris: OECD.

"OECD Data Declaration Started." (1982). *Transnational Data Report* 5, no. 1: 57-59.

Oettinger, A. G., et al. (1977). *High and Low Politics of Information Resources for the 80s.* Cambridge, Mass.: Ballinger.

Owen, B. (1970). "Public Policy and Emerging Technology in the Media." *Public Policy* 18, no. 3: 539-52.

Panitch, L. (1980). "Recent Theorizations of Corporatism: Reflections on a Growth Industry." *British Journal of Sociology* 31, no. 1: 159-87.

Parkman, N. (1981). "The FCC's Allocation of Television Licenses: Regulation with Inadequate Information." *Albany Law Review* 46: 22-58.

Patterson, T. E. (1985). *Toward New Research on Communication Technologies and the Democratic Process.* Queenstown, Md.: Aspen Institute.

Pepper, R., and Brotman, S. N. (1987). "Restricted Monopolies or Regulated Competitors? The Case of the Bell Operating Companies." *Journal of Communication* 37, no. 1: 64-72.

Picard, R. G. (1985). *The Press and the Decline of Democracy: The Democratic Socialist Response in Public Policy.* Westport, Conn.: Greenwood Press.

Pipe, G. R. (1984). "Searching for Appropriate TDF Regulation." *Transnational Data Report* 7, no. 1: 1-10.

Ploman, E. W. (1982a). *International Law Governing Communications and Information.* Westport, Conn.: Greenwood Press.

_____. (1982b). "Transborder Data Flows: The International Legal Framework." *Computer/Law Journal* 3: 551-62.

Pond, W. (1983). "Restraining Regulatory Activism: The Proper Scope of Public Utility Regulation." *Administrative Law Review* 35: 423-50.

Pool, I. de S. (1983). *Technologies of Freedom.* Cambridge: Belknap Press of Harvard University Press.

Porat, M. U. (1978). "Communication Policy in an Information Society." In G. O. Robinson, ed., *Communications for Tomorrow: Policy Perspectives for the 1980s,* 3-60. New York: Praeger Publishers.

_____. (1977). *The Information Economy: Definition and Measurement.* U.S. Department of Commerce, Office of Telecommunications (OT) special pub. 77-12, no. 1.

Potter, W. C. (1980). "Issue Area and Foreign Policy Analysis." *International Organization* 34, no. 3: 405-27.

Pound, A. (1926). *The Telephone Idea: Fifty Years After.* New York: Greenberg.

Renaud, J. (1987). "The ITU and Development Assistance: North, South, and the Dynamics of the CCIs." *Telecommunications Policy* 11, no. 2: 179-92.

Rosati, J. (1981). "Developing a Systematic Decision-Making Framework." *World Politics* 33, no. 2: 234-52.

Rosenau, J. (1984). "A Pre-Theory Revisited: World Politics in an Era of Cascading Interdependence." *International Studies Quarterly* 28, no. 3: 245-306.

Rowland, W. D. (1982). "The Process of Reification: Recent Trends in Communications Legislation and Policy-Making." *Journal of Communication* 32, no. 4: 114-36.

Rutkowski, A. M. (1983). "The Integrated Services Digital Network: Issues and Options for the Future." *Jurimetrics Journal* 24, no. 1: 19-42.

_____. (1981). *United States Policy Making for the Public International Forums on Communication.* New York: Communications Media Center, New York Law School.

Sampson, M. (1982). *Issues in International Policy Coordination.* Denver: University of Denver Monograph Series.

Schiller, D. (1982). *Telematics and Government.* Norwood, N.J.: Ablex.

Schiller, H. J. (1986). "The Erosion of National Sovereignty by the World Business System." In Traber, *The Myth of the Information Revolution,* 21-34.

Schmitter, P. C. (1985). "Neo-Corporatism and the State." In W. Grant, ed., *The Political Economy of Corporatism,* 32-62. New York: St. Martin's Press.

Schwartz, B. (1977). "Administrative Law: The Third Century." *Administrative Law Review* 29: 291-319.

Siff, A. (1984). "ISDNs: Shaping the New Networks that Might Reshape FCC Policies." *Federal Communications Law Journal* 37: 171-201.

Skocpol, T. (1985). "Bringing the State Back In: Strategies of Analysis in Current Research." In P. B. Evans, D. Rueschmeyer, and T. Skocpol, eds., *Bringing the State Back In*, 3-37. New York: Cambridge University Press.

Skolnikoff, E. B. (1967). *Science, Technology, and American Foreign Policy.* Cambridge, Mass.: MIT Press.

Smythe, D. W. (1981). *Dependency Road: Communications, Capitalism, Consciousness, and Canada.* Norwood, N.J.: Ablex.

Snow, M. S. (1986). *Marketplace for Telecommunications: Regulation and Deregulation in Industrialized Democracies.* New York: Longman.

_____. (1985). "Arguments for and against Competition in International Satellite Facilities and Services: A U.S. Perspective." *Journal of Communication* 35, no. 3: 51-79.

Soma, J. T.; Peterson, R. D.; Alexander, G.; and Petty, C. W. (1983). "The Communications Regulatory Environment in the 1980s." *Computer/Law Journal* 4: 1-54.

Spero, J. E. (1982). "Information: The Policy Void." *Foreign Policy* 48 (Fall): 139-56.

_____. (1981). *The Politics of International Economic Relations,* 2d ed. New York: St. Martin's Press.

Sprehe, J. T. (1987). "Implementing the Government's New Information Policy." *Information Services and Use* 7, no. 4/5: 139-44.

Sterling, C. H. (1982). "The FCC and Changing Technological Standards." *Journal of Communication* 32, no. 4: 132-47.

Stern, J. A.; Krasnow, E. G.; and Sunkowski, R. M. (1983). "The New Video Marketplace and the Search for a Coherent Regulatory Philosophy." *Catholic University Law Review* 32: 529-602.

Stoil, M. J. (1983). "The Executive Branch and International Telecommunications Policy: The Case of WARC '79." In J. J. Havick, ed., *Communications Policy and the Political Process*, 89-108. Westport, Conn.: Greenwood Press.

Straus, R., ed. (1982). *Communications and International Trade: A Symposium.* Washington, D.C.: International Institute of Communication.

Sullivan, J. A. (1985). "Study Slams U.S. Embargo." *Government Computer News* 6.

Trauth, E. M. (1986). "An Integrative Approach to Information Policy Research." *Telecommunications Policy* 10, no. 1: 41-50.

_____, Trauth, D. M.; and Huffman, J. L. (1983). "Impact of Deregulation on Marketplace Diversity in the United States." *Telecommunications Policy* 7, no. 1: 111-20.

Tunstall, J. (1986a). "American Communication Deregulation: How to 'Copy' and Misunderstand It." *Nordicom Review*, no. 1: 31-35.

_____. (1986b). *Communications Deregulation: The Unleashing of America's Communications Industry.* New York: Basil Blackwell.

Ullmann, J., and List, K. (1985). "An Analysis of Government Cost Estimates of FOIA Compliance." *Journalism Quarterly* 62, no. 3: 465-73.

Underdal, A. (1981). "Issues Determine Politics Determine Policies" (unpublished rev. ed.). *Cooperation and Conflict* 1 (1970): 1-10.

U.N. Conference on Trade and Development. (1984). *Services and the Development Process.* TD/B11008. New York: United Nations.

U.S. Congress, Office of Technology Assessment (OTA). (1981). *Computer-based National Information Systems: Technology and Public Policy Issues.* Washington, D.C.: U.S. Government Printing Office.

U.S. General Accounting Office (GAO). (1986). *Telephone Communications: The FCC's Monitoring of Residential Telephone Service.* PB86-216802. Washington, D.C.: U.S. Government Printing Office.

_____. (1982). *The FCC's International Telecommunications Activities.* Washington, D.C.: U.S. Government Printing Office.

U.S. National Research Council. (1986). *The Policy Planning Environment for National Security Telecommunications: Final Report to the National Communication System.* Washington, D.C.: National Academy Press.

U.S. National Telecommunications and Information Administration (NTIA). (1985). *Issues in Domestic Telecommunications: Directions for National Policy.* Special pub. 85-16. Washington, D.C.: U.S. Government Printing Office.

U. S. Senate, Committee on Government Operations. (1982). *Maintaining the Network: Rural Telephone Service and FCC Actions.* 97-922. Washington, D.C.: U.S. Government Printing Office.

Von Weizsacker, C. C. (1986). "Free Entry into Telecommunications?" *Information Economics and Policy* 1: 197-216.

Wall, S. (1984). "The British Telecommunications Decision: Towards a New Telecommunications policy for the Common Market." *Harvard International Law Journal* 24, no. 2: 299-328.

Webster, F., and Robins, K. (1986). *Information Technology: A Luddite Analysis*. Norwood, N.J.: Ablex.

Wenders, J. T., and Egan, B. L. (1986). "The Implications of Economic Efficiency for U.S. Telecommunications Policy." *Telecommunications Policy* 10:33-40.

Wiley, R. E., and Leibowitz, D. E. (1987). "The Electronic Communications Privacy Act of 1986 Moves Privacy Protection Towards the Twenty-First Century." *Telematics* 4, no. 2: 1-12.

Woolcock, S. (1984). "Information Technology and Atlantic Trade Relations." In R. Cruise O'Brien, ed., *The Impact of Informatization on International Relations* (published by the Humphrey Institute) (workshop report). Minneapolis, Minn.: Hubert H. Humphrey Institute of Public Affairs.

Zimmerman, W. (1973). "Issue Area and Foreign Policy Process: A Research Note in Search of a General Theory." *American Political Science Review* 67, no. 4: 1204-12.

Economy of Thought in the Age of Information Overload: Toward an Organic Nucleus of Knowledge

JERE W. CLARK AND JUANITA STONE CLARK

COUNTING THE TOLLS

As the volume of information continues to double each decade, the need to face the threat of being drowned in tidal waves of unassimilated information continues to mount. In his article "Managing Modern Complexity," Sir Stafford Beer expressed his concern this way: "The problem of information management is now a problem of filtering and refining a massive overload of data" (Beer 1985, 59).

The paradox of this data overload and its instantaneous communication, according to Walter B. Wriston, is that "information, the thing that eliminates uncertainty, now increases everybody's feeling of insecurity because of the failure to convert data into knowledge" (Wriston 1986, 59).

Making things worse, Morton F. Meltzer has suggested, is the tendency of the quality of information to vary inversely with its quantity because of such factors as redundancy, superficiality, and incomprehensibility, each of which takes its toll (Meltzer 1971, 5).

Perhaps the most costly toll stems from incompatibility – not only of software and hardware systems, but also of one-field languages in the emerging interdisciplinary world of interdependent "thought-ware systems" (Beer 1985). Added to the incompatibility toll for "thought-ware models" within each field must be the cost of seeking compatibility between the models of objective analysis, on the one hand, and the equally important models of subjective synthesis, on the other (Fuller 1969).

ECONOMY OF THOUGHT

This paper is based on the assumption that the time has come to rediscover the embryo of a solution to the problem of information overload suggested by Ernst Mach around the turn of the century. In *The Science of Mechanics,* Mach said simply: "The object of science is economy of thought." To us, this means optimizing the benefits of scarce intellectual resources such as information, know-how, habits, skills, and time within the "scientific domain of objectivity" (Mach 1902, 1).

In the late 1920s, Alfred North Whitehead extended the basic idea behind the phrase "economy of thought" to embrace the "aesthetic sense of style" of the arts and humanities when he said:

> It is an aesthetic sense, based on admiration for the direct attainment of a foreseen end, simply and without waste. Style in art, style in literature, style in science, style in logic, style in practical execution have fundamentally the same aesthetic qualities, namely, attainment and restraint. . . . Style, in its finest sense, is the last acquirement of the educated mind; it is also the most useful. It pervades the whole being. The administrator with a sense of style hates waste, the engineer with a sense of style economizes his material, the artisan with a sense of style prefers good work. Style is the ultimate morality of the mind. (Whitehead 1929, 24).

The subconscious quest for this kind of aesthetic style led the two of us independently to switch our undergraduate majors while sophomores in college. In both cases, we had originally been attracted to the "hard sciences" and math as bases for our commitment to the quest for universal pattern and order. In both cases, we soon discovered that what we really were seeking was the meaning behind the pattern and order that dominated the scientific thinking of that day.

Our four decades of researching and experimenting that followed, with various forms and extensions of the concept of economy of thought, have led us far beyond the confines of our graduate school specialties of economics and art into the relatively new interdisciplinary research fields of general systems theory, "whole-brain education," "grass-roots creativity," and futures research.

Throughout that experimental quest we have been guided by what we call the "economy-of-thought interpretation" of the logic of economics, or "optimizing" in its broadest sense. In a report on a 1980 research project, we expressed the belief that "the greatest chapter in the history of economic thought" was in the process of being written: "This is a chapter in which generic extensions of the basic principles of economics are being used to integrate all fields of thought at the qualitative level."

Later in the same report we added:

What is involved is nothing less than the opportunity to do for the economizing process what Descartes did for mathematics more than three centuries ago when he showed that the need for mathematics is universal. One difference: whereas the need then was for quantitative description, the need today is for qualitative explanation. (Clark and Clark 1985, 56).

We now define the broadened image of economy of thought as resourcefulness in using the intellectual resources we have to tap the intellectual resources we need to do what we commit ourselves to do (Clark 1965, 31). In this qualitative context we add to the intellectual resource inventory such subjective elements as imagination, sensitivity, beliefs, commitments, expectations, and metaphorical perspectives.

This proactive, teleological concept focuses on the challenge of mapping alternative pathways from where we are today toward where we hope to be in the future. The process begins with the question, where do we want (or need) to go? rather than the question, where will our limited resources permit us to go?

In terms of resources, this approach leads with the question, what resources do we need? Only then does it ask, what resources do we have? Once the needed resources and those that are available have been inventoried, the key is to devise a strategy for transforming our available resources into those that are needed. The stage then is set to devise a grand strategy for transforming the total endowment of actual and potential resources into the results we are seeking.

THE INTERPRETIVE APPROACH TO ECONOMY OF THOUGHT

In calling attention to the need for a special type of social intelligence for dealing with the changing expectations of an individual actor under conditions of uncertainty, complexity, and change, Frank H. Knight, founder of the Chicago school of economic thought, used the phrase "an interpretive study" (Knight 1956, 177).

In *The Integration of Human Knowledge*, Oliver L. Reiser called attention to the need for an analogous approach to managing social intelligence that he called "a science of social cybernetics" (Reiser 1958).

It is our purpose to sketch in a heuristic, representational way an interpretive approach to helping students and practicing executives in industry and in the arts and sciences learn to be resourceful in evolving their own interpretive approach to managing social intelligence. We hope to be able to help students and field executives alike learn to use the intellectual resources they have to identify and tap the intellectual resources they need to do what they (and their organizations) commit themselves to do. We think this is one of the most promising approaches to resolving the problem of information overload while advancing more effectively toward professional goals.

CONSTANT REORIENTATION OF ONE'S MIND

Matthew B. Kibbe provides an instructive interpretation of the interpretive approach for the general reader in a review essay of Ludwig Lachmann's book *The Market as an Economic Process* (1986):

> In a world of constant change, the "economic problem" faced by the individual actor is essentially an interpretive one. Because the knowledge needed to adjust one's plans is not an objective stock existing "out there," individuals cannot improve their existing knowledge simply by "purchasing" it. An individual must continuously interpret the new events he experiences and reorient his plans accordingly. This reorientation of the mind is an unending process. (Kibbe 1987, 4).

Kibbe quotes Lachmann on the importance of heuristic probes and plausible reasoning on the frontiers of entrepreneurship: "What men adjust their plans to are not observable events as such, but their own interpretation of them and their changing expectations about them" (Kibbe 1987, 4).

To be one's own interpreter of complex and rapidly moving events on the frontiers of knowledge requires that the executive be able to use the mental eye of not only the objective, nuts-and-bolts mind-set, but also that of the subjective, intuitive mind-set. When we blend the images of a situation provided by both mind-sets to form a workable image of the whole, we have what we call "bifocal intellectual vision," or "bifocal vision," for short.

In discussing the need for balancing these two mind-sets, Chester Barnard, in *The Functions of the Executive,* said back in the 1930s that what is needed is "better use of the non-logical mind to support" the capacity for rigorous reasoning. "'Brains' without 'minds' seem a futile unbalance," he added (Barnard 1938, 302-3).

Our four decades of experimental efforts in this area suggest that the key to bifocal vision is to learn to frame short-range, objective images of situations within long-range, intuitive perspectives (Clark 1977, 38-46, 1985, 34-40; Clark and Clark 1979, 112-13, 1980a, 140; Ferguson 1980, 40-41, 352). By adding the intuitive dimension of what Barnard called "the corrective of the feeling mind," we have a basis for providing what we call "qualitative perspectives for quantitative analysis" (Clark and Clark 1979, 110-18).

The fact that the intuitive mind-set can be reawakened, disciplined, and harnessed in policy-level thinking by many–perhaps most–healthy-minded men and women in some areas of endeavor provides an element of confidence in appropriate education programs committed to the ideal of bifocal vision (Ferguson 1980, 40-41, 352).

Also, the fact that both of these mind-sets seem to use appropriate adaptations of the logic of economy of thought makes basic economics courses a fertile area in the curriculum for introducing the idea of modeling one's world picture for one's self (Clark 1969, 1985, 34-40; Judge 1970, 2; Judge and Clark 1970, 1-5).

THE NEED FOR AN ORGANIC NUCLEUS OF KNOWLEDGE

The central concept in this interpretive, economy-of-thought approach to information management is our own version of what Kenneth E. Boulding, in 1956, called "an indispensable minimum of knowledge," as introduced in his book *The Image: Knowledge in Life and Society* and as explicated in some of his subsequent public lectures.[1]

To reflect the bifocal, organic emphasis of our lifetime work, we use the label, "organic nucleus of knowledge."[2] This is essentially an exploratory, heuristic approach to learning to constantly reorganize and refocus one's thinking and entire knowledge system around each of the varied challenges of a lifetime of work on the cutting edge of action. Like the nucleus of a cell, this intellectual nucleus, when fully developed, will be analogous to a communications nerve center and control tower in the mind of the decision-maker on the cutting edge of knowledge. It will be charged with responsibility for optimizing the benefits of efforts to select, acquire, organize, and use information required to meet more or less any need in any field at any time.

This organic, results-oriented nucleus is an interactive blending of beliefs, attitudes, perspectives, concepts, skills, sensitivities, habits, and expectations that are required to determine in relatively unfamiliar – as well as familiar – situations what information to look for and how to acquire, organize, and use it to best advantage. More specifically, it is an introspective, metaphorical frame of reference for crystallizing beliefs, evoking attitudes, setting priorities, making decisions, shaping expectations, focusing actions, and tracking progress in the arts, humanities, and the natural and social sciences.

From a structural point of view, this intellectual nucleus consists of common denominators of the patterns of communications flows that control organized activity in all fields of thought from the hard and soft sciences to the arts and humanities. Of special interest are the patterns of interactions of six of the simplest, most common, most basic, most flexible, and most learnable elements of qualitative communications – namely, goals, guides, motivations, expectations, decisions, and feedbacks.

Equally important are the common denominators of the principles of economic logic, such as the laws of opportunity costs and comparative advantage in shaping, implementing, and assessing policies and strategies for any purposive organization. The potential role of these "common denominators of economy-of-thought communications" is to serve figuratively as a genetic code of the intellect. They are all flexible, accessible, recognizable, and more or less universal building blocks for developing rational images, or models, of economic and social organizations.

This intellectual nucleus consists not so much of content as it does of structural guidelines for organizing one's expectations, perceptions, and thoughts about situations with a view toward determining what content is needed and how best to locate, acquire, organize, and use it (Clark 1969, 1970b, 1972a, 1972b; Clark and Clark 1980b).

This interpretive nucleus is anything but a substitute for the precision and rigor, or for the "content," of objective, one-field models. As a supplement to these indispensable, objective anchors for policy thinking in any field, this nucleus aims to provide open, flexible, and artistic perspectives that can be expected to keep the objective, one-field models relevant and viable as we move toward the anticipated turbulence of the twenty-first century. It is a question of being able to visualize any one-field model as a special case of the organic, metaphorical nucleus of knowledge. As Alfred North Whitehead has put it, "the aim of scientific thought" is to "see what is general in what is particular" (Whitehead 1948).

CRAFTING THE ORGANIC NUCLEUS

Using the common denominator approach, we have developed our version of this intellectual nucleus around three strategic control functions that are common to the communications processes that control all purposive ecosystems in virtually all fields. These are the functions of *mapping* the environment in ecosystems communications terms, *scanning* that environment to identify problems and opportunities, and *choosing* between alternative courses of action. Each of these three control functions is assumed to be performed through its own unique arrangement of six invisible communications elements that are common to all purposive communications systems of control: *goals, guides, motivations, expectations, decisions,* and *feedbacks.*

We are now ready to show how these six elements can be combined and recombined to form a symbolic model of each of the three control functions of mapping, scanning, and choosing. We can then blend the models of the three control functions mutualistically, or *organically,* to form the embryo of the master interpretive model we call the organic nucleus of knowledge.

Mapping the Communications Controls

Mapping the firm's environment in terms of communications controls is introspectively interpreting the company and related organizations as interactive networks of information control systems of goals, guides, motivations, expectations, decisions, and feedbacks. This bifocal control map, or model, interprets objective, analytical perceptions of decision-making units and market processes in the language of information control systems extended to embrace the subjective, qualitative side of the control process.

For example, consider the functions of money. In the language of objective analysis, its main functions are to serve as a medium of exchange, a yardstick of value, and a store of value. The subjective communications language of control focuses on the higher level of organizational functions that enable money to serve these indispensable, behavioral functions. In this purposive context, money serves as a *goal* to show the preferred direction of movement, as a *signal* to show when and where to turn, and as a *motivation* to encourage the decision-maker to take the indicated route.

A schematic, introspective framework for mapping the qualitative communications elements that control XYZ Corporation is shown in Figure 1.

Figure 1: Communications Control Map: A Teleological View of Ecosystems Controls

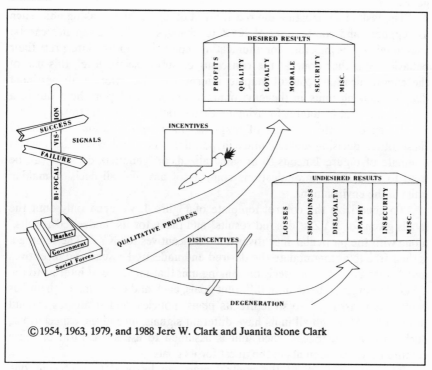

The crossroads represent the need to make a decision. The signpost symbolizes a set of guides, or signals, for informing individuals who know the bifocal communications code what is expected of them. Market prices of things bought and sold are portrayed as the most tangible set of signals, with governmental edicts and directives and social custom and tradition playing important supportive roles.

The carrot represents incentives such as a high income, recognition, and pride in doing a good job. The stick represents disincentives such as low income, frustration, and chagrin. The incentives and disincentives are intended to motivate individuals to heed the signals and take the road of qualitative progress for the corporation as well as for themselves and to avoid the road of degeneration. The goal sections at the end of the two roads obviously represent the organization's positive goals and unwanted results, or "negative avoidance goals," as they are sometimes called. A feedback loop, not shown on the map, can be added to make visible the feedback process whereby ongoing evaluative messages are sent to the CEO indicating how well the company is hewing to the anticipated trajectory toward its composite goals.

The task of anticipating the reactions of other decision-making units such as suppliers and competitors of XYZ to changes in XYZ strategies can be simplified by using the communicating control map to interpret their behavior. Whether done at the conscious or subconscious level, this use of the communications control map to interpret the behavior of all pertinent decision-making units in the environment amounts to laying them out in a parallel way that facilitates focusing on their strategic control patterns.

To expedite this process of mapping the communications controls of these other decision-making units in parallel, functional ways, the control template of Figure 1 needs to be generalized, or "genericized," so it can be used to map the communications controls of any and all decision-making units in the environment.

To genericize the control template of Figure 1, we need only omit the labels given for XYZ's "desired results" and those for its "undesired results," along with the particular incentives and disincentives for XYZ. The template is then free to accommodate the desired and undesired results and incentives and disincentives for any decision-making unit that might be of interest to the CEO. Although all units have different goals, each and every one of them has goals and is assumed to structure its plans, policies, and strategies around those ends. Although all units have different signals, incentives, expectations, decisions, and feedbacks, each unit is assumed to use some form of these communications elements in the quest for its goals.

The generic form of the control map can be used to represent one person, firm, union, or other organized group. In that case the individual decision-maker would portray his or her long-range aspirations in the "desired results" section and his or her relatively tangible, short-range objectives in the "incentives" section.

Scanning for Strategic Potentials

Strategic potentials imaging is an introspective way of scanning the environment in search of hidden means for advancing one's organization toward its goals, or objectives.

The process of qualitative scanning is a bifocal extension of the age-old process of objectively scanning the environment seeking evidences of threats and opportunities and clues for designing strategies to face the challenges that are posed. It interprets bifocally the goals, guides, motivations, expectations, decisions, and feedbacks of the varied ecosystems that inhabit the environment with a view toward identifying and exploring the behavior of ecosystems that are deemed to be especially pertinent to the success of one's own firm from time to time.

Figure 2: Strategic Image Focuser for Transforming Quantitative Facts into Qualitative Images

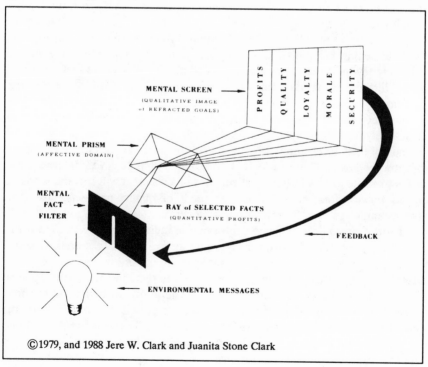

©1979, and 1988 Jere W. Clark and Juanita Stone Clark

The "strategic image focuser" represents our attempt to portray metaphorically what we believe to be the process through which one's bifocal mental eye is enabled to crystallize hidden, as well as visible, clues that problems and/or opportunities may be evolving. This interpretation of the strategic image focuser's role is based on the assumption that philosopher Oliver Reiser was right when he said that the human mind is "like a prism that breaks up the white radiance" of truth into "all colors of the rainbow" (Reiser 1960).

As illustrated in Figure 2, this focusing template portrays these mental processes in the mind of the CEO of XYZ Corporation in identifying quantitative profits as a strategic item to be interpreted. For that interpretation to qualify as a qualitative one, it must be transformed into the hues of the figurative rainbow of qualitative progress – that is, the goals shown on the CEO's mental screen.

In that figure, the light bulb represents "reality" as a multitude of unorganized environmental messages that are more or less competing for the CEO's attention. Except for these unorganized messages represented by the light bulb, the rest of this template represents what is assumed to be inside the CEO's mind when probing for new insights into what the future might hold for XYZ.

The CEO's mental fact filter of beliefs, attitudes, and expectations is at work screening out all unwanted types of messages and filtering in the relatively few pertinent facts that are needed. The illustrative fact shown as being filtered in is the quantitative figure for XYZ profits from the traditional, objective income statement prepared by the firm's chief accountant. As this "black-and-white" figure for profits is filtered in, it is figuratively refracted by the mental prism of the affective, or "feelings," domain of the CEO's mind into the hues of the qualitative image of the firm's rainbow of goals. This executive has assumed that the XYZ Corporation wants to make profits in the short run, but in a way that will sow the seeds of profits for the long run – that is, the seeds of quality products, customer loyalty, employee morale, and corporate security.

From time to time evaluative information indicating how well the firm is progressing toward – or moving away from – its goals is fed back to the CEO.

In preparing to make decisions that are both important and complex; the strategic image focuser is especially important in the quest for fertile options to consider. To be eligible for serious consideration, an option must show promise as a potential "producer," or generator, of the desired results, or goals, that make up the qualitative image on the CEO's mental screen.

The mental prism of the affective domain is the key to triggering the intuitive mind-set to do its qualitative work. We agree with Willard Gaylin that feelings are keys to effective imaging, or modeling, rather than deterrents: "Feelings are the instruments of rationality, not – as some would have it – alternatives to it. . . . Feelings become guides to . . . choice" (Gaylin 1979, 5-17).

The role of subjective thinking in this kind of focusing operation was emphasized also by psychologist Carl Jung when he said that the intuition "explores the unknown and senses possibilities and indications which may not be readily apparent" (Jung 1921).

In identifying intuitive thinking as "the most valuable coin of the thinker at work, whatever his line of work," Jerome Bruner stressed the importance of intuitively seeking "the shrewd guess, the fertile hypothesis, [and] the courageous leap to a tentative conclusion" (Bruner 1963, 13-14). The strategic potentials focuser is simply a device for coaxing the intuition out of hiding and putting it to work to uncover what John Maurice Clark called "the electric potentials of purpose" hidden in Reiser's "white radiance" of a black-and-white purpose such as making profits (J. M. Clark 1957, 37).

To transform the particularized form of the strategic image focuser for the XYZ Corporation in Figure 2 into a universal, or generic, template, we need only block out the specific list of "refracted goals" in the mental screen. In that case the refracted goals of any organization can then be inserted.

Choosing Qualitatively

The qualitative process of choosing is a bifocal extension of the traditional, objective decision-making process with emphasis on identifying and fusing "hard" and "soft" information within the mind of the decision-maker. It structures goals, guides, motivations, expectations, decisions, and feedbacks interactively to facilitate the process of putting goals, priorities, and expectations in command of the quest for quality.

The quality optimizer index is a variation and extension of the age-old, multiattribute matrix for making consumer decisions. In its simplest decision-making form, this index is a commonsensical, ad-hoc blending of two indexes involved in making any multicriterion decision at the intrapersonal level.

The first is a weighted index of goals being used as criteria for making a decision. The other index is an introspective scale for measuring the benefits, or expected results, of each option being considered in terms of each criterion.

An example of a decision-making quality optimizer index being used by XYZ Corporation to decide on a corporate strategy is featured in Figure 3 (Clark and Clark 1988, 901).

In its planning form, the structure of the matrix is modified to facilitate the process of planning. In this context, the weighted index of goals, or criteria, is not used to make a decision. It is used, rather, to identify where the firm is relative to its goals today, on the one hand, and to suggest a realistic set of expectations of progress toward each of those goals by some future date, on the other.

Figure 4 is an example of a planning quality optimizer index being used to design the mission of XYZ Corporation. That figure identifies not only where the firm was in 1981 in terms of its goals and priorities, but also where it expected to be a decade later, given a resourceful effort throughout that decade.

Both the decision-making and the planning forms of the optimizer index provide a simple, introspective way to focus Stanley Davis's "future perfect approach" to management outlined in his book *Future Perfect*–that is, "managing in the future perfect tense–as a way of measuring the consequences of events that have not yet occurred" (Davis 1987, 8).

One of the structural advantages of the optimizer index is that it can be used to focus what is, in effect, a dialogue between the objective and subjective mind-sets within the mind of the decision-maker. In the case of challenges on the frontiers of knowledge, the intuitive mind-set is believed to take charge of raising to the level of consciousness the relatively subconscious criteria of column 1 and the priorities of column 2.

The objective mind-set is believed to take charge of doing the research for the performance coefficients and making the calculations for the remaining columns of both the decision-making and the planning optimizer indexes (Ferguson 1980, 295-300).

A generic form of either the decision-making or the planning matrix can be generated simply by omitting the criteria shown for XYZ Corporation in column 1 and the figures in the other columns of the matrix to create a blank form of the template. This universal format can be adapted to accommodate any multicriterion decision made by anyone, anywhere, any time.

Interactive Nature of the Communications Templates

What is more important than the role of each of these three interpretive communications control templates is the way they can be used interactively to reinforce each other. All three are teleological in that they are oriented around goals, priorities, and expectations that are translated into policies and strategies for navigating toward company goals. In all cases the signals and incentives–in some cases more implicit than explicit–flow from and are oriented around the goals.

Figure 3: Decision-making Quality Optimizer Index (QOI) for Choosing Corporate Strategy

Option A:	To adapt present management style and organizational structures				
Option B:	To reconceptualize global challenge of becoming "better than the best"				

PRIORITIES			PERFORMANCE EXPECTATIONS		
PERFORMANCE CRITERIA (Long-range aspirations expressed as results to be achieved)	QUALITY WEIGHTS		WEIGHTED MERITS of EACH OPTION		
			A. Adapt		B. Reconceptualize
	Q	P*	QP	P*	QP
(1)	(2)	(3)	(4)	(5)	(6)
PROFITS (ROE)	30	5	150	9	270
QUALITATIVE GROWTH	25	6	150	10	250
RESPONSIVENESS	20	3	60	9	180
WORLD-CLASS LEADERSHIP	10	4	40	9	90
CUSTOMER LOYALTY	5	6	30	9	45
STEWARDSHIP	5	9	45	8	40
SYNERGY	5	5	25	9	45
TOTALS	100 %	xxxx	500	xxxx	920

© 1953, 1984, and 1988 Jere W. Clark and Juanita Stone Clark   * P = 1 to 10; with 10 = best

Figure 4: Planning Quality Optimizer Index (QOI) for Mapping Mission Design

PRIORITIES			PERFORMANCE EXPECTATIONS		
PERFORMANCE CRITERIA (Long-range aspirations expressed as results to be achieved)	QUALITY WEIGHTS		WEIGHTED MERITS of EACH OPTION		GAP
		1981		1991	
	Q	P*	QP	P*	QP	QP
(1)	(2)	(3)	(4)	(5)	(6)	(7)
PROFITS (ROE)	30	6	180	9	270	90
QUALITATIVE GROWTH (Becoming world's most valuable corporation re market capitalization)	25	5	125	10	250	125
RESPONSIVENESS (Adapting to change by staying lean and agile)	20	4	80	9	180	100
WORLD-CLASS LEADERSHIP (Dreaming, reaching, and daring to shape the future)	10	5	50	9	90	40
CUSTOMER LOYALTY (Attracting repeat customers through quality goods and services)	5	7	35	9	45	10
STEWARDSHIP (Evoking responsible behavior by employees to company and society at large)	5	8	40	8	40	0
SYNERGY (Capitalizing on unity in diversity through sharing)	5	5	25	8	40	15
TOTALS	100 %	xxx	535	xxx	915	380

* P = 1 to 10; with 10 = best

© 1953, 1984, and 1988 Jere W. Clark and Juanita Stone Clark

What is important is that when we blend the communications control templates for mapping, scanning, and choosing interactively and bifocally, we have the embryo of the organic nucleus of knowledge (Clark and Clark 1985).

Thus, we see that crafting this intellectual nucleus can begin with learning to view the communications elements of goals, guides, motivations, expectations, decisions, and feedbacks bifocally, while constantly reorganizing them in one's own mind to shift from mapping to scanning, or from scanning to choosing, or from choosing to mapping.

INTEGRATIVE PROBLEM-SOLVING FLOW DIAGRAM

The acid test of a conceptual model is a question of how effective it is in the field helping to solve problems and capitalize on opportunities that face an organization from time to time. More specifically in the context of this paper, it is a question of how well the model helps the field executive use the information available to get the information needed to take care of whatever problems and opportunities emerge from time to time.

In the final analysis, it is in the realm of being conceptually prepared to solve many types and levels of problems in many areas of work that the need for compatibility of problem-solving models becomes acute. To provide one iterative template for identifying, processing, and resolving all kinds and levels of problems and opportunities, Juanita Stone Clark and Andrew Esposito have developed the generic diagram of Figure 5 (Clark and Clark 1985, 166).

This generic map of feedback loops is structured to provide a results-oriented, iterative frame of reference for identifying and processing problems and opportunities on an ad-hoc basis, ranging from the simple, familiar, and tactical to the complex, unfamiliar, and strategic.

The simple, familiar, and tactical types of problems can be handled in routine ways by moving almost automatically and instantaneously through the six rectangles shown above the controller's observation point near the middle of the template (beginning with the one labeled "problem definition"), while relying on the short, straight arrows for feedback. Few, if any, of the policy-level competencies would be needed in these routine situations. More baffling and important problems require more and wider feedback loops to represent broader probes into more areas of knowledge to seek clues.

The continuous, open-ended nature of the process can be highlighted by imagining the bending of the template from top to bottom to form a cylinder. The concept of the quality of living reminds us that there are ever higher ideals latent in the quest for progress to induce us to take on still greater challenges.

Figure 5: Generic Process of Resourceful Problem Solving "Using the means one has to get the means one needs to do what needs to be done."—Jere W. Clark

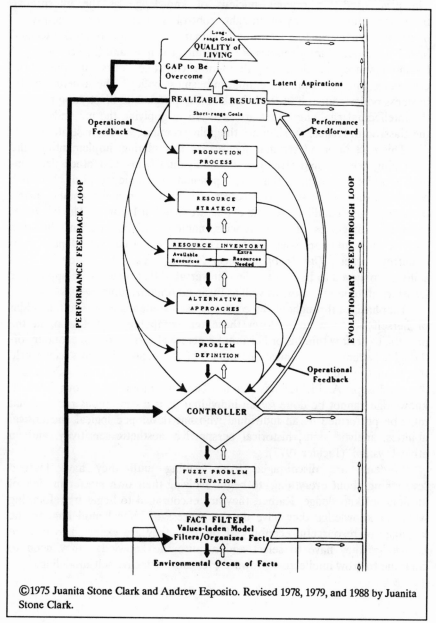

GRADUATE SEMINAR IN BUSINESS POLICY

We have used the organic nucleus of knowledge as the interpretive framework for economy-of-thought control processes in a variety of university courses ranging from the freshman to the graduate level. Included have been the freshman courses of economic principles and the economics of human resource development, the senior capstone course in managerial economics, and the graduate seminar in business policy.[3] The structure of the business policy course best lends itself to the purpose of illustrating many of the intellectual challenges that are involved in applying the methodology in the classroom. Hence, we shall use the policy seminar as our illustration.

This case-oriented seminar focuses on formulating, implementing, and evaluating policies and strategies for individual firms and other decision-making units operating in the interdependent economic world of electronic communications. The seminar revolves around the ten policy competencies, or "information handling literacies," that are listed in Figure 6. The labels for the three categories of competencies, namely, "mission design," "mission control," and "mission assessment," have been borrowed and adapted from Geoffrey Vickers, *The Art of Judgment* (1970). These information handling skills are believed to be more or less universal in that they can be applied, or transferred, to nonbusiness as well as business organizations.

Emphasized throughout the course is each student's efforts to teach him or herself not only to perform these ten competencies but also, in the process, to craft within his or her mind a personal version of the economy-of-thought, systems communications model of the economic and social world that he or she inhabits.

As Joseph A. Pichler has put it, "The integration of various fields of knowledge cannot be done *for* an individual. It is a continuous process that must be performed *by* an individual who has developed logical and critical abilities, analytic skills, historical perspective, aesthetic sensitivity, and an ethical system" (Pichler 1977).

Students are discouraged from waiting until they have learned "everything about everything" to begin evolving their own master models of all fields of knowledge. Rather, they are encouraged to begin by refocusing whatever knowledge they have on the process of bifocal modeling. In the language of resourceful economy of thought, they are expected to use the knowledge they have to select and acquire the knowledge they need to continue to grow intellectually toward ever more effective self-modeling.

Figure 6: Policy Level Competencies for Qualitative Planning

A. MISSION DESIGN: Destination Setting

   1. <u>Imaging Goals</u>: Crystallizing workable goal configurations

   2. <u>Setting Priorities</u>: Showing relative importance of goals

   3. <u>Targeting Mission Expectations</u>: Crystallizing challenging, but realistic, sets of prioritized expectations

B. MISSION CONTROL: Problem Solving

   4. <u>Defining Problems Coherently</u>: Focusing relevant quantitative and qualitative aspects of situations into coherent images of performance gaps between what is and what might be

   5. <u>Setting Criteria</u>: Organizing prioritized criteria for choosing strategy with greatest potential

   6. <u>Weighing Options</u>: Using prioritized criteria to assess the potentials of each of the most promising strategies

   7. <u>Targeting Operational Expectations</u>: Crystallizing expectations of progress toward prioritized, operational goals

   8. <u>Tracking Progress</u>: Measuring progress toward goals

C. MISSION ASSESSMENT: Course Correcting

   9. <u>Setting Standards</u>: Certifying prioritized, evaluative yardsticks for measuring long-range progress

   10. <u>Assessing Mission</u>: Using prioritized standards to appraise, reappraise, and adapt design of mission

Elsewhere we have characterized the challenge of intellectual growth through self-modeling in the metaphor of intellectual navigation:

> Today the student must be viewed as a potentially self-propelled, self-guided navigator. He needs to be able to chart his way not only through the relatively familiar, static, and simple world of today, but also through the relatively strange . . . and complex world of tomorrow. He must be able to program his mind in a way that will enable him to re-program it whenever necessary throughout his lifetime. (Clark 1972a, 171).

The competencies listed in Figure 6 are practiced in the briefing of weekly cases pertaining to problem situations faced by real firms and in a field research project in which students select and map the policy thinking of a local business or other appropriate organization of their choice.

The design specifications for the case briefs are shown in Figure 7. We have found that the quality optimizer index, in both its planning and decision-making forms, provides a simple and practical focus not only for learning these information-handling skills individually, but also for integrating them into a coherent whole.

Figure 7: Design Specifications for Case Briefs*

A. MISSION DESIGN: Direction Finding

   1. One-page, mission-oriented introduction to the firm and the context in which the problem emerges.

   2. Quality Optimizer Index No. 1: A planning QOI portraying the firm's goals priorities, present position, and long-range expectations.

B. MISSION CONTROL I: Problem Processing

   1. A functional, positive, "one-sentence" definition of the overarching problem/ opportunity. Begin with an infinitive--e.g., "to reconceptualize our mission so as to focus more on..."

   2. A coherent definition of the problem/opportunity expressed as the total weighted quality points (QPs) in the performance gap targeted in QOI No. 1.

   3. Analysis of the inventory gap--i.e., the difference between available and needed resources.

   4. Rationale for each of the two strategies you think have greatest potential for resolving the problem or enhancing the opportunity.

C. MISSION CONTROL II: Decision Making

   Quality Optimizer Index No. 2: A decision-making QOI using prioritized criteria to choose optimal strategy.

D. MISSION CONTROL III: Decision Implementing

   Quality Optimizer Index No. 3: A planning QOI targeting operational expectations.

E. MISSION CONTROL IV: Commitment Building

   A proactive statement of rationale for recommended action.

F. MISSION ASSESSMENT: Course Correcting

   Quality Optimizer Index No. 4: A planning QOI for assessing the long-range effectiveness of the company mission in terms of targeted expectations and the possible need to change direction.

---

* Excerpt from the syllabus of the graduate seminar, BUE 560: Business Policy, Southern Connecticut State University, 1988.

INVITATION TO A DIALOGUE

This heuristic exploration of economy of thought as a basis for resolving the problem of information overload obviously is subject to many limitations inherent in experimental probes into the subjective domain of the human mind. For that reason, over and beyond any errors of omission and commission that may have been made, great caution must be exercised in interpreting this exploration.

Because the subjective qualities highlighted here are to be found, like beauty, in the eye of the beholder, we feel very strongly that the time has come to experiment more openly, as well as more cautiously, with these subjective wellsprings of economy of thought in the individual mind. Our hope is that this paper might play some part, however small, in keeping the dialogue on this type of research alive and responsive to the emerging needs of the twenty-first century.

With that thought in mind, we want to close this paper with a statement we penned some years ago highlighting resourcefulness in the quest for thought patterns appropriate to the challenge of resolving the problem of information overload for the twenty-first century:

> Economy of Thought at its best consists of dreaming up the best world that has a chance of coming to be, identifying its landmarks, blueprinting its structure, and developing operational strategies for reaching the goal. The approach is a resourceful one with as much emphasis on evoking the will as on charting the way. It begins with the world that needs to be, that might be, and, indeed, can be.

> It then inventories the resources that are required and compares them with those that are available. The strategic step then is to develop an operational strategy and supporting system of tactics for transforming available resources into the required resources. At that point, objective rationality again becomes critical. (Clark, Clark, and Esposito 1971, 13)

Notes

1. So profound was the impact of The Image on our thinking that we predicted in 1958 that that monograph would prove to be one of the twentieth-century books with the greatest influence in shaping the twenty-first century. Reading *The Image* and listening to a few of Boulding's public lectures on this and related epistemological issues indirectly led us to begin thinking around 1967 of shaping our evolving master model of knowledge in the direction of this "indispensable minimum," but with a bifocal emphasis and a different label.

2. Between 1967 and 1971, we focused four national and international conferences around various aspects of what we are now calling the organic nucleus of knowledge. All four of these conferences were sponsored by the Center for Interdisciplinary Creativity at Southern Connecticut State College and cosponsored by the (SGSR) Task Force on General Systems Education (which was spawned by and coordinated through the center). The fourth one, an international workshop, was cosponsored also, by the Brussels-based Union of International Associations. The last three of the conferences were funded by the Calvin K. Kazanjian Economics Foundation.

In some of our earlier writings during the last two decades, we have used the label "metalanguage" for what we are now calling the organic nucleus of knowledge. Within the context of a given spoken tongue, the metalanguage is viewed as being primarily a "master metaphorical grammar" that is capable of subsuming the grammatical ways of structuring expectations and observations in the various fields of thought to form a more or less coherent and artistic whole at the metaphorical level (Clark 1969, 1970b, 1971, 36-38). In 1975, at the initiative of the USOE/HEW, we used the basic model to design a high school careers planning project under the label, "The General Ecology of Knowledge." This label was intended to convey not only the idea that basic ideas and ideals are organic in nature and can be "germinated and grown," but also the idea that each student could "grow" his or her own ecology of career concepts in his or her own mind (Clark 1972a, 168-69).

3. At the freshman level, the interpretive model of the organic nucleus of knowledge is used to help students organize their thinking about the intellectual world they are going to be studying the next four years. It is intended to help students understand why they need to take courses in many areas that may appear to be foreign and how they can evolve "a living place" in their minds for each specialty. At the senior and graduate levels and in in-house executive training programs, the focus is more on helping students reorganize and reconceptualize "what they already know," so as to be able to identify and learn better what they still need to learn.

References

Barnard, Chester I. 1938. *The Functions of the Executive.* Cambridge, Mass.: Harvard University Press.

Beer, Stafford. 1985. "Managing Modern Complexity." *Futures Research Quarterly* (Fall).

Boulding, Kenneth E. 1956. *The Image: Knowledge in Life and Society.* Ann Arbor: University of Michigan Press.

Bruner, Jerome S. 1963. *The Process of Education.* Cambridge, Mass.: Harvard University Press (quoted in Zoa Rockenstein, "Intuitive Processes in Executive Decision Making." *Journal of Creative Behavior,* 2d Quarter 1988, 78).

Clark, Jere W. 1965. "Creativeness–Can It Be Cultivated?" *Business Quarterly* (Spring) (condensed in *Management Review,* June 1965).

_____. 1969. "Quantum Leaps in Education." *Connecticut Industry* (May).

_____. 1970. "The Nature and Purpose of a Metalanguage." In Milton Rubin, *Man in Systems.* Boston: Gordon and Breach.

_____. 1971. "The Nucleus of a Unified Curriculum." *Educational Technology* (November).

_____. 1972a. "The General Ecology of Knowledge in Curriculums of the Future." In Ervin Laszlo, ed., *The Relevance of General Systems Theory.* New York: George Braziller.

_____. 1972b. "Systems Philosophy and the Crisis of Fragmentation in Education." In Ervin Laszlo, ed., *Introduction to Systems Philosophy.* Boston: Gordon and Breach.

_____. 1977. "General Systems Perspectives." *Journal of Creative Behavior* (1st Quarter).

_____. 1985. "Broadening Our Image of Rationality." *Futurics* 9, no. 1.

Clark, Jere W., and Juanita S. Clark. 1979. "The Art of Soaring." *Journal of Creative Behavior* (2d Quarter) (reprint of ch. 3, *From Quantity to Quality*, 3d experimental ed., 1979).

_____. 1980a. *"Bi-Focal Vision: Qualitative Perspectives for Quantitative Analysis."* Concept Outline Series no. 1, Center for Interdisciplinary Creativity, Southern Connecticut State College.

_____. 1980b. *Coherence in Designing Policy.* 1st experimental ed. (photocopied for our classes).

_____. 1985. *Strategic Potentials Imaging: The Heuristics of Entrepreneurial Policy Design*, 1st experimental ed. (photocopied for our classes).

_____. 1988. "A Qualitative Framework for Defining, Measuring, and Improving Productivity." In Canadian Council for Productivity, *Learning from Experience: Proceedings of the Sixth World Productivity Congress* 2. Montreal, Canada (September 27), 887-913.

Clark, Jere W., Juanita S. Clark, and Andrew Esposito, eds. 1971. *Launching Operation Man to Mankind: Toward Grass-roots Involvement in Designing the Global Democracy of the 21st Century.* Kazanjian Economics Foundation.

Clark, John Maurice. 1957. *Economic Institutions and Human Welfare.* New York: Knopf.

Cleveland, Harlan. 1986. "Educating for the Information Society." In H. F. Didsbury, Jr., ed., *Challenges and Opportunities: From Now to 2001.* Bethesda, Md.: World Future Society.

David, Stanley M. 1987. *Future Perfect.* Reading, Mass.: Addison-Wesley.

Drucker, Peter F. 1968. *The Age of Discontinuity: Guidelines to Our Changing Society.* New York: Harper and Row.

Ferguson, Marilyn. 1980. *The Aquarian Conspiracy: Personal and Social Transformation in the 1980s.* Los Angeles: J. P. Tarcher.

Fuller, Buckminster. 1969. *Operating Manual for Spaceship Earth.* New York: Simon and Schuster.

Gaylin, Willard. 1979. "Feelings: Our Vital Signs." *Science Digest* (June), 15-17 (from Willard Gaylin, *Feelings: Our Vital Signs.* New York: Harper and Row, 1979).

Judge, Anthony J. N. 1970. "Editorial Comment: General Systems and International Organizations and the United Nations International Education Year." *Associations Internationales*, no. 1, p. 2.

Judge, Anthony J. N., and Jere W. Clark. 1970. "Development of Trans-Disciplinary Conceptual Aids" (Occasional paper published in English and French). Brussels: Union of International Associations (April).

Jung, Carl G. 1921. "Psychological Types." In H. Read, M. Fordham, and G. Adler, eds., *Collected Works of C. G. Jung*, vol. 6. Princeton, N. J.: Princeton University Press (quoted in Zoa Rockenstein, "Intuitive Processes in Executive Decision Making." *Journal of Creative Behavior*, 2d Quarter, 17).

Kibbe, Matthew B. 1987. "Escaping the Paretian Paradigm." *Market Process* (Fall).

Knight, Frank H. 1956. *On the History and Method of Economics.* Chicago: University of Chicago Press.

Lachmann, Ludwig. 1986. *The Market as an Economic Process.* Basil Blackwell.

Mach, Ernst. 1902. *The Science of Mechanics: A Critical and Historical Account of Its Development*, translated from the German by Thomas J. McCormack. Chicago: Open Court Publishing Co.

Meltzer, Morton F. 1971. *The Information Imperative.* New York: American Management Association.

Pichler, Joseph A. 1977. "Ibsen and the Business Schools." A "Point-of-View" editorial, *Chronicle of Higher Education* (September 26).

Reiser, Oliver L. 1958. *The Integration of Human Knowledge.* Boston: Gordon and Breach.

_____. 1960. "Magnetic Moments in History" (source and exact date of publication – c. 1960 – not available).

Vickers, Geoffrey. 1970. *The Art of Judgment: A Study of Policy Making.* New York: Basic Books.

Whitehead, Alfred North. 1929. *The Aims of Education.* New York: Macmillan.

_____. 1948 (originally published in 1911). *Introduction to Mathematics.* New York: Oxford University Press.

Wriston, Walter B. 1986. "The World According to Walter." *Harvard Business Review* (January-February).

Information Filtering

MARY F. HABAN

When an entity or commodity that is important in human life expands so greatly that it is said to surround us, to saturate our environment, does it become *more* important to us, or *less* important? When we consider that question, we realize that the *phrasing* of the question does not quite fit the kind of response the question evokes. For the change that takes place in our perception of the entity because of its great growth is not a change in the *importance* it has, but is rather a change in the way we *react* to the entity. Food, for example, is a very important component of human life. When it becomes so plentiful that a community or nation cannot use it all, however, it does continue to be very important but the *approach* to it changes. While earlier people made strong efforts to obtain it, seeing it as a desirable goal, people now turn their efforts to coping with it, managing it, controlling it.

At present, we are said to have entered an "information age." Information surrounds us – some say we are bombarded by it, some say we are in danger of being submerged by it. Despite some hyperbole on the subject, there is general agreement that we have access to *far* more information today than ever before in history, and that its already high growth *rate* will not only continue but even increase. So our gaze into the twenty-first century shows us a society permeated by information, a society that must expend more effort in managing its information, controlling it, coping with it.

Indeed, that situation exists already in some environments, to some degree. But in the current decade we still must give strong attention and efforts to extracting *more* information from available data and from expressed ideas. We still must give strong efforts to expanding the *access* to the information that is generally available. By the twenty-first century, however, with the advances in communications technologies and in computer capabilities, we can expect that the extraction and communication of *more* information will require far less attention and effort, and that the priority will have shifted strongly to the *management* of information – and more specifically, to the problems of the *individual* who must deal with a situation of easy access to far more information than he or she can absorb.

These thoughts bring us to the concept of information filtering, the topic of this paper. Many of these ideas individually will not be new to readers of this book, but perhaps the way they have been brought together will be useful and will spark further thoughts along the lines of reasoning to be presented here.

INFORMATION OVERLOAD

Readers may remember the paper by the Spanish philosopher José Ortega y Gasset in which he traced the importance of the book in human society and expressed the idea that books had then (he was speaking in the 1930s) become so important and so prevalent that they posed a problem to humans. "There are already too many books," he said.

> The quantity of books [a man] must absorb is so enormous that it exceeds the limits of his time and his capacity of assimilation. Merely the work of orienting oneself in the bibliography of a subject today represents a considerable effort for an author and proves to be a total loss. For once he has completed that part of his work, the author discovers that he cannot read all that he ought to read. This leads him to read too fast and to read badly. It moreover leaves him with an impression of powerlessness and failure, and finally skepticism towards his own work.

Ortega went on to refer to "the raging book" and concluded by saying, "I imagine the librarian of the future as a filter interposed between man and the torrent of books."[1]

I am not using Ortega's remarks in the 1930s as a basis for my discussion of information filtering in the twenty-first century. But there is something appealing about the voice crying in the wilderness, with its strong and sincere plea and the perceptiveness of his concern from within the framework of his times.

This "overload" problem is our focus here. It is a problem that is significant already but that will grow enormously by the twenty-first century, in tandem with all our vastly improved means of gathering and communicating information. A number of thinkers from the precomputer era spoke on this overload problem, but the expressions of concern are now becoming widespread within the library and information science professions. It is a concern that arises as the "flip side" of the record of technological advances in information retrieval.

From the user's perspective, the overload problem is one of unnecessary repetition. Many documents retrieved for the user contain repetitive information, and he or she must waste valuable time sifting through the material to isolate the information that is unique or treated in a unique manner. It is this "sifting through" that is meant by "information filtering."

This idea may raise fears of similarities between "filtering" and "censoring." But such filtering should be no more threatening than the *selection* that has always had to be exercised by those who purchase materials for collections. The effect of the activity is to provide only limited access through *some* services or service centers – not to limit the access (or publication) available to those who desire the fuller access.

The *Encyclopedia of Library and Information Science* says, "Neither information nor access to it solves problems. Increasingly, the *volume* of information in itself can constitute a problem."[2] Indiana University's Herbert White has written about users' "very real fear that 'better' information systems will bring them *more* information, when their real hope is for less but more germane information."[3]

But of course our advances in information technology *are* bringing users *more* information. Today the information explosion includes not only the high rate of growth of publications but also the high rate of growth in the number of *databases* made available – and, beyond that, significant advances in the *linking* of databases so that a search can move across multiple databases.

In a recent article in *Database* magazine, Stephen Arnold speaks of the database explosion:

> "In electronic publishing, it is obvious that the creation of electronic files of information is one of the hottest areas across all sectors of professional life in the U.S. . . . Databases are being built by academic institutions, governmental agencies, service companies, manufacturing firms, trade associations, non-profit organizations, and individuals."[4]

Among the principal effects of this situation he includes his prediction of "continued proliferation of databases online and in CD ROM form for public, sponsored, and proprietary applications."

These trends towards more and more databases and better linking of databases to make searches across multiple databases possible and feasible, lead to concern about the end-user. In the journal *Online*, Elizabeth Eddison says, "Information products in the online world will become increasingly customized, shaped to match the requirements of a particular customer. People will be able to get subsets of commercial databases, or to ask for customized front ends with particular software packages."[5]

Carlos Cuadra, in the same journal, says:

The history of online database services, as I see it, involves a 20-year period of development that has taken users from limited, do-it-yourself, in-house database use into an environment of timeshared centralized database services and now promises or threatens (depending on one's point of view) to bring those users back to in-house use of databases. But this time, the in-house database will be *online*. And this time the user, not the data processing department, will be in control.[6]

In *College and Research Libraries*, David Crawford points out another concern – about the proliferation of *specialized* databases: "Another cautionary note needs to be kept in mind with regard to the discipline-oriented bibliographic database: not all disciplines are similarly well served by the databases that presumably support them. Books, editions, and journals are dutifully reviewed in a discipline's literature, but public databases seem to be subjected to less critical review, if any at all."[7]

It is not only the database explosion that will intensify the overload experience of the user. As *electronic publishing* has developed, we see concern already in the scholarly and information professions about the commercial ventures into electronic journals, which might bypass the quality checks (editorial policy statements, refereeing of articles, etc.) that are such an important part of standard journal practices. John Sack notes that a report of the Carnegie Foundation for the Advancement of Teaching gave attention to this matter, and that the report *emphasizes* that "the refereeing and public criticism found among printed works is not part of the electronic journal article."[8] In other words, the *current filtering process* for scholarly communications can be bypassed entirely.

So we look into the twenty-first century and we see two seriously problematic results of our highly developed information retrieval systems: we see that better information filtering is a crucial need; and we also see that electronic publishing could make obsolete some of our twentieth-century methods of information filtering.

ANOTHER ROLE FOR COMPUTER TECHNOLOGY

What needs to be done between now and the twenty-first century to lessen the chances of widespread misinformation and overload of information? Let us consider first how the computer technologies that *aggravate* these problems can be used to *alleviate* these problems.

Can computer technology be used to identify the information that is truly new, or uniquely expressed? Can it determine what articles or what books, in Patrick Wilson's terminology, truly add to "the store of public knowledge"?[9] Can it determine what information submitted to the system is merely repetitive, and then filter it out?

Information scientists have worked along lines that relate to these questions. A study by the University of Chicago's Don Swanson has led him to conclude that "new knowledge *can* in principle be extracted from the body of existing published knowledge."[10] His studies on "objective relevance" offer hope, for if he or others can develop and verify an accurate and precise definition of objective relevance, then computers can be programmed to identify that which is objectively relevant and then filter out that which is not. William Cooper and Wilson have each worked on a related concept, "logical relevance." Wilson speaks of seeking a precise method of determining the "retrieval worthiness" of a document.[11] Cooper wrote pessimistically about the matter of designing an information retrieval system that could identify that which is valid. He said, "The system designer cannot do much to ensure that only the most credible material will be retrieved; such a goal lies largely beyond the state of the art at present." But he goes on to say, "Logical relevance is almost the only factor in utility which the designer does know how to deal with very effectively at present."[12] Swanson says, "For the most part, bibliographic retrieval systems are topic oriented, and topics are presumed to be objectively defined and applied."[13] Arnold speaks of new information sources "with different 'angles' on *similar* information."[14]

What we certainly will need in the twenty-first century are objective definitions of relevance, uniqueness, and validity, so that the computer can recognize each of these. Computer technology and developments in machine analysis of textual information make it possible that by the twenty-first century the computer can be used to analyze all forms of text, to identify all combinations of topics, levels of meaning, disciplinary approaches, and conclusions, so that *lack* of uniqueness of information, for example, can be at least *tentatively* determined by machine. Such documents can then be referred to human experts to judge whether these should indeed by filtered out because of their repetitive nature.

In summary, we can now envision various levels of databases and indexing services, both filtered (for various levels of audiences) and unfiltered.

EDUCATION OF THE INFORMATION USER

Let us now look beyond the computer to the end-user, the individual for whom information filtering may be a necessity. What must educators do so that users will become proficient in filtering information for themselves? Toni Bearman says, "There is . . . an increasing awareness that information, itself, is not a panacea. The ability to find and use information effectively, to analyze and synthesize it is critical."[15] Swanson refers to

> the widespread but mistaken idea that online searching is interactive by definition and highly effective simply because a very large bibliography on

almost any topic under the sun can be produced quickly. [Effectiveness requires] applying human imagination, creativity, and ingenuity to the search process – qualities that can be brought to bear only through sufficiently intensive and repeated interactions with a retrieval system, whether online or not.[16]

An article by Mary Jo and Joel Rudd in the *Journal of Academic Librarianship* suggests, "Users must . . . refine their abilities to efficiently and effectively select and evaluate information to avoid overload."[17] We should note that the Rudds are critical of the many commentators on the negative effects of the information explosion. They say we have *mythologized* an information overload problem, that there is not an empirical research base to support such comments. Yet the empirical studies they do cite seem to lend support to the existence of an overload problem, although the studies then focus on the methods users employ to *avoid* overload. The Rudds claim that users *adapt* their information *processing* to deal appropriately with the amount of information retrieved.

All of these scholars give us clear ideas of the kinds of objectives that should be part of information literacies for the twenty-first century. The information literacies required in information users will be (1) the ability to recognize their own *level* of need, and (2) the acuity to judge the validity of the information found.

As information proliferates, the user's methods of dealing with it must become more sophisticated, even as the information retrieval system itself becomes more "intelligent." Though the information retrieval system will become much more accurate in identifying the information relevant to a particular problem or expressed need, a matter that Swanson calls "subjective relevance" enters into the information retrieval process; it is the *user* who must be sophisticated enough in information handling to act or express his or her information need in the appropriate way to elicit information at the appropriate level. The user must clearly understand in a very concrete way that, for any topic, there is likely to be information available for many different levels of interest and expertise. The user must be astute in recognizing and expressing the level of information appropriate for his or her information need on a specific topic at a particular time. The user must be familiar with the difference between *new* information and information not new but uniquely expressed or synthesized. Users recognizing their own level of *need* will be able to choose the database filtered to the right level to match their need.

EDUCATION OF THE INFORMATION PROFESSIONAL

Finally, let us consider the implications in all this for the education of information professionals. Certainly we need continued research in the areas mentioned above: computer identification of textual relevance, validity, and uniqueness of information. Secondly, if information filtering is to be effective, the education of information professionals will need to focus more intensely on developing *their* skills in analysis of textual content. Finally, more attention must be given to the information professional's growth in subject expertise. Information filtering of textual material will not be done by computers alone; it is likely that reference to human subject experts will be an essential component. Skills in analysis of textual content and extensive subject knowledge may be expected to replace the current emphasis on technological expertise. And so may the information professional master at least a segment of the "torrent of raging information."

Notes

1. José Ortega y Gassett, "The Mission of the Librarian," *Antioch Review* 21 (1961): 133-54.

2. James I. Penrod and Judith V. Douglas, "Information Technology Literacy," in *Encyclopedia of Library and Information Science* 40, suppl. 5 (New York: Marcel Dekker, 1986), 89.

3. Herbert S. White, "The Other Barriers to Information Access," *Library Journal* 111 (November 15, 1986): 60.

4. Stephen Arnold, "Private or Independent Databases: A New Trend?" *Database* 10 (October 1987): 9.

5. Elizabeth Bole Eddison, "Choreography for Technology and Humans," *Online* 11 (1987): 50.

6. Carlos A. Cuadra, "History Offers Clues to the Future: User Control Returns," *Online* 11 (1987): 46.

7. David Crawford, "Meeting Scholarly Information Needs in an Automated Environment: A Humanist's Perspective," *College and Research Libraries* 47 (1986): 573.

8. John R. Sack, "Open Systems for Open Minds," *College and Research Libraries* 47 (1986): 537.

9. Patrick Wilson, *Public Knowledge, Private Ignorance* (Greenwich, Conn.: Greenwood Press, 1977).

10. Don R. Swanson, "Subjective Versus Objective Relevance in Bibliographic Retrieval Systems," *Library Quarterly* 56 (1986): 392.

11. Patrick Wilson, "Some Fundamental Concepts of Information Retrieval," *Drexel Library Quarterly* 14 (April 1978): 18; and Patrick Wilson, "Situational Relevance," *Information Storage and Retrieval* 8 (1973): 457-71.

12. William S. Cooper, "A Definition of Relevance for Information Retrieval," *Information Storage and Retrieval* 7 (June 1971): 36.

13. Swanson, "Subjective Versus Objective Relevance," 397.

14. Arnold, "Private or Independent Databases," 9.

15. Toni Carbo Bearman, "The Information Society of the 1990's: Blue Sky and Green Pastures?" *Online* 11 (1987): 84.

16. Swanson, "Subjective Versus Objective Relevance," 397.

17. Mary Jo Rudd and Joel Rudd, "The Impact of the Information Explosion on Library Users: Overload or Opportunity?" *Journal of Academic Librarianship* 12 (1986): 306.

Information: Who Will Corner the Market?

MICHAEL S. AMEIGH

Today, as they have over the centuries, scholars go off on pilgrimages to the world's great libraries to study and engage in research. They do so to gain access to documents, manuscripts, and other materials often unavailable elsewhere yet essential to the process of accumulating knowledge and passing it along to future generations. The very foundation of scholarship is built upon the premise that the library is the official house of knowledge, and that a traditional procedure for selecting, cataloging, displaying, and retrieving information will make the best writings in all disciplines available to everyone over time.

Public libraries have drawn record numbers of users in recent years, often by employing innovative techniques designed to increase circulation of materials. These materials are often held in large, central libraries and transported among smaller satellite facilities in outlying communities via library networks. Large university library systems are often of similar design, with the most complete collections housed in libraries on big central campuses that act as the hub of a wheel whose spokes lead to smaller campuses with more modest collections.

The role of the library has been expanded over the years to include art exhibits, poetry readings, and other high-minded events that serve to reinforce the view that the library, in concert with schools and universities, is the repository of knowledge in the community. Sponsorship of concerts, plays, even trips to the zoo are designed to increase visibility for library services and encourage scholarly endeavor.

But the most important factor in the evolution of the library concept has been its accessibility. Young and old, rich and poor, highly educated and marginally educated, have access to the library free of charge in large measure. All that is required is a modest degree of literacy and a fertile curiosity.

In recent times, governmental entities, academic institutions, and philanthropies have consistently accepted responsibility for the support of libraries and their related programs on the assumption that access to literature is in the public interest. In the not too distant future, however, free access to some forms of information may no longer be the rule as new technologies coupled with changing patterns of activity in the home and workplace create new markets for it. Even among scholars, the convenience of the electronic database is leading to a reappraisal of the way information is analyzed, cataloged, stored, and retrieved.

The electronic creation and storage of information is providing remarkable new opportunities for entrepreneurs to acquire and resell it. The future impact of this developing technology, just now beginning to come into focus, may be manifested in changes in the way libraries have traditionally served specific constituencies. The public may find itself paying for certain kinds of information that have heretofore been readily and freely accessible to those willing to look for it in the traditional library environment.

Consider this example: Recently, the publisher of the *Buffalo News*, a daily newspaper that serves several hundred thousand readers in western New York State and southern Ontario, Canada, announced that he has authorized installation of equipment to provide an electronic library like those of the *Wall Street Journal* and other newspapers whose back files are stored in electronic databases and distributed by electronic information gateways such as CompuServe, Dialogue, and BRS. The experience of a very few years in the marketplace by several such newspapers has demonstrated that this service will begin to generate significant new revenues for the *Buffalo News* in just two years. Customers will include scholars, researchers, clipping agencies, and commercial and legal entities of every stripe who will gladly pay to avoid the time-consuming task of poring over stacks of newspapers or microfiche at the local library. They will dial the database from their homes or offices, connect their computers to the mainframe, and, using search strategies, locate the materials they seek in a fraction of the time without many of the inconveniences associated with traditional research techniques.

Since almost all publications are created electronically today, electronic text storage is an obvious next stage in the evolution of the technology for those not already doing so, particularly when there is an enticing payback potential down the road. Most of the nation's leading consumer periodicals are already available in electronic form, via an increasing number of electronic information gateways.

Once this computer-based information retrieval market has developed fully, one wonders whether back files of the *Buffalo News* and thousands of similar publications will be available in formats that are currently freely accessible to the public at no cost.

The most intriguing characteristic of the current market for such electronic information services is the relatively small customer base. By contrast, the potential market, once the masses come on-line, is staggering. Yet, revenues are already significant enough to encourage investment in such systems by many publishing companies.

In some disciplines, the need to stay informed about changing conditions requires constant, systematic attention to current published information. Researchers are increasingly finding electronic databases to be an efficient time-saver. Academics are also discovering the on-line advantage. No longer bogged down by the dreary chore of slogging through mountains of irrelevant material in search of specific information, scholars in some disciplines are finding the busywork of research is reduced exponentially. Many are paying the telecommunications costs and on-line fees happily despite the fact that the vast bulk of scholarly literature is not available electronically, at least not yet.

Changes in the information marketplace are also resulting from a breakdown in the traditional system of information management. The information explosion is taxing the ability of libraries to store vast quantities of material, forcing many to be increasingly more selective in what they acquire, a risky endeavor at best. This development alone is eroding the confidence some scholars have in the system. And there are other problems. A recent article in the *Chronicle of Higher Education* reported that many of the nation's leading university libraries have cut back on the acquisition of scholarly journals and publications by as much as 25 percent because of an inability to meet escalating subscription fees. To scholars who consider these journals to be the compendia of premier scholarly research, this development alone is alarming. The alternative, of course, for those willing to pay the costs, is to access such publications from electronic databases. In many cases, subscription charges are increasing because circulation is decreasing, so that publishers are looking for ways to generate revenues sufficient to continue publication. Some scholars are speculating that on-line formats like electronic mail may increase opportunity for academic discourse in ways that will significantly erode the status of the academic journal.

A related issue that is currently attracting the attention of Congress has to do with the huge flow of information from the federal government. In October 1988, the Office of Technology Assessment (OTA), a joint committee of the House and Senate, issued a report entitled *Informing the Nation: Federal Information Dissemination in an Electronic Age*. Among the highlights is a finding that federal depository libraries set up under the Depository Library Act of 1962 are failing in their attempt to keep up with the never-ending stream of information from the federal government. In many cases, these libraries are in chaos, unable to make portions of important collections available for lack of space and manpower. This situation is defeating the intended purpose of the regional depository program, which is to make federal documents, reports, rule-makings, and the like available to the general public throughout the nation in a consistent and timely manner. The report also states that primary users of such information are putting pressure on the government to make it available electronically. The report states:

> OTA has concluded that congressional action is urgently needed to resolve Federal information dissemination issues and to set the direction of Federal activities for years to come. The government is at a crucial point where opportunities presented by the information technologies, such as productivity and cost-effectiveness improvements, are substantial. However, the stakes, including preservation and/or enhancement of public access to government information plus maintenance of the fiscal and administrative responsibilities of the agencies, are high and need to be carefully balanced by Congress. (OTA 1988, 1)

The report goes on to say that over the next three to five years the overall demand for paper formats in the dissemination of federal information will decline modestly, and that the demand for microfiche will drop rather markedly as the demand for electronic formats skyrockets. In fact, federal agencies are increasingly relying on electronic formats for internal and interagency information transfer, which will eventually influence the nature of and amount of information available to the public in paper form. The report concludes that if the depository program is to retain free access to government information, Congress must set in motion a process for meeting the additional expense of equipping depository libraries with the hardware and software required to continue providing fee access to such information.

The issue is far from resolved, however. The report goes on to declare:

> At the most basic level, a fundamental crosscutting issue is public access to Federal information. Debate over the use of electronic formats, privatization, and the like is obscuring the commitment of Congress, as expressed in numerous public laws, to the importance of Federal information and its dissemination in carrying out agency missions, and the principles of democracy and open government, a renewed congressional commitment to public access in an electronic age may be needed. (OTA 1988, 17)

While the library remains the center of the academic universe today, the modern age is bringing other fundamental challenges. University undergraduate and graduate seminars are increasingly subscribed by foreign nationals, many of whom challenge traditional notions about the evolution of civilization as professed in Western classrooms. The history of civilization is, they say, but a tradition handed down over the millennia by

114

librarians–gatekeepers who, throughout history, have made decisions as to what is and what is not the true literature of the ages. Often these decisions have been political rather than scholarly exercises. Occasionally, great collections have been purged at whim or caught up in wartime destruction. Increasingly, students and scholars are expressing interest in what has been missed, lost, or ignored, rather than what has been retained. Ongoing globalization will increase interest in the literature of other cultures, and demand for electronic access to it will create opportunities for new, nontraditional libraries. This issue is being studied around the world.

Recently, the president of France, François Mitterand, called for the building of the "largest and most modern library in the world" on French soil. He indicated it would be connected to all of the great libraries of Europe and would include electronically formatted information in all disciplines. His statement came at a time when academicians in France were complaining that that nation's university libraries are in serious decline.

Perhaps not coincidentally, France is also where the first successful application of on-line information services for the mass consumer market has occurred. In the early 1980s, the French government agreed to subsidize an ambitious national telecommunications system called Minitel that combines the telephone with a small computer terminal for accessing a national on-line telephone directory. Now boasting three and a half million users, Minitel is very successful, having evolved into a vast network of public, private, and commercial electronic databases that are accessed by millions of users daily. The French government's subsidization of Minitel has stimulated public use of it, and users are now paying for information that was, and in many cases still is, available in the traditional library environment.

Among the parties who have visited France to inspect the Minitel system are representatives of the seven Bell operating companies, which have recently been allowed by U.S. District Judge Harold Green to begin offering gateway services for the first time. Judge Green, who ordered the breakup of AT&T and has assumed the role of trustee in the telecommunications environment that was created by that action, has also visited Minitel and appears to favor a loosening of the regulatory constraints currently placed on the phone companies in this country. He cites the success of the French system and has voiced concern that unless the "baby" Bells are allowed to participate in the development of videotex in this country in a more direct way, the United States will continue to fall behind in that area. In fact, should the Bell operating companies provide such services, the technical process of going on-line will probably become much simpler for the average consumer and truly universally available. Today, a large segment of the potential market for on-line services must make a long-distance call to the nearest phone exchange that can access a specific gateway, then pay access and online fees. The telcos, as the Bell companies are called, have the ability to make that process less cumbersome and less expensive.

There are, of course, critics of on-line communication technology today. Some point to the failure of videotex in this country as demonstrated in experiments like Knight Ridder's Viewtron in Florida. Others recognize that the actual amount of information accessible from all of the electronic databases currently available is a very small fraction of what can be found in the stacks of even a modest library of paper. The publisher of the *Buffalo News* told me in our conversation that newspapers have failed in attempts to transfer the contents of issues that were not saved electronically as they were being created, which suggests that electronic libraries are essentially archives of contemporary information at this time. Of course, with each passing day that becomes less the case.

Perhaps the most common criticism of such services is the often Neanderthal technical complexity of getting on-line. To do so, the user must know about modems, value-added networks, gateways, databases, and where to find specific kinds of information. BRS, among the favorite electronic gateways in the academic community, offers access to some 200 databases, all identified by acronyms that often fail to offer even the slightest clue as to what they contain. Many overlap in the types of information they provide, and many store woefully incomplete files. NTIS, the National Technical Information Service, for example, is described as the electronic database of the federal government specializing in scientific and technical data prepared by federal agencies and contractors, along with related indices and bibliographies. The OTA report mentioned previously points out, however, that from one-third to one-half of all such reports are never provided to NTIS, since agency participation is strictly voluntary. The NTIS collection is becoming increasingly incomplete, it would seem.

It is true that all of these criticisms and others have slowed the growth of demand for such services, but the situation could change quickly. In France, whose national telephone system was the laughingstock of Europe just a decade ago because of inefficient and inconsistent service, many of the technical obstacles to mass on-line communication were avoided with the creation of a national standard and a commitment to nationwide deployment by the government. Everyone got the same hardware, software, and access to everyone else in the country. The result has been that users have begun to design the programming for the system, and development of Minitel has been remarkable.

In the United States, there is no standard at this time. This has given the on-line marketplace a character similar to that of the home computer market, with every manufacturer building some degree of propriety into its particular system to ensure a future market for its products and services. This free-market approach has led to a bewildering array of constantly changing products and services that may in fact work against the application of on-line technology in this country.

This situation may change soon. Once the privately owned telcos are allowed to begin providing on-line services, the potential will exist for the emergence of a national technical standard that will provide simpler, more convenient access to on-line services, which will provide information merchants with continuous nationwide access to millions of potential information customers located within the telephone system and beyond.

Will the information merchants be able to entice the public to come on-line? Indications are that the public will eventually be forced on-line in increasing numbers as the true efficiencies of the technologies become more apparent.

In California, for example, 200 state employees are currently engaged in a telecommuting experiment that is designed to study the productivity of those who work at home during at least part of the week in comparison to counterparts who commute to the office daily. In a state where at least half of the 140,000 state employees are information handlers, the success of the experiment could result in a dramatic shift away from centralized, office-based activity to home-based activity for thousands of workers. In a commuter-clogged state like California, the potential benefits would appear to extend to all concerned. And it follows that once this new group of users becomes comfortable with the on-line process, it will seek other services, many personal in nature.

Recently, two corporate giants, Sears and IBM, committed to a new on-line videotex service called Prodigy that will eventually allow consumers across the nation to access the Sears catalog, the J. C. Penny catalog, and hundreds of other services on-line. In San Francisco and Atlanta, grocery shoppers too busy to visit stores are already making weekly purchases via computer, while others are checking stock quotes, making airline reservations, and communicating with colleagues and friends nationwide on electronic mail networks.

Recently, a U.S. Postal Service official, describing the effect of overnight delivery, electronic mail, fax mail, and other services on first-class delivery, indicated that the Postal Service has become just another player with its own particular niche in the marketplace: a massive financial transaction network, delivering invoices and returning checks. Overnight, a multibillion-dollar market has developed as an alternative to the U.S. Postal Service simply because it provides greater convenience. As the French have demonstrated, the same opportunity exists in the area of information services – and it is out there, looking for a way into the American marketplace. Belatedly, information generators and policymakers are beginning to ask important questions about the nature of the information distribution process in the future: Who will sell it, grant access to it, distribute it – and ultimately, who will own it?

References

Burgess, John. "Cutting off the Electronic Cottage." *Washington Post*, national weekly edition, November 2, 1987, 21.

Dordick, Herbert S. *Understanding Modern Telecommunications*. New York: McGraw-Hill, 1986.

Flemming, David. "A Design for Telecommuting." *Personal Computing* 12, no. 10 (October 1988): 148-50.

Johnson, Robert M. "Electronic Publishing: Use It or Lose It." *Presstime* (February 1988): 10-12.

Kleiner, Art. "Child Prodigy." *Adweek's Marketing Week* 29, no. 44 (October 3, 1988): 22-25.

Lewis, Peter H. "BellSouth Opens an Electronic Mall." *New York Times*, September 26, 1988, F9.

Marchand, Marie. *The Minitel Saga*, translated from the French by Mark Murphy. Paris: Larousse, 1988.

Rogers, Everett M. *Communication Technology: The New Media in Society*. New York: Free Press, 1986.

Salvaggio, Jerry L. *Telecommunications: Issues and Choices for Society*. New York: Longman, 1983.

Sherman, Barry L. *Telecommunications Management: The Broadcast and Cable Industries*. New York: McGraw-Hill, 1987.

U.S. Congress, Office of Technology Assessment, *Informing the Nation: Federal Information Dissemination in an Electronic Age*. Washington, D.C.: U.S. Government Printing Office, GPO stock no. 052-003-01130-1.

Williams, Frederick. *Technology and Communication Behavior*. Belmont, Calif.: Wadsworth, 1987.

Beyond "The Chicken and the Egg" Dilemma: Designing a Hospitable Universal Information Utility

ROBERT JACOBSON

In discussing the coming "information age," which comes first, the audience or the information service? This "chicken and the egg" dilemma is crucial. If information services are developed only in response to the needs of existing, well-defined audiences, then the emergence of a universal information utility may have to wait.[1]

A concerted, long-term effort to define a broader information literacy and, simultaneously, create a matching utility is a fit challenge for our times. If we can broadly define *functional information literacy*, we can apply this definition to the design of an information utility that is truly useful and accessible to the general public.

This paper proposes that three nonresidential design methodologies – *sense-making, wayfinding,* and *open planning* – may be particularly useful in this enterprise of defining functional information literacy and designing an information utility to serve it.

The most ambitious general-interest information services in the United States, CompuServe and Prodigy, have yet to find an audience markedly larger than the population of computer enthusiasists.[2] The processes by which they are designed are obviously flawed. These massively expensive information services, which require ownership and some facility with a personal computer, generally are marketed only to consumers with high disposable incomes.[3]

We stand in very real danger of never getting over the hump of popularizing information services or developing a functional information literacy on a nationwide basis. This does not have to be the case. It is possible to create a popular information utility: the public library is its proof.[4]

119

The enterprise of defining a broader information literacy might resemble a modern-day "Edison's laboratory" where *understandings*, not products, are the goal. The mission of this laboratory would be to describe a functional information literacy and to use this description as the design parameter for the new technology.

How can designers of the universal information utility identify, understand, and meet the information needs of the citizenry at large? Obviously, we must resist the temptation to design the universal information utility in the image of hierarchical, corporate information systems.[5] Most individuals do not process insurance forms, use CAD-CAM systems to build homes, or plan physics curricula. These are not unworthy projects, but they are extraneous to the experience of ordinary people (Childers and Post 1975).

People live in a complex web of social and material relations. The essential design question is: How can information utility help people to better understand their predicament and better their lives?

Knowledge is the act of moving with purpose through the information environment, the data matrix that constitutes the social world (Jacobson 1984). A successful information utility would help its users to map, model, and move through the *information environment* with beneficial effect.[6] The principle of *personal empowerment* is more than an advertising slogan: the hope of personal empowerment is what compels people to use technologies without duress (Athanasiou 1985).

Sense-making, wayfinding, and open planning are three nonresidential design methodologies that are exceptionally well suited to this purpose. Taken together, these very different methodologies help people to understand the surrounding (and internal) environment and to produce desired change. They hold great promise as tools for the design of information services.

Sense-making is how people understand the world (Dervin 1984; Dervin and Nilan 1986). For most people, the "world" is a collection of domains: the home, the neighborhood, the workplace, where one spends leisure time, and just possibly, the region. Understanding this personal world is not easy, even if we share with the subject an objectively similar situation in the material world. The sense-making researcher studies the "gaps," "barriers," and "bridges" that deny or allow people to acquire necessary information (which the people themselves consider useful). Sense-making can provide novel tools – "knowledge devices"[7] – for making sense of the intangible information environment.

Dervin has refined sense-making research techniques to a high level of sophistication (Dervin and Clark 1987). Subjects are interviewed and observed to determine, to a high degree of precision, their ability to find information in the environment that is useful to them. The value of this methodology to the endeavor of designing the components of information services (databases, conferencing systems, and so forth) is obvious (Wurman 1989).

Wayfinding is sense-making applied to the built environment. Lynch's ground-breaking work in the area of urban design (1964, 1981) is the foundation of wayfinding practice. Wayfinding practitioners, including the Canadian Romedi Passini (1984) and Paul Arthur, and the Swedish research team of Garling, Book, and Lindberg (1986, 1985, 1984), are developing a comprehensive picture of the built environment as it affects perception. They are quickly building a repertoire of rules by which physical environments can be made understandable and navigable.

Wayfinding theories of location, navigation, and guidance are fascinating and have been incorporated into official guidebooks for the design of public spaces (Passini and Shiels 1987). Wayfinding "scripts" are programmatic, resembling decision "trees," and can be adapted to the creation of artificial intelligence "agents" capable of helping people traverse unfamiliar information spaces.

Open planning is a variation of participatory planning that integrates policymakers, planners, and their clients through the process of designing technological systems. Open planning first emerged in Australia as a philosophical orientation for long-range studies on the appropriate form and capabilities of the national telecommunications network (Newstead 1975; Australian Telecommunications Commission 1976).

In theory, open planning, as an intensely democratic design process, will result in a greater social intelligence and, ultimately, technological systems responsive to popular need (Barber 1984; Wilden 1980). In the context of the information environment, open planning would prescribe continuous interaction and uncorrupted communications between system designers and their clients as they proceed toward a common goal: the design of a successful, practical, and attractive universal information utility (Jacobson 1989).

By combining these three streams of cutting-edge social research with tested engineering design methods, it should be possible to enunciate service-design principles and parameters for the construction of an actual information utility.[8]

These relationships – the Laws of Information Design, so to speak – will have to be carefully designed into the universal information utility. For example, one may speculate that its interface will have to adapt to its users' individual traits and habits, rather than the other way around (as is the case today). The machinery powering the information utility will have to parallel in function its users' personal information-acquiring and information-using behaviors. Its data architecture may even feature artificial intelligence agents, generated by the user's own activity, that create knowledge templates for sizing up and navigating the information environment.

Ideally, the overall impression on entering into this novel information environment might be that of entering a hospitable, friendly place that is part library at Alexandria, part museum of natural history, part town plaza, and part helpful-plumber-dispensing-advice – all rolled into one.

A research program employing these novel technologies of knowledge will not be the usual neat and orderly research ritual of which Big Business and Big Government are so enamored. Interaction among persons with uniquely different methods but a common goal may be praised in the literature of technology management. However, this combination of elements will probably not be found in the institutional settings where, regrettably, our technological future is being constructed.

Moving from design parameter specifications to prototypes may require years. But the "window of opportunity" for this enterprise is not infinite. The information environment in which we will live is being designed today (Vitalari and Venkatesh 1987).

Engineers and marketeers can try to divine what it is that the public wants from technology. But the idea that one can design useful products for the general public, with the public's participation in the process, while perhaps appropriate for the fast-food business, is quite fallacious when applied to the design of information services.

If we want to design a universal information utility that has mass appeal, we will have to go where the masses live, work, and play. Then we must learn from them. Design methodologies suited to that enterprise can produce a universal information utility that fulfills essential information needs and really gives people power over their lives.

Notes

1. By *information service* I mean the functional operations of an information system, as they are perceived by the end-user. The information system – technology and organization – is the invisible machinery that supports the information service. The distinction between *service* and *system* is not trivial, and information designers should keep it in mind.

2. Ironically, the French Teletel ("Minitel") service, the most successful general-interest information service (with three million customers), is a product of planning "ad-hocism."

3. Some estimates put the development cost for the IBM/Sears Prodigy system at over $500 million.

4. For a discussion of the evolution of the public library in the information age, see Hayes (1985) and Dowlin (1984).

5. For examples of this bias in action, see Barudi, Olson, and Ives (1986); Consel and McKendree (1987); Williams (1986); and Whiteside and Holtsblatt (1987). The managerial perspective that may be useful in institutional settings hinders a broader outlook on the usefulness of information services for the public.

6. Rheingold (1987) describes the "virtual community" that grows up within a successful computer conferencing system, meeting its members' practical, social, and spiritual needs.

7. Dennett (1986a, 1986b) uses the phrase *concept piano* to describe a category of learning systems that can be adapted to this purpose. Interestingly, Australian Aborigines use learning devices "in reverse": their "information services" are "dreamtime" experiences used to map and interpret the sparse resources of the physical environment in which they live (Michaels 1985).

8. There is also a spiritual dimension to the design of successful conferencing systems, alluded to earlier. Johnson-Lenz and Johnson-Lenz (1988) have designed conferencing processes that stimulate noncognitive cooperation and emotional closeness – "removing blocks to the flow of energy" – via what is often looked upon as cold technology, the computer.

References

Athanasiou, Tom. "High-Tech Alternativism: The Case of the Community Memory Project." In *Making Waves: The Politics of Communications*, ed. Radical Science Collective, 37-51. London: Free Association Books, 1985.

Australian Telecommunications Commission. *Telecom 2000*. Melbourne: Government Printer, 1976.

Barber, Benjamin. *Strong Democracy*. Berkeley: University of California Press, 1984.

Baroudi, Jack F.; Olson, Margrethe H.; and Ives, Blake. "An Empirical Study of the Impact of User Involvement on System Usage and Information Satisfaction." *Communications of the ACM* 29, no. 3 (March 1986): 232-38.

Childers, Thomas, and Post, Joyce A. *The Information Poor in America*. Metuchen, N.J.: Scarecrow Press, 1975.

Consel, John M., and McKendree, Jean. "Interface Design Issues for Advice-Giving Systems." *Communications of the ACM* 30, no. 1 (January 1987): 14-31.

Dennett, Daniel. "What Is a Concept Piano?" Mimeograph, Curricular Software Studio, Tufts University (March 1986a).

_____. "Information, Technology, and the Virtues of Ignorance." *Daedalus* (1986b): 135-53.

Dervin, Brenda. *The Information Needs of Californians.* Sacramento: California State Library, 1984.

Dervin, Brenda, and Clark, Kathleen. *Alternative Tools for Information Need and Accountability Assessments by Libraries.* Belmont, Calif.: Peninsula Library System, 1987.

Dervin, Brenda, and Nilan, Michael. "Information Needs and Uses." *Annual Review of Information Science and Technology* 21 (1986): 3-33.

Dowlin, Kenneth E. *The Electronic Library.* New York: Neal-Schuman Publishers, 1984.

Garling, Tommy; Book, Anders; and Lindberg, Erik. "Spatial Orientation and Wayfinding in the Designed Environment." In *Journal of Architectural Planning and Research* 3 (1986): 55-64.

_____. "Adults' Memory Representations of the Spatial Properties of Their Everyday Physical Environment." In *The Development of Spatial Cognition,* ed. R. Cohen, 144-84. Hillsdale, N.J.: Erlbaum, 1985.

_____. "Cognitive Mapping of Large-Scale Environments." *Environment and Behavior* 16, no. 1 (January 1984): 3-34.

Hayes, Robert M. "Introduction." In *Libraries and the Information Economy of California.* Los Angeles: Graduate School of Library and Information Science, and UCLA, 1985.

Jacobson, Robert. *An Open Approach to Information Policy Making.* Norwood, N.J.: Ablex Publishing, 1989.

_____. "Design and the Information Environment." Paper presented at the Twelfth Annual Telecommunications Policy Research Conference, Airlie, Va., April 22-26, 1984.

Johnson-Lenz, Peter, and Johnson-Lenz, Trudy. "Beyond Cognitive Exchanges: Computer Support for Non-Cognitive Cooperative Process." Paper presented at the Second Conference on Computer-Supported Cooperative Work, Portland, Ore., September 1988.

Lynch, Kevin. *Good City Form.* Cambridge, Mass.: MIT Press, 1981.

_____. *The Image of the City.* Cambridge, Mass.: MIT Press, 1964.

Michaels, Eric. "Constraints on Knowledge in an Economy of Oral Information." *Current Anthropology* 26, no. 4 (August-October 1985): 505-10.

Newstead, Anthony. "Open Planning for Telecommuncations." *IEEE Transactions on Communications* COM-23, no. 10 (October 1975): 1059-64.

Passini, Romedi. *Wayfinding in Architecture: A Design Guideline*, AES/SAG 1-4:87-2. Ottawa: Public Works Canada, July 1984.

Rheingold, Howard. "Virtual Communities." Topic in "Information" conference, the WELL computer conferencing system, Suasolito, Calif., 1987. Modem telephone number 415-332-6106.

Vitalari, Nicholas P., and Venkatesh, Alladi. "In-home Computing and Information Services." *Telecommunications Policy* (March 1987): 65-81.

Whiteside, John, and Holtsblatt, Karen. *Usability Engineering: Our Experience and Evolution*. Unpublished manuscript, Digital Equipment Corporation, 1987.

Wilden, Anthony. *System and Structure*. New York: Methuen, 1980.

Williams, Martha E. "Transplant Information Systems through Gateways, Front Ends, Intermediaries, and Interfaces." *Journal of the American Society for Information Science* 37, no. 4 (1986): 202-14.

Wurman, Richard Saul. *Information Anxiety: The Disease of the Eighties and Beyond*. New York: Doubleday, 1989.

Information Literacy: Concepts of Literacy in a Computer Age

BARBARA H. KWASNIK

As we move into an age where information plays an increasingly central role in our personal, social, and professional lives, reading and writing, long regarded as the cornerstones of literacy, may well come to be seen as instances of the far more generic concept of information-processing competencies. It is likely that, in retrospect, we will conclude that even today's "innovative" concept of computer literacy often refers to only the most superficial and transitory of the skills and competencies that will eventually define *information literacy*.

Before we can discuss information literacy and the skills required of such competency, it might be helpful to take a close look at literacy itself. What does the term encompass, why does it always represent an emotional investment, and why can't it be pinned down to a neat definition, even though each of us knows perfectly well what it is?

For most of us, literacy, however we define it, implies a positive value, and as such we tend to view it as a desirable goal in itself, without much thought as to what we specifically mean by it. We have a personal definition of literacy when we use the term, but we readily accommodate a variety of usages:

- Computer literacy is the key to a good job.

- She is more literate than the average college freshman.

- Public spending aims to achieve 100 percent literacy.

The concept of literacy is fluid and changes depending on the historical and social context in which it is considered. Furthermore, defining literacy

127

objectively is difficult since we are unable to study it except from the viewpoint of "literate" participants in a "literate" society. "Literacy is unique among technologies in penetrating and structuring the intellect itself, which makes it hard for scholars, whose own skills are shaped by literacy, to reconstruct the mental changes which it brings about" (Clanchy 1979).

At the very least, most people define literacy as "reading and writing," or the ability to encode and decode the graphic medium of our language. Throughout history, however, these basic requirements were not always the ones that defined literacy. In the Middle Ages, the concept of *litteratus* was not associated with the mechanical skills we think of today. A literate person was one who had the ability to read, understand, compose by dictation, make verse, and express him or herself in the Latin language. Reading and writing were not automatically coupled. Since books were commonly read out loud until the advent of printing, and scribes could be hired to do the writing, these skills were not absolute prerequisites of the *litteratus*. In the broader sense, scholarly and learned people (usually clerics) were considered literate (Clanchy 1979).

Gradually this concept changed and literacy, now defined as the skills of reading and writing, became embedded in social theories, particularly those that stressed mass schooling and "the unquestioned necessity of literacy for mobility, citizenship, democracy, progress, development, and civilization" (Graff 1981). In fact, literacy became synonymous with these terms, as it once had been synonymous with the *clerici* (learned religious). Literacy acquired utilization value in spreading practical information as well as aesthetic and spiritual messages.

Contemporary society views literacy as a commodity. We want our children to be literate so they can be successful. We bemoan the "functional illiteracy" of our high school graduates. Many writers, however, now take a two-sided view that does not automatically assume literacy to be better than illiteracy (Cressy 1980). They tend to describe literacy in a broader way, defining it as primarily "consciousness of problems posed by language" (Pattison 1982), or as a "technology of the mind" (Ong 1982), and only secondarily as the specific skills used to express such consciousness. Literacy is seen as but *one aspect* of knowledge, or progress, or human development. Writers now acknowledge the relative significance of literacy in different cultures and the fact that different cultures apply varying standards and definitions to it.

ASPECTS OF LITERACY

Even within the contemporary consciousness of literacy as more than just reading and writing, however, there is a rich array of approaches to the concept. Generally speaking, there is no disagreement about what reading and writing are per se, but the interpretation of "more than" depends on the intellectual framework and intention of the author. These approaches can be roughly organized into four broad (and, of course, overlapping) categories:

1. Literacy as a *primary academic skill*

2. Literacy as a *cognitive* and *developmental* factor

3. Literacy as inextricably embedded in a *social context*

4. Literacy as an *abstract concept*

Literacy as a Primary Academic Skill

At the simplest level of mechanical skill, literacy means the ability to decode printed messages (reading), and the ability to physically make graphic symbols (writing). Even these tasks are hardly "simple," cognitively speaking, and it is difficult to precisely define the parameters by which we distinguish between a mechanical/perceptual task and the process of cognitive interpretation. For instance, if a person is able to decode French but not English, we do not say he or she is illiterate. Such a person is able to decode in *some* language and therefore has internalized the patterns of reading skills, which consist of the ability to: recognize shapes as letters, identify groups of letters as words, match up words to a known lexicon of words, and so on. Literacy is defined as "merely" a mechanical skill by those who wish to emphasize a qualitative difference between such a skill and the more sophisticated mental processes (thinking) that, according to this point of view, chronologically follow the acquisition of reading and writing. By such a definition, an illiterate is simply one who does not know the alphabet.

Using a similar distinction, Bloomfield states that writing itself is not language at all but "merely a way of recording language by means of visible marks." According to him, spoken language is the more appropriate subject for scientific study (cited in Raymond 1982). Such a view is a departure from the tradition in which written English constitutes the norm for the language, while varieties of spoken English are considered deviations.

Most writers, however, do not conceptually limit their definition of literacy to the mechanical skill of reading and writing, even though in fact they frequently refer only to this aspect of literacy when they use the term. Thus, a two-tiered usage is common. One tier refers to the skill (with *speaking* and *computing* sometimes thrown in), and the other to the cognitive or social context.

By far the most common blend of these two tiers is the concept of *functional literacy*. It means the ability to read and write *and* apply these skills to everyday life (Copperman 1978). By implication, the term includes the functions of interpretation and integration, as expressed in such skills as "reading with understanding," or "rhetoric."

It is in the context of functional literacy that literacy becomes equated with *education*. An uneducated person is "unlettered" even if he or she is physically able to decipher words. Such a concept also brings with it the notion of a *norm*, that is, "good" English (correct word usage and grammar) (Simon 1982).

Literacy as a Cognitive and Developmental Factor

Viewed as a cognitive and developmental factor, literacy "embraces not only skills of reading and writing, but the ways in which they are used to extend an individual's intellectual and emotional range" (Goddard 1974). This point of view assumes a psychological urge to communicate by recording events and feelings for oneself and others. Literacy, then, creates an environment that can liberate the imagination by "providing a friendly condition for linguistic innovation" (D'Angelo 1982). By writing down thoughts after consideration, and by reading such recorded thoughts, we have a way of "relating the human interior to an exterior world" (Ong 1982).

Literacy is seen as a developmental experience. According to this point of view, and in direct contrast to the view of literacy as mechanical skills only, the condition of literacy is seen as subtly permeating our use of language and our cognitive style. Literacy enables us to free ourselves from the constraints of concrete and specific thinking. Instead, we are able to think conceptually and to make imaginative connections that do not necessarily occur in real time and space. We can classify experienced phenomena based on qualities or attributes that can be mentally detached from their objects (D'Angelo 1982). In this way, literacy extends us.

Not everyone agrees that literacy in this sense is necessarily a positive attribute. Once in the literate mode, for instance, we have difficulty extricating ourselves. According to Olson, "Literacy is simply a means to a specific kind of knowledge that has its own biases, not knowledge in general, not universal knowledge" (cited in D'Angelo 1982). A distinction is made between knowledge acquired by reading and knowledge acquired by "common sense" or action.

Literacy in a Social Context

No aspect of literacy is context-free. Even the deciphering of an alphabet relies on a knowledge of the socially agreed upon conventions governing the range of shapes that will be interpreted as a given letter. Nevertheless, there are some aspects of literacy that particularly stress the social context in which it appears, and which it, in turn, helps shape.

Primarily, literacy in this sense connotes *power, progress,* and *civilization,* but particularly power. Archives in written form constitute a permanent record and can be used as "proof" when a question of validity arises. Orally transmitted and individually remembered data rely on a different social context. Such "power" over data is in fact only an aspect of the political and social power that is attributed to literacy.

Literacy is viewed as an avenue to human liberation and a catalytic force for social change (Mackie 1981; Kozol 1981). Literate people are "informed" and can therefore express dissent and participate in the political processes that affect their lives (Pattison 1982). This view permeates every literacy campaign, whether it is in Third World countries or in American high schools. It assumes that words matter, that words can be dangerous or useful (Kozol 1981). It assumes that self-expression and consciousness *via* words are indispensable to a better world. Pattison notes that it was Christianity that imbued the concept of "the Word" with such resonance and as such has "helped to shape the direction of our culture, and is probably more important itself than the advent of print technology" (Pattison 1982).

Proponents of the social-context point of view agree that literacy is not an abstract, reified, neutral concept. Literacy (like education) is *always* a political event; it is always connected to language, politics, and consciousness.

Literacy as an Abstract Concept

To say that literacy is an abstract concept does not necessarily deny that it is also embedded in a social context. Such an approach, however, views literacy as a technology of the mind (a mental process, as it were) to be treated as any other technology—that is, as value-free until applied in a given setting. It is a consciousness of language that allows us to separate the reception of data from its production. An author writes (imagining an audience); readers re-create a new world. Writer and reader (even if they are the same person) are isolated from each other by the production of words. Ong points out that such distancing "fosters analytic management of knowledge" (Ong 1982). As such, literacy is a strategic interface between the mind and the world.

It is clear that literacy defies comprehensive definition. We know that the concept changes historically and from culture to culture, where it may have different status and priority. Nevertheless, in our culture, literacy is a key to success and development, both personal and societal. It is intrinsic to our style of inquiry and our communication of practical information and aesthetic values. Literacy permits us to connect socially, politically, conceptually, and economically in a way that is denied to us if we are "illiterate," whether the term is defined broadly or narrowly.

LITERACY	ILLITERACY

Academic Skill

Ability to encode and decode the *graphic medium* of the language	Illiteracy = ignorance of alphabet
Functional literacy: reading/writing (perhaps also speaking and computing) *and* application to every day life	Functional illiteracy
Representing a norm of "good" or "correct" Use of language literacy = education	Unlettered Unschooled

Cognition and Psychological Development

Method of *extending* emotional and intellectual range	
Communication: recording of events/feelings for self and others	Silence
"Friendly condition for linguistic innovation"	
Liberation of the imagination – "way of relating human interior to exterior world"	Introversion
Literacy producing a different cognitive style – the proclivity to think conceptually	Tendency to concrete/specific cognitive style
Reading as a mode rather than listening	

Literacy can be dysfunctional,
constricting us with
complicated syntax

Only *one kind of knowledge*　　　　　　　　　Knowledge gained by other
　　　　　　　　　　　　　　　　　　　　　　methods, such as action or
　　　　　　　　　　　　　　　　　　　　　　common sense

Social Context

Archives used as *proof* and to　　　　　　　Oral transmission; personal
ensure *permanence of records*　　　　　　　memory

Literacy = civilization　　　　　　　　　　　Primitiveness

Literacy as a tool for the
dissemination of useful and
aesthetic information

Human liberation –　　　　　　　　　　　　　Social failure
enfranchisement is catalyst for
change – means of expressing
dissent; literacy = a political
event

Abstract Concept

Literacy as technology of the
mind; "consciousness of
problems posed by language"

A further step of abstraction　　　　　　　　Spoken language, art
from other methods of
expression (e.g., a dog, a
picture of a dog, the word *dog*)

OVERLAPPING CONCEPTS OF LITERACY AND COMPUTER LITERACY

Given the deeply penetrating value of literacy in our society, it is no surprise
that we choose to attach this term to our newest "muscle extender," the

133

computer. Since literacy is associated with a new technology in the term *computer literacy*, it has also somehow assumed the status of a new concept. While it is true that the computer has changed our organization and manipulating of data, and perhaps even our patterns of perception and cognition, our basic underlying human information processing skills remain the same. And while computer use may have widespread social and political impact, the basic underlying issues of human/machine interface also remain the same.

It is, in fact, interesting that "computer literacy" as used by academic and popular writers shares with literacy many of the same conceptual frames. Thus, if we sort out all the common and implied usages, we can organize them into: (1) computer literacy as a basic (academic) skill; (2) computer literacy as a cognitive and developmental factor; (3) computer literacy in a social context; and (4) computer literacy as an abstract concept.

Computer Literacy as a Basic Skill

At this level it is useful to distinguish between those aspects of computer literacy that stress the machine and those that stress the person or the process. Just as literacy can be partially defined as the ability to encode and decode the graphic medium of a language, at the level of basic skills having to do with the machine, computer literacy can be defined as the knowledge of how to make a computer work (Zemke 1983). Within this knowledge, we can include an awareness of basic computer history, terminology, and general operations. Parallel to functional literacy is the ability to assign specific tasks to specific machines (including software literacy), simple programming, and an understanding of how programs and subprograms fit together (Penrod 1983).

Computer Literacy as a Cognitive and Developmental Factor

It is obvious, however, that computer literacy is more than just the acquisition (by training) of the ability to make a computer function properly. A computer, which stores, retrieves, computes, and manipulates large amounts of data, is nothing more than a fancy typewriter, calculator, or filing cabinet unless the user has the ability to competently use these capabilities in a new and imaginative way.

Such awareness, of course, focuses on the individual and the *process* of computer literacy. The computer is seen as an extension of the mind, an extension that enables the *analysis* and *organization* of large amounts of data, which the human mind could theoretically process but for lack of time and stamina.

An awareness of "computing concepts" rather than "computing skills" presupposes knowing how to use the computer for solving problems

(Johnson 1983; Penrod 1983; Zemke 1983). It assumes that use is not "prewired," but that the individual is able to recognize and produce creative relationships (for example, the results of postcoordinated index searches) and to design and understand models and simulations. Such skills rely on a subject knowledge in addition to the ability to apply computing concepts in the formulations of the problem.

As important as knowing what a computer can do (as well as how to make it do it) is knowing what it cannot do. It cannot, for instance, make judgments; it cannot formulate a problem, or comment on the significance of a revealed relationship.

Just as literacy changes people, some would say that computer literacy also has the power to change the basic way in which problems are approached (Johnson 1983). It is difficult to isolate those skills that aid computer-style reasoning and problem-solving, but clearly, such skills must be related to any information processing skills, namely, a large body of subject knowledge, a flexible problem-solving attitude, and the ability to recognize, organize, discard, and reorganize data in the process of making useful decisions.

Computer Literacy in a Social Context

Computer use is popularly viewed as indispensable to modern life. Other methods of data management, in fact, are viewed as primitive or archaic. The outcome of such an attitude (aside from its validity) has far-reaching social impact, manifested in particular in educational and political institutions.

Computer literacy assumes *power* over data and its management. As such, it enfranchises (informationally speaking) those who have access to computers and disenfranchises those who do not–clearly a matter of some political import.

As literacy enabled access to disseminated information, computer literacy brings with it a new technique of communication. Both the channel and the medium are altered by the convergence of communication technology (as exemplified by networking, electronic bulletin boards, and computer publishing), but in addition, the altered time framework and the deluge of data available at once force the receiver to switch from a predominantly data-accumulating mode to a predominantly data selection mode.

When societies first adopted written records in response to a need for permanent, archival representations of both day-to-day and historical events, they did so precisely because of the permanence of such records, and because of the fact that they were relatively exempt from the vagaries of human memory and changing purpose. The spread of computer literacy brings with it a changing view of records. First of all, the records are relatively ephemeral, that is, they are saved until no longer useful, and then they are *easily* destroyed. Records are easily available, easily centralized, relatively easily changed, and therefore easily censored. By contrast, it is much more difficult to destroy all the copies of a printed newspaper, or to access an individual's private correspondence.

Computer Literacy as an Abstract Concept

If we view literacy as a "technology of the mind" and a "consciousness of problems posed by language," then computer literacy (and in particular, that aspect we might call *computer fluency* [Zemke 1983] can be viewed as a consciousness of problems per se, that is, as the ability to see a problem in its parts *and also* as part of a system. Such a consciousness is neutral until applied, and furthermore, since it is abstract, it can only be defined operationally.

LITERACY	COMPUTER LITERACY
Basic Skills	
Ability to encode and decode graphic medium	Knowledge of *how* to make a computer do what you want it to do
Functional literacy	Knowledge of general operations Software literacy
"Correct" use of language	Terminology Specific tasks for specific machines Simple programming How programs fit together

Cognitive and Psychological Development

Extension of emotional and intellectual range	Using computer to extend mind for analysis and organization of large amounts of data
"Friendly condition for linguistic innovation; liberation of imagination	Modeling, simulation Ability to recognize and produce creative relationships among data
A different cognitive style; thinking conceptually	"Computing concepts"; knowing how to use computer for solving problems
Only *one kind of knowledge* attained by literacy	Knowing what cannot be done by computer; it cannot make judgments or "imaginative" applications

Social Context

Written archives as *proof;* permanence of records	Records ephemeral, changeable, and not secure; vulnerable to censorship
Literacy = civilization	Computer literacy seen as indispensable to modern life – other methods of data management seen as archaic, primitive

Dissemination of information	New way of communicating; convergence of communication technology
Human liberation; enfranchisement; social equity; expression of dissent; literacy = political event	Information "haves" and "have-nots" based on access to computers *and* ability to use them; computer literacy = *power* over data and its management
Literacy = survival in society	Computer literacy popularly viewed as new key to success
Literacy = education crosses all curricula	Computer literacy crosses all curricula; aim is to "learn well as the technophiles do"

Abstract Concept

Literacy = "technology of the mind"; consciousness of problems posed by language	Computer *fluency* = consciousness of problems per se; ability to see a problem in its parts and also as part of a system
Neutral (socially speaking) until applied	Neutral until applied

LITERACY AND COMPUTER LITERACY AS INFORMATION COMPETENCE

What emerges from the above summary is a clear profile of both literacy and computer literacy defined primarily as *information competence* rather than mechanical competence alone. We may tend to view them in a social or cognitive context, but either way, their positive value relies on their usefulness to us in dealing with our environment. Being literate empowers us to deal with data impinging on us either from the outside world or from within ourselves. Just as the medieval *litteratus* was a person who had integrated and managed a particular realm of knowledge without necessarily possessing the mechanical skills of reading and writing, the modern concept treats the mechanical skills as but one part, albeit a necessary part, of a kind of literacy that changes the possessor of such skills irrevocably.

When literacy, generally taken, is defined as information competency, we need to elaborate on the components of such competence. We know that merely possessing the skills of reading and writing, or computer use, is "not enough," but we need to identify the other factors that enable us to be functionally literate, that is, able to interact in a special and consequential way with the environment.

At the core is an acceptance and an understanding of the fact that to be exposed to the potential information in data, however generated, is not necessarily to "be informed." To be informed requires the use of our minds and of information-processing skills that are more generic than the skills generally put forward as indispensable to the successful person in a modern environment. Yet it is easy to be seduced by the facility with which we can manipulate data, retrieve a bibliography, or simulate a chemical reaction. Formerly, we borrowed a stack of books from the library, or photocopied endless journal articles, and thought we "had information." Now, we can instantly retrieve and continually update data, but we have no more information in a computer graphic per se than we do in a photocopied article, except to say, "Oh, how nice that the machine can do that for me!"

Just as the terms *literacy* and *computer literacy* overlap conceptually, the operational competencies associated with modern technology begin to overlap. The acquisition of basic skills presents issues that transcend individual devices.

These information skills are components of a processing system that is not static in either time or dimension. Each component changes the system and is in turn changed by it. For purposes of discussion, however, we can divide information skills into those dealing with (1) attention to and selection of data; (2) the individual processing of data in the human mind; and (3) how the skills enable the individual to interact with the environment.

Attention to and Selection of Data

The primary skills of selection and attention deal with perception, which we define here as an individual's sensory *and* conceptual interface with data. Perception, therefore, includes memory in the form of recall and recognition, as well as the ability to reject data.

Although *memory* plays a part in all aspects of information competence, it is at this stage that the skill of *recognition* is utilized. We recognize data in the context of other images in our memory. In turn, we remember in terms of what we already know. Thus, data is not stored in discrete particles, but in chunks. Furthermore, what is in memory is not what the senses perceived, but what the mind made of it, that is, our individual version of it. Our memory, then, as a skill, relies on previous information and in turn enhances future information processing. The ability to recognize letters of the alphabet and words of a vocabulary is an example of such a process. *Recall* as a function of memory relies on the same ability to make a connection, or analogies. The information must be located in some sort of organized context in order to be retrieved.

Selection of data implies a recognition of the problem, or put another way, a recognition of the parameters of the situation. The process is of particular importance with respect to computer use. In theory, the ability to read and write has always presented us with an overload of data, and we have always had to select and reject, but the proportions have changed with the introduction of computers. Furthermore, the computer's ability to generate large quantities of data has been popularly accepted as one of its marvels, rather than one of its serious drawbacks. Whether in the print or computer mode, we still need to resolve the problem of having more than we can meaningfully use. Why do our imaginations lag behind technological advances? How do we determine what is meaningful, what is useful? Obviously, considerable skills of interpretation are used at this stage. The individual selects from a vast array of possibilities on the basis of previous knowledge and anticipation of future applications. In addition, considerable interpretation is needed to reject data that is considered irrelevant.

Processing of Data

As already noted, processing occurs at all points and is defined here as those mental skills that permit *categorization, conceptualization,* and *organization* of data. Thus, if recognition of a problem comes first, then the mental representation of such a problem – the definition of problem space (Hunt 1982) – occurs here.

The individual is able to categorize data and organize it in hierarchies (that is, personally defined systems of organization). To do this, he or she must be able to see similarities between specific items and recognize where such items might fit within existing classification systems in the mind. The greater the store of knowledge (the mental databank, as it were), the more possibilities there are for making connections and ordering material.

Processing of information involves reasoning, which is the system by which connections and relationships between items are recognized. An example is the relationship expressed as cause and effect. As humans, we do not think deductively. Instead we use *plausible reasoning* (Hunt 1982). We leap from insufficient data to a conclusion that may be formally illogical but is plausible based on our experience and knowledge. We do not do this serially, following all possible decision-making paths. Instead, we shortcut to a decision before there is ample evidence, and without even knowing quite how we did it. We call it "informed intuition." Our frame of reference, our integrated system of rules, permits us to do this successfully in many cases. The richer our experience, the more "informed" are our plausibly reasoned conclusions.

Our flexible mental abilities also permit us to *reorganize* material in order to find new connections. Such flexibility prevents us from being stuck in a rigid mode of conceptualization.

Interaction with the Environment

Interaction with the environment entails the use or application of information. An individual using "interpreted" data is enabled to not only repeat certain mental activities but to also perform new ones. Through such a learning process, an individual is able to adapt and adjust to new experience and to fresh incoming data. In fact, the ability to *apply* technology in a useful (i.e., problem-solving) manner may prove to be more crucial than the acquisition of the skill itself. It is far simpler to teach programming than to teach imaginative or even appropriate applications of programs. Part of the difficulty is the inability to envision technological capabilities as part of an ongoing learning interaction with the environment. Each skill, whether it involves print technology or computer graphics, is seen as an end in itself.

Regularity vs. Anomaly

If we describe human information-seeking behavior as an ongoing tension between a search for regularity and no variance on the one hand and the recognition of anomalous elements on the other, we see that it is advantageous for an individual to be able to utilize and balance both. Regularity enables the individual to accommodate and organize a large body of knowledge. The larger the body of knowledge, and the better organized it is, the easier it is for the individual to select and integrate new knowledge. A large and organized body of knowledge provides all the more material for varied connections and alternatives, and it enables more successful plausible reasoning.

On the other hand, the ability to accommodate and recognize the unusual enables the individual to be creative in applying a body of knowledge to his or her interaction with the environment. Flexibility and tolerance for ambiguity steer the mind toward alternatives rather than toward a prescribed, right mode of problem solving.

We might summarize the information skills as follows:

1. The acquisition, through experience, of a large body of knowledge within which to integrate new knowledge (Griffith and King, no date). Such knowledge includes subject-specific knowledge as well

as knowledge of processes and methods, such as computing and rhetoric.

2. An ability to organize existing knowledge conceptually, to remember it, to recognize it, and to reorganize it. This is the basis for recognizing and producing relationships (for instance, theories or metaphors).

3. Conceptual flexibility to allow alternative methods of organization and different, creative avenues of formulating and solving problems, as well as to avoid a rigid mind-set.

4. An ability to not only analyze a problem into its components but to also view it in a larger context; an ability to switch from one viewpoint to another.

5. To use the above to define one's information requirements effectively, to choose appropriate problem-solving aids, and to know their limitations; the ability to translate an inchoate information need into the "language" of the system so that the system (computer, library, index) can be utilized to advantage.

The information skills described only briefly above constitute a catalytic, dynamic system by which experience, a body of knowledge, the ability to organize, and conceptual flexibility reinforce and enhance each other. Literacy viewed in this light acquires a new dimension. Reading, writing, and computer skills are necessary components of the process for data gathering and dissemination, but what happens to the information acquired and transmitted in the "literate" mode is far more significant.

References

Clanchy, M. T. *From Memory to Written Records; England 1066-1307.* Cambridge, Mass.: Harvard University Press, 1979.

Copperman, P. *The Literacy Hoax: The Decline of Reading, Writing, and Learning in the Public Schools and What We Can Do about It.* New York: Morrow, 1978.

Cressy, D. *Literacy and the Social Order: Reading and Writing in Tudor England.* Cambridge, Eng.: Cambridge University Press, 1980.

D'Angelo, F. J. "Loury on Literacy: The Cognitive Consequences of Reading and Writing." In *Literacy as a Human Problem*, ed. J. C. Raymond. Tuscaloosa: University of Alabama Press, 1982.

Goddard, N. *Literacy: Language-Experience Approaches.* London: Macmillan, 1974.

Graff, H. J. *Literacy in History: An Interdisciplinary Research Bibliography.* New York: Garland, 1981.

Griffith, J.-M., and King, D. A. "A Framework for Describing Information Processional Competencies." No publisher or date.

Hunt, M. *The Universe Within.* New York: Simon and Schuster, 1982.

Johnson, R. R. "Computer Literacy: A Longer View." *Educom* 3, no. 4 (Fall/Winter 1983): 2-3, 8.

Kozol, J. "Foreword." In *Literacy and Revolution: The Pedagogy of Paolo Friere,* ed. R. Mackie. New York: Continuum, 1981.

Mackie, R., ed. *Literacy and Revolution: The Pedagogy of Paolo Friere.* New York: Continuum, 1981.

Ong, W. J. "Reading, Technology, and Human Consciousness." In *Literacy as a Human Problem,* ed. J. C. Raymond. Tuscaloosa: University of Alabama Press, 1982.

Pattison, R. *On Literacy: The Politics of the Word from Homer to the Age of Rock.* New York: Oxford University Press, 1982.

Penrod, J. I. "Information Technology Literacy: Initiatives at Pepperdine University." *Educom Bulletin* (Summer 1983): 11-15, 29.

Raymond, J. C., ed. *Literacy as a Human Problem.* Papers presented at the Sixth Alabama Symposium on English and American Literature, University of Alabama, 1979. Tuscaloosa: University of Alabama Press, 1982.

Simon, J. "Why Good English Is Good for You." In *Literacy as a Human Problem,* ed. J. C. Raymond. University of Alabama Press, 1982.

Zemke, R. "How to Conduct a Needs Assessment for Computer-Literacy Training." *Training* (September 1983): 24-27, 30-31.

Humans 10 – Computers 6

JAMES V. BIUNDO

Humans 10–Computers 6. That was the score of a three-day chess tournament that pitted selected college students against computers.

The exercise seems innocuous enough; but at a time when the spotlight is increasingly on technology, it might be well to let the light splash onto the human element. In the chess game report, the top human score was 3½ by a computer science student at the University of Pittsburgh, and the top computer score was a 2 by Northwestern University's "Nuchess" computer. People have been winning, but a 1½ point spread is not a comfortable margin in any contest. Carnegie-Mellon's "HI-TECH" computer met a retired Grand Master in a four-game match in New York in September 1988.[1] "The tide is turning somewhat," said Ann Watzman, Carnegie-Mellon's university relations official. This time, the computer beat the human Grand Master. It would do well to look for a moment at that changing tide and its impact on society.

This is, indeed, a time of sophisticated technology. Robotics, computerization, telecommunications, genetic engineering–all are a real part of the everyday world and affect society at all levels. The term *computer literacy* is already viewed by some as a redundancy. Basic literacy will include knowledge of computers, and those not possessing that fundamental knowledge will be thrust into the "functionally illiterate" category. Some institutions are requiring computer literacy for a degree. Seventeen of the twenty-six private colleges in Iowa reported three years ago that computer literacy will eventually be required. "If you don't know anything about computers, you're going to be lost," warned the director of the Iowa State University Computer Center. At Yeshiva University, it has been suggested that a computer course might satisfy the foreign language requirement. The medievalist attitude that theology was the "queen of all thought" translates

145

into the twenty-first-century view that technology is the "queen of all thought." Tom Peters and Nancy Austin reaffirm this notion as they speak of "technical hubris" – the idea that technological superiority is the only thing that really counts.[2]

Some, however, are approaching the whole issue tongue-in-cheek. Witness this example of a modern rejection letter:

Dear Mr. Johnson:

Thank you for your interest in our job opening; the selection committee, however, has announced that the position has been awarded to an Apple II computer. This computer has been serving in a management capacity at this firm for the past two years, so an internal promotion was in order. Please do not interpret this decision as a reflection on your qualifications. It is not. In fact, the entire committee was impressed with you. But let's be realistic. An Apple II does not haggle over salary increases, doesn't request additional vacation days, and doesn't groan at the thought of having to work overtime.

I wish you continued success in your subsequent job searches.

Sincerely,

There is, of course, little humor in this for those who have been displaced.

Technology *is* increasingly evident in education. Art students in the ten-member consortium of East Coast arts schools and the Boston Architectural Center learn to design with computers at a visual-technology center. At Harvard, fuzzy telescope images caused by atmospheric distortion are being eliminated by computers. At the University of Iowa, a professor of religion is using a computer to write a commentary on the Jewish apocalypse. More recently, Carnegie-Mellon developed the first commercial intelligent tutor, which went on the market in 1986. It was designed not only to drill, but to evaluate how far along a student is in subject mastery. In 1986, Ball State University researchers developed a program to scan limericks. The program counts the number of stressed syllables and checks the rhyme scheme. "Alternate reality kits" were developed at the Xerox Palo Alto Research Center. Students build miniature universes and, at will, alter the laws of nature and then watch the effect.

The technocracy is quite evident in education. The challenge is to control that technocracy so it does not become an end in and of itself. In short, the challenge is to prevent the technology from displacing the art of being human. When *Time* magazine made the computer its "man of the year" for 1983, it created quite a furor. It was the first time that a thing, not a person, had been selected. The competition came from Margaret Thatcher, E.T., Paul Volcker, and Menachem Begin.

Time's criteria for selection are:

Is the candidate in the news a lot?

Does the candidate affect the lives of millions of people?

Could the candidate be said to have represented a trend?

Has the candidate exerted an influence for good or evil?

Many writers, from the beginning of the Industrial Revolution to the present day, have reminded society about the impact of technology. The poet e.e. cummings wrote, "A world of made is not a world of born."[3]. H. Ross Perot, the computer magnate and philanthropist, paid $15 million dollars in 1986 for one of the world's most important private collections of English works – including the first English Bible, eighteen Shakespearean quartos and four folios, and first editions of works by Milton, Spenser, and Ben Jonson – and donated it to the University of Texas at Austin. When asked if it wouldn't have been better to strengthen the university's resources in high technology, he said, "No. I have spent my entire adult life in advanced technologies. The worst mistake we could make is to turn out large numbers of technological robots. . . . The memory of the race, the rights for the next generation, cannot be taught by advanced technologies."[4]

In *The Third Wave*, Alvin Toffler summarized the personality of the future as follows: "As Third Wave civilization matures, we shall create not a utopian man or woman who towers over the people of the past, not a superhuman race of Goethes and Aristotles (or Genghis Khans and Hitlers). But merely, and proudly one hopes, a race – and a civilization – that deserves to be called human."[5] One of Toffler's points was that people need balance in their lives: balance between work and play, abstract and concrete, and objectivity and subjectivity.[6] His theory of balance is consistent with that espoused by Plato centuries earlier, with that reflected in the notion of the "Renaissance man," with that evident in nineteenth-century Samuel Butler's "theory of moderation." Surely, it is also appropriate to advocate balance between the technological and the human.

Those in private enterprise know the value of relating sophisticated technology to human dimensions. Initially, the advertising of technological products had a dramatic, new "wave of the future, don't get left behind" tone. Quickly, however, there was an attempt at more identification with traditional foundations and values: "Computers can help kids learn basics," said Centurion. "The tube talks with them, not at them," said Computerland.

Sams Books have a basic programming primer, a CP/M primer, a microcomputer primer, and a Pascal primer. Apple's new "Schoolbus" allowed several Apple II's to "share peripherals." Some manufacturers assured us that their computer product is "user friendly." "Let it be your pal," said Universal Systems. More and more, the advertising language conveyed images of traditional education within the framework of nonthreatening technology.

The next phase of advertising was one of power and simplicity: IBM said that "College and University Business Systems" (CUBS, for short) is a *total* solution to academic record-keeping and accounting. Zenith claimed that its PC "is the only option. To measure up is to reach beyond the pursuit of academic excellence." Besides, it has a "smarter" keyboard. Honeywell offered unsurpassed freedoms: "Freedom to maximize, freedom to work in any language, freedom to grow or change, freedom to access," and so on. AT&T presented a "world of in-laws" in our family. "Good providers" and a "supportive environment" provide a base for compatibility with other vendors' products. Wang could do all of it. Toshiba had the touch. And Decision Laboratories gave us a spreadsheet so simple that it "ends spread sheet impotency" and "thinks like an administrator."

Now in the current advertisements, the image of power continues, but it's coupled with speed and vision: IBM's "fast" has become "much faster," "extraordinarily fast," and "can store mountains of information." WordPerfect has people of "vision to nurture and refine" its product. Apple's strength is in "creating visions of the possible." Zenith "moves both your career and your imagination." Toshiba has the *"largest number* of high-powered PCs." And though Toshiba had the touch before, Digital "has it now!"

The "new things" are here, and the talent to devise all the systems is here. If one believes in the importance of balance, the time is a propitious one for those in leadership positions in business, industry, and education to initiate a new campaign to balance the challenges of the increasingly technological world – the *technocracy* – with the challenges of the art of being human. It is time to emphasize *anthropocracy* – to counter the anthropomorphism that has crept into the ads and discussions of technology. In short, it is time to acknowledge *people* as the focal point and fulcrum of society.

Herbert Simon, professor at Carnegie Mellon, stated in an interview, "We are beginning to understand ourselves as a part of nature, as subject to natural law. We are going to survive and thrive if we learn how to live in harmony with nature and not by devoting all of our efforts to distancing ourselves from the world we live in. We'd better understand how to survive as part of the system and not say, 'Well, here we are and there it is and we're the master of it all.' I don't think we're the master of anything."[7] To describe the technology as user friendly does not create that harmony. That harmony is not fostered when Writer's Workshop and DECTalk software programs at North Iowa Area Community College read aloud student compositions. "While the DECtalk software program has many voices," we're told, "students most frequently use the voices of Perfect Paul and Beautiful Betty."[8] The world is not populated with PPs and BBs.

Even more frightening are such innovations as "Housecall '86," a program that proposes to diagnose your illnesses (for $105) by turning your PC into an M.D., or statements like that by Pete Jordan, professor at Tennessee State University, who believes that the games which manufacturers have produced programs based on novels that "transcend the rigid, sequential experience of reading a book."[9] Namco Ltd. in Tokyo has a robot receptionist to greet visitors – a woman painted in soft pink and gray, perpetuating a sexist stereotype. Television gave the world a new electronic persona in Max Headroom. Finally, it was announced just this year that biogenetic scientists are capable of creating an anthropoid with a chimpanzee mother and human father. Brunetto Chiarelli, dean of Anthropology at Florence University, suggested that the new species could be used "for labor chores or as a reservoir for transplant organs."[10] In summary, the inference here is not that technology is all bad; it is that the human perspective within the technological world must be recognized. It is not an either-or inference. Just as some speak of the "romance" of life, others speak of the "romance" of technology.

The call, again, is to launch a series of activities that can reaffirm *people* as the fulcrum of society. What can be done?

- Establish "human awareness councils" with the same fervor and intensity with which high tech councils have been established.

- Schedule "celebrations of the human spirit" lectures, poetry readings, drama productions, seminars.

- Introduce special classes into the curriculum patterned after the theme of a recent conference at the University of Akron, entitled "The Human Future in a Brave New World" ("The Human Future in a Technological World," perhaps). Virginia Tech, for example, has an urban history course into which has been added the component, "technology assessment," which addresses discussions of how to arrive at a sustainable world economically, environmentally, ethically, and humanly (humanely).

- Support the science-technology-society (STS) interdisciplinary movements now gaining momentum but in critical need of faculty-administrative encouragement, involvement, and financial support.

- Seek "integration grants." Humanities courses are often stand-alone courses. George Bugliarello, president of New York Polytechnic University, has stated, "It is the rare professor of optics who uses paintings to help explain the theory."[11] William Paterson College has integrated telecommunications into the humanistic curriculum. The unique aspect is that "the study of the technology of telecommunications will be presented only in a context of humanism. In other words, students will be taught first to understand communication situations from an interpersonal and theoretical perspective and *then* to seek appropriate technological applications to improve those situations."[12] The Fund for the Improvement of Postsecondary Education has funded "Writing and Speaking Across the Curriculum." Wellesley College developed seventeen interdisciplinary courses with a $250,000 Sloan Foundation grant. Institutions have "internationalized" the curriculum through grants; how about an integration grant to humanize the curriculum.

- Sponsor "protest poetry" contests.

- Ask corporate friends to hire or underwrite a humanist to work with their employees.

- Institute "Technology and . . ." series of special workshops, conferences, and/or summer institutes: "Technology and the Theatre," "Technology and the Small Business," "Technology and Teaching," "Technology and Survival."

- Ernest Boyer and John Gardner were on the Southeast Missouri State University campus to help inaugurate the new university studies program. The entire program, which replaces the traditional general education component, has nine objectives, each representing the knowledge and skills that all educated people should possess and that are essential to improve one's quality of life and sustain success in a chosen career:

    1. Locate and gather information.

    2. Demonstrate capabilities for critical thinking, reasoning, and analyzing.

    3. Demonstrate effective communication skills.

    4. Demonstrate an understanding of human experience and the ability to relate them to the present.

    5. Demonstrate an understanding of various cultures and their interrelationships.

6.   Demonstrate the ability to integrate the breadth and diversity of knowledge and experience.

7.   Demonstrate the ability to make informed, intelligent decisions.

8.   Demonstrate the ability to make informed, sensitive aesthetic responses.

9.   Demonstrate the ability to function responsibly in one's natural, social, and political environment.[13]

- In the excitement of networking campuses, let us be sure that we network *people*. Humanize the delivery system. Deliver the support services.

This kind of awareness of the "human condition" provides a context in which people can distinguish the "world of born" from the "world of made." That "world of born" is not the exclusive domain of any segment of society. It has its roots in education, in the home, in religion, and in the business world. It is a world in which we can have the time of our lives in the way that William Saroyan describes:

> In the time of your life, live – so that in that good time there shall be no ugliness or death for yourself or for any life your life touches. Seek goodness everywhere, and when it is found, bring it out of its hiding-place and let it be free and unashamed. Place in matter and in flesh the least of the values, for these are the things that hold death and must pass away. Discover in all things that which shines and is beyond corruption. Encourage virtue in whatever heart it may have been driven into secrecy and sorrow by the shame and terror of the world. Ignore the obvious, for it is unworthy of the clear eye and the kindly heart. Be the inferior of no one, nor of anyone be superior. Remember that every person is a variation of yourself. Despise evil and ungodliness, but not people of ungodliness and evil. These, understand.
>
> In the time of your life, live – so that in that wondrous time you shall not add to the misery and sorrow of the world, but shall smile to the infinite delight and mystery of it."[14]

Notes

1. "Computer Chess Machine Achieves Master Status," *Chronicle of Higher Education*, March 8, 1989, A14.

2. Tom Peters and Nancy Austin, *A Passion for Excellence* (New York: Random House, 1985), 44.

3. e.e. cummings, "Pity This Busy Monster, Manunkind," *The Many Worlds of Poetry* (New York: Alfred A. Knopf, 1969), 81.

4. "U. of Texas Is Beneficiary of Largest Rare Book Sale," *Chronicle of Higher Education*, January 29, 1986, 3.

5. Alvin Toffler, *The Third Wave* (New York: William Morrow and Co., 1980), 407.

6. Ibid., 403-5.

7. "Artificial Intelligence," *The Arizona Republic*, July 28, 1986.

8. "Inspiring Iowa Writers," *What's New On Campus*, 1986, 14-16.

9. Pete Jordan, *Online Today*, August 1985, n.p.

10. "Apeman Embryo Aborted at Embryo Stage, Scientist Says," *Arizona Daily Star*, May 15, 1987.

11. Judith Axel Turner, "Professors Find Many Obstacles to Combining Technology and Liberal Arts," *Chronicle of Higher Education*, March 4, 1987, A-16.

12. Barry Morganstern and Diana Peck, "Integrating Telecommunications into the Humanistic Communication Curriculum" (Paper presented at Conference on the Networked Campus, SUNY, Farmingdale, May 27, 1987).

13. John Hinni, "University Studies Program at Southeast Missouri State University" (Unpublished paper, 1988).

14. William Saroyan, *The Time of Your Life* (New York: Harcourt, Brace and Company, 1939), 15.

Numeracy: An Imperative for the Information Age

BILL H. WASHBURN

The issue of "numeracy" is succinctly stated in Clarke's Third Law (otherwise known as Murphy's Law of Technology): "Any technology, sufficiently advanced, is indistinguishable from magic." Of course, few of us would acknowledge magic in any form as an explanation for the scientific, medical, or technological feats of this century. But for a majority of citizens in this country, the words *magic* and *technology* are, in truth, indistinguishable. How many people, for instance, will fly in a jet airliner today without the faintest idea how or why any of it works? If these jet passengers were asked to explain what they know about airplanes, I doubt any of them would resort to describing jet travel as magic. However, most of them may feel perfectly comfortable saying that it is a matter of technology, or engineering, or science, at work. Nevertheless, if we do not understand or comprehend the basic principles and phenomena underlying airplane travel, then – for us – saying it is science at work is no more satisfactoy than saying I got here on a magic carpet.

Well, so what? you might ask. What difference does it make if otherwise literate people can't explain why or how airplanes fly? What does it matter if you and I don't understand the risks and pharmacology of recreational alcohol and drug use? And what difference does it make if we fail to comprehend the biochemical bases of cancer? And does it really matter if you and I don't know anything about the epidemiology of Acquired Immune Deficiency Syndrome? Or is it really important for us to understand the probable long-term consequences of careless disposal of radioactive and other hazardous waste material? Or what about "Star Wars"? Does it matter if most of us find it impossible to understand or participate in the debate about whether satellites and "space stations" should become the newest weapons for defense, confrontation, and military one-upsmanship? Then there's the idea of using nuclear fusion as a possible new source of energy in the next 50 or 100 years. Who among us has the capability to participate in that debate? Have you thought about the possibility of literally transplanting human brains in the next century? Is that an important question for public discussion?

I hope these questions make the point evident and clear. Even if you find none of today's medical, technical, or scientific debates worrisome, it is a virtual certainty that even more difficult dilemmas will compel your attention tomorrow. And herein lies the rub. No one can have it both ways. If we choose steadfastly to remain scientifically illiterate, that is, innumerate, we will have no alternative but to watch from the sidelines while new public policies regarding technology, medicine, and science are debated without us. And as technology pushes us headlong into the twenty-first century, more and more of what we must judge regarding public priorities, policies, and prohibitions will necessarily be highly technical in nature. So, eventually those of us who are today content to get on and off airplanes without any knowledge of how or why they fly will one day discover we can neither understand nor contribute to many of the most important societal questions because, for us, the technical issues will be so advanced we will unable to distinguish science from magic.

"How will numeracy (scientific literacy) make a difference in public policy and debate in the twenty-first century?" is the question I pose and propose to address here.

Consider the printing press revolution and the renaissance of classical learning as a metaphor for today's "computer" or "information" revolution. Consider especially the possibility of another renaissance in the twenty-first century.

Five hundred years ago the development of movable-type printing presses and improvements in paper manufacturing provided the basis for what we might call the First Information Technology Revolution.

Today, the computer – along with the telephone, the camera, the radio, and the television – clearly signify a second momentous revolution – the Second Information Revolution.

Soon after the Gutenberg "technology" emerged, the printing, distributing, and selling of books, bibles, manuscripts, journals, dictionaries, indulgences, calendars, maps, and so forth became a large, important industry that substantially changed Western societies. In part, the appearance of commercial printing and publishing helped demark the end of the Middle Ages and the beginning of the modern era.

In just the last forty years, computing has already become the third largest commercial enterprise in the world, surpassed only by oil and automobiles in revenues. To be sure, the educational, economic, political, and cultural consequences of the blossoming computer age are only now becoming apparent. Perhaps in the twenty-fifth century this era will be remembered as the beginning of the Information Age.

Five hundred years ago, with massive increases in printed material, literacy gradually became a widely useful and needed skill. Books were no longer the exclusive possession of churches, universities, schools and the high-born. Elementary reading and writing increased rather slowly at first, but by 1875 some countries had literacy rates approaching 90 percent. As we now see, the printing press made "language literacy" imaginable, possible, and eventually achievable for everyone. Indeed, who among us today would dispute the goal of "universal literacy" as a fundamental objective of society? It is not an exaggeration to say that in the twentieth century universal literacy is a definitive characteristic of modern nations. It would be difficult to find anything more basic than the book as the building block that laid the foundations for today's postindustrial societies.

Perhaps the microcomputer represents today what the book represented 500 years ago – a powerful, promising new tool and a potential means of vast knowledge for every person. Microcomputers are now becoming widely utilized and in the coming decades will be as universally available as books. And, as much as with books, microcomputers will soon give each of us an unimagined tool for exploring and understanding the principles and concepts of science, advanced mathematics, engineering, and technology. Microcomputers will soon be so miniaturized, so compact, so portable, and so powerful that we will have them with us all the time – just as we love to live with books.

At the time of Gutenberg, the idea of "literacy" or "illiteracy" was not deemed a significant social issue. The resources for providing general language literacy were simply unavailable, and people carried on other traditions (such as "giving one's word and a handshake," town criers, public ceremonies, oral histories, troubadours, religious festivals, etc.) to give, receive, and preserve knowledge. Monarchies, magistrates, and religious authorities in pre-printing press societies must have long assumed that reading and writing could be neither learned nor used by anyone but themselves – the self-perpetuating, socially dominant, and "chosen" elite.

Today, "numeracy" is only barely a public issue. When it comes to technical matters, scientific reports, and mathematical formulas, most of us believe that only a small, intellectually superior segment of the population has the capacity to become fully numerate. Moreover, we assume that science and math education is intrinsically difficult, expensive to provide, and somehow irrelevant with little value for most individuals. So, contradictory as it is, today our society, on the one hand, is convinced that universal language literacy is virtually a God-given right and, on the other hand, we are casually persuaded that numeracy is only for the few, the intellectually superior among us. It would appear that most people in the United States think science and math are quite beyond their powers and are irrelevant anyway. But I, for one, think we can now begin to imagine microcomputers that will make universal numeracy entirely possible, just as Gutenberg's books made universal literacy an achievable objective.

Five hundred years ago, written language had always been the exclusive domain of the "high priests": the religious, economic, political, royal, and military leaders or authorities of society. Indeed, before Gutenberg, the written word and the spoken word were literally (no pun intended) different modes or forms of communication.

Today, the language of advanced math and science remains the domain of an intellectual high priesthood–professors, scientists, doctors, engineers, a few businesspeople and some scholars. Mostly male, mostly white, these high priests of science necessarily exert substantial influence on our lives, our public institutions, and society overall. Politicians, business executives, and private citizens all worship at the altar and kneel to hear the counsel of our elite scientists and technocrats. We have little choice but to rely on their expertise, their ethical vision, and their presumed benevolent wisdom. How many citizens today have the background to understand, let alone evaluate, Reagan's Strategic Defense Initiative ("Star Wars")? Is transplanting human brain tissue an acceptable medical practice or research procedure? To what extent is genetic engineering environmentally safe? By what means can public policy delimit the domain of scientific inquiry? By what means *should* it do so?

Like it or not, most of us today live in a situation intellectually analogous to that faced by our ancestors in Gutenberg's day. Just the onslaught of jargon from science and technology is enough to confound our communication and conversation. There is a sense in which many of us may feel utterly bewildered and ignorant about many of the most significant issues of the day–ignorant no matter how advanced we may be in total number of years of education. As it was 500 years ago, once again we have two kinds of language in our society: the language for everyday discourse and the language of mathematics and science–in which parlance many of the most crucial technical, economic, and political decisions are made. The trouble is, 95 percent of us don't speak, read, or write the language of science. Just as people in the middle ages probably didn't think of themselves as backward or illiterate, we do not consider ourselves ignorant. But ignorant we are, nevertheless.

Today the book stands as a metaphor for Western civilization during the last 500 years. Over the centuries of the modern era, books have laid much of the foundation on which virtually every revolution has been built, be it economic, political, scientific, religious, educational, or social. Isn't it true that the ever-increasing availability of books and the concomitant expansion in the exchange of ideas fueled and fomented most of the change we have seen since 1450?

With time, perhaps some advanced version of the personal microcomputer will symbolize this dawning age of information. And just as books are the tool we have used to develop universal language literacy, it seems quite possible that the microcomputer may serve as the tool to give every human being the chance to become truly numerate.

Before Gutenberg's movable type, only a few very fortunate individuals could ever hope to enjoy the fruits of literacy. But for the past few centuries, books have quickened our hearts, nourished our minds, and sustained our souls by the millions. Today we see universal literacy as a highly desirable, entirely achievable, and, indeed, essential objective of society.

Today microcomputers hold the promise of astounding possibilities for the twenty-first century. The personal microcomputer can be a drafting table, a typewriter, a calculator, a telephone, a game room, a printing press, a television, an orchestra, a laboratory, a camera, a library, and a fax machine. The personal microcomputer may become the fundamental tool for bringing numeracy to everyone. If microcomputers can become as easy to use as books, then we can start with children before kindergarten and they all may have the chance to learn to think in numbers as well as pictures and words. What might really happen if all of our children become fully numerate, just as we expect them to become devotedly literate? In what unimagined ways will they begin to transform anew our world and our lives?

But becoming a nation of highly numerate, as well as highly literate, citizens surely isn't just a matter of technological innovation driving us into the twenty-first century. The United States seems to have a cultural mind-set that may take an entire generation to change, no matter how great the scientific advances. Here are a few of the more egregious problems we must resolve.

1. Our society has long been convinced, apparently, that science literacy, or numeracy, is something that only the elite or elect few among us can achieve. We must move far beyond the "advanced math is too tough for ordinary people" syndrome. Just as we now realize that literacy is universally possible, we must see that numeracy is a universal imperative for tomorrow.

2. We should no longer casually accept the commonplace "fact" of a pervasive double standard for college education in the United States. The de facto acceptance of a high standard of numeracy for the bachelor of science student and yet virtual scientific illiteracy for the bachelor of arts student must be abandoned before the year 2000.

3. Educators today don't think science should be taught until high school. Here again we face the ingrained presumption that only the select few can master the concepts and principles of science and advanced math. Numbers and science must be as pervasive as words and pictures and language in the primary education of all our children.

4. For generations we have used introductory science and math courses in high school and college as barriers, as insurmountable hurdles, as academic brickbats for convincing most students to avoid at all cost any further study of or interest in science and math. In a demented and really tragic move to maintain or protect elite status, many of the high priests of science, engineering, and math have unwittingly achieved our worst fear – a nation where even most of the college-educated adults loathe math and turn comatose or catatonic in any discussion of science-related issues. Basically, we have convinced most adults that they are not smart enough to become numerate and to avoid science and technology, no matter what the price.

5. We need to abandon the false dichotomy taken very much for granted in higher education that computers constitute either (1) a luxury that wastes our limited resources, or (2) an invidious threat to replace classroom teachers with machines. If technology can stimulate students, help them learn more, enable them to be more productive in doing homework, and assist them in breaking conceptual bottlenecks in science and math, then we must use all the tools available to us. Teachers remain quite irreplaceable. However, we must give both professors and students the means to become far more productive in teaching and learning.

Even without the benefit of a magician's crystal ball, it seems apparent that a number of current trends will continue, at least for the next two or three generations: (1) the population will keep increasing; (2) scientific discoveries will continue to support a vast, indeed an unprecedented, array of technological innovations; (3) speeds of communication and travel will continue to shrink our globe; (4) we will face tougher and tougher ethical dilemmas as medical and genetic "advances" present us with unimagined questions about life and death; (5) ecological conundrums such as acid rain, the greenhouse effect, deforestation, and ozone depletion will become more acute concerns, and (6) the militarization of space exploration will add to the threat of global annihilation.

In conclusion, I hope you would agree with me that solving the challenges we face today and the even greater difficulties we anticipate tomorrow will require far more than the wave of a sorcerer's magic wand. It is just as foolish as waving a magician's wand, however, to think we can or should take our nation's future out of our own hands and hand it over to scientists, engineers, technocrats, doctors, or scholars, no matter how benevolent, wise, good, and kind we may consider them to be. Rather, we must deepen and broaden dramatically the math and science education opportunities for all of us. And perhaps the microcomputers of tomorrow will hold the keys of numeracy for all of us who will live in the twenty-first century.

Think of the vast change that has occurred around the world as the push to establish universal literacy came to fruition. This world has been transformed – both for good and for ill – as books have brought the power of knowledge and ideas to millions upon millions of human beings. Perhaps this is only the very beginning of the history and the story of humanity. Realizing what we do today, how can we aspire to anything less than universal numeracy? How can we wait? How can we ever accept less? Let me finish by suggesting to you another Murphy's Law – Murphy's Law of the Future: not only is the future more challenging than we imagine, it is more challenging than we *can* imagine.

Bibliography

Bloch, Arthur. *Murphy's Law and Other Reasons Why Things Go Wrong*. Los Angeles: Price/Stern/Sloan. 1979.

Copperman, Paul. *The Litercay Hoax: The Decline of Reading, Writing, and Learning in the Public Schools and What We Can Do About It*. New York: Morrow, 1978.

Erlich, Elizabeth. "Needed: Human Capital." *Business Week*, September 19, 1988, 100-136.

Harman, David. *Illiteracy: A National Dilemma*. Cambridge: Oxford University Press, 1977.

Westheimer, Frank H. "The Education of the Next Generation of Nonscientists." *Chemical Education News Journal* 66, no. 26 (July 4, 1988): 32-38.

Section Two

LITERACIES FOR THE INFORMATION AGE

These papers suggest the broader definition of literacy that will be appropriate in the new information age. The papers first discuss the predominant literacy of the current era, print, as well as its immediate predecessor, oral literacy. Oral literacy is linked to print literacy. Finally, the newer literacies, visual and computer, are discussed.

Renee Tjoumas examines the literacy programs associated with three metropolitan public libraries in "Libraries and Librarians as Social Change Agents: Three Case Studies in the Battle against Adult Illiteracy." This paper concludes with recommendations for future action that could be implemented by the information professional. In "From Oral Tradition to Printed Format: Australian-Aboriginal Legend and the Work of Dick Roughsey," Karen Smith traces the evolution of an Aboriginal author's work from its original oral format to print, re-creating in this essay the themes of the transformation experienced by Western civilization in ancient Greece. The impending changes in the art of storytelling made possible by the computer and other interactive media are reported by Hilary McLellen in "Storytelling via Technology in the Information Age." Another development related to storytelling is the recreation of printed stories in oral form on "bookcassettes." This is the subject of Virgil Blake's "Something New Has Been Added: Aural Literacy and Libraries." Further consideration of the role of aural literacy and the introduction of the concept of visual literacy in the unique setting of the court system is detailed by Joseph Fulda's "The Evidentiary Quality of Taped Evidence." Jennifer Shaddock's "The Alien Space of (M)other: The Female Gothic and *Aliens*" demonstrates the use of visual literacy in the more relaxed setting of popular culture. In his "From Orality to Literacy to Electronic Technology: Conceptualizing Classical Rhetoric in an Age of Word Processors," John Frederick Reynolds contends that the teaching of writing by means of the five canons of classical rhetoric

161

developed in the oral tradition of ancient Greece leads to improved writing skills and an enhanced comprehension of the printed word. Wayne State University's program in assisting medical students achieve computer literacy is outlined in Faith Van Toll's "Librarians, Faculty, and Students: An Integrated, Interdisciplinary Team Approach to Medical School Computer Literacy." These essays demonstrate that the realities of the next century will require a far more sophisticated "reader" to effectively utilize the broader spectrum of available information products.

Libraries and Librarians as Social Change Agents: Three Case Studies in the Battle against Adult Illiteracy

RENEE TJOUMAS

The consequences of illiteracy profoundly affect American society. Millions suffer loss of self-esteem in constantly confronting the limitations imposed by the inability to read. The financial losses are also enormous. Six billion dollars are spent yearly on welfare and unemployment compensation due to illiteracy. To counteract illiteracy, a number of library organizations have become involved in implementing innovative activities for adult learners. The unrealized earnings relinquished by the undereducated is estimated at $237 billion yearly. Crime and illiteracy are also linked to $6.6 billion spent annually on 750,000 illiterate prison inmates.[1]

The literacy programs of three public library systems within the metropolitan New York area are examined. The investigation is based upon on-site visits, interviews with key personnel, and a review of institutional documents of the Queens Borough Public Library, the New York Public Library, and the Brooklyn Public Library. This study identifies unique programs, the use of technology, the development of unusual learning packages, and other imaginative activities that could provide valuable examples of what other libraries might do to confront the problems of illiteracy. The closing remarks present recommendations for combating illiteracy more effectively as the twenty-first century approaches.

INTRODUCTION

Any discussion pertaining to adult illiteracy in the American context needs to be based upon some attempt to elucidate relevant terminology. Conventional literacy has been defined as "the ability to read, write, and comprehend texts on familiar subjects and to understand whatever signs, labels, instructions, and directions are necessary to get along within one's environment."[2] Illiteracy, in contrast, is the inability to read and write. Individuals who are illiterate lack coding and decoding abilities "to recognize letters, associate them with the sounds they represent, and combine them into words, sentences, and texts."[3] The concept of functional literacy is far more complex and difficult to describe. One of the better explanations has been formulated by Carmen St. John-Hunter and David Harman in their ground-breaking study, *Adult Illiteracy in the United States*. They define functional literacy as

> the possession of skills *perceived as necessary by particular persons and groups* to fulfill their own self-determined objectives as family and community members, citizens, consumers, job-holders, and members of social, religious, or other associations of their choosing. This includes the ability to obtain information they want and to use the information for their own and others' well being; the ability to read and write adequately to satisfy the requirements *they set for themselves* as being important for their own lives; the ability to deal positively with demands made on them by society and the ability to solve the problems they face in their daily lives.[4]

Some estimates suggest that twenty-three million Americans lack the reading and writing abilities needed to handle the minimal demands of daily life.[5] In addition, forty-six million adults read on a limited level, but far below what is required to function effectively in a technologically advanced society, and therefore, they are considered marginally literate.[6] To make matters worse, the pool of adult illiterates continues to grow at an annual rate of 2.3 million persons each year.[7]

The roots of this problem are deeply intertwined in the social, economic, and cultural elements of our society. Some of the reasons most frequently cited include a dropout rate that in some urban areas reaches as high as 55 percent,[8] the oversimplification of textbooks,[9] ineffectual teachers, and overdependence on television for both recreational and informational purposes. The home environment is another important factor because nonreading parents often transmit the legacy of illiteracy to their children.[10] Immigration is also a critical ingredient with one million people entering this country illegally and 400,000 legally on an annual basis.[11] Many of these individuals may be able to read one or more languages, but lack any proficiency in handling English-language materials.[12]

THE NEW YORK REALITY

There are 1.5 million people in the New York metropolitan area who are functionally illiterate. These New Yorkers cannot:

■ Read a newspaper

■ Read a menu in a restaurant

164

- Write a check a bank can process

- Address an envelope that will be delivered by the post office

- Read road signs, bus schedules, or a subway map

- Understand the instructions on a medicine bottle

- Compare prices of groceries or check change against a receipt

- Fill out a job application, an insurance form, or income tax return

- Read a written petition or an election ballot[13]

The three New York City public library systems, Queens Borough Public Library, New York Public Library, and Brooklyn Public Library, have assumed some of the responsibility for educating adults who lack reading skills.

Queens Borough Public Library

Recognizing the needs of the local community, Director Constance B. Cooke was the prime catalyst in initiating the literacy program of the Queens Borough Public Library (QBPL). The program began in 1977 with seed money provided by a grant from the Library Services Construction Act (LSCA). Financial support since that time has come from a variety of other sources, including the New York City Municipal Assistance Corporation (MAC) and the New York State Education Department.[14]

The literacy program is associated with the Programs and Services Department, operating as part of the Adult Learning Center of the Central Library, with nine participating branch sites.[15] The foundation of the program's structure is based upon the one-to-one learning configuration maintained between adult learners and tutors. The support staff fulfills an essential role in selecting materials, training and supervising tutors, keeping records, and submitting reports to funding agencies.[16]

Enhanced literacy services beyond the tutorial arrangement are clustered in six key locations, with the Adult Learning Center at the main branch performing a pivotal coordinating role. The five additional sites are adult learning centers established at the Flushing, Elmhurst, Rochdale, Peninsula, and Forest Hills branches. Two centers (Elmhurst and Flushing) have a "comprehensive" program providing both English as a second language (ESL) and literacy assistance, while the remaining sites work only with adult illiterates. Greatly facilitated through MAC funds, these centers provide computer-assisted instruction opportunities for both literacy and ESL students, writing skills workshops, comprehensive collections of high/low materials for leisure reading, and professional development collections geared specifically to meet the needs of adult basic education (ABE) instructors and ESL teachers.[17]

Highlights of the QBPL literacy program include:

(1) *Transitional Classes*

After beginning their tutoring program, adult learners are tested with each fifty-hour block of instruction. Adjustments in the curriculum are then made to reflect the evolution of their reading abilities. Students who have advanced beyond the fifth-grade reading level are often referred to local ABE programs; however, many individuals resist leaving the library. This reluctance is often based upon negative experiences in the formal school environment or apprehension in confronting a group learning situation. In response to these needs, transitional courses were formulated. They consist of ten or twelve literacy graduates who meet with a teacher and two paraprofessionals. Reading skills are emphasized, but mathematics, science, history, geography, and current events are also included in the curriculum. Writing activities and group interaction are emphasized.[18] These classes continue to attract new students, and they have proven to be quite successful in assisting adult learners transfer to more advanced ABE programs.

(2) *Read-Aloud Project*

Supported by LSCA funds, an eight-week pilot program was organized to teach literacy students how to read aloud to their children. Participants were organized into groups and were introduced to materials. Helpful techniques in reading aloud to children were explained. Some participants brought their children to a few sessions in order to practice as well as demonstrate their newly acquired skills. Parents wrote stories that they later shared with their children. Participants and their children were introduced to other library facilities, programs, and resources during tours that were tailored to their needs and interests. The twofold purpose of this program was to encourage personal contact between parent and child and to nurture the reading habit for both generations.[19]

New York Public Library

The literacy program of the New York Public Library (NYPL) was initiated in 1977 with financial assistance from an LSCA grant. Volunteer tutoring programs and small specialized collections for adult learners were established at branch locations in Staten Island and the Bronx. Aided tremendously by grant monies furnished by the Municipal Assistance

Corporation, the library established eight centers for reading and writing in neighborhood libraries in Manhattan, Staten Island, and the Bronx.[20] Services at these centers include:

- One-to-one and small-group tutoring for adult new readers

- English classes for adult speakers of other languages at some centers

- Microcomputers for self-instruction

- The Lifelong Learning Collection, which includes books and other materials for adult new readers, non-English speakers, and other professionals[21]

The ESL program has been developed for non-English-speaking adults over the age of sixteen who need to develop basic conversational skills. Funded by federal and state monies, the program is coordinated by the NYPL, with classes taught by ESL specialists from the Riverside Adult Learning Center, which is an independent agency that is not part of the library system. ESL classes are offered at three centers for reading and writing, as well as at ten other branch libraries where language training of this type is most needed by local communities.[22]

Highlights of the New York Public Library's approach to combating adult illiteracy include:

(1) *Deposit Collections*

The library purchases materials geared to the new adult reader in bulk quantities. Located at the centers for reading and writing, these materials are reviewed by ABE teachers, who borrow up to 250 items for an extended period of time to use in their classrooms. A variety of fields are represented, with over 1,300 titles available in both fiction and nonfiction categories.[23]

(2) *Meet-the-Authors Program*

Authors of mature trade books speak to students about the creative aspects of writing and share personal glimpses of how they became writers. Among the authors who have participated in these activities are Claude Brown, Brenda Wilkinson, Judy Simmons, and Joyce Hanson. The purpose of this enrichment program is to expand students' horizons regarding the creative aspects of the literary world, as well as to motivate them to continue their efforts in improving reading proficiency.[24]

(3) *Saturday Morning Writing Workshops*

Open to literacy students and to other members of the community, the objective of this program is to help individuals improve their writing abilities. An unusual feature of this workshop is that it is used as a training component by ABE teachers and literacy tutors who desire additional strategies in assisting adult learners. Students, teachers, and literacy tutors meet together for two hours in a classroom atmosphere. Two learning professionals are responsible for conducting the workshop. In the third hour, team teachers meet with the other learning professionals and tutors to discuss their observations and the insights gained during the previous time period. Plans and instructional methodologies are then formulated by this group for the next workshop meeting.[25]

Brooklyn Public Library

The literacy program at the Brooklyn Public Library (BPL) began in 1977 and consisted of one staff person who worked on a volunteer basis. This individual coordinated the efforts of several volunteers who tutored literacy students in the Central Library. Funds, provided by a grant from the Older Americans Act in 1980, were utilized to pay the volunteer coordinator. Two years later, additional monies dedicated specifically to community development activities were received from the Office of the Mayor. With these funds, satellite literacy locations were established in seventeen branches identified as "community strategy areas." Specialized collections containing hi/low materials and survival skills information were also purchased and placed at these sites.

Dramatic growth and strengthening of the literacy program began in 1984 with the receipt of grant monies from the Municipal Assistance Corporation. These funds were used to establish five adult literacy centers, currently operating at the Central Library and at four branches: Eastern Parkway, Williamsburgh, Coney Island, and Bedford. Even though literacy tutoring and materials are still available at satellite sites, enhanced services and coordinating functions are located primarily at these centers.[26] The centers contain computers that are used by students, and space is available for one-to-one as well as small-group tutoring. Support services for tutors include in-service training sessions and consultations with a reading expert. Students' programs are monitored, with evaluations occurring at the initial stage of implementation and after each fifty hours of tutoring. Special materials housed at these centers are in three interrelated areas: A major segment called the "Adult New Reader Collection" consists of books and other resources of interest to adults who are beginning to read. The second component consists of ESL materials, and professional books for teachers and tutors make up the third portion.[27]

Innovative features of the Brooklyn Public Library's literacy program include:

(1) *Study Table Groups*

This concept was developed in an effort to retain literacy students who approach the library for assistance but must wait for a tutor. A six- to nine-month delay is not unique because there are many more individuals interested in learning how to read than there are people available to instruct them. Study tables are made up of six or seven adult learners who work with a teacher on a specific topic of interest. Two popular areas of focus are citizenship information and driver's education. In this manner, students become integrated into the program and also formulate new social relationships while they learn new skills and concepts.

(2) *Subject-Oriented Curriculum Kits*

Since 1984, MAC funds have also been awarded to other community-based organizations within the New York metropolitan area in support of their literacy efforts. Among the stipulations enumerated in the MAC grants was the mandate that these agencies utilize the resources of neighboring libraries.

Striving to facilitate this connection, the staff prepared curriculum kits consisting of videotapes, instructional materials, and handouts on topics such as citizenship, AIDS, New York City government, and how to use newspapers effectively. Library personnel introduce the packets to ABE instructors teaching in locally based service operations. The compilation of these kits serve a twofold function: (1) providing instructors with resource materials that can be incorporated into classroom activities, and (2) introducing the educators to the library's services. The personal contact also creates an opportunity to encourage both students and teachers to register for borrowers' cards and to promote the library as a viable information center.[28]

(3) *The Student Council and the National Issues Forums*

Funded by grants from Time, Inc., the Student Council offers an avenue for more experienced students to provide a support system for each other and to assist newer learners as they adjust to the program. The council is composed entirely of students and meets on a monthly basis. Officers are elected and agenda items are selected based upon students' interests and concerns. This organization serves as an important communication vehicle for conveying suggestions to staff members regarding the literacy program. The Student Council is also the structure by which literacy students have participated in the National Issues Forums (NIF), which are sponsored by the Domestic Policy Association. Citizens gather in their communities, each fall and winter, to discuss policy issues of outstanding national concern. These meetings are organized by local groups and organizations and offer an opportunity for people to discuss selected topics and express their opinions. Three yearly themes are selected by NIF in close collaboration with local organizers. NIF also provides materials and coordinates follow-up meetings to share citizens' opinions with policymakers. These encounters, held in Washington, D.C., include briefings of congressional and White House staffs. Participating communities also convey summaries of informed judgments arrived at during local forums to regional and state policymakers. Topics selected for 1988-89 were: "Coping with AIDS: The Public Response to the Epidemic," "Health Care for the Elderly: Moral Dilemmas, Moral Choices," and "The Public Debt: Breaking the Habit of Deficit Spending."[29]

Central to the NIF program are issue books written on each of the three topics selected yearly. Produced by the Public Agenda Foundation and the Kettering Foundation, NIF issue books present a nonpartisan, nontechnical analysis of each issue. Booklets contain questionnaires that participants complete both before and after reading and discussing each topic. These responses are mailed to NIF, where they are compiled into a report that is presented to policymakers.[30]

The Brooklyn Public Library, along with other library institutions across the country, has established forums for literacy students. Utilizing abridged editions of the NIF books prepared on 4.5- to 6.5-grade levels, adult learners have been introduced to major issues confronting American society. These booklets are incorporated into the instructional materials used by tutors and students. Crossword puzzles based on the vocabulary of the issue books have been prepared and incorporated into the program.[31] Small-group and roundtable discussions are also organized.

At the Brooklyn Public Library, other resources and activities have been developed to encourage student involvement. For example, when dealing with a topic related to freedom of speech, skits were organized and presented at monthly student meetings that featured both the literacy staff and the learners. Three scenarios were presented: (1) a debate between Jerry Falwell and Larry Flint on freedom to publish pornography; (2) a dialogue on whether or not Nazis should have had the right to march in Skokie, Illinois; and (3) a discussion about music with suggestive lyrics between a rock musician and a distressed parent.

Thousands have learned to read in the New York metropolitan area through the staff efforts of these three public library systems. The success of their literacy services can be traced to some fundamental ingredients that characterize their program activities. In all three instances, literacy projects have been developed that not only teach individuals how to code and decode messages, but also strive to assist them in developing self-expression, esteem, and confidence. Library personnel have created nonthreatening and nurturing environments for adult learners who have often been bruised by the social system. In fact, for some, these libraries are the only avenues open for literacy instruction because very few adult education courses are available for students who read below the third-grade level. Opportunities for self-governance, socializing, and sharing ideas through the publication of student journals not only reinforce newly acquired skills but provide new avenues of expression. Empowerment, the ultimate goal of these literacy efforts, is fostered by removing self-imposed and societal barriers that hamper the blossoming of each person's potential. Therefore, these programs provide a bridge for the disenfranchised to become active participants in directing the destiny of their local communities and, ultimately, the nation at large.

Another component that has contributed to the success of these programs is the availability of local, state, and federal funding. The importance of the MAC grants in strengthening and extending literacy services to a broader based audience cannot be underestimated. Without these funds, the three library systems could not have created specialized centers, workshops, and collections. Programs would have remained small, and many innovative ideas would have been aborted because of the lack of financial support to implement them.

Beginning in 1988, MAC literacy funds were incorporated into the annual library city budget as a separately designated line item. These monies were allocated specifically for literacy activities and cannot be expended on other programs or materials. This step is more than a political gesture by the New York City government; it is the recognition, supported by a firm financial commitment, of the public library as a potent and viable combatant in the war against adult illiteracy.

Staff commitment is the third element that exemplifies the work of these three libraries. Initially, personnel associated with these programs encountered resistance from other librarians as well as educators. Patience, persistence, creativity, and a willingness to experiment have contributed to a profound transformation. The public library as a passive, archival institution has been reshaped into a learning, information hub of the community. Literacy services were designed based upon the needs and characteristics of the local populace. This approach is a dramatic break from the past, when librarians often imposed program activities that did not fit the community but exemplified some artificial ideal.

The success of these literacy programs can be demonstrated by the close working relationships that have been formed between these library systems and ABE agencies throughout the New York metropolitan area. Library personnel now experience less resistance and more acceptance from other adult education professionals. Further evidence of the confidence that has evolved in the ability of these libraries to assist the new adult reader resides in the extensive and on-going financial support provided by a variety of government agencies on the local, state, and federal levels.

RECOMMENDATIONS AND SUGGESTIONS

As the twenty-first century approaches, the number of adult illiterates will continue to increase. The public library should function as a vital key in unlocking the literacy barriers that block many from realizing the full range of their talents and gifts. The examples provided by the Queens Borough Public Library, the New York Public Library, and the Brooklyn Public Library prove that library institutions and staffs can be social change agents in assisting new adult readers to realize their human potential. However, much more needs to be done to facilitate this work in the New York area and throughout the nation. The recommendations proposed by the author can be grouped into four categories.

(1) *Recruitment of New Tutors*

There are many more adult learners waiting for instruction than there are available tutors. A pool of talent that can be tapped is the college community. Students could tutor adult learners for a minimum of one year and receive course credit towards graduation. This idea may seem farfetched, but negotiations of this type have begun between the Queens Borough Public Library and the Queens College Department of Linguistics.

(2) *Library and Information Science Education*

Throughout this researcher's encounters with literacy personnel working in the three public library systems, the need for employees who were equally proficient in librarianship and adult learning was expressed. Administrators believe that individuals with the dual background would be more effective on the job and require less in-house training in either area. Furthermore, the job market will increasingly demand candidates of this type as more public libraries become involved in literacy activities.

In response, library schools can actively recruit students who have an expertise in adult reading skills, adult basic education, or English as a second language. Another option would be to develop a cross-disciplinary program that combines classes in librarianship with graduate courses in these specialty areas.

(3) *Research*

More investigatory research is needed in examining the literacy programs operating in library settings. Among some of the relevant questions that could be explored are:

- What factors contribute to the retention of the adult learner in a library program? What additional services could be designed based upon variables of success?

- Are there any additional measures or procedures that could be formulated to assess and evaluate library-related literacy programs?

- Hard facts and statistically sound analyses that demonstrate program success would enhance requests for funding.

- After literacy students have gained the skills to read self-sufficiently, do these learners continue their association with the library as an informational and recreational source? What are the variables that reinforce this relationship? What additional resources or services need to be furnished in responding to their needs?

(4) *Literacy Center for Research, Information, and Referral*

The major purpose of such an organization would be to serve as a resource center for literacy programming in the library environment. Holdings could consist of elements such as:

- Grant proposals

- Bibliographies of software programs and reading materials suitable for literacy students

- Examples of learning games, quizzes, and word puzzles

- Curriculum guides

- Annual reports

- Student publications

- Research projects, surveys, and reports

Such a collection could be utilized by library personnel across the country to serve as models for planning activities and to stimulate ideas. A directory would also be compiled of literacy specialists willing to act as consultants in assisting project directors establish and/or strengthen local programs.

These suggestions are but a few that could be formulated and implemented. As the twenty-first century draws closer and the demand for reading assistance increases, libraries will be forced to develop multifaceted programs. Imagination, human caring, and funding will be three essential components needed by public librarians in their arsenal to combat adult illiteracy.

Notes

1. Stanley N. Wellborn, "Ahead: A Nation of Illiterates?" *U.S. News and World Report* (May 17, 1982), 53.

2. Carmen St. John-Hunter and David Harman, *Adult Illiteracy in the United States: A Report to the Ford Foundation*, paperback ed. (New York: McGraw-Hill, 1985), 7.

3. David Harman, *Turning Illiteracy Around: Agenda for National Action*, Business Council for Effective Literacy, working paper no. 2, (May 1985), 2.

4. Hunter and Harman, *Adult Illiteracy in the United States*, 7-8.

5. Wellborn, "Ahead: A Nation of Illiterates?" 53.

6. Howard Fields, "A View from Washington," *Publishers Weekly* 277 (May 24, 1985): 31.

7. U.S. Congress, Joint Committee on the Library of Congress, *Books in Our Future: A Report from the Librarian of Congress to the Congress* (Washington, D.C.: U.S. Government Printing Office, 1984), 10.

8. Robert A. Carter, "Mobilizing Business for Literacy," *Publishers Weekly* 277 (May 24, 1985): 35.

9. U.S. Congress, *Books In Our Future*, 11.

10. Eleanor Touhey Smith, "Adult Functional Illiteracy: A Pervasive Problem," *Catholic Library World* 55 (October 1983): 118.

11. Henry Drennan, "Libraries and Literacy Education," *Catholic Library World* 52 (April 1981): 380.

12. William L. Cohn, "Meeting Adult Literacy Needs," *Catholic Library World* 52 (September 1980): 54.

13. New York City Adult Literacy Initiative, "Mission Statement" (no date).

14. Catherine Kavanagh, "Queens Literacy Volunteers: Beyond the Basics," *Bookmark* 43 (Summer 1985): 177.

15. Ibid.

16. Evelyn Wolf and Catherine Kavanagh, "Adult Illiteracy: A Public Library Responds," *Catholic Library World* 55 (October 1983): 125-26.

17. Renee Tjoumas, "Innovation and a Touch of Human Kindness: The Queens Borough Public Library's Approach to Combating Adult Illiteracy," in *Unequal Access to Information Resources: Problems and Needs of the World's Information Poor*, ed. Jovian P. Lang, OFM (Ann Arbor, Mich.: Perian Press, 1988), 31.

18. Kavanagh, "Queens Literacy Volunteers," 178; Queens Borough Public Library, Adult Learning Center, "Annual Report 1981-1982," Jamaica, New York (typewritten), 4-5.

19. Interview with Catherine Kavanagh, Edith Branman, Jeanette Tillman, Queens Borough Public Library, Programs and Services Department, Jamaica, New York, August 19, 1988.

20. Interview with Donald Walker, New York Public Library, Programs and Services Division, New York, July 22, 1988.

21. New York Public Library, "The New York Public Library Centers for Reading and Writing: Fact Sheet," (November 1986), 1.

22. Ibid.

23. New York Public Library, "Books to Go!: Bring the Library to Your Classroom" (no date).

24. Telephone interview with Mildred Dotson, New York Public Library, Special Services Division, New York, September 19, 1988.

25. Telephone interview with Charlene Di Calogero, New York Public Library, Project Literacy, New York, September 30, 1988.

26. Interview with Patrick M. Fiore, Brooklyn Public Library, Collection Development Department, Brooklyn, New York, August 12, 1988.

27. Brooklyn Public Library, "The Literacy Program" (no date).

28. Telephone interview with Patrick M. Fiore, Brooklyn Public Library, Collection Development Department, Brooklyn, New York, September 30, 1988.

29. National Issues Forums, "Special Report: Literacy Program" (no date), 7.

30. National Issues Forums, "Special Report II: NIF Community College Network Grows!" vol. 1, no. 2 (Spring 1988), 1, 3.

31. National Issues Forums, "Special Report: Literacy Program," 3-4.

Bibliography

Alford, Thomas E. "There Is a Need for a Larger Adult Literary Effort." *Catholic Library World* 56 (April 1985): 379-81.

Anthony, Carolyn. "Literacy Programs in Action." *Publishers Weekly* 277 (May 24, 1985): 39-41.

Axam, John A. "The Library's Role in Eradicating Illiteracy." *Catholic Library World* 55 (October 1983): 122-23.

Bearman, Toni Carbo. "Situation Report: NCLIS." *Wilson Library Bulletin* 59 (October 1984): 122-23, 158.

Bolle, Sonja. "The Bookseller Effort." *Publishers Weekly* 277 (May 24, 1985): 42-43.

Brooklyn Public Library. "The Literacy Program." Informational brochure (no date).

Carter, Robert A. "Mobilizing Business for Literacy." *Publishers Weekly* 277 (May 24, 1985): 35-38.

Caskey, Mary Lou. "Microcomputers and Illiteracy: A Starter Kit." *Bookmark* 43 (Summer 1985): 189-92.

Cathcart, Jane, and Graczyk, Mark. "In the World of Literacy: The Onondaga County Public Library." *Bookmark* 43 (Summer 1985): 181-84.

Cohn, William L. "Meeting Adult Literacy Needs." *Catholic Library World* 52 (September 1980): 54-56.

Coleman, Jean E. "Libraries, Learning, and Literacy–A Tradition of Involvement." *Public Libraries* 23 (Winter 1984): 108-9.

Di Calogero, Charlene. New York Public Library, Project Literacy, New York, New York. Telephone Interview, September 30, 1988.

Dotson, Mildred. New York Public Library, Special Services Division, New York, New York. Telephone Interview, September 19, 1988.

Drennan, Henry. "Libraries and Literacy Education." *Catholic Library World* 52 (April 1981): 376-85.

Fields, Howard. "The View from Washington." *Publishers Weekly* 277 (May 24, 1985): 31-34.

Fiore, Patrick M. Brooklyn Public Library, Collection Development Department, Brooklyn, New York. Interview, August 12, 1988.

Fiore, Patrick M. Brooklyn Public Library, Collection Development Department, Brooklyn, New York. Telephone interview, September 30, 1988.

Fleming, Joseph E. "Adult Illiteracy in the United States During the Twentieth Century: A Selected Annotated Bibliography." *Public Libraries* 21 (Summer 1982): 54-56.

Harman, David. *Turning Illiteracy Around: Agenda for National Action.* Business Council for Effective Literacy, working paper no. 2. May 1985.

Heiser, Jane C. "The Coalition for Literacy." *Public Libraries* 23 (Winter 1984): 110-14.

"How to Form a State or Local Literacy Coalition." *Public Libraries* 23 (Winter 1984): 115.

Jackson, Andrew P. "A Multi-Edged Sword Fighting Illiteracy." *Bookmark* 43 (Summer 1985): 185-87.

Kavanagh, Catherine; Branman, Edith; and Tillman, Jeannette. Queens Borough Public Library, Programs and Services Department, Jamaica, New York. Interview, August 19, 1988.

Kavanagh, Catherine. "Queens Literacy Volunteers: Beyond the Basics." *Bookmark* ,43 (Summer 1985): 177-79.

Kozol, Jonathan. "A Nation's Wealth." *Publishers Weekly* 227 (May 24, 1985): 28-30.

Kozol, Jonathan. "A Plan to Reach and Teach Twenty-Five Million Illiterate Adults." *Wilson Library Bulletin* 54 (June 1980): 640-44.

Lyman, Helen Huguenor. "Libraries and Literacy Education: Looking Forward." *Public Libraries* 23 (Winter 1984): 120-21.

McCallan, Norma J. "What State Libraries Can Do to Eliminate Illiteracy." *Catholic Library World* 52 (September 1980): 71-74.

Malecki, Paul M. "Putting Computer Software in the Literacy Tutor's Toolbox." *Bookmark* 43 (Summer 1985): 193-96.

Markarian, Rita. "'I Can Read!' Literacy Articulated in the Mid-Hudson Library System." *Bookmark* 43 (Summer 1985): 173-75.

National Issues Forums, "Special Report: Literacy Program" (no date), 1-8.

National Issues Forums, "Special Report II: NIF Community College Network Grows!" vol. 1, no. 2 (Spring 1988), 1-8.

Nelson, James A. "Kentucky's Coalition for Literacy." *Public Libraries* 23 (Winter 1984): 119.

"The Public Library Association Response to 'A Nation At Risk.'" *Public Libraries* 23 (Winter 1984): 122-23.

New York City Adult Literacy Initiative. "Mission Statement" (no date).

New York Public Library. "Books to Go!: Bring the Library to Your Classroom." Informational brochure (no date).

New York Public Library. "The New York Public Library Centers for Reading and Writing: Fact Sheet" (November 1986).

Queens Borough Public Library, Adult Learning Center. "Annual Report 1981-1982." Jamaica, New York.

Ruby, Carmela. "'It's Bad When You Can't Get Your Dreams': The California Literacy Campaign." *Public Libraries* 23 (Winter 1984): 116-18.

Smith, Eleanor Touhey. "Adult Functional Illiteracy: A Pervasive Problem." *Catholic Library World* 55 (September 1983): 117-23.

Smith, Eleanor Touhey. "Advocates for Literacy? The Library Situation." *Catholic Library World* 52 (September 1980): 65-70.

Smith, Kevin. "Literacy Volunteers of New York State." *Bookmark* 43 (Summer 1985): 165-67.

Steiner, George. "Books in an Age of Post-Literacy." *Publishers Weekly* 277 (May 24, 1985): 44-48.

St. John-Hunter, Carmen, and Harman, David. *Adult Illiteracy in the United States: A Report to the Ford Foundation*, paperback ed. New York: McGraw-Hill, 1985.

Strong, Gary. "Public Libraries and Literacy: A New Role to Play." *Wilson Library Bulletin* 59 (November 1984): 179-82.

Tabor, Janet M. "Developing a Rural Literacy Program." *Bookmark* 43 (Summer 1985): 197-200.

Tjoumas, Renee. "Innovation and a Touch of Human Kindness: The Queens Borough Public Library's Approach to Combating Adult Illiteracy." In *Unequal Access to Information Resources: Problems and Needs of the World's Information Poor*, ed. Jovian P. Lang, OFM, 29-34. Ann Arbor, Mich: Perian Press, 1988.

U.S. Congress. Joint Committee on the Library of Congress. *Books in Our Future: A Report From the Librarian of Congress to the Congress*. Washington, D.C.: U.S. Government Printing Office, 1984.

U.S. Department of Education. *Alliance for Excellence: Librarians Respond to "A Nation at Risk."* Washington, D.C.: U.S. Government Printing Office, 1984.

Walker, Donald. New York Public Library, Programs and Services Division, New York, New York. Interview, July 22, 1988.

Wellborn, Stanley N. "Ahead: A Nation of Illiterates?" *U.S. News and World Report* (May 17, 1982), 53-56.

Wolf, Evelyn, and Kavanagh, Catherine. "Adult Illiteracy: A Public Library Responds." *Catholic Library World* 55 (October 1983): 125-28.

Young, Diana. "Literacy, Libraries, and the Whole Child in North Carolina." *Catholic Library World* 52 (September 1980): 60-64.

From Oral Tradition to Printed Format: Australian-Aboriginal Legend and the Work of Dick Roughsey

KAREN PATRICIA SMITH

It is believed that ancestors of the Australian-Aboriginal people first migrated to the Australian continent from Asia some 40,000 years ago. At that time, the population consisted of approximately 300,000 individuals representative of several hundred tribes, speaking more than 200 languages. S. A. Wurm, in *Languages of Australia and Tasmania*, states the existence of 260 languages from which emanate numerous dialects.[1] A. P. Elkin, in his study *The Australian Aboriginees: How to Understand Them*, states the number of dialects as being at least 500.[2] The culture that white Europeans first encountered during the waves of settlement beginning during the eighteenth century was an oral culture. The variety of languages and dialects, the fact that none of the beliefs or customs of the Aboriginal people had been recorded by themselves in print, as well as the relative complexity of many of the traditions and the lack of affiliation with Western traditions, served to act as paradoxical forces for both cultural isolation of the people and fascination for the race, by those outside the culture. This fascination led to the recording of observations and the traditions of Aboriginal culture in print by those involved with the earliest explorations of the eighteenth century and to the scholarly anthropological studies that proliferated during the nineteenth century and onwards.

The value of the "outside" recorder has been both recognized and historically encouraged. Over the centuries the Aboriginal people have become accustomed to (and at times, resentful of) the continuing desire of those outside their culture to study and examine what is deemed to be one of the world's oldest cultures.

In the preface to the 1964 edition of *Australian Legendary Tales* (collected by non-Aboriginal author Mrs. K. Langloh Parker), Wandjuk Morika, chairman of the Aboriginal Arts Board, cited the importance of the collection as a way of making it possible for people everywhere to know something of the inner self of the Aboriginal people – a cultural self strongly connected to a mythic past.[3] The need for accuracy in scientific, social, and artistic studies of the Aboriginal perspective is imperative. Ironically, what have at times proven to be biased and/or inaccurate viewpoints have not been aided by the fact that up until the 1970s the Aboriginal people were not recording their own traditions and stories in print. This was due to their position as a "minority" within a now overwhelmingly Western culture, and to the economic, political, and educational difficulties that accompany that status, as well as the dominant oral nature of Aboriginal culture, as stated earlier. In recent years, however, as literacy has become more widespread in Australia, and as the Aboriginal people have become more aware and demanding of their political and social rights, they have expressed a greater interest in taking a more active role in the personal preservation of their culture in written form.

Dick Roughsey (1920-85) is one such individual who successfully recorded and illustrated the traditions and legends of the Aboriginal people in written form. His work is outstanding for both its quality and its pioneering nature, as well as the substantial success he achieved during his lifetime for his contributions within Australia. Roughsey, whose Aboriginal name was Goobalathaldin, was a full-blooded member of the Lardil tribe of Langu Island, located in the Gulf of Carpentaria off the northeast coast of Australia. His upbringing included a combination of grounding in tribal belief and Western-style schooling, which was provided by the mission school that Aboriginal children were obliged to attend through the fifth grade. Roughshey's early life is well detailed in his autobiography, *Moon and Rainbow: The Autobiography of an Aboriginal*. While he speaks of his schooling at the mission as being hardly pleasant, it did provide him with the skills that enabled him to successfully write the texts of his own works later on. When *Moon and Rainbow* was published in 1971, it was the first autobiography written by an Aboriginal. It was not, however, the first attempt to record the life of an Aboriginal individual. In 1962, *I, the Aboriginal* was published. This work was unique in that it offered in print the recorded life of an Aboriginal, Waipuldanya of the Alawa tribe, who grew up in the Port Roper area, not far from the Gulf of Carpentaria. Although the work is written in the first person, it was recorded by a non-Aboriginal, Douglas Lockwood. Lockwood recorded more than 100 hours of interviews with Waipuldanya. After receiving Waipuldanya's verification, Lockwood wrote down the story, based upon the interviews. This work, therefore, is a form of autobiography, but not an autobiography in the classic sense of the word.

Waipuldanya was apparently literate but did not, for reasons of his own, elect to undertake the actual writing of his story. The story was immensely popular, being the first such endeavor of its kind. *I, the Aboriginal* is a fascinating account. In 1962, it won the Adelaide Festival Arts Award.[4]

Roughsey's work was encouraged through his friendship with Percy Trezise, a friendship that was to continue until the death of Roughsey in 1985. *Moon and Rainbow* is Roughsey's own written account of his life. The significance of the work lies not only in its vivid, and at times frank, discussion of Aboriginal life and traditions, but also in the unique presentation of the second part of the book, which consists of Roughsey's retellings of Aboriginal myths known to the people of his tribe. The style of both sections of the work is clear and to the point. Roughsey emphasizes the importance of the sea to the hunting and gathering Lardil community. The sea is significant as a provider of food. Tradition states that the ancestors of the Lardil tribe traveled to Mornington Island (connected to Langu Island by a sandbar) from the west, over the sea, and founded the tribe. Further, the Lardil people believe that the small bubbling holes that can be seen along the seashore contain baby spirits, and that the capture of a creature from the sea heralds the entry of the baby spirit into the body of the human mother. (The union of men and women simply prepares the way, according to traditional belief, rather than initiating life.) Roughsey also mentions in his autobiography the importance of the capture of fish, turtles, and dugong – a type of whale. These literary images are important. Several would later reappear in the pictures as well as in the texts of Roughsey's picture books for children.

Roughsey also relates tales of Gidegal (the Moon Man) and the Rainbow Serpent in his autobiography. These are significant stories found within the Aboriginal tradition of northeast Australia. It is from these stories that *Moon and Rainbow* takes its name. The Rainbow Serpent myth is found throughout Australia, though the Serpent is known by different names in various locations. In Roughsey's acclaimed picture book, *The Rainbow Serpent*, the Serpent took the name Goorialla, as he is known to the people of Cape York, also located in northeast Australia. According to legend, the Serpent is believed to be the creator, the life-giving force, sometimes male, sometimes female, at times benevolent, and at other times, malevolent. The Serpent is of tremendous size, power, and influence. He is not a being to be offended. Young children were taught from childhood to have great respect for the Serpent. They were even warned that loud crying might arouse his anger. Gidegal, or the Moon Man, was held to be the originator of the all-important circumcision ceremonies. Both legends are strong representatives of the Dreamtime, the cosmological past of the Australian-Aboriginal people.

Roughsey's account of his life (spent on Mornington Island), of his upbringing and growth into adulthood, as told in his own words, goes beyond the obvious benefit of providing valuable factual material about the life of an individual who is part of a culture generally unfamiliar to Westerners. The book also provides the literary representation of legend at risk. Roughsey's work is filled with the pathos of a writer relating traditions that, at the time of the writing of the book, were dying out as a result of the meeting of Western and Aboriginal cultures and the overpowering influence of the former. The legends of the Rainbow Serpent and Gidegal, among others, were later to be told from the point of view of the people of Cape York and would be transformed from simply told narrative tales into Roughsey's illustrated stories. In these works, the visual image was to be central, accompanied by a concise text.

Bob Hodge, in his article "Aboriginal Myths and Australian Culture," makes a strong case for directly translating Australian-Aboriginal myth into English, rather than rewriting the myths to suit European-Australian tastes.[5] He also addresses the concern of attributing Aboriginal myths to a specific tribe and author. He uses as an example a popular text entitled *The Dreamtime,* compiled by anthropologist Charles Mountford. Hodge concedes that Mountford's text has brought the knowledge of Aboriginal myth into European households, but at the expense of authenticity. Roughsey's retellings do not seem to suffer from these difficulties. While his stories are written in "traditional" English, they come as a result of the oral tradition experienced personally by, and related to, Roughsey during his upbringing. Other stories were communicated to him by the Cape York people. Roughsey's unique position of being part of one culture and simultaneously an individual who by acculturation had become knowledgeable about the tenets and conventions of Western civilization enabled him to bring to his material an informed literary and artistic voice.

Roughsey learned and mastered the art form of bark painting. This medium was not indigenous to Roughsey's environment. Styles of painting were heavily influenced by the properties of the natural environment (the availability of certain materials needed for the artistic work), as well as by tradition and custom. Aboriginal art, in general, was strongly practical, both in terms of immediate needs and spiritual motivations. It was used as a way of instructing young initiates in tribal concerns. Many of these concerns were of such a secretive nature that, upon completion of the occasion, the artistic work, so carefully wrought, would be destroyed. Certain tribes over the years have shown a distinct preference for specific artistic expressions. Arnhem Land, part of the Northern Territory, shows perhaps the greatest diversity. Joseph Campbell in *The Way of the Animal Powers* indicates that cave painting and bark painting are popular there.[6] Styles of painting vary as well. Arnhem Land is best known for its "X-ray" technique, in which the inner skeletal components of men and animals are carefully detailed in the reproduction. Natives of eastern Arnhem Land tend to create visually complex backgrounds in their art work, in which figures assume a more static stance. In western Arnhem Land, however, the figures are more important and are often animated, appearing against less complex backgrounds.[7]

In 1962, while working at a tourist fishing lodge, Dick Roughsey met Percy Trezise, captain of the DC-3 rom Cairns. Roughsey had by this time seen the work of Albert Namatjira, the most successful Aboriginal artist of the time. Roughsey also wished to become an artist. He shared his career goals with Trezise, and the friendship was begun. Trezise advised Roughsey to begin by painting the legends of his people on bark, and then gradually master the European oil-on-canvas technique. Since bark painting was not an art form indigenous to Mornington Island, it was new to Roughsey. Trezise arranged to have bark flown into the island for Roughsey, since none was available there. Within a year, Roughsey had mastered the form and was able to make a living from sales of bark paintings.[8] One painting done in three panels depicts the story of Mornington Island and shows Roughsey's particular strength for portraying the human figure both in action and at rest.[9] The background is white and detailed with dark dots resembling an almost pointillistic style. Figures are black and are outlined in part using a yellowish tint. This technique suggests a two-dimensional effect. Various birds and fish adorn the extremities of the painting, giving it a unique sense of detail and balance.

The cave galleries of Cape York, an area northeast of Mornington Island, are well known for their incredible preservation of Aboriginal cave art. Roughsey toured these galleries extensively with Trezise and conversed with the Gugu-Yalanji Aboriginal people living there. In return for sharing their legends with Trezise and Roughsey, the people requested that the two agree to preserve the stories for posterity by recording them in book form. This request on the part of the people illustrates not only the desire to share their culture with others, but also their recognition that use of the printed medium is one way to ensure the preservation of tradition for all foreseeable time. The oral tradition and the illustrated printed medium were soon to be successfully united in a series of picture books for children. Roughsey wrote later:

> It was a very proud day for me when my book Moon and Rainbow was published. Later when I was Chairman of the Aboriginal Arts Board and travelled around Australia, I saw what a wonderful impact our picture books were having with children everywhere, and I was even prouder.[10]

For purposes of this discussion, only *The Giant Devil Dingo* (1973), *The Rainbow Serpent* (1975), *Turramulli the Giant Quinkin* (1982), *Gidja* (1984), and *The Flying Fox Warriors* (1985) will be considered. These works are significant representatives of their genre for many reasons. Here, however, we shall examine the nature of the retellings, the textual-visual treatment of human and mythical characters as well as the representations of the environment, and the use of the transformation theme.

In all of the works mentioned, Roughsey (and the team of Roughsey and Trezise, when they collaborated) designates the location of the tales as in or near Cape York. This is crucial, since the retellings vary from tribe to tribe. Roughsey relates several tales in his autobiography that make use of the characters later used in the picture books. However, in some cases, such as that of the Rainbow Serpent, whom the Lardil people call Thuwathu and the Gugu-Yalanji call Goorialla, names may change and/or stories about these figures may vary completely.

The narrations of Roughsey's tales involve the use of vigorous plots that are quickly developed. In *The Rainbow Serpent,* the Serpent is immediately engaged upon a search northward for his own people. As he makes his journey, his tremendous girth and weight create various features of the natural landscape – mountains and creeks among them. Upon finding his own people, he instructs them in various traditions. At the approach of a storm, all take cover, including the Serpent. He is asked to take in some relatives and does so, though against his will. He swallows them and is later pursued by the men of the tribe. They cut him open, thus releasing the boys – but he turns on them in his wrath and kills many of them before going into the sea. *The Giant Devil Dingo* opens with a devious old woman trying to entice two brothers into camping in her area. She plans to have them taken unawares by her giant devil dingo dog companion. Later, the boys must fight the dog, who is truly fearsome in aspect, and kill him. From his bones, kidneys, and head are created smaller dingoes who will be friendly companions to men. *Gidja* is a more complex tale. Here, a young boy is being made fun of because of his short, round, moon-like figure. He is later faced with the dilemmas of obtaining a wife, dealing with the accidental death of his daughter, and being expelled from his tribe because of that death. He is later thrown up into the sky by the tribe. But he has the last word. He places a curse of mortality upon them and, at the same time, announces his own immortality, for he has become the moon and will wax and wane – but never die.

Turramulli the Giant Quinkin is the story of two children who are pursued by an evil giant Quinkin who would eat them. When two friendly Timara, gentle Quinkins, intercede, the children are saved. The giant Quinkin is later killed by the tribesmen. *The Flying Fox Warriors* is the story of a dispute between two tribes – the Bird people and the Flying Fox people. During the ensuing battle, the Bird people are forced into a cave. Again, a Timara Quinkin intervenes and leads them through the darkness of the cave to safety. When the battle is resumed, the Bird people set fire to the land and many of the Flying Fox people are burned to death. Those that remain transform themselves into various types of birds.

The stories vary in degree of complexity. *The Giant Devil Dingo* and *Turramulli the Giant Quinkin* are the simplest of the group. The conflicts are immediately apparent. They are stories of pursuit in which children and young people are the intended victims. All of the tales are serious in nature, with horrible consequences awaiting those who are caught by their pursuers. Roughsey's style is clear and straightforward. While the stories are action-packed, the weight of the action is carried by the illustrations. The stories themselves read fluidly and seem designed to be comprehended by a young audience, and one that may not be acquainted with the traditions and legends of the Aboriginal people.

The textual-visual treatment of human and mythical characters is one of the strongest points of the stories. The text does not attempt to explain or match the terror of the visual depiction. In fact, the simplicity of the text serves to underscore the riveting action in the illustrations. In *The Giant Devil Dingo,* we are told, "And Eelgin set her devil-dingo on the tracks of the butcher-bird brothers."[11] Ah! but what a devil-dingo. For the scene before the reader is one of a massive dog with clawed feet and heavily emphasized white teeth. A lolling red tongue and bright red eye encircled by black are fixed upon the treacherous old woman. The use of perspective is deftly managed, with the boys' tracks and the forest trees receding into the background. The old woman takes an instructive stance; the dog dominates the foreground and is rigid with anticipation. The reader senses that this will be a formidable chase. Even those totally unfamiliar with Aboriginal tradition come away with a sense of the magnitude of the legend and the power it must hold for the young Aborigine.

When the issue of collaboration arises, an immediate question always develops regarding precisely who is responsible for what. Neither Trezise nor Roughsey make this clear within their collaborative works. However, the question was answered in a videotaped discussion recorded in *A Journey to Quinkin Country,* part of the "Story Makers" series. In this tape, Trezise states that he generally was responsible for the landscapes while Roughsey did the figures, birds, and animals.[12] The contrasts between landscapes and figures are often striking. In *Turramulli the Giant Quinkin,* an opening pastoral scene showing the quiet environment of the Gugu-Yalanji people is followed by a scene inside one of the cave galleries. The galleries are adorned with numerous paintings. Amongst illustrations of dingo, emu, and various other animals and birds, we find the imposing Imjim, who, we are told, bounce about on knob-like tails. Next to this stands a tall thin Timara Quinkin who holds his arms in a protective fashion around two children. To his right we find Turramulli, the Giant Quinkin with white eyeballs. He is the largest creature on the cave walls. It is interesting to note that only the Imjim and Turramulli have staring white eyes, thus differentiating them from all other creatures. (Human figures are seldom painted with clearly defined eyes.

185

Sometimes there are dark indications of eyes. Eyes, however, are generally meant to take secondary place to the figures themselves. The well-defined eyes of both the Imjim and Turramulli may represent the heightened awareness of evil beings who are alert to all about them.) The scene on the cave wall portends the action to follow and in itself seems alive with action, in marked contrast to the preceding pastoral scene. Indeed, the two children do find themselves confronted by Turramulli and later protected by good Timara. The scene that follows brings the cave representations to life. Turramulli stands in the midst of a forest and beside a quiet pool. Birds and animals flee his presence; a Timara scrambles to get out of his way; an Imjim hops up and down on its knobbed tail as if in wicked anticipation. Turramulli himself, now come to life and no longer a painting on a wall, has bright red eyes. In his hand, upside down and helpless, he holds a recent victim – a kangaroo. The frightened parents of the two children hide them in a hollow log. Sometime later, Turramulli passes by, but pauses long enough in front of the log in which the children are hidden to strike terror into their hearts. Here, the artist changes his perspective to that of the two children. The outer edges of the log occupy the illustration. Center vision is dominated by a huge hairy foot with three claws on it. In the distance, a terrified Timara runs by. We do not see the children; we are seeing through their eyes. The contrast between the distant scenery and the hugeness of the feet of Turramulli makes the scene more terrifying. Roughsey and Trezise have carefully created the scene and have achieved maximum effect.

In *The Rainbow Serpent,* the legendary creature rises huge and brilliantly hued in tones of red, black, green, yellow, and blue against a very slender and fragile background. He is a formidable being even to those whose heritage does not include an understanding of his powers. He has a brilliant red eye and an equally red tongue; the use of red eyes again seemingly denotes a creature to be feared. Roughsey spares no attempt to make this most important of creatures from Aboriginal tradition imposing. However, the Serpent is not merely terrifying. There is a textual ambivalence at work here as well. The narration informs the reader that the Rainbow Serpent is searching for his people. The search begins as a sympathetic one. The desire to find one's own people is certainly reasonable. When the creature does locate people, he refuses to share his shelter with them. Later, the reader wonders if this refusal comes about more as a result of knowledge of its own nature than out of selfishness. The Rainbow Serpent serves the roles of both creator and adversary in Aboriginal belief. In Roughsey's story, the Serpent greets the boys with a wide-open, fiercely red mouth. However, even though the Serpent is indeed in serpent form, the sense of "oneness" with the people is still there. He fears the reaction of his people to this act of cannibalism. He takes flight. The depth of this sense of oneness is more fully realized when one considers the search he is making for his people and the fact that his sheer size, which dominates every illustration, precludes his need to be truly fearful of anyone. Goorialla has violated the trust of his kinsmen and knows the price will be stiff. He flees to avoid payment.

Roughsey's human figures are fragile. Always, one is aware of the largeness of the environment and the feeling that people are at risk in that environment. The human figure is portrayed with grace. The artist concentrates on form rather than facial expression. In fact, the majority of his figures have no discernible facial features at all. Bodies are clothed in limited fashion with loincloths and decorated with painted body decorations. Figures are shown sitting, dancing, running, and standing in a listening pose. Roughsey conveys the feeling of the scene through the stance of his figures then, rather than through facial expressions.

Roughsey uses the rich colors of red, yellow, white, and black primarily. These are the colors most often used in Aboriginal bark paintings, and the ones obtained from the environment. In that environment, red and yellow are obtained from pipe clay and gypsum. Black is created from charcoal, soot, or manganese ore.[13] His picture-book art is smooth and highly polished, reflecting his mastery of oil painting techniques as well. Because of his use of the colors of the environment, Roughsey's work presents a natural appearance. One realizes immediately that the stories are set in the Australian environment.

The appearance of bodies of water is also an integral part of Roughsey's art. In his brief autobiography in *The Story Makers*, he says that blue is his favorite color and his favorite foods are those that come out of that blue: turtles, dugong, prawns, fish, and crabs.[14] Images of oceans and smaller bodies of water appear in both *The Rainbow Serpent* and *The Giant Devil Dingo*, as well as in the which he coauthored. Water is crucial to all men at all times. To a people living solely from the environment, water becomes the all-important factor of existence. Water always has a benign aspect in these works; that is, bodies of water are never seen as raging or hostile. The Rainbow Serpent himself is connected to water imagery. As a creator-being, he is often credited with etiological powers. It is through his movement across Australia from south to north that the beds for creeks, rivers, and lagoons were made. He is often said to reside at the bottom of a body of water. At the conclusion of *The Rainbow Serpent*, Goorialla disappears and goes down into the sea where, it is said, he still remains. Jennifer Isaacs comments that when one is flying above places such as northern Arnhem Land, one notes that

> the ground below becomes a maze of winding rivers with their tributaries and water channels forming vein-like patterns across the crystal salt pans. The sinuous bends of the Alligator and Liverpool Rivers as they carve through valleys, gorges and open plains, remind us that this is the home of the great serpents, in particular the powerful Rainbow Serpent.[15]

The Rainbow Serpent is a powerful representation of man's most crucial life-maintaining resource.

Besides natural environmental features, animals and birds indicative of the Australian landscape appear prominently. Crocodiles, pelicans, wagtail birds, kangaroo, dingo, butcher birds, and flying foxes, as well as other creatures, are in evidence. These creatures are integral to Aboriginal existence. They provide food and, in some cases, companionship. In Roughsey's books they are often onlookers, passively overseeing the action. While some may be less helpful than others, most of them are at peace with the people. There is a sense of harmony and even fellowship. When Turramulli enters the scene in *Turramulli the Giant Quinkin*, birds and animals flee. He is the unnatural element and, as such, is at odds with all creatures. Only the Imjim seems in no great hurry, for his intent matches that of Turramulli. He does not share a bond with nature. According to tradition, animals and birds are killed for purposes of providing food and never for the joy of the hunt. Certain creatures may indeed be fully off-limits to certain individuals. This is connected to strong totemic beliefs and the understanding that animals are descended from men. To eat or kill one's totem would be strictly taboo.

The natural environment is strongly linked to the transformation theme, which is present throughout the books. All of the stories take place during the Dreamtime, that period in which the natural landscape and the creatures of the environment were going through the process of formation. The reader is frequently told that, as the result of some action or event, a feature of the landscape or a creature of the environment is formed. It is also common for the narration to inform us that people are transformed into part of the landscape, or more commonly, into animals and birds. In *The Flying Fox Warriors*, a mountain of dead warriors is turned to stone and becomes the Black Mountains near Cooktown. In *Gidja*, Gidja is transformed into the moon; his daughter becomes the Morning Star, and his wife Yalma, the Evening Star. The eye of Goorialla becomes a shooting star, watching, we are told, everyone. According to tradition, people inhabited the earth prior to the appearance of bird and animal life – and some natural features. These came about as a result of people undergoing transformation.

When Goorialla in *The Rainbow Serpent* becomes enraged upon discovery of the loss of the boys he has swallowed for dinner, he hurls down huge portions of mountain at his people. As they flee his wrath, some of them turn themselves into animal and plant life. The visual image is arresting; huge chunks of mountain are flung at a people in flight. Some have already changed into birds. One warrior on the ground is in the process of turning into a dingo.

The Flying Fox Warriors contains two remarkable transformation scenes. While this book is particularly striking visually, these scenes are outstanding in the brilliant use of color. In the first scene, the Joonging people, who are also called the Flying Fox people, transform themselves into flying foxes. Arms are changed to wings. Little children as well as adults are in the crowd. Some flying foxes have taken flight, others are hanging upside down in trees, while still others look on with an expression of anticipation. In the second scene, the Bird people warriors, astonished at the transformation of the Flying Fox people, decide to undergo transformation themselves. A bit more planning, however, goes into it, as each bird clan decides what kind of bird it would like to be. The result is a profusion of birds and people changing into birds. Various stages of the process are evident. Some individuals have bird heads; others have wings. The story line is also used to explain observable phenomena. Flying foxes, we are told, naturally avoid contact with birds; while many birds come out during the day, flying foxes come out after dark.

In *The Giant Devil Dingo,* Gaiya the Dingo is killed by the tribe. His spirit, however, returns to bite the old woman Eelgin who, he feels, has used him. The visual images are eerily rendered. Only the transparent form of Gaiya exists, though his eyes and tongue still glow red. We look through that image and it is possible to see parts of the landscape.

Roughsey's repertoire includes three single-authored books, seven collaborations with Percy Trezise, and one collaboration with his wife, Labamu. Ironically, he died in 1985 at a time when Western interest in the Australian-Aboriginal literary-cultural heritage was taking a more personalized turn. That is, there was more interest in the accomplishments of Aboriginal individuals, as compared with the previous interest in the Aboriginal as the representative of a "unique" culture. Roughsey's contributions, which succeed in introducing adults and young people to his world and make evident his unusual talent combined with his personal perspective, stand as a permanent record of oral heritage and tradition.

As the age of information and technology moves us steadily forward into the twenty-first century, we must continue to promote the richness of the past. Distribution of literary and artistic resources must be further encouraged both within and outside countries of origin. Sharing the heritage of past and present cultures is an important outcome of access to and mastery and control of the information-sharing mediums of the arts and the printed word.

Notes

1. S. A. Wurm, *Languages of Australia and Tasmania,* Janua Linguarum: Studia Memoriae Nicolai Van Wijk Dedicata, Series Critica, ed. Werner Winter, no. 1 (The Hague, Paris: Mouton and Co., 1972), 10.

2. A. P. Elkin, *The Australian Aboriginees: How to Understand Them* (Sydney: Angus and Robertson, 1964), 17.

3. Mrs. K. Langloh Parker, *Australian Legendary Tales, Being the Two Collections, Australian Legendary Tales, and More Australian Legendary Tales* (London: Bodley Head, 1978), 7.

4. Douglas Lockwood, *I, the Aboriginal* (London: Cassell and Co., 1962), preface.

5. Bob Hodge, "Aboriginal Myths and Australian Culture," *Southern Review* 19 (November 1986): 277-90.

6. Joseph Campbell, *The Way of the Animal Powers,* vol. 1 (San Francisco: Harper and Row, 1983): 138.

7. Helen M. Groger-Wurm, *Australian Aboriginal Bark Paintings and Their Mythological Interpretation,* vol. 1 (Canberra: Australian Institute of Aboriginal Studies, 1973), 9-10.

8. Margaret Dunkle, ed., *The Story Makers: A Collection of Interviews with Australian and New Zealand Authors and Illustrators for Young People* (Melbourne: Oxford University Press, 1987), 62.

9. Douglas Baglin and Barbara Mullins, *Aboriginal Art of Australia* (New South Wales: Shepp Books, 1988), 28.

10. Quoted in Dunkle, *The Story Makers,* 62.

11. Dick Roughsey, *The Giant Devil Dingo* (Sydney: Collins, 1976), 4.

12. *Percy Trezise and Dick Roughsey: A Journey to Quinkan Country,* Story Makers series, part 2. 17 min. Film Australia, 1987.

13. Groger-Wurm, *Australian Aboriginal Bark Paintings,* 6.

14. Dunkle, *The Story Makers,* 62.

15. Jennifer Isaacs, ed., *Australian Dreaming: 40,000 Years of Aboriginal History* (Sydney: Lansdowne Press, 1980), 62.

Bibliography

Baglin, Douglas, and Barbara Mullins. *Aboriginal Art of Australia.* New South Wales: Shepp Books, 1988.

Campbell, Joseph. *The Way of the Animal Powers.* Vol. 1. San Francisco: Harper and Row, 1983.

Dunkle, Margaret, ed. *The Story Makers: A Collection of Interviews with Australian and New Zealand Authors and Illustrators for Young People.* Melbourne: Oxford University Press, 1987.

Elkin, A. P. *The Australian Aboriginees: How to Understand Them.* Sydney, Australia: Angus and Robertson, 1964.

Groger-Wurm, Helen M. *Australian Aboriginal Bark Paintings and Their Mythological Interpretation.* Vol. 1. Canberra: Australian Institute of Aboriginal Studies, 1973.

Hodge, Bob. "Aboriginal Myths and Australian Culture." *Southern Review* 19 (November 1986): 277-90.

Isaacs, Jennifer, ed. *Australian Dreaming: 40,000 Years of Aboriginal History.* Sydney: Lansdowne Press, 1980.

Lockwood, Douglas. *I, the Aboriginal.* London: Cassell and Co., 1962.

Parker, Mrs. K. Langloh. *Australian Legendary Tales, Being the Two Collections Australian Legendary Tales and More Australian Legendary Tales.* London: Bodley Head, 1978.

Roughsey, Dick. *The Giant Devil Dingo.* Sydney: Collins, 1976 (first published in 1973).

_____. *Gidja.* Sydney: Fontana Picture Lions, 1987 (First published in 1984).

_____. *Moon and Rainbow: The Autobiography of an Aboriginal.* Sydney: A. H. and A. W. Reed Pty, 1971.

_____. *The Rainbow Serpent.* Sydney: Collins, 1975.

_____. *Turramulli the Giant Quinkin.* Sydney: Collins, 1982.

_____, and Trezise, Percy. *The Flying Fox Warriors.* Sydney: Collins, 1985.

Storytelling via Technology in the Information Age

HILARY MCLELLAN

How can education be designed to promote the new literacies needed in the twenty-first century? Our understanding of literacy is at a turning point that is driven by new technologies and a new worldview. As we move from the industrial age, with its mechanistic view, to the information age, which is predicated upon a systems view of the world, we have a tremendous opportunity to redefine literacy in ways that empower the individual. The new information literacies for the twenty-first century will be linked to information technologies with their interactive capabilities; these literacies will also be premised on higher order cognitive abilities. With electronic technologies, there is an unprecedented attempt to model technological capabilities around human abilities, rather than assuming that humans should adapt to the technology. I suggest that the emerging interactive technologies have the potential to shape new literacies that are based around, and highly resonant with, natural human capabilities. In particular, these new literacies will be linked to our distinctively multimodal perceptual and cognitive abilities. The new literacies will be more diverse and multimodal than in the industrial age, and at the same time more flexible and mutually supportive and interlinked. This paper will explore this issue – the transition from print to interactive electronic media and the literacies thereby engendered – focusing on the metaphor of media as a tool for storytelling.

Electronic media such as the computer provide a new kind of tool for storytelling. With this tool of the intellect, storytelling becomes interactive, nonlinear, and highly participatory. Thinking of the computer in education as a tool for storytelling provides an evocative and powerful metaphor: it involves creativity, critical thinking, and effective communication. And computer storytelling makes it possible to explore rich contextual information in ways that are highly meaningful. All of these skills – creativity, critical thinking, interdisciplinary thinking, effective communication, and contextual understanding – are vitally important for the emerging information age.

Jerome Bruner (1986, 13) has put forward a model of storytelling: he speculates that we have two modes of storytelling (another way of conceptualizing the "two modes of thinking"). Bruner identifies the paradigmatic and narrative modes of storytelling. The paradigmatic mode leads to "good theory, tight analysis, logical proof and empirical discovery." The narrative mode leads to "good stories, gripping drama and believable historical accounts." These are two kinds of literacies that will be needed in the twenty-first century. And they will need to be linked together so that it is possible to move fluidly from one to the other, integrating different literacies that are more and more interconnected. We often assume that these two modes of storytelling are opposites, unconnected, but often they are highly complementary.

Traditionally, literacy has been linked almost exclusively with print. Literacy has meant both an ability to read and a condition of being well read (Williams 1983). Literacy has meant facility with and active use of the print *medium*. But before print, there were other literacies associated with other media or channels of communication.

In ancient Greek times, literacy meant storytelling – oral communication. This storytelling emphasized the narrative mode: narrative literacy was of paramount importance in explaining the world, in bringing the unknown into relation with the known. This oral mode of storytelling involved "literacies" such as memorization and knowledge of cultural context (i.e., myths, history, metaphors, common wisdom), as well as responsiveness of the storyteller to an audience. This involves a highly dynamic form of literacy, person to person.

Literacy in Greek times also involved a form of "visual literacy": a highly trained visual memory, used in tandem with oral storytelling. In the absence of written notes, Greek speakers relied on a locus of memory system to remember what they wanted to cover (White 1987). In their mind's eye, these speakers "walked through" a building; different landmarks along the path reminded them of points they wanted to make and of topics to cover.

As Mary Alice White (1987, 46) of Teachers College points out, "For 10,000 years, humans learned from images and from speech. For the last 500 years, humans have learned primarily from print." With print, literacy meant understanding how to read and comprehend written text. With print literacy, we learn to structure information in accordance with the structure inherent in the technology: left to right, top to bottom. The structure of the print medium, which emerged during the Renaissance, is linear. The linear structure of this medium of communication dominated the industrial age.

Now, again, a fundamental change in technology is under way: a shift to electronic media. This includes television, computer, videodisk, optical technologies such as CD-ROM, and hypermedia, as well as other technologies. All of these technologies are merging together, integrating, forming new, more powerful crossover technologies or multimedia systems; this is what the term "hypermedia" means: multimedia systems. We are coming around again full circle: our literacies again match more fully the multimodal nature of human perception.

Shavelson and Salomon (1985) suggest that information technologies can be characterized by three fundamental attributes: information, the symbol systems in which the information is cast (e.g., language, numbers, pictures), and the activities that the technologies call forth. They further suggest that unlike other technologies, the computer is limited to neither particular kinds of information or symbol systems nor a restricted set of activities. Similarly, Dickson (1985) focuses his attention on formal symbol systems that are culturally valued and allow relatively direct translation between themselves. He identifies nine paired juxtapositions of symbol systems present in several different computer applications: (1) oral-pictorial, (2) written-pictorial, (3) oral-written, (4) mathematical-graphical, (5) procedural-graphical, (6) arithmetic-pictorial, (7) musical-graphical, (8) verbal-spatial, and (9) logical-pictorial. Shavelson and Salomon argue that the power of representing information in more than one symbol system lies in the ability to: (a) provide a more complete picture of a phenomenon than any single symbol system can; (b) increase the chances of linking new information to the learner's preferred mode of learning (i.e., to the learner's preferred symbolic representation); and (c) cultivate cognitive skills in translating or shifting among symbol representations. These ideas are largely speculative, but I believe they offer exciting possibilities in education.

As we move into the twenty-first century, "the information age," our literacies must be geared to electronic media with their dynamic, interactive, and multimodal capabilities. The interactive power of the computer and related electronic technologies changes the nature of storytelling. Instead of the teller and audience playing separate roles, the two roles are blurred together (Krasney-Brown 1985). One indication of how this has affected our conceptualization of storytelling comes from literary theory: contemporary theorists are exploring the role of the reader's imagination in "creating" literature (Eco 1984). In this model the reader has become an active partner with the writer; this new collaborative model of storytelling is very much in synchrony with our emerging electronic technologies and how they can be expected to shape our thinking and our style of storytelling.

We usually think of stories in terms of beginning, middle, end. Problem, resolution, outcome. This is a highly linear model, familiar in connection with print media. Even the stories of the Greeks followed relatively unchanging story scripts. As a result, contextual understanding could be attained fairly easily. But the world is no longer as static as it was in the days of ancient

Greece; today, change is the constant. Thus, we need scripts that can be changed, adapted to meet new criteria. Our traditional model of learning has been to improve effectiveness under constant conditions. This is a closed system model. The twenty-first century will need learning that includes adaptive skills so that people can maintain or improve effectiveness under changing conditions: an open system model that accounts for change. The new interactive storytelling via electronic technology involves scripts that can be changed and reviewed from different points of view and different levels, providing important benefits for learning. Both the imaginative narrative mode of storytelling and the analytical, evaluative paradigmatic mode will be needed.

Storytelling with electronic media tools is nonlinear, in contrast to print media. The computer's nonlinearity fundamentally changes the idea of the story as something fixed, with beginning, middle, and end predetermined. With the computer, it is possible to explore different sequences of events and outcomes. This may have extremely valuable potential, given what is known about experts' thinking (Resnick 1986). Recent research in science problem solving shows that, in contrast to novice problem solvers who attempt to pursue a straightforward linear path toward a problem solution, experts "dance" around a problem looking at it from many different vantage points. The experts do not respond to problems as they are presented. Instead, they reinterpret the problems, recasting them in terms of general scientific principles until the solutions become almost self-evident.

The nonlinear, exploratory perspective offered by the computer and other electronic media tools promotes critical thinking. Edward Weeden of the Xerox Corporation suggests that this kind of thinking includes the ability to see things developmentally: perceiving trends rather than just "facts." It also includes the ability to see patterns in time, not just as isolated events. This kind of critical thinking includes the ability to look forward and backward with some degree of balance, and to unravel cause and effect, implications over time, and conditional alternatives. And it includes the ability to scan from side to side, to engage in comparative evaluation of alternatives in any number of situations. Also, critical thinking includes the ability to handle situations that are almost always neither black nor white: many times they are not even any recognizable shade of gray. Dealing flexibly with complex situations and concepts that are often nonquantifiable is also an aspect of critical thinking. In a complex world, a critical thinker has a distinct advantage over anyone more accustomed to formula, prescriptive solution, and pat answer. Critical thinking also includes the ability to take facts or concepts and perform critical evaluation and analysis.

With electronic media, it is possible to examine different "perspectives" in several ways. First, it is possible to shift between symbol systems, from text to visual, to graphic, and so on. Second, it is possible to simulate different courses of action and explore the possible ramifications of different options. Third, with hypertext and related resources, it is possible to explore multiple levels of information, to branch off onto sidelines, exploring contextual information as deeply as you want at any time, conveniently, using different modes of interaction (browsing, grazing, and hunting) before returning to the point of detour. These terms describe different modes of interaction with electronic media, related to different goals. Electronic media provide not only different viewpoints, but also different kinds of descriptions, using different symbol systems, depending on our purposes. And, ideally, these media also facilitate different modes of interaction, thereby supporting user goals.

Unlike print with its linear structure, the structure of the new technologies is still under design and is linked to an exploration of the structure and operation of the human mind so that it will be as "user-friendly" as possible. The goal is to make the structure of the new information technologies similar to that of the human mind. Marvin Minsky (1986, 286), one of the founders of artificial intelligence, explains: "A mind is too complex to fit the mold of narratives that start out here and end up there; a human intellect depends upon the connections in a tangled web – which simply wouldn't work at all if it were neatly straightened out." Some analysts suggest that the way to find out what needs to be done to improve communication via media is through exploring the human sensory and cognitive system and the ways that humans most naturally interact. This quest is a mix of two rapidly evolving and very different fields: information technologies and the human sciences. This is exciting because it means that the human rather than the machine is the ultimate focus of attention, and ultimately the final arbiter of literacy goals. Technologies are being refined to adapt to human needs and capabilities, rather than being developed under the assumption that humans need to adapt to technology.

This trend has its roots in developments dating back to World War II. Since that time, the model of technology has become the biological process, the events inside an organism, rather than the mechanical processes of a machine. In an organism, processes are not organized around energy in the physicist's meaning of the term; they are organized around information. Thus, the need for "information literacy" in all the forms it may take.

The ability to look at, analyze, synthesize, and evaluate things from different but highly interrelated points of view is a cluster of the most important literacies we will need in the twenty-first century. The Renaissance invented perspective (together with the printing press). Today, technology provides ready access to different "perspectives," or points of view.

John Sculley (1987), president of Apple Computers, has put forward the idea of the computer as a "knowledge navigator." We think of a navigator as "one who explores by ship; one who is qualified to navigate." The original

Latin meaning of the word *navigate* is "to steer a course through any medium." We can think of storytelling as a kind of journeying, with a starting point and a destination. Navigation is the science of getting from place to place: the method of determining position, course, and distance. The notion of navigating is very apt here; computer tools make it possible to explore and test the possibilities of different courses and positions for arriving at a destination – a destination of knowledge and relational understanding. The computer allows us to navigate back and forth between information presented in several modes: between text, graphics, and numbers; between levels of detail; and between different scenarios of interrelated actions and events. Furthermore, the computer "knowledge navigator" helps us to navigate across disciplinary boundaries. Interdisciplinary thinking is vital to the information age.

Along similar lines, Howard Rheingold (1985, 190) has put forward the image of the computer as a vehicle for navigating "information space." Rheingold speculates, "Imagine that you are in a new kind of vehicle with virtually unlimited range in both space and time. In this vehicle is a magic window that enables you to choose from a very large range of possible views and to rapidly filter a vast field of possibilities – from the microscopic to the galactic, from a certain word in a certain book in a certain library, to a summary of an entire field of knowledge." This territory "is not the normal landscape of plains and trees and oceans, but an *informationscape*." The features consist of words, numbers, graphs, images, concepts, paragraphs, arguments, relationships, formulas, diagrams, proofs, bodies of literature, and schools of criticism. The computer vehicle provides a catalyst for fundamentally changing our old ways of organizing information. This new information space is a system modeled on the way the human mind processes information. We can consider "navigating information space" as one of the critical new literacies needed for the twenty-first century.

I suggest that interactive media can help provide learners with both paradigmatic and narrative modes of storytelling, thereby enhancing contextual understanding and the meaningfulness of the information encountered. The work of J. R. R. Tolkien provides an example of how this can be approached. Tolkien began with databases: words in imaginary languages (Elfin, Hobbit, etc.). His love of linguistics and language history drew him to imagine a mythical world--Middle Earth--where he could put his databases into context to see whether they could function as languages and fulfill their intended purpose. Can you imagine creating this kind of world via hypermedia? Tolkien's work invites detours, side trips to find out more background information about history, legends, characters, geography, natural history, ethnic studies. Granted, Tolkien's imagination is highly exceptional, but perhaps the networking of information via accessible electronic tools can promote similar kinds of exploration and creativity on the part of learners. This kind of multifaceted learning activity may be facilitated with electronic media. Ideally, it should be a goal of education for the twenty-first century to promote this kind of learning.

One goal of education is to train learners in the literacies and skills they will need to function effectively in and contribute to the world. Given the nature of the changes taking place as we enter the information age, it is essential for learners to become "literate" in interactive, adaptive approaches to learning and exploration. This interactive mode is very new. It requires continuous learning and continuous evaluation and modification. It is an open-ended, unfolding, adaptive process. The interactive mode is predicated on system change.

Electronic technologies appear to offer special potential as tools for interactive storytelling. This is where the learner has the most directiveness in both roles – teller and audience – because the learner rather than the program sets the goals (Krasny-Brown 1985). This responsibility for goal setting on the part of the learner enhances commitment and is likely to enhance the contextual understanding that can be brought to bear upon a problem, since it has more personal significance. Tolkien's activities are an example of the importance of this kind of goal setting and the amazingly diverse and imaginative results that can come about.

Electronic media tools do not too narrowly presuppose the questions and the problems people will want to address in using it. Instead, it is designed as a fairly "open" system. Formulating the question or clearly defining the problem is usually by far the most difficult task in any endeavor, not the least in education. Questions are formulated for computers by people. With "educational" software, this is now done by instructional designers who are usually the ones to formulate which questions a program will ask the learner, based on a closed system rather than an open-system model. But questions, wanting to know, to understand, to find meaning, are at the heart of learning and discovery. Ideally, electronic tools can be designed to support rather than impose questions and goals.

Electronic technologies such as the computer and hypermedia are interactive, nonlinear, transformative tools for the intellect. These tools provide us with the opportunity to explore a story from many different vantage points. Thus, it is context-intensive. And these electronic media provide instant feedback together with a great flexibility that makes it possible to change the script, change the focus of attention, the outcome of events, or the proposed solution to the problem.

In this exploratory paper, I have examined the potential of electronic media as both a catalyst and tool for the emerging literacies of the information age. I used the metaphor of media as a tool for storytelling. Storytelling is a vital component of every culture, stretching back in time before recorded history. Stories are systematic representations of experience–for individuals and entire societies–that provide both an interpretation or structuring of the past and a system for anticipating the future. Stories provide a mirror but also a prism for focusing meaning, for helping us to explore and comprehend where we stand in the world. As culture changes, so do our stories. And so do our conceptions of literacy.

We are moving from a mechanistic closed-system model to an open-system model of the world. Under this open system, we will need learning for a context of rapidly changing conditions. For the twenty-first century, learning must be adaptive; it is no longer sufficient to learn how to improve effectiveness under constant conditions–the world is changing too fast. To adapt means to improve effectiveness under changing conditions.

The ideas that I have presented are highly speculative; however,they point the way to research and development activities. I am embarking upon research with videodisk and hypermedia to explore some of the potential I see with these ideas. It is important to remember that with these exciting visions of interactive learning and empowerment with technological tools, I have not addressed existing problems of poverty and inequitable access to technology. I see potential for technology both as a catalyst for new literacies and for enhanced learning. But I hope this potential vision will not merely build upon existing inequities. These are vitally important considerations in assessing and attempting to project the potential of interactive technologies in education for shaping and enhancing literacy in the twenty-first century.

References

Bruner, J. (1986). *Actual Minds, Possible Worlds*. Cambridge, Mass.: Harvard University Press.

Dickson, W. P. (1985). "Thought Provoking Software: Juxtaposing Symbol Systems." *Educational Researcher* 14, no. 5 (May): 30-38.

Eco, U. (1984). *The Role of the Reader: Explorations in the Semiotics of Text*. Bloomington: Indiana University Press.

Krasny-Brown, L. (1985). *Taking Advantage of Media*. Boston: Routledge & Kegan Paul.

Minsky, M. (1986). *The Society of Mind*. New York: Simon and Schuster.

Resnick, L. (1986). *Education and Learning to Think*. Report prepared for the Commission on Behavioral and Social Sciences Edication, National Research Council.

Rheingold, H. (1985). *Tools for Thought: The History and Future of Mind-Expanding Technology*. New York: Simon and Schuster.

Sculley, J. (1987). Speech presented at the EDUCOM Conference (October 21). See also his *Odyssey*, 403 (1987). New York: Harper & Row, 403.

Shavelson, R., and Salomon, G. (1985). "Information Technologies." *Educational Researcher* 14, no. 5 (May): 8.

Tolkien, J. R. R. (1966). *The Hobbit*. Boston: Houghton Mifflin.

Tolkien, J. R. R. (1974). *The Lord of the Rings*. Boston: Houghton Mifflin.

Weeden, E. (1987). "In a Multidimensional World, Humanists Think Multidimensionally." *Chronicle of Higher Education* 34, no. 3, A52 (September 16).

Williams, R. (1983). *Key Words: A Vocabulary of Culture and Society*. New York: Oxford University Press.

Something New Has Been Added:
Aural Literacy and Libraries

VIRGIL L. P. BLAKE

The era in which monographs and serial publications constituted the predominant element of library collections has passed. Library collections now include a wide variety of formats to better serve their publics. In this paper I will discuss the emergence of another new medium, the "bookcassette," and its acceptance into the library's repertoire. The concept of listening comprehension is then introduced, and the implications of research in this field for library service is then indicated.

THE BOOKCASSETTE – ORIGINS

Spoken-word sound recordings have been a feature of the recording industry since Thomas Edison first recorded "Mary Had a Little Lamb" in 1877. Edison, however, soon lost interest in the phonograph and recordings. Further development of sound recordings as a medium was the result of the efforts of Emile Berliner and others. Many commercial recordings through the golden age of sound recordings, 1900-30, were spoken-word recordings. Only with the improvement of recording equipment that ushered in the "electric age," 1925-48, did musical recordings with complete orchestras become the mainstay of the emerging recording industry.

Spoken-word sound recordings never completely disappeared. There has been a sizable educational market with annual sales of more that $62 million.[1] Even within the commercial sector of the recording industry, spoken-word recordings of comedians such as Bob Newhart and Bill Cosby have been quite popular.

Another type of spoken-word recording with a long history is the recording of books and periodicals as a service to the blind, visually

203

handicapped, or physically disabled. The Library of Congress began its talking-book program in October 1934. These recordings were on disk, and later on reel-to-reel tape. Both of these formats presented problems for patrons because the record players were large and cumbersome, while the reel-to-reel tape had to be threaded.

In 1963 the Phillips Company of the Netherlands invented the cassette, a tape recording format that held promise for these users because they were small, easy to handle (no threading), and required a relatively small and easily operated player.

The first bookcassettes were used by the Library of Congress. Its National Library Service for the Blind and Physically Handicapped began distributing cassette tapes in 1969. At approximately the same time, the Canadian National Institute for the Blind began recording books on cassette as well.

Shortly thereafter, others began to take advantage of this new recording format. The American Bar Association began in 1970 to develop continuing education materials on cassette. *Law Library Journal* started to include in each issue a list of all legal education materials available in cassette form. Titles were listed alphabetically by state, and within each state by title. Each entry indicated the source and price of the cassette.

Business also discovered the advantages of the audiocassette in the early 1970s. At that time, Valerie Noble identified eight audio-publishers of business information cassettes. This format was regarded as especially useful for salespersons who spent a large amount of time traveling. Through cassettes, they could receive updated training and memos from the home office. The topics ranged from *Managing and Selling Companies* (12 cassettes, $300) from Advanced Management Resources, Inc. to *Executive Seminar in Sound*, a series of sixty-minute cassettes from Nation's Business.

Others discovered the cassette format in the 1970s. The Idaho State Library had 1,000 books on cassette and began recording on cassette some local interest periodicals – for example, *Idaho Wildlife Review, Idaho Yesterdays,* and *Incredible Idaho.* Distribution was limited, however, to the blind and physically handicapped. A more innovative use of the cassette was devised by the Southwestern Library Association's Continuing Education for Library Staffs in the Southwest Project. In 1976 the association began distributing the *Current Awareness Journal,* a sixty-minute cassette that included news of the profession, abstracts of current articles of interest, and new service ideas. The recording was done by professional actors.

In its first decade, the use of the cassette to record and distribute information was limited to the blind and physically handicapped, or to precisely defined audiences with precisely defined information needs. Patricia Lawson foresaw the potential of this new format but lamented the lack of titles then available for use with a broader audience. Lawson noted, though, that Voice Over Books had "begun the production of best sellers on cassettes. These condensations are dramatized by professional actors and cost about the same as hardcover books."[2]

Other commercial companies began to publish titles in the cassette format. Recorded Books and Books on Tape, pioneers in this new sound recording format, recorded unabridged versions of books on cassette. These recordings, lasting up to twelve hours, consisted of eight to twelve cassettes and were fairly expensive at $80-100 per title. Income was generated from the sale of these cassette versions of books to the institutional market, libraries, schools, and so on, and from rentals (at $11-12) to individuals. Into the early 1980s, the recording of unabridged versions of plays, poetry, drama, and fiction remained a very small business. Within even that circumscribed world, the focus remained on serving the needs of the blind, visually handicapped, and elderly.

Barriers in the form of time, price, and convenience would have to be overcome before the bookcassette would become a more significant medium. The time required to listen to a book was the easiest to resolve. Rather than record the complete text, one could record an abridged version of the print original. The abridging strategy, in turn, would result in a product that was convenient and less expensive than the unabridged recordings. Further technological developments, however, were required before the bookcassette in its current mode would emerge. The first of these was the introduction of the compact, lightweight cassette player, such as Sony's Walkman. The second step was the inclusion of cassette players in cars as standard equipment. These twin developments made it possible to listen to cassettes at any time – walking, jogging, sitting in a bus or subway, commuting in a car, or working in or outside the home. These technological advances virtually assured the emergence of the bookcassette.

BOOKCASSETTES DEFINED

The bookcassette is a one- or two-cassette item that is generally an abridgement of a book. It has a duration of three hours maximum. They are currently priced at approximately $14.95. Excluded from this definition are single cassettes with identical material recorded on each side (one with an advance tone for page turning), issued with the original book, either in hardcover or paperback. These items are known as book-and-cassette packages and are usually designed for the preschool through junior high school age groups. Bookcassettes are not released with the book or accompanying activities and are released as separate entities.

Not all bookcassettes are abridgments. There are some audio-publishers who only release complete versions of print titles on cassette. Bookcassettes may be a reading by the author of the work, or a reading of the work by a professional actor. Other bookcassettes are multivoiced recordings. Some are dramatizations complete with sound effects and background music. Multivoice recordings are done by actors who can assume a variety of voices for a greater number of characters. Published print titles featuring both dialogue and action are better suited for dramatic recordings. Authors relying on the narrative to develop their stories are more often read.

THE EMERGENCE OF THE BOOKCASSETTE

While Walden Books had introduced a line of twenty-four titles in the book cassette format earlier, observers of publishing first began to note its development in 1984, when David Blaiwas identified eleven audio-publishers. These were small companies, such as Caedmon, Metacom, Newman Communications, and Recorded Books, that offered children's stories, classics, fiction titles, poetry, and a few biographies and nonfiction titles. The largest of these firms offered 200 titles. Bookstores did make them available to patrons, but they were not a significant portion of total sales.

In 1984 the bookcassette emerged. A new company, Brilliance, developed a technique for recording unabridged versions of works that reduced by half the number of cassettes required. Authors such as Jean Auel and Mario Puzo, who had refused to permit abridgments of their work to be recorded, could now be accommodated. The solution was to record on each of the two channels of each stereo track. Recording engineers invented a device to adjust the speed of the recording. Fewer cassettes were required, and the price for an unabridged recording of a title could be reduced. Brilliance began by recording fiction titles but has recently added some nonfiction titles in its "Health Talk Self Help" line.

By September 1985 *Publishers Weekly* could identify twenty-one audio-publishers. A number of major book publishers, such as Harper and Row, Random House, and Warner Communications, were entering the market and offering consumers classics and recent best-sellers in this new format. One bookcassette title, *Iacocca,* sold an impressive 50,000 units.

The next year, 1986, was really the turning point for the bookcassette. A number of rapid events ensured it would no longer be a curiosity. Audio-publishers formed a trade association, the Audio-Publishers Association. Sales were greatly aided when book clubs began to offer their members bookcassettes. Time-Life offered its members twenty-five titles from Caedmon, Listen for Pleasure, and Warner Audio. Book-of-the-Month club regularly offered its members audio titles, whereas Literary Guild did this only twice a year. Even specialty book clubs like the Get Rich Club, History Book Club, and Nostalgia Book Club began offering members audio titles in 1986. Book clubs for children operated by Scholastic and Harcourt Brace Javonovich included bookcassettes in their offerings as well. Secular publishers and religious publishers began releasing religious and inspirational titles in bookcassette format and placing them in both trade and Christian bookstores. Overall, 1986 was a very good year for audio-publishers. Even those specializing in unabridged recordings of titles did exceedingly well. Duval Hecht, founder of Books on Tape, reported a 25 percent growth rate, with sales of $2.8 million in 1985 and $3.5 million in 1986.

By May 1987 *Publishers Weekly* recognized the significance of audio-publishing by initiating a regular column to cover events and activities there. Houghton Mifflin consummated a deal with Brilliance for the publication of some of its titles in unabridged form. Even small presses – Butterfly Publishing, for example – began to issue bookcassette titles on self-hypnosis, subliminal persuasion, martial arts, as well as recorded lectures.

New marketing strategies were designed to broaden the consumer base for the medium. Simon and Schuster launched bookcassette versions of the "Star Trek" titles in the hope that the Trekkies would not only snap these up but, once exposed to the format, would return to purchase other audio titles. Other publishers began to release a bookcassette edition of their titles with each title's publication in paperback. Celebrity autobiographies – by Carol Burnett, Vanna White, and Chuck Yaeger, for example – were simultaneously released in hardcover and bookcassette formats.

Simultaneous publication of hardcover and bookcassette editions of titles was expanded to well-known authors such as James Michener and John Jakes. Authors such as these had good records in the past and might attract others to the bookcassette form. Even a nonfiction title like Bob Woodward's *Veil: The Secret Wars of the CIA 1981-1987* was simultaneously published in hardcover and bookcassette. The narrowing of the time gap between the publication of the book and the bookcassette, combined with some cross-promotion, has been successful. By the end of 1987, bookcassettes were an estimated $200 million market. Bookcassettes were being sold in 75 percent of the regional and independent bookstores surveyed by *Publishers Weekly.* The August 5, 1988, issue of *Publishers Weekly* contained the announcement of the fall titles. John Zinser identified more than forty audio-publishers. The listing of the individual titles to be released occupied fifteen pages. The bookcassette had arrived.

LIBRARIES AND BOOKCASSETTES

Libraries generally had little to do with audiocassette recordings of books until recently. Libraries with the mission of serving the blind and physically handicapped had the most enduring relationship with the bookcassette. But these libraries restricted the use of recorded books and periodicals on cassettes to that carefully defined clientele. Few libraries offered recorded books on cassette to other patrons, but there were some exceptions.

In the spring of 1969 the Los Angeles Public Library began an experimental program of circulating cassettes to patrons, but use was restricted to the library itself. The first report of the circulation of bookcassettes is at the Veterans Memorial Public Library in Bismark, North Dakota. James L. Denton, in the spring of 1972, made available to users three cassette series–First National City Bank's *Sound of the Economy*, *Fortune* magazine's *Executive Voice*, and Nation's Business's *Executive Seminars in Sound*. At the same time, the Suburban (Illinois) Library System established a cassette program by placing 6,279 cassette tapes in eight member libraries. Two-thirds of these were spoken-word recordings. The program was judged an immediate success, with an average circulation of between 3,500 and 4,000 per month for the first year.

Other innovative programs were begun by libraries in the 1970s and early 1980s. A local public library in England started to acquire cassette recordings of lectures by experts in areas of concern for local governments. These cassettes were made available to local government officials as another means of acquiring sufficient background information to vote intelligently on matters brought before them. The Cumberland County (North Carolina) Public Library introduced its "Information to Go" program in 1983. The library itself produced and distributed a series of cassettes on health, American literature, politics, the Bible, and other topic of interest. All of these were made available to all patrons. However, real strides in the use of spoken-word audiocassettes only took place after the technological developments had made the bookcassette a viable commercial medium.

In 1984 the Oskaloosa (Iowa) Public Library began to purchase and circulate bookcassettes made available by the then-emerging new audio-publishers. The idea was deemed an immediate success. "In the first six weeks the tapes circulated 175 times or an average of 3.7 circulations per title."[3] During its first full year of operation, the bookcassettes, reported Davis, "have accounted for a steady 2 percent of the total circulation though representing . . . .5 percent of the total collection."[4]

Subsequently, *Library Journal* has conducted a series of national surveys on the place of audiocassettes in library collections. The 1986 survey of public and academic libraries concluded, "What began as a craze had become a library."[5] Circulation of audiocassettes was substantial, often nearly 20 percent of the total circulation of the responding libraries, with average increases of 15-30 percent each year. In 1987 *Library Journal* broadened the scope of its survey to include some special libraries. The eighty public, academic, and special libraries responding indicated that their materials budgets allocated for the purchase of both audio and video materials was increasing an average of 12 percent per year, that the size of their collections continued to increase, and that circulation increased 13 percent over the previous year. The bookcassette had become a fixture in library collections.

LISTENING AND READING

Listening to a book or journal is not quite the same as reading the printed book or journal. They are related but not identical experiences. Both involve the reception of a message through some bodily earth station, the transmission of that message to the brain, and the decoding of the message by the brain into something meaningful to that individual. In reading, the bodily earth station is the eyes, the message is a series of symbols on a white page, and understanding occurs when the brain perceives that this particular group of symbols (cat) stands for a concept stored in its memory (a small, furry, four-legged animal with a long tail that drinks milk and purrs). In listening, the bodily earth station is the ear, the message is a sound or series of sounds in the open air, and comprehension occurs only if the brain associates the sound with an idea in its memory. Beyond the similarity in framework, these two communication activities are dissimilar.

Roger Sutton points out that "listening to a book requires an enormous amount of effort."[6] When you are reading print, you can afford to lose some concentration because you can always go back to an earlier point in the chapter or article and reconstruct, by rereading, any information that might have been lost. An additional advantage with print is that you can "backtrack to check a character name, go over a difficult (or enjoyable) passage two or three times, scan ahead to see if there is enough time to finish the chapter."[7] With a book or journal on cassette, there is no such cushion. The cassette tape will inexorably move along at one and seven-eighths inches per second. Even if the listener wanted to go back and pick up the threads of the narrative or information being presented, the lack of either an index or a table of contents for the bookcassettes makes the process difficult. For children, Sutton points out, this is more critical because they "can't look back at any page or a picture to clear up any confusion."[8]

There is some research that indicates that Sutton is correct in contending that different modes of presentation evoke different responses from individuals. To determine whether there were some persons who learned better from visual materials and others who learned better from oral presentations, Carol DeBoth and Roger Dominowski conducted an experiment with 160 college students. These investigators developed six lists of words that were randomly assigned to their subjects. One-half (eighty) were exposed first to an oral presentation, via a tape recorder, and then to a visual presentation, via a slide projector, of two lists of words. The other half of the subjects were first exposed to a list in the slide format, and then to a second list of words in the oral format. In both modes, the students were instructed to learn the words in the lists they were exposed to. They were then to list all the words that they were able to recall. If there were students who learned best from auditory presentations, their scores for the number of words they could recall from the list they heard on the tape should be significantly higher than their scores indicating the number of words they could recall from the list seen on a slide. The data did not support this hypothesis. These subjects did not fall into neat categories of audio and visual learners. On the basis of these findings, DeBoth and Dominowski suggested that the selection of format should rest on its effectiveness (i.e., its ability to relay information).

Marshall McLuhan, William Allen, and Lester Ashiem have all suggested that the identification of each medium's strengths and weaknesses is the key to its most effective use. Unfortunately, Schramm's analysis of research indicated that "there is almost a complete lack of studies to ascertain under what circumstances or for what purposes one medium may be superior to another."[9] In the last decade, however, there has been some research that tends to indicate that oral presentation of information is a different experience from other modes of presenting the same information.

Meringoff addressed this issue with a study of children's reactions to a story both read to them and seen as a film. Meringoff hypothesized that children experiencing the film version of the story would be more aware of the action and characters. Those to whom the story was read would remember more of the language and make more inferences about the story.

Twenty-four 6-8-year-olds and twenty-four 9-10-year-olds were the subjects. "A Story, a Story" in both picture-book form and film form was selected. The subjects were randomly assigned to a reading of the picture book or to a viewing of the film. After each child had either listened to or seen the story, she or he was asked to put in sequence pictures from the story, to comment about the story, to estimate the length of time that transpired in the story, and, finally, to estimate the distances between the places mentioned in the story.

As expected, the children who had seen the film recalled actions, and those read to remembered the language. Younger children who were read the story were better able to place the pictures in proper sequence than those who had seen the film. Among the older children, the 9-10-year-olds, this situation was reversed. Those children exposed to the film version made more inferences based on visual information, estimated that the story took place over a shorter period of time, and estimated the distances depicted in the story as much shorter than did those to whom the story was read. Meringoff's results indicated that children limited to the oral rather than the visual format had significantly different responses to items in the post-test. Listening seemed to be a unique experience.

Beagles-Roos and Gat replicated the Meringoff study. The subjects here were forty-eight children in two age groups, 6.5-8-year-olds and 9-10.5-year-olds. In this study, two stories were used, "A Story, a Story" and "Strega Nona." Both stories were recorded on cassette and were available as animated films. Children were randomly assigned to the audiocassette format or film format of one story in one session, and to the opposite medium for the second story in their second session. In this study, one of the investigators left the room while the child listened to the cassette or saw the film and returned upon its conclusion to ask the child about the story. The responses were recorded and then analyzed.

These investigators expected that, when exposed to the cassette version of one story, the children would recall more of the language and dialogue. When exposed to the film of the second story, the same children would recall the action more vividly. The ordering of pictures, it was anticipated, would be more accurate when done after the subjects had viewed the film. Inferences made after viewing the film of the story would be based on actions. When the subject had just listened to the cassette version of a story, it was expected that inferences would be based on language, dialogue, and outside sources.

The data suggested that, when experiencing the cassette version of a story, the children were more aware of the language and this was the basis of their inferences. After seeing the film of either story, subjects recalled more characters and more details. They also more accurately organized pictures based on the story and made more inferences based on actions. This replication of Meringoff had similar results and adds weight to the contention that listening results in different perceptions than other modes of relaying information.

Horowitz and Samuels were primarily interested in examining the unity theory, which suggests that reading and listening are identical skills. Good readers, it follows, are those persons who can decode print as easily as they do sound. If it could be demonstrated that this might not be the case, the linking of reading and listening comprehension would require reexamination.

These investigators selected thirty-eight sixth-graders, twenty of whom were judged to be good readers. The remainder were considered poor readers. These subjects were first to listen to and then read selected passages – one judged easy, the other judged difficult – from four texts. After reading or listening to one of the passages, each of the students was asked what he remembered. Each idea indicated was recorded as a score.

The data suggested that, when the easy passages were considered, there was no difference between the groups of readers in listening comprehension, but a significant difference in recall for reading comprehension. A similar pattern developed with the more difficult passages.

Horowitz and Samuels concluded that good and bad readers do not have significant differences in general comprehension. The major difference between the two groups of readers seemed to lie in the area of decoding skills. Listening comprehension, it follows, is not identical with reading comprehension. These are allied but not identical skills.

These three investigations suggest that listening comprehension will require separate attention. This skill cannot be overlooked. The Crittendens point out that people are communicating seven of each ten minutes they are awake. Forty-five percent of that seven minutes is spent listening. Still, researchers have estimated that we comprehend only about one-fourth of all that is said to us.

LISTENING COMPREHENSION

Listening comprehension is not just hearing. Beyond the physical ability to hear, listening involves "understanding what is sent to the brain, evaluating the information the brain has received, and, finally, reacting or responding to what has been said."[10] To this basic definition Strother adds detecting the speaker's attitude, making inferences, and drawing conclusions. Effective listeners, note Pearson and Fielding, have four basic skills: (1) phonology (i.e., the ability to distinguish between sounds and to recognize words); (2) syntax (i.e., the ability to pick up clues in the sounds, to recognize statements, questions, and exclamations, to detect the key words and phrases, to determine the end of one word and the beginning of the next, and to use the right meaning when a sound can have more than one); (3) semantics (i.e., knowing what the word represented by the sound signifies); and (4) text structure (i.e., having a sense of how narratives, drama, poetry, etc. are organized). Samuels has identified other qualities associated with effective listening: (1) the intelligence of the listener (i.e., does the listener have the ability to comprehend the message; (2) motivation (i.e., does the listener care enough to work at listening); and (3) kinesics (i.e., does the listener have the ability to decode the nonverbal cues of the speaker).

Different types of listening seem to exist. At the lowest level of the hierarchy is listening at the "phatic communication" level. It involves small talk: "How are you doing?" "How do you figure them Jets?" Listening at this level is done for enjoyment or to gather impressions. The involvement of the listener is related to whether or not he or she has any interest in the Jets or the speaker. The second type of listening is labeled "cathartic communication" by Collins. Here, the listener's role is simply to listen while the speaker airs his or her complaints, discusses a problem, and so on. The listener is passive, merely serving as a sounding board. A third level is "informative communication." At this level, information is shared, new ideas are introduced for consideration, arguments are developed, and agreements are sought. The listener is more involved in two activities. First, he or she must comprehend the speaker's messages. Secondly, he or she must discriminate between facts and opinions, as well as develop a sense of the line of thought being presented. At this level, the listener must remain involved and expects to respond with messages of his own. The most complex listening activity, the "persuasive communication" level, calls for the listener to evaluate critically and decide to accept or reject the message.

Bookcassettes operate at the latter two levels of listening— informative communications and persuasive communications. To be an effective medium, the listener must be actively involved and concentrate, just as Sutton suggests.

In their review of research on listening comprehension, Pearson and Fielding found that researchers had been most active in the 1950s and 1960s. Nearly all the findings reported were offshoots of investigations focused on the reading of print. Research in the 1960s revealed a great deal about the process of listening and the prerequisites for effective listening. These researchers also suggested that listening comprehension was a skill that could be taught. Nevertheless, oral communication skills did not receive federal funding until the 1978 amendment to the Elementary and Secondary Education Act (ESEA). However, states were still not required to set aside monies for such programs. A 1985 survey by the Speech Communication Association revealed that only eleven states had identified listening skills as a priority and developed a curriculum for teaching them. Seventeen states had no such curriculum and had no plans to develop one. The remaining states were in various stages of planning. By and large, progress has been left in the hands of individuals such as Gold and Vukelich, who have developed and published individual approaches to the teaching of listening skills. There has been no concerted effort to teach this unique skill.

CONNECTIONS AND CONCLUSION

The connection between listening comprehension skills, the library, and the emergence of the bookcassette should now be made clear. The bookcassette, in the last five years, has become a $200 million enterprise that is broadening its offerings to include nonfiction titles. This format has become readily accepted by consumers. It has also become, as the *Library Journal* surveys have shown, an important segment of the library's collection; these titles often represent a disproportionately large share of the library's total circulation. Listening, research indicates, is a distinct skill that requires concentrated effort. Listening skills, however, are not systematically being taught.

In the past, libraries have been associated with literacy programs. But the emphasis in these activities has always been on the reading of printed matter, the mainstay of library collections. No reason exists for the library to limit its attention to a single type of literacy associated with only one type of information package. The emergence of the bookcassette and the inclusion of these new information packages in library collections, it would seem, call for a response from the libraries on aural literacy. The addition of nonfiction titles by new audio-publishers and the existence of professional journals in law, medicine, and so on in the cassette format add emphasis to the need to address aural literacy in the same fashion libraries have attended to print literacy.

This is not to suggest that libraries become the primary agent in the development of listening skills. That job more properly belongs to the school systems, just as reading does. But the library can still play a role that is analogous to the one the library seems willing to undertake in traditional literacy programs. First, libraries should become aware of groups concerned with aural literacy and programs available for the development of listening skills. Offering publicity and the use of meeting rooms to such groups is a minimal supportive activity. Secondly, librarians need to be made aware of the results of research in listening skills in order to be able to select materials and guide patrons to more useful materials in this format. Thirdly, library education in courses such as storytelling and media services needs to build into the course syllabuses the concept of listening comprehension and the findings of relevant research to better equip new professionals to perform their information-brokering function.

If librarians are to seriously take on the role of omnimedia information centers and broaden their service base, they must be willing and eager to take on new responsibilities. Failure to rise to an opportunity such as that presented by the development of the bookcassette may lead to the final irony. The omnimedia information age arrives, and we are still at the bookstore.

Notes

1. Tom Hope, "AV Materials and Equipment: Spending Trends," in *Educational Media Yearbook 1983,* ed. James W. Brown (Littleton, Colo.: Libraries Unlimited, 1983), 124-29.

2. Patricia Lawson, "Tape Cassettes," *Booklist* 70, no. 8 (December 15, 1973): 436.

3. Bryan Davis, "Books (on Cassette) Are Better than Ever," *American Libraries* 15, no. 3 (March 1984): 165.

4. Ibid.

5. Susan Avallone and Bette Lee Fox, "A Commitment to Cassettes," *Library Journal* 111, no. 19 (November 15, 1986): 35.

6. Roger Sutton, "Hear! Hear! Books on Cassette," *School Library Journal* 32, no. 10 (August 1986): 21.

7. Ibid.

8. Ibid.

9. Wilbur Schramm, *Big Media, Little Media: Tools and Technologies for Instruction* (Beverly Hills, Calif.: Sage Publications, 1977), 73.

10. Bertha Collins, "Are You a Listener?" *Journal of Business Education* 58, no. 3 (December 1982): 102.

References

"Audio Preview: Best Sellers on the Way." *Publishers Weekly* 232 (July 31, 1987), 53-55.

Avallone, Susan, and Fox, Bette-Lee. "A Commitment to Cassettes." *Library Journal* 111, no. 19 (November 15, 1986): 35-37.

Barkholz, Gerald R. "Audiotapes." In *Nonbook Media, Collection Management and User Services.* Edited by John W. Ellison and Patricia Ann Coty. Chicago: American Library Association, 1987.

Beagles-Roos, Jessica, and Gat, Isabelle. "Specific Impact of Radio and Television on Children's Story Comprehension." *Journal of Educational Psychology* 75, no. 1 (1983): 128-37.

Blaiwas, David. "Sideline Update: Books on Cassette." *Publishers Weekly* 225, no. 13 (March 3, 1984): 36-40.

"A Bountiful Season for Audiocassettes." *Publishers Weekly* 228, no. 12 (September 20, 1985): 75.

Brown, E. G. "The Talking Book." *Feliciter* 21, no. 5 (1974): 19-20.

_____. "Cassettes on Legal Subjects for Continuing Legal Education." *Law Library Journal* 63, no. 3 (August 1970): 315-17.

Collins, Bertha. "Are You a Listener?" *Journal of Business Education* 58, no. 3 (December 1982): 102-3.

Crittenden, Vicky L., and Crittenden, William F. "Improving Listening Skills – A Three Step Process." *Journal of Business Education* 58, no. 6 (March 1983): 226-28.

Davis, Bryan. "Books (on Cassette) Are Better than Ever." *American Libraries* 15, no. 3 (March 1984): 165-69.

DeBoth, Carol, and Dominowski, Roger L. "Individual Differences in Learning: Visual Versus Auditory Presentation." *Journal of Educational Psychology* 70, no. 4 (1978): 498-503.

Dertien, John. "Specialized Business Sources on Cassette." *Unabashed Librarian* no. 3 (Spring 1972): 6.

Ditlow, Timothy P. "Recording Danziger on Young Adult Cliff Hangers." *Top of the News* 41, no. 4 (Summer 1985): 321-25.

Egan, Carol M. "Establishing a Cassette Program for a Public library." *Illinois Libraries* 56, no. 3 (March 1974): 239-43.

_____. "Tape Cassette and Framed Art Print Collections in the Public Library." *Catholic Library World* 46, no. 2 (September 1974): 52-57.

Gold, Yvonne. "Teaching Attentive Listening." *Reading Improvement* 18 (Winter 1981): 319-20.

"Good News for the Holidays." *Publishers Weekly* 232, no. 25 (December 18, 1987): 29-30.

Havens, Shirley E.; DeCondido, Grace-Ann; and Fox, Bette-Lee. "Audio and Videocassettes: Patron Demand = Library Response." *Library Journal* 112, no. 19 (November 15, 1987): 33-35.

Hope, Tom. "AV Materials and Equipment: Spending Trends." *Educational Media Yearbook 1983*. Edited by James W. Brown. Littleton, Colo.: Libraries Unlimited, 1983.

Horowitz, Rosalind, and Samuels, S. Jay. "Reading and Listening to Expository Text." *Journal of Reading Behavior* 17, no. 3 (1985): 185-97.

"Houghton Mifflin, Brilliance Collaborate on Two Audio Lines." *Publishers Weekly* 231, no. 18 (May 8, 1987): 42-44.

Lawson, Patricia. "Tape Cassettes." *Booklist* 70, no. 8 (December 15, 1973): 436.

"Libraries Produce Talking Books, Provide Information to Aging." *Library Journal* 102, no. 19 (November 1, 1977): 2206.

Loeb, Marion C. "Choice Magazine Listening." *Serials Librarian* 7, no. 4 (Summer 1983): 77-80.

Long, Donna Reseigh. "Listening Comprehension: Need and Neglect." *Hispania* 70 (December 1987): 921-28.

Maitland, Laura. "When the Teacher's Away, the Students Will Learn." *American Biology Teacher* 46, no. 5 (May 1984): 275-76.

Majeska, Marilyn Lundell. *Talking Books: Pioneering and Beyond.* Washington, D.C.: National Library Service for the Blind and Physically Handicapped, 1988.

Masello, David. "Audio Abridgers." *Publishers Weekly* 229, no. 3 (January 17, 1986): 51-53.

_____. "Audio and Video in the Book Clubs." *Publishers Weekly* 230, no. 22 (November 28, 1986): 51-54.

_____. "Children's Publishing: Book and Audiocassette Packages." *Publishers Weekly* 230, no. 4 (July 25, 1986): 161-63.

_____ . "Tracking the Audio Market." *Publishers Weekly* 229, no. 21 (May 23, 1986): 83-85.

"McGraw-Hill Gets Serious about Audio." *Publishers Weekly* 232, no. 3 (July 17, 1987): 36-37.

McIntyre, Annie. "Enter, Speaker Right." *Publishers Weekly* 232, no. 2 (December 11, 1987): 39-41.

Meringoff, Laurene Krasny. "Influence of the Medium on Children's Story Apprehension." *Journal of Educational Psychology* 72, no. 2 (1980): 240-49.

Mitchell, Morton, and Strickland, Martha. "The Current Awareness Journal Cassette Project." *Journal of Education for Librarianship* 18, no. 3 (Winter 1972): 229-33.

"New Media for a New Age." *Publishers Weekly* 232, no. 13 (September 25, 1987): 60-61.

Nobel, Valerie. "Chatty Chatty Bang Bang: Business Information Cassettes." *Special Libraries* 62, nos. 5/6 (May/June 1971): 231-33.

Pearson, P. David, and Fielding, Linda. "Listening Comprehension." *Language Arts* 59, no. 6 (September 1982): 617-29.

Postman, Andrew. "Celebrity Autobiographies on Cassette." *Publishers Weekly* 231, no. 21 (May 26, 1987): 56-57.

_____ . "Commercial Fiction on Tape." *Publishers Weekly* 232, no. 10 (September 4, 1987): 27-28.

_____ . "In the Beginning There Was Caution." *Publishers Weekly* 230, no. 14 (October 13, 1986): 70-77.

Purdue, Bill. "Talking Newspapers and Magazines." *Audiovisual Librarian* 10, no. 2 (Spring 1984): 82-85.

Riding, R. J., and Vincent, D. J. T. "Listening Comprehension: The Effects of Sex, Age, Passage Structure, and Speech Rate." *Educational Review* 32, no. 3 (1980): 259-65.

Samuels, S. Jay. "Factors Influencing Listening: Inside and Outside the Head." *Theory into Practice* 23, no. 3 (Summer 1984): 183-89.

Schramm, Wilbur. *Big Media, Little Media: Tools and Technology for Instruction.* Beverly Hills, Cal.: Sage Publications, 1977.

"Simon and Schuster Audio Launch Star Trek Series." *Publishers Weekly* 231, no. 18 (May 8, 1987): 44-45.

Spain, Tom. "Ingram Announces Monthly Audio Promotions for Fall." *Publishers Weekly* 229, no. 40 (March 17, 1986): 60-61.

_____ . "Wiley Introduces New Audio Line." *Publishers Weekly* 229, no. 24 (June 13, 1986): 39-40.

"Spring Audio Cassettes." *Publishers Weekly* 229, no. 11 (March 14, 1986): 52.

Stewart, Barbara. "Making Book on Book and Cassette Packages." *Publishers Weekly* 222, no. 22 (November 27, 1987): 51-55.

Strother, Deborah Burnett. "On Listening." *Phi Delta Kappan* 68, no. 8 (April 1987): 625-28.

Sutton, Roger. "Hear! Hear! Books on Cassette." *School Library Journal* 32, no. 10 (August 1986): 21-24.

Tangorra, Joanne. "Working a Niche That Works." *Publishers Weekly* 231, no. 1 (January 16, 1987): 52-54.

Tripp, Pat. "Audio Cassettes for Local Government Information." *Assistant Librarian* 70, no. 1 (January 1977): 6-7.

Tuman, Myron C. "A Comparative Review of Reading and Listening Comprehension." *Journal of Reading* 23, no. 8 (May 1980): 698-704.

Vukelich, Carol. "The Development of Listening Comprehension through Storytime." *Language Arts* 53, no. 8 (November/December 1976): 889-91.

Wise, Kathryn. "Idaho State Library Talking Book Program." *Idaho Librarian* 28, no. 1 (January 1976): 15-16.

Zinser, John. "Comedy on Cassette." *Publishers Weekly* 232, no. 23 (December 4, 1987): 31-34.

_____ . "Fall Audio Cassettes." *Publishers Weekly* 234, no. 6 (August 5, 1988): 35-50.

_____ . "Testing the Waters." *Publishers Weekly* 232, no. 18 (October 23, 1987): 35-36.

_____ . "Word-for-Word." *Publishers Weekly* 231, no. 6 (February 20, 1987): 52-54.

The Evidentiary Quality of Taped Evidence

JOSEPH S. FULDA

The criminal justice system is increasingly and successfully relying on audio and videotapes, especially videotapes, as evidence of criminality, particularly in "sting" operations. In this paper, we hope to cast considerable doubt on the very high evidentiary quality commonly attributed to taped evidence, using concepts drawn from truth-functional logic. Truth-functional logic is a good mechanism for this because the necessity of fixing a precise meaning to natural language constructs – in order to determine truth or falsity – brings unresolved questions of meaning to the fore, questions that might otherwise go undetected. For (the classic) example, consider the sentence, "It is raining." Resolution of this sentence into a true-or-false statement requires making it less ambiguous. It is raining – where? When?

We make use of two logical points to support our thesis: (1) Tapes record sentences, linguistic entities that may or may not be uttered; evidence requires statements, logical entities that are true or false. Thus, whether taped discourse has, in truth, been uttered is a logically distinct question from whether the discourse uttered is truthful; (2) Tapes are produced (inevitably) from a perspective and are (necessarily) presented as context-free; evidence requires "the whole truth" (which includes context) and no admixture of facts with interpretation – "nothing but the truth" (which excludes perspective). While upon direct statement these points appear self-evident, experience shows that in specific instances they are readily forgotten or ignored. The examples we shall present will join the reader's own experience in convincing him of this.

The principal difficulty with the use of tapes as evidence is that tapes provide a static picture in a limited frame, whereas witness-provided testimony is subject to that awesome tool of the law, cross-examination. Cross-examination forces the witness, willy-nilly, to go beyond whatever frame direct examination has artfully constructed. Thus, with witness-provided testimony, cross-examination can translate context-free sentences into in-context statements, can resolve ambiguous sentences into truth-functional statements, and can bring out and put before the court and the jury background details and perspective-related matters hidden from direct view. With a tape, however, there is no way to do this, and sentences that do not make unambiguous statements capable of bearing a truth value remain linguistic (non-truth-functional, and therefore nonevidentiary) rather than logical (truth-functional, and therefore evidentiary) entities. Furthermore, and beyond mere ambiguity, tapes are naturally presented as context-free and therefore must reflect a particular perspective – the perspective of the (unknown) context in which they were recorded.

Physical perspective, the angle from which the camera is focused, is the most obvious, and the classic example is that of a confession taped where the police officer with a stun gun is outside the field of vision of the camera. Likewise, temporal perspective is lacking when a prior beating is not taped along with the subsequent confession. But there does not have to be a deliberate attempt to frame someone as in the above cases. Our point is that *all* taped evidence comes within a static, limited frame.

In addition to physical and temporal perspective, there is linguistic perspective, the angle, as it were, of the conversation. For example, it is not unusual for a conversation between friends to proceed along a hypothetical course, with the hypothetical not directly expressed. Needless to say, a tape of the conversation without the hypothetical will result in the listener's taking both the hypothetical and the conversation that is predicated on it as indicative and true. "If you were to burglarize the corner grocery store, how would you do it?" the conversation opens. The detailed fantasizing that follows by an innocent but suspected man may well doom him if it is taped because the conversational angle is unrecorded and therefore unknown.

Consider as a second example of linguistic perspective the student's response to the following question on a teacher evaluation form: "Did the professor show uniformly professional conduct?" The response: "He singled me out in front of the whole class and said to me that were he to marry me he'd like as not end up divorcing me." Certainly this seems like a grossly inappropriate, unprofessional remark and one unlikely to have been fabricated in such detail by the student. Now consider that the perspective is one of a hopelessly inept student who has been appropriately flunked and that the context is a lecture on discrete mathematics introducing the concept of probability. The teacher, wishing to motivate probability, relates it to frequency. First, he points out, concretely, that the divorce rate is 50 percent and that this is a frequency. Second, he points out that the particularization of this to the arbitrary individual is probability, and then, pointing innocently to a student in the front row, says, "Thus, if I were to marry her, like as not we'd get divorced." The lecturer concludes by saying, with professorial overtones, that probability is the reduction of frequency and frequency is probability writ large. Anyone familiar with the philosophy of mathematics will agree that this is an oversimplification, but that – and not unprofessionalism – is the only fault to be found. When context is provided and perspective sheds light on motivation, a highly incriminating remark is seen as totally innocent.

Finally, let us put into logical notation the central question that we have been facing: does $T(X) => X$? Does the fact that a tape records X mean that X is true? This question requires decomposition. First, does $T(X) => S(X)$? and, second, does $S(X) => X$? Namely, does the fact that a tape records X mean that a speaker said X, and does that, in turn, mean that X is true? The answer to the first question is a qualified yes. Qualified, for it is true only when X is at least a statement, as a less ambiguous rendering of a sentence, and, as we have seen, it may be a serious undertaking to recover from a sentence the statement it was uttered to assert. (Parenthetically, we note that this task is the principal job of the appellate judiciary.) The answer to the second question is, of course, what finders of fact must decide. It is the primary purpose of cross-examination to test the connection between $S(X)$ and X vigorously, by clarifying ambiguities, bringing out relevant background details, finding out perspective, and providing context omitted from the testimony itself (i.e., X). After all this is accomplished, one must ask whether X conjoined to whatever was learned during cross-examination, and further conjoined to the remaining body of evidence, is consistent and credible.

Because one cannot cross-examine a tape, its perspective and context are forever hidden from direct view. To the question, then, does $T(X) => X$? what most quickly comes to mind is that it is almost certainly true that $T(X) = S(X)$, making it psychologically easy to overlook the fact that that hardly resolves the question, does $T(X) => X$? because the connection between $S(X)$ and X has not been tried in the manner of ordinary courtroom testimony.

In summary, the use of taped evidence is fraught with epistemological difficulties and is by no means as simple a matter as is commonly supposed. Videotapes, especially, are hard to view with skepticism. We learn so much from sight and sound, and especially sight, that rejection of what we see and hear *ex machina* is psychologically difficult, even when logically indicated.

This paper is dedicated to Lieutenant Patrick J. Vincent, USN.

The Alien Space of (M)other:
The Female Gothic and Aliens

JENNIFER SHADDOCK

At a recent conference, "The Future of the Public Library," keynote speaker Robert Olson claimed that what libraries need is not merely agencies to provide access to information but "agencies to *select and interpret* [the] rising mountain of data in a way that leads individuals to *knowledge and wisdom*" (Hennen 1988, 390). This statement begs two crucial questions: what are knowledge and wisdom, and what information sources lead to them? These questions simply will not get answered today, but I do hope by using a feminist analysis of the 1986 popular culture horror film *Aliens* to point toward a few of the enormous interpretive problems and responsibilities that Olson's remark presages.

The Rutgers University film library, for one, does not own *Aliens*, ostensibly because the film is relegated to the category "entertainment" rather than that of "education." And yet, it is precisely because *Aliens* purports to be merely entertaining, because it is so unself-conscious of its own cultural biases, that it can tell us so very much about the cultural assumptions and the power structures that form the pervasive foundation of our society.

Aliens opened in 1986 to blockbuster audiences across America, promising to reveal the identity of the mysterious alien whose offspring wreaked havoc in the original film, *Alien*. Upon the sequel's release, critics hailed writer and director James Cameron for rehabilitating a worn genre through his inspired use of a woman protagonist within a sci-fi horror film. This "wonder woman" heroine, an intelligent and resourceful gunslinger, ultimately overcomes a slew of obstacles in order to save herself, her adopted daughter, and her wounded lover from annihilation by the alien–hence the widespread perception of *Aliens* as a feminist film. *Village Voice* critic David

Edelstein (1986, 56) goes further, not only citing *Aliens'* feminist appeal but dubbing the film, a "paean to motherhood."

Ironically, it is through this very representation of motherhood that *Aliens* reveals its latent yet powerful cultural misogyny, for the alien world within the film is depicted as the terrifying space of the (m)other. I am interested here in applying the paradigm of the "Female Gothic" formulated by literary critic Ellen Moers to illustrate the self-perpetuating misogynist construct of motherhood and woman's sexuality as patriarchally defined and reflected in the popular culture film *Aliens*.[1]

Moers defines the Female Gothic essentially as any narrative mode that provides an image for the fear of self as woman.[2] She locates the beginning of this tradition in the classic, eighteenth-century Gothic novel – works like Ann Radcliffe's *Mysteries of Udolpho* and *The Italian*, as well as later works such as Mary Shelley's *Frankenstein* and Christina Rossetti's poem, "Goblin Market." We readily associate the following plot conventions with the Gothic novel: a motherless heroine is compelled to penetrate a dark, womblike, labyrinthian space; as if living out a nightmare, she is subjected to fearful pursuits, dangerous confinement, and insidious if not overt sexual harassment; the heroine finally escapes, however; she triumphs and restores order. Typical interpretations by male critics of this Gothic narrative focus on the villain as the source of the Gothic experience. Leslie Fiedler, for example, reads the Gothic as "the son's rebellious confrontation with paternal authority" (Kahane 1985, 336). Recently, however, feminist critics have begun to excavate many Gothic texts to reveal a psychological narrative form that challenges these traditional interpretations of the Gothic novel by exposing the heroine's central conflict as occurring not with a male protagonist at all, but rather, with the mother.[3]

Film critic Linda Williams (1984, 87) suggests a similar shift in perspective in her analysis of the horror film:

> The power and potency of the monster body in many classic horror films . . . should not be interpreted as an eruption of the normally repressed animal sexuality of the civilized male (the monster as double for the male viewer and characters in the film), but as the feared power and potency of a different kind of sexuality (the monster as double for the women).

Both Moers and Williams depend upon the work of a handful of influential feminist psychoanalysts who argue against the patriarchal oedipal model and assert instead that the development of an infant's identity depends upon the repressed problem of the ambivalent identification of children with their mothers.

Basically, this model argues that during a child's pre-oedipal stage, from birth to about eighteen months, she has not developed ego boundaries and thus is not conscious of herself as an autonomous individual. Entirely dependent on her mother, she perceives with both desire and fear that her mother is omnipresent and omnipotent. In order to facilitate the child's progressive assumption of subjectivity, however, the maternal space must be perceived by the child as less and less a protective habitat and more and more an annihilating prison. At this point, the mother necessarily becomes increasingly associated with insatiability, with images of (s)mothering, so that the child feels compelled to separate from the mother. Thus, women in general become charged with the ambivalence of fear and desire that is the inevitable by-product of the process of mothering a young child – providing an other against which the child defines itself. Woman becomes the carnal scapegoat for what are pervasive, vestigial human fears of annihilation of self by the all-devouring (m)other.

For girls this process becomes complicated in that they internalize the fear and dread associated with their own sexuality. Relating this fear to the narrative structure of the Female Gothic, Eleanor Fleenor (1993, 11) suggests that "in the Female Gothic the ambivalence toward the female (good and evil) has been internalized."

In *Aliens* these latent feelings of self-disgust and self-fear are externally embodied in a material form as a grotesque (m)other monster with horrible devouring and contaminating reproductive needs. The division, then, between the chaste heroine, Ripley, and the sexual (m)other, the alien monster, is precisely the dichotomy basic to the Female Gothic. Ripley sees what she herself will become if she heeds her sexual self.

Aliens' interest in the terror of procreation is evident from the opening scene of the film. The heroine Ripley is reborn from the glass, coffinlike freezer in which she has been adrift in outer space for fifty-seven years. By chance, she is found and "reanimated" into society by her previous employer, the Company. In an odd way, then, Ripley is, like most Gothic heroines, motherless, though birthed by the patriarchal order. While resting in bed under medical observation at the Company's "deep way station" hospital, and looking much like a healthy, young expectant mother, Ripley has a seizure. Her body suddenly contorts. As though in the throes of labor, she groans, and the heavy, rhythmic sound of a beating heart crescendoes. The film warps into slow motion. Ripley lifts her shirt, and in a scene reminiscent of the gory deaths in *Alien*, when alien babies explode from the stomachs of infected crew members, we watch as Ripley's stomach begins, grotesquely, to protrude. Ripley screams and wakes up. The thematics of the entire film depends upon this sequence of distorted birth imagery, as it looks back to the original events in *Alien* and foreshadows those to come in *Aliens*, and yet the film undermines the significance of this establishing scene by discounting it as merely a nightmare.

Ironically, a "real" and sustained nightmare occurs as a result of a similar repression of the narrative of the (m)other. The Company's unwavering, bottom-line, bottom-dollar capitalistic interests, its phallic expansionism, necessitate that it delegitimate the terrifying alien experience of its employee, Ripley, and silence her about the potential for dangerous future encounters with the alien. Thus, the Company ignores Ripley's prophetic warnings, demoting her from flight officer to forklift operator. It is specifically this patriarchal repression of the terrifying vision of the alien (m)other that actually *produces* the subsequent nightmarish outbursts of alien monsters from within human bodies, as well as the ultimate confrontation with the all-devouring (m)other. Had the Company listened to and legitimated Ripley's account of the alien (m)other's power, the horror story would not have been enacted.

The feminist appeal of *Aliens* resides in the subsequent triumphant validation of Ripley's story and the concomitant castration of the patriarchal powermongers who scorned her. Ripley has been called in as an adviser to a Marine unit assigned to check out a possible "zenomorph" (bug) that has seemingly wiped out a large group of colonists that the Company recently had sent to the alien planet. At first, Ripley is subjected to the same humiliating belittlement from the Marines that she received from her employers. After the crew's first disastrous confrontation with the alien, however, the survivors soon realize that they will need more than military might to fight the (m)other, and they turn for help to Ripley, who has lived through a previous encounter with the alien. The roles rapidly reversed, Ripley from here on barks orders, pacifies hysterical men, skillfully maneuvers military machinery, and, while men drop dead around her, manages to gun into oblivion an army of alien babies.

However, the terror of the procreative forces of the (m)other at the heart of the Gothic story belies *Aliens'* seemingly liberating narrative. The role reversal that apparently creates a new feminist order within the film does so only on the film's most rudimentary level. Significantly, it is immediately after Ripley adopts the nine-year-old girl, Nute, the only survivor left in the original colony, that she aggressively establishes herself as the group's leader and protector, a militaristic mother. In assuming the role of mother, Ripley becomes the appropriate and self-appointed match for the alien (m)other. Clearly, this maternal confrontation enacts the characteristic motif of the Female Gothic: dread of female sexuality as an annihilating force. The film inscribes the self-hatred of the heroine toward her own body as a struggle between the good, chaste mother and the corrupt, sexual (m)other. Ripley, the nonbiological mother of Nute, assumes the chaste role, while the monster, a metonymy for the vagina, represents the terrifying terrain of female sexuality.

The visual images chosen to flesh out the maternal space of the alien (m)other within *Aliens* is, in fact, disgusting, reflecting extreme societal apprehensions surrounding female reproductivity. As Claire Kahane (1985,

345) asserts, pregnancy and childbirth "can arouse fears about bodily integrity that are intimately related to one's sense of self. . . . In pregnancy the woman's very shape changes as she feels another presence inside her, growing on her flesh, feeding on her blood." As the military crew penetrates the labyrinthian passages leading to the secret center, the origin of reproductivity, the surrounding environment assumes the disquieting form of the interior workings of a female body. The Marines pass, for example, what appears to be, through the dripping, dank mist, a rib cage, and perhaps something resembling intestines. The walls secrete a sticky resin, and eggs enveloped in a protective, gooey coating lie scattered across the floor. A huge cocoon, within which fester human bodies, looms in front of them, blocking their path. A bloated, sweating woman wrapped within the cocoon raises her drooping head, and as she begs to be killed, an alien baby, having gestated within her, bursts out of her stomach, splattering blood on the horrified Marines who watch as the squealing baby monster scuttles by. The crew penetrates no farther, for it is attacked by huge black monsters with engulfing mouths and multiple rows of teeth dripping a sticky white resin. These vaginal man-eating monsters gnash the imprisoned victims in an oral frenzy that leaves the frame subsumed in a red, bloodlike image of fusion with the devouring (m)other.

Faced with images of, in Claire Kahane's (1985, 346) words, "the womb as the mummy's tomb," of female sexuality and reproductivity as Gothic terrors relegating "women to an imprisoning biological destiny that denies the autonomy of the self," Ripley must penetrate to the mysterious center of the maternal space. In other words, in order to preserve both herself and her daughter from the threat of obliteration by the (m)other, the chaste mother must displace the dangerous sexual (m)other. While the greater part of the diegetic space of both *Alien* films is dedicated to destroying the seemingly indestructible, terrorizing alien (m)other, Ripley finally succeeds. After rescuing the cocooned Nute, whose alien impregnation was imminent, Ripley stumbles on the alien (m)other's nursery. Here, at the heart of the maternal space, the alien (m)other sits laboriously occupied in laying eggs. A standoff ensues, from which Ripley and Nute escape by blowing up the nursery, infuriating the (m)other monster, who now doggedly pursues them. Just as the alien (m)other reaches out to repossess Nute, Ripley emerges from behind a massive steel door. Protected within her metallic forklifting suit, she cries out with the instinctive authority of a desperate mother protecting her child, "Get away from her, you bitch!" After a savage struggle, Ripley blows the (m)other monster through the spacecraft's open access chute into the vacuum of outer space (an ironic reversal of maternal territory since this is where Ripley impotently floated when the film began). Thus, Ripley figuratively aborts the (m)other, ensuring that no more unwanted pregnancies occur in the future.

There is, seemingly, a new terrain established within the film in which to envision and potentially experience motherhood. The film appears, for example, to deliver poetic justice to those who victimize the female body. Carter, the Company man who unsuccessfully plots to let an alien impregnate Ripley and Nute so that he can make a buck, is himself killed later in the film by an alien. Carter, in being devoured by the monster, seems to be representative of the film's insistence that those who use the female body to oppress and incapacitate women will be punished.

What is insidious about *Aliens*, however, is that in destroying the alien (m)other, the film seems to suggest that the heroine achieves freedom over motherhood's victimizing threat to her own body. Yet the film's apparent establishment of a maternal virginal terrain paradoxically occurs at the expense of female sexuality. While Ripley has surmounted the Gothic threat of becoming the passive or unwilling victim of one's own body, she does so by aborting the maternal body, by blowing her figurative vagina into outer space. Afterwards, she resumes a quiescent role, denying the Gothic force of the sexual (m)other that she has just confronted. Appropriately, then, at the conclusion of the film Ripley is left with an incapacitated male lover and a nonbiological daughter.

Moreover, her relationship to her daughter begins to take on ominous overtones. In the sterile confines of the spacecraft navigating its way home, Ripley, dressed only in her underwear, escorts the now clean and feminized Nute to her glass freezer. Perhaps it is the possessive way that Ripley touches Nute's shoulder, perhaps the resemblance of the enveloping glass freezer to an alien cocoon, but the sight of Ripley's seminude body towering over Nute now invokes a slight, yet uncomfortable disgust. Concluding with a shot of the face of the daughter uncannily mirroring that of the (m)other as the two proceed to fall into a deep-freeze hypersleep, a futuristic pre-oedipal state, the final sequence of the film provokes an unsettling sense of the inescapable process of woman's reproduction of motherhood and the self-abnegating oppression inherent in that process as the patriarchy defines it.

Posing the question, "What is a mother?" psychiatrist Monique Plaza (1982, 78) answers: "It is, above all, the function of material and affective attendance on the children in the heart of the family. . . . "Mom" is neither a woman nor an individual, it is someone whom I perceive as (or rather whom *I represent to myself* as) closely linked to myself, quasi-instinctively."

By redefining "mother" as a function rather than "a female parent," as the *Oxford English Dictionary* would have it, Plaza and the other feminist theorists I have cited here argue that the conflated role of woman and mother is, in fact, a construction of a patriarchy that depends upon woman's identity as mother to ensure her domination by men.[4] As such, the conception of motherhood represents, in Plaza's words, "one of the most prodigious and effective bastions of misogyny" (1982, 78).

Aliens has been interpreted as creating an alternative feminist view of the woman-mother. Yet it simply has at its service sophisticated techniques to cover up its identifying traces as it works all the while to reconstitute the patriarchal construction of motherhood. In never questioning the basic patriarchal assumption that the maternal function is the undisputed biological destiny of women, such a Female Gothic film echoes the patriarchal injunction that "woman must define herself by maternity, pregnancy must be associated with mothering, 'dependence' must be posed as the antinomy of 'autonomy.'" As Plaza concludes, this construction is "a phantasm and not a given of nature" (1982, 88).

The ambivalence of *Aliens'* definition of motherhood – its overt feminism and its covert misogyny – raises serious questions not only about the kinds of narratives capable of moving us beyond old ways of seeing female sexuality and reproductivity, but, more disturbingly, about the very potential for alternative narratives to produce significant change in the gendered definition of motherhood – the conflation of woman and mother – that now often confines women's lives.

In this paper, I analyze just one predominant cultural assumption in just one American popular culture film. The embodiment in film of cultural perspectives can at best be a transformatory, even a potentially radical, process for both an individual viewer and society at large. It can also, as in the case of *Aliens*, be reactionary in ways that we often cannot recognize immediately from the literal, narrative level. Films such as *Aliens* must therefore be "read" with the same seriousness as a classic novel, and perhaps even with more urgency since millions of viewers daily absorb the cultural biases of such "entertaining" films. *Aliens* is educative in its very posture as entertainment and, like many similarly neglected sources of information, needs to be affirmed alongside self-consciously serious art as a valid cultural analogue.

Notes

1. I wish to thank Elaine Showalter not only for introducing me to the theories of the Female Gothic, but also specifically for suggesting the connection between the Female Gothic and *Aliens*.

2. See the chapter, "Female Gothic," in Moers (1972) for the original formulation of the Female Gothic.

3. I am indebted to Juliann E. Fleenor's introduction to her collection of essays, *The Female Gothic*, for much of my own formulation of the definition of the Female Gothic.

4. See Nancy Chodorow, *The Reproduction of Mothering* (Berkeley: University of California Press, 1979), Dorothy Dinnerstein, *The Mermaid and the Minotaur* (New York: Harper and Row, 1976), and Adrienne Rich, *Of*

Woman Born (New York: Harper and Row, 1976) for further discussions of patriarchal constructions of motherhood.

Works Cited

Aliens. Dir. James Cameron. Twentieth-Century-Fox, 1986.

Edelstein, David. "Lovers and Other Aliens." *Village Voice* (July 22, 1986): 56.

Fleenor, Juliann E. *The Female Gothic*. Montreal: Eden Press, 1983.

Hennen, Thomas J. "Public Librarians Take Cool View of the Future: Leadership, Not Technology, May Be the Issue." *American Libraries* 19 (1988): 390-92.

Kahane, Claire. "The Gothic Mirror." In *The (M)other Tongue: Essays in Feminist Psychoanalytic Interpretation*, eds. Shirley Nelson Garner, Claire Kahane, and Madelon Sprengnether, 334-51. Ithaca, N.Y.: Cornell University Press, 1985.

Kaplan, E. Ann. *Women and Film: Both Sides of the Camera*. New York: Methuen, 1983.

Moers, Ellen. *Literary Women: The Great Writers*. New York: Doubleday, 1972.

Plaza, Monique. "The Mother/The Same: Hatred of the Mother in Psychoanalysis." *Feminist Issues* 2 (1982): 75-99.

Williams, Linda. "When the Woman Looks." In *Re-Vision: Essays in Feminist Film Criticism*, eds. Mary Ann Doane, Patricia Mellencamp, and Linda Williams. Los Angeles: American Film Institute, 1984.

From Orality to Literacy to Electronic Technology: Conceptualizing Classical Rhetoric in an Age of Word Processors

JOHN FREDERICK REYNOLDS

I want to preface my remarks with an acknowledgment that should not be relegated to footnote status. Given my undergraduate and graduate studies in both English and speech communication, my experiences as a high school debate coach, and my work as a corporate writer in the computer services industry, I am indebted to biographical circumstance for my nearly equal interests in speaking, writing, and computers. But for my exposure to and interest in the exciting but complicated relationship between orality, literacy, electronic technology, and classical rhetoric, I am indebted to Dr. Kathleen Welch of the University of Oklahoma and Dr. Winifred Bryan Horner of Texas Christian University. I can best recommend their work to you by saying, to employ a figure of speech appropriate to the occasion, that their writing speaks for itself.

The seven centuries of Greek and Latin work that we call "classical rhetoric" articulated an approach to information literacy that remains valuable today. "Although classical rhetoric was conceived in a primarily oral culture," Professor Horner (1988, 2) has pointed out, "the underlying principles remain valuable in a literate society. The classical orator and the contemporary writer share and rely on the same basic precepts." The center of the classical approach lay in its five interactive canons: invention, arrangement, style, memory, and delivery. These five functions or parts or faculties of the classical system were first canonized in Latin rhetoric as *inventio, dispositio, elocutio, memoria,* and *pronuntiatio* or *actio,* but they were "existent, important, and apparent" (Welch 1988, 4, 5) even earlier in Greek rhetoric as *heurisis, taxis, lexis, mneme,* and *hypocrisis*.[1] The five canons pervaded classical rhetorical theory (as Professor Welch has demonstrated, tracing important work done by Yates, Nadeau, and Scaglione) not only as a system for the *critical analysis* of information, but also as a system for the *production* of information. This combination, that the classical canons can function for both *encoding* and *decoding,* makes classical rhetoric unique as a language and literacy system. Professor Welch has argued, in fact, citing Eagleton, that the classical canons constitute "the most complete [though not infallible] critical system that has ever been devised" (1988a, 3). The five canons pervade modern rhetorical theory as well, but in a truncated form, with "two-fifths of this system – memory and delivery – . . . deleted without a word of explanation" (Welch 1987, 270), a "removal [that] is not an adaptation but a wholly new structure" containing "only remnants of the original theory" (Welch 1988b, 9, 18).

Though others see larger and more sinister agendae, I contend that the truncating of the five canons into three was one inevitable result of the lost focus on memory and delivery that accompanied the Western world's shift from oral dominance to writing dominance. And, similarly, I contend that the restoration of the two lost, removed, abandoned, misunderstood canons is an inevitable result of the new focus on memory and delivery that will accompany the Western world's shift-in-progress from writing dominance to word-processing dominance. As we meet to confer about information literacies for the twenty-first century, I will argue that there is good news and bad news. The bad news is that the reduction of the classical canons from five to three still forms the dominant theory behind most university writing textbooks, and that it is far from benign, since the removal of memory and delivery destroys the classical system by robbing it of its context and power, of its completeness and connectedness, of its usefulness for both information *analysis* and information *production.* The good news is that the age of electronic technology offers us exciting opportunities to reconceptualize classical rhetoric, especially its lost canons of memory and delivery.

Here I will focus on the exciting opportunity that lies in exploring the effect of word processing on the fifth canon – "delivery" in English, *pronuntiatio* or *actio* in Latin, *hypocrisis* in Greek. Specifically, I will report results from my own work teaching delivery as presentation[2] in several experimental university writing courses where we taught students to use the classical system and to conceptualize *pronuntiatio* or *hypocrisis* as the analysis and production of the extra-textual features that can and usually do accompany word-processed text. But first, I want to take us from orality to literacy to electronic technology.

"The theory of orality, literacy, and secondary orality developed by Walter J. Ong and Eric A. Havelock over the last twenty-five years," Professor Welch has noted, "reveals one of the primary reasons that rhetoric and composition acquired so much power in fourth century B.C. Greece and in 20th century North America" (Welch 1988a, 1). The theory identifies three stages of human consciousness in regard to information literacy.

Ong and Havelock call the first stage "primary orality." It is a stage in which human knowledge and culture are encoded, transmitted, and decoded orally. It is a stage best revealed in the oral-formulaic epic poems that manage everything from the art to the history, to the religion, to the governmental regulations, of oral cultures.

Ong and Havelock call the second stage "literacy." It is a stage in which knowledge and culture are encoded, transmitted, and decoded in writing. It is a stage in which technologies like alphabets and printing presses with movable print type create political, economic, and social tensions, as well as changes in consciousness for oral cultures. Havelock (1973,9) has written that "simplified as much as possible, the process is one in which language managed acoustically on echo principles is met with competition from language managed visually on architectural principles."

Ong and Havelock call the third stage "secondary orality." It is a stage in which knowledge and culture are encoded, transmitted, and decoded by bits and bytes – electronic sound and electronic print. It is a stage in which technologies like computers and television create further political, economic, and social tensions, as well as further changes in consciousness for oral cultures still trying to cope with the competition between speech and writing.

Ong and Havelock argue that the three stages are recursive and dependent, rather than discrete and chronological. One stage does not cancel or replace the other. Each builds upon the previous stage, changing it gradually by adding to it by way of competition with it. And each stage alters human consciousness, Ong and Havelock tell us, by changing the way people think, know, store, and transmit information as they interiorize the new technology.

The tensions and changes in concepts of information literacy brought on by speech, then alphabets, then printing presses, word processing, desktop publishing, Fax machines, and even MTV are, as Professor Welch has put it, "analogues." "We must face," she says, "the interiorization of electronic media as Plato faced the interiorization of the alphabet" (1988a, 3, 6). Consequently, she argues, "classical rhetoric has taken on a significance that it has not had for hundreds of years. . . . Orality once again has become central; but this time the orality is electronic" (1988a, 8-9). Professor Horner agrees. "Plato actually criticized writing," she notes, "by saying that people would grow lazy and use it as a substitute for memory. In not having to train and use their memories, he warned, students would lose a very important mental ability.

His criticisms," she points out, "sound much like those levelled against calculators and computers today" (1988, 3-4).

Much of the criticism of this new interiorization surely results from human reluctance to have its consciousness altered by technologies that demand more and more that hearing dominance yield to sight dominance. As speech yields to writing, which in turn yields to print, which in turn yields to typewriter, which in turn yields to computer, which in turn yields to video, concepts of information literacy must change. Just as the effect of print technology was "diversified" and "vast" (Ong 1982, 117-18), so are the effects of electronic media. Electronic print, for example, situates words in space "more relentlessly than writing ever did" and "deepen[s] the commitment of word to *space*" causing readers to "pick up a sense of word-in-space quite different from that conveyed by writing" (Ong 1982, 135, 122). I wonder, sometimes, if those of us so relatively new to the electronic can adequately conceptualize this difference that the interiorization of the new technologies makes in our consciousness. I first felt my own conceptual inadequacy when my fourteen-year-old nephew asked me last year if I had *seen* Michael Jackson's new song yet.

I want to focus now on the fifth classical canon, delivery, or presentation, and how it can be restored and made more meaningful by reconceptualizing it in this age of word processing and her more elaborate cousin, desktop publishing.

In an important work entitled "McLuhan in the Light of Classical Rhetoric," Patrick Mahoney reported that "the very history of [*pronuntiatio*] has yet to be written," but that "classically speaking, [it] consisted of voice and gesture" (1969, 13, 12). Marshall McLuhan, Mahoney contended, "broadened" the fifth canon with his "far more complex and expansive" conception of *pronuntiatio* as *medium* (1969, 12). McLuhan has even revealed, he said, the "vital alliance between memory and [delivery]," an important contribution, since, "in part, the history of rhetoric consists in changing relationships between the five rhetorical categories" (1969, 14).[3] Professor Welch agrees with this Mahoney-McLuhan notion of *pronuntiatio* or *hypocrisis* as *medium*. "If delivery is regarded as medium," she has said, "then the dynamics of the canon are reinvested with the original power" (1988b, 8), and teachers and researchers are offered "new possibilities in contemporary rhetoric" (1988a, 6).

I contend, however, that even better possibilities are offered by regarding delivery as *presentation*. When rhetoric was oral, *pronuntiatio* involved observing and using strategies for delivery enhancement, not selecting a delivery medium. To conceptualize delivery as medium is intellectually exciting, and certainly one up from ignoring or deleting the canon, but it is not particularly useful pedagogically. That is, to think of delivery as medium works well for the *analysis* of discourse, but it is of precious little help for the *production* of discourse. From a theoretical point of view, I contend that the full original power of the classical canons is restored only if they can be used for both encoding and decoding. And from a practical point of view, as a writing teacher, I contend that I must help my students discover not merely their medium but what to do when using that medium.

Until word processing and desktop publishing, our rhetorical repertoire, our pedagogical arsenal of ways in which writers could be taught to manage and analyze language (as Havelock put it) "visually on architectural principles" has been fairly limited. At the macrorhetorical level, we have perhaps talked about using – and noticing the use of – paragraphing, margins, signposters, and thesis- and topic-sentence placement. At the microrhetorical level, we may have talked about using – and noticing the use of – certain stylistic features (repetition, parallelism, tropes, balanced-periodic-cumulative-parenthetical sentences), as well as certain mechanical features (capitalization, punctuation). I contend that it is useful for both encoding and decoding to expand this repertoire and arsenal to include the analysis and production of headers, footers, paragraph markers, inset windows, illustrations, and font/pitch/type/layout manipulations.

In short, I believe technology now makes it easy for us to teach students to notice extratextual features in others' work and to use extratextual features in their own. In effect, technology now makes it easy for us not only to allow students, but also to teach students, to "publish" their own pieces. Technology allows them to deliver or present their written work with the visual features that they believe enhance their message. As Professor Welch has noted, the illustrative excerpts in most writing textbooks "derive their authority implicitly from perfect pages. The *ethos* each shares as a validated (published) discourse resides even in the beauty of the typeface" (Welch 1987, 272). I believe rhetorical extratextuals offer the student writer access to this implicit authority, validation, and beauty, at the same time that they restore the full context, power, completeness, and connectedness of the five canons of classical rhetoric.

If we deliver "delivery" as "presentation," as format and packaging, as the written equivalent of voice and gesture, we will have "found a way to restore [what] the invention of writing and printing [had] made superfluous" (Corbett 1988, vi) to many rhetoricians. And if we use classical rhetoric in writing classes, with all five canons restored and appropriately reconceptualized as necessary, we will get good results. In several experimental writing courses, I found this approach to *pronuntiatio* to be powerful in three ways.

First, I found it to be powerful theoretically. I could effectively restore the fourth and fifth canons to the classical system, which in turn allowed me to restore the interactive possibilities of all five. One student commented, for example, that he thought using presentational devices was, in a sense, part of the canon of memory, to the extent that it provided a mnemonic dimension for readers of a written text. Another asked me in class one day if I thought it would change the way writers revised their work if they started spending more time on their "look" than on their "sound."

Second, I found it to be powerful for my students. I could effectively offer them more tools and, better yet, the same tools they can observe being used by the writers of the published, perfect, beautiful pieces in their textbooks. Students in these experimental courses came to view their written work as equivalent to – not lesser imitations of – the work they see daily in books, newspapers, and magazines.

Finally, I found it to be powerful for me. When a student said during a conference, "But look where I put that word," I knew I was going to have new clues into student intent. When others repeatedly said things like, "This is the hardest I ever worked on a paper," or, "This is the most fun I ever had writing a paper," or, "Why don't we sell advertising in our blank space," I knew I had generated new interest and enthusiasm. When one student said in class one day, "I think you should always put your thesis sentence in a highlighter box," I knew I had succeeded at explaining the importance of thesis. And when, on an end-of-term evaluation form, one student wrote, "This was the first English course that taught me things I could really use, you know, in letters and resumes and reports and stuff," I knew I had bridged that often-perceived gap between academic and "real" writing.

To many, the notion of offering student writers the power of *pronuntiatio* in this form is a mistake. Teaching rhetorical extratextuals prompts complaints (as did some of the work of the ancients) that the view relegates rhetoric to decoration. To others, however, reconceptualizing and then teaching the fifth classical canon in this form will, I hope, be viewed as one more case for the vitality of the classical system, and one more demonstration that delivery is "not a secondary consideration of language manipulation but a central and defining aspect of encoding and decoding of all kinds" (Welch 1988a, 4).

Notes

1. In a stunning new writing textbook, *Rhetoric in the Classical Tradition* (1988), Professor Horner calls students' attention to some of the important implications imbedded in the meanings of modern English cognates for these Greek names of the five canons.

2. The new Horner new text is, I believe, the first to treat delivery as presentation. In her chapter on presentation, Horner focuses on monitoring overall appearance and conforming to conventions associated with context (e.g., research papers).

3. Mahoney (1969, 14) cites Yates (1966) for treatments of the "deep interrelationship . . . between invention and memory," and Ong (1958) for memory's "subsumption" under arrangement.

References

Corbett, Edward P. J. 1988. Foreword to Winifred Bryan Horner, *Rhetoric in the Classical Tradition*. New York: St. Martin's. Pp. v-vii.

Havelock, Eric A. 1973. *The Literate Revolution and Its Cultural Consequences*. Princeton, N.J.: Princeton University Press.

Horner, Winifred Bryan. 1988. *Rhetoric in the Classical Tradition*. New York: St. Martin's.

Mahoney, Patrick. 1969. "McLuhan in the Light of Classical Rhetoric." *College Composition and Communication* 20: 12-17.

Ong, Walter J. 1982. *Orality and Literacy: The Technologizing of the Word*. New York: Methuen.

_____. 1958. *In Ramus: Method and Decay of Dialogue*. Cambridge, Mass.

Welch, Kathleen E. 1988a. "Classical Rhetoric and Contemporary Writing Pedagogy: Orality, Literacy, and the Historicizing of Composition." Manuscript of paper presented at the Conference on College Composition and Communication, St. Louis (March).

_____. 1987. "Ideology and Freshman Textbook Production: The Place of Theory in Writing Pedagogy." *College Composition and Communication* 38: 269-82.

_____. 1988b. "The Platonic Paradox: Plato's Rhetoric in Contemporary Rhetoric and Composition Studies." *Written Communication* 5: 3-21.

Yates, Frances. 1966. *The Art of Memory*. Chicago: University of Chicago Press.

Librarians, Faculty, and Students: An Integrated, Interdisciplinary Team Approach to Medical School Computer Literacy

FAITH VAN TOLL

In 1984 the Association of American Medical Colleges issued a series of twenty-seven recommendations for improving the quality of medical school education in its landmark report, *Physicians for the Twenty-first Century* (the GPEP report). A key concern of this report was the general lack of computer literacy skills among medical school graduates. The report noted that "the use of computer systems to help physicians retrieve information from the literature and analyze and correlate data about patients can be expected to grow. At present, the use of computers in medical education and patient care is limited."[1] The report then recommends that "medical schools should designate an academic unit for institutional leadership in the application of information sciences and computer technology to the general professional education of physicians and [should] promote their effective use."[2]

This same concern with the absence of a computer literacy component in the medical school curriculum had been voiced in 1982 by Matheson, Cooper, and Wilson in their publication, *Academic Information in the Academic Health Sciences Center: Roles for the Library in Information Management*. This report observes that "the continuing discovery, transmittal and utilization of information and knowledge depends on the capability of faculty, clinicians and students to tap these new systems and to exploit them effectively as memory extenders, consulting knowledge systems and decision aids."[3] The report goes on to propose the role that the library should and could play in the creation and maintenance of educational programs that deal with computer literacy. "The library should, in association with other educational programs, become a focus for ensuring the computer literacy and information handling capabilities of the academic health sciences centers, faculty, staff and students."[4]

Following the publication of these two Association of American Medical Colleges reports, medical schools, which had yet to incorporate computer skills/computer literacy elements into their curricula, began to reexamine their curricula in efforts to incorporate new modules or to revise existing programs to overcome this weakness.

Such efforts at Wayne State University's School of Medicine began in 1983 with the appointment of the Committee on Medical Computer Science Curriculum, composed of faculty and students. The major objective of this committee was the development of a broad strategic plan to integrate computer and information science skills into the medical school curriculum. The committee met several times in 1983 and again in 1985. Its report, issued in 1985, recommended that: (1) training of WSU medical students in medical computer science be accomplished by integrating this into the existing curriculum; (2) students should be given the means by which they could experience the ways in which computers are used in medicine and become comfortable in their use; (3) brief instruction in basic computer operation be provided in Years I and II; (4) Year III curriculum in medical computer science be designed in conjunction with the clinical rotations; (5) an elective consisting of instruction (lecture and lab) in specific topics of computer applications to medicine be offered to a limited number (16-32) of Year IV students; (6) each of the sixteen multidisciplinary labs and the Self-Instructional Center be equipped with a computer workstation consisting of the following: (a) IBM-XT microcomputer with 640 K RAM, 1DSDD diskette drive, one 10-megabyte fixed disk drive, one parallel printer port, one communications port, graphics, adapter, color display, 8087 coprocessor and clock/calendar; (b) IBM Prowriter printer; (c) Hayes 1200B modem; (d) mobile workstation cabinet; (e) security locking mounts; (f) a basic library of software including word processing, spreadsheet, database management, decision-maker, DOS Version 2.1. Underlying these recommendations were three basic assumptions: (1) The existing medical school curriculum would not be modified to accommodate a discrete unit on medical information science; (2) The success of a WSU medical information science program would be dependent upon the integration of the program into existing teaching modules. That is, students would have to use computer skills to complete assignments, develop specific skills, learn procedures, and so on, within existing teaching modules; (3) Emphasis would be placed on using computer technology and how this technology fits into the practice of medicine. The technology itself would not be taught. Students would be taught how computers work and what they are supposed to do with them.

These assumptions would force the utilization of an integrated, interdisciplinary team approach to computer literacy.

Acting on the recommendations in this report, the dean for curriculum affairs at the School of Medicine authorized the purchase of eighteen microcomputer workstations complete with the accompanying software, which became available for use in early 1987. At the same time, he revamped the Committee on Medical Computer Science Curriculum to become the Task Force on Computer and Information Science Curriculum for the School of Medicine. Membership was expanded to incorporate people with a greater variety of backgrounds. It was at this time that the director of Shiffman Medical Library was added to the task force as an ex-officio member. It marked the first time that a librarian had been appointed to a task force or committee in the School of Medicine. (Note: Shiffman Medical Library reports to the University Libraries, not to the School of Medicine). It also provided the opportunity for librarians to play a key part in an integrated, interdisciplinary team approach to the development of information literacies for the twenty-first century.

DEVELOPING AN INTEGRATED, INTERDISCIPLINARY APPROACH TO COMPUTER LITERACY

By the time the revamped task force began its work in the spring of 1987, it was apparent that the provision of computer workstations was only the first step in the multistep process of integrating computer and information science skills into the medical school curriculum. Definitive plans for the actual integration of skills into the curriculum had to be developed. The Task Force on Computer and Information Science Curriculum for the School of Medicine was divided into the following four subcommittees, each concerned with a particular aspect of the information science curriculum: basic information science curriculum (computer literacy), graphics and imaging, simulation and modeling, and computer-assisted instruction. Each committee was charged with developing a curriculum proposal addressing needs, educational goals, resources required, and implementation strategy.

As each subcommittee initiated its work to meet this charge, common questions and concerns began to be raised, such as: (1) Who will teach students use of the software located in the multidisciplinary labs? (2) What level of skill should be presumed? (3) Should faculty use existing commercial subject software or create their own? (4) If existing commercial software is used, can it be modified by faculty to reflect their particular subject emphasis? (5) If faculty create their own software, how can consistency in programming, format, and so on, be ensured? (6) If faculty use existing commercial software, how is such software identified, evaluated, and selected for purchase? (7) Where will software, whether created or purchased, be housed, and to whom will it be accessible? (8) How many copies of software will be purchased, and who will pay for it? (9) How many kinds of software should students be exposed to?

It was during the discussions of these generic questions that the integrated, interdisciplinary team approach to computer literacy emerged. Faculty and students worked together, as did computer experts and librarians.

At this juncture, the relevance of student and librarian participation on the task force became apparent. Students suggested that medical students who were computer experts be used to instruct freshmen in the use of word processing software, spreadsheets, and database management programs. This approach would take advantage of existing skills and free faculty to work on integrating the use of such programs into the curriculum. Students also identified student association networks that could be tapped for identification and evaluations of existing software or for input on various ways to utilize software/hardware most effectively. Students also volunteered to assist in the loading, testing, and debugging of any software obtained for the program.

Questions raised by the librarian included: (1) How will conceptual issues involved with computer use be presented in the curriculum, and who will be responsible for this segment of the curriculum? (2) Will the programs offered by the university's Computer Information and Technology Center be duplicated? (3) How can human resources be shared so available resources are fully used and unnecessary duplication is avoided? (4) What national resources, such as the National Library of Medicine, have been investigated as possible sources of support, bibliographically via interlibrary loan, through grant support, or staff expertise? Solutions offered by the librarian were: (1) Since Shiffman Medical Library had already started its development of the Computer Resource Lab, this lab could be used to house computer software for the medical information science program. The library's operating hours would provide eighty-five hours of access to the software per week. Availability of the software within the library would also eliminate the need for multiple copies of expensive items. (2) Shiffman Medical Library could purchase software as part of its collection. Software is a nonprint medium appropriate for the library's collection. Ownership by the library would prevent territoriality and/or access restrictions that could occur if departments within the School of Medicine owned the software. Ownership by the library would also result in bibliographic access and location information access via the on-line public access catalog. The library would also coordinate purchase of software so that all disciplines would be appropriately represented in the collection. (3) Librarians could provide instructional sessions to develop library computer literacy, expanding the scope of the medical information science curriculum. (4) Librarians could provide a variety of information on computer literacy, educational programs, trends, and so on, as part of a selective dissemination of information (SDI) developed especially for the task force.

DEFINING THE LIBRARY'S ROLE IN INFORMATION LITERACY

The librarian's ability to identify a variety of solutions for many of the questions and to raise additional generic questions focused attention on the coordinating role that the library and its staff could play on the task force. This coordinating role became a multifaceted one. It's four major components were: (1) developing the Computer Resource Lab; (2) establishing a library computer literacy educational package; (3) providing resource materials on all phases of computer literacy to the task force; (4) marketing the library and its services to the medical school community. To fulfill the expectations of these diverse responsibilities, the library utilized the skills of the members of the task force. Through this process, the team approach to computer literacy for the medical school was further reinforced.

Computer Resource Lab

From its inception, the Computer Resource Lab was designed to supplement the medical school curriculum in the areas of computer literacy and medical decision-making. With this tenet as a foundation, the collection development plan for the software for the lab focused on five topics: (1) tutorials; (2) patient simulation/medical decision-making; (3) database management/reprint file management; (4) authoring systems; (5) aids for searching bibliographic databases. Interpretation of these five topics is very liberal, as well as pragmatic.

The initial selection of software was simplified for the library staff by two of the student members of the task force. The students scoured the computer literature for descriptions, reviews, and evaluations of relevant software. They also contacted their colleagues in the American Medical Student Association and the American Association for Medical Systems and Informatics for their recommendations. As a result of their investigative work, a list of recommended software was prepared, complete with evaluations. After input from the other members of the task force, librarians selected the titles to be purchased as the first set of software for the lab.

It is important to note that final selection of software is the responsibility of librarians. While task force input plays a significant role in the selection process, the librarians' responsibility is never abrogated. It is the librarians who have in-depth knowledge of our collection, its scope, breadth, and depth. They are also, in effect, disinterested selectors whose primary role is to develop a balanced collection of quality materials that serves the needs of our primary clientele.

243

The ongoing selection process is initiated either by task force members (or other faculty and students) or by the librarians. When software titles of interest are identified, information about the titles is shared with all task force members. Then the viability of each recommended title is assessed by librarians in terms of potential use, content, type of application, and cost.

If it appears that a recommended title will have a limited audience, librarians will contact the faculty in several departments to ascertain the title's potential usefulness. An example of the value of this procedure can be seen in our selection of a nutrition program. Initially, at its $500 price, it did not seem to have a large enough potential use to justify purchase. However, discussions with the oncology, pharmacology, and internal medicine departments revealed that the diet therapy and/or influence of drugs on nutrition were important to all departments. The program was recommended because it can be used to determine appropriate food levels/diets for patients with a multiplicity of conditions or multiple drug therapies. The software package just described has, in fact, been ordered. The content of the recommended software must fall within the five topics of the library's software collection development plan and must not represent subjects already included in the collection. Since software ordinarily is expensive, duplication of subject content is kept to an absolute minimum.

Because one of the goals of the task force is to show students how computers can be used in medicine, the type of computer application is assessed. If the recommended software presents a new use of computers, subject content may become much less significant.

Cost plays the same decisive role in the selection of software as it does in the selection of other nonprint media. The purchase of several high-priced pieces would make it difficult to provide the scope, depth, and breadth essential for the computer literacy program. Consequently, expensive software must be more critically evaluated before its purchase is considered. The significance of an expensive program must be compared with the significance of the other programs that would not be available if the expensive program is purchased.

Concurrent with the establishment of a collection development plan and a selection process for the Computer Resource Lab was the procurement of physical space, equipment, and hardware for the lab. Because no finances had been allocated for a lab, creative decisions about space, equipment, and hardware had to be made both philosophically and practically. Philosophically, the traditional concepts and procedures of developing and designing a lab had to be set aside. Instead of waiting until a special room was provided and funds allocated, existing resources had to be used. Space previously occupied by the Technical Services Department, which had been transferred to University Libraries, was selected because it was available and had appropriate wiring for a lab. With no funds available to purchase computer workstations, the desks and tables previously used by the Technical Services Department were rearranged to create pseudo-workstations. Except for the purchase of power surge-protected outlet strips, no other changes were made in the physical space allocated to the lab. While the area functions as a computer lab, it still looks like the technical services area of an academic library.

Because Wayne State University is an IBM institution, initially it was agreed that only IBMs would be purchased for the lab. In discussions with task force members, especially the students, it became apparent that several significant software titles were available only for the Macintosh, while others were available only for the IBM/IBM clones. Consequently, the decision was made to purchase two IBMs and two Macintoshes. Since some software titles require hard-disk drive, graphics, and a color monitor, all computers for the lab are purchased with all three of these features. As with the physical space and equipment, no funding was available for computer hardware. Existing gift monies were used in a matching instructional equipment program sponsored by the university. All four computers were purchased through this matching program.

Most of the hesitancy staff has had about offering the services of a computer facility focuses on the staff's lack of computer training or experience. None of the staff have used any of the software that has been ordered. None have had any experience in loading software to a hard disk. None have had any computer training other than database searching or use of our NOTIS integrated library system. The staff was reluctant to offer service under such circumstances. As with all other aspects of the Computer Resource Lab, no funding or line position was available to employ a librarian or a paraprofessional with the appropriate experience to staff the computer facility. Once again, pragmatism and the availability of medical student computer experts provided solutions. Since library staff would be unable to provide substantive assistance with the use of the software, the medical students offered to load all software into the hard disk, creating easy-to-use menus at the same time. The library staff only have to show patrons how to turn on the computer and how to select an item from the menu. If a patron needs additional help, manuals are available for all software. No other assistance is provided by library staff. Since software is not kept in the lab and does not have to be handled by the patron, the lab is open whenever the library is open. Service is self-mediated. As new software is acquired, the medical students continue to load to hard disk and to test and debug the software for us.

Library Computer Literacy Educational Package

The involvement of the Shiffman Medical Library staff with the School of Medicine's Task Force on Computer and Information Science Curriculum provided the segue for library instructional programs on database searching. Building on the work of the task force, the librarians designed an initial program that focuses on the concepts involved in library computer literacy. The program was intentionally limited to one session lasting two to three hours, to accommodate the existing medical school curriculum and class schedule. The primary objective of the program is to introduce students to the concepts of database searching rather than to the "how-to" of database searching. Knowledge of the concepts underlying computer searching enables the patron to ask the right questions so that the best results possible will be generated in a search. Such questions are important no matter who performs the search – the patron or a trained professional.

The first step in the development of the course content was the selection of the concepts to be included in the presentation. Given a time frame of two to three hours, only overview concepts that presumed no exposure to computer searching were selected. These were clustered into four general topics. The first topic is the importance of database searching. Emphasis is placed on the growth of medical information, the time-consuming nature of the medical profession, and the efficiency of computer searching. The second topic was a description of the nature and types of databases accessed by libraries. Four types of databases – bibliographic, informational, knowledge, and locator – are defined, with examples of each type provided. The third topic focuses on the preparation that should be done to generate the optimum results from a database search. The nature of medical literature, with its reliance on journal publications, is explained. Next, guidelines for the appropriate definition of a search topic are elaborated. Key concepts of this discussion are specificity, flexibility, search expectations, time frame, critical elements of the topic, and alternative descriptions for the topic. At this point in the presentation, database demonstration of these concepts is incorporated. Definition of the search topic is followed by an introduction to database protocols. The differences between free text vocabulary and controlled vocabulary are elaborated. The logical connectors used in database searching (*and, or, not*) are described using Venn diagrams and then are illustrated via the computer. The computer mode of matching, which prevents the identification of relationships between terms, is discussed. The final topic is a comparison of the advantages of end-user searching and the advantages of trained professional searching. The objective of this comparison is to demonstrate that neither type of searcher is the best but that each offers particular skills. The circumstances of the search request will determine which kind of searcher is most appropriate.

While "Introduction to Library Computer Literacy" is the only course currently offered by Shiffman Medical Library staff, a second course on reprint file management is in development. This course, like "Introduction to Library Computer Literacy," will concentrate on concepts rather than "how-to."

Provision of Resource Materials

The role that has been the easiest for the library to assume in the School of Medicine's information literacy program has been that of provider of resource materials. Publisher blurbs, reviews, evaluations, and so on, on any and all phases of information literacy, are routinely routed to the Task Force on Computer and Information Science Curriculum. Articles on authoring systems, evaluation techniques for assessing software, and descriptions of computer literacy programs at other medical schools have been sent to task force members. Materials are routed in anticipation of task force member interests, not just in response to specific requests. As task force members have become acquainted with this library service, more requests for information are made and greater recognition of the library as an information resource develops.

Marketing of the Library

An unexpected benefit of membership on the Task Force on Computer and Information Science Curriculum has been the opportunity to market the library and its services. Since a report from the library is routinely an agenda item, the librarian member of the task force is able to publicize the library's service on a regular basis. The librarian can also answer questions about policy and procedures, accept suggestions for new, expanded, or improved services, obtain input on proposed new services, and so on. This improved visibility has simultaneously improved the image of the library and its staff.

PROGRAM ASSESSMENT AND FUTURE PLANS

As Shiffman Medical Library's computer literacy program enters its second year, there is growing evidence of its success. The "Introduction to Library Computer Literacy" course will be offered for all freshmen medical students for the third time between January and April 1989. Because this course is an elective, squeezed into already overloaded schedules, attendance will continue to be low. However, additional requests for this course have been made by faculty for their graduates and fellows. In September 1988 a mailing was sent to all department chairs announcing the availability of this course for faculty, researchers, graduates, and fellows. Ten departments have scheduled the course.

More significantly, members of the Task Force on Computer and Information Science Curriculum submitted a proposal to the dean of curriculum affairs recommending that training in medical literature searching be incorporated into the medical school curriculum. Key elements of the proposal are: (1) training in medical literature searching should be included in the formal training requirements for all medical students; (2) the minimal time required to introduce students to medical literature searching would be one four-hour, half-day session that would include an overview of search strategy, logging on and entering the search, and reviewing search results; (3) the most cost-effective manner for teaching literature searching is to use the CD-ROM available at Shiffman Medical Library; (4) the Shiffman Medical Library staff would be best suited to provide instruction for this type of literature searching.

Use of the Computer Resource Lab continues to increase. Prior to the start of this academic year, a description of all software available in the lab was prepared and included in the freshman orientation package and placed in all Year II student mailboxes. Since this material was distributed, student use has intensified. Several faculty members have become regular users of the lab and have, in turn, assigned students work in the lab.

In fiscal year 1987-88, sufficient acquisitions funds were allocated to acquire fourteen software programs. In the 1988-89 fiscal year, allocations will be increased by 10 percent by shifting funds from monographs to software. Two additional computers have been acquired through the university's instructional equipment matching funds.

The involvement of the library staff in the Task Force on Computer and Information Science Curriculum publicized the informational and instructional expertise of that staff, which has now been invited to participate in the continuing education programs of two medical school departments. One of these two programs has a national audience. Staff presented a CME (continuing medical education)-approved workshop at the Thirty-ninth American Association for Laboratory Animal Science, which was an international conference for the first time in October 1988.

The recognition that the library has earned through its participation in the School of Medicine's Task Force on Computer and Information Science Curriculum has positively affected the relationship between the School of Medicine and the library. The library and its staff are now viewed as an integral part of the school's educational program. At the start of each semester, departments contact the library to schedule classes; it is no longer necessary to launch a massive publicity campaign to entice an audience for the library programs. Because requests for additional programs have been made, library staff is developing a course on reprint file management.

The availability of the Computer Resource Lab has increased use of the library by the medical school students. Once in the library to use the lab, students discover and use other library resources. More students are repeat users of the library, and greater numbers of students frequent the library.

The success of Shiffman Medical Library's Computer Literacy Program has indeed illustrated the viability of instituting new library programs under less than optimal conditions. Simultaneously, this same success has demonstrated the importance of planning for the ongoing support of such programs with appropriate resources. The future success or failure of these programs will be determined, in large measure, by the library's long-term level of commitment to the programs. In the case of Shiffman Medical Library, a long-term commitment will address the following. First, current staffing levels do not permit the designation of one staff member on at least a half-time basis to the Computer Resource Lab. As a result, no one has acquired the expertise to adequately handle the hardware/software questions or problems that occur. As the users of the lab become more sophisticated and have greater expectations of the program, these questions and problems will become more complex and will demand even greater staff expertise. Consequently, more staff, assigned to the lab, should be added to existing staff. Staff will also need specialized training to develop and maintain expertise. Second, reliance upon student volunteer help to load software or develop user-friendly menus or other program enhancements is, at best, risky. As a student's schedule becomes increasingly demanding, the student is available less and less frequently for assistance. Software may become inaccessible to the user simply because the volunteer has been unable to find the time to work in the lab. When a volunteer student resigns or graduates, a new volunteer has to be identified and trained. Considerable time can be spent familiarizing a new student with the existing program protocols – time that could be better used in direct patron assistance. Use of a trained computer technician working for the library would be a more effective and efficient mode of operation. Third, the space currently allocated for the lab should be renovated. Since the lab occupies part of the Acquisitions Department, anyone who uses the lab has access to library offices, materials, books, phones, and so on. Patrons also impose on acquisitions staff for assistance, taking the staff away from their primary assignments. The space allocated to the lab should be physically separated from the library space. Computer workstations should be purchased, as well as file cabinets, shelving for materials, and other miscellaneous equipment and supplies. Fourth, plans for ongoing funding of the lab and its supporting programs must be developed and implemented. Development and/or grant funds should be sought for the one-time expense associated with the lab. Acquisitions allocations should include a line item for software for the lab. Additional monies should be incorporated in the personnel budget to ensure additional positions for the lab. Fifth, publicity and informational materials for and about the library's Computer Literacy Program should be prepared. The materials developed to date have been minimal and of a quality that could be improved. Marketing and graphics personnel should be employed to produce these materials. Sixth, regular communication linkages with the students, faculty, and administration will have to be maintained. These linkages will provide an input/feedback channel for the library's clientele, as well as an information channel for the library. Such a channel is particularly important in the area of computers because of the diverse sources of information about computers, equipment, and software. Seventh, an evaluation mechanism should be established that will identify when new types of equipment or software, such as interactive videodisks and players, should be acquired, or when existing equipment, software, or programs should be discontinued. The rapidity of change in both hardware and software, along with the expense of both, mandates frequent review of the appropriateness of each for a library computer lab.

SUMMARY

The urgency for change in the medical school curriculum provided the opportunity for Shiffman Medical Library to become involved in an integrated, interdisciplinary computer literacy program. Through its aggressive response to this challenge, the library staff initiated a computer literacy program that established the library's role as a significant member of the team responsible for the medical school's computer and information curriculum. To build upon this initial success and continue its reputation as a leader in computer literacy, the library should secure the appropriate resources to upgrade the program to a level of excellence.

Notes

1. Panel on the General Professional Education of the Physician and College Preparation for Medicine, *Physicians for the Twenty-first Century* (the GPEP report) (Washington, D.C.: Association of American Medical Colleges, 1984), 14.

2. Ibid.

3. Matheson, Nian W.; Cooper, John A. D.; Wilson, Marjorie P. *Academic Information in the Academic Health Sciences Center: Roles for the Library in Information Management* (Washington, D.C.: Association of American Medical Colleges, 1982), 13.

4. Ibid, 94.

Section Three

THE ROLE OF EMERGING TECHNOLOGIES IN THE NEW INFORMATION ENVIRONMENT

The gathering and sorting of information is a basic element in the management of an organization in any setting. The utilization of new technologies in the new information environment to seek out and make sense of information for the purpose of decision-making is the focus of these papers.

After demonstrating that technological developments can facilitate the handling of information, Herbert K. Achleitner and Martha Larsen Hale, in "Dissolving Certainties: Managing Information in the New Information Environment," consider the implications of these changes for the management of organizations. This theme is reiterated in Leena Siitonen's "Communication Systems for Managing the New Information Environment," which focuses upon the interactive and more intimate nature of microcomputer technology. She explains how the microcomputer has the potential of reducing formal, chain-of-command communication patterns typically found in organizations and of restoring more informal channels. Like Siitonen, Gerald P. Miller points to the more fluid communication linkages made possible by the new information technologies. As a result, he points out in "An Overview of the Impacts of Microcomputers on Organizations," administrators will face new problems and challenges in the twenty-first century. Organizational changes created by the development of local area networks (LANs) are described by Marlyn Kemper in "Managerial Strategies for Local Area Networks." Managerial changes in library administration are the focus of John Vinson Richardson, Jr.'s "The Role of Microcomputers in Library Decision-Making." The ramifications of digital networks use is detailed by Harry Mayanja Kibirige in "The Role of the Integrated Services Digital Network in Promoting Information Literacy." Anthony Debons and his coauthors in "Electronic Means for Human

Resource Research," demonstrate that the new information technologies may provide better means of gathering the data needed for decision-making. These papers suggest that technology will provide the tools for facilitating the decision-making process in the new information age.

Dissolving Certainties: Managing Information in the New Information Environment

HERBERT K. ACHLEITNER AND MARTHA LARSEN HALE

> There is no sun without shadow, and it is essential to know the night.
>
> —Camus

Is the twentieth century more chaotic than other times in history? Indeed, one can argue that it is a distraught age in which rules are breaking down under the pressure of events. The economic, political, and social certainties of the industrial age are being undermined by information and the increased application of technology. A continuing scientific revolution fueled by the exponential growth of information is disturbing the conventional view of human progress. Curiously enough, however, this age may not be much different from the medieval world, which seems to have been equally turbulent. Barbara Tuchman, in her insightful book *A Distant Mirror* (1978, xiii), refers to the fourteenth century as a time of "economic chaos, social unrest, high prices, profiteering, uncertain morals, lack of production, industrial indolence, frenetic gaiety, wild expenditure, luxury, social and religious hysteria, greed, avarice, maladministration, decay of manners."

In order for us to understand and appropriately respond to the changes taking place in today's society and the reflective shifts occurring in disciplines, it is instructive to review the concepts of paradigm and metaphor. This paper will then attempt to illustrate the shifts by culling the managerial literature.

PARADIGM

In *The Structure of Scientific Revolutions* (1970), Thomas Kuhn defines *paradigm* in a variety of ways; the term is not easily reduced to a precise definition. For the purpose of this paper, a paradigm can be best described as concepts, values, methods, and perceptions of reality held in common by a group of people (Achleitner and Hale 1988, 3). Simply stated, a paradigm is a lens through which a community views the world. For the researcher, the lens directs what will be studied (concepts), which evidence will be admissible (research methodologies), and which values will influence the interpretation of the findings.

The collapse of certainty in society is also evident in the intellectual revolution taking place in the sciences, even in the paradigms of fields such as physics or chemistry. The revolution of Einstein's theory of relativity, Max Planck's quantum theory, and Heisenberg's uncertainty principle in modern physics began the destruction of the neat Newtonian image of a machine world. Inevitability has been replaced by probability; relativism and an emphasis on uncertainty have undermined the notion of a harmonious and predictable universe. Interestingly enough, it is also the notion that information is distinct from matter and energy that undermines Newton's deterministic future (Boulding 1988, 4-6).

The collapse of deterministic science is further analyzed in an excellent work by Peter Schwartz and James Ogilvy, *The Emergent Paradigm: Changing Patterns of Thought and Belief* (1979). They document emergent patterns common among disciplines and discipline-like areas such as physics, chemistry, brain theory, ecology, evolution, mathematics, philosophy, politics, psychology, linguistics, religion, consciousness, and arts. While Kuhn focuses on scientific paradigms, Schwartz and Ogilvy present ample evidence that we are experiencing paradigm shifts not only in science but also in the humanities and social sciences. The arts have reacted to the concept of "stable form": art now captures the changing reality in its fluid form.

Linguistics has also shifted from finding meaning in a word itself to determining meaning as a result of linguistic structure (Schwartz and Ogilvy 1979, 9-10).

The shift in many disciplines from the dominant to the emergent paradigm can be summarized as follows:

1. From simple toward complex views of phenomena being investigated

2. From hierarchic toward heterarchic views of order inherent in the world being studied

3. From mechanical toward holographic metaphors used to describe the phenomena being studied

4. From a view that the unknown can be determined toward an acceptance that the future is indeterminate

5. From a linear cause/effect toward views of mutual causality

6. From a view of change as a planned assembly of events toward a sense that change is ongoing and spontaneous, that is, morphogenetic change

7. From a belief in objective research toward an acceptance of perspective research (Achleitner and Hale 1988, 5)

METAPHOR

According to one dictionary, a metaphor is a figure of speech in which one object or idea is used in place of another to suggest a likeness. As a figure of speech, a metaphor is a means that we use to communicate. By likening something less known to an image more familiar, the unknown begins to take shape. A metaphor can be used to clarify our views or thinking or to shield us from alternative views, images, or ideas.

Burrell and Morgan (1979) propose that within each paradigm multiple metaphors are used to form and communicate the paradigm. They suggest that, in fact, most of the differences evident in organization studies and sociology, for example, have been metaphor shifts, not paradigmatic shifts. The metaphor that influences how a manager acts in the practical world colors the way she understands the environment, what she perceives the organization to be, and the activities that she chooses to engage in and endorse in others. When an emerging paradigm reshapes disciplines, the metaphors certainly shift, but it is possible that the metaphors that are more concrete shift first and direct our understanding toward a new paradigm. We may want to view a metaphorical shift as a preparadigmatic cluster of images; that is, metaphorical shifts eventually bring a realization of a new paradigm.

In the old paradigm, machines were the metaphors used to create images of the universe. However, the machine metaphor is inaccurate when the concepts of complexity and heterarchy are accepted as a part of the phenomena being studied. A hologram is suggested as a more accurate metaphor for the patterns evident in the universe as we see it through the lens of the new paradigm.

THREE MANAGERIAL METAPHORS

The following section reviews three shifts within managerial literature and analyzes how each influences the view of organization and the accompanying tasks of the managers for the age of information. Many other illustrations could have been chosen to demonstrate metaphorical changes, but the following were chosen because they can be briefly explained and are familiar to many.

This paper discusses the machine metaphor with a hierarchical approach to organizational structure and managerial activities (Anthony and Dearden

255

1980). A shift begins as a greater awareness of swampy conditions in the organizational environment is seen to influence organizational and job design (Biller 1981). Finally, the metaphor of a hologram is introduced. Throughout this discussion the terms used in the previous description of the shift from the dominant to the emerging paradigm will be used to call the emerging paradigm to the reader's attention.

The mechanistic approach to management views an organization as a machine and the people in it as cogs in the wheel. The language used in this metaphor is often militaristic: chain of command, strategy and tactics, wage campaigns, gather intelligence, code of conduct, staff and line, and so on. (Weick 1978). The dominant image for this metaphor is the bureaucratic triangle. Anthony and Dearden (1980) have contributed a great deal to this image by identifying succinctly three major divisions in the hierarchical triangle: strategic, management and operational. Responsibilities, frequency of tasks, time frame, types of issues, information needs, and perspective can be drawn for each level in the organization once one accepts an organization as a triangle (see Table 1). The logic is tidy in this simple view of an organization. The inferred recipes make one feel that order is inherent in organizations, that the future can be predicted or at least determined, and that change can be planned.

Managerial activities of the former paradigm focused on PODSCORB (planning, organizing, directing, staffing, coordinating, reporting, and budgeting) (Gulick and Urwick 1937) and stressed prediction and control. The intent was to predict future conditions and control the organization's behavior in order to achieve certain objectives. The emergent paradigm rejects the notion of singular prediction and instead suggests that heterarchical structures and ever-changing events are more evident in the current environment. In the new paradigm, causal linear models in which action leads to predictable results must be replaced by multifaceted models that at best reveal trends.

The contingency theorists, dominant in the sixties and seventies, added consideration of the organization's environment to the machine metaphor. The awareness of the difference between stable and uncertain environments stems from Burns and Stalker's 1961 work (Morgan 1986) but is perhaps most dramatically described by Robert Biller. The swampy environment that he described as being realistic for most organizations is contrasted with the stable environment in which the bureaucratic hierarchy works well. For organizations that are in swampy conditions, Biller recommends emergent managerial activities. By the early seventies, there were fewer proponents of the "one best way" of managing, reminiscent of Frederick Taylor, though the new view retains the same perception of what makes up managerial work. Column 1 of Table 2 illustrates the approaches to some of the managerial activities identified with PODSCORB that would be found in the machine metaphor, and column 2 identifies Biller's suggestions for how those activities would be conducted in a swampy environment.

To the contingency theorists, an organization is not a simple triangle. An organization should adapt its structure and purpose to the environment and consider the needs of the individual workers. The order within the organization, according to those within this metaphor, is more complex, sometimes a matrix of approaches to completing tasks. The predictability of the future in this metaphor hinges on an understanding of the environment and an ability and willingness to alter the structure of the organization to match what is needed in the environment. However, change is still viewed as something that can be planned and controlled. It is this view of organizations that may have led to action research, the precursor to the qualitative, perspectival research dominant in the new paradigm.

Table 1: Bureaucratic Triangle

ANTHONY'S TRIANGLE	Primary Responsibilities	Frequency	Time Frame	Issues	Information Needed	Perspective
STRATEGIC	*objectives of the business *policies to carry out the business * role of the business in the environment *planning *change	exceptions	long range	unstructured	specific to needs	overview external
MANAGEMENT	most effective allocation of resources to accomplish objectives	cyclical	one year	more structure	summary MIS (management information systems)	operation whole internal
OPERATIONS	activities that accomplish tasks	repetitious	immediate task	precise procedural	details	task small internal

Source: Based on Anthony and Dearden, *Management Control Systems,* 1980.

Table 2: Managerial Activities in Two Environments

MANAGERIAL ACTIVITY	STABLE ENVIRONMENT	SWAMPY ENVIRONMENT
PLAN	Holistic, comprehensive, long-range, flexible, anticipatory	Particularistic, short-range; attend to the present; save resources
Planning sequence	Set goals and objectives; act/implement; evaluate	Quickly evaluate; act without consensus; react to the action; plan new goals
ORGANIZE	Permanent hierarchy; large-scale system	Temporary structure; small, less costly bureaucracy
	Sparce communication system	Redundant communication system, lots of sharing and problem solving, errors recognized early
MANAGE/EXECUTE	Deal with exceptions; delegate	"Murphy's law"
	Minimize conflict	Maximize conflict before action
CONTROL	Set standards and compare performance to them	Performance primary criterion
	Create roles and fill with qualified people	Hire personality and share responsibilities
	Future predictable from knowledge of past	Uncertainty

The appropriate model for the contingency theorists is not a triangle but a two-by-two (Figure 1), or Kast and Rosenzweig's (1973) well-known drawing that points out the interaction of subsystems rather than the singularity of the bureaucratic triangle (Figure 2).

Figure 1: Contingency Theory Model I

	Stable Environment	*Swampy Environment*
EMERGENT METAPHOR	Ineffective; wasteful	Perfect match
BUREAUCRATIC METAPHOR	Perfect match	Ineffective

Figure 2: Contingency Theory Model II

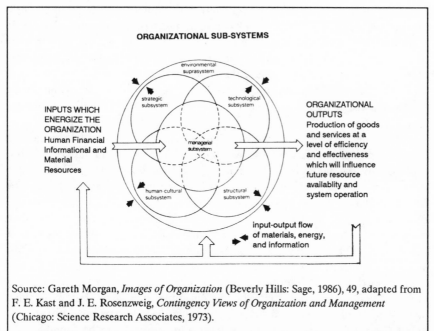

Source: Gareth Morgan, *Images of Organization* (Beverly Hills: Sage, 1986), 49, adapted from F. E. Kast and J. E. Rosenzweig, *Contingency Views of Organization and Management* (Chicago: Science Research Associates, 1973).

In the late sixties, Henry Mintzberg broke new ground by studying what managers actually do. He found that managers act as information-processing systems, receiving, disseminating, and restructuring information (Mintzberg 1972). This provided not just a variation on the PODSCORB theme but a redefinition of what managers' activities are. The third approach to management and organization has been popularized by Tom Peters in his newest book *Thriving on Chaos* (1987). Many of Peters' ideas stem from more theoretical work done by Karl Weick. Weick writes of *organizing* as a verb, not of *organizations*, the noun. The action inherent in verbs is stressed rather than the stability of a "person, place, or thing." The complexity of organizing is found not merely in the attempt to match the structure to that which best suits the environment, but in Weick's realization that the organization makes the environment and the environment makes the organization. In fact, the existence of the organization is in the eye of the beholder. The multiple views of order lead to the question of whether order is possible. The predictability of the future is in even greater doubt and leads to the discussion of whether planning is a justification of the past more than a blueprint for the future. Change is seen as being a given – a constant, unpredictable and spontaneous (Peters 1987).

The primary activity of the manager within the most recent metaphor is brokering information. More specifically, the manager must listen intently and contribute to the broad repackaging and redistribution of information. It is important that all the smaller units have as much, not as little, information as the manager. The manager uses information to envision the future amidst constant change and to distribute that vision widely. The manager must also maintain the focus of subordinates who are organizing people in the larger world, and the manager must value, measure, and reward quality, flexibility, and innovation.

The emerging view of reality is most succinctly described by the change in metaphor used to describe the new image. The machine metaphor is being replaced by the metaphor of the hologram, which appears to be a truer likeness of the organization. Holograms are created by a dynamic process of interaction and differentiation. Any portion of a hologram contains the information needed to create the whole. Holography is photography that records information of the whole in the parts. Interacting laser beams record patterns of interference waves from an object, which is recorded on a film. What is important is that a hologram can re-create the original image even when a portion of the inference pattern is lost (Morgan 1986). Schwartz and Ogilvy (1979, 14) note that the holographic metaphor has important attributes: information is distributed throughout the system; information about the whole is contained in the part and the part can be found in the whole; and everything is interconnected.

CONCLUSION

In fact, an intellectual revolution is taking place and the concept of information is playing a fundamental role in reshaping our views of reality (Wright 1988, 30). It is information in the form of know-how that has made us aware of complexity. The metaphors of use in the new paradigm are altering how we understand society, governments, science, individuals, and technology. The paradigmatic shift has opened new perspectives and new possibilities for reexamining structures, relationships and human interaction. As part of society, managers are also affected by this shift to a more complex view of reality.

The impact of the greater availability of information has shifted managerial activity. The primary activity of the manager in the information age is brokering information. Organizations in the new age must be structured to distribute information so widely that any subportion of the organization reflects the total available knowledge, like a hologram. Information must be distributed throughout the system rather than concentrated at a specific point.

An image of organizations that is gaining some popularity among organizational theorists is the view that organizations are garbage cans, organized anarchies, loosely coupled assemblages, entities that keep falling apart, or units that make themselves up as they go along (Weick 1977, 7).

Bibliography

Achleitner, H. A., and Hale, M. L. "Information Transfer: Educating Information Professionals in the Emergent Paradigm." In Rejean Savard, ed. *Proceedings of the First Joint Meeting between the Association Internationale des Ecoles de Sciences de l'Information (AIESI) and the Association for Library and Information Science (ALISE)*, Montreal, Canada, May 25-27, 1988.

Anthony, R. N. and Dearden, J. *Management Control Systems*. Homewood, Ill.: Richard D. Irwin, 1980.

Biller, Robert P. "Bedrock and Swampy Ways of Action." Unpublished manuscript, 1981, 4 pp.

Boulding, K. *Information: The Source and the Enemy of Knowledge*. Speech presented at the School of Library and Information Management, Emporia State University, Emporia, Kansas, March 28, 1988 (available from the School of Library and Information Management).

Burrell, G., and Morgan, G. *Sociological Paradigms and Organizational Analysis*. London: Heinemann Educational Books, 1979.

Gulick, L., "Notes on the Theory of Organization." In L. Gulick and L. Urwick, eds. *Papers on the Science of Administration*. New York: Institute of Public Administration, 1937.

Kast, F. E., and Rosenzweig, J. E. *Contingency Views of Organization and Management*. Chicago: Science Research Associates, 1973.

Kuhn, T. S. *The Structure of Scientific Revolutions*. 2d ed. Chicago: University of Chicago Press, 1970.

Mintzberg, H. "The Myths of MIS." *California Management Review* 15 (1972): 92-97.

Morgan, G. *Images of Organization*. Beverly Hills, Calif.: Sage, 1986.

Peters, T. J. *Thriving on Chaos: A Handbook for a Management Revolution*. New York: Knopf, 1987.

Schwartz, P., and Ogilvy, J. *The Emergent Paradigm: Changing Patterns of Thought and Belief*. Menlo Park, Calif.: SRI International, 1979 (cited with permission of the authors).

Tuchman, B. *A Distant Mirror: The Calamitous Fourteenth Century*. New York: Knopf, 1978.

Weick, K. "The Metaphors of Business." *Cornell Executive* 4, no. 2 (1978): 2-4.

_____. *On Generating Better Organizational Theories*. Minneapolis: Industrial Relations Center, 1977.

Wright, R. "Did the Universe Just Happen?" *Atlantic Monthly* 26, no. 4 (April 1988), 30.

Communication Systems for Managing the New Information Environment

LEENA SIITONEN

COMMUNICATION SYSTEMS

The current era has been called the "era of person-to-person communication." It centers, in fact, on two-way media that have been made possible by computers since 1946, when ENIAC, the first mainframe computer, was invented in Philadelphia. Thirty years later, miniaturized, low-priced microcomputers became available. The era of personal computers had begun.

A person's communication behavior has changed remarkably. A shift has occurred from mass media to the new communication technologies that require a high degree of individual involvement; a person must be actively involved in choosing the information he or she wants. Many options are at hand if a person has a modem attached to the microcomputer: for instance, searching an online bibliographic database via BRS or DIALOG, checking an airline schedule via The Source or CompuServe, or interacting with other members of a computer bulletin board. Clearly, as Everett M. Rogers reminds us, this approach requires individual activity, not a passive media audience.[1] The shift in emphasis to the role of the individual has been remarkable.

The new electronic technologies are causing an integration of formerly separate media. In France, the Minitel system combines a microcomputer function, a TV screen, and a telephone wire in order to provide an electronic telephone directory of 100,000 pages of listings. In the United States, experiments with similar devices are being made. Also, the integration of computers and communication systems in computer teleconferencing is being paralleled by the integration of media corporations such as AT&T and Warner Communications with companies that manufacture and sell computers. In other places, such as Japan, France, West Germany, and Scandinavia, similar developments are occurring.

The integration of media involves individuals at yet another level: they need to interpret to themselves and, possibly, to others the steps required in accessing and processing when using these media and the outcome of new combinations of media and communication technologies. The new media with computer-mediated systems include several different technologies: microcomputers, teleconferencing, teletext, videotext, interactive cable television, and communication satellites.

Microcomputers are stand-alone units that provide for individual use of software and for connection with other units into a network. Teleconferencing allows interactive electronic communication among three or more people in two or more separate locations. The three main types are video teleconferencing, audio teleconferencing, and computer teleconferencing.

Teletext is an interactive information service that allows individuals to request frames of information for viewing on a home television screen. A user can choose a frame using a keypad and, after decoding, can view it on a television screen. Videotext is also an interactive information service; it allows the request for frames of information to be made from a central computer for viewing on a video display screen, usually a TV screen. The capacity of the computer limits the number of frames. As online teletext, videotext requires a request channel for responses and feedback.

Via a cable, text, graphics, and video pictures can be sent to a TV set in answer to a request. Again, only the head-end computer's capacity limits the amount of content. Interactive communication is established by the cable also serving as the request channel. The responses that poll and tabulate, as well as those that accept orders for services or products, are system functions. The Qube system in Columbus, Ohio, has used interactivity for polling on a variety of issues.

For long distances, communication satellites relay telephone messages, television broadcasts, and other messages and have been effectively linked to distribute television programming to cable television systems.

Everett M. Rogers of the Annenberg School of Communications at the University of Southern California described the range of the existing communication technologies on the continuum of interactivity. Interactivity, the capability of a communication system to "talk back" to the user, is relatively low or nonexistent in the traditional mass media of newspapers, radio, film, and television, whereas the several varieties of computer communication are relatively high in their degree of interactivity, for example, computer communication via videotext, computer bulletin boards, electronic messaging systems, computer teleconferencing, and interactive cable television.[2]

PRODUCTIVITY AND CHANGES IN MANAGEMENT SYSTEMS

Although the specific nature of technology varies from one work system to another, each work system has one core technology. The core technology is what carries out the transformation process that must be performed if the work system is to survive. More complex systems may contain several additional technologies that carry out other transformation processes.[3]

In the United States, the typical approach to selecting and designing technology has been to choose the technology and to leave workers' responses and the working environment as dependent variables.[4]

The idea of communicating with computers has its roots in the fact that mainframe computer power was very expensive. Until the mid-1970s, when the microcomputer started to become popular, computers were owned and operated by the Establishment: government, big corporations, universities, and other large institutions. These mainframe computers were mainly used for data-crunching tasks such as accounting, record-keeping, research and data analysis, and airline ticketing.

When a computer communication structure was created, the mainframe computer could be shared. Several users would join a time-sharing system in which a single mainframe was so wired that it would perform more than one task simultaneously, thus sharing its time with several users. These users could communicate with large computers over telephone lines. It did not take long to realize that these telephone connections could be utilized for user-to-user communication. The potential of computers as a special means of communication had become evident.

COMPUTER NETWORKS

Networks emerged linking users and computers in such a way that users could communicate with each other and share a common collection of information, such as a database. During the 1980s, miniaturization, decreased costs, and the popularization of microcomputers led to a tremendous explosion in computer networking. Computers have now become a special medium of interactive communication. Computer networking is illustrative of the new type of human communication that is the hallmark of the information society.

At present, about one-quarter of home computer owners have a modem to connect a microcomputer via a telephone system to an information bank, for example, The Source or CompuServe, to another computer or to a network of other microcomputer users. About 20 percent of American households have a microcomputer. Individuals who have access to a microcomputer or a computer terminal can access computer-based databanks in order to obtain information rapidly and at a relatively low cost. Some databanks, such as The Source and CompuServe, are provided for use by the general public; others are aimed at specialized users such as libraries, information services, and information brokers. Computer communication has some special characteristics. However, it is not an impoverished attempt to emulate personal interaction. It has several advantages over face-to-face communication. One of these is *asynchronicity:* messages can be sent and received at any time. Computer communication suffers from its lack of a nonverbal band, which computer designers try to create via user-friendliness.[5] Users, on the other hand, are getting faster and better adjusted to the demands of computer communication in terms of accuracy, inflexibility, and nonindividuality. Recent advances in computer security have increased computer communication by individuals in spite of threats from hackers and viruses.

Computers have become the printing presses of the twentieth century. Publishing is becoming electronic for both convenience and cost reasons. Large information bases can be edited, stored, transmitted, and searched with a speed and flexibility impossible for ink records on paper.[6]

Figure 1: The Diffusion Process: An Innovation Is Communicated through Certain Channels over Time among the Members of a Social System

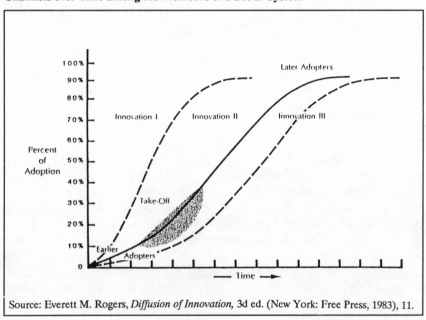

Source: Everett M. Rogers, *Diffusion of Innovation,* 3d ed. (New York: Free Press, 1983), 11.

ADOPTION AND IMPLEMENTATION OF COMMUNICATION TECHNOLOGIES

Research on adoption of new media is largely based on a contemporary application of the theory of diffusion of innovations. The interactive nature of the new communication technologies means that the value of the innovation to the adopter becomes greater with each succeeding adopter. As an extreme example, an electronic messaging system is worthless to the initial adopter until there is at least a second adopter. Further, the *degree of use* of a new communication technology becomes an important variable, in addition to whether or not adoption has occurred.[7]

The main elements of an innovation in the diffusion of new ideas are: communication through certain channels, over time, among the members of the social system (Figure 1).

An *innovation* is an idea, practice, or object perceived as new by an individual or other unit of adoption (e.g., a library). The characteristics of an innovation, as perceived by the members of a social system, determine its rate of adoption. Five attributes of innovations are: relative advantage, compatibility, complexity, reliability, and observability.

A *communication channel* is the means by which messages get from one individual to another. Mass media channels are more effective in creating knowledge of innovations, whereas interpersonal channels are more effective in forming, and changing, attitudes toward a new idea, and thus, more effective in directly influencing the decision to adopt or reject a new idea. Most individuals evaluate an innovation that they are considering adopting, not on the basis of scientific research by experts, but through the subjective evaluations of near-peers who have previously adopted the innovation. The near-peers thus serve as social models whose innovation behavior tends to be imitated by others in their system.

The *innovation decision process* is described by Rogers as a mental process in which an individual (or other decision-making unit) passes first from knowledge of an innovation to forming an attitude toward the innovation, to a decision to adopt or reject, to implementation of the new idea, and finally to confirmation of this decision (Figure 2). Five steps in this process are: (1) knowledge, (2) persuasion, (3) decision, (4) implementation, and (5) confirmation. An individual seeks information at various stages in the innovation-decision process in order to decrease uncertainty about the innovation.[8]

Rogers found that the diffusion of communication technologies differs from the spread of other innovations in at least three aspects: (1) the critical mass, (2) a relatively high degree of reinvention, and (3) the focus on implementation and use rather than just on the decision to adopt (Figure 3).

Figure 2: A Model of Stages in the Innovation-Decision Process

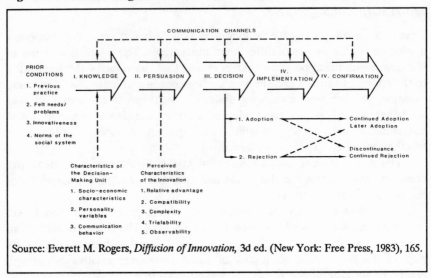

Source: Everett M. Rogers, *Diffusion of Innovation,* 3d ed. (New York: Free Press, 1983), 165.

Figure 3: The Distribution of Degree of Use of a New Communication Technology

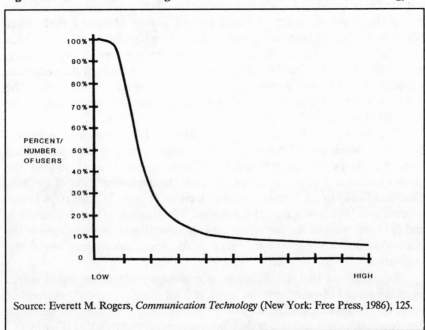

Source: Everett M. Rogers, *Communication Technology* (New York: Free Press, 1986), 125.

Also, the adopters of new communication technologies have been found to have certain definite characteristics: they tend to be highly educated, especially those who are employed in information work such as R&D, education, and the professions.[9] A higher status individual may be especially likely to adopt the new media because they are seen as status symbols. Those who adopted new communication technologies earlier than others are relatively more active information-seekers about such innovations, to the extent that they pursue such information from more expert sources and they range far afield in their travel, reading, and friendships.

Figure 4: A Model of Stages in the Innovation Process in Organizations

Stage in the Innovation Process	Main Behavior at Each Stage in the Innovation Process
I. Initiation:	All of the information gathering, conceptualizing, and planning for the adoption of an innovation, leading up to the decision to adopt.
1. Agenda-setting	General organizational problems, which may create a perceived need for an innovation, are defined; the environment is searched for innovations of potential value to the organization.
2. Matching	A problem from the organization's agenda is considered together with an innovation, and the fit between them is planned and designed.
— — — — — — — The Decision to Adopt — — — — — — — — —	
II. Implementation:	All of the events, actions, and decisions involved in putting an innovation into use.
3. Redefining/ Restructuring	(1) The innovation is modified and reinvented to fit the situation of the particular organization and its perceived problem, and (2) organizational structures directly relevant to the innovation are altered to accommodate the innovation.
4. Clarifying	The relationship between the innovation and the organization is defined more clearly as the innovation is put into full and regular use.
5. Routinizing	The innovation eventually loses its separate identity and becomes an element in the orgnaization's ongoing activities.

Source: Everett M. Rogers, *Diffusion of Innovation,* 3d ed. (New York: Free Press, 1983), 363.

Earlier adopters also differ from later adopters in certain personality variables: they have greater empathy, less dogmatism, a greater ability to deal with abstractions, and more rationality. Rogers also indicated that, perhaps, there are two other personal characteristics of adopters worth mentioning: age and sex. Children are much more receptive to the new communication technologies than adults. They are able to learn how to use them with much greater facility. Individuals past middle age, especially women, encounter great difficulties in learning to use computers and other new media.

The innovation process in organizations is usually considered successful if it leads to implementation, not just to the adoption decision per se. Recent studies of the innovation process in organizations are guided by a model of the innovation process in organizations, which is conceptualized as consisting of five stages, each characterized by a particular type of information-seeking and decision-making behavior. It is important to notice that later stages in the innovation process usually cannot be undertaken until earlier stages have been settled.

There is a logical sequence to the five stages in the process, although there are exceptions. The five stages are organized under two broad subprocesses, initiation and then, after the decision to adopt is made, implementation (Figure 4).

ADJUSTING THE WORK PLACE TO TECHNOLOGY

In the 1980s, remarked Wickham Skinner, James E. Robinson Professor of Business Administration at the Graduate School of Business Administration, Harvard University,

> Technological changes will undoubtedly affect working environments massively, powerfully, often unpredictably, often perniciously.... Nevertheless, some new forces may begin to alter the consistent historical pattern, a pattern in which technology has been an irresistible prime mover that inevitably defines working tasks and working environments. Many companies have recently begun to try to manage this process instead of simply letting it happen. For example, the need for technologies that save materials and energy is rising relative to the traditional labor-saving motive. At the same time, management assumptions, values and techniques may be shifting in the direction no longer taking for granted that the quality of working life (QWL) must be subordinated to the choice of equipment and process·[10]

Skinner listed a number of interdependent issues that are involved: "For example, what technological changes will take place? How will these changes bear on the working environment? What is the process by which technology affects the work environment? When these impacts take place, what is the result? ... The QWL depends not only on the equipment and process technologies (EPT) but on . . . the web of procedures, such as work rules and pay systems." The working environment is a function of EPTs and the network of operating policies and procedures. These must be both designed and managed so that they are internally consistent with the technologies in use, and they must also support technological processes.

Informed managers who are beginning to make the quality of working life a criterion in choosing EPTs may influence the efforts and directions of scientists and engineers who design technology by sharing a manager's experience with them. Of course, the quality of a work environment is a human perception, and Skinner emphasizes that it depends "on each worker's personal sense of what makes a good working life."

According to Skinner, the effects of an EPT take place on three levels:

- *Primary* – Direct effects on the work, worker, working environment, product, costs, investment, and basic requirements

- *Secondary* – Demands on the operating system infrastructure: wage and work force management, production planning, scheduling, and control, quality control, production organization

- *Tertiary* – Effects on the performance ability of the operating system, that is, what the system can and cannot do well[11]

The reduction of tedious, repetitive work has probably been the major fringe benefit of mechanization and automation. Numerically controlled machine tools, computers, word processing systems, direct telephone dialing, and so on, are examples of technologies that have reduced tedious and strenuous operations. Yet, none of these technological innovations, it seems safe to say, were developed primarily for the purpose of improving working environments. Nevertheless, that turned out to be a major and primary effect of these new EPTs.

There is inherent conflict between high productivity and high QWL. Both the working environment and productivity are dependent on the technical, human, and workplace infrastructure. These complex interdependencies and relationships deserve much more attention from information professionals who have chosen libraries and information services as their field. Skinner provides a long list of influences that can change the future impact of technology on the workplace:

- Scientific and engineering knowledge and skills leading to new technologies

- Sociological/ideological forces inducing new technologies

- Economic forces inducing new technologies

- New objectives for management selection of EPTs

- New criteria for management selection of EPTs

- New weighting of criteria for management selection of EPTs

- New operating policies and practices to cushion or improve the impact of existing EPTs

- Legal and governmental influences on EPT choices and operating policies and practices

- New perceptions of existing workers about what makes a good working environment

- Perceptions of new workers about what makes a good working environment

- New worker reactions to working environments they perceive as poor[12]

It is ultimately necessary to look at these critical factors identified by Skinner in the technology-work environment interface: How is the impact of technology on work managed? What motivates and influences the development of new EPTs? How are EPTs selected by management? Future changes will be a result of changes and choices made now.

Many forces are inducing the development of important new intellectual and analytical concepts that are providing useful frameworks for management to develop tools and techniques for improving the working environment. In particular, there is now a rich literature that describes how work may be "restructured" within given technology. Work restructuring generally includes changing job tasks and content, compensation schemes, the scope of workers' responsibility, social structure, status hierarchy, and procedures for vertical and horizontal mobility. How well grounded and how effective are these changes? It is now clear that many managers are making modest but increasing progress in learning how to improve working environments created by technologies that were developed or chosen without regard to the working environment. The explosion of computers and communication systems shows promise for a favorable effect on QWL. The effect is fortuitous. The main purposes of such technology are improved production and inventory controls, cost and quality controls, and information systems. But side effects are already beginning to be seen at the workplace. Workers can respond intelligently to the information they need for doing their jobs better and more easily. Classical "supervision" is superseded by an information system that answers questions and gives rapid feedback about the workers' own improvements of performance. Thus, the supervisor becomes a helper, colleague, teacher, or coach. Providing continuing education by coaching fellow workers is again in vogue.

SOME WORK RESTRUCTURING CRITERIA IN THE DESIGN OF MACHINES AND PLANT LAYOUT

The necessary knowledge for restructuring the workplace is developing very rapidly. Certainly, many years of experimentation and refinement will pass before EPT designers will be as effective at producing good working environments as they are at reducing direct labor and increasing volume and quality. But the criteria they must use have already been defined and are available:

1. Knowledge and skill will be required (not eliminated) by complexity and challenge in the task.

2. Variety will be allowed in operations performed, skills required, physical location, and working conditions.

3. Judgment and discretion will be permitted.

4. "Free space," that is, time, is created, for example, by buffer inventories between stations, permitting meetings, self-pacing, action independent of others, teaching-learning interchanges, and so on.

5. Operations will be grouped so as to allow team responsibility for an integrated task, incorporating support activity such as scheduling, maintenance, and inspection.

6. Jobs will be similar to avoid a hierarchy of jobs and to allow a pay scheme based on "what you know."

7. Interpersonal contact and communication will be facilitated by layout, noise level, and free space.

Skinner predicted that, to make the effect of changing technologies on the working environment acceptable and livable, managers will slowly begin to react to existing technologies and to whatever technologies come along with better operating policies and practices. Then they will gradually provide better working environments.

SOCIAL IMPACTS OF COMMUNICATION TECHNOLOGIES

A general principle about the social impacts of the new communication technologies can be stated as follows: "Impacts that are desirable, direct, and anticipated often go together, as do the undesirable, indirect, and unanticipated impacts."[13]

Figure 5: Social Impacts of the New Communication Technologies in Work Organizations

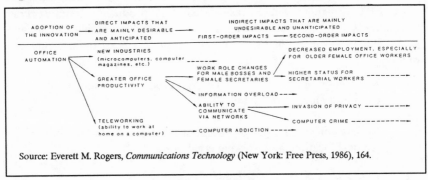

Source: Everett M. Rogers, *Communications Technology* (New York: Free Press, 1986), 164.

The special precaution to those who introduce the new media is to see beyond the desirable, direct, and anticipated impacts, and to realize that undesirable, indirect, and unanticipated impacts usually follow. Communications research can often help detect these less visible and less immediate consequences of a new communication technology. Figure 5 shows the numerous social impacts of the new communication technologies on work organizations. Computers can be used to supervise employees very closely. In contrast to such an electronic sweatshop, computers can be utilized as tools for employee independence and responsibility, allowing an individual to work with greater autonomy. Computers can have a centralizing effect on communication patterns in an organization. Usually, however, microcomputers especially have a decentralizing impact.

The one major impact of the new communication technologies, especially computing, videotaping, and photocopying, is *to make information more accessible.* The unique and the secret become more difficult to keep away. What happens to the issues of individual privacy and organizational security? What happens to information and its gatekeepers – librarians?

Notes

1. Everett M. Rogers, *Communication Technology* (New York: Free Press, 1986), 35.

2. Ibid., 33-34.

3. Rupert F. Chisholm, "Introducing Advanced Information Technology into Public Organizations," *Public Productivity Review* 11, no. 4 (Summer 1988): 39-56.

4. Wickham Skinner, "The Impact of Changing Technology and the Working Environment," in *Work in America: The Decade Ahead*, eds. C. Kerr and J. M. Roscoe, 204-30 (New York: D. Van Nostrand, 1979).

5. Rogers, *Communication Technology*, 45.

6. Ithiel De Sola Pool, *Technologies of Freedom* (Cambridge, Mass.: Harvard University Press), 190.

7. Rogers, *Communication Technology*, 116.

8. Ibid., 119-20.

9. William Dutton, et al., "Computing in the Home: A Research Paradigm," *Computers and the Social Sciences* 1 (1985): 5-18.

10. Skinner, "The Impact of Changing Technology."

11. Ibid., 209-12.

12. Ibid., 215.

13. Rogers, *Communication Technology*, 162.

An Overview of the Impacts
of Microcomputers on Organizations

GERALD P. MILLER

As John Diebold (1987, 5) stated, "The corporations which will excel in the 1980s will be those that manage information as a major resource." In their study of excellent companies, Peters and Waterman (1982) reiterated this theme by emphasizing the central role that communications and information systems play in successful corporations. Information's role is well realized, but not fully understood, by organizations, many of which have attributed their ability to maintain a competitive edge to their maintenance of a comprehensive information management system.

Some managers specifically attribute their increased productivity to the increased utilization of microcomputers (PCs). Other managers are not so optimistic and indicate the serious organizational problems that they have experienced (Chester 1987). Additionally, findings from many studies reveal mixed results (Attewell and Rule 1984). Like the organization itself, the impact of microcomputers is unique to each organization and may vary between departments. In the midst of this confusion, articles in popular computer magazines continue to lure the efficiency-driven managers with the guarantee that productivity will be increased by both installing a powerful PC, such as Compac's Deskpro 386-20, and sending inefficient workers to intensive and costly training sessions. Despite these efforts, managers still encounter unforeseen, complicated problems. The search for the all-encompassing solution or the sophisticated, predictive algorithm continues. This search is often lead by highly rational managers or newly appointed corporate information officers (CIOs) who were programmers in MIS departments. Although this scenario may be simplistic, the point is, the impact of microcomputers, as with most technology, cannot be easily rationalized or accurately predicted. The impact of any activity can be realized at various levels within an organization. The effects of an information technology are more extensive, since information applications function in many organizational settings. The influences of a multi-functional technology that is used in multiple settings are not easily identified, especially when organizations are viewed as static and rigid.

The purpose of this article is to place the impact of microcomputers within the broader context of the open systems theory. By viewing information as an integral resource in systems, information technologies, and PCs in particular, are key tools in promoting information flow. Approaching impact from this perspective more clearly exposes the fluidity of information, its technology, and the resultant behavioral effects. Because of management's persistent drive toward effectiveness, efficiency, and high profit margins, these effects are often overlooked. In other instances, management may be acutely aware of the complexity and pervasiveness of these effects, which are evident at the organizational, functional, managerial, task, and individual levels. The rational perspective that is seeking to discern causality cannot encompass the breadth of change (Argyris 1971). Therefore, examining impact from a multilevel approach demonstrates its fluidity and instability.

The article will first lay the foundation of the open systems theory and indicate the place of information and its technologies. To further frame the principal discussion, a brief sketch of the history of microcomputer use within organizations will follow. The impacts of microcomputers will then be examined from the macro (organizational) to the micro (individual) level.

DEFINITIONS AND CLARIFICATIONS

The following definitions will clarify the discussion: *Data* are conventional symbols of communication (e.g., numbers, letters, images, sounds) that, if interpreted, become functional for the user. The interpretation, to which data is subjected, is based upon the user' values and purposes. *Information* is any data that have been interpreted, processed, and/or transformed by the user into a meaningful form. A *resource* is a reserve source of supply or support that may be utilized when needed. *Information resources* are any communication media (e.g., telecommunications, documents, images, voice and audio reproductions), as well as other organizations (e.g., information brokers, legislative bodies, public service organizations) from which data are gathered. The information resources of a specific organization may include any of the following processes: telecommunications, computer systems, voice and image processing, mail room functions, electronic and paper file maintenance, library services, document storage and retrieval, microform processing, and interpersonal communication. An *information processing system* includes both the personnel and technology that transform the data into usable information. The basic functions of any system would include the storage, retrieval, and dissemination of information. An *organization* is understood to be "a coalition of shifting interest groups that develop goals by negotiation; the structure of the coalition, its activities, and its outcomes are strongly influenced by environmental factors" (Scott 1981, 45). Since this discussion focuses on an organization as an open system, the terms *organization* and *system* are often used interchangeably.

Systems Theory

An organization as an open, natural system depends upon its external and internal environment for continual flow of energic input from sources such as personnel, raw materials, working capital, and/or information (Katz and Kahn 1978; Thompson 1967; and Scott 1981). Without this continual input, the cyclical nature of an organization entropies and eventually ceases to function. An open system is greatly concerned with maintaining its own energic cycle and its relationships with other systems that are both internal and external to the organization. To sustain negentropy, the organization strives to maintain both its intra- and interrelationships.

The intrarelationships of an open system are found among its subsystems, whereas its interrelationships are derived from those external sources that form its suprasystem. The internal sources emanate from the subsystems, or intrarelationships, of the organization. Internal sources monitor the organization's utilization of energic input and provide the feedback necessary for further adaptation. External sources indicate both the receptivity of the environment to the organization's output and the social effects of the organization upon the suprasystem and its pressures.

Each organization, as a unique system, maintains a distinct purpose, or domain (Thompson 1967); therefore, an organization cannot be completely open. Each organization chooses those external sources, and maintains those interrelationships, that it perceives as necessary for its survival. An organization whose industry experiences extreme fluctuations and whose external environment is highly uncertain must respond rapidly to change in order to counteract entropy. To accommodate these fluctuations, the dynamic system may respond by adjusting its distinct purpose, or domain, and by increasing the comprehensiveness and complexity of its structure and design. As a result of this adaptation, the organization's subsystems incorporate the energic input from the environment to maximize the acceptance of its output. Subsystem adaptation also increases an organization's complexity, causing further differentiation and specialization. Subsequent internal changes demand that an organization's internal functions be adapted to monitor throughput processes (i.e., production techniques). By furnishing information to the external environment, the organization can more accurately respond to the adjusted output. This information will maintain the environment's receptivity to the output (i.e., sales) and assure continued energic input (i.e., working capital) to sustain the system.

In the midst of rapid change and uncertainty, the organization must integrate and coordinate its internal processes. Through these efforts, the values of the organization are communicated. This articulation often takes the form of various control mechanisms that address the core problem of an organization: the reduction of the variability and instability of human actions to patterns of uniformity and dependability (Katz and Kahn 1978). In other words, "the ultimate goals of an organization [are achieved by circumscribing] idiosyncratic behaviors and [keeping] them conformant with the rational plan of the organization" (Tannenbaum 1962, 236-37). In an uncertain environment that causes functional differentiation and role modifications, stabilization of behavior is effectively achieved through increased coordination and control of the system's processes. Consistent behavior also affects the quality of output and the eventual energic input that reenters the system. Throughout this uncertain environment, the organization as an open system is concerned with viability in the society. Its characteristics are communicated to all its constituents in both its internal and its external environments (i.e., personnel, customers, suppliers). This outreach maintains interest in the system's output. When the organization maintains a stable image, sources of additional resources (i.e., raw materials, capital) may be acquired, and assurance may thus be projected to skeptics.

Information in an Open System

The organization as an open system is sustained by core energic resources. Information, as one such resource, is drawn from both internal and external sources. The internal sources of information are integrated throughout the structure of the organization, helping to sustain its internal processes. The external sources of information from the environment form the boundaries of the organization and, therefore, delineate its outermost limits. As an open, living, and natural system, an organization assimilates external sources of information, thus assuring further energic input.

As a source of control, information maintains the proper utilization of other resources, generating a maximum amount of energic output from a minimal amount of energic input. To maintain a profitable ratio and to reduce slack, information sources can also reduce the behavioral instability of personnel resources by various means, including the encouragement of participative decision-making processes. Such participation not only increases commitment but also reduces behavioral variations. The sharing of information relative to the organization's operations and to the communication of the acceptable values and norms of the organization assures a steady flow of energic output. Therefore, for an organization functioning as an open system, information serves as a resource of energy, a source of control, a stabilizer, and a boundary marker.

When administrators view organizations from the open systems perspective, they can appreciate information and its management as a resource of energic input (Meltzer 1981). If information is valued, and if its significance is understood and accepted, its usefulness is reflected in adequate levels of funding, personnel, and technological applications. Only those organizations whose environment and industry are stable need not emphasize the information function. In highly volatile organizations that have adopted the open systems perspective but have not allowed information to assume its rightful role within the system, feedback might not be received, information's boundaries might not be accurately defined, other resources might not be effectively controlled, and the organization, as an open system, might not survive.

During this century, when financial, material, and personnel resources have been threatened, a comprehensive management system has been implemented to more effectively utilize the newly valued resource (Beniger 1986). Various commentators, such as Donohue (1985) and Horton (1982), indicate that a strategic management perspective must be instituted to fully exploit the benefits of information. Particularly for those organizations that experience considerable uncertainty, internal and external information sources must be maintained. External input must be quickly assimilated, opportunities evaluated, and effective decisions made and communicated via internal information sources. To respond to rapid change and uncertainty, an organization must establish a comprehensive information management system. Depending upon the extensiveness of the organization's boundaries, a thorough telecommunications system can quickly channel the incoming energies into the system. An extensive local area network (LAN) of microcomputers and internal communication channels facilitates integral monitoring and decision-making functions.

A decentralized database and an expert system promote analysis and synthesis of disparate information sources from various corporate sectors. Since all information sources bear energic input for the system, a comprehensive information management system channels this energy to its appropriate receptor. The extensiveness of this management system is dependent upon the degree of environmental uncertainty that is experienced by the organization (Morgan 1986). Regardless of the comprehensiveness of the information system, each function must be equally equipped to ensure an even transfer of information throughout the organization. In addition to these recent innovations in electronic information technology, an extensive information management system also includes the more conventional techniques of information transfer (e.g., communication skills, mail room operations, document storage, and publishing).

Technological Trends

Computers were first utilized in corporations to manipulate data. As both hardware and software developed, computer applications became more varied. Since information and its technologies were not integrated into the overall purposes of organizations, managers were not able to harness the benefits of information resources. When managers experienced both failures and successes in conjunction with information technologies, and with PCs specifically, they attempted to develop a comprehensive approach to harness this technological power.

Information technologies include a broad variety of interconnected devices and skills that access, analyze, disseminate, and store information. The data may be graphic, textual, video, bit-mapped, audio, and/or numeric; it may be printed, microformed, magnetically recorded, and/or digitized; and it may be stored on optical or magnetic disks, on reels, and within binders or files. Today's powerful PCs can manipulate highly compressed data, such as color graphics that require upwards of 500,000 bytes per image.

Microcomputer power continues to grow at staggering rates. In 1981, IBM's original PC ran at 4.77 million cycles per second and stored data on floppy disks that accommodated 160,000 bytes. Currently, the most powerful microcomputer runs at 25 million cycles per second and stores 300 million bytes on its optical disk. Corporations are the largest buyers of these powerful tools. Although accurate estimates are nearly impossible to obtain, *Datamation* estimated in 1985 that approximately 300,000 PCs had been purchased by the top 100 buyers of PCs among the Fortune 500 companies (Rubin 1985). Another estimate indicated that 3.3 million PCs were shipped in 1986 to all segments of the market of which corporations commanded the largest share. IBM still dominates the market, although its market share has slipped in the past few years. It controls the corporate segment of the microcomputer market because of the volume of its mainframe installations. Corporate allegiance to IBM is attributed not only to sales but also to the maintenance of systems, compatibility of its products, and the ease of dealing with a single vendor. Although various technological gurus dispute these reasons, IBM's market dominance gives executives a sense of stability and assurance. Aware of its advantage, IBM nurtures its corporate accounts by promising that total integration, compatibility, and connectivity will be achieved in the near future (Cummings 1987).

Computers were first utilized in financial and accounting departments, where their power was applied to the massaging of large data sets. Inventory, sales, manufacturing, and ordering applications soon followed during the

1970s. As applications became more diverse, the need for corporatewide integration increased. Management established MIS (Management of Information Systems) departments to regulate hardware, software, and databases – the entirety of corporate data processing. During the same period, software designers began to manipulate words and texts as they had numeric data. After the introduction of word processing, computerization began to permeate office functions with the processing of mass mailings, schedules, and other corporate communications (Murljacic 1987).

With the introduction of PCs, MIS directors moved many costly functions off the mainframe. Vendors hastily developed software to meet the growing numbers of corporate PC users. Software applications became easier to learn and apply to specific needs. In some instances, this change was unknown to MIS managers. Although they were aware of the advantages of microcomputers, they were fearful of losing control over their technological progress and, therefore, hesitated in approving the installation of stand-alone PCs.

As information technology applications increased, costs grew. In the midst of a fluctuating economy, executives were faced with these rising costs and demanded hard justifications from their MIS managers. Depending upon the corporate posture regarding information technology in general, and PCs in particular, executives pressed MIS departments to evaluate the benefits of their PC installations. Managers began to assess PC benefits, which included:

- Low cost

- Increased individual and departmental efficiency

- Consolidation of data from various databases

- Increased internal communications

- User-generated applications

- Broadening of corporate capabilities

- Better quality of corporate data

- Productivity gains

- Freedom for personnel to confront more complex issues

- Enhancement of services to specific customers

- Better utilization of data in multiple formats

The disadvantages included:

- Difficulty in maintaining data standards

- Increased threat to data security

- Poor service contracts

- Inconsistent program logic

- Costly software licensing fees

- Poor training manuals and in-service sessions

- Unqualified local support staff

- Lack of vendor support

- Poor installation

- Inadequate warranties

- Short-term dependability of vendors

- Inability to address unique needs

- Inaccessibility of data

- Poor compatibility with existing technology

In fact, a study of seventeen large U.S. corporations found that eleven companies had experienced considerable difficulties with their PCs (Cougar 1986). Another study of 526 companies revealed that 70 percent had serious problems (Chester 1987). By implementing a corporate policy for microcomputer acquisition, they might have achieved their goal of increased productivity through the introduction of PCs. A study of 319 companies revealed that 72 percent had not devised such a policy (Bryant 1985).

Information technology is intended to promote productivity. Although the present focus is on PCs, knowledgeable managers whose goal is the exploitation of corporate resources must understand the benefits of any viable technology. The organization that adopts either a strategy of adherence to dated technology or one of excessive permissiveness is an organization that is not effectively managing information. Traditionally, the corporate posture regarding PC utilization has been based upon: (1) a tight control over their acquisition, or (2) a moderate approach, whereby a specific department justified the need and was then free to select the appropriate products from an approved list, or (3) a policy of noninterference, under which management encouraged departments to devise applications and select packages that could best achieve their specific needs. Ideally, a philosophy of integration and coordination must temper technological adaptation and, specifically, PC acquisition. As an outgrowth of a corporation's approach to information and its technology, a policy (1) coordinates information technology, (2) provides a comprehensive set of data processing requirements, (3) establishes standards of compatibility, and (4) stresses accountability that is beneficial for cost-benefit purposes (Keen and Woodman 1984). Guidelines not only must indicate the hardware and software parameters, but also must designate the lines of responsibility for the successful utilization of information as a corporate asset. A strategic approach includes:

1. the appointment of a CIO and staff that integrate information with corporate goals;

2. the development of long- and short-term strategies that would permit the corporation to harness information in order to maintain (or obtain) a competitive advantage;

3. the establishment of an effective procedure to evaluate the benefits of specific information processing functions; and

4. the formulation of an effective participatory framework that encourages user interaction.

Traditionally, managers have viewed information and its technologies as part of operating procedures. The successful corporation knows the strategic importance of information and maintains fluid lines of internal and external communications to monitor both the constant fluctuations in the industry and its own corporate response to these shifts (Hussain and Hussain 1988). Having established such limits, the successful company analyzes the increasing amount of data in an effort to maximize its position in the market and to further develop its lines of communication (Urkowitz 1987). This connectivity and analytical ability is greatly enhanced throughout carefully designed technological architecture that establishes standards for the various information functions that occur within the company. Although these procedures may be centrally coordinated, the responsibility for their effective functioning is equally distributed. The key to coordination lies in the ability of these functions to interact with one another for an integral flow of corporate information. As end-user computing continues to flourish, the success of this strategy lies in the interdepartmental functionality of user-generated applications. If each department develops its own application with the use of fourth-generation languages, individual effectiveness is often achieved. But if these functions are not interrelated, and if their databanks and reports cannot interact with other applications, the company cannot capitalize on the volume of information that it is generating. Successful businesses do not overlook the central role that information and interconnected PCs have in the maintenance of their competitive advantage (Wiseman 1988). On the other hand, those businesses that underestimate the strategic significance of information and connectivity will often find themselves missing the mark and eventually losing out in the marketplace (Porter and Millar 1985; and McFarlan 1984).

IMPACTS ON ORGANIZATIONAL BEHAVIOR

Microcomputers are tools that, if effectively managed, may assist the company in achieving a competitive advantage. At one level, analysts show that applications may generate an ROI of 6:1 (Cougar 1986). More pervasive changes occur at less tangible levels. Information technology is not only transforming an organization's functions but, more importantly, its design and the behavior of its constituents (Zuboff 1988).

In an effort to seize the potential of PCs, researchers have attempted to evaluate computer impacts. At first glance, one might deduce that the innate power of computers is capable of changing an organization—a concept that resurrects the false assumptions of technological determinism (Davis and Taylor 1976). Organizational psychologists emphasize that changes are the result of the interaction of systems with existing organizational factors, such as job design, hierarchy, structure, culture, and so on. Various studies have revealed some broad areas in which changes are likely to occur.

Impacts may be observed at the *managerial* level. Managers who are very familiar with departmental operations indicated that their interaction with staff decreased as system users increased. Executives, on the other hand, expressed a greater need to consult with staff to better comprehend the advantages of computer systems. Ideally, such organizations will find a common ground with respect to the level of participation of their managers. It is important to note that systems do not impose a common style of leadership. Rather, managers incorporate systems into their own, unique leadership styles. Therefore, changes are more likely to be evident on a broader basis, depending upon the size of the organization, rather than focused on a small segment or unit (Bjorn-Anderson, et al. 1986).

If the majority of personnel have access to workstations, they will have equal access to the information. By raising the quality of information, the entire company benefits. If workstations are *not* equally distributed, users could perceive that their access to information is in direct proportion to their level of power and influence in the organization or, even if these users may not have legitimate authority, they could perceive and in actuality obtain a greater amount of control. If system access is equally distributed, this level of power could be viewed as a reflection of the individual's role in the functioning of the entire information system. Those who coordinate the system could also gain greater power and influence. The possibility of power shifts and the creation of the gatekeeper role are very interesting phenomena of the information revolution (Bjorn-Anderson 1986).

Organizational impacts may also be examined from a functional perspective (Markus 1984). Systems may effect different organizational changes, depending upon the application. According to Markus, applications may be grouped into five major categories: (1) operational, (2) monitoring and control, (3) planning and decision-making, (4) communication, and (5) interorganizational. These five areas are significant because they provide a comprehensive framework in which to study the many organizational features of the growing number of computer-based systems. In addition, an increased awareness of these impacts is beneficial for managers and system designers. Some impacts, in fact, may be planned in conjunction with system development.

Operational applications coordinate data, structure procedures, and promote more effective use of resources. Examples would be word processing and data entry. The drive toward efficiency may shift responsibilities and modify job structure and design. Computerization may create the need for greater specialization. This shift will further affect the movement of functions within a department or unit, which will cause additional changes in informal relationships. These organizational characteristics may increase or decrease the value of specific roles and jobs. As jobs are restructured, the habits and customs of the work unit will be affected.

Monitoring and *control* applications measure productivity and efficiency. Examples might be quality control and/or time management systems. Systems must accurately monitor those responsibilities that have been assigned to employees. Considerable gaming and resentment often arise when systems improperly gauge a laborer's performance (Goleman 1988). These negative aspects may be overcome by permitting personnel to participate in establishing realistic standards, measures, and related feedback mechanisms. Employee input may also influence better acceptance of control applications. This type of system may also impact job structure and social interaction, as well as change both individual and collective autonomy and control.

An example of an operational and monitoring application that had a considerable organizational impact was a relatively simple database product utilized by a small school district. The district implemented this system to better monitor student registrations and attendance patterns. As the attendance clerk's responsibility for accurate data entry increased, so did her influence and power over this information. This task removed her from the congenial office atmosphere and modified her job design, which included the role of pressing instructors for their grade books and attendance rosters. She reprimanded delinquent teachers for inaccurate and inconsistent attendance records because these were used by administrators to justify the level of state support. Delinquent students, many of whom were welfare recipients, were reprimanded not only by school authorities but also by social service agents who would discontinue financial support. This seemingly small system had profound repercussions on job design, social interaction, autonomy, performance, organizational culture, and power distribution.

Planning and *decision* applications are used by corporate analysts to evaluate data and the benefits of possible options. Decision support systems are good examples. Fourth-generation language applications increase management's ability to frame data within new parameters and to discover possible strategies and opportunities for increased productivity. In addition to the obvious impacts that possible differentiation has on jobs, these systems may decentralize decision-making and spread it horizontally within the organization. Such movement can cause power shifts and intersperse gatekeepers throughout a company. Depending upon management's reaction, considerable corporate politicking may result.

Communication applications, such as electronic mail, can change the information patterns of organizations and expand information boundaries (Culnan and Markus 1987). Among the organizational impacts, remote work locations have received considerable attention (Olson 1982). Social scientists suggest, though, that alternative job settings may isolate the worker not only from the social context that an organization furnishes, but also from the benefits that employees receive through serendipitous interchange.

The expansion of boundaries has brought the concept of organization as open system into greater focus. Businesses can observe corporatewide production, monitor market conditions and resource allocation, and quickly respond to consumer needs, regardless of their location. More aggressive companies whose expanded product lines reflect their close attention to fluctuating conditions exploit numerous opportunities. The benefits of increased contact with external information sources give larger businesses a competitive edge that smaller, less diversified companies find difficult to achieve.

Corporate directors may utilize *interorganizational* applications to form more dynamic links with the external environment. Because increased productivity and maintenance of one's competitive advantage is the driving force behind corporate growth, these applications impact the broader economic and industrywide factors. The heightened corporate dependence upon information has been cited as one factor that may have caused the blurring of industries and the rise of large multinational businesses. This broadened organizational base has also increased the interdependence of many businesses. For example, a hospital supply company's decision to install terminals at the sites of its major accounts resulted in both the staff's placement of large orders with a single vendor and the supplier's increased ability to react to customer demands.

In addition to Markus's functional perspective, impacts may also be examined at the *human interface* and *social interaction* levels. Most software developers are not sensitive to cognitive issues, yet the human-computer interface is the very level at which users interact with the systems. When applications fail to consider a user's mental abilities, system effectiveness is severely limited. Many displays are cluttered, illogical, and too slow for most users. Methodologies for increasing interaction are aggressively being developed and tested. These provide engineers with tools with which to design successful systems and increase the potential of this technology.

Impacts result from *hardware* and *spatial* designs. System designers often dismiss behavioral changes as luxurious fringes. Organizational and cognitive psychologists realize the significance of these factors upon performance. Although managers may often assume that PCs can simply be placed at the same setting that was once occupied by the electric typewriter, improper placement will cause body fatigue, which, in turn, negatively influences attention and performance. An individual's stress at a workstation may be caused by:

1.   *Screen glare* – poor hardware design, reflective surfaces, and improper lighting

2.   *Workstation design* – stationary tabletops and inadequate space to accommodate additional hardware

3.   *Keyboard layout* – improper location of function keys and the outmoded nature of the "qwerty" keyboard

4.   *Conventional chairs* – lack of adjustable back, leg, and arm supports

5.   *Lighting* – overhead lighting affects perception of screen displays and user ability to read original copy

Solving some of these issues is the responsibility of hardware engineers, but many may be easily rectified by minor structural changes and equipment purchases.

As with technology in general, a PC application will be used by individuals who perceive it as offering some assistance to fit their tasks. User-generated applications often meet this criterion. Older systems were not designed from the user's perspective. Ease of use is another factor that influences acceptance of technology. If users perceive *and* experience the system as being beneficial to the task and complementary to their behavior, the technology may be more readily adopted. User support is a related factor that greatly influences adoption. Manuals written by highly trained engineers usually do not incorporate the many principles from cognitive psychology and often offer very little guidance. Some vendors are attempting to alleviate this problem by hiring writers who are trained in educational psychology. Since some studies have indicated that users prefer personal support, large organizations are encouraging the MIS staff to become involved with end-users to better understand their problems and to more accurately respond to their needs. Smaller organizations often may find the desired level of support via the vendor's toll-free phone number. As applications become less complicated and more responsive to user needs, workers have indicated that the task complexity and uncertainty have decreased. Furthermore, managers are free to analyze corporate issues at a broader and more complex level (Bjorn-Anderson 1986).

Impacts upon *social interaction* also reveal the inappropriateness of office architecture in which workstations are incorporated. The design of most offices still reflects the traditional conception of individual, permanent work areas. Offices should reflect the associative nature of the many jobs that require settings for group interaction. This is not to discredit the importance of an individual's psychological space, but rather to stress the importance of decreasing the size of many separate offices and utilizing the space for group interaction.

At the *psychological level*, impacts are more intangible, but highly influential. As indicated, microcomputer applications routinize many labor-intensive tasks. When more external information is incorporated into the organization, administrators challenge employees to broaden their perspectives in order to accommodate new input and to address the subtle implications of their tasks. When system designers utilize sophisticated communication applications to join disparate corporate sectors, employees' interactions become more transparent, both to fellow workers and to authority figures. By utilizing effective monitoring systems, data regarding workers' productivity is dispersed throughout the organization to key decision-makers. By incorporating multifunctional information technologies into an organization, management demands that employees adopt new intellectual abilities. Supervisors evaluate employees not only on their output levels but also on their ability to synthesize, analyze, and creatively respond to complex information.

Employee response to these new pressures and expectations are inevitably mixed. Some employees readily embrace the challenges; others fearfully resist them. As workers are released from menial tasks and given greater challenges, their perception of self-worth and personal satisfaction varies considerably (Zuboff 1988). While some workers feel greater personal fulfillment, others agonize under the pain of failure.

The adapters make the adjustment and find themselves with a new level of expertise and authority in relationship to their task. Because they now share the knowledge and ability that was previously restricted to managers, adapters may threaten existing authority structures (Zuboff 1988). They may also place greater demands on labor unions to negotiate increased compensations for their new responsibilities. Adapters wield a newfound power.

Resisters attempt to reskill but feel frustrated and incapable of understanding the complexity of the highly praised electronic technology. The underskilled quickly conclude that they lack the intellectual qualifications to succeed in their redesigned jobs. They feel displaced, abandoned, and angry. They perceive the organization's leaders as reneging on the long-held assumptions and competencies on which they based their livelihood and identity. The underskilled grasp at the promises in negotiated settlements that abate any possible layoff. Resisters cower under the vast potential of information technology.

Administrators must respond to both extremes and to the intervening continuum. Corporate leaders must redesign the system to sustain higher skilled employees, but they may not be capable of adequately addressing the complex problems of underskilled employees. Continuing education programs may be part of the corporate response to these employees, but the needs of the underskilled are not fully met by short-term methods. Social agencies must therefore address the inevitably growing number of displaced workers.

Information technology, and the PC in particular, has the capability of influencing corporate functions at many levels. Administrators can harness this potential to promote efficiency and effectiveness, to achieve a competitive advantage, and ultimately, to survive in the marketplace. Management can strategically position microcomputers to either focus corporate systems and the company's throughput functions or to fracture the organization into competing segments of turf protectors pursuing personal advancement. It can utilize technology positively by focusing on the life of the corporation and its constituents, or negatively by strengthening its own power at the expense of the corporation and its resources. An organization as an open system relies on its interrelationships to survive. Core technologies can strengthen or weaken these linkages.

CONCLUSION

Like any organism, organizations survive by adapting their internal processes to external environmental forces. Information and its technologies play a central role in this ongoing process. Information facilitates an organization's selection of inputs, throughput methodologies, and output strategies. Information also serves as a gauge in monitoring both the external environment's receptiveness to an organization's products and the extent of adaptation required to maintain its competitive advantage. Similarly, information and its technologies function as the organization's nervous system in stimulating ongoing adaptation.

Organizations utilize microcomputers to facilitate constant modification and adaptation. This increasingly powerful technology promotes greater efficiency and effectiveness if properly designed for the organization and its constituents. To achieve this goal, system designers and managers must be aware of microcomputers' numerous impacts on internal structures, organizational boundaries, tasks, and individual and collective behavior.

By approaching impact analysis at the functional level, administrators may more readily identify potential problems and unforeseen changes. Since computerization, specifically the microcomputer, affects tasks, workers must be reskilled, and their jobs, their work setting, and the organization must be redesigned. The reskilling must occur at the intellectual level, since workers now synthesize vast amounts of previously unconnected data. If reskilling and redesigning do not occur at the individual level, microcomputer technology will leave workers as mere morlocks of electronic devices. Because this reskilling and redesigning will cause fundamental changes at the managerial level, it will also affect authority structures. If modifications are not made here, the promised technological efficiency will not be realized, information's potential will not be utilized, and the organization will not survive.

Ultimately, impacts are a result of managerial planning and design. Administrators make decisions that reflect their values and assumptions relative to the organization. Open systems theory positions information technologies as important resources that sustain organizational linkages. From this perspective, decision-makers implement microcomputers with an understanding of their relational importance on the total organization. From this perspective, managers must view microcomputers as tools for organizational survival.

Effective organizations look beyond microcomputers' increasing abilities to the potentially pervasive changes that may transpire. Adaptive organizations install machines and encourage commitment, motivation, and enthusiasm in the work force. John Diebold may have been more accurate if he had said, "The corporations which will *survive* in the 1980s will be those that manage information as a major resource."

Bibliography

Argyris, Chris (1971). "Management Information Systems: The Challenge to Rationality and Emotionality." *Management Science* 17, no. 6: b275-b292.

Attewell, Paul, and James Rule (1984). "Computing and Organizations: What We Know and What We Don't Know." *Communications of the ACM* 27: 1184-92.

Beniger, James R. (1986). *The Control Revolution: Technological and Economic Origins of the Information Society*. Cambridge, Mass.: Harvard University Press.

Bjorn-Anderson, Neils, Ken Eason, and Daniel Robey (1986). *Managing Computer Impact: An International Study of Management and Organizations*. Norwood, N.J.: Ablex Publishing Corporation.

Boulding, Kenneth E. (1956). "General Systems Theory: The Skeleton of Science." *Management Science* 2: 197-208.

Bryant, Susan (1986). "Are Corporate PCs Earning Their Keep?" *PC World* 4, no. 8: 173-79.

Bryant, Susan Foster (1985). "Corporate Micro Users Speak out." *Computer Decisions* 17, no. 30: 30, 34.

Bugg, Phillip W. (1986). *Microcomputers in the Corporate Environment*. Englewood Cliffs, N.J.: Prentice-Hall.

Cartwright, D. (1965). "Influence, Leadership, and Control." In *Handbook of Organizations*, ed. J. March, 1-47. Chicago: Rand-McNally.

Chester, Jeffrey A. (1987). "IBM and OS/2 Take on the Clones." *Infosystems* 34, no. 8: 34-36.

Clemons, Eric K., and E. Warren McFarlan (1986). "Telecom: Hook up or Lose out." *Harvard Business Review* 64, no. 4: 91-97.

Cougar, J. Daniel (1986). "E Pluribus Computum." *Harvard Business Review* 64, no. 5: 87-91.

Culnan, Mary J., and M. Lyyne Markus (1987). "Information Technologies." In *Handbook of Organizational Communication: An Interdisciplinary Perspective*, eds. Frederic Jablin, et al., 420-43. Newbury Park, Calif.: Sage.

Cummings, Steve (1987). "Buying IBM: The Mainframe Is the Message." *PC World* 5, no. 8: 186-91.

Davis, L. E., and J. C. Taylor (1976). "Technology, Organization, and Job Structure." In *Handbook of Work, Organization, and Society*, ed. R. Dubin, 379-90 Chicago: Rand-McNally.

Diebold, John (1987). "Competing from Strength." *Infosystems* 34, no. 9: 26-27.

Donohue, Joseph C. (1985). "Information Resources Management: Passing Fad or New Paradigm." *Information Management Review* 1: 67-77.

Ein-Dor, Phillip, and Carl R. Jones (1985). *Information Systems Management: Analytical Tools and Techniques*. New York: Elsevier.

Er, M. C. (1987). "The Impact of Information Technology on Organizations." *Journal of Systems Management* 38, no. 4: 32-36.

Fleischer, Mitchell, and Jonathan A. Morell (1985). "The Organizational and Managerial Consequences of Computer Technology." *Computers in Human Behavior* 1: 83-93.

Forester, Tom (1987). *High-Tech Society*. Cambridge, Mass.: MIT Press.

Foster, Lawrence W., and David M. Flynn (1984). "Management Information Technology: Its Effects on Organizational Form and Function." *MIS Quarterly* 8, no. 4: 229-35.

Freedman, Beth, and Jim Forbes (1987). "Increasingly, Corporate Users Acquire a Taste for Macintosh." *PC Week* 4, no. 33: 1, 6.

Freedman, David H. (1987). "Pushing Computers out the Door." *Infosystems* 34, no. 3: 30-32.

Galbraith, Jay R. (1974). "Organizational Design: An Information Processing View." *Interfaces* 4: 28-36.

Gold, Jordan (1986). "Move over, Mainframes." *Computer Decisions* 18: 56-58.

Goleman, David (1988). "Why Managers Resist Machines." *New York Times*, February 7.

Horton, Forest Woody (1982). "Human Capital Investment: Key to the Information Age." *Information and Records Management* 16: 38-39.

_____ (1985). *Information Resources Management*. Englewood Cliffs, N.J.: Prentice-Hall.

Hulin, C. L., and M. Roznowski (1985). "Organizational Technologies: Effects on Organizations' Characteristics and Individuals' Response." *Research in Organizational Behavior* 7: 39-85.

Hussain, Donna, and K. M. Hussain (1988). *Managing Computer Resources*, 2d ed. Homewood, Ill.: Irwin.

"Information Systems Are the Key to Managing Future Business Needs" (1986). *Marketing Needs* 20 (May 23): 12.

Innon, William H. (1986). *Managing End User Computing in Information Organizations*. Homewood, Ill.: Dow Jones-Irwin.

Katz, Daniel, and Robert L. Kahn (1978). *The Social Psychology of Organizations*, 2d ed. 1-68. New York: Wiley.

Keen, Peter G. W., and Lynda A. Woodman (1984). "What to Do with All Those Micros." *Harvard Business Review* 62, no. 5: 142-50.

Krasnoff, Barbara (1987). "Managing Technology in the Changing Workplace." *PC Week* 4, no. 39: 59-60.

Malone, Thomas W. (1985). "Designing Organizational Interfaces." *Proceedings of the 1985 Conference on Computer-Human Interaction.* New York: ACM, 66-71.

Mankin, Don, Tora K. Bikson, and Barbara Gutek (1985). "Factors in Successful Implementation of Computer-Based Office Information Systems: A Review of the Literature with Suggestions for OBM Research." *Journal of Organizational Behavior and Management* 6: 1-20.

Marchand, Donald A., and Forest W. Horton (1986). *Infotrends: Profiting from Your Information Resources*. New York: John Wiley.

Markus, M. Lynne (1984). *Systems in Organizations: Bugs and Features.* Boston: Pitman.

_____, and Daniel Robey (1988). "Information Technology and Organizational Change: Causal Structure in Theory and Research." *Management Science* 34, no. 5: 583-98.

Mass, Rita (1982). "Records, Words, Data . . . Whatever You Call It, It's Still Information." *Information and Records Management* 16: 18-20.

McFarlan, E. Warren (1984). "Information Technology Changes the Way You Compete." *Harvard Business Review* 62, no. 3: 98-103.

Meltzer, Morton F. (1981). *Information: The Ultimate Resource*. New York: AMACOM.

Miller, J. G. (1978). *Living Systems*, 1-29. New York: McGraw-Hill.

Morgan, Gareth (1986). *Images of Organization*, 39-76. Beverly Hills, Calif.: Sage.

Murljacic, Tony (1987). "The Evolution of Automated Office Systems." *Infosystems* 34, no. 8: 48-49, 52.

Nickerson, Raymond S. (1986). *Using Computers: The Human Factors of Information Systems*. Cambridge, Mass.: MIT Press.

Nilles, Jack, Omar El Saway, Allan Mohrman, and Thierry Pauchant (1986). *The Strategic Impact of Information Technology on Managerial Work: Final Report*. Los Angeles: Center for Futures Research, University of California at Los Angeles.

Olson, Margrethe H. (1982). "New Information Technology and Organizational Culture." *MIS Quarterly* 6: 71-92.

Peters, T.J., and Waterman, R. H. (1982). *In Search of Excellence*. New York: Harper & Row.

Poppell, Harvey L., and Barnard Barnard (1987). *Information Technology: The Trillion Dollar Opportunity*. New York: McGraw-Hill.

Porter, Michael E., and Victor E. Millar (1985). "How Information Gives You a Competitive Edge." *Harvard Business Review* 63, no. 4: 149-60.

Rohm, Wendy Goldman (1987). "The Overused, Underused, Better-Used Micro." *Infosystems* 34, no. 4: 60-63.

Rubin, Charles (1985). "Blossoming Productivity Linked to Micros." *InfoWorld* 7, no. 20: 31-41.

Scott, W. Richard (1981). *Organizations: Rational, Natural, and Open Systems*, 3-54, 102-20. Englewood Cliffs, N.J.: Prentice-Hall.

Simon, Herbert A. (1973). "Applying Information Technology to Organization Design." *Public Administration Review* 33: 268-78.

Tannenbaum, Arnold S. (1962). "Control in Organizations: Individual Adjustment and Organizational Performance." *Administrative Science Quarterly* 7: 236-37.

_____ (1980). "Organizational Psychology." In *Handbook of Cross-Cultural Psychology* 5, eds. Harry C. Triandis and Richard W. Brislin, 281-334 Boston: Allyn and Bacon.

Thompson, J. D. (1967). *Organizations in Action*. New York: McGraw-Hill.

Tushman, Michael L., and David A. Nadler (1978). "Information Processing as an Integrating Concept in Organizational Design." *Academy of Management Review* 3: 613-24.

Urkowitz, Michael (1987). "Automating for Information." *Bankers Magazine* 170, no. 2: 78-80.

Verity, John W. (1986). "Minis, Micros, and Maturity." *Datamation* 32: 65, 72-74.

Whisler, Thomas L. (1970). *The Impact of Computers on Organizations*. New York: Praeger.

Wiggins, Bob (1985). "The Evolving Information Manager." In *Information Management: From Strategies to Action*, ed. Blaise Cronin, 39-54. London: Aslib.

Wiseman, Charles (1988). *Strategic Information Systems*. Homewood, Ill.: Irwin.

Woodman, Lynda (1985). "Information Management in Large Organizations." In *Information Management: From Strategies to Action*, ed. Blaise Cronin, 97-114. London: Aslib.

Zmud, Robert W. (1983). *Information Systems in Organizations*, 53-78. Glenview, Ill.: Scott, Foresman.

Zuboff, Shoshana (1988). *In the Age of the Smart Machine*. New York: Basic Books.

Management Strategies for Local Area Networks (LANs)

MARLYN KEMPER

INTRODUCTION TO COMPUTER COMMUNICATIONS AND NETWORKS

Advances in computing technologies and data communications have come together, facilitating information transfer, accumulation, and selection on a broad scale in one of the most profound technical mergers since the invention of movable type and the printing press. Optical fiber and the semiconductor laser form communications links that economically carry voice and data traffic in major urban areas. Electronic mail networks consisting of voice-grade lines join corporate locations to communication centers where computers switch messages to their destinations. Virtually any communicating workstation, terminal, or personal computer can be linked via terrestrial telephone lines to online databases.

Recent technological developments in solid-state power amplifiers, low-cost frequency converters, and digital processing techniques that manipulate and interweave signals have paved the way for satellite communications based on VSAT (very small aperture terminal) networks as cost-effective alternatives to terrestrial data communications networks. A VSAT satellite channel resource-sharing system can interlink computer terminals to facilitate high-bit-rate information exchange among large numbers of remote users requiring special services, such as automobile dealerships, retail stores, banks, hotels, airlines, and brokerage firms.[1]

In the present-day, volatile computing communications environment, managers who are responsible for designing and expanding applications must keep pace with technological developments, increasingly sophisticated organizational computing, user demand for high performance and enhanced transmission speed, shifting carrier regulations, and vendor claims and promises. As computer and communications industries enter an unprecedented period of transition, traditional ways of thinking about electronic media are also changing. Boundaries between these media are fuzzy.

Orbiting geosynchronous satellites are employed as major mechanisms for terrestrial communications. Voice and video messages, electronic photographs and newsprint, and business transactions are passed in and out of space by satellite transmission. Innovations in electronic message transfer technology enable individuals to access electronic libraries and information databases, to shop and bank electronically, to receive home educational instruction and entertainment, and to utilize work-at-home microcomputers and terminals. Such phrases as "paperless office," "neurocomputing," "voice mail," "intelligent workstation," "telecommuting," "satellite videoconferencing," "wired city," and "distance-based learning" have been coined to mirror the impact of computing and communications in the library, home, and school and in the corporate and government environments.

Neural networks, defense networks, and music networks are presently undergoing dramatic changes by taking advantage of recent developments in computer communications technology. Based on a nonalgorithmic approach to information processing modeled on the gross structure of the human brain, neural networks that parallel-process large quantities of data and create mappings or associations between objects in response to their environment are employed in prototype systems for speech and image recognition, for scheduling airline flights, and for scoring applications for bank loans.[2] Managed by the Defense Communications Agency, the Defense Communications System (DCS) includes packet data networks using radio, terrestrial, and satellite transmission capabilities supplied by commercial and military carriers to maintain connectivity between critical users.[3]

An international standard in the musical applications field, MIDI (musical instrument digital interface) provides parameters for interlinking devices ranging from computer sequencers to a hundred pieces of equipment in the studio or on the concert stage to facilitate musical and nonmusical data exchange on a computer communications network.[4] Using innovative architectures, this music network can be optimized to support specific topology, applications, device characteristics, and management requirements.

The potential of data communications for processing data into information can be realized in the application of computer networks or structures that make available to an end-user at one geographic locale some service performed at another geographic locale. Capabilities exist to transform at increasingly lower costs textual information, television pictures, speech, and music to a common digital representation. Technically, computer networks have evolved from dedicated private networks to those utilizing multiplexed links or accessing hosts from multiple vendors.

LOCAL AREA NETWORKS

Just as they have become prime resources, computer networks have grown in size, in number, and in complexity, power, and versatility. During the past decade, the local area network (LAN), a special type of computer network, has become a viable alternative for joining together resources for sharing and backup, and as a mechanism for implementing distributed data processing in order to enhance productivity both intraorganizationally and interorganizationally.[5] A combination of evolving technologies, economic circumstances, and the need to improve access to decision-making data has led to the emergence of LANs as cost-effective solutions for optimizing information exchange. LANs offer a bonanza of new services for users. Their integration into the work environment is driven by capital and expense containment requirements and by user demand for integrated services.

Featuring an abbreviation that has filtered into everyday language, LANs have been dubbed one of the hottest advances on the digital landscape. Like other highly touted technologies, LANs have grabbed their share of headlines. Since the creative use of computer networks such as LANs makes the volume of knowledge, which is growing exponentially, manageable, local area networking commands the attention of those involved with information technology in disciplines ranging from librarianship and information science to education and engineering.

A LAN is a privately owned, user-administered data communications system, rather than a publicly available or commercial utility spanning a limited geographical area, and it facilitates communications between a number of independent devices, thereby enabling information and peripheral equipment to be shared.[6] Networked devices can include:

- Computers

- Facsimile units

- Telephones

- Terminals

- Printers

- Plotters

- Scanners

LANs can involve numerous components interlinked in complex ways. Since a LAN supports total connectivity, every user device on the network can communicate with every other user device.

Local area networking is a relatively new phenomenon; presently, there is no single, universally accepted definition of a LAN. Nonetheless, a few general concepts delineate the topic. As implied by its name, a LAN is a facility providing data communications within a geographically restricted space. Most LANs operate over distances less than ten kilometers at speeds up to 10M bps.

A LAN is a mechanism for transmitting bits of data from one attached device to another in a network that is limited to a single building or several buildings, such as on a college campus or a military base. The LAN can support a wide variety of applications, including:

- Document filing and retrieval

- File editing and transfer

- Graphics

- Word processing

- Electronic mail

- Database management

- Desktop publishing

- Electronic calendar

BACKGROUND AND DEVELOPMENT

LAN development has responded to demands for greater transmission speed and resource-sharing capacity. Among the user advantages provided by a LAN are enhanced reliability, faster response time, flexibility in programming applications, better supported facilities, and internetworking capabilities for multiple remote locations.

Press coverage, advertising hype, and the profusion of new announcements accompanying the introduction of LANs into the marketplace engender confusion and challenges for library practitioners. A wealth of new computer applications and user capabilities has been fueled by the recent boom in microcomputer and workstation usage and by decreasing costs for electronic equipment. Confronted with a burgeoning new technology, potential users are typically mystified by local networking techniques, concepts, and terms and dazzled by the perceived capabilities of networking products and highly visible networking schemes. Much confusion stems from attempts to evaluate the array of new commercial offerings and recent technological solutions. It's a rough world out there for anyone attempting to make an educated buying decision. The challenge involves establishing the LAN as a central contributor to productivity in the library setting. Changing computer communications technology, regulations, and user requirements are sources of both present-day problems and opportunities in LAN design.

Over the past few years, factors such as these have contributed to the rapid growth of LANs:

- Dismemberment of AT&T, deregulation, and the movement of the telecommunications industry from a monopolistic to a competitive structure

- Advances in microelectronics and transmission media such as fiber optics and satellite communications

- Commitment to distributed processing – the microprocessor fostered both significant opportunity for fully distributed data processing at the local level and concomitant demand for the allied capability to tie back to centralized data processing resources and databases

- Falling prices of information technology equipment, including data storage devices

- Growing popularity and dependence on computer networks

THE NEED FOR NETWORK PLANNING

In the early days of local area networking, managers generally focused on facilities equipment and costs instead of on delineating opportunities and strategies for exploiting them. With incorporation of desktop workstations, intelligent terminals, programmable devices that control groups of terminals, and minicomputers into the LAN as costs of microelectronic devices plunged, these networks now feature a blend of old and new technologies and have become increasingly diverse and complex.[7] Managers are presently charged with creating an environment for the peaceful coexistence of multiple generations of technologies within the boundaries of the LAN. The increased maturity of networking is mirrored in a shift away from purely technical issues to broader questions of enhanced services, user support, economic analysis, pricing, compatibility, connectivity, and planning for future needs.

LANs, like the institutions they serve, are dynamic entities. LAN development is characterized by a staggering number of available technologies and claims of vendor superiority. Since LAN hardware and software are interlinked with a computer's operating system, the potential for incompatibilities exists everywhere. Troubleshooting can be exceedingly difficult, calling for interface cards, cables, and connectors to be unplugged and replugged networkwide to trace a problem to its source. Generally, there is no single best LAN solution. The optimal LAN is typically a trade-off between data rates required, the number of users, their geographical location, and the applications that must be supported.[8]

LAN analysis and design constitute a process for determining networking requirements, investigating options for LAN implementation, and selecting the most appropriate alternative to supply the necessary capability. A purchasing decision calls for detailing the costs and support required in building, installing, operating, and maintaining the LAN. LAN technology should be mastered to convert its promise into a useful reality.

LAN PROJECT LIFE CYCLE

Since LAN implementation can be extremely difficult, careful planning is required. Every LAN project has certain phases of development. An understanding of these phases facilitates the achievement of desired goals and objectives. Developmental phases that constitute the LAN life cycle include:

1. The *conceptual* phase, or preliminary evaluation of the LAN idea: The conceptual phase involves problem definition. Existing needs or potential deficiencies should be determined, goals and objectives discussed, and answers provided to the following questions:

- What are the costs involved?

- How will the LAN be integrated into the environment?

- What are the human and nonhuman resources necessary to support LAN technology?

2. The *definition* phase, or a firm identification of the resources needed, along with the establishment of realistic cost, time, and performance parameters: This phase involves the preparation of a feasibility study that is designed to establish with greater accuracy, precision, and certainty the potential of the project and its likelihood of success. Types of questions that should be considered include the following:

- Are the total costs of equipment, facilities, and materials for LAN technology known?

- Are delivery costs for the proposed LAN, including acquisition, hardware, and maintenance costs, available?

- Will use of the LAN culminate in annual savings over existing systems in-house?

3.   The *planning* phase, or the establishment of objectives or targets to be accomplished by a certain time, as well as strategies or specific actions for achieving them: All work required can be delineated in a planning document, which should include descriptions or statements of the following:

- Goals and objectives

- Personnel requirements

- Equipment

- Facilities

- Expenditures

- Service options

- Hardware

- Software

- Analysis of costs

- Timetable for implementation

4.   The *implementation* phase, or a testing and standardization effort to ensure that operations proceed smoothly, including:

- Verification of specifications

- Final preparation of procedural reports and policy

- Documentation to operationally support the LAN

- Delineation of resources needed to facilitate installation

- Active involvement of all participants

5. The *conversion* phase: Once the LAN is installed, operations commence. Modifications may be minor, involving only maintenance, or major, calling for redevelopment and redesign. Conversion involves the following steps:

- Preparation of resources

- Testing the technology

- Changing over from employing the present system to utilizing the new one

6. The *evaluation* phase: The LAN can be assessed in terms of the following criteria:

- Reliability

- User perception of service and quality

- Frequency of errors or discrepancies

- Throughput and response time

- Software and hardware performance

- Vendor service and support

- Achievement of objectives and goals

STAFFING

Investing in a LAN does not guarantee successful operation. Like other new technologies, a LAN can disturb and change an existing environment. Change triggers discontinuity and stress and should be accommodated. Acceptance of LAN technology requires management commitment and clear objectives coupled with ongoing staff training and education. These steps can enhance acceptance:

- Involvement of key staff members in decision-making

- Progressively reassuring and informing professionals and paraprofessionals

- Fitting LAN responsibilities and capabilities to user perceptions of job tasks

LAN DEPLOYMENT

A library's individual situation, including its experience with data communications, its size, and the complexity of its information systems, should determine whether an individual project manager or an executive committee or project team assumes responsibility for LAN deployment.[9] Generally, project teams include a project manager, administrators who will be users, representatives from top management, and librarians with computer and telecommunications expertise.

Effective LAN leadership calls for a manager with a proven track record of administrative, technical, interpersonal, and communication skills, decision-making and problem-solving expertise, and a sense of mission, enthusiasm, and commitment to the project. LAN training and orientation should be given on a continuing basis to those monitoring LAN activity. Clearly written LAN documentation facilitates the smooth operation and control of the LAN project and helps minimize the adverse effects of staff turnover during LAN implementation.

As the LAN architect, the project manager should provide complete task definitions, resource requirements, major timetable milestones, and criteria for performance measurement. Strategies for exploiting computer and communications technology for quality service should be well thought out.

COMMUNICATIONS MEDIA

In designing a LAN, the manager must consider the overall network architecture, including conformity to international standards, as well as several basic technical issues. These issues include the network's physical medium and transmission technique, its topology (the logical arrangement of its stations), and its access method (the way it arbitrates among its stations for the use of the shared medium). Effective project planning and control involve carefully balancing money, time, and resources so that all networking components work together harmoniously.

A LAN should be economical and easy to use. The process of putting a LAN together ultimately depends upon the selection of a suitable cabling medium.[10] Three media are presently practical in terms of cost and performance for local area networking: twisted copper wire, coaxial cable (baseband and broadband), and optical fiber. Also known as "twisted pair," twisted copper wire is common telephone cord and the least expensive medium available in the marketplace for LAN installations. Although extremely sensitive to electrical interference, twisted copper wire is well suited for short-distance, low-cost LANs, particularly for small networks linking microcomputers. Twisted copper wire can carry data at rates up to 1M bps over distances spanning 100 meters.

A reliable proven technology with a high bandwidth for carrying lots of data at burst speeds of 1M to 10M bps, coaxial cable is used most frequently in high-speed LANs. For local networking, the cable supplies a simple economical mechanism for transmitting voice, data, text, and images in a digital form, along with analog control signals. Distinguished by layers that are concentric around a common axis, coaxial cable includes a central conductor, or the portion of the cable carrying the signal, which is surrounded by a nonconducting or a dielectric insulator, then by a woven or solid metal shielding layer, and finally by some outer protective coating.

The two general types of coaxial cable are baseband and broadband. Baseband cable transmits one signal at a time. The cable used in broadband networking is identical to the cable commonly used for cable television. While baseband networks handle only data traffic, broadband networks can carry voice and video as well as data. Hybrid broadband and baseband configurations are generally used for large applications.

Demand for enhanced transmission speeds in networked facilities with a greater aggregate capacity has contributed to the popularity of fiber-optic products and the emergence of the 100M bps ANSI standard called FDDI (fiber distributed data interface). Optical fiber, the newest medium in the commercial LAN market, transmits light through thin strands of glass or clear plastic and can handle many times the bandwidth of coaxial cable.[11] Among advantages of fiber-optic cable over copper-based LAN media such as coax and twisted pair are the following:

- Security: Since fiber does not emit electromagnetic signals, the cable must be tapped physically, causing a decrease in light level and thereby making intrusions in high-security applications easier to detect.

- Distance: Signals on a copper cable and light in a glass fiber travel at the same speed, yet the light meets less resistance as it moves along. Fiber-optic LANs can extend over a greater distance without calling for repeaters. Whereas Ethernet is geographically limited to 2.7 kilometers, for instance, a point-to-point fiber link can expand the distance to five kilometers.

- Immunity and reliability: Fiber is impervious to lightning, signals generated by computers and machinery, and radio frequency interference.

- Speed: Speeds on fiber-optic LANs can range from 35M to 100M bps.

While planning begins with strategy formation, the process ultimately must be translated in terms of boxes and cables, thereby calling for the manager to deal with the nuts and bolts of the technology. For instance, managers should understand different cabling impacts on LAN operation, since the right kind of cable directly affects LAN functions and adaptiveness in satisfying the changing needs of mobile staff. LAN cabling ideally should be flexible, strong, inexpensive, reliable, and lightweight. LAN wiring design reflects compromises in factors such as speed, cost, security, efficiency, and maintainability. Requirements issued by various governmental bodies and standards organizations should be accommodated in the cabling process.

LAN TOPOLOGY

A network's topology is the logical and physical arrangement of its stations or nodes in relation to each other. Three basic LAN topologies are bus, ring, and star.

The stations in a bus are arrayed along a single length of cable that has the capability of extension at one of the ends. A tree is a complex linear bus in which the cable branches at either or both ends; a tree features only one path of transmission between any two stations. Many baseband networks and all broadband networks use a bus or tree topology.

The stations in a ring topology are arrayed along the transmission path so that a signal passes through one station at a time prior to returning to its originating station. The stations in a ring topology form a closed circle. A ring in which one master station controls transmissions is a loop network.

A star network is characterized by a central node that connects to each station via a single point-to-point link. All communications between one station and another station pass through the central node.

ACCESS METHODS

Techniques by which the network allocates transmission rights among its participating stations or nodes to employ the shared communication channel are known as the network's access method. The access method typifies the network's mechanism for controlling traffic and guaranteeing throughput, even with a very heavy network load, to facilitate error-free data transmission.[12] Generally, access control can be:

- Centralized: In centralized access control, the terminals are polled in sequence for their transmissions.

- Distributed: In distributed access methods, each station participates in controlling the LAN equally. Most LANs employ distributed access. The two general categories of distributed access are random and deterministic.

NETWORK ARCHITECTURE

The exact definition of functions that a computer network and its components perform is termed network architecture. Explosive LAN development has been accompanied by a strong market pull toward an open network architecture that requires equipment vendors to follow generally agreed upon standards in order for end-users to mix and match network equipment. This movement toward standardization has culminated in the reference model for open systems interconnection (OSI) of the International Standards Organization (ISO).

The OSI reference model features strict definitions of protocols for communications between pairs of peer-level layers and separates the functions necessary for two computer systems to communicate into a seven-layer hierarchy. LAN characteristics that are defined by standards present users with a uniform, consistent interface for information transport.[13]

LAN EVOLVEMENT

Generally, LANs originate as small, manageable entities, only to expand rapidly in capabilities and functions. In most organizations, a LAN typically begins as a homogeneous set of equipment obtained from a single vendor. Usually, this LAN has one primary application, such as host communications, desktop publishing, or electronic mail. Small-scale LANs are generally easy to install and deliver substantial benefits.

LAN popularity in the workplace triggers additional networking applications and subsequent emergence of the LAN as a critical part of an organization's daily operations. More peripherals, internetworking, and multivendor and multiprotocol configurations transform a simple LAN into a maze. Detecting problems and enhancing performance in complex, large-scale LANs can confound even sophisticated LAN managers.

Call reports that supply a measure of resource utilization and traffic statistics correlated with user complaints of downtime, poor service, or system slowdowns are used for evaluating LAN performance and for planning network reconfiguration.[14] To provide fast response time and consistently high throughput, queuing models can be developed based on transmission speed, normal operating hours per day, peak hours, calls per day per terminal, connect time per call, messages per call per terminal, and average characters transmitted per message per terminal.

Automated aids for network monitoring, reporting, and control maximize the use of skilled technical personnel and limited resources to optimize LAN performance.[15] Popular packages for automatically tracking data flow, displaying traffic statistics, and analyzing protocol layers to determine software and hardware problems include tools such as:

- ARC-Monitor Plus and E-Monitor, distributed by Westcon Associates, Inc., 140 Marbledale Road, Eastchester, N.Y. 10707, (914) 779-4773.

- EtherProbe, distributed by 3Com Corporation, 3165 Kifer Road, Santa Clara, Calif. 95052, (408) 562-6400.

- LAN MAP, distributed by Computer Communication Company, 151 New Park Avenue, Hartford, Conn. 06106, (203) 236-5873.

- LANWatch, distributed by FTP Software, Inc., P.O. Box 150, Kendall Square Branch, Boston, Mass. 02142, (617) 868-4878.

- LT Auditor, distributed by Blue Lance, P.O. Box 430546, Houston, Tex. 77243, (713) 680-1187.

LAN INTERCONNECTIVITY

Increased multivendor LAN installations in the work environment can spearhead the development of network interconnectivity that exceeds individual LAN design restrictions, such as physical extent and number of stations or nodes supported.[16] Obstacles involved in creating extended LANs include joining subnetworks supplied by different vendors with different proprietary techniques and communications protocols, and operating on different media using different internal architectures.

Often, LANs evolve on an as-needed basis in response to specific requirements. Design decisions are made without a rigorous analysis of the entire LAN framework, since only incremental expansion is initially addressed.

To ensure interoperability, information sharing, interconnectivity between devices, resource availability, service quality, and an appropriate level of performance in the dynamic LAN environment, the project manager's responsibilities include:

- Equipment selection and acquisition

311

- Design of networking applications

- Benchmarking or modeling to determine an appropriate computer architecture

- Adherence to standards

- Development of guidelines, policies, and procedures

- LAN installation, maintenance, and administration

LAN MANAGEMENT FUNDAMENTALS

Proper planning precedes every successfully designed network. The network plan is a road map facilitating the development of a LAN solution that meets present and projected future requirements of the user organization.

Accommodating the expansion and complexity of interconnected LANs and accurately forecasting networking requirements in a multiuser, multitasking setting can be difficult. The project manager can enhance LAN productivity with an understanding of:

- Current capabilities based on computer capacity considerations and an inventory of hardware, software, applications, and personnel

- Communications technologies involved

- Network design techniques to promote system availability so that individual component failures minimally affect network operation

- Network configuration and topology for determining the present capacity for handling an increased load and hardware changes for supporting additional networking tasks

- Network control based on a capability to monitor LAN status, react to overloads and failures, and plan intelligently for future growth

- Problem detection and accurate diagnostics

- Implementation of planned alternatives in case of downtime

- Network security, such as protection of resources against unauthorized disclosure, modification, use, restriction, or destruction

The project manager's administrative functions involve resolving LAN problems such as bottlenecks, response-time spikes, and traffic patterns prior to initiating network optimization based on applying network design tools, evaluating design options through a cost performance analysis, and configuring communications lines to maximize LAN performance. Evaluation of alternative design techniques for addressing LAN requirements reflects capacity, accessibility, reliability, manageability, maintainability, and economy, thereby allowing for orderly expansion. Whether implementing an individual LAN or a linked LAN, the resulting network should provide consistent service quality, maximize network benefits, and minimize costs.

By boosting work-group productivity, LANs make it easier for personnel to:

- Cooperatively perform tasks, thus fostering wider participation in creating and reviewing job assignments

- Exchange data and relevant facts quickly

- Schedule meetings, thus eliminating the time tyranny of telephone calls

A LAN employs the high-technology glue for binding together terminals, microcomputers, and other communications equipment and for providing distributed information processing and management, as well as the sharing of common databases and other information sources. With its ability to incorporate diverse functions, a LAN supplies a framework for strategically implementing applications involved in organizational growth. The capability for joining incompatible software and hardware systems quickly and easily constitutes a powerful mechanism for joining resources between all sectors of the information community.

Once the LAN is in place, proposals for adding or deleting resources such as terminals, controllers, multiplexers, protocol converters, and front-end processors, redesigning applications software, or changing routing strategies can be assessed. Each of the various possible configurations will have associated costs and response times, so that the final selection of a configuration is generally based upon operational trade-offs left to the manager responsible for balancing budget constraints against user service levels.

Notes

1. D. M. Chitre and J. S. McCoskey, "VSAT Networks: Architectures, Protocols, and Management," *IEEE Communications* 26 (July 1988): 28-38.

2. Robert Hecht-Nelson, "Neurocomputing: Picking the Human Brain," *IEEE Spectrum* 25 (March 1988): 36-41.

3. S. M. DiSilvio and J. D. Edell, "Automating System Control Functions in the Defense Communications Systems," *IEEE Communications* 26 (August 1988): 8-12.

4. K. Sakamura, K. Tsurumi, and H. Kata, "Applying the uBTRON Bus to a Music LAN," *IEEE Micro* 8 (April 1988): 60-66.

5. M. Kemper, *Networking: Choosing a LAN Path to Interconnection* (Metuchen, N. J.: Scarecrow Press, 1987).

6. W. Stallings, *Local Networks*, 2d ed. (New York: Macmillan, 1987).

7. F. J. Derfler, Jr., "Connectivity: LANs and Beyond," *PC Magazine* 5 (December 9, 1986): 119-26.

8. D. N. Chorafas, *Designing and Implementing Local Area Networks* (New York: McGraw-Hill, 1984).

9. M. Kemper, "Local Area Networking: The Management Problem," in *The Library Microcomputer Environment: Management Issues*, ed. S. S. Intner and J. A. Hannigan, 187-206 (Phoenix: Oryx Press, 1988).

10. D. N. Hatfield, "Transmission Media," in *Data Communications, Networks, and System*, ed. T. C. Bartee, 15-32 (Indianapolis, Ind.: Howard W. Sams & Co., 1985), 15-32.

11. M. A. Wernli, "The Choices in Designing a Fiber-Optic Network," *Data Communications* 15 (June 1986): 167-75.

12. J. L. Hammond and P. J. P. O'Reilly, *Performance Analysis of Local Computer Networks* (Reading, Mass.: Addison-Wesley, 1986).

13. S. Wakid, "Coming to OSI: Network Resource Management and Global Reachability," *Data Communications* 16 (December 1987): 137-50.

14. M. Schwartz, *Telecommunications Networks: Protocols, Modeling, and Analysis* (Reading, Mass. : Addison-Wesley, 1987).

15. F. J. Derfler, Jr., "Administrative Relief for LAN Managers," *PC Magazine* 7 (June 14, 1988): 247-72.

16. G. T. Koshy, "Understanding Multiple LANs: The Why and How of Linking up," *Data Communications* 15 (May 1986): 221-27.

The Role of Microcomputers in Library Decision-Making

JOHN VINSON RICHARDSON, JR.

THE ROLE OF MICROCOMPUTERS IN LIBRARY DECISION-MAKING

Microcomputers are increasingly prevalent in library settings, and thus available to support a more analytical decision-making process (Hernon and McClure 1986). However, their role in supporting this process is not always apparent to many librarians, department heads, and even library directors. Consequently, this chapter examines the changing computing environment, the potential shift from a more intuitive-based decision-making process, and the role for microcomputers in this transition.

Interest in the Topic

Obviously, the technology exists. Libraries have widely adopted microcomputers (Howell 1987). Furthermore, we are also witnessing a change in the structure of library organizations that may be due in large part to the introduction of microcomputer technology. At the same time, large opportunities exist for reducing the risk inherent in making decisions whenever alternative courses of action present themselves. Microcomputers allow directors to take control of these library situations. Furthermore, an opportunity also exists for library staff to increase their personal job satisfaction, as well as their positional power, by adopting microcomputer applications such as database management, spreadsheet and statistical analysis, and graphic presentation.

315

DEVELOPMENT OF COMPUTING RESOURCES

Need for Mainframe Power

In the early to mid-1960s, the library profession adopted mainframe computers for manipulating large cataloging data sets (Library of Congress 1963). The introduction of expensive electronic computing equipment in this period led to the centralization of computing resources. It simply did not make economic sense for most libraries to buy their own computers. Rather, they could achieve an economy of scale by cooperation–with the entire school district, with other departments on campus, or with other government agencies.

A new field, called electronic data processing (EDP, or simply DP), emerged as a result (Lankau 1982). And in short order, EDP managers took control in this new environment. They accepted the responsibility for maintaining the machinery, backing up data, and restoring archived data sets. Along with this assumption of responsibility came the associated power and authority. On college and university campuses, EDP managers received the go-ahead from university administrations to implement their ideas, which resulted in a hegemony of power. This one group took control by possessing the technical sophistication lacking in many other groups, librarians included. Interacting indirectly with the computer via the EDP professionals, librarians became passive users.

Some benefits of the mainframe are obvious (Hickman 1986). Specifically, the mainframe supported many users, and it could run many different applications at the same time. Furthermore, large data sets could be stored on it. Most of the software offered for the mainframe possessed superior accuracy. It had been time-tested and thoroughly debugged.

However, substantial costs existed. Mainframe users were accustomed to computing costs based on: (1) storage, specifically the number of data sets, (2) the actual use of a certain number of CPU machine units, (3) the total number of pages of output, (4) the time of usage, depending upon (a) daytime, weekdays, (b) evenings and weekends, or (c) graveyard, and (5) total connect time. Because many of these factors were hard to predict, costs were often unknown or hard to project. Such was life with the mainframe computer.

There were other risks as well. First was something called system saturation, a familiar situation in academic environments, especially at the end of a quarter, when so many users tried to log on to the system that it could not accommodate everyone. The dissatisfied mainframe users had no option because no alternative presented itself until the late 1970s.

Lack of access due to downtime occurred occasionally as well. System maintenance had to be done, and while operators scheduled it for the least inconvenient time, such as late night or on weekends, the computer was still unavailable during these times. Then, too, unscheduled downtime due to equipment malfunctions also happened.

The last major disadvantage to full utilization of the mainframe was that it required a sophisticated user. Designers of the existing software used a command-driven interface that users found difficult to use on an occasional basis. In some cases, the software had to be programmed and debugged by a highly trained and technologically sophisticated librarian – a rather unlikely situation, given the other responsibilities of librarians that seemed more directly related to getting the job done.

Mainframe technology satisfied librarians' needs for massive computing power and storage, especially in the area of technical services. Huge cataloging or bibliographic databases emerged in the late 1960s and early 1970s (Maruskin 1979). Librarians found additional uses for mainframe computers. For example, librarians responsible for interlibrary loan (ILL) found that, with mainframe computers, they could keep better track of the borrowing and lending patrons. Circulation librarians found that their massive charging systems ran more effectively on a mainframe computer (Matthews and Hagerty 1984). Based on an analysis of the data provided by these systems, thoughtful implications could be developed for collection building.

Front-line librarians ventured relatively infrequently into any kind of statistical analysis because they lacked quantitative preparation. Most new library recruits came from history, English, or foreign-language backgrounds (Fasdick 1986). So, librarians required the assistance of an outside statistical consultant, although librarians seemed hesitant to rely upon consultants or rarely saw the advantages of these experts.

DEVELOPMENT OF MICROCOMPUTERS

The situation began to change in the late 1970s and early 1980s with the introduction of small personal computers (PCs), or more formally, microcomputers. Realizing that if they did not share their knowledge and authority they would lose control, DP managers adapted to this changed environment and established microcomputer information centers (MICs). These centers feature recommended hardware and display demonstration copies of major software products. Librarians, however, need special applications and receive little support from this group at present.

Libraries were among the innovators and early adopters of this new technology, adopting it for word processing and spreadsheets in particular; articles began appearing in the professional literature promoting the use of microcomputers (Malinconico 1984). Consistently, if not rapidly, declining costs contributed to the successful rise of powerful microcomputers. Equally attractive was the marked increase in computing power. Admittedly, the first machines possessed small memories, storing only 8K.[1] Compared to the mainframe power, storage, and data-handling capabilities, early microcomputers such as the Radio Shack TRS 80 seemed almost like toys. Indeed, some library staff and other early adopters found them more useful to run arcade games, such as Larry Ashmun's "INVADERS-PLUS with Stereo Sound"! (However, "personal computers promote a sense of playfulness" that can lead to creativity [Geis 1987a].) When IBM introduced its microcomputer, the PC-1, it soon came with more memory, 64K. By the mid-1980s, manufacturers commonly installed 640K on the motherboard, or at least on add-on boards.[2] With increased memory, microcomputers could finally run applications useful in many library settings.

There was a low buy-in cost for micros, especially because they do not require special air conditioning units and they consume about the amount of electricity it takes to power a 100-watt bulb. By comparison with the mainframe, the personal computer offered fixed storage costs for data. Small or even relatively large data sets cost the same, that is, the cost of the diskette.

The low price for the hardware and fixed, predictable costs for storage meant that a library could easily amortize the cost of the microcomputer and its attendant software over the course of a single, medium to large-sized project. With the increasing speed of the newest PCs, more library projects could become automated.

Another advantage of the microcomputer was that it allows local control of data. Relatively instant analysis via databases, spread sheets, and statistical packages becomes available, allowing more sophisticated manipulations of data. Users grow more accustomed to shorter time frames, and small-scale projects, such as reports, can be finished sooner.

Of course, some hardware, as well as software, disadvantages exist. Microcomputers are largely single-user and single-purpose machines, while mainframes, by contrast, support many users running different applications at the same time. Alternatively, local area networks (LANs) can link several microcomputers together, and micros can be used to upload and download information from mainframes. Another disadvantage, however, is that someone has to service these microcomputers; formerly, the EDP people took care of that problem. While most of the microcomputer's components possess an extraordinarily long mean time between failure (MTBF) for a piece of high technology, libraries will probably need to replace this equipment every seven to ten years. Anticipating this eventual capital replacement, the library might establish a reserve or sinking fund for this as part of its budget.

Other risks include data security and data redundancy or integrity. Microcomputers are readily accessible. Previously, the mainframe required the use of passwords, and unauthorized users had a much more difficult time gaining access. Now, however, almost anyone capable of booting the microcomputer has access to local records. Secondly, departments can create their own databases, which may duplicate existing files elsewhere in the library. In some more extreme cases, librarians have started a sort of internal "black market" for needed databases within the library but outside of the approved administrative channels.

Finally, some software, especially new releases, simply does not perform as advertised or possesses algorithms of questionable accuracy. Nevertheless, the perceived benefits began to outweigh the risks in the early 1980s, and all types of libraries began to acquire the technology.

APPLICATIONS FOR THE PRESENT AND FUTURE

With the advent of microcomputers, front-line librarians wishing to undertake their own analysis could do so with a resultant improvement in the library's planning process. Among the other potential outcomes were better and more interesting jobs, as well as potentially lower costs of performing some highly repetitive tasks. However, some library managers and directors have probably not adopted microcomputers because the tasks undertaken with it appeared too clerical for their tastes.

Due to the declining cost of microcomputer technology, libraries have adopted it for several different applications: word processing, database management, spread-sheet analysis, statistical analysis, and graphic presentation (U.S. Department of Commerce 1984).

Word processing, or the ubiquitous office automation (Goldfield 1985), appears in many library departments. No doubt, libraries have experienced improvements in the timeliness of reports. Otherwise, some rather unreasonable expectations still exist in this area. Word processing on a microcomputer really only evidences significant gains in productivity if the report goes through several drafts, and editing and reformatting is necessary. Some companion writing aids, such as spelling checkers, thesauri, and grammar correctors, are available on microcomputers, too. Short memorandums and envelopes may be prepared faster on the typewriter, but long mail listings are easier with a micro. Nonetheless, the effectiveness of library managers can be improved by delegating these clerical tasks.

So-called islands of automation exist when it comes to database management systems. These islands include departments such as cataloging and circulation, which have large-scale projects. Indeed, all of these islands have worked against cooperation. Self-sufficiency has been encouraged to some degree. Yet, there is a situational irony when bibliographic utilities started to appear in many libraries. The IBM PC became the de facto technology in many libraries by 1985 when all the bibliographic utilities, including UTLAS, WLN, RLIN, and OCLC, settled upon this machine; although there is a notable exception, school libraries have adopted Apple computers and other machines. With dBASE or similar programs, corporate executives (Geis 1987b), and now librarians with microcomputers, have allowed automation to move into other relatively unexplored areas. Reference, unless you include ILL, has probably lagged behind in this application area. However, expert systems serving as decision support for front-line reference librarians can answer basic or fact-type questions and consequently offer great possibilities (White 1981; K.F. Smith 1986; Waters 1986; L. Smith 1987). In this area of database management, the long-term objective should be linking otherwise disparate departments. Library directors must make policies regarding the integrative use of databases.

Library managers have also adopted spread-sheet programs, such as VisiCalc, the first commercially available spread sheet (1978), and more recently, Lotus 1-2-3 (LeBlond and Cobb 1986). In fact, this software really demonstrated the power of microcomputers. Consequently, this kind of software has found a place in accounting, the budgetary process, payroll operations, and any of the more business-oriented aspects of library operations. Spread sheets, like the previous type of software, have encouraged librarians to collect "personal" and departmental data sets. However, spread sheets are ultimately limited in highly complex situations. (If no easy course of action is suggested, then the situation must be labeled complex.) Although simple modeling and "what-if" scenarios can be undertaken, most spread sheets provide only a two-dimensional (i.e., rows and columns) analysis of the world.

Statistical analysis, on the other hand, has the power to transform raw data that are readily available into valuable information for a three-dimensional world (Madron, Tate, and Brookshire 1985; Stahr 1984). No doubt, the term *statistics* has a variety of meanings to users, but in any definition it means the manipulation of numbers, a fact that seems to disturb many librarians. Although there are numerous reasons why librarians should have quantitative analysis skills, some reasons stand out. Increasingly, the professional literature in librarianship uses statistical methods for testing hypotheses and drawing conclusions. As consumers, librarians must understand the statistical assumptions behind hypothesis testing. Secondly, librarians themselves need to adopt a problem-solving approach and support their own conclusions about relationships in their day-to-day work on a statistical basis.

Statistics enable librarians to accomplish more; specifically, Edward Tufte (1974) identifies five such tasks:

- *Test* theories and explanations by confronting them with empirical evidence

- *Summarize* a large body of data into a small collection of typical values

- *Confirm* that relationships in the data did not arise merely because of happenstance or random error

- *Discover* some new relationship in the data

- *Inform* readers about what is going on in the data

Librarians are continually confronted with situations in which numerical analysis would be beneficial. For instance, librarians are often asked to display data in some fashion, usually with descriptive statistics (i.e., measures of central tendency, or averages). More quantitatively sophisticated librarians could test their "educated guesses" about the results of their decision-making by collecting raw data and processing it with a statistical package.

Of course, there are some risks to using quantitative techniques, for instance:

- The raw data may not be available

- The existing data may not be reliable (undetected errors can lead to costly and erroneous decisions)

- Having reliable numbers available can lead to "paralysis by analysis" (where no decision is made)

- Some statistical packages allow only simplified assumptions, which limit the effectiveness of the results

- Misusing a statistic (applying an inappropriate statistical test to data)

Most importantly, however, statistical results still need interpreting; that is, according to one's judgment, what do the results mean? Library directors should have competent staff who know how to collect data, who know how to select the appropriate statistical test, and who understand how to interpret it. These staff members should not be willing to say that the data support an otherwise desirable decision path when in fact the data will not support it.

Graphics, the last category of microcomputer application, combines the latter two areas of spread sheet and statistical analyses. Library managers have experienced an information overload in the form of specific statistics with reams of computer printouts. The data chunked out by mainframes might not have been provided in a very useful format; unfortunately, these mainframe computers generated massive amounts of data but did not distill them. Microcomputer-based presentations of graphs and charts offer vivid representations of data, and as such, they can be a cost-effective aid in reducing the information overload. As an added benefit, some of these graphics packages can be quite convenient to use.

Graphic presentations reveal trends not readily apparent in complex situations. Graphics can also show ratios effectively. Empirical evidence shows that decisions come quicker (Benbasat and Dexter 1986), are better (DeSanctis 1984), may result in shorter meetings (Keepper and Pridmore 1982), and result in exploring other alternatives rather than simply accepting the first solution (Lucas 1981). Nevertheless, graphics are not categorically superior to the written word (Ghani and Lusk 1982). Graphics "do not always lead to better decisions, but they can help to pinpoint problem areas that need more research" (Needle 1985).

Librarians who have become middle managers realize how much time they spend: (1) presenting information, (2) organizing activities, and (3) supporting group decision-making. Consequently, graphical presentation of information could be a real boon to them. Such graphics may help convince colleagues who are otherwise overwhelmed by numbers generated from a statistical analysis; in fact, it may be a highly acceptable alternative when people understand that the presentation is as important as the information.

In summary, though, microcomputer hardware and software are only a tools means to an end. As the old cliche states so well, "If garbage goes in, then garbage comes out" (GIGO). Analysis by way of a spread sheet or statistical software requires a well-educated user. If assumptions are violated, the software will still calculate an answer – an invalid answer, of course, and one that can lead to an erroneous decision. Thus, any technique will only be as good as the people using it.

DECISION-MAKING

Perhaps it is obvious how microcomputer-based spread-sheet and statistical analysis could improve decision-making in libraries, but let us examine the process as it is widely practiced now. Librarians, from front-line staff to directors, are routinely involved in problem solving. Just some of the decisions that must be made are:

- Automation decisions (making choices among alternative systems)

- Decisions about selecting a book, cataloging it, and helping the user find it (Bundy 1961)

- Structural decisions (centralization or decentralization of technical services)

- Preservation decisions (whether and how to convert a portion of the collection to microfilm)

- Decisions during the renewal of periodical subscriptions, especially when 50 percent of the library's budget is devoted to this area (Woodward 1978)

- Storage decisions (whether to store a portion of the collection in a depository facility)

- Departmental decisions regarding how to improve the quality of reference service (McClure and Hernon 1983)

- General staffing decisions (how many persons, at what level, will be needed to provide a new service)

Of course, not every situation requires decisive action. Occasionally, librarians may wish to avoid taking any action because of the stress involved, the facts not being available, or for fear that later the decision may not turn out to have been a good one. Sometimes a problem can be "solved" by not doing anything; merely procrastinating will sometimes allow the problem to go away (Evans 1983, 112).

Nevertheless, the work environment more frequently requires a judgment, and delayed decision syndrome (DDS) will not help. In this event, librarians must identify the alternatives, select the best one, and implement the decision effectively. These judgments are often creative and are nearly always highly subjective and based on an ad hoc response to the situation.

Intuitive Approach

Consequently, intuition plays a large role. Carl Jung defines intuition as that which "explores the unknown, and senses possibilities and implications which may not be readily apparent"; all of which makes intuition sound rather mysterious (Agor 1986). Less formally, intuition is simply *feeling* that a particular action is correct. Intuition is an unstructured approach based on informal observation and perhaps advice from others. Based largely on previous experience, intuition is backward-looking (Einhorn 1987). It also contains a large element of common sense, which may not be all that common in group settings.

In *Management Techniques for Librarians*, Evans argues that "each individual has a different idea of what common sense is, so it is best not to rely on intuition to find solutions for problems" (Evans 1983, 120). Intuition certainly is not systematic and should be characterized as essentially nonrational. Librarians probably are more strongly intuitive than analytical, and perhaps because it is mysterious, they have made it a popular approach to solving problems. Nevertheless, there are only illusory reasons for its superiority, the primary one being that people believe that the decision based on intuition has a better outcome than one based on fact. So what is the alternative to an inductive style?

Analytical Approach

The intuitive is often contrasted with a deductive or analytical approach. Some writers characterize the analytical approach as more "left-brained." No doubt, it is a more fact-oriented approach, encouraging an empirical or linear, cause-and-effect thought pattern. (Quantitative software is the machine equivalent or complement to left-brain thinking.) In *The Rational Manager*, the authors have articulated the quintessential analytical approach, listing seven steps that should be followed in arriving at a decision (Kepner and Tregoe 1965). This approach requires that the decision-maker define the situation, detail the component parts, examine each alternative, and implement at least a tentative solution.

The traditional objection to adopting the analytical decision-making style has been its cost. Apparently, the assumption is that this approach may require more time than is available and that it will be more expensive, as well as more difficult, because it requires data that will have to be collected and analyzed. While there is a certain face validity to this assumption, it should be thoroughly tested. Furthermore, accountability–having to justify library decisions–will promote analytical decision-making because reasons, not feelings, must be presented for why certain actions were taken (Hagaford and Brehmer 1983).

Merging of the Two Styles

Ideally, there should be some way to merge these two differing, but valuable, approaches to decision-making. Although they have not provided a method, several management specialists have suggested merging these two styles (Agnew and Brown 1985; McGinnis 1984). In other words, a library manager must pay attention to the "small voice inside one's head" but also look for the facts that support the initial inclination. One way to do this is to adopt a new technology–a tool, in other words. Because the microcomputer technology already exists in many library settings, it makes sense to look at its potential. Spread sheet and statistical analysis accompanied by graphical presentation of data on a PC allows managers to discern trends and to test the validity of their "gut-level" feelings. Thus, the microcomputer can augment their intuition and lead to more reliable predictions.

Frankly, there are some strong personal advantages to librarians, especially middle managers, in adopting personal computers in their strategic decision-making. Such librarians can "leverage" their personal power in the process, which can lead to competitive advantages.

SUGGESTIONS AND RECOMMENDATIONS

The adoption of statistical analysis techniques that can run on a microcomputer has implications for four different groups: researchers, educators, practitioners, and library directors.

Researchers

The field of microcomputer-supported decision-making appears ripe for researchers (Geis 1987a). Some ideas are for descriptive or comparative studies – for instance, describing differences in each stratum (staff, department heads, and directors), or comparing and contrasting academic versus other types of libraries. Historians might look at the emergence of data-processing professionals and their hegemony on authority in this field. Opinion researchers might ask librarians about their perceptions: who is in charge, and what is the perceived role of microcomputers. Other researchers, organizational theorists, for example, might study the change in organizational structure brought on by the introduction of microcomputers. The evaluation of library services and performance measures should be pursued. Certainly, a cost/benefit analysis should be conducted for libraries. Another study might examine the executive style of library directors and their adoption of personal computers. Finally, other fields, such as manufacturing, have experienced a 20-30 percent gain in productivity; a similar study of librarianship would be informative.

Educators

The preceding discussion certainly has curricular implications for faculty teaching in schools of library and information science. These educators should examine their entrance requirements and determine whether students should not have at least a basic statistics course before entering the program. One justification for this requirement is the increasingly quantitative presentations in the professional literature. A related concern is about where students actually learn about microcomputers. Many colleges and universities started by requiring a computer literacy course but are now considering dropping the requirement because their incoming students are being introduced to the computer at an earlier age. Nevertheless, faculty may still wish to examine whether their existing curriculum makes use of microcomputers and statistical packages. How well integrated into the program is such use? In courses such as research methods, do students have an opportunity to use statistical packages? Finally, for the library community, does the faculty teach any extension courses on the role of micros or systems analysis that would help keep interested practitioners up-to-date in this area?

Practitioners

For several reasons, middle managers, whether librarians or not, compose the largest segment of the potential market for microcomputers. These individuals have a substantial role in the decision-making process and could profit most from the introduction of microcomputer-based statistical analysis. By developing these analytical skills and merging them with their intuitive abilities, librarians are likely to become better leaders.

Of course, these individuals must first see the value of analytical thinking in their library department and, secondly, be willing to devote the time to learning microcomputer technology. A self-assessment of one's own role in the organization, as well as one's own ratio of intuitive versus analytical skills, is necessary (Agnew and Brown 1985); librarians might consider taking a personality test such as the Meyer-Briggs, which is based on Jung's ideas (Slocum 1983). Successful managers are people-oriented most of the time, so they may not be as interested in working with a technology that appears to be isolating (Goldfield 1985). Furthermore, "people tend to put more faith in human judgment than in statistical models" (Einhorn 1987). Nevertheless, managers can become more valuable employees, even a technological elite, within their library organization if they adopt analytical thinking supported by microcomputers.

Several outcomes are possible with the adoption of statistical software. Library employees may gain more independence in their work because their managers do not understand the techniques. Indeed, such statistical users can leverage their expertise and become mediators between the data and the library's top management. Microcomputer users may also be perceived as more competent in their jobs. On a smaller scale, for instance, departmental committee meetings and presentations would undoubtedly be enhanced by the graphics capabilities of some of these spread-sheet and statistical programs. While informal agendas may encourage intuitive thinking, more formal presentations should be considered. Indeed, the presentational aspect of information is growing in importance; some writers even argue that it is as important as the information itself. The potential downward shift in the control of the organization that could occur may explain the lack of enthusiasm from above for this technology.

Library Directors

Directors and other senior managers should welcome this new technology for a couple of reasons. First, the potential of the existing hardware has not begun to be fully tapped. This may be because staff see minimal payback for the effort to learn; or, it may be that the existing library staff are not familiar with the technology (Koehler 1986). If it is the latter case, then directors should support attendance at professional conferences where this topic is discussed. They should also encourage staff to take extension courses to further enhance their computer skills; or, they could simply provide the existing staff with the needed training in-house by bringing in a consultant. Armed with the skills they need to accomplish their jobs, library management staff should be more satisfied in their work environment.

Directors might also think about the type of new staff they will be needing. People who can think, who are intuitive as well as analytical, who can use the newest technology, are highly desirable. Directors must also be willing to delegate some authority, as well as responsibility, to these new staff members. Directors should not be surprised if the organization structure shifts somewhat. Studies of other organizations that have adopted microcomputers suggest that the organization becomes more decentralized, less hierarchical, less divisional, and more dynamically able to reshape itself to meet new environmental and technological challenges (Geis and Kuhn 1987).

This situation, however, should not be threatening. The micro or personal computer is quite likely to broaden staff access to strategic management information. A by-product of this increased access will be a concomitant commitment to the organization and its objectives. Ideally, microcomputer-supported statistical packages will increase the quality of decisions. To accomplish this end, directors must hire skilled, creative staff members.

One final caveat: statistical packages running on microcomputers are no panacea. Nevertheless, microcomputers are powerful tools that can facilitate organizational excellence when a fit is achieved between a lean structure, participative management processes, and tightly focused strategies within an organization (Miles and Snow 1984).

Notes

1. K, the abbreviation for Kilobytes – 1,000 bytes – is a basic measure of computer processing and storage space.

2. Add-on boards plug into special sockets on the computer's motherboard and offer additional features, including increased memory or clock-calendars that will automatically inform the system of the current time and date.

References

Agnew, Neil M., and John L. Brown. "Executive Judgment: The Intuitive/Rational Ratio." *Personnel* 62 (December 1985): 48-54.

Agor, Weston J. "The Logic of Intuition: How Top Executives Make Important Decisions." *Organizational Dynamics* 14 (Winter 1986): 5-18.

Benbasat, Izak, and Albert S. Dexter. "An Investigation of the Effectiveness of Color and Graphical Information Presentation under Varying Time Constraints." *MIS Quarterly* 10 (March 1986): 59-83.

Bundy, Mary Lee. "Decision-Making in Libraries." *Illinois Libraries* 43 (December 1961): 780-93.

DeSanctis, Gerardine. "Computer Graphics as Decision Aids: Directions for Research." *Decision Sciences* 15 (Fall 1984): 463-87.

Einhorn, Hillel J., and Robin M. Hogarth. "Decision-Making: Going Forward in Reverse." *Harvard Business Review* 65 (January/February 1987): 66-70.

Evans, G. Edward. *Management Techniques for Librarians*, 2d ed. New York: Academic Press, 1983.

Fasdick, Adele. "Library and Information Science Students." *Library Trends* 34 (Spring 1986): 607-21.

Geis, George T. (1987a). "Databases for Managerial Creativity." *Ashton-Tate Quarterly* (April/May/June 1987): 31-33.

-----. (1987b). "Microcomputer Enhancement of Creative Management." Presentation at the Third International Conference on Creative and Innovative Management, Carnegie-Mellon University, June 1-3, 1987.

_____, and Robert L. Kuhn. *Micromanaging: Transforming Business Leaders with Personal Computers*. Englewood Cliffs, N.J.: Prentice-Hall, 1987.

Ghani, Jawaid, and Edward J. Lusk. "Amount of Information on Decision Performance." *Human Systems Management* (the Netherlands) 3 (December 1982): 270-78.

Goldfield, Randy J. "Aiming OA [Office Automation] towards the Top." *Modern Office Technology* 30 (February 1985): 55-68.

Hagaford, Roger, and Berndt Brehmer. "Does Having to Justify One's Judgments Change the Nature of the Judgment Process?" *Organizational Behavior and Human Performance* 31 (April 1983): 223-32.

Hernon, Peter, and Charles R. McClure. *Microcomputers for Library Decision-Making*. Norwood, N.J.: Ablex Publishing Co., 1986.

Hickman, Linda J. *Freedom from the Tyranny of the Campus Main-Frame: Handling the Statistical Analysis of a Ten-Year Survey Research Study with a Personal Computer*, ED 270 463. Bethesda, Md.: ERIC Document Reproduction Center, 1986.

Howell, Karen M. "Microcomputers and Public Services of College and Research Libraries: A Preliminary Analysis," Council on Library Resources supporting study grant no. 8001, MLS specialization paper, University of California at Los Angeles, Winter 1987.

Keepper, Lester H., Jr., and Jay Pridmore. "Graphics Boost Chances of a Favorable Outcome." *Cash Flow* 3 (November 1982): 46-49.

Kepner, C. H., and B. B. Tregoe. *The Rational Manager*. New York: McGraw-Hill, 1965.

Koehler, Kenneth G. "Using Micros as a Decision Tool." *CMA: The Management Accounting Magazine* 60 (November/December 1986): 12.

Lankau, Walter E. "Decision-Support Systems Clearly Explained." *ComputerWorld* 16 (September 1, 1982): 5-12.

LeBlond, Geoffrey T., and Douglas Ford Cobb. *Using 1-2-3*, 2d ed. Indianapolis, Ind.: Que Corp., 1986.

Library of Congress, *Automation and the Library of Congress*. Washington, D.C.: 1963.

Lucas, Henry C., Jr. "An Experimental Investigation of the Use of Computer-Based Graphics in Decision-Making." *Management Science* 27 (July 1981): 757-68.

Madron, Thomas W., C. Neal Tate, and Robert G. Brookshire. *Using Microcomputers in Research*, Sage University Papers (Quantitative Analysis in the Social Sciences) series 07-082. Beverly Hills, Calif.: Sage Publications, 1985.

Malinconico, S. Michael. "Decisions under Uncertainity." *Library Journal* 109 (November 15, 1984): 129-31.

Maruskin, Albert F. "An Historical Analysis of OCLC, Inc.: Its Governance, Function, Financing, and Technology." Ph.D. dissertation, University of Pittsburgh, 1979.

Matthews, Joseph R., and Kevin Hagerty, eds. *Automated Circulation: An Examination of Choices*. Chicago: American Library Association, 1984.

McClure, Charles R., and Peter Hernon. *Improving the Quality of Reference Service for Government Publications*, ALA Studies in Librarianship, no. 10. Chicago: American Library Association, 1983.

McGinnis, Michael A. "The Key to Strategic Planning: Integrating Analysis and Intuition." *Sloan Management Review* 26 (Fall 1984): 45-52.

Miles, Raymond E., and Charles C. Snow. "Fit, Failure, and the Fall of Fame." *California Management Review* 27 (Spring 1984): 10-28.

Needle, David. "Deciding about Decision Support." *Personal Computing* 9 (June 1985): 85-91.

Slocum, John W., Jr. "A Look at How Managers' Minds Work." *Business Horizons* 26 (July/August 1983): 58-68.

Smith, Karen F. "Robot at the Reference Desk?" *College and Research Libraries* 47 (September 1986): 486-90.

Smith, Linda C. "Artificial Intelligence and Information Retrieval." *ARIST* 22. Washington, D.C.: American Society for Information Science, 1987.

Stahr, Lisa B. "Working with Statistical Analysis." *Personal Computing* 8 (October 1984): 97-107.

Tufte, Edward R. *Data Analysis for Politics and Policy*. Englewood Cliffs, N.J.: Prentice-Hall, 1974.

U.S. Department of Commerce, National Bureau of Standards. *Microcomputers: Introduction to Features and Users*. NBS Special Publication no. 500-110. Washington, D.C.: Government Printing Office, 1984.

Waters, Samuel T. "Answerman, the Expert Information Specialist." *Information Technology and Libraries* 5 (September 1986): 204-12.

White, Howard D. "Measurement at the Reference Desk." *Drexel Library Quarterly* 17 (Winter 1981): 3-35.

Woodward, A. M. *Factors Affecting the Renewal of Periodical Subscriptions: A Study of Decision-Making in Libraries with Special Reference to Economics and Interlibrary Lending*. London: Aslib, 1978.

The Role of the Integrated Services Digital Network in Promoting Information Literacy

HARRY MAYANJA KIBIRIGE

Integrated services digital network (ISDN), as currently conceived and projected, promises to add an extremely important dimension to information processing and management. The changing outlook on literacy, from the traditional "read and write" mode to the more sophisticated multimedia and electronic mode, makes ISDN an attractive conduit for communicating literacy-oriented messages. In this respect, it is likely to be invaluable for both corporate- and government-sponsored literacy programs. Information literacy is the core of modern conceptual perceptions and definitions of literacy. When all pieces are in place and ISDN technology has spread to a larger user community, literacy projects programming will inevitably be influenced by ISDN.

The conventional notion of literacy has changed in the last two decades, owing to the widespread use of computers and other electronic devices. Prior to the computer age, now the information age, a literate person was one who could read and write. Many scholars of literacy and its concomitant societal problems thus focused on the printed word. They convincingly argued that the whole social, economic, and political community depends on the assumption that every citizen can communicate and be communicated to in writing.[1] Among the often-quoted elements of society that require basic literacy are reading bus signs, completing job application forms, and reading instructions for taking medication.

Some scholars have traced the spread of literacy in the preelectronic era to the invention of printing with movable type in Europe in the middle of the fifteenth century.[2] Elizabeth Eisenstein discussed the printing press as an agent of change, for early printers acted not only as businessmen but also as editors, translators, lexicographers, and cultural impresarios. According to her, printing ushered in a revolution that affected traditional Christian faith, literature, and science.[3] Eisenstein's analysis shows the impact of the printing press to have been comparable to the pervasive influence of electronic media and its effect on modern society. ISDN that embraces all the media will thus take on a higher level of magnitude in influencing the flow of information in the United States and the rest of the industrialized world.

TRENDS IN THE INFORMATION ARENA

The 1990s will bring interesting trends to the information arena. The first, started in the 1970s, is the gradual blending of computers and telecommunications.[4] It has resulted in computers that can communicate and telecommunications systems that can compute. This marriage of computers and telecommunications not only has blurred the demarcation lines between the roles of computer scientists and telecommunications engineers, but has also called for the coinage of technical terms to describe the blended functions.

The second major trend, which has been around for almost two decades, is the increasing importance of information in both national economies and organizational productivity and competitiveness. Since Daniel Bell's promulgation in the early 1970s of the coming of the postindustrial society, the concept of the "information age" has become pervasive in the industrialized countries.[5]

The final trend to discuss in setting the stage for ISDN is the ubiquitous microcomputer. Since they became popular in the 1970s and early 1980s, microcomputers have played three major roles on the information scene. First, they have spread computer literacy to the individual and in organizations because they are smaller, less intimidating, more user-friendly than large computers, and thus easier to handle. Second, they have compelled information systems designers and vendors to develop systems for the layman with no computer-science training. Third, they have continued to expand the concept of distributed processing, from the departmental computing unit to the individual user's desk.

Microcomputer users have realized that a lot of the data they need cannot be obtained on a stand-alone micro. Consequently, they have demanded connectivity on the local, regional, and in some cases, international levels. Local area networks (LANs) have sprouted in several organizations to cater to the local information link requirements. Using gateways and bridges, LAN users have been provided with links to other computer networks, such as metropolitan area networks (MANs) and the nationwide wide area networks (WANs).[6]

All these trends mean that the United States and other industrialized countries have a very strong infrastructure for information transfer. It is composed of: the societal need for fast information, accentuated by the high premium on current information; the presence of high-powered computer and communications systems; and finally, the sophisticated microcomputer and associated networks. Such an infrastructure is ideal for the various literacies that are needed for U.S. citizens. The source of information or medium to be used in literacy programs is insignificant as long as the information obtained is accurate, timely, and relevant. Information access media that can be used include the telephone, telex, facsimile, and workstation. Such media and their interoperability constitute a significant component of the raison d'être of ISDN.

Figure 1: ISDN Schematic

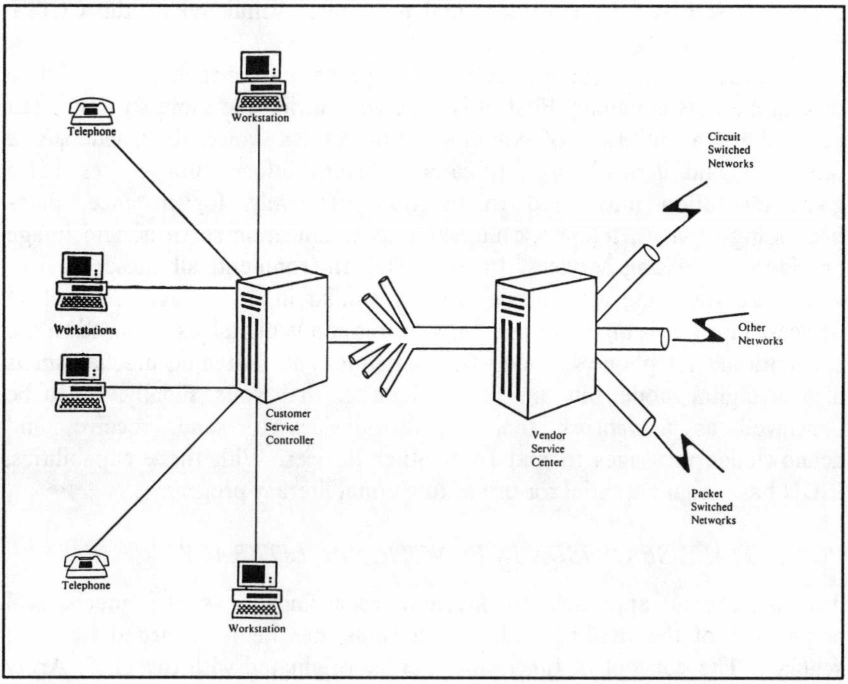

ISDN TECHNOLOGY

The most influential single technology in information processing for the next decade or so is likely to be ISDN (see Figure 1). The concept of ISDN embraces the totality of information as evidenced by the component parts of the term. It is a state-of-the-art network that has evolved from the telephony integrated digital network (IDN) that provides an end-to-end connectivity for supporting a broad range of services, such as voice, video, data, telemetry, and facsimile.

There are several definitions in literature; John Ronayne's is adopted as it equates that of the Consultative Committee for International Telephone and Telegraph (CCITT), a division of the International Telecommunications Union (ITU), one of the specialized agencies of the United Nations.[7] He defines ISDN thus: An ISDN is a network, in general evolving from a telephony IDN, that provides end-to-end digital connectivity to support a wide range of services, including voice and nonvoice services, to which users have access by a limited set of standard, multipurpose user network interfaces.[8] ISDN's origins may be traced to the mid-1970s when AT&T and later the Bell Operating Companies (BOCs) successfully changed their switching technology from analog to digital. It is part of the results of that change. It is based on interfaces and protocols formulated by the CCITT Study Group No. 18.

In order to fully comprehend the scope of the concept, it is useful to disaggregate its elements. First, it is *integrated* in that the same structure can be used for a multitude of communication modes – voice, data, video, and others. Second, it can be used to cater to several information *services* that a given institution may need to function effectively, for instance, data-processing services, telephone message communication services, and image or video processing services. In an ISDN environment, all these services would use the same transmission media, similar input, storage, and output devices. Third, it is *digital* in that its transmission is digital, as opposed to the conventional telephone's analog transmission. The switching mechanism is also in digital mode; bits are switched rather than volts. Finally, it can be conceived as a *network* that permits devices to send, receive, and acknowledge messages to and from other devices. With these capabilities, ISDN has a high potential for use in functional literacy programs.

POTENTIAL USE OF ISDN IN FUNCTIONAL LITERACY

The traditional approach to literacy, regarding it as the mechanical acquisition of the reading and writing skills, has been discarded by most scholars. The concept of functional literacy originated with the U. S. Army during the Second World War. The Army coined the term *functional literacy* to indicate the capability to understand written instructions necessary for conducting basic military functions and tasks, comparable to the fifth-grade reading level.[9]

The corporate world has capitalized on and expanded this concept in light of the complexity of modern working environments. Illiteracy has been characterized as a growing economic problem in the United States and has been associated with lack of competitiveness. It is estimated that 45 million adults are too limited in the basic skills of reading, writing, and arithmetic to be able to cope with their daily environment. A number of large corporations have instituted training programs of all types to remedy the situation for their employees. Travelers Corporation and Polaroid Corporation are among the leading ones. Harold McGraw, a leading proponent of literacy programs in the corporate world, has warned:

> If American business is to regain its competitive edge in the world, we must develop a far better-educated workforce. I hope we won't wait for demographics to force us to act, but that all of us – and not the least our personnel professionals – start now to get involved, both for our own future and the future of this country.[10]

Many modern scholars see literacy in a broader perspective. However, much of the literature is slanted towards the influence of technology. It is argued that in highly complex and technology driven-societies, technologies and technocrats shape the nature and potential of society. Thus, Paul DeVore asserts that "if we are to maintain our freedom and our democracy we have only one choice, a technology literate citizenry."[11] In a similar view, Suzanne DeCastell and her coauthors would rather see literacy analyzed not only in context but unlimited by the demands of interpersonal and vocational practice, in light of the broader literacy needs for social and political practice, as determined by the demands of a truly participatory democracy.[12]

Another way of looking at literacy in the electronic age is to extend our horizon beyond the computer to the understanding of information resources. William Neal calls this "information literacy," which he defined as "the ability to manage the effective use of information technology and information resources, rather than merely an understanding of computer hardware and software."[13] It implies that individuals should be able to understand a number of technologies to be effective workers and citizens.

Closely related to the concept of information literacy is what some analysts have referred to as "world knowledge," or "cultural literacy."[14] Competitiveness, which is the concern of business and economists, has to be seen on a world scale. American workers have to be aware of the fact that the market for their product is no longer the "home" market but the "global" one. Similarly, some of the toughest competitors are beyond the confines of the United States. There is therefore an urgent need to be conversant with both the global and the home environments.

Some literacy analysts have argued that the focus should be moved from print to a multifaceted media perspective. They argue that, in the electronic age, print is just one of the many media that can promote the various types of literacies discussed in this chapter. Peter Wagschal's observation is instructive:

> As we move faster and faster into the electronic age, the skills required to be informed, critical, responsive citizens of a democratic society become further and further removed from literacy as we have known it in the past. We may spend our time bemoaning the passage of the Age of Print, and clinging to a set of outmoded skills which we continue to insist on using as a way of distributing power and wealth in America, or we can move boldly forward. That would require us to identify a whole new range of information gathering skills which apply to our new technologies, and make sure that they are fairly and equitably distributed to our children, while at the same time making sure that the artificial hold which print continues to have over power and status is allowed to wither away.[15]

These perceptions of literacy have an important bearing on the potential of ISDN, which is an information highway that accommodates various types of media that can be used in literacy projects sponsored by government or corporations. Since it supports data, video, voice, and facsimile, it has a tremendous potential in exchanging information between agencies and units in a corporate environment.

HOW DOES ISDN OPERATE?

Unlike other network architectures such as IBM's system network architecture (SNA) and Digital Equipment Corporation's network (DECNET), ISDN is not proprietary to any single vendor. It is based on international principles. Steps to encourage ISDN development and implementation into viable products can be traced to 1980 when CCITT decided to devise standards to accommodate it. Using special CCITT interfaces, devices developed by telephone and computer companies can transmit and receive data, voice, or image to and from other designated devices, for instance, workstations, fax machines, and telemetry-controlled meters.

Currently, ISDN has two levels of interfaces, the low-volume basic rate interface (BRI) and the high-volume primary rate interface (PRI) (see Figure 2). The low-volume mode is composed of a four-wire loop between the vendor's central switch and the user's premises, terminating onto an ISDN-compatible device. Two 64K/bps "B" (bearer) channels and one 16K/bps "D" (data) channel are multiplexed over a single 192K/bps pair of wires. This format is often referred to as "2B+D." It is full duplex. The B channel may be utilized for either voice or data, while the D channel is for signaling only (call setup and acknowledgment), not for voice.

Figure 2: BRI and PRI Formats

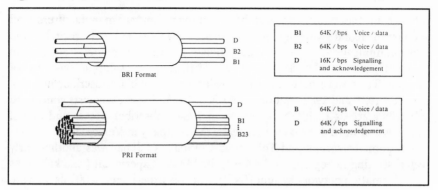

B1	64K / bps	Voice / data
B2	64K / bps	Voice / data
D	16K / bps	Signalling and acknowledgement

BRI Format

B	64K / bps	Voice / data
D	64K / bps	Signalling and acknowledgement

PRI Format

PRI is comparable to BRI in composition in that it has both B and D channels. However, one PRI may support twenty-three B 64K/bps channels and one 64K/bps D channel multiplexed over 1.544M/bps digital interface, known as a "23B+D" format. PRIs are normally connected to high-volume sources like PBXs or CBXs. The essential difference between the BRI and the PRI is the volume of throughput. These operation modes are the results of intensive research in industrialized countries.

DEVELOPMENT OF ISDN

Another 1990s trend will be more research to develop hardware and software for ISDN by telecommunications corporations. Such a trend would not be surprising since the concept is an outcome of the digital telephone. At the international level, the cast of main actors in the ISDN arena reads like the international who's who in the telecommunications industry. Almost all the major industrial giants in telecommunications are developing products for ISDN. The United States is dominated by AT&T and the Regional Bell Operating Companies (RBOCs), although IBM/ROLM is also a major contender. The leading international operators include Nippon Telegraph and Telephone Co. (Japan), Northern Telecom Canada Ltd., Siemens (West Germany), British Telecom (United Kingdom) and Ericsson Information Systems (Sweden).

Since the early 1980s, trials testing ISDN prototypes have been under way in Europe and Japan. Within the United States, trials started later but have been very comprehensive. Most field trials have tested the 2B+D or BRI. As to scope, field trials have covered: the public network, or the main-trunk transport segment of the network; the private network, or the PBX/CBX component; and the different types of terminals and other devices to be used on the network as a whole.

Field Tests

Interest in the field tests has been rampant among manufacturers and vendors of digital switching systems because ISDN promises to revitalize the telecommunications industry. The pioneer in studying digital transmission problems associated with ISDN was Ericsson Information Systems of Sweden. Tests were performed in Sweden on the public subscriber network between 1981 and 1982, and on a PABX in 1983. These early tests concerned subscriber access to ISDN. Later on in 1984, subscriber access and digital transmission were done concurrently by the company in Venice, Italy.

Nippon Telegraph and Telephone Company of Japan was another early tester, starting in September 1984 with its Mitaka experiment (also known as the information network system [INS]). For this experiment, 2,000 users were given free terminals. In addition, 250 information services providers cooperated. The INS also had a broadband component of ISDN that was used to test video conferencing, high-speed facsimile, and color facsimile. The broadband sector used optical fiber.

Another interesting early tester was United Kingdom's British Telecom, whose UK integrated digital access (UKIDA) experiment started in June 1985. For the experiment, the corporation used a lower bandwidth than the one recommended by CCITT. It was initially concentrated within London subscribers, and access as well as transmission were tested. UKIDA was offered on a commercial basis in 1986, thus making British Telecom one of the first European corporations to do so.

Within the United States, field tests have been carried out by AT&T, the RBOCs, and a number of switching systems manufacturing companies.[16] The earliest tests were done by Ameritech and its operating companies, starting in 1985. Wisconsin Bell in conjunction with Siemens conducted an interesting experiment in 1985-86 to test ISDN hardware and customer reaction in thirteen cities. Using Siemens' EWSD (from the German Elektronik Wahl System Digital) exchange on a mobile trailer, over 100 major customers were permitted hands-on experience with ISDN applications. Reactions were mostly positive, though many customers indicated they had special requirements, which led to custom-tailored ISDN services. The McDonald's Corporation project started in 1986 in Chicago was Ameritech's earliest and most profound test trial. It has been used for several aspects of ISDN, incorporating voice data and video. Telephone caller identification, modem pooling, security monitoring, and high-speed file transfer are among the specific activities that have been tested. Illinois Bell is the operating company involved. In addition, a number of customer premises equipment (CPE) manufacturers, such as AT&T, Hayes, NEC, Fujitsu America, and Telrad, are participating.

US West RBOC and its BOCs, starting in 1986, have run several tests based in Phoenix, Arizona. Several customers are connected via the central office switch and three ISDN remote switches. Among the customers are the Arizona state government and Honeywell. Mountain Bell is the main operator in Phoenix. The other two BOCs, Northwestern Bell and Pacific Northwestern Bell, are also engaged in similar projects.

Other RBOCs and/or BOCs are involved in equally interesting programs. As indicated earlier, the main difference between U.S. and international trials is that the American ones are more comprehensive and competitive. Since ISDN promises a large consumer market, it is not surprising that many U.S. telecommunications corporations are scrambling to get a piece of the pie. Practical applications of research efforts are relatively recent. Presently, testing and implementation are proceeding concurrently.

IMPLEMENTATION OF ISDN

Some information systems market analysts had predicted that ISDN products would not be commercially available until the 1990s. Such predictions were proven wrong when American telephone companies filed for ISDN tariffs in 1988. The year 1988 was thus the turning point, the year when ISDN products were declared to be commercially marketable in the United States. Illinois Bell Telephone Company was the first to file for an ISDN tariff, on March 29, 1988. It was followed in the following month by Southern Bell Telephone Company and AT&T. Among U.S. long-distance telephone companies, AT&T was thus the first to implement ISDN. These announcements were followed by other RBOCs declaring commercially available products. By the mid-1990s, most telephone companies should have a basic product or two to offer.

Initially, the RBOCs offered the 2B+D format or BRI. AT&T, on the other hand, offered the 23B+D format, or PRI, which divides a 1.54M/bps T-1 line into twenty-four channels. The RBOCs' target market is varied; while AT&T first concentrated on its Accunet T-1 digital transmission service customers. Whereas several large corporations were participants in the trials, McDonald's Corporation, the giant fast-food chain, stands out; in mid-1988 it became the first American corporation to make ISDN a corporate standard for information transfer. One may question the immediate practical relevance of this new network to the day-to-day information management functions. Is it a network only for the super-giant corporations like AT&T, Exxon, McDonald's and IBM? This may initially be true, but ISDN'S influence should eventually be felt in small and medium-sized organizations as well.[17]

ISDN IMPLICATIONS FOR INFORMATION LITERACY

The impact of ISDN on information literacy can be analyzed in several ways. First, the integration of data, video, and voice is likely to become popular among information-intensive industries and businesses. ISDN interface adapter boards are now available to modify existing workstations. When ISDN becomes user-friendly and familiar to the majority of intensive information-using sectors of society, it will enhance user access to online information. Some of the institutions that will be deeply influenced are finance, insurance, retail, telemarketing, research, libraries and information centers, the U.S. government, and education. Information databanks that currently provide citations online should be able to give full text, including video or graphic images. Current estimates put the cost of ISDN at one and a half times that of regular telephone service. Cost per se is not likely to be a limiting factor for adoption of ISDN. Information demand will most likely outstrip the cost factor.

Second, creation of a multitype transparent network will simplify the process of online information access for the user. ISDN should facilitate efficient use of the user's time by reducing the number of devices the user has to learn to use. The ideal system should eliminate the user's effort to learn the various protocols of the various devices. This would enable the user to concentrate on using information accessed for the professional functions. Too often, a prospective user is deterred from using an information device because of its apparent complexity. Multiply this by the number of devices to learn to use and a formidable barrier to information is created resulting in inadequate usage.

Finally, ISDN will improve online information throughput since it is based on digital transmission. In most operations, modems will be eliminated at both the CPE end and the information providers center. Increase in the use of T-1 digital communication lines will further accentuate throughput. Several colleges, business corporations, and governmental organizations use T-1 dedicated lines especially for data. Use of ISDN allows multiplexing data, video, and voice messages onto these lines, which improves multimedia and multimode throughput. The literacies discussed in this chapter will be immensely enhanced by these features of ISDN as an information highway.

SUMMARY

ISDN promises to be a vital component of the information infrastructure and will affect information literacy. Modern perceptions of literacy have gone beyond an emphasis on the basic mechanical knowledge of reading and writing to an emphasis on functional literacy. Illiteracy has been linked to the drop in American productivity, and corporations are now organizing remedial programs to address staff writing, reading, and mathematical deficiencies.

The complexity of industrialized countries demands a high level of literacy, which in effect means developing skills in information literacy involving several media and technologies. ISDN has several attributes relevant to information literacy: integration of data, video, and voice; creation of a multitype transparent network; and improvement of information throughput.

When ISDN technology has spread to corporate, government, and other institutions, the various types of literacy projects will take advantage of it. We live in an environment in which literacy has a new meaning that is continuously evolving. As Zirinsky put it:

> The literate person of the future will be one who can use language to perform higher order thinking tasks, who can read to interpret and predict, who can evaluate contradictory sources and understand links between ideas when not explicitly stated, who can read and write collaboratively to solve problems and propose solutions. Who in short, is literate not in a basic or mechanical sense, but who can use language to continue learning.[18]

Such an individual will need to use several types of media and technologies, including data, voice, and video. ISDN will be invaluable as the highway to access the multimedia.

References

1. Jeffries, Sir Charles, *Illiteracy: A World Problem* (New York: Praeger, 1967), 3-14.

2. Clanchy, Michael T., "Looking Back from the Invention of Printing," in *Literacy in Historical Perspective*, ed. Daniel P. Resnick, 7-22 (Washington, D.C.: Library of Congress, 1983).

3. Eisenstein, Elizabeth L., "On the Printing Press as an Agent of Change," in *Literacy, Language, and Learning*, 19-33 (Cambridge, Eng.: Cambridge University Press, 1985).

4. Marchand, Donald A., and Horton, Forest W., *Infotrends* (New York: John Wiley, 1986).

5. Bell, Daniel, *The Coming of the Post-Industrial Society* (New York: Basic Books, 1973).

6. These networks are elaborately discussed in the author's book entitled *Local Area Networks in Information Management* (Westport, Conn.: Greenwood Press, 1989).

7. Rosenwald, Jeffrey, "ISDN: Reinventing the Telephone," *Administrative Management*, October 1987, 41-42.

8. Ronayne, John, *The Integrated Services Digital Network: From Concept to Application* (New York: Wiley, 1988), 1-2.

9. DeCastell, Suzanne, et al., "On Defining Literacy," in *Literacy, Society, and Schooling: A Reader*, eds. De Castell et al. (Cambridge, Eng.: Cambridge University Press, 1986).

10. McGraw, Harold W., "Adult Functional Literacy: What to Do about It," *Personnel*, October 1987, 42.

11. DeVore, Paul W., "Technology–An Examen," *Journal of Industrial Teacher Education*, Spring 1988, 10.

12. DeCastell, "On Defining Literacy," 12.

13. Neal, William G., "Beyond Computer Literacy: Information Literacy," *Business Education Forum*, December 1987, 13-14.

14. Hirsch, E. D., Jr., *Cultural Literacy: What Every American Needs to Know* (Boston: Houghton Mifflin, 1987), 1-32.

15. Wagschal, Peter H., "Literacy in the Electronic Age," *Educational Technology*, June 1987, 9.

16. Pirani, Judith, "The ISDN Field Trials," *Telecommunications*, January 1988, 72, 74, 104.

17. Leonard, Donald, "ISDN–The Next Decade," *Telecommunications*, August 1987, 39-42,

18. Zirinsky, Driek, "Facing Our Own Literacy Crisis," *English Journal*, December 1987, 62.

Electronic Means for Human Resource Research

ANTHONY DEBONS, DONALD L. SHIREY, MARIANO MAURA-SARDO,
AND ANNE F. THOMPSON

During the past several decades the increasing complexity of problem solving by individuals and institutions (both public and private) has accentuated the importance of information: its acquisition, processing, and use. The rapid development of technology has provided new options for generating, processing, and distributing data–increasing individual and collective awareness, with concomitant potential for understanding and knowledge. As a result, old vocations associated with clerical functions have been entrusted with new definitions. New vocations based on the new applications of data and knowledge have emerged. These developments have challenged and continue to challenge institutions in their charge to prepare individuals for such vocations.

The problem exists as to how the challenge to institutions presented by the advances in technology can be translated into academic programs that prepare individuals with the skills, both conceptual and practical, that are either implicit or explicit in the new vocations. A second dimension of the problem is the determination of the human resources needed to meet the demands of employers for the new and redefined vocations appropriate for the information age.

Many academic programs presently exist that attempt to provide the skills required of information professionals. The following are some of the questions that can be asked about such programs:

- To what extent do the courses meet the needs of the real-world working environment, in terms of both theory and practice?

- Upon completion of the respective programs, to what degree does the competence of the graduate relate to the position titles recognized by those who hire suggested graduates? In other words, to what extent do the position titles adopted by the institution correlate with the designations of the vocation provided by the academic institutions?

- What is the extent of the human resource need for information professionals in public and private institutions?

Academic institutions need these data to support faculty recruitment, to establish background requirements for student admission policies, and to develop standards for the updating of course curricula, for the development of research programs, and for many other requirements that are part of the creation, development, and maintenance of academic departments. Other private and public institutions benefit from such data by providing their personnel departments with guidelines for the recruitment, placement, and training of personnel engaged in information work.

It is these considerations that constitute the motivation for research that attempts to establish the nature, character, and extent of the resources required to meet the demands for information professionals. In a 1980 study conducted by the University of Pittsburgh and supported by the National Science Foundation, it was found that there were at least 1.6 million information professionals in the United States who performed the following functions:

- Managing information operations, programs, services, or databases

- Preparing data and information for use by others

- Analyzing data and information on behalf of others

- Searching for data and information on behalf of others

- Operational information functions not included above

- Information system analysis

- Information research and development

- Educating and training information workers[1]

Individuals who performed such functions were identified by numerous (1,500) occupational titles. It is obvious that trying to identify the type of work an information professional engages in by his or her job title is an extremely tenuous and risky task since it is a many-to-one mapping.

The motivation for the 1980 study remains relevant to the present; as indicated, there is an important need to know the number and the intellectual and technical competencies of the work force that is engaged in acquiring, processing, and using information. The experience with the 1980 study did reveal some basic problems with this kind of research:

1. It is costly and difficult to obtain funding. Unfortunately, the importance of the outcome of this research remains to be fully realized, despite the fervor from the field.

2. The follow-up required for conducting the survey through a paper-pencil instrument is time-consuming, costly, and error-prone.

3. In a new field, definition of terms is a matter of considerable technical difficulty because of the tendency by respondents to translate the new terms into concepts or perceptions of the terms that do not correlate with those established by the creators of the survey. Applications of seemingly related terms blur distinctions that are critical to identifying functions that are important in a new field.[2]

An approach to alleviating these problems is to examine the feasibility of using electronic (computer) means in the conduct of the survey. By presenting the survey instrument electronically, the direct processing of the data gathered from the survey could be expedited. The margin of error due to the handling of the data could be reduced. Follow-up cost (telephonic referral, correspondence to ensure compliance, etc.) could be reduced and, conceivably, survey instrument reliability and validity could be increased through programming and other techniques. Further, electronic means provide the potential for developing computer-human dialogue when explanation and more explication of terms and concepts are demanded by the respondents.

As part of an overall effort to update the 1980 study, the Commonwealth of Puerto Rico, under the auspices of the Graduate School of Librarianship, University of Puerto Rico, engaged in an effort to determine whether electronic means are suitable to conducting a survey on human resource requirements for information professionals. Puerto Rico enjoys excellent telecommunications capabilities that connect a number of academic, governmental, and industrial institutions in a network over the island. The first phase of the project was to select a small sample of respondents from government, industry, and academia to demonstrate the applicability of electronic procedures. The results of such a demonstration would then serve to guide a more comprehensive accounting of the needs of the commonwealth for information professionals. The data from the Puerto Rico study would serve as a guide to a survey of the United States that would be conducted later.

As part of the preparation for the demonstration study, an advisory committee was established, consisting of representatives from industry, government, and academia, to oversee the efforts and provide recommendations to the investigators. The advisory committee was briefed on the objectives, the plans for the conduct of the survey, and the need to ensure its implementation.

The committee together with the present investigators addressed the following technical issues:

- Accounting for the bilingual character of the island's population and the influence of this factor in the construction of an electronic survey instrument

- Procedures to be undertaken to ensure adequate documentation of all variables critical to the credibility of the demonstration

- Mechanisms (documentation) for obtaining data on the time taken to generate the electronic support system (i.e., programming, network synthesis, etc.), and for ensuring that data were collected on the amount of time taken by respondents in completing the survey electronically

- Mechanisms for accounting, electronically, respondents' reaction to the survey

The following procedure was applied in developing the demonstration:

1. Using the survey from the 1980 Pittsburgh study, the content of the form was translated into Spanish. The translation was checked to ensure that it conformed to the idiomatic demands representative of the local culture.

2. A professional systems analyst developed the computer program for presenting the survey items electronically.

3. A manual, in Spanish, was developed to explicate in detail the procedures that governed the proper execution of the survey electronically.[2]

4. Thirty-six respondents were identified and notified orally and in writing of their role and function in the survey.

5. The manual, together with the time and place to report for completing the survey, was mailed to all respondents one week prior to their scheduled time. Each respondent was asked to read the manual at least twenty-four hours prior to the scheduled time for completion of the survey. The respondent was permitted to bring to the survey site the manual and any other data required.

Table 1

	Respondent's Position/Title	Sector*	Respondent's Major Prof. Activity	Respondent's Location
1.	Dept. of Education/ Supervisor III	G	Training/Education	San Juan
2.	Dept. of Education/ Supervisor III	G	Librarian	San Juan
3.	Engineer	I	Consulting	San Juan
4.	Dept. of Education/ Supervisor	G	Librarianship	Mayaguez
5.	Librarian IV	A	System Librarian	Mayaguez
6.	Librarian	A	Librarian/Education	Mayaguez
7.	School Librarian	G	Librarian/Education	Arecibo
8.	Head Librarian	A	Info. Services/Education	Arecibo
9.	Teacher/ School Librarian	G	Education	Humacao
10.	Director of Computer Center	A	Education	Humacao
11.	Materials Supervisor	I	Supervising Manufacture	Humacao
12.	Librarian	I	Indexing	Humacao
13.	Computer Operator	A	Operation	Aguadilla
14.	Head Librarian	A	Education	Aguadilla
15.	School Librarian	G	Education	Aguadilla
16.	Director of Computer Center	A	Education	Aguadilla
17.	University Professor	A	Education	San Juan

*Brief Respondents' Profile:
G = Government
I = Industry/Private
A = Academia

Table 2: Number of Information Professionals by Their Sector of Employment and by Their Information Functions: 1988

Sector of Employ-ment	System Analysis	System Design	Data Prep.	Data Analysis	Search for Data Info.	Remain. Oper. Func.	Info. Mgmt.	Educ./ Training	Re-search	TOTAL	%
Gov't (DPE)	2		1	4	14	37		18		76	9.4
Colleges & Univ.'s	2				32	408		222		664	81.9
Industry	15	45		1		10				71	8.7
Totals	19	45	1	5	46	455		240		811	100

Source: *Pilot study of Information Professionals in Puerto Rico, 1988, University of Pittsburgh and University of Puerto Rico.*

Table 3: Number of Information Professionals by Their Geographical Locations and by Their Information Functions: 1988

Geographi-cal Locations	System Analysis	System Design	Data Prep.	Data Analysis	Search for Data/ Infor.	Remain. Oper. Functions	Info. Mgmt.	Educ./ Training	Research	TOTAL	%
San Juan	2		1	4	12	37		18		74	9.1
Mayaguez					24	150		42		216	26.7
Arecibo					9					9	1.1
Humacao	17	45		1	1	10				74	9.1
Aguadilla						258		180		438	54.0
Ponce*											
Totals	19	45	1	5	46	455		240		811	100

Source: *Pilot study of Information Professionals in Puerto Rico, 1988, University of Pittsburgh and University of Puerto Rico.* *No data received. System was down because of maintenance.*

Table 4: Number of Information Professionals by Their Workfield and by Their Geographical Locations: 1988

Workfield	San Juan	Mayaguez	Arecibo	Humacao	Aguadilla	Ponce*	No. of Info. Prof.	Proportion of Info. Prof. (%)
Library	13	24	9	1			47	5.8
Education & Training	59	192					251	30.9
Computer	2			72	438		512	63.2
Information Services				1			1	0.1
Totals	74	216	9	74	438		811	100

Source: *Pilot study of Information Professionals in Puerto Rico, 1988, University of Pittsburgh and University of Puerto Rico. *No data received. System was down because of maintenance.*

The demonstration study was initiated in the middle of June 1988. The last data from the respondents who completed the survey were completed in August 1988.

Seventeen of the thirty-six completed the survey as asked. Table 1 provides data on the affiliation of those who did complete the survey. The fact that those who responded came from the library community is to be expected inasmuch as the investigators conceded that many of the information professions would represent that aspect of the community of professionals.

Table 5: Number of Information Professionals by Their Occupations: 1988

Selected Occupations	Number of Information Professionals
Computer/SystemAnalyst	19
Librarian	46
Archivist	1
Electrical/Electronic Engineer	25
Engineer (others)	20
Personnel Specialist	10
Educator	240
Supporting Specialist	445
Financial Analyst	5
Total	811

Source: Pilot study of Information Professionals in Puerto Rico, 1988, University of Pittsburgh and University of Puerto Rico.

The data on the specific functions are contained in Tables 2-5. Table 2 shows the distribution of the 811 information professionals over the nine functions and by their sector of employment. Table 3 distributes the same 811 professionals by function and by the geographic area from which they came. In Table 4 the professionals are organized into occupations and the data are presented in Table 5. An assessment of the data can be considered as inconclusive for reasons that we will allude to later in this chapter. It is important to stress at this point that the purpose of the present work was not to obtain human resource data per se but rather to determine the feasibility of obtaining such data electronically. In this connection, we can propose the following:

1.   The survey asked the respondents to indicate their reaction to the experience of responding to the survey electronically. By and large, the respondents stated that the interaction with the computer was difficult and not friendly; that the survey was too long; that the response time by the computer to their actions was sluggish; that the terminology was too technical and at times obscure; that the manual to guide the process was unclear, leaving some questions unanswered; and that the program should allow some sections not applicable to the respondent to be omitted.

2.   Follow-up on the nineteen individuals who did not respond to the survey electronically was undertaken by letter, asking for reasons for noncompliance to the survey. Replies clearly indicated that they were asked to comply at a time when they were on vacation. One respondent indicated that he could not comply when he realized that the computer system available to him would not make possible the interlink with the mainframe located at the University of Puerto Rico.

What does this demonstration effort portend for the use of electronic means to the conduct of surveys of the sort demanded of human resource requirements for information professionals?

RESPONDENT'S COMPETENCE

1.   The computer experience level of the respondent is a variable that will influence the respondent's ability to undertake and complete the survey. Thus, it is not simply a matter of identifying a respondent (as in paper-pencil surveys) and placing such a respondent in front of a computer terminal.

2.   Because of the fixed scheduling required of a survey conducted electronically (i.e., availability of computer, system tie-in, etc.), compliance with such scheduling should acknowledge respondent's personal commitments, seasonal limitations (i.e., weather), vacations, and so on.

3.   Unless all respondents share the same level of computer literacy, the necessity of intermediaries to support the user's ability to comply seems mandated.

SURVEY INSTRUMENT

An examination of the survey data would suggest that the ability of the respondents to make distinctions between functions is influenced by a number of linguistic and cultural variables. For example, when the functions are described in a language that is familiar or clear to the respondent, no problems exist in the ability of the respondent to provide valid data. But conversely, when the language is unclear, the respondents tend to project their own uncertainties by putting their responses in a "catch-all" category, thus obliterating the utility of the data. In addition, the catch-all category can indicate a disagreement with the classification established by the survey instrument. This observation may be particularly relevant when cultural differences exist. The established classification of functions may not correspond to those held by some of the professionals of the culture.

SYSTEM CONSTRUCTION

1. Programming: Twenty-two hours of programmers' time was consumed in generating the software. No particular problem was experienced in this task, other than the variable availability of personnel resources required in the effort.

2. Response time of respondents: The program did include a provision for recording the amount of time taken by each respondent to complete the survey. Unfortunately, it was not possible to collect reliable data on this part of the demonstration. We learned that to be able to collect data on total response time, one needs to possess control of all the system variables that will influence the overall network, namely, reliability in terms of downtime, respondents' preparation prior to the execution of the survey, and so on.

A few conclusions can be advanced regarding our attempt to determine whether electronic means can be applied to the study of human resource requirements:

1. Subjects who are engaged in executing surveys via computer should have a nominal level of literacy. This does not seem to be a factor for individuals undertaking surveys by paper-pencil instruments.

2. Depending on the level of experience of respondents, the need exists for a monitoring agent to aid the respondent during the survey.

3. A serious impediment to electronic means for survey execution is the aborting of the survey because of system breakdown. Surveys conducted electronically are sensitive to system breakdown.

4. The need for program testing to determine flows in data sequencing prior to survey execution is critical.

5. Written aids given to respondents should be carefully tested with the respondents prior to the execution of the survey.

In general, there seems to be a significant difference between paper-pencil and electronic means in the administration of a survey of the sort attempted in this study. Because of the extra support that such activities require, it is doubted that electronic means offers a cost advantage, although it is clear that it does provide a distinct advantage in reducing errors in data collection. Respondent preparation is a prime consideration, as well as having a network support system that is both user-friendly and reliable.

Notes

1. Debons, Anthony, Donald W. King, Una Mansfield, and Donald L. Shirey. *The Information Professional.* New York: Marcel Dekker, 1981. (This study was conducted in 1980.)
2. Ibid.

Acknowledgment

Grateful appreciation for the valuable support provided in the initiation and conduct of this work is extended to Dr. Roberto Loran, director of the Information Systems Office, University of Puerto Rico, and Mr. Francisco J. Principe, systems analyst, Information Systems Office, and the staff of the School of Library and Information Science, University of Pittsburgh. Particular mention and acknowledgment should go to Mrs. Aiza Leon, Graduate School of Librarianship, University of Puerto Rico, who translated the survey form into Spanish.

Section Four

TECHNOLOGICAL APPLICATIONS FOR LITERACY IN EDUCATIONAL SETTINGS

The new information age will require an educational system that equips its graduates with more sophisticated information-seeking and -processing skills. The papers included in this section all address that theme.

Educators and other information professionals ought to be "Adopting a Critical Stance toward Technology," states Pierrette Jamison. Schools, in particular, should embrace new information technologies only when they assist the school in attaining its goals, not simply because they exist and are available at a good price. Linda Main and Char Whitaker describe "Learning the Hypertext Way." The development of hypertext, its advantages, and its potential for teaching writing skills in high school are discussed. At the collegiate level, the "Impact of Electronic Information Technology on Learning: Some Examples" are reported by Steve Alford and Barry Centini. Innovations such as on-line access to class readings and electronic mail as a means to contact faculty are included. Nick Eastmond demonstrates in his essay, "Information Technologies for Foreign-Language Learning for the Twenty-First Century," how computers, video, and CD-ROM can be integrated into the instruction of foreign languages within institutions of higher learning.

"Information Literacy: Only a Beginning" is James Healey's account of the curriculum revision process at San Jose State University's Division of Library and Information Science. The integration of information technology into the curriculum was undertaken to ensure that all future librarians/information scientists graduating from this program would be information-literate. Sheila Smith-Hobson concludes this section with her paper "New Pedagogies and Methodologies for the Teaching of Writing to Remedial Students" who have begun their college or university program. These developments at the college/university level of education show great promise but must be introduced at the primary and secondary levels to have their maximum effect.

Adopting a Critical Stance toward Technology

PIERRETTE KIM JAMISON

> The expert in any technology bears no special responsibility for how others use it, and his share of the blame for any abuse is no greater than anyone else's. Atomic weapons are not detonated by scientists, but by politicians and soldiers. And if IT is abused for evil, rather than used for good, that will not be the fault of the IT experts. . . . My own view is that, like every other technology, IT is morally neutral. . . . Everything will depend on what people do with it. (Sieghart 1982, 9, 15)

Paul Sieghart raises two issues that I believe are crucial to a fuller understanding of technology. The first is that technology is neutral and exists independently of those who create it. The second, by implication, is that "experts" themselves are neutral. However, technology is not developed blindly or without purpose. Technology is developed in response to particular interests within a society and is influenced by both those who create it and those who use it. Therefore, I believe an expanded concept of technology is necessary, one that places technology within the processes (historical, political, social, cultural, and ethical) that generate, and subsequently construct, the knowledge and practices of a society. This reconceptualization of technology asks for a critical analysis of technology.

As information technology (IT) and related fields such as educational technology and instructional technology (which I will collectively refer to as instructional development, or ID) exert influence in education, and as technology increasingly mediates human interaction and learning, questions such as, "What is the relationship between technology and society?" and, "Whose interests will be served by information literacies in the twenty-first century?" are relevant and necessary.

In this paper, I will identify the assumptions and practices in IT/ID that I believe prevent an expanded view of technology and prevent the adoption of

355

a critical stance towards technology. This paper does not outline answers to the questions posed. Instead, it offers a starting point for others, from which further discussion and criticism regarding technology, and its uses in society, may be generated. Drawing upon the work of critical theorists, I hope to illustrate the urgent need for critical analysis, discussion, and responsibility when developing and using information technology in education.

A CRITICAL ANALYSIS OF TECHNOLOGY

The benefits of critical analysis lie in its ability to identify elements of the relationship between technology and society not typically addressed in the theory and practice of IT/ID.

> Not only are more complex causal factors involved in relating technology and society, but the interpretation which turns the chronicle of technological history into the narrative of social history inevitably brings into play human values and questions about the nature of man. (Mitcham 1973, 168)

Once technology is placed in a social context, it becomes a construction of society, and a part of constructed reality. Berger and Luckmann (1966) discuss the importance of acknowledging the social construction of reality and the biases that affect this construction due to historical, political, social, cultural, and ethical knowledge and practices, which are a part of every society.

Critical analysis makes available alternative thought and activity concerning technology and society because it develops a philosophy that "frees us of attachment to specific models and doctrines" (Drengson 1985, 25), such as those supported by IT/ID. Paul Sieghart's statements at the beginning of this paper ignore the knowledge and practices in the IT/ID fields that "legitimize" or dictate what knowledge and values are of most worth in a society and, as a result, what is taught in schools. I believe there are several factors that veil the associated assumptions and presuppositions IT/ID hold about the nature of society and the benefits (or lack of) that IT can provide society. In addition, these factors contribute to and instill the belief that IT is neutral. Therefore, IT and ID legitimize particular interests and professions, capitalize on certain values and knowledge, and limit or ignore other values and knowledge.

Critical analysis asks "hard questions about the source of our values, the image we have of humanity, the duties of the makers and users of technological systems and artifacts, and how to balance long-range goals with those that are short-range" (Hickman 1985, 5). In short, critical analysis generates debate about the meaning and consequences of technology in society.

FACTORS THAT SERVE TO LEGITIMIZE IT/ID THOUGHT AND PRACTICES

The factors I wish to address, which I believe need to be critically discussed and reflected upon, are the following:

1. The language of IT/ID

2. The concepts of "progress" and "change" in IT/ID

3. The roles of "expert" and "nonexpert"

4. The separation of the development of content and materials and the execution of them

5. The selection and presentation of certain values and knowledge, and therefore a construction of a particular reality in the classroom

Language of IT/ID

Language shapes and reflects reality, and therefore knowledge and values. It reveals what an individual thinks about reality, how that individual sees reality, and how he or she believes reality operates. Often, the connection between language and the construction of reality is overlooked. Moreover, although language is obviously present in educational materials, and in inquiry about teachers, students, and learning, the role of language in determining the purposes and processes of education is neglected.

The acceptance of language without analysis implies that one accepts the "worldview" embedded in the language (Skolimowski 1973, 330). In education, this worldview is often characterized by three sets of "metaphors": military, industrial, and disease (Dobson, Dobson, and Koetting 1985, 8). Examples of language associated with the military metaphor are *information systems*, *training*, and *strategy*. The industrial metaphor uses language such as *management*, *cost-effectiveness*, *efficiency*, and *feedback*. Finally, *treatment*, *remediation*, and *prescription* are examples of language used in the disease metaphor (Dobson, and Koetting 1985, 8). Borrowing from military, engineering, and medical fields, these metaphors illustrate a use of language that foregrounds IT/ID's desire for prediction and control. The preference for language that objectifies and orders reality is an attempt to define a particular classroom environment while appearing to remain neutral, or outside of judgment. However, language is value-laden, although IT/ID tries to convince us otherwise. "In education for example, such notions as 'achievement,' 'failure,' 'progress,' 'ability,' (and 'education' itself) are neither objective, nor natural, nor disinterested terms. Rather, they are categories constructed by, and serving the interests of, certain groups" (Gibson 1986, 4).

357

Furthermore, by co-opting language from the military, industrial, and medical fields, education may further distance itself from the values and cultures of a society. For example, in education the term *information* has become an objectified replacement for the term *knowledge*: the phrase *information literacy* is preferred over *knowledge literacy*. Havelock (1986) argues that "information" must be understood to be rooted in a knowledge perspective, regardless of its implied objectivity. "Somehow or other, 'information' has come down to us as a purer term than 'knowledge,' something more acceptable and manipulable in scientific terms, less freighted with cultural baggage" (14).

My analysis of terms like *information* illustrates how language can reinforce the interests of certain groups, such as IT/ID. The worldview dictated by the language of IT traditionally emphasizes industrial, militaristic, and medical approaches to the teacher-learner relationship in the classroom and promotes a focus in education that reflects the underlying ideas and values of IT/ID. In order to develop alternatives to the IT/ID worldview, an alternative language that suggests the aesthetic, ethical, and dialectic in teaching and learning is necessary. A critical analysis of the language currently in use (and more importantly, not in use) in information technology and the classroom is necessary to uncover the effects IT/ID have on the knowledge base, values, and cultural practices of a society.

"Progress" and "Change" in IT/ID

I would like to continue my analysis of language and relate it to differing views of the concepts of "progress" and "change." I discuss the two together because change is often thought of as "an agent of progress" (Skolimowski 1973, 325).

IT/ID promote "technological determinism," or a reliance on technology as necessary for continued growth and advancement. Consequently, IT/ID view change as technical in nature. This type of change results in quantitative, material, and visible progress. However, it ignores the nontechnological components of change and the qualitative, invisible, and immeasurable effects of progress on society.

Pacey (1983) contrasts two kinds of progress: "linear progress" and "contextual progress." Linear progress focuses on the development of technology to complete a particular task, or in some cases, to complete a task faster. This kind of progress, then, is mechanical and technical and is viewed as stable, regular, and homogeneous. In the linear definition of progress, machines perform work more efficiently and effectively because the irregularities and ambiguities characteristic of human performance are controlled or removed (24). Therefore, the focus of linear progress is on the technical or mechanical component rather than the human element. In contrast, "contextual progress" concerns itself with the effects of technological innovation on the organizational aspect of human affairs. This view emphasizes the interaction between social, cultural, and technical factors in society. In addition, the ambiguities and irregularities of human activity are accounted for. Thus, the focus in the contextual analysis of progress is the effects of change on the organization of work, roles, and tasks.

Progress and change in IT/ID, as described by C. A. Bowers (1988) in "Teaching a Nineteenth-Century Mode of Thinking through a Twentieth-Century Machine," are characteristically technical or linear. Bowers suggests that technology strengthens a nineteenth-century cultural tradition based on positivism, whereby the social world and the social experience are reduced to the "observable and measurable" and to "objective knowledge" (45). Therefore, the use of microcomputers in classrooms reinforces a worldview (the worldview of IT/ID) that is based on nineteenth-century patterns of thinking. For example, much of the literature about educational computing highlights the technical problems associated with using technology, while "a discussion of the metaphorical nature of thought, how educational computing reinforces a masculine mode of thinking, or the difference between analogue and digital knowledge" is ignored (44). As a result, alternative or "contextual" views that have been developed, such as those of Berger and Luckmann and the "social construction of reality" school, are put aside. Also, alternative views of the roles of teacher and student, resulting from alternative thought and activity in educational studies, are ignored. Finally, questions about the impact of technology on the environment and on race, class, and sex are given low priority or not discussed at all.

In "Does Improved Technology Mean Progress?" Leo Marx (1987) uses a historical analysis to trace the development of technology and beliefs about "progress." Like Pacey, he identifies two different views of progress: the critical view and the "technocratic" view. The critical view, which can be traced to the writings of individuals such as Thomas Jefferson and Benjamin Franklin, holds that progress should be politically and socially liberating. This view is in line with Pacey's "contextual" description of progress. The technocratic view, represented by Daniel Webster (a spokesperson for business interests and industrialists during the 1840s, who disregarded the political uses of technology) and Frederick Winslow Taylor (author of *Principles of Scientific Management*, 1911, who believed that a task could be reduced to a series of steps and therefore made more efficient), promoted "a belief in the sufficiency of scientific and technological innovation as the basis for general progress" (39). Bowers' criticisms are directed at the technocratic view of progress.

What Leo Marx describes as the "critical view" has been consistently challenged by the technocratic view. As a result, the concepts of progress and change are accepted as offshoots of science and management, and manageability and scientific determinism provide the framework that all change is constructed in and measured against. The technocratic view of progress subordinates the human to the machine. Alternatively, the critical view holds that progress is a human and social/political activity characterized by resistance, divergence, and creativity, not mechanical efficiency.

IT/ID consistently seek technical progress and change that "legitimize" their worldview, industries, and professions. "Computer literacy" and "information literacy" are good examples of a "legitimized" change in education from the viewpoint of a growing industry, the computer industry, and endorsed by the fields of information technology and instructional development. Shor (1986), Giroux (1988), and Magrass and Upchurch (1988) emphasize that the term *literacy* implies judgment about what knowledge or values make an individual "literate" and discuss how "literacy" is used to profit certain industries and support particular values.

A recent advertisement by John Roach of the Tandy Corporation (1988, 30), published in *Newsweek* provides an example of how the technocratic view of progress and change is being promoted in schools. The leading statement of the ad reads, "Global competitiveness in an age of technology begins in the classroom."

Tandy emphasizes the future of America in the world marketplace and the role American teachers and students must play if America is to be competitive.

> For students and teachers demonstrating excellence in high school math, computer science and the sciences, Tandy Corporation wants to reward, honor and encourage you to become Tandy Technology Scholars. We know our future and America's competitiveness is dependent on those who attain excellence in rigorous disciplines. (30)

It is important to critically analyze the language and ideas presented in the Tandy ad. For example, what do words such as *competitiveness*, *excellence*, and *rigorous* refer to? Did Tandy create the ad out of a concern for education, students, and teachers, or out of a concern for its role in the future world marketplace? Will information technology ignore the humanities because they are not "rigorous"? The ad leads the public to believe that excellence requires technological progress. Again, it envisions technological solutions to human affairs and to national and global problems.

My analysis of the technocratic or linear view of the concepts of progress and change leads me to four conclusions. First, progress within the technocratic framework is equated with technical advances or changes. Secondly, the technocratic view of progress relies on observable measures of progress, efficiency, and effectiveness, the result of comparing the external capabilities of a machine with those of a human. Thirdly, the technocratic or linear view of progress ignores the importance of the human dimension in "progress" and the nonmaterial effects of technology on society. And, finally, progress and change within the technocratic framework occur regardless of the costs to society.

The Roles of "Expert" and "Nonexpert"

IT/ID create an artificial separation between "experts" (IT/ID persons, or those who theorize and design) and "nonexperts" (teachers, or those who are required to execute the designs). Teachers are becoming merely "managers" of technology and less practitioners of education. Today, the "practice" of education is increasingly absent from the classroom as commercial enterprises design and package learning media and mass-produce them.

In *Instructional Media and the New Technologies of Instruction* (1985), Heinich and his coauthors argue that the effectiveness of media is dependent on how media "are integrated into the larger scheme" of the classroom (13). They maintain that "the way in which teachers perceive their students" determines how students will behave (28). This view characterizes IT as neutral and is contradictory, since the role of media (and therefore the role of the teacher) is assigned "prior" to its use in the classroom. Ideas such as these (and Sieghart's at the beginning of this paper) are used to legitimize the expansion of IT/ID into the areas of teacher education and practices.

Will teachers be held accountable for students' failure to learn from IT, while the experts are let off the hook? Philip Jackson (1987) argues that the medical and engineering models of teaching supported by IT/ID are ignorant of the teaching experience. He asks for a "rejuvenation" of courses in the foundations of education and in the history and philosophy of education. Jackson echoes the sentiments of many critical theorists when he says that teacher education should "make available to all teachers the rich traditions of thought and practice that are legitimately theirs" (79). Popkewitz and his coauthors (1979) also warn that teaching must be seen as a political, social, and ethical enterprise, not as a site for "industrial production." The irony of the criticisms flung at the profession of teaching by IT/ID experts is clearly evident in the following passage:

> Those who are most noisy about the lowering of standards, about the lack of discipline, about teachers failing their students, are the very same people who have preached the necessity of our fullest subservience to the ethics of the marketplace. Those who attack the teachers most vigorously for their shortcomings and lack of professional commitment are the very same who preside over a system which makes money and profit the ultimate arbiters of morality. (Blackwell and Seabrook 1988, 46)

Separation of Development and Execution

In the classroom, teachers and students use curricula, technology, and other materials that are designed outside of the classroom. Many of these materials, such as textbooks, instructional videos, computer languages, and software programs, are commercially developed and designed by IT/ID "experts." These materials, as well as their content, resources, activities and objectives, are based on the knowledge and values of IT/ID experts. As a result, instructional planning is not based on the unique qualities of different classrooms and on teacher and student relationships, but on "universal" rules, principles, and processes of learning generated by the theory and practice of IT/ID. The teacher and student behaviors (or actions) are generalized and preconceived without knowledge of the individual characteristics of the persons who are present in the classroom.

Thus, the separation of the development and execution of educational materials by IT/ID parallels a belief in the separation of theory and practice found in the positivistic paradigm. Diana Coole (1988) describes theorizing in the positivist paradigm as a "a form of domination, whereby the theorist conceptually appropriates the objects of knowledge" and imposes his or her own laws (267). As a result, the content is "impoverished and fragmented" and stems from the theorist (developer) "lacking any interaction with the world" (267). Her analysis illustrates that the separation of development and execution ignores the necessary relationship between learning processes and learning purposes.

Gibson (1986) and Nunan (1983) state that an emphasis on "processes" is central to the worldview of IT/ID. In this way, any debate on the "purposes" of learning—which calls into question values and judgment about what is of most worth to learn—is limited to the values and knowledge of IT/ID experts. Since IT/ID value the "design rather than the implementation end of curriculum" (Nunan 1983, 47), the focus shifts to the "means" of learning rather than the "ends." Gibson refers to this preoccupation with "means" or learning processes as "instrumental rationality" (7).

> It is concerned with method and efficiency rather than with purposes. Instrumental rationality limits itself to "How to do it?" questions rather than "Why do it?" or "Where are we going?" questions. It is the divorce of fact from value, and the preference, in that divorce, for fact. (79)

Therefore, the separation of the development and execution of educational materials, or the separation of learning processes and learning purposes, reduces learning to the preconceived goals and activities stated by IT/ID experts, which may have little or nothing in common with the purposes of learning articulated by the teacher and student in the classroom.

362

Selection and Presentation of Values and Knowledge in the Classroom

IT/ID's separation of the development and execution of content and materials subsequently designates the values and knowledge made available in the classroom. Teachers and students should be in control of their lives and "able to determine their own destinies" (Gibson 1986, 2). Yet, often in the classroom, knowledge and values are defined in terms of preselected (and contrived) objectives, presentation strategies, and results. Thus, IT/ID effectively remove and censor teacher and student interests and deprives them of power to choose what is of most worth to learn.

Two important elements that IT/ID control in the classroom are behavior and time. "Behavior," according to the worldview of IT/ID, is trainable and observable and is an indicator of achievement of an assigned task or goal. "Time" is something externally manipulated by objectives, the amount of material to be covered, scheduling, or time management. Alternatively, these two elements can be constructed very differently by each teacher or student and utilized for different purposes. These elements may reflect abstract experiences, beliefs, and knowledge, as well as concrete ones. For example, behavior (or action) can be the "actualization of one's hope, one's intent to direct the course of his/her life through the use of human freedom" (Dobson, et al. 1985, 12).

Often, an individual will try to protect his or her beliefs about reality. Gibson (1986) cites the work of Giroux, who refers to this concept as "resistance" (60). In one sense, an individual's construction of reality empowers him or her by providing a set of beliefs that can be used to plan and organize his or her experiences. However, resistance can also prevent an individual from realizing alternatives. For example, teachers are sometimes resistant to the amount of freedom students should have in the classroom. In such cases, teacher resistance hinders positive change for both the teacher and student. Ted Sizer (1988, 5-7) identifies this problem and states that teachers must reflect upon and change their own self-definition, that they must allow students the opportunity to govern themselves. Unfortunately, though, instead of examining teacher resistance (or student resistance) through dialogue with teachers and/or students, resistance and alternative ways of knowing are constrained in the IT/ID-designed classroom, and as a result remain an untapped source of knowledge about (and for) teachers and students.

The effects of the selection and presentation of values and knowledge on an individual's learning, experiences, and construction of reality are evident in computer-assisted instruction. Although many in IT/ID emphasize the effectiveness and efficiency of learning from computers, others such as Michael Striebel (1986) have questioned the kinds of gains in learning from computers and are worried about the technologizing of education. After examining the three major approaches of computer-assisted instruction in education–drill and practice, tutorial, and programming and simulation–Striebel discovered that learning from computers may actually prevent alternative knowledge and experiences.

Drill-and-practice programs "introduced a technological framework into the classroom culture" and lessened the value of nonbehavioral educational goals. Tutorial programs extended the "behavioral and technological approach to learning." The learner "was still treated as a means toward someone else's ends and only given a form of pseudo-control in the interaction." Therefore, tutorials ignored personal and intellectual choice, and they directed learning. Computer programming and simulations "limited the learner's mental landscape to objective, quantitative, and procedural 'intellectual' tools." As a result, the "qualitative, dialectical, and experiential domains of natural and social events" are left underdeveloped (158).

I believe reality is continually emerging, opposing, and changing for the individual. Therefore, the IT/ID view of a controllable and trainable action/time reality is in conflict with the lived world of the individual. Furthermore, by believing it can and should specify, and as a result, select what is valuable to society, IT/ID make choices for us all.

CONCLUSION

The work of Striebel and others indicates a need for critical analysis of the thoughts and practices of IT/ID. IT/ID envision the complexity of learning as a problem of efficiency. Through guarantees, certainty, and closure, IT/ID try to "make explicit as many aspects of people's activity as possible, be it the researcher, educational decision-maker or student" (Apple 1979, 109).

In addition, IT/ID, using a quasi-scientific belief system, move towards centralization, order, and conceptual emptiness. Scientific rationales act as "symbolic canopies" (Popkewitz 1984) that hide the fact that IT/ID do not meet the needs of society or education and, instead, serve the interests of industry and profit.

"Experts" in IT/ID are responsible for the use of technology and must begin to critically analyze its use in society. I believe IT/ID experts should not act as "milk nurses" for IT/ID industries (Rogers 1983, 101). IT/ID so-called experts must adopt a critical stance towards technology and "see beyond the machines themselves to the social system" in which they are used (Forty 1986, 51). Technology is a part of a historical, political, social, cultural, and ethical context, and it must be looked at in this way.

> The important issue to realize is that there are options open to us, and that we should not allow ourselves to be swept along by the internal dynamism of the technology. The future is not "out there" in the sense in which America was out there before Columbus went to discover it. The future is not pre-

determined, nor does it have prescribed boundaries and forms. It is yet to be made by human beings, and as we start to construct it we must never allow ourselves to be so fascinated by the technology and the systems that we forget what it is really about, which is people. (Cooley 1982, 91)

References

Apple, M. *Ideology and Control*. London: Routledge and Kegan Paul, 1979.

Berger, P., and Luckmann, T. *The Social Construction of Reality: A Treatise in the Sociology of Knowledge*. Garden City, N.Y.: Doubleday and Co., 1966.

Blackwell, T., and Seabrook, J. *The Politics of Hope: Britain at the End of the Twentieth Century*. London: Faber and Faber, 1988.

Bowers, C. A. "Teaching a Nineteenth-Century Mode of Thinking through a Twentieth-Century Machine." *Educational Theory* 38, no. 1 (1988): 41-46.

Coole, D. H. *Women and Political Theory: From Ancient Misogyny to Contemporary Feminism*. Boulder, Colo.: Lynne Rienner Publishers, 1988.

Cooley, M. "Computers, Politics, and Unemployment." In *Micro-chips with Everything: The Consequences of Information Technology*, ed. P. Sieghart, 72-97. London: Comedia Publishing Group, 1982.

Dobson, R. L.; Dobson, J. E.; and Koetting, J. R. *Looking at, Talking about, and Living with Children: Reflections on the Process of Schooling*. Lanham, Md.: University Press of America, 1985.

Drengson, A. R. "Four Philosophies of Technology." In *Philosophy, Technology, and Human Affairs*, ed. L. Hickman, 25-39. College Station, Tex.: Ibis Press, 1985.

Forty, A. *Objects of Desire: Design and Society from Wedgwood to IBM*. New York: Pantheon Books, 1986.

Gibson, R. *Critical Theory and Education*. London: Hodder and Stoughton, 1986.

Giroux, H. "Literacy and the Pedagogy of Voice and Political Empowerment." *Educational Theory* 38, no. 1 (1988): 61-75.

Havelock, R. "The Knowledge Perspective: Definition and Scope of a New Study Domain." In *Knowledge Generation, Exchange, and Utilization*, eds. G. M. Beal, W. Dissanayake, and S. Knonshima, 11-34. Boulder, Colo.: Westview Press, 1986.

Heinich, R.; Molenda, M.; and Russell, J. D. *Instructional Media and the New Technologies of Instruction*. New York: John Wiley and Sons, 1985.

Hickman, L. *Philosophy, Technology, and Human Affairs*. College Station, Tex.: Ibis Press, 1985.

Jackson, P. "Facing Our Ignorance." In *Reforming Teacher Education: The Impact of the Holmes Report*, ed. J. F. Soltis, 74-79. New York: Teachers College Press, 1987.

Magrass, Y., and Upchurch, R. L. "Computer Literacy: People Adapted for Technology." *Computers and Society* 18, no. 2 (1988): 8-15.

Marx, L. "Does Improved Technology Mean Progress?" *Technology Review* (January 1987): 33-41, 71.

Mitcham, C. "Philosophy and the History of Technology." In *The History and Philosophy of Technology*, eds. G. Bugliarello and D. B. Doner, 163-201. Urbana: University of Illinois Press, 1973.

Nunan, T. *Countering Educational Design*. London: Croom Helm, 1983.

Pacey, A. *The Culture of Technology*. Cambridge, Mass.: MIT Press, 1983.

Popkewitz, T. S. *Paradigm and Ideology in Educational Research*. New York: Falmer Press, 1984.

_____; Tabachnick, B. R.; and Zeichner, K. M. "Dulling the Senses: Research in Teacher Education." *Journal of Teacher Education* 30, no. 5 (1979): 52-60.

Roach, J. "Global Competitiveness in an Age of Technology Begins in the Classroom ... America's Challenge" (advertisement). *Newsweek* (October 10, 1988): 30.

Rogers, E. *Diffusion of Innovations*. New York: Free Press, 1983.

Shor, I. *Culture Wars: School and Society in the Conservative Restoration 1969-1984*. Boston: Routledge and Kegan Paul, 1986.

Sieghart, P. "IT in Our Times: Or down among the Baboons." In *Micro-chips with Everything: The Consequences of Information Technology*, ed. P. Sieghart, 7-20. London: Comedia Publishing Group, 1982.

Sizer, T. "Putting Ideas into Practice: An Interview with Ted Sizer." *Harvard Education Letter* 4, no. 4 (July/August 1988): 5-7.

Skolimowski, H. "Philosophy of Technology as Philosophy of Man." In *The History and Philosophy of Technology*, eds. by G. Bugliarello and D. B. Doner, 325-36. Urbana: University of Illinois Press, 1973.

Striebel, M. "A Critical Analysis of the Use of Computers in Education." *Educational Communication and Technology Journal* 34 (1986): 137-61.

Learning the Hypertext Way

LINDA MAIN AND CHAR WHITAKER

The computer has affected the way we structure, access, process, and present information. Just as the printing press had an immense impact on the distribution and availability of information, so the computer has had an immense impact on the ease and convenience of using information. Nevertheless, until recently we have had a one-dimensional perception of information. Attempts to make information retrievable in other ways have been limited, partly by technology and partly by the linear model built into our heads since childhood. The reading of the written word is a linear process—we must perceive each word serially, one after the other. Even though new printing techniques allow greater use of graphic methods for communication, we are forced, at least subconsciously, into a one-dimensional perception of information. As we move toward the twenty-first century, a logical progression is to move toward a multidimensional perception of information. Hypertext is just that—a move away from linear, serial-based modes of information perception and a move toward new dimensions of information understanding.

Hypertext is a type of software in which information is stored in discrete nodes that can be given individual addresses or labels. The nodes of data can be displayed on the computer user's screen, and direct software links can be created to connect any file with any other. So, while viewing one file, it is possible to call up any of the linked files through clicking on key words. When a user reads on the screen, "See also a related work by . . . ," it is not necessary to head for the bookshelf or the library. Simply hit a key or click a mouse and the referenced item will appear. It is possible to follow further links or return to the original document. Hypertext is thus a way to link disparate fragments of information, a way to link ideas in separate documents, more like human thought.

If we view hypertext as the ultimate in making the computer interactive, the roots of hypertext go back to Vannevar Bush and his Memex, as outlined in his July 1945 article, "As We May Think."[1] In Bush's Memex, it was possible to store and look up an infinite amount of information and to shift in seconds from one document to another. The technology, however, was not available in the 1940s to enable the Memex to be more than a dream. As technology developed, Bush's ideas resurfaced. The new leaders of the field were Douglas Engelbart (working at Stanford Research Institute, Menlo Park, California) and Ted Nelson, who coined the word *hypertext* in 1965 and founded the Xanadu Operating Company (acquired in May 1988 by Autodesk, developers of computer-assisted design [CAD] software for personal computers [PCs]). Nelson argues that hypertext lets users structure their data based on intuitive associations. Every piece of text, every word, can be treated as a linkable element of an information system. Nelson points out:

> In the same way that we acquire knowledge and begin to consider its relationship to other groups of knowledge, hypertext tools let users gather information and construct relationships, including links with already established bits of information.[2]

At its most ambitious, hypertext will link the whole universe of print and online information.

The reality of hypertext is closely bound up with developments in software and hardware that have occurred in what is regarded as the fifth generation of computers. The fifth generation of computers has been characterized by work with artificial intelligence (AI). AI in its purest sense of making computers do what we do – when we are being intelligent – is still very much at the laboratory stage of development. The future of AI seems to be that it can be built, or embedded, into other applications. As Adam Osborne says, "Hypertext is only made possible because of AI lurking in the background, waiting for the occurrence of a key [?] ex word in a field. When such a word occurs a sequence of events will then be triggered."[3]

AI deals with fuzzy logic, with subjective reasoning made objective, and with a gigantic set of rules. Its development has been closely tied to hardware development in fifth-generation computers: 80386-based CPUs for faster processing; parallel processing (using multiple CPUs to do different pieces of a problem in chunks, simultaneously); the breaking of the 640K memory barrier, first by Apple computers and now by IBM with its OS/2; and CD ROM, which has given us huge volumes of space in which to put information. One technical problem that has not yet been totally overcome is that of file incompatibility, but strides are being made in this direction.

Perhaps the biggest impact of the work done in the fifth generation of computers is the fact that hypertext systems can now run on microcomputers, whereas earlier hypertext programs had to use mini- or mainframe computers.[4] "Guide" is available for micros, as is "Hypercard," which does not claim to be a full hypertext system, but which does contain many characteristics of hypertext. A user as a reader can follow associative links between elements of nonsequential text, and a user as an author can draw such connections, leaving associative links for readers to pursue.[5]

It can be argued that in a hypertext system, there are few commands to learn, a low level of user sophistication, and more direct interaction with information. But it can also be argued that hypertext is a way of storing information in a computer so that you can jump from one item to any other item remotely associated with it, until you reach a state of total befuddlement:

> If you want to move instantly from an economic analysis of diamond mines to a picture of a baseball diamond to a recording of "Diamonds Are a Girl's Best Friend," then hypertext is for you. It is for people whose attention span is no wider than a computer screen.[6]

Perhaps, with ever-developing technology, in the twenty-first century our attention span will be just that. Eric Drexsler of Stanford University has a solution. He wants hypertext materials to carry their own votes and voting system with them, for example, a button to say, "Glad I read this," and a button to say, "This stinks." There could be a button saying, "The *New York Times* liked this."

There is, however, a real danger in hypertext systems. We have the technical ability to establish a complex stream of links between information elements, but where should the links be placed? By the time all the data are computerized and linked, sooner or later there will be so many paths that users will end up spending most of their time guessing which ones might actually be useful. In a hypertext system, the links between pieces of information are just as important as the information itself. Those who make the links in a hypertext system will shape the way knowledge evolves. The links that are embedded determine the kind of information readers will browse through, with all the possibilities for censorship and bias that implies. It is true that it would be possible to set up a number of different paths through the same materials, for example, one for the reader interested in technical detail, another for a reader interested in social implications, and so on. But an illogical guideline could send you on the road to electronic oblivion; the essential fact you are looking for might be hidden down some alternate route or concealed under some text you didn't move the cursor over. If humans do the work, errors and omissions, deliberate or otherwise, will occur. We might also ask, is this any different from relational databases that provide "random" access to information, except that the relationships must all be planned for ahead of time? Access to the content may be spontaneous, but the use of the data must be mapped out during system design. Perhaps by the twenty-first century we will have hypertext systems where the computer will algorithmically broaden searches, estimate the relevance of the material it finds, and establish links.[7]

Another point to consider is that, in a hypertext environment that is truly interactive, the line between the editor, the writer, and the reader blurs. So, where does that leave copyright? How will we establish pricing structures for information on hypertext systems? Will we have to reconsider the old issue of processing information based on its value? Also, people will become familiar with a new way of handling knowledge. Research patterns will change and will concentrate on comprehension and performance based on the *format* of the information.

In the twenty-first century, one of the biggest uses of hypertext will be as a new concept of programmed learning in schools, where students can learn by following a multiplicity of paths instead of just one, and where a teacher can set up word, conceptual, and visual associations. Indeed, a start has already been made along that path.[8] The second part of this paper will outline an application of hypertext in teaching composition that may well be commonplace in the twenty-first century.

In the last ten years, a "back to basics" approach has been instituted in many high schools throughout the United States. The core curriculum for secondary schools has stressed writing, reading, and mathematics. Nevertheless, these basic skills among high school students still seem to be sadly lacking. Remedial classes have been set up to review the "fundamentals" in order to produce better qualified college freshmen, as well as better prepared young adults entering the work force. Students have found themselves confronted with detailed lessons on nouns, verbs, sentence structure, and the construction of concise, coherent paragraphs. This is the usual sequential formula leading to writing of the well-organized three- to five-paragraph composition.

Instruction in writing/grammar can be very mundane and repetitious, but necessary. The perennial worksheet – write out a five-paragraph composition in forty-five minutes every week – becomes a turn-off! An alternative to this rote, boring technique is hypertext. The following discussion and examples illustrate the appropriateness of using hypertext in teaching composition.

A tenth-grade student is assigned to write a five-paragraph descriptive composition on a subject of his or her choice. Before going to the computer, the student makes the decision to look at the definition of the basic elements of a composition, and then to more specifically examine the definition of the descriptive composition. At the computer, he or she types in the word *composition* – or highlights it from a menu – and the following appears on the screen.

A paragraph is a group of sentences that deal with a single topic or idea. Usually, one sentence, the topic sentence, states the main idea of the paragraph. The single idea of the topic sentence is then supported with other related sentences.

The definition of the composition is only slightly different:

A composition is a group of paragraphs dealing with a single topic or idea. Usually, one paragraph, called the *introductory paragraph*, states the main idea of the composition. The *body*, or middle paragraphs, are related to the introductory paragraph. They further explain or support the main idea. The *conclusion*, or final paragraph, pulls all of the information together.[9]

The student feels a further explanation of introductory, body, and concluding paragraphs is important to grasp the composition concept. He or she then highlights or types out the word *introductory* and another screen brings up examples of introductory paragraphs by well-known writers with accompanying explanations.

TYPES OF INTRODUCTORY PARAGRAPHS

There are many types of introductory paragraphs. Each provides a different approach to the material that will be presented in the composition. When choosing the approach that will be the most effective, the writer must consider both the subject and the purpose of the composition.

Four types of introductory paragraphs are illustrated by the following examples.

The Paragraph That Makes a Direct Appeal

Have you ever felt embarrassed because you didn't know what to say? If the answer is yes, you're not alone. If you've ever felt tense, timid, or tongue-tied in social situations – or if you've been so frightened that you've gone out of your way to avoid them – you need some advice on how to deal with them. (Alice Fleming)

In this type of introductory paragraph, the writer speaks directly to the reader. The subject of the composition is introduced. This approach is particularly effective for involving the reader in your topic.

The Paragraph That Uses a Personal Approach

Halloweens I have always considered wilder and richer and more important than even Christmas morn. The dark and lovely memories leap back at me as I see once again my ghostly relatives, and the lurks and things that creaked stairs or sang softly in the hinges when you opened a door. (Ray Bradbury)

In this type of introductory paragraph, the attitude of the writer toward the subject is immediately apparent. A composition that begins with this approach will probably go on to describe a personal experience and the writer's feelings about the experience.

The Paragraph That Describes an Overall Effect

November chills. Raw rain flays the sullen fields and black roofs. Sunlight touches the earth, but shyly. Most mornings are dusted with frost. Storm sashes rattle in the wind. Snow flurries swirl from a lonely sky and whip the flinty earth. It is the time for man-made warmth. (Herb Daniels)

This type of paragraph is effective in "setting the scene" for a composition. It often is used as the opener for a description or for a narrative based on a real or imaginary experience. A writer who uses this approach must be careful to evoke a mood that will be consistent with the content of the composition.

The Paragraph That Arouses Curiosity

Suppose there were no critics to tell us how to react to a picture, a play, or a new composition of music. Suppose we wandered innocent as the dawn into an art exhibition of unsigned paintings. By what standards, by what values would we decide whether they were good or bad, talented or untalented, successes or failures? (Marya Manners)

This type of paragraph invites the reader to find the answers to a question by reading the rest of the composition. It is especially effective for compositions whose purpose is to explain an idea.[10]

The student then has the option of returning to the original screen by typing or highlighting the word *body*, which then transports him or her to the following:

THE BODY

The major part of a composition is the *body*. It is in these paragraphs that the idea indicated in the introductory paragraph is developed or explained.

Sample

It is now seven o'clock and the sun begins to hide behind the hills. Its rays reflect the heat that beat upon the day. But it is cooler now, and both the sun and I begin "to rest." As it darkens, something that catches my eye is the blinking light of the lighthouse. Up ahead the trees clumped together down the side of the hill stand still like soldiers at ease.

In the distance, sounds of the oar boats loading and unloading their wares in the nearby harbor. Above the squawking of gulls and the flapping of their wings is present. The rush of waves at my feet keeps a constant roar, like a drummer beating out the same notes over and over. These sounds blend into one beautiful, mystical melody.

As I walk on, my toes grip the damp, hard-packed sand. I continue ahead as the fresh air surges into me, giving me a burst of new life. Feeling that I am no longer alone, I turn around to see my dog creeping behind me like a detective searching for clues.[11]

The student types or highlights the word *conclusion* – and studies the final concept in the element of composition. Ready then to start the assignment, utilizing the same command procedure as described in the previous sentence, "Winter Happening" by Josephine Johnson and a definition of *descriptive composition* appear on the screen.

Winter Happening

Once in the year there comes *the snow*. There are all manners of snow, both cruel and kind, but there is one snow that people think of as *the snow*. It is the symbol of all snows, the childhood miracle that remains forever an image larger than all the bitter snows that come before and after.

The snow falls slowly in soft clusters like fairy snowballs. The clusters are so slow, so far apart that children can stand and catch them on their tongues. The snow clings where it falls, pure as wool blankets. The thistles become flowers. The wild carrot blooms again. Everything is unbelievably still.

The snow falls to the proper depth, to the exact moment when all ugliness is covered, to the weight that the twig and branch can bear without breaking. It knows precisely when to stop. All night *the snow* remains motionless unless a twig is shaken by an owl or a weasel. It hardens a little with a light crust, to bear the weight of the wild things walking in the night.

The morning comes slowly and begins with a gray whiteness. The ground is stitched with tiny tracks that end suddenly in round, damp holes, or vanish where a small thing flew upward. Rabbit tracks wander along the raspberry thickets, and the sycamore balls have little caps of fur. It is best in this white grayness before the sun has come through the ascending clouds. The brooding, silent, closed-in world of *snow* and whiteness, motionless except for the birds, a timeless moment like an enormous pearl, a moment of stillness before the sun, and the thousand-diamond glitter and the rainbowed sound of light.

Even children, whose first thought is to tramp it and scrape it into balls, stand for a moment in awe. They drink in the miracle that is to become forever *snow, the snow* that is almost too beautiful to be borne. (Josephine W. Johnson)

MOOD

The mood of a *descriptive composition* often depends on the mood a writer was in as he or she viewed a scene. Suppose you are looking down at a city street. The sky is dark. Heavy, black clouds are moving in from the west. The wind is blustery, and thunder rumbles in the distance. You may feel depressed, melancholy. This is the mood that will be reflected in your description of the scene. To achieve this mood, you would use words such as *dismal, oppressive, dreary,* or *cold*.

On the other hand, suppose the sight of an oncoming thunderstorm fills you with excitement. The details of the scene would remain the same, but your description of them would change. Now you would use words such as *powerful, brisk,* and *electric* to create an entirely different mood.

A *descriptive composition* is a type of *essay* – a short composition in which the writer expresses some sort of opinion or personal view. In contrast to the description, the artistic description is primarily subjective. Therefore, the mood the writer creates is very important.

Read the following artistic description.[12]

Now the student feels ready to begin writing. By typing the letters *WP*, a menu comes on the screen offering a word processing program. The student can then begin to create on the computer. While composing, he or she perhaps is unable to remember when the word *west* should or should not be capitalized. However, by typing or highlighting the word *capitalization*, a list of capitalization rules appears with examples. The student is then able to zero in on the one rule that will solve the problem. For example:

Capitalize names of sections of the country but not of direction of the compass.

Cotton was king in the South.

Cities in the Southwest are flourishing.

It is just north of Paris.

They flew east through the storm.

She lives on the north side of the street.

The lake is west of our cottage.

The hurricane moved northward.

Capitalize proper adjectives derived from names of sections of the country. Do not capitalize adjectives derived from words indicating direction.

an Eastern school; southerly course

a Western concept; an eastern route[13]

Then, by typing *WP*, he or she is back at the word processing screen to continue with the descriptive composition assignment. The student decides to take another look at the sample introductory paragraphs. By typing the word *composition*, the screen with the paragraphs appears. The student rereads the Ray Bradbury paragraph and decides he or she would like to know more about this writer. By highlighting or typing the writer's name, a biographical sketch appears with a complete annotated bibliography of his works. In a fully developed hypertext program, a student could read a short story or an abridged version of one of Ray Bradbury's novels. What in fact the student has done is move from language to literature without realizing it.

The end result of these examples is that the teacher constructs the lessons that can be good, or not so good, depending on how the lesson on composition is formulated. However, utilizing the computer and the linking process provides the student with instant access to areas of weakness or interest in order to proceed with the assignment.

Notes

1. Vannevar Bush, "As We May Think," *Atlantic Monthly* 176 (July 1945): 106-7.

2. Ted Nelson, *Computer Lib/Dream Machines* (Berkeley, Calif.: Tempus Press, 1987), 17.

3. Remarks made by Adam Osborne, president of Paperback Software International, Berkeley, California, at a reception in April 1988.

4. Examples of hypertext systems available for microcomputers with CD ROM drives are "Hyperties" and the "Electronic Encyclopedia," developed by the University of Maryland; "Intermedia," developed by Brown University; and "Notecards," developed by Xerox PARC.

5. "Guide," is produced by Owl International, Bellevue, Washington, and "Hypercard" by Apple Computer, Cupertino, California. The Boeing Aircraft Corporation and several auto manufacturers have also set up manuals on hypertext systems on micros for their technicians.

6. Edward Mendelson, "Electric Language: A Philosophical Study of Word Processing," *New Republic* 198, February 22, 1988, 37.

7. A program called "Personal Librarian" has been developed to attempt just this.

8. Gregory Crane, "Extending the Boundaries of Instruction and Research," *T.H.E. Journal* (MacIntosh Special Issue) 16, no. 2 (September 1988): 51-54; Mia McCroskey, "MacIntosh and Multimedia," *T.H.E. Journal* (MacIntosh Special Issue) 16, no. 2 (September 1988): 71-72; Andrew Phelan, "The Albers Project: A Model for Multimedia Coursework," *T.H.E. Journal* (MacIntosh Special Issue) 16, no. 2 (September 1988): 73-75.

9. Joy Littell, ed., *Building English Skills – Blue Level* (New York: McDougal, Littell & Co., 1985), 180.

10. Ibid., 197-98.

11. Ibid., 199.

12. Ibid., 227-29.

13. Ibid., 647.

Impact of Electronic Information Technology on Learning: Some Examples

STEVEN E. ALFORD AND BARRY AUSTIN CENTINI

Education has moved from an era of movable type to movable digits, from nonvolatile, portable memory (print) to volatile electronic storage devices. This movement has caused a change from a more or less static system of books with stable authorship, ownership, and copyright to a system of dynamic knowledge bases whose contents can be altered at will, moved at the speed of light, and copied without the original owner losing possession of the original document. While erasers, overnight mail, and photocopying can achieve similar results, the online environment combines these powerful capacities in tools that may or may not be used wisely by any individual with a personal computer, a modem, and a communications line. With the advent of "information" as a global concept that includes language as a communicative tool, the switch from movable type to movable digits has fundamentally altered the semantic relation of word to meaning: digits can represent sentences, graphics, video, or audio. If digits are the basis of information, if the online environment has, consciously or unconsciously, changed our understanding of our relation to words as radically and democratically as did movable type, how must we rethink our responsibility as educators?

OUR EXPERIENCE WITH ELECTRONIC LEARNING

Entire organizations are being redesigned with "information" as the core structural concept (Penrod 1983). With the development of systems such as "Andrew" at Carnegie Mellon University (Morris 1986), the use of networked computers to take education out of the classroom and into the home and dormitory will increase dramatically. Alford (1985-88), Centini (1985-88), Scigliano (1985-87), and their coauthors have described Nova University's use

379

of personal computers, the TYMNET packet switching network, and a Nova campus-based VAX 8550 running Unix (Ultrix 2.3) to deliver both undergraduate and graduate-level programs of study. With students (from twenty-three states and Canada) pursuing their course work through telecommunication links, Nova has become one of the leaders in computer-based distance learning.

The electronic tools that enhance computer-based learning include:

- Electronic mail

- Teleconferencing

- Relational database management systems

- Analytical writing packages

- Statistical packages S and SPSSx

- Simulation languages

- Electronic spread sheets

- Course authoring systems

- Language compilers and interpreters

- C-based educational tools and services

- Unix information management tools

Standard Unix tools satisfy many of the students' requirements. However, continued efforts to meet online students' needs have provided enough challenges to warrant unique software development. Using Unix shellscripts and C programs, the staff of Nova University has produced the following software tools:

1. ECR – the "electronic classroom," an interactive learning environment that can accommodate up to twenty-four students per classroom. The design and application of this program have been discussed elsewhere (Scigliano 1987).

2. Electronic management tools – A series of programs has been developed for filing student work and keeping track of progress. A system, "electronic student," allows automatic storing and record-keeping, with proper student/instructor notification, to be

in effect at all times with minimum supervision. A "grader" program allows instructors with minimum computer expertise to read assignments and make comments, select sections of text for discussion, and mail their critiques to the student.

3. Electronic curriculum guides–Menus, tutorial drivers, tutorial expert systems, and other student aids have been designed so that students can choose the level of "system help involvement" and find the electronic learning style that best suits their needs.

TRADITIONAL EDUCATION

Traditionally, the term *education* has been equated with *liberal education* – one appropriate to a free man, meaning one who is not a slave. Being liberally educated means learning what it means to be free. In turn, freedom, generally conceived, manifests itself in three ways: political freedom, moral freedom, and intellectual freedom. At the university, students learn about these freedoms by experiencing what we loosely call "human culture," artifacts whose sole purpose is to nourish and stimulate the soul toward a greater appreciation of its freedom. (In turn, the educated person can then create new artifacts, furthering the development of human culture.) We can also say that universities are repositories of culture, and that one of the university's principal functions is to maintain and transmit culture to maintain human freedom.

There are several things to note about this pre- or antibehavioral description of education. Principally, education's function is to form something, an ill-defined but generally agreed on something within the student, the mind or soul. The purpose of what we might call "educational media," such as books or writing instruments, was to facilitate this inward formation. That is, education was in no way principally oriented toward developing mechanical skills, although a well-formed soul may be in a better position to quickly and independently develop those manual skills.

Hence, *knowledge* functioned to change the person; the person did not use knowledge to change the world, or rather, the person did change the world as a by-product of another, inner change. In a pure sense, education was practically useless, since it concentrated on forming the soul, although it could become useful, since, for example, a student with a well-founded understanding of what it means to be free had a good chance of becoming a skilled politician.

Also, it is worth noting education's moral force: a person who knew what it meant to be free was somehow morally better than a person who did not, although we may reserve judgment on the relation between knowledge and practice. In any event, education was not a neutral enterprise; it sought moral elevation in students.

To summarize: liberal education changed the inner self of the student, the function of the knowledge acquired during education was to effect this change, and this change was viewed as moral improvement.

INFORMATION THEORY'S CHALLENGE TO EDUCATION

It is worth reviewing this classical understanding of education to contrast it with the challenge it has received from the various forms of information theory. Originating with a series of papers by Claude Shannon of Bell Laboratories in the late 1940s, and then restricted to a mathematical solution to problems in telephony, information theory has now become a full-blown metaphysical system. Seeing all nature as matter, energy, and information permits information theory's metaphysical claims to range from the microscopic to the cosmic. The DNA molecule is an information system, with a message, a channel, noise, and entropy. Both computers and brain neurons are two-state entities. The universe may well be one giant cellular automaton. Claims such as these, combined with the physical presence of computers at the university, are bound to influence the definitions of critical terms used in universities, such as *knowledge, understanding*, and, indeed, *education*. Hence, the presence of computers on campus is not primarily an issue of budgets, training, and technique, to be solved by administrative committees, but a genuine intellectual force whose symptoms are computers, but whose cause is information theory itself.

A better understanding of the conflicts between liberal education and information theory as it seeks to redefine education will allow educators to make more intelligent practical decisions about curriculum, distribution of funds, training, and administration. Let's review some common issues in education and how they have been changed by the intersection of information theory with the traditional understanding of education, issues regarding information ownership, students' expectations of faculty, the impact of computer-based learning on extracurricular faculty issues, the changing nature of a student paper, and the loci of information resources.

INFORMATION AS PROPERTY

Our understanding of property has its roots in Locke, and more recently, Marx. Used by them as a political term, its meaning has extended into the legal system and, within the academy, to the notion of "intellectual property": one can "own" one's writing through copyright. But unlike traditional property, property on the computer is a constantly renewable resource. If I sell you a plot of land, I had the land and now you have it. If I sell you a piece of information, I had the information and now you have it, and yet I still have it. While the same phenomenon obtained with the advent of the photocopy machine, the range of computers, both for sending information (through modems) and for manipulating it (changing the information once it comes into another's possession), challenges the imagination.

For the teacher, the issue arises with respect to plagiarism. To plagiarize is to "take ideas, writings, etc. from another and pass them off as one's own." Many teachers fear the integration of computers into the curriculum, since they would allow a student to incorporate another student's work without leaving a trace. Rather than retyping a term paper, the student, armed with an electronic copy, need not retype it, and the student can modify it so that the new paper does not resemble the old one enough to be immediately identifiable.

However, while computers may seem to introduce a dangerous new level of possibilities for plagiarism, two things need to be observed. First, computers may make copying other work easier, but that does not change the recurrent problem: prior to computers, students could retype term papers, have their girlfriend or boyfriend do the work, or buy a paper from a term paper company. The teacher had no more assurance before computers that the work was the student's own than after computers. The presence of computers does not threaten to complicate issues of plagiarism any more than their absence; it just makes plagiarism a little easier for the student. Second, while computers may make plagiarism a little easier for the student, they also make it easier to detect for the teacher. Armed with search commands for a single file, and comparison commands for two files, a teacher need no longer rely on visual inspection to determine similarity between two papers. The possibility of searching and comparing files gives the teacher extra power in determining whether a text was plagiarized. Generally speaking, this problem only reminds us that all classes should combine home assignments with in-class assignments. Having students do supervised work in class gives the teacher a basis for comparison with work done at home.

Our experience has been that students have shown great restraint in "sharing resources," if we restrict the use of that concept to sharing with another user. "Reusing their own resources," the practice of writing a paper for one subject and reformatting it for another, can occur. Here the importance of networking computers, particularly developing common faculty access to student databases, becomes apparent. If faculty are encouraged to "search" student databases for similar papers, the practice of autoplagiarism will be greatly diminished. To our knowledge, most traditional academic settings do not provide a mechanism for such oversight.

STUDENT "PAPERS"

In our online environment, we have created an option for students to post papers in a menu-driven system that fundamentally changes the idea of a "paper." The options that affect our definition of a paper are as follows:

1. The ability to change the paper at any time, that is, to add new bibliography, update material, and so on

2. An option for the reader to add comments to the paper that, in effect, become part of the online paper itself—these comments are mailed electronically to the author to encourage a dialogue

3. An option to "talk" directly to the author who is online at the time of reading—this creates a "live" interactive dialogue

These three simple options appear more innovative if one tries to picture them being available to a library patron. To pick up a book by a living author and add comments to the book, send a letter immediately, or even talk to the author directly, are options that exist only in fiction. In the online world, they are not only possible but easily done.

FACULTY ACCESS

In an online environment, the student never needs to wait for classtime or office hours to communicate with a faculty member. Instead, electronic mail and real-time, online communication commands mean that the student can communicate with the teacher instantly. This possibility, however, can create two opposing problems. First, students can assume that instantaneous communication implies instantaneous evaluation or reply. If their messages reach the teacher immediately, why does it take the teacher two days to reply, or one week to evaluate work? Here, it is important to separate the notion of communication from reply or evaluation. Teachers, finding themselves with a "stack" of electronic mail messages, can feel compelled to reply instantly, creating an expectation in the students that will cause problems over time. These same teachers would not have treated a stack of papers or exams similarly.

However, an opposing problem also occurs. In the online environment, it is possible that the teacher sees the students in person less than in a conventional educational environment. Some teachers, not having to "face" their students, take the opportunity to avoid replying to students at all; they find it easier to simply not log in, much easier than walking into a classroom and listening to students' questions about when their papers will be returned. Teachers with this attitude create problems for student perceptions of the overall online environment. When they receive no response, they feel adrift and alone, not a healthy educational situation. The solution to both these problems is to establish a set of expectations at the outset. Faculty, among themselves, can arrive at standards for reply: forty-eight hours for a mail message, ten days for a paper, or a note saying the evaluation will be delayed. This way, both students and faculty share expectations. Teachers should be made aware of these problems, of too compulsive a reaction to the computer's "demands," or a too lackadaisical attitude, given the ease with which the demands can be ignored.

FACULTY RESPONSIBILITIES

A related problem concerns the relation of an online faculty member to the administration. If, as is the case at some institutions, faculty are considered laborers who must occupy their offices a certain number of hours a day, what does the possibility of being online do to such considerations? Should faculty be allowed to move to an "electronic cottage" relation with their students? Or, are faculty who continue to work during the day but interact extensively with students online during the evening, working the equivalent of two jobs? There are no easy or general answers to such problems, given the differences in institutions and individual work patterns. However, once an online environment has been introduced, a correlative understanding of what constitutes faculty "free time" should be established as well.

Several ways of approaching the problem present themselves: online time could be used as an equivalent to office time, or online time could be considered an equivalent of the time all teachers spend concentrating on student work outside the workplace. Online "office hours" could replace regular office hours, or merely supplement them. An online "homework hotline" could be considered part of the job duties, or replace other duties. In any event, the important issue is that administrators and faculty alike should arrive at an understanding about what constitutes "free time." One complicating factor is the various ways that faculty react to computers: for some it is a compulsive activity, one that they think should be rewarded; for others, computers should be avoided for everything except the most necessary tasks. Should the compulsive faculty member be rewarded for following the compulsion? To repeat, there are no easy answers to these problems, but they do need to be worked out between administration and faculty.

Faculty can also react negatively to computers because computers provide students with tools that make certain tasks much easier than in the past, such as spelling checkers or thesauri. Faculty think that these tasks should not be made easier, that part of the formation of the students' minds is involved in doing the tasks. Two things need to be kept in mind. First, a spelling checker does not find spelling errors; it finds words that do not match a master list in the computer's memory. Hence, the student still must determine if a word is indeed misspelled and take steps to correct the spelling. Second, much was made a few years ago of the entrance of calculators into math classes. Calculators have not spelled the doom of undergraduate math education, and it is unlikely that a spelling checker, a thesaurus, or any other similar tool will reduce students' intellectual abilities.

LIBRARIES, TEXTBOOKS, AND THE ELECTRONIC ENVIRONMENT

Finally, the presence of computers on campus has affected the concept of the library and the textbook. One means of dealing with online information services is to rethink the concept of the library and conceive of it as an "information center," with access to online search services, an online "card" catalog, and so forth. In the not-too-distant past, other media became fashionable, such as audiotapes, films, and other resources, and were adapted to students' individual "learning styles." Then, the push was for the library to become a "media center," with books being one of many available media for education. Despite the pundits' prognostications, books will remain the central focus of education; paper will not disappear in a cloud of electrons. In the library, computers should be used as tools for research, but it should also remain clear that they are ancillary equipment to the central concern of the library: books.

One exciting possibility exists, however, in the relation of the online environment to the textbook. Traditionally in, for example, literature, teachers have made do with massive survey textbooks for many courses, such as the Norton editions of world, American, and English literature. No teacher ever would or could assign the entire book, but students had to carry a tome that would make a good boat anchor. Conceivably, in an online environment, rather than order the entire book, the teacher could order a set of copies of a book, picking from an available list of authors. The works of the authors picked by the teacher could then be printed and bound, saving the company much paper and meeting the teacher's needs directly. The students would have a tailor-made book that covered the course's aims and no more. While we should remind ourselves that the Bobbs-Merrill reprint series sought to achieve this goal in an analog, rather than digital, fashion, it remains a possibility worth considering.

Clearly, educators dedicated to both the economic and pedagogic success of their institutions cannot afford to either reject computer technology on romantic grounds or embrace it as the technocratic key to educational success. Educators must recognize that the presence of computers on campus reflects a more profound challenge to education than the immediate budgetary implications. Computers themselves are symptomatic of a larger phenomenon: the conflict of traditional, humanistic views of education with information theory. Careful thought will be required at all levels of the university system to ensure that the curricular needs of the students and the budgetary needs of the institution are improved by electronic learning.

References

Alford, Steven. 1985. "Practical Implementation of Unix in Writing Instruction." *National Issues in Higher Education* 18: 19-26.

Centini, Barry, and Alford, Steven. 1988. "A Computer-Networked Environment for Developing Composition and Math Skills." Paper presented to the George Mason Conference on Nontraditional/Interdisciplinary Programs, Virginia Beach, Virginia, 1988.

Centini, Barry. 1987. "Telematics and Education." Paper presented at the Conference on the Impact of Telematics in the Development of Costa Rica, San Jose, Costa Rica, 1987.

Centini, Barry, and Rafferty, M. 1987. "Extending Field-based Learning through the Use of Telecommunications: A Paradigm." Paper presented at Kansas State University's Conference on Innovation in Higher Education, Fort Lauderdale, Florida, 1987.

Centini, Barry; Scigliano, John; and White, A. 1987. "Online Training for Trainers: A Working Model Based on UNIX." Paper presented at the Annual Conference of the Association for Development of Computer-based Instructional Systems (ADCIS), Oakland, California, 1987.

Centini, Barry, and Scigliano, John. 1986. "Telecommunications-based Learning: The Final Educational Frontier?" Paper presented to the George Mason University Conference on Nontraditional/Interdisciplinary Programs, Arlington, Virginia, 1986.

Centini, Barry. 1986. "Telecommunications in Education." Paper presented at the Caribbean Telecommunications Council Annual Meeting, San Juan, Puerto Rico, 1986.

Centini, Barry, and Maddock, Jeremy. 1986. "Networked Training for Information Scientists." Paper presented at the Annual Conference of the American Society of Information Science (ASIS), Chicago, Illinois, 1986.

Morris, James H., et al. 1986. "Andrew: A Distributed Personal Computing Environment." *Communications of the ACM* 29, no. 3 (March): 184-201.

Penrod, James I. 1983. "Information Technology Literacy: Initiatives at Pepperdine University." *EDUCOM Bulletin* 18, no. 1: 11-15.

Scigliano, John A., and Centini, Barry. 1988. In *The Unix Microcomputer Environment*, eds. Sheila S. Intner and Jane A. Hannigan, Phoenix, Ariz.: Oryx Press.

Scigliano, John A.; Joslyn, Don; and Levin, J. 1988. "An Online Classroom in Unix." Paper presented at the Florida Instructional Computing Conference, Orlando, Florida, 1988.

Scigliano, John A.; Joslyn, Don; and Centini, Barry. 1987. "The Electronic Classroom." Paper presented to the IEEE Southeastcon '87, Tampa, Florida, 1987.

Scigliano, John A. 1987. "Artificial Intelligence and Expert Systems in Instructional Design." Paper presented at the Florida Instructional Computing Conference, Orlando, Florida, 1987.

Scigliano, John A., and Mizell, Al. 1986. "Telecommunications: The Online Frontier for Media Educators." Paper presented at the Annual Conference of the Florida Association of Media Educators, Orlando, Florida, 1986.

Scigliano, John A. 1986. "Local Area Networks: The Computer Condominium." *American School and University* 58, no. 8 (April): 12.

Scigliano, John A., and Centini, Barry. 1985. "Unix in a Community of Scholars." Paper presented at the Mid-year Conference of the American Society of Information Science, Fort Lauderdale, Florida, 1985.

Information Technologies for Foreign-Language Learning for the Twenty-First Century

JEFFERSON NICHOLLS EASTMOND, JR.

The age of information is bringing our world together, through communication and improved transportation. As former Secretary of Education Terrill H. Bell has stated, "No country has a separate future." Levels of interdependence are increasing. The farmer in the American Midwest has much at stake in the weather and harvests occurring in other countries, as does the automobile manufacturer or dealer. Our world has become interdependent and can be expected to become more so in the coming decades.

While many barriers to improved communication among nations have been removed, a major one that remains is the barrier of language. In addition to the challenge of the linguistic code is the set of differences imposed by culture. Attaining fluency in another language – with the ability to listen, speak, read, and write effectively – represents a major task, requiring years of study and continued practice.

This paper will explore the technological means now coming of age to shrink this task. Some of us who thrive on the joy of foreign-language learning cringe at even calling it a task, but the fact remains that considerable and dedicated effort is required to bridge the gaps of language and culture. New technologies are now available to make language learning more enjoyable and more efficient. The examples given in this paper will be drawn primarily from French, since this has been my particular area of interest. Similar materials have been under development in other languages as well; these instances will be cited when they exist only in another language.

The recent experience at the U.S. Air Force Academy will be highlighted as well. At the present time, seven languages are taught to cadets: French,

Spanish, German, Russian, Arabic, Chinese, and Japanese. Where possible, the academy's experiences with technology will be generalized to other modern languages as well.

The various media forms and their application to foreign-language instruction will be examined in light of a model proposed by the Corporation for Public Broadcasting (Johnston 1987, 18). This model classifies technologies according to increasing levels of sophistication–audio, video, and electronic text and graphics, from passive, linear, interactive communications to interactive user command and control. Video technology, building upon nearly a century of progress in the cinema, will be examined first, followed by a discussion of computer technology, which came after World War II but became readily available to individuals and schools in the form of the microcomputer mainly within the last decade. The final technology, videodisk, combines both previous media–the visual advantages of video with the interactive capability of the computer–and has only become available for training applications in the past five years.

Additionally, the terms *second-language learning* and *foreign-language learning* will be used synonymously, recognizing that there are differences in the difficulty of the language task for those studying another language for which native speakers are easily found (e.g., Spanish) and those for which they are seldom encountered (e.g., the languages labeled "strategic"–Arabic, Russian, Chinese, etc.).

One additional assumption ought to be made clear at this point. While it is assumed that much learning of foreign language occurs with individuals acting as autonomous learners, the value of the language classroom, with the teacher serving as a role model and source of motivation, is not to be overlooked. As learners become more sophisticated, as more people are exposed to a second language and begin working on a third or a fourth, it can be anticipated that learners will be more capable of learning greater amounts independently. However, in this paper both the language classroom and the outside activities will be considered.

THE IMPACT OF VIDEO

The use of video for foreign-language instruction is a topic that frequently excites the teacher of foreign language. Bringing in foreign-language films, scenes of actual life in the target culture, and idioms from actual speech–all these are exciting.

Actually implementing video instruction in the classroom turns out to be more difficult than many would anticipate, as the language seldom comes in the order the teacher wants to teach it or the learner is prepared to learn it. Most video is more comparable to watching a foreign film or foreign television than to the measured pace of the foreign-language lesson. In video, the words come out rapidly and in a order dictated by the patterns of the native speaker.

The most prominent theory of second-language learning (Krashen 1981) would suggest that the learner is best served by frequent exposure to "comprehensible input," namely, expression in the target language that is just slightly above the current ability of the language learner, thus challenging him or her to listen with curiosity and to infer the meaning of unknown words from context. For the teacher using video, the task is often to somehow slow down the flow of words and to keep the utterances understandable to the student.

Video-based Instruction via Television

Probably the most prominent use of video to teach has been the "French in Action" series. Speakers of French were delighted to see this Annenberg Foundation/CPB-funded series developed by Pierre Capretz and his colleagues at Yale University and broadcast over PBS in the United States beginning in the fall semester of 1987. The series consists of fifty-two half-hour television programs, accompanied by a full set of course materials – including audiotapes, text, student workbooks, and study guides (Capretz 1987). It was targeted at the college-level teaching of French and covers material equivalent to two years of college French. It has been designed to be used as part of a college class or as a telecourse, with the learner working independently.

The course has received considerable attention among teachers of foreign languages, in part because of the professional manner in which the work was carried out and in part because of the modest pricing structure required for purchase. The videotaping was done on location in France, with quality video production and current situations and language usage. The story line, which carries through the entire series, features a college-age American (Robert) who makes the acquaintance of a Parisian girl (Mireille), shown as a student at the Sorbonne. The story line resembles a small soap opera but allows for an exposition of family members, daily situations, and considerable culture along the way; for example, it includes visits to scenic spots in Paris, a ride on the TGV (high-speed train), a tour of the cathedral at Chartres, and so on.

Pricing of this series, as mentioned above, has been subsidized by Annenberg and is most reasonable. For example, the rights to off-air copying of all fifty-two half-hour programs, for use as supplementary materials for out-of-class work, cost a mere $200, good for the life of the tapes. With that type of pricing structure for quality materials, many teachers of French have been interested.

If all goes according to plan, an experimental version of the "French in Action" series will be made available on videodisk for the first twenty-six lessons, yielding thirteen double-sided videodisks. Production should be completed prior to the end of 1988.

Videocassettes Distributed Separately

With the widespread distribution of videocassettes, independent or classroom use of video is increasingly promising. The use of video in the classroom on videocassette is often favored by teachers, as it is completely under teacher control and can readily bring in television or film of the target country.

One recent development aimed at the home viewer is the "France Panorama" series. This service offers a monthly videocassette mailed directly to the home of the subscriber, who can view one program summarizing recent news and cultural events of France. The cost of subscription is modest, similar to subscribing to a magazine. The series appears to be targeted at an audience with considerable experience and fluency with the language. However, teachers of foreign language at the college level are quick to catch hold of this sort of material and to make it available to their students.

Another development making extensive use of videocassette technology, also funded by the Annenberg Foundation, has been the Project for International Communication Studies (PICS). Begun as a consortium of five American colleges with interest in foreign-language video, the project has received national recognition and funding to bring recent video material of quality to teachers of foreign language. PICS obtains the video material, obtains copyright permission for use in the United States, transfers the material from the foreign video standard (e.g., PAL or SECAM) to the North American standard (NTSC), and distributes a catalog of available materials. Most developed at present in French, its catalog also includes video material in Spanish and German.

Satellite Transmissions

Another prominent use of foreign-language video has been the growth of off-air recording from satellite transmissions. Capturing authentic video from satellite appears to be the equivalent of recording shortwave radio broadcasts in the 1950s, except that now more of the nonverbal cues are recorded. Many college campuses now have the capability of receiving stations in commonly studied foreign languages; the more exotic languages are available in some parts of the United States. In particular, the U.S. Naval Academy at Annapolis has made extensive use of satellite recordings. While the advantages of such material are obvious–immediacy and topics of interest–the disadvantages are also considerable: obtaining copyright clearance is difficult, and the problem of editing for classroom use can be time-consuming.

IMPACT OF COMPUTERS

The microcomputer revolution has transformed the American office and is presently transforming the academic community. The uses of computers for language instruction are many. However, it does not take long to find examples of poor use of the technology. The most prominent uses at present are:

1. Computer programs for drill and practice – The student can review and be tested on an unending series of grammatical points with an infinitely patient mechanical tutor.

2. Computer programs that allow simulations – An example of such a program now available would be Blue Lion Software's "Trip to Paris" program (available for Apple or IBM), which allows the student to visit various parts of Paris vicariously, to make actual decisions about where and when to eat, and to obtain certain bits of cultural knowledge.

Certain new varieties of computer applications promise to have even more impact on the teaching of languages:

1. Just as the addition of a spelling checker program to word processing in English is a powerful combination, the same sort of tool for writing in a foreign language is powerful. An example would be the recently developed "Systeme D" program in French, which allows the user to create sentences in French, complete with accent marks, and then to have them checked by computer. Particularly as the student becomes more sophisticated, this approach has promise.

2. Electronic mail and teletex, two innovations that have seen more use in U.S. businesses than in U.S. homes, are used extensively in France. The Minitel system, a national arrangement for electronic mail administered by the national telephone system, deserves greater use with language learners. Just as teachers have organized pen pals with students in the foreign country, the means now exists to allow communication over electronic mail, allowing major time savings.

3. Finally, hypertext programs allow access to information as needed in any part of a program and promise to provide far more

information resources to the user of a computer program for foreign-language learning.

While each of the above applications of computer technology has promise, the merger of computer and video formats as described below appears even more promising.

INTERACTIVE VIDEODISK COMBINES FEATURES OF COMPUTERS AND VIDEO

The technology promising the most sophisticated language learning capability at the present time is the interactive videodisk. When used alone, the videodisk can be used as a demonstration device for the capable classroom teacher (Sutherland 1986; Reese, Eastmond, and Sutherland 1988). When coupled with a microcomputer for use as an interactive workstation, with the learner working independently, the system allows access to still or full-motion video, dual-language tracks for translation or explanation, and virtually all of the interactive advantages of the microcomputer (DeBloois 1982; Schwier 1987).

Those of us who have used microcomputer-based instruction have frequently found ourselves thinking how limited the graphics screens are. For example, in the microcomputer simulation "Trip to Paris" described above, the experience would be much more meaningful if actual street scenes of Paris were available for the learner to view, supplemented with actual conversation rather than simply a written message. Similarly, the microcomputer program "La Carte de France" (Gessler Educational Software) could provide a much richer view of the various French provinces if only video could be provided. Videodisk allows just such a use, giving the learner control by computer of video scenes and actual conversation, repeatable on command and augmented with computer graphics.

The experience of using videodisk at the Air Force Academy illustrates how such sophisticated hardware can be used for language learning. After several years of experimenting with microcomputer and video systems, the academy equipped its language lab with thirty-two Sony Advanced VIEW workstations. Cadets have access to videodisk materials in Spanish, German, and French. Authoring of lessons is done using a sophisticated "icon"-based authoring system, entitled "Icon-Author" (Aimtech Corporation, Nashua, New Hampshire). Using a template approach, it is possible to create a full hour of student instruction on the microcomputer, using previously mastered videodisks, in roughly three hours of instructor time.

Existing templates use a segment of video – usually ten to fifteen utterances – as an overview, and then allow the learner to review words, see a written transcription, and access a translation for every utterance given. Then learners may select various options for practicing usage, including scrambled sentences, scrambled words, translation exercises, and the like. The powerful feature of this program from a teacher's point of view is that much of the programming is handled by the authoring system itself. Teachers need only select the sequences for use, enter the transcript and translation, and select specific frame numbers for viewing segments.

A second template now being developed uses the technique of "total physical response," which allows the learner to simply point to objects pictured in a still frame image. Following a period of practice, the learner is expected to demonstrate mastery of the vocabulary by correctly labeling the objects pictured.

Obtaining quality videodisk material to begin with is becoming easier. For the French language, it appears that the "French in Action" series will soon be available on videodisk for experimentation and tryout, which will offer the possibility for application of sophisticated instructional design for interactive learning.

CONCLUSIONS

Current information technologies that have impact on foreign-language learning have been examined in detail, using an abbreviated form of the CPB model. Video media as televised instruction, as distributed foreign-language cassettes, and as off-air satellite recordings have been considered. Similarly, the impact of the computer–through computer-aided instruction, electronic mail, and computer simulations–has been considered. The final step, combining the strong points of both media, has been considered in examining the applications of interactive videodisk. Particular attention has been focused upon the experience at the U.S. Air Force Academy, given its progress in applying this most recent and most powerful technology.

Future directions for these technologies are still hazy. As is frequently the case, the gap between the latest available technology and the tools actually available to the practitioner is large. In the domains of higher education and public education, it may be expected to increase. The new technologies of compact disc ROM (CD ROM) and compact disc interactive (CD-I) can be expected to make the videodisk applications described above more powerful and more portable.

The use of intelligent tutor systems is seen by many as the wave of future language learning programs with videodisk. While it is true that language learning does progress according to some well-established guidelines (Ariew 1987), it appears that considerable practice, both mental and vocalized, is necessary to use a foreign language fluently. Thus, to be useful, an "intelligent tutor" must be more than simply an expert system that diagnoses the learner's current level and areas of deficiency. It must also provide the means to practice, review, and creatively reconstruct the language structures as they become more familiar.

Such information would resemble a large database and would include interactive features and information in a variety of formats. One idea proposed at the Air Force Academy allows a videodisk user to access a visual dictionary, currently available on CD ROM, in which words are shown pictorially as well as pronounced by a native speaker. Again, access to information must be rapid and the data source must be vast. New technologies of information storage, including holography and optical memory systems, promise much in future years.

An exchange between two of my colleagues at the Air Force Academy, both teachers of French, makes a fitting note for closing because it points up the contradictions inherent in using technology in a field where human interaction is the final outcome. Speaking of the proper place for technology, the conversation went as follows:

> B: "Just remember, technology comes and goes, but the professor is there forever."

> W: (offhandedly) "Some of the ones I had were there forever."

The foreign-language teacher is and must remain a key element in the language learning equation. However, teachers' knowledge and techniques do become dated. Technology offers promise both for independent learning by students and as promising tools for the foreign-language teacher. And the future possibilities for technology's contribution are well beyond our present limited vision. The field of foreign-language learning is now and will increasingly become a fertile field for advancing information technologies.

Sources

Ariew, Robert. 1987. "Integrating Video and CALL in the Curriculum: The Role of the Foreign Language Education: ACTFL Guidelines." In *Modern Media in Foreign Language Education: Theory and Implementation*, ed. W. Flint Smith, 41-66. Lincolnwood, Ill.: National Textbook.

Capretz, Pierre J.; Beatrice Abetti; and Marie-Odile Germain. 1987. *French in Action: A Beginning Course in Language and Culture*. New Haven, Conn.: Yale University Press.

DeBloois, Michael L. 1982. *Videodisk/Microcomputer Courseware Design*. Englewood Cliffs, N.J.: Educational Technology Publications.

Doyle, Buford. 1986. *Videodisk Techology in Education at USAFA*, Working Paper (November 6). Colorado Springs, Colo.: Directorate of Visual Information Services.

Johnston, Jerome. 1987. *Electronic Learning: From Audiotape to Videodisk.* Hillsdale, N.J.: Lawrence Erlbaum Associates.

Krashen, Stephen D. 1981. *Second Language Acquisition and Second Language Learning.* New York: Pergamon Press.

Reese, L. Grant; J. Nicholls Eastmond, Jr.; and Richard Sutherland. 1988. "Integrated Use of Videodisk for Intensive Spanish Language Learning." *CALICO Journal* 6, no. 1 (September): 69-81.

Reigeluth, Charles M. 1987. *Instructional Theories in Action: Lessons Illustrating Selected Theories and Models.* Hillsdale, N.J.: Lawrence Erlbaum Associates.

Rubin, Joan, and Irene Thompson. 1982. *How to Be a More Successful Language Learner.* Boston: Heinle & Heinle Publishers.

Schweir, Richard. 1987. *Interactive Video.* Englewood Cliffs, N.J.: Educational Technology Publications.

Sutherland, Richard. 1986. "Inexpensive Use of the Videodisk for Proficience: An Attempt to Link Technology and Teachers." *CALICO Journal* 4, no. 1 (September), 67-80.

Information Literacy: Only a Beginning

James S. Healey

In the gospel according to Naisbitt, Drucker is quoted as saying, "The productivity of knowledge has already become the key to productivity, competitive strength, and economic achievement."[1] Still later, the guru of the future states, "We are drowning in information but starved for knowledge."[2] In a more recent article on the new supercomputers, in my local paper, I read the following: "It seems that as computers grow in power, so do the problems that their users want to solve with them. Scientists now have problems relating to weather forecasting, the spread of airborne pollution, space weapons systems, and molecular biology that require systems 100 times more powerful than what's now available."

Into this discussion one introduces the sad counterpoint of Norman Howden in the most recent issue of JELIS: "The environment [libraries] seems ready for users schooled in microcomputer techniques."[3] Contrasting Howden's (one hopes) tongue-in-cheek assessment of the position of libraries against the spectra of information needs and the demands being made upon new technology, it is not hard to understand why library education might be accused, as McLuhan might have put it, of approaching the future by looking in a rearview mirror. The difficulty is even more starkly set out when Howden states, "Approximately 11 of the 60 ALA-accredited schools list courses that encompass microcomputer technology."[4] In some ways, Howden's work makes it nearly impossible to consider the topic of this conference, when the very technology upon which the literacy is practiced is missing in so many places. Nonetheless, one must attempt what one can.

The title of this conference has to do with information literacies for the twenty-first century. But what do we mean by the phrase "information literacies"? William Paisley introduces the subject in this way: "Reading literacy is defined narrowly as the ability to decode a system of

399

communication symbols such as a language. Writing literacy is defined as the ability to produce a message in such a system that can be decoded by others."[5]

That statement would hardly lead one to equate the ability to decode symbols with the ability to read, understand, and grasp the significance of Shakespeare, Jane Austen, or the Bible. And computer literacy, given the mass of nonsense written about it, is no different. Again from Paisley: "Computer literacy taught as a set of mechanical skills misses the point. It is the algorithms of information seeking, problem solving, decision-making and other tasks of learning, working and everyday life that need to be taught."[6] And Paisley cites Alan Perls with what he, Paisley, considers the correct view of computer literacy: "teaching people how to construct and analyze processes."[7]

Obviously, how you phrase your question, how you view the underlying symbols and concepts, has much to do with the answers you get when you ask the question. For example, if you are interested in a very limited view of computer literacy, you will be more than pleased to have a few students learn a bit of word processing, some online searching – if you don't consider that, as some do, unfit work for information professionals – and maybe take a tour of a great big computer operation so you can ooh and aah over the wonderful blue machines that don't seem to be doing very much at all.

Or you can be concerned, as we are at San Jose State, with teaching process and growth. You can be concerned, as we are, with teaching people not to settle for being information-literate but rather to insist upon being an information intellectual.

At San Jose, we proudly recognize the reality that we are a professional school. It is we who must prepare those who will work in the information economy that all of the futurists have been describing for the last ten years. By acknowledging that our educational mission is to educate not researchers but practitioners who would go forth to practice our profession, we established the key concept that provided the foundation for the rest of our program. We next moved to implement the medical school model of library education. The model's title "medical school" precisely describes what the model is and does. The student is immersed in theory and practice the way medical students are. The student is exposed to concepts, issues, and theories on which he and she will build future responses to the needs for new processes and growth. At the same time, students are exposed to greater and greater hands-on opportunities. Within the first five courses of our core curriculum, students are expected to not only become familiar with the computer but to incorporate the computer into their total academic effort.

For example, in the first organization/cataloging course, the student naturally encounters OCLC, RLIN, and UTLAS, all online. They encounter online catalogs and catalogs on CD ROM, and how to use them. They meet

CDs again in the basic reference course, in which they are also exposed to online searching. That course has been adjusted to place electronic resources alongside Sheehy and Winchell. Training in online work is also dealt with, in technical terms, in the microcomputer course.

The micros course–which serves as the primer, if you will, for our students' quest for technological intellectualism–is responsible for teaching more than a group of software packages. The most important lesson that course attempts to teach is that computers are tools and should be used as such. San Jose has at least its share of humanities-educated undergraduates for whom the computer is all too frequently a symbol of the evil of the modern world. The students must be encouraged to lose their fear and loathing of the machines and to learn to view the technology as far less life-threatening than, say, their motorcar. And if the instructor in this class has done her work well–and she generally does–in addition to becoming at ease with the technology the student learns to use spread sheets and management software for the management class, database software for the database management courses, and the basic use of technology for the automation courses.

They are equally ready to move into advanced courses in reference and resources and online searching. In those advanced courses, the faculty has the luxury of not having to deal with elementary issues because those issues have already been dealt with at a lower level. The beauty of this foundation building is that it only has to be done once. Even though there are those who need help throughout their programs, the majority of students are able to move quite rapidly up the technological ladder. This strong technical preparation at the beginning provides the student with a very firm foundation on which to build the framework of their technological intellectualism.

Given the firm foundation, the faculty has been able to explore new ideas, one of which was to do away with the "literature of" courses. In this day and age, trying to retain such omnibus courses is the height of folly. How one course can deal with the literatures of biology, exo-biology, and microbiology, let alone physics, chemistry, and the other hard sciences, is beyond imagination. Attempting to emphasize only the literature aspect of the vast arrays of available information resources is equally hard to fathom. In the place of the three old warhorses, San Jose developed nine courses dealing with business and economics, the fine and performing arts, engineering and technology, the law, and so on. In the place of the old and terribly weary way of dealing with literature, the student, again, is taught process. This process includes how to learn a discipline, the sociology of information, who produces and uses information, how it is transmitted, and how it is stored. Within the process, the student is made continually aware of the totality of resources. Paper resources are considered alongside electronic resources. The serial is investigated, as is the database. Electronic search strategies particularly applicable to a discipline are considered within the total context of information resources, and resource barriers are removed.

Throughout the curriculum, another process is unobtrusively taking place; the student is consistently brought into contact with the computer and its software. As the student moves beyond the basic courses, awe of the equipment first diminishes and then disappears. It is not quite that familiarity breeds contempt, but familiarity does remove awe. In the beginning courses, the student is acutely aware that he is using a brilliant new technology. The glow of satisfaction on the face of the student whose paper is being typed on the laser printer, as it comes from the disk that he himself has created, is a joy to behold. But as the student moves into other courses and finds himself confronting software that makes the computer bend to so many directions, he begins to feel his mastery of the machine. I liken this process, the process of technical mastery, to the process of learning the symbols of language, assembling those symbols into simple combinations, and later, learning to take them apart and reassemble them in new ways. The child does this with the primer and easy reading book and gradually moves up to the point where he can reassemble those symbols into the words of Hawking as he describes time and space. Or the stark pain of Lear on the heath. Or Anna's feelings before she falls beneath the wheels of the train. Just as the student moves beyond literacy to the threshold of intellectualism and beyond, the library school student at San Jose moves beyond technological literacy to a state of technological intellectuality by the time he graduates. For example, 70 percent of the courses in the curriculum make some or much use of the computer. Computer avoidance is impossible.

It is almost as difficult to avoid the CD ROM. The student is given the opportunity to build his online sophistication before he goes online by searching on one of the growing number of disks that more and more vendors are wisely making available. Thus, much of the stumbling and uncertainty we all experience at the beginning of any new technical acquisition is conquered in a no- or low-cost mode. The student is given a chance to make mistakes when it doesn't cost anything. Later, online, the student discovers what it's like to experience the frustration of coming up empty-handed from a search because the logic was wrong, or because he didn't use the correct terms. As with language acquisition, with practice comes competence, and then, it all works, from practice comes brilliance.

This approach has resulted in at least one curious result. At one time, the online course was the sexy course of the division. By that, I mean that many students wanted to take the course because it seemed to offer them the most exciting part of the curriculum. But now we see that changing. Because we have built courses around highly specific disciplines and have included equally specific electronic search strategies, students are enrolling more frequently in those courses, leaving behind the more general online searching course. I view this as a very clear indicator of the students' greater interest in process and subject knowledge – as opposed to interest in bells and whistles – in itself, a mark of sophistication.

I happen to emphasize the online aspects, but it must be understood that opportunities for technological excitement extend to courses in cataloging, automation (naturally), database management, and development. And even children's services.

This involvement with technology is carried into the field as students move to get not only hands-on experience but practical experience as well. The medical school model requires not only that students be allowed to deal in theory but that those students be placed in situations where their work has real-life consequences. While the issues in library school are not as serious as they are in medical school, being placed in situations where one's work will have costly results if one does not succeed is a critical experience for a student. Think of what that can mean in a learning situation. We encourage students to reach out to do projects that make extensive and innovative use of the technology. One of the papers delivered at these sessions is coauthored by Professor Linda Main, one of the San Jose faculty, and Ms. Char Whitaker, one of Professor Main's students. Ms. Whitaker's project involved the use of "Hypercard" in the development of a program to teach reading. Nice bit of irony there, using the new process to teach the old.

There are those who wonder whether our education program has sold its value-soul by so strongly emphasizing the technology. Such an issue must be continually confronted, but I doubt we have given anything away. I suspect that a similar kind of nonsense was a burden Gutenberg had to carry as he installed his technology – the printing press. As far as how Dewey might have seen the issue, I suspect Melvyl would have encouraged us to press on even further beyond the barriers. And we will. Whoever is responsible for the idea that it must be either the book or the computer was a fool. The issue is not which technology is the only orthodoxy, but how to integrate the new with the old and well-tried.

Does it work? Are we successful in developing a more technologically aware and able information professional? Those who are hiring our graduates seem to think so. They find our graduates comfortable with the use of technology, from their first days on the job. Since most of the libraries to which our students gravitate – from little public and school libraries to the information centers of Apple Computer and FMC, to Dialog and beyond – make extensive use of the PC, our students are prepared to function effectively from day one.

We had questions. After all, we had set out on a different tack, proudly declaring ourselves a professional school. What kind of library school does that? Then, we had developed a curriculum that made technology and theory cocenterpieces. It turned out that we have apparently touched an important chord. The response of the California library community has been enthusiastically supportive. Our graduates are actively recruited. More recently, with our newly developed types of library courses, the professional community has taken on the role of coinstructor.

Perhaps the most satisfying indicator of our success is the recently signed agreement between the division and the Stanford University Libraries, establishing an internship program. More recently, there has been an inquiry from the library at Berkeley to suggest possible internship opportunities at the Moffitt Undergraduate Library. You will forgive my obvious pride when I remind you that these are two of the most prestigious members of the ARL.

So, yes, it has worked.

But that was the past, and we must be concerned with the future. The division will continue its process as we expect our students to continue theirs. The progression of an educational program into an uncertain future is fraught with uncertainty and potential for failure. There is no guarantee that there will be funds with which to provide the growing array of required tools. There is no guarantee that all will work out in the end. And there is always the tendency to try to hold onto that which one has, to become conservative and protective. Yet down such a road lies the end of process and the death of growth.

Library education must take a more life-enhancing stance. We have it in our power to produce the technologically intellectual elite who will serve the nation's information needs into the twenty-first century. The success we seek depends on our willingness to risk and grow, to take chances, to build a process for the future. Our professional potential is enormous. Will we, this time, realize that potential, or will we wait mutely for a never-arriving future, sadly wondering, like Shaw's St. Joan, "How long, oh Lord, how long?"

Notes

1. John Naisbitt, *Megatrends: Ten New Directions Transforming Our Lives* (New York: Warner Books, 1982), 7.

2. Ibid., 17.

3. Norman Howden, "Advanced Preparation in Microcomputer Systems," *Journal for Education for Library and Information Science* 29, no. 1 (Summer 1988): 17.

4. Ibid., 18.

5. William Paisley, "Rhythms of the Future," in *Libraries and the Information Economy of California: A Conference Sponsored by the California State Library,* ed. Robert M. Hayes (Los Angeles, Calif.: GSLIB-UCLA, 1985), 171.

6. Ibid., 172-73.

7. Quoted in ibid., 173.

New Pedagogies and Methodologies for the Teaching of Writing to Remedial Students: A Five-Tiered, Integrative Approach Using Interactive Computing (ENFI), Word Processing, Writing, and Literacy Theories, and Peer Tutoring (FTIA)

SHEILA SMITH-HOBSON

The once secret issue of illiteracy in America has finally gone public. However, for educators and other literacy workers who have been toiling long and hard in educational and communal vineyards throughout the nation, there has been no secret, only the sense of being, at times, overwhelmed in their attempts to stem an ever-swelling tide. That illiteracy is at the heart of so many of the problems that face our society has long been a reality in these circles.

While the growing attention to the problem of illiteracy is to be applauded, one would hope that that attention groundswells into a more national and local commitment to the problem. One would also hope that that commitment will entail something more than the usual quick fixes that governmental and political factions have continually forced upon educators and community activists. These quick fixes, such as the return to the so-called basics movement, and Hirsch's "modest proposal" for a "cultural literacy," have done little but obscure the depth of the problem and, ironically, have perhaps contributed to a real functional and functioning illiteracy.

The opening of a national dialogue that seeks to offer realistic and truly *democratic*, nonelitist solutions rather than cast blame is immediately needed. Some aspects of that expanded discussion must include a broadening of the definitions of literacy and illiteracy. Nineteenth-century Eurocentric understandings of literacy as "reading, writing, and arithmetic" and the solely Western great books can no longer suffice in an interdependent, multicultural world that is nearing its twenty-first century.

Implicit in this discussion should be the development of new methodologies and pedagogies in the teaching of literacy, and methodologies and pedagogies that use innovative approaches that borrow various concepts from an eclectic and integrative realm of knowledge and that boldly avail themselves of the "miracles" and virtually untapped potentialities of the new technologies. This critical pedagogy and new methodology of literacy is centered in praxis, where theory and practice not only coexist but merge into a pedagogy of possibility and hope.

What follows is an attempt at praxis. This model, called FTIA (for five-tiered integrated approach), has been evolving over my seventeen years of teaching college writing, much of it in the last decade to underprepared students. As is common to all such evolutionary processes, much of it was developed unconsciously and rather intuitively. It was not until the last three years that the current model began to take its present shape. A brief explanation of the whys and wherefores of that conceptual shaping might be instructive to other teachers–secondary and university level–who are searching for pedagogies and methodologies that might assist them in the herculean task of teaching writing to a similar audience.

THE PROBLEM

The persistent problem of retention at City University of New York (CUNY) is well known. At Lehman College, the problem has become a major one. For instance, 70 percent of its entering students are underprepared and require remediation in at least one subject area. Most of those students find themselves in at least one remedial and/or developmental writing course. The following statistics bear out the urgency of the problem. In 1983, approximately 62 percent of the entering students failed the CUNY Writing Assessment Test (WAT). (The WAT is an essay that must be written in 50 minutes; it determines placement. If students pass, they take English courses at the "college level," generally those courses that give equivalent credits for equivalent hours. If they do not pass, they are placed in remedial and/or developmental courses, where two credits may be given for an eight-hour course or two credits for a five-hour course. They cannot enter any "college-level" courses until they successfully pass the WAT.)

This led the department of Academic Skills/SEEK Program to initiate an innovative curriculum that integrated the teaching of writing–integrated language studies: reading, writing, thinking–with content courses. (SEEK–Search for Excellence, Elevation, and Knowledge–is a program housed in Academic Skills that offers intense remediation to underprepared students from economically deprived backgrounds.) This Skills Development Program (SDP) blocks students into courses taught separately by two to three teachers working in close collaboration. This curriculum recognizes that language is the medium for studying various disciplines; therefore, it follows that one learns a subject best by using language about it. (I might add that one first learns to write by writing *and then* by talking about that writing.) In sum, the SDP approach is an integrative, interactive one that asserts that reading, writing, and thinking are not discrete skills, but all part of the communicative process.

As a result, by the fall of 1984, 80 percent of the students who entered the program at Level II–those who enter with WAT scores of 5 or 6 (8 is a passing grade) and passing RAT (Reading Assessment Test) scores–had successfully completed all of the blocked courses. However, about 40 percent of this group failed to pass the WAT or RAT in one semester. In fact, after two or even three semesters, this population, numbering about seventy each semester, cannot exit remediation and must spend an extra semester in preparation for the WAT and RAT. A significant number have demonstrated the ability to write acceptable essays in writing courses and in other academic courses. The WAT remains the sticking point. In fall 1984, the Department of Academic Skills/SEEK Program initiated intersession workshops to help these particular students. That project in two years has had some success in moving these students into the college mainstream.

These two innovative programs in Lehman's Department of Academic Skills/SEEK Program are bold steps taken toward the retention of students. However, the problem still persists. Simply put, too many students who have the potential to eventually succeed in the academic environment are lost before they have the opportunity to mature and demonstrate fully that potential. Their failure to pass the WAT, and later the College Writing Examination (CWE), which must be passed in order to receive the baccalaureate degree, seems to play a major role in that reality.

BACKGROUND OF THE DEVELOPMENT
OF AND RATIONALE FOR FTIA

The FTIA approach addresses this problem from a different perspective. "042: Integrated Language Studies III" is an unofficial Level III of the SDP. Many of its students are those students, especially SEEK, who have failed to pass the WAT after one, two, and even three semesters. (In reality, 042 is a rather complicated course. It is a catchall course containing transfer students from community and senior colleges, as well as new and returning students, all of whom have failed to pass the WAT. In addition, one of the tasks of 042 is to find ways to assist those students who must pass the WAT within the semester or face possible dismissal from the college for failing to fulfill the BSAT [Basic Skills Assessment Test] requirements within three semesters and/or sixty credits.)

I alone taught this newly created course for the first two semesters of its existence (beginning spring 1986), six sections in all. We (teacher and students) quickly dubbed 042 "the course of last recourse." It was obvious to the teacher (and to the students!) that the traditional methods of teaching writing had proved ineffectual. Most unsuccessful are those that focus on such techniques as: (1) multiple, shotgun topics assigned by teachers, (2) the regimented five-paragraph theme (an anthem to the WAT), (3) constant revision of those minimalist essays, which obviously do not allow for such an exercise, (4) rote instruction in grammar and mechanics separated from the context of the student's writing, and (5) selection of texts and themes that present such culturally unfamiliar contexts that the opportunities for discourse so important to the learning of language for students of multicultural, multilinguistic, and in some cases, multidialectic backgrounds are all but effectively removed. Writing in these traditional methods is seen discretely as either a skill, a state, or an action (Langer 1988), not as the integrative, interactional, collaborative state/skill/action that it is.

Consequently, I began to look at new ways of teaching writing. The first semester "tutors in the classroom" were introduced. Four to five peer tutors visited the five-hour class once a week for two hours. They worked with students one to one or in small groups and at times participated in the general classroom dialogue.

The following conceptions emerged from this informal experiment: (1) Peer tutors seemed to relate to the students on levels that the teacher could *and* should not. (2) With peer tutoring, issues of hierarchy and authority are generally resolved, and more even give-and-take results. Students allow each other their own voices, thus creating a relatively stress-free and more candid environment for dialogue and learning. (3) Also, the peer tutors, many of whom had gone through remedial/developmental writing courses, understood firsthand the emotional, psychological dilemma faced by these students. More importantly, since all peer tutors have passed both the WAT and CWE, they have often developed various methods and approaches that can improve upon and even, in some instances, surpass some teacher methods and approaches. (4) Finally, peer tutors who have become part of the class better understand the issues involved in that particular class and have some idea of the teaching methodology and academic demands and expectations of that teacher. In short, they are privy to the dialectics that develop in the class.

Students of those first 042 classes quickly judged the peer tutoring experiment successful in that it (1) provided them with readily accessible consultation, and (2) offered options and different approaches to the traditional writing conference with the traditional teacher-student dyad. Tutors also expressed their liking for being in the classroom. (It was seen as an important and vital expansion beyond their usual bailiwick of the writing center – an ethnographic excursion, if you will, into the field.)

The next innovation introduced into 042 was word processing. I had noticed over the years (usually in the wee hours of the morning when correcting student efforts) that when student papers were typed (which was a rare occasion) they were greatly improved in content, organization, grammar, and mechanics. Since I had been trained to compose on a keyboard, a result of my high school journalism major and experiences on the school newspaper, I decided that henceforth all papers from my students would be typed. Then the idea expanded, as do most two o'clock-in-the-morning ideas. My students and I would learn word processing and use the computers in the college Academic Computing Center.

(As an informational sideline, I might add here that the obvious advantages and effects of type, or most accurately, the printed word, on cognitive processes have been well cited in the literature. Focus and attention are reinforced by the more visual and spatial aspects of the typed [printed] word.)

Strangely enough, while many more students have developed keyboard skills over the years (owing to high school vocation courses and the general accessibility of the typewriter, and now of the computer), few writing instructors have insisted upon typed work. Therefore, students and teachers alike are left to struggle over the deciphering of handwriting and the ensuing mess that results in same-page revisions. In addition, revision often entails moving to a new sheet of paper, a "starting over." In doing this, students have a tendency to either discard much of the original text and begin anew and/or fail to see the connection of the "new" or additional material to the old, thus resulting in disjointed and incoherent essays. This frustration, for student and teacher, obviously adds to the "physical drudgery of writing." Writing on the computer would soon change all of that.

The college Academic Computing Center is equipped with various user-friendly word processing programs. "BankStreet Writer," judged the friendliest of all of the programs, was chosen. Students after several weeks of instruction and practice with online tutorials (one hour each week in class and whatever time students could spare on their own) were "up" and writing. The teacher was a colearner in this process. (Up to this point the teacher had never used a computer!)

After overcoming the usual technological pitfalls and frustrations, the majority of the class by the fourth week was producing essays on the computers. Several things became immediately noticeable: (1) The levels of collaboration and interaction between students and teacher increased (owing to the common task of learning together). (2) Also, students tended to ask more questions of the teacher and of each other. What initially would begin as an informational inquiry about the technology often became extended and elaborate interchanges into the context of the writing at hand. (3) Students spent more time writing and, eventually, revising and discussing the work at hand. (4) Essays increased dramatically in length, three to four computer-written double-spaced pages with appropriate margins for teacher and peer comments and with last-minute writer-revised pages became the norm. (5) More time was spent proofreading. (Various functions, such as spell-check and editing, help students to better focus on their texts and to physically manipulate texts more easily.) (6) Students seemed to enjoy the class more and, therefore, seemed to be more conscientious about their work.

Students reported that, since the course was different and did not simply go over the old ground of their previous writing experiences, it helped to hold their interest. Also, the learning of a new skill—word processing—was for them a valuable experience that could be carried over into their lives outside of the class. Brice Heath and Branscombe (1983) contend that learners learn, become more literate, when they see something of personal value in it all. In this very first use of computers in the teaching of writing it became clear that with proper and specific methodologies the use of the computer could become an invaluable tool in the writing class.

The next components of FTIA, the introduction of ENFI (Electronic Networks for Interaction) and the specialized training of peer tutors, were then added to the teaching of 042. In 1987, through the efforts of the director of the college writing center, ENFI was acquired. There are now two dedicated online classrooms, comprising thirty computers, in the college Academic Computing Center. ENFI is an interactive, networked computer system that was developed in 1985 at Gallaudet University to help teach English and writing to deaf students. It has a forty-channel capacity. Of its many features, perhaps the most effective is its split screen, on which students writing on separate channels can send messages to one another (a sort of visual and linear CB) and have extensive discussions. The lower part of the screen, which is totally student-controlled, is for the composing of the message. Until it is transmitted, other students cannot see it, allowing the writer the time to compose, reconsider, and revise before committing it to the channel. The larger upper portion of the screen displays by name the transmitted messages from all the various members of the channel. The resulting "emerging text" supplies further opportunities for yet more innovative methodologies and heuristics. (For further discussion and description of ENFI, see the bibliography. Also see my article, "Special Interest Channels," in D. Beil, *Hooked on Writing.*)

The first year of its existence at Lehman, ENFI was used in my 042 classes and later that same year in English 282, the peer tutor class in which a colleague and I train the tutors for the college writing center. (English 282 as presently taught was a natural outgrowth of "tutors in the classroom." While the course itself predated FTIA, it did not specifically train tutors in integrative theory. As drafted by its original framers, there was little or no emphasis on praxis. The focus was more on the further development of the tutor's own writing rather than on the tutor-tutee (colearner) relationship and the teaching of literacy skills. Consequently, the course was revamped with new theoretical concerns and new goals. Presently, all English 282 tutors are trained and well versed, theoretically and practically, in all five components of FTIA.) So ENFI was initially tested in this diverse arena. As one could predict and suspect, the use of ENFI elicited different results.

At the more advanced level, it served as a rich mode for the dissemination and exchange of ideas among English 282's above-average and often gifted students. Its interactive capability only enhanced and quickened the written communication that took place between the tutors. The transcripts (a laser printer provides for next-day copies of the ENFI dialogue/interaction) served as additional text for the course, often helping to amplify and illustrate ideas and issues under study.

At the 042 level, the effect of ENFI is not so easily seen.

Obviously, as the literature has shown, new techniques and methodologies only enhance the better student. It follows that we need to develop more structured ways of using ENFI at a remedial or developmental level, and, in particular, methods that consider the wide range of skills that are seen in such a class. However, judging from two years of observation and from student comment, it is apparent that the use of ENFI served a positive role at this level.

Some students commented that ENFI helped them to focus better on what they were "talking about," that it allowed them to compare their writing to that of others (role modeling), thereby helping them to *see* their errors and, consequently, to correct them. One student had this to say: "In many ways ENFI gives you a leap in your research paper. It's kind of like cheating with the teacher's permission because you always get more information on your topic from the people you are working with on ENFI." Finally, one said that ENFI was a "great social tool." (I hope "social" was meant in an educational way. Come to think of it, any way that it was meant is acceptable, considering the general tensions and negative attitudes that too often exist in remedial classrooms.)

Apparently, the interactivity of the system offers immediate feedback to written ideas. Also, students are able to see something that rarely happens in the average college writing course–the teacher writing. With ENFI, the teacher can "show" students what is meant, or join in discussions on channels, or go one on one with a student–thus operationalizing the concept that writing is best taught through writing.

Finally, writing process (Berthoff 1978; Horton 1982) and literacy theory—especially that of Paulo Freire—which have always been used by this teacher/researcher as the theoretical underpinnings in her teaching of writing, were added as a metacommunication component of the course. Students were encouraged to actively and interactively enter the theoretical dialogue and debate about the hows, whats, and whys of literacy acquisition. Student talk about writing was focused and informed by various theories about writing. Colearners had become coresearchers and coinvestigators.

In the three years since the conceptualization of FTIA, these theories have moved more and more to a conscious and intentional level for both students and teacher. Further, the use of computers and tutors has altered and expanded upon some of those theories. For instance, the Freirean concept of the "culture circle," where participants learn to codify their daily worlds for the purposes of reading, writing, and thinking, can be applied to what has become a sort of "electronic speech community" via ENFI and the use of the computer as a word processor. Working on what I have named "special interest channels," students of like interest can discuss and share their ideas and research in depth.

The concept of writing as a collaborative and social activity is further extended by the use of tutors and computers. Brice Heath's (1986) contribution, that students should be made "coresearchers" into the causes of their own writing problems, has new significance with the addition of computers and tutors. Therefore, it would appear that certain writing and literacy theories marry well with the new technologies.

REVIEW OF THE LITERATURE

In proposing and understanding any new pedagogy, a review of the literature is necessary. By the very nature of FTIA, that literature is eclectic, wide-ranging, and interdisciplinary. Therefore, this brief review will look at selected articles and books in these four areas: computers and composition, ENFI, writing and literacy theories, and peer tutoring. (The extensive, but hardly complete, bibliography offers some background for the rationale of FTIA and is offered as an aid to those who are interested in developing other pedagogies and methodologies.)

The first microcomputer was introduced into the American classroom only ten years ago (Bozeman and House 1988). Since that time, CAI (computer-assisted instruction) has rapidly grown in areas such as mathematics and science. The growth of computers in the social sciences and humanities has been slower, although computers are beginning to find a constituency here as well. The use of computers in the teaching of writing is a fairly recent activity. A review of the literature shows that most articles and books have emerged only in the 1980s. It is rather understandable that computers would come slowly into use in the teaching of writing. Theories of writing as an interactive process have only recently emerged.

Many teacher/researchers (Langer 1986; Lyman 1984; Riel 1983) have written of the collaborative nature of writing on the computer. This concept ties in with those literacy scholars who see writing as a socially oriented activity that creates a sense of community—a speech community (Heath and Branscombe 1983). Others have written of the sense of community and interactivity established when students write on computers that are networked (Schnaldt 1987; Sirc 1988). Some researchers have even said that the process of writing on the computer leaves the text in a more fluid mode than does the more traditional form of writing with pen or pencil. This fluid mode not only permits but encourages experimentation so that the full expression of the idea may be tried and settled upon. The way one thinks, they opine, and the way one writes are more nearly becoming the same process (Balestri 1988). Brannon (1984) has reported that the introduction of word processing has been changing writers' habits in unique and unpredictable ways.

There are those who purport that word processing can be compared to oral composition, in which the flow of words is continually reshaped or redirected to follow the thread of intent. This makes word processing seem more like discourse (Noblitt 1988). Wheeler (1987, quoted in Noblitt 1988, 56) has boldly considered that the "computer 'instantiates' a virtual third hemisphere of the brain. Word processing turns into Hypertext processing and that becomes knowledge processing."

The excitement felt by researchers and teachers who study and use computing in the teaching of writing is also felt by students. New and surprising student attitudes turn the "mess and mystery" (Horton 1982) of writing into "ecstasy and adventure" (Riel 1983). But despite the excitement in the field, the utilization of computers in the teaching of writing is still in its infancy.

ENFI, the interactive, networked computer system, is barely three years old. The research in the area has been limited to date to the less than twenty colleges in the country that have been using the system. (Lehman is a beta-site for ENFI.) ENFI is an intriguing tool when wedded with the concept of writing process.

Batson (n.d., 11-12) puts it this way:

> Linguists pointed out that skill in language use is best learned through a complex process of constant interaction, similar in some ways to the natural language acquisition process between parent and child. Since this basic human process succeeds so brilliantly, they argue that many of its features (instant feedback, non-critical acceptance, "scaffolding,"' eliciting of production, modeling topic extenuation and so on) should be built into writing instruction.

Other composition researchers, borrowing concepts from anthropology and sociology, believe that writing is essentially a social activity, like speaking. According to these theorists, writing in isolation doesn't make sense. They advocate writing as some kind of group activity. They also point to the world of work, where cooperative writing is as much the norm as solo writing.

In all these areas of theory, ENFI has the potential to carry theory one step further toward full realization. . . .

To know anything about that process (cognitive, social, linguistic, etc.) teachers have to either rely on what students tell them after they write (retroactive protocol analysis) or on what the student texts *seem* to tell them (text analysis), both of these analyses occurring *after* the fact.

However, if there were a way to better monitor thinking processes *while they're occurring,* teachers would have a more direct way to put current composition theory into practice. This is precisely what writing interactively on the ENFI network makes possible. It makes thinking processes (1) more visible, (2) more accessible, (3) more captureable, and therefore (4) more modifiable.

Various literacy theories say that learners must be treated as subjects and not objects (Freire 1981). Brice Heath (1983, 1988), as previously mentioned, boldly extends the concept and proposes that learners be made coresearchers. Collaboration and interactivity are once again stressed in those learning processes that seek success. To this end, ironically, Freirean concepts, originally developed for the so-called Third World, are amenable to the integrative approach proposed here, which uses the latest in electronic technology. The concepts of collaboration and interactivity are indeed ideas of and for the immediate future.

Freire's concept of the culture circle can be compared to computer networking and to the activity that takes place on ENFI (Freire 1983). The idea of a popular library (Freire 1987) created by members of that community is made possible by the relative ease and speed that the computer adds to writing, not to speak of what the laser printer adds (Freire 1987). Students can write for real audiences (each other) and gain immediate feedback and access to each others' ideas. Also, the basic Freirean concept of the "generative theme" (those concepts, symbols, beliefs, concerns, and aspirations around which the everyday reality of students turns) can be translated using the FTIA approach via student-student computer interaction, as well as via the dialogue that takes place between student and tutor in the classroom and the writing center and on the computer.

Other scholars suggest that social contexts also must be focused on if literacy is to occur (Bloome 1987). They posit that literacy is learned as people have an opportunity to use language as a tool to mediate meanings in both the personal and social world. Olsen (quoted in Bloome 1987) says that students need to learn to work out the relationship between the text and their own lives. Tannen (quoted in Olson, Torrance, and Hildyard 1985) questions the oral/written distinction, arguing instead that there are not two forms of discourse: one that is context-based and requires reader/listener participation, and a second that is information-based and requires a form of discourse that is more explicit.

Finally, the literature on peer tutoring supports several concepts presented in FTIA, such as that students learn cooperatively through collaboration and interaction with each other and with their tutors (Slavin 1986). Segal and Segal (1986) support the idea that peer relationships are essential to learning, socially and academically. They substantiate the concept that certain "transactions" occur in peer groupings that could not occur in more hierarchial groups of students and teachers. Levine (1986) has found in her research that the importance of training tutors is generally acknowledged, but that there is no strong empirical evidence of its value. Those who work with tutors agree that training in how to provide positive feedback, give directions, and play a supportive teaching role is important. Opportunities for tutors to discuss their activities with peers appear to improve their cognitive skills and their ability to solve problems and to increase their empathy for those they tutor. (I would add here that the fact that student and tutor are colearners only aids the process of learning for all concerned. FTIA offers the opportunity to further investigate this aspect of peer tutoring.)

CONCLUSION

As stated earlier in this paper, it has become evident that traditional methods of teaching writing to remedial and developmental students have not resulted, in general, in success for a significant portion of the CUNY student population. Universitywide statistics attest to this. Large numbers of students are not passing the basic requirements in writing. As a result, individual college and universitywide retention rates are directly affected. New and innovative approaches to the teaching of writing that specifically address the uniqueness of this population are sorely needed. Since this population is diverse culturally, linguistically, and in prior educational preparation, an integrative, interactional approach is needed because its flexibility offers support to these students at the many levels of group and individual need.

It should not be overlooked that integrative theory also addresses and helps to unite both the cognitive and the affective. When this integration is successful, it has been shown that student academic growth and retention are more certain.

HYPOTHESES

To those ends, FTIA poses the following hypotheses:

First, an integrative, interactional approach to the teaching of writing (FTIA) will more substantially help develop and then strengthen the writing/thinking/reading (cognitive) skills of remedial and developmental students than do more traditional writing approaches.

Second, the attitudes of remedial students who have undergone such instruction will improve because the interactional and dialogic modes of this model also contribute to the affective. Thus, there will be less resistance on the part of students. (The role that learner resistance plays in students who find themselves in academic difficulty is well known.)

Third, because an integrative, multilevel approach is flexible and is geared to operate at the level of group and individual need, students will have more opportunities to improve upon their skills than they would have in more traditional, less flexible methods of teaching.

Fourth, the development of specific classroom methodologies and heuristics that seek to integrate all of the parts of the model will help students develop new epistemologies, new ways of knowing in writing/thinking/reading, which will therefore aid them in achieving more academic success.

Fifth, the new methodologies made possible by the computer – word processing and ENFI – integrated into appropriate pedagogy can only serve to strengthen and expand that pedagogy.

While only continuing research and investigation can support these hypotheses, FTIA is offered as a viable model for the present and for the twenty-first century.

Bibliography

Arnheim, R. (1969). *Visual Thinking.* Berkeley: University of California Press.

Balestri, D. P. (1988). "Softcopy and Hard: Wordprocessing and Writing Process." *Academic Computing* 2, no. 5 (February): 14-17; 41-45.

Batson, T. (n.d.) *Computer Networks in the Writing Classroom: The ENFI Project,* Gallaudet University, Washington, D.C. (Unpublished paper).

_____. (1988). "The ENFI Project: A Networked Classroom Approach to Writing Instruction." *Academic Computing* 2, no. 5 (February): 32-33; 55-56.

Beach, R., and Bridwell, L. (1984). *New Directions in Composition Research.* New York: Guilford Press.

Beil, D., ed. (1989). *Hooked on Writing: Resource Guide – Using Realtime Writer Software*. Washington, D.C.: Realtime Learning Systems

Belanoff, P.; Rorschach, B.; Rakijas, M.; and Millis, C. (1986). *The Right Handbook*. Upper Montclair, N.J.: Boynton/Cook Publishers.

Berthoff, A. (1978). *Forming/Thinking/Writing*. Rochelle Park, N.J.: Hayden Publishing.

Bloome, D., ed. (1987). *Literacy and Schooling*. Norwood, N.J.: Ablex Publishing Corporation.

Bozeman, W., and House, J. (1988). "Microcomputers in Education: The Second Decade." *T.H.E. Journal* 15, no. 6 (February): 82-86.

Bradley, V. (1982). "Improving Students' Writing with Microcomputers." *Language Arts* 59,(8): 732-43.

Brannon, L. (1984). "Composing and the Word Processor: A Case Study of Two Professional Writers." Paper presented at Modern Language Association Convention, 1984.

Bruffee, K. (1984). "Collaborative Learning and Conversation of Mankind." *College English* 46, no. 7 (November): 635-52.

Clark, I. L. (1985). *Writing in the Center*. Dubuque, Iowa: Kendall/Hunt Publishing Co.

Cooper, C. R. (1984). "Studying the Writing Abilities of a University Freshman Class: Strategies from a Case Study." In R. Beach and L. Bridwell, eds., *New Directions in Composition Research*. New York: Guilford Press.

De Castell, S.; Luke, A.; and Egan, K. (1986). *Literacy, Society, and Schooling*: Cambridge, Eng.: Cambridge University Press.

DeLoughry, T. (1988). "Remote Instruction Using Computers Found Effective in Classroom Sessions." *Chronicle of Higher Education* (April 20): A19, 21.

Freire, P. (1981). *Pedagogy of the Oppressed*. New York: Continuum Publishing Corp.

_____. (1983). *Education for Critical Consciousness*. New York: Continuum Publishing Corp.

_____. (1985). *The Politics of Education*. South Hadley, Mass.: Bergin and Garvey Publishers.

_____. (1987). *Literacy: Reading the Word and the World.* South Hadley, Mass.: Bergin and Garvey Publishers.

Gerrard, L. (1987). *Writing at Century's End: Essays on Computer-Assisted Composition.* New York: Random House.

Giroux, H. (1983). *Theory and Resistance in Education.* South Hadley, Mass.: Bergin and Garvey Publishers.

_____. (1988). *Teachers as Intellectuals: Toward a Critical Pedagogy of Learning.* South Hadley, Mass.: Bergin and Garvey Publishers.

Goodlad, J. (1983). *A Place Called School.* New York: McGraw-Hill Publishing Co.

Heath, S. B. (1983). *Ways with Words: Language, Life, and Work in Communities and Classrooms.* Cambridge, Eng.: Cambridge University Press.

_____. (1986). "Taking a Cross-cultural Look at Narratives." *Topics in Language Disorders* 7, no. 1: 84-94.

_____. (1988). *Inside Learners: Participants as Observers.* New York: Teachers Press.

_____, and Branscombe, A. (1983). "Intelligent Writing in an Audience Community: Teacher, Students, and Researcher." In S. W. Freedman, ed., *The Acquisition of Written Language.* Norwood, N.J.: Ablex Publishing Corp.

Horton, S. R. (1982). *Thinking through Writing.* Baltimore, Md.: Johns Hopkins University Press.

Jacobs, S., and Karliner, A. (1977). "Helping Writers to Think: The Effects of Speech Roles in Individual Conferences on the Quality of Thought in Student Writing." *College English* 38 (January): 489-506.

Kagan, S. (1985). *Cooperative Learning: Resources for Teachers.* Englewood Cliffs, N.J.: Educational Technology Publications.

King, D., and Flitterman-King, S. (1986). "The Tug-of-War Is on between Writing Approaches: Emphasis on Process Challenges the Five Paragraph Essay." *ASCD Curriculum Update* (December): 1-7.

Kleiman, G., and Humphreys, M. (1982). "Wordprocessing in the Classroom." *Computer* no. 22 (6): 96-99.

Kreeft, J. (1984). "What Is Dialogue?" *Dialogue* 1, no. 1: 1-2.

Langer, J. A. (1986). "Musings . . . Computerized and Conversation." *Research in the Teaching of English* 20, no. 2: 117-19.

Langer, J., ed. (1987). *Language, Literacy, and Culture: Issues of Society and Schooling.* Norwood, N.J.: Ablex Publishing Corp.

Langer, J. (1988). "The State of Research on Literacy." *Educational Researcher* (April): 42-46.

Levine, M. (1986). "Docemur Docendo (He Who Teaches, Learns)." *American Educator* 10, no. 3 (Fall): 22-25, 48.

Lyman, P. (1984). "Reading and Writing and Word Processing: Toward a Phenomenology of the Computer Age." *Qualitative Sociology* 7, nos. 1-2 (Spring/Summer): 75-89.

Madden, N. A.; Slavin, R. E.; and Steven, R. J. (1986). *Cooperative Integrated Reading and Composition.* Baltimore, Md.: Johns Hopkins Team Learning Project.

McDonald, J., and Naso, P. (1986). *Teacher as Learner: The Impact of Technology.* Cambridge, Mass.: ETC.

Meyers, M. (1980). "A Procedure for Writing Assessment and Holistic Scoring." *NCTE-ERIC* (National Council of Teachers of English-Educational Resources Information Center) Document.

Noblitt, J. S. (1988). "Writing, Technology, and Secondary Orality." *Academic Computing* 2, no. 5 (February): 34-35; 56-57.

Odell, L. (1977). "Measuring Changes in Intellectual Processes as One Dimension of Growth in Writing." In C. S. Cooper and L. Odell, eds., *Evaluating Writing.* Urbana, Ill.: National Council of Teachers of English.

Oller, J. (1983). "Some Working Ideas for Language Training." In J. Oller and P. Richard-Amato, eds., *Methods That Work.* Rowley, Mass.: Newberry House.

Olson, D.; Torrance, N.; and Hildyard, A. (1985). *Literacy, Language, and Learning: The Nature and Consequences of Reading and Writing.* Cambridge, Eng.: Cambridge University Press.

Ong, W. (1982). *Orality and Literacy: The Technologizing of the Word.* London and New York: Methuen Publishers.

Peyton, J. K. (1987). *Classroom Networking: Developing a Communal "Tongue."* Paper presented at the CCCCs (Conference on College Composition and Communication). Louisville, Kentucky, March, 19.

_____, and Batson, T. (1986). "Computer Networking: Making Connections between Speech and Writing." *ERIC/CLL News Bulletin* 10, no. 1 (September): 1; 5-7.

_____, and Mackinson-Smyth, J. (in press). "Writing and Talking about Writing: Computer Networking with Elementary Students." In D. H. Roenl, and D. M. Johnson, eds., *Richness in Writing: Empowering Minority Students.* New York: Longman.

_____, and Michaelson, S. (1987). *The ENFI Project at Gallaudet University.* Washington, D.C.: Gallaudet University.

Resnick, D. L., and Resnick, L. R. (1977). "The Nature of Literacy: An Historical Exploration." *Harvard Education Review* 47, no. 3: 370-85.

Riel, M. (1983). "Education and Ecstasy: Computer Chronicles of Students Writing Together." *Quarterly Newsletter of the Laboratory of Comparative Human Cognition* 5, no. 3: 59-67.

Rose, M. (1985). "The Language of Exclusion: Writing Instruction at the University." *College English* 47, no. 4 (April): 341.

Rumford, J. (1988). "Using a CAI Network for Statewide Remediation: GRI in South Carolina." *T.H.E. Journal* 15, no. 7 (March): 70-73.

Schnaldt, P. (1987). "Write on: How a University Teacher Writes on a Lan." *LAN Magazine* (December): 86-87.

Scribner, S., and Cole, M. (1980). *The Psychology of Literacy.* Cambridge, Mass.: Harvard University Press.

Searle, J. (1975). *Speech Acts.* New York: Academic Press.

Segal , J., and Segal, Z. (1986). "The Powerful World of Peer Relationships." *American Educator* 10, no. 2 (Summer): 14-17, 45.

Sharan, S., and Sharan, Y. (1976). *Small-Group Teaching.* Englewood Cliffs, N.J.: Educational Technology Publications.

Shor, I. (1987). *Freire for the Classroom: A Sourcebook for Liberatory Teaching.* Portsmouth, N.H.: Boynton/Cook Publishers.

Shuy, R. (1984). "The Function of Language Functions in the Dialogue-Journal Interaction of Non-native English Speakers and Their Teacher." In J. Kreeft, et al., eds., *Dialogue Writing: Analysis of Student-Teacher Interactive Writing in Learning of English as a Second Language.* Washington, D.C.: Center for Applied Linguistics.

Sirc, G. (1988). "Learning to Write on a LAN." *T.H.E. Journal* 15, no. 8 (April): 99-104.

Slavin, R. (1986). "Learning Together." *American Educator* 10, no. 2 (Summer): 6-13.

Smith, F. (1982). *Writing and the Writer.* New York: Holt, Rinehart & Winston.

Sommers, N. (1982). "Responding to Student Writing." *College Composition and Communication* 33, no. 2: 148-56.

Staton, J. (1981). "Literacy as an Interactive Process." *Linguistic Reporter* 24, no. 2: 1-5.

_____; Shuy, R.; and Kreeft, J. (1982). *Analysis of Dialogue Journal Writing as a Communicative Event,* vol. 1 (report no. NiE-G-80-0122). Washington, D.C.: Center for Applied Linguistics.

_____; Shuy, R.; Kreeft, J.; Peyton, J.; and Reed, L. (in press). *Dialogue Journal Communication: Classroom, Linguistics, Social, and Cognitive Views.* Norwood, N.J.: Ablex Publishing Corp.

Stotsky, S. (1986). "On Learning to Write about Ideas." *College Composition and Communication* 37, no. 3: 276-93.

Thompson, D. (1987). "Teaching Writing on a Local Area Network." *T.H.E. Journal* 15, no. 2 (September): 92-97.

Vygotsky, L. S. (1962). *Thought and Language,* edited and translated by E. Hanfmann and G. Vakar. Cambridge, Mass.: MIT Press.

_____. (1978). *Mind in Society,* edited by M. Cole, V. John-Steiner, and E. Souberman. Cambridge, Mass.: Harvard University Press.

Wells, G. (1981). *Learning through Interaction: The Study of Language Development.* Cambridge, Eng.: Cambridge University Press.

Wheeler, H. (1987). *The Virtual Library: The Electronic Library Developing within the Traditional Library.* Los Angeles: University of Southern California University Library.

Wilson, B. (1986). "When Technology Enhances Teaching." *American Educator* 10, no. 4 (Winter): 8-13, 46-47.

Wolff, D. E.; Desberg, P.; and Marsh, G. (1985). "Analogy Strategies for Improving Word Recognition in Competent and Learning Disabled Readers." *Reading Teacher* 38, no. 6: 412-15.

Writing Lab Newsletter 11, no. 10 (June 1987).

Writing Lab Newsletter 12, no. 1 (September 1987).

Writing Lab Newsletter 12, no. 1 (March 1988).

Zoellner, R. (1969). "Talk-Write: A Behavioral Pedagogy for Composition." *College English* 30 (January): 267-320.

Section Five

LITERACY, TECHNOLOGY, AND LIBRARIES

The implications of the new information age for libraries are the concern of these authors. Libraries, like schools, have traditionally been an inexpensive, if not free, source of information for their intended users. Whether they can or will remain so is the focus of these papers.

S. D. Neill's concern in "The Drift from Art to Science: A Profession in Transition: The Evidence of Collection Development" is that the general acceptance of science and the scientific method as the model for all fields, including librarianship, is altering the way service librarians view themselves and their profession. He centers his discussions on one aspect of library education, collection development, to demonstrate this transformation and its effect on library service. This growth of information and the variety of formats in which it is now available is the focus of Rhoda Channing's "Looking Back at the Twentieth Century: Implications of Our Format Choices on Libraries and the Preservation of Information." Channing centers her discussion on the information that will be lost unless steps are taken to preserve traditional media. Another form of information loss, according to Channing, is one that results from the continuous updating of electronic databases and reference works. The material deleted can be lost unless it is maintained in some other format. John Blegen, in "Beyond Access: Implications of the Information Age for the Public Library," provides an overview of developments constituting the information age and speculates on the role the public library can play in this rapidly changing social context. Online databases and their role in reference services in the public library are discussed by Janice Helen McCue in "Impacts, Implications, and Possible Future Scenarios for Public Libraries as a Result of Online Database Searching in Reference Departments." McCue advocates fees for online services and indicates that the key element in online service is the well-trained reference librarian. School librarians, according to Julie Tallman in

"School Library Media Center Networking for the Year 2000," have been the forgotten entity in the new information environment. New York State, Tallman reports, has mandated the inclusion of school library media centers in multitype library networks. The development of CD ROM and LAN technology has the potential to provide school students access to more information than ever before. The issue of access to information led Florence DeHart and Karen Matthews, in "OPACs: Context for the Development of Cataloging and Classification Theory," to suggest that the application of hypertext to online public access catalogs (OPACs) would create a more powerful catalog and enhance access to the resources in the library's collection. Similarly, in "Librarians and Archivists: Coming Together," Bradford Koplowitz points out how both librarians and archivists are employing new technological tools to both preserve materials and improve the catalogs and indexes to improve access to these materials.

Through the selection of materials, the preservation of these same materials, and the development of more powerful access tools, the library has the resources to remain "the people's university" if it so decides.

The Drift from Art to Science: A Profession in Transition: The Case of Collection Development

S. D. NEILL

It is generally conceded that when Descartes had the notion that the mind was different from the body, he started folks thinking of themselves as beings in opposition to nature – the world "out there." From that position it was not hard to see nature as something to be studied and something to be used. The goal then was to reduce all explanations to the physical (Guignon 1983, 37).

Emptied of the subjective, the physical world is viewed as disconnected from human beings and is reduced to a collection of mere objects; so we chop down forests, gouge out mines, and smother the good earth in concrete and effluents.

It has not been until recently that we have become conscious that perhaps we humans are not quite as separated from the earth, or our bodies, as all that; that part of our subjective nature is the world in which we find ourselves, without which we are unimaginable as humans – aliens, perhaps.

But alienation is just what happened to us during the Industrial Revolution when we began our exploitation of the unthinking earth in earnest, using the harnessed powers of nature turned against herself. Tied body and mind to the rhythms of the machine, we were truly alienated from both land and flesh.

The success of the industrial and scientific enterprises created the great technologies of control: bureaucracies to control complex human interactions, standardized forms to control information (the computer only making these more sophisticated and commodious), scientific management to control work, psychology to control and even make our own personalities, and market analysis to control consumption and keep the machine turning over (Beniger 1986). In all of these technologies there is a necessity to reduce or eliminate the peculiarities and eccentricities of individuals – both individual items on an assembly line and human individuals. Massive amounts of data about any one person have to be ignored if any kind of control is to be achieved in the complexities of the social and economic organizations we have built around us. Any science must reduce what it studies to what can be measured.

The motor invented to drive the discovery and exploitation of the physical world was the scientific method – objective, impartial, freed from subjectivity and emotion and bias (or so we believed for hundreds of years). It was this method and the attitude of separateness and superiority it fostered toward all creation and creators that became the ultimate technology, *the* way to do things.

Because it is, in its ideal form, free from bias, the scientific method is a democratic technology. Ideas and facts are free to speak their significant piece. Which brings us to the institution designed to enable all citizens to educate themselves freely without being pressured by a standardized, preprocessed curriculum to take a certain direction. I speak of the public library as it has been idealized.

What effect has the scientific method had on those responsible for the maintenance and development of the public library? To what extent has their thinking been influenced by the culture of control? Struggling into existence in the first half of the eighteenth century, along with the idea of universal and compulsory education, this great humanistic enterprise has always fought hard against the pressure to measure mathematically and scientifically, in spite of such technocentric characters as Melvil Dewey.

Even after the leaders of the profession finally succumbed in the 1930s, there was resistance (Harris 1986). Research and its results found little room in the hearts and actions of librarians and their instructors (Houser and Schrader 1978), and science lost that battle to art (Karetzky 1982). The initial research project of the Chicago Graduate Library School, to investigate the humanistic activity of reading, lost ground to research into administrative problems – one technology investigating another. It was not until after the first half of the twentieth century, with the example and under the threat of information science, that librarians became resigned to the use of the scientific method.

This paper will explore a few square miles of the territory of librarianship to see how research and the attitudes embodied in the scientific method are at work in our field.

426

PARALLELS BETWEEN THE DEMOCRATIC FRAME OF MIND, SCIENTIFIC ATTITUDES, AND LIBRARIANSHIP

I implied in the introduction that democracy and the scientific method shared similar attitudes toward the world. In this section I will briefly lay these parallels before you. I do not wish to press them too hard, although I suggest that there is some interrelation. My purpose is to identify them in order to have them available for application to librarianship as we know it today and have known it over the past hundred years.

The attitudes and traits commonly understood to make up the democratic frame of mind are described below (based on Barbu 1956, and Bobbio 1987) and, where appropriate, are linked to science and to librarianship.

1. Democracy is dynamic, always in the process of becoming. Despotism is static and always essentially the same. One of the basic traits of the democratic frame of mind is a feeling of change, the feeling shared by members of a community that their lives are in a permanent state of readjustment. The individual, therefore, sees his society as open.

This clearly parallels the scientific attitude of being open to accept whatever presents itself as a "result" as true or factual or real.

One can then ask, for example, is librarianship open to change, or does it cling unreasonably to traditional habits and instincts and traditional authorities (or tradition as authority)? Do we find librarians breaking the rules based on custom?

2. Because change is seen as a direct result of their own activities, people who are democratic by nature or nurture believe that society grows from within by the activity of its members, both individuals and corporate bodies. With this comes the feeling of confidence in the ability of all people to learn and thus make decisions intelligently. Any citizen can become president.

A democracy must assume that all its members are capable of learning about the issues confronting them and of making choices. Barbu (1956) related this characteristic to the scientific method or way of studying nature: "This flexible character of mind is expressed by a particular structure whose function is to relate the data of environment, to compromise between their various aspects, to organize them so as to make adjustment possible. This structure has been called reason" (22).

Belief in the ability of each member of society to use information materials has been the keynote of much library literature over the past century and a half. However, there seems to be some question about the clarity and consistency of the sound of that note. Harris (1986) has called the pluralistic library philosophy a myth. Nauratil (1985) quotes a study of book selectors in which most of the selectors paid lip service to an "egalitarian" philosophy of book selection, but in actual practice the majority applied an "elitist" philosophy. That is, they chose books for their intrinsic worth and their contribution to the collection, not for their relevance to any specific individual need (161).

3. Action in a democratic pattern requires deliberation before any decision is taken. Such deliberation demands a critical mind. For the mind to be critical, it must also be objective. I speak here, of course, of ideals, realizing that ideals are hard to achieve. It is necessary to have ideals, however, for they set the tone of debate, they teach attitudes, and they describe goals.

As a society of individuals, not a collective, a democracy is composed of a multitude of self-contained units, persons, or things, which are formally related to each other. The adjustment to such a world requires objectivity. In the medieval world, adjustment in social and political life was dominated by the power of habit and tradition. The impact of the new discoveries during the Renaissance sowed the seeds of rapid change and the need for reliance on something other than the rules for solving old problems.

Objective knowledge is the individual's most important step towards making adjustments in a swiftly changing world. Instincts and habits won't work, so the individual has to "observe" the environment to grasp specific structures and connections. Modern science is in many ways the embodiment of this objective spirit.

When librarians fully accept such an objective spirit, when they accept fully the critical *attitude* of science (methods being less important because always under scrutiny for flaws), then the heavy hand of the tradition will be lightened. They will look at what they do openly, objectively, and scientifically, and what they look at will include their old instincts and habits. The process is already under way.

4. Leisure is a necessary condition for the functioning of the critical mind, for contemplation and speculation. Democracies must build leisure time into the social structure if each individual is to be given the chance to absorb and understand the necessary information to act responsibly. A long period of education supports the individual's ability to do so.

Librarians have been aware of the need for leisure. Sidney Ditzion (1947) discussed the move to the eight-hour day, arguing that libraries would be used if the workers had more time (125). On the other hand, Andrew Carnegie funded libraries for workers and preached their use, while his own foundrymen worked a hard, exhausting, dangerous twelve-hour day (Neill 1986).

5. The democratic attitude toward authority closely parallels the scientific attitude toward the authority of accepted truths. This attitude is linked to the feeling for and acceptance of change. Power and authority are, in the democratic way of thinking, relative and unstable. The trust once given to kingly and divine authority has gradually been transformed into confidence and reliance on the powers of human reason and conscience.

Government by an individual or an elite is replaced in a democracy with government by the participation of the masses and conditional delegation of power. If I ask how often we have mass participation in the selection of materials for a library, you will think me mad. But if we do not construct procedures toward such participation, we deserve the elitist brand. No book selector, in a democratic library, can be above the original holders of power – the taxpayers.

A democracy is rule-governed. It is a technology for controlling procedures, as is the scientific method. It establishes rules and procedures for arriving at collective decisions in a way that facilitates the fullest possible participation of interested parties. Librarians with such democratic attitudes, and applying their powers of reason objectively, would (1) find methods to teach people how to select, (2) establish procedures for implementing citizen selection of items, and (3) ensure, on the other side, that the sources from which the selections were made represented all varieties of publishers, not just the powerful established houses that dominate the reviewing journals and the conference exhibit booths.

IN CONTRAST: THE COMMUNIST WAY OF THINKING

Given the reluctance of librarians to accept the scientific way over the subjective (visionary, imperative, artistic) way, there is a case to be made that librarians are closer in their attitudes and beliefs to the communist way of thinking about things.

Smith (1987) identifies three basic principles for thinking like a communist. The first is the necessity to abolish private property and establish a collective ownership of the means of livelihood. Of course, collective ownership of information resources is the foundation of modern public librarianship. We do hear librarians talking about "my library" and acting as if it were true, but they usually catch themselves before it is too late. At least they try.

The second principle of communist thought is that history is the history of class struggles and the correct way to understand the course of history is through a "scientific" analysis of social forces defined in class terms (Smith's quotes). Note that this "science" is not objective, because it accepts a point of view (class terms) on the authority of the leader or the party or the doctrine. So library book selectors, on their own authority or the authority of tradition, ensure that the collection is defined in terms of certain criteria for assigning "quality" – literary criteria and certain truth values (see appendix). No other criteria are allowed, unless to choose "bait." As we shall see, the literary criteria are now being questioned.

The third principle is that the party holds the doctrine, has total control, and is unaccountable to the people. There is no consensus and no approved political action by the people. The party and its leaders have a teaching function, since, as Che Guevara said, "the vanguard is ideologically more advanced than the mass; the latter understands the new values, but not sufficiently" (quoted in Smith [1987, 224]). Lenin held the same view, and I tend to think those of us who see our work as a mission to uplift and enrich the unenlightened have accepted this principle and this attitude toward our compatriots as the right and only way to go.

THE CASE OF COLLECTION DEVELOPMENT

The contemporary malaise assigned to professional librarianship by informationists and by librarians themselves (Giuliano 1979; Harris 1976; Heilprin 1980; Kilgour 1987; Lynch 1984; Mason 1980; Tague and Austin 1986) is deserved. It is deserved because librarians have been unable to maintain a clear view of their purpose while undergoing the transition from ad hoc, seat-of-the-pants, artistic decision-making to a research-oriented method of operation.

This is particularly obvious in the reluctant abandonment of the belief that librarians are able to choose "good" books. Research has told us that the effects of any one book on any one person are unpredictable, that, for instance, popular novels can have good effects (Emery and Csikszentmihalyi 1981; Haney, Harris, and Tipton 1976; Mann 1982; Radway, 1984). We conclude that only the reader can judge what is good, and that we must abdicate our responsibility for selection based on criteria of literary quality and conformity with the academic canon (Bloom 1987). We must go along with current reader interests, whatever they may be.

With that abdication we realize that we are also abandoning our mission, our felt responsibility to future patrons who will expect our libraries to contain the best – the best of our culture and the cultures of the world. Perhaps even worse, by abdicating the authority to decide what is "good" for a community, we believe we have lost our mission completely. We are in disarray because we have lost our nerve. Alfred North Whitehead (1933) said that a coordinating philosophy gives a sense of importance that nerves all civilized effort and that without it there is decadence, boredom, and a slackening of effort – and, I might add, a worried thrashing about for a new direction. Without the mission to uplift and enrich, we have lost what philosophy we had. We need to replace the old mission with a new one. The search is exemplified in the indecision surrounding the question of whether or not to get into the information business, stick stubbornly with the tradition, or find some way of redefining the tradition to make it a more legitimate enterprise.

It is not surprising that librarians have begun to drift away from the authoritarian values implicit in judgmental book selection. The rest of

Western culture seems to have given up any firm view about the nature of society. Absolutist moralities are on the defensive, and there is no accepted moral authority confronting or controlling the diverse subjective experiences and orientations of groups and individuals. Value pluralism and ideological relativism are the norm (Stanley 1978, 153). Even the idea of progress that empowered the industrial program of the nineteenth century is on its deathbed (Nisbet 1980), shattered by the destructive and negating power of many of the conveniences of our time. The potential of pollution and weaponry to take us through barbarism to a new primitivism, if not annihilation, is all too clear.

There is, nevertheless, a need for authority, inasmuch as our decisions must be authoritative. That is, they must be sound. They must be legitimated in some way. Librarians are as reluctant as any to give authority to other individuals or to organizations such as church, state, or school. They are also concerned about the inherent danger in the culture of control (the hidden domination by an elite of experts). They are at last, however, seemingly prepared to give that authority to research, to the scientific method.

Witness to the attitude change in our field is found not only in position papers (Heilprin 1980; Lynch 1984; Tague 1987), but also in the content of professional education and the textbooks written to support it. Within the past twenty years courses in research and quantitative methods have been added to library school curricula (Grotzinger 1976), and library school faculty have moved, or have been moved, to make research as important an activity as teaching (Heim 1986). This does not mean that the practical nature of education for librarianship has changed. Research methods courses are, after all, courses in methodology.

In the past such technocentrism was relieved and nerved by the sense of mission. That is no longer generally true. I will illustrate this by looking at collection development, which, in the days when the mission to uplift was unquestioned, was called book selection. It is in collection development that we face the controversy over selection by quality or demand. In collection development we cannot avoid thinking about the reason for the collection – the purpose of the library. In addition, all of the other activities of librarians are targeted on the collection – acquisitions, classification, reference. All are meaningless without a collection. Of course, the quality of the collection is of no relevance to cataloging or classification or systems processes, but answering reference questions without considering the criteria of quality would be an exercise in futility if not perversity. The question we must ask is, are the criteria based on democratic (and scientific) or authoritarian principles?

I could find no studies of book selection or collection development texts, but Metzger's (1986) historical overview of texts recognizes the content of texts as "codifiers and standardizers of knowledge in the field," which may also reveal "a great deal about attitudes and approaches of a discipline at a particular time" (486). This is not to say that the instructor in the classroom will not add to the information in the texts and even counter the attitudes found in the texts with her own and different opinions. But multiedition texts have been accepted, not rejected, and I think we can assume that the attitudes and values, as well as the factual information, have also been accepted. I have therefore chosen to examine those texts that have gone into several editions, mentioning others in passing.

Marcia Pankake's (1984) review of the change from book selection to collection management is itself evidence of the move from the subjective to the objective, from art to science. Pankake does not compare texts, indeed does not mention any of the standard texts on collection development. She does cite Helen Haines's *Living with Books* (1950) as part of a past literature – a literature that was, she notes, sure of itself and of the professional's goals in society.

That assurance has gone. In the 1974 introduction to the fourth edition of their text *Building Library Collections*, Carter, Bonk, and Magrill wrote in response to questions about what principles or guidelines they thought to be true: "We do not believe that there are such great, unshakable truths, which can be enunciated in such a form that the librarian as selector can be saved the difficulty of making judgments" (xiv). Judgments on what criteria? What guidelines? What secured rules? What authoritative position? Carter, Bonk, and Magrill had not abandoned the idea that librarians would have to make personal judgments. They just were not prepared to lay down the rules. On the other hand, they did not advocate research as the sole means of making decisions. Instead, they compiled a list of statements illustrating every possible opinion and principle from 1876 to 1956 and left it open – up for grabs. To present such a list implies that any profession operating on such a diversity of principles, some in opposition to others, is highly subjective – and I would infer that such subjectivity is not a good thing.

A new approach can be found in the much expanded chapter on studying the community in Curley and Broderick's sixth edition of *Building Library Collections* (1985). Curley and Broderick say they do not intend to deprecate the importance of book selection; on the other hand, they tell us book selection has been "(a) judgmental, (b) restrictive, (c) passive" (25). Collection development, on the other hand, is active, going beyond the conventional sources to get off the beaten path, to get to the edges of the community. It is democratic. To do this, of course, one must study one's community, be scientific.

However, Curley and Broderick seem to be caught in the transition period, arguing for the use of research yet unwilling to let go of the traditional. For example, they cite the case of a library that based its selection on statistical analysis of circulations and market studies (31). One sensed from the opposing argument that followed that the authors did not really approve. They did not take sides, naturally, being objective in their presentation of evidence.

Marcia Pankake (1984) concluded: "Librarians have lost the certainty evident in the past, and have substituted a spirit of inquiry and a need to seek objective evidence for verification of their work" (206). Observe the words she uses – *the spirit of inquiry* and *need*. Research has not yet been done, but its spirit has arrived. Curley and Broderick are witnesses to this uncertainty and are directly in line with the relativistic approach to truth enunciated by their predecessors. Nobody knows, anymore, what the truth is, and those who said they knew were elitists and more often wrong than not.

Curley and Broderick (1985) provide us with the democratic argument: "The evolution of collection development philosophy over the past century has involved considerable reaction against a presumed elitist past. Defense of the public's right of access to popular materials of essentially entertainment value has been part of a larger pattern of evolution toward a more democratic service" (32).

However, Curley and Broderick are only paying lip service to the democratic philosophy. Their real philosophical position is much more that of the business world, in which reasons for action are based on expediency – on winning and keeping customers. Managers, Wright (1979) tells us, use research "as a means of coping with entrepreneurial problems" (72), but this is the use of research with an ulterior motive, much as Lenin would use "science" to gain already proclaimed ends. Strangely, or not so strangely at this time in librarianship's history, Curley and Broderick seem to adopt a similarly skewed view of an ideally unbiased scientific attitude. They write:

> Members of the community whose taste level is "low culture" will never find in the library the materials they want most. These people will have to continue to buy *Hustler* and the daily racing form and the tabloids found at the check-out counters of supermarkets. The question is not whether this is fair or unfair to this segment of the population; it is a fact of life that most libraries could not withstand the outrage they would find expressed by the majority of their patrons who are at higher cultural taste levels. (1985, 36-37)

There are several things happening in these three sentences. One is the elitist position of the authors in labeling the reading matter of a large segment of society as "low culture." There is the assumption that only "low culture" types read such materials, whereas the racing form, at least, is "read" by a very wide range of cultural types. Do we know who reads skin magazines and the tabloids? Under a democratic philosophy, does it matter?

But the most astounding lesson we take from these sentences is that the reason for rejecting materials not only has nothing to do with quality but also has nothing to do with the democratic principle of objectivity–fairness to all. The only reason is to keep the customers we already have. If the argument against the traditional method of selection is that it was judgmental and restrictive, then surely the argument for the democratic method is that it is not judgmental and restrictive. Curley and Broderick can't have it both ways. Of course, we have a strong suspicion from the work of Michael Harris (1986) that the open, neutral, impartial, pluralistic stance of the library profession is a myth. This remark by Curley and Broderick supports Harris in a most disconcerting way. Here we have advocates of community studies already rejecting a whole section of society prior to the research act.

TAKING THE SWING POSITION

Curley and Broderick quote Charles Coffin Jewett's remark on opening the first national conference of librarians in 1853: "We meet to provide for the diffusion of knowledge of good books and for enlarging the means of public access to them" (1985, 24). Jewett's "exhortation" was both intended and understood as a "dynamic, humanistic statement of mission" (25). The access part of Jewett's statement is now the main focus of the profession and the schools. In a time when what is "good" is no longer known for sure, and the word must always be placed in quotation marks to indicate its questionable meaning, we must rely on what we *can* know if we are to decide anything at all. For us, as well as our society, that is economics–cost-benefits. We must rely on what can be measured. Naturally, therefore, access systems are more comfortable to work with and to study. We have moved from "selecting," say Curley and Broderick, "to providing 'access' to the widest range of ideas, opinions, and informational resources–as determined by the user's need, not just the librarian's judgment" (1985, 25-26). Except, of course, for those users who need *Hustler* and the daily racing form.

The mission to diffuse a knowledge of good books is quickly squelched, for in it the seeds of subjectivism can be clearly seen. Curley and Broderick write: "Sadly, in certain social circumstances, selectors of 'good' books too easily become judges of goodness, defenders of traditional values or the established order, and unwitting champions of mediocrity and censorship" (25). Note the rapid slide down the ladder from selecting "good" books to censorship. It is also clear that anyone who defends traditional values or the established order is a purveyor of mediocrity and a champion of censorship. How casually it is proclaimed that anyone who is not a rebel is a censor–the most vituperative utterance one can level at a librarian.

Curley and Broderick are as subjective as those they pillory, regardless of the degree of truth in their statement. The point to be made here is surely that any confrontation with the established order comes, and can only come, from those who can think, who know themselves, who are informed, and who have the power of language to speak. In a democracy and in a democratic library system, the goal must be to bring those communication powers and abilities to everyone in the community. Where the schools have finished, or failed, the public library must continue. To do so democratically, the profession must call on objectively gathered facts and keep an open mind. The problems of applying scientific methods in social situations must be understood as well, and procedures adopted to reduce the influence of subjectivism.

In a radically democratized library system, the swarm of beasts would be seen as intellectually capable individuals who not only must be let in to the garden but also must be part of the process of choosing the plants to grow there. Using literary and truth-value criteria as *sole* guides means that other criteria, such as interests and needs of groups with diverse experiences and orientations, are, if used at all, always the exception and always subjected to the derision of the criteria of the tradition.

Most texts on book selection list the traditional criteria (Broadus 1981; Gardner 1981; Katz 1980) and discuss them in the context of the quality versus demand debate. None seem prepared to abandon the criteria that Curley and Broderick label elitist and that, in their view, are prone to lead to subjectivism and censorship. The authors merely acknowledge that in practice librarians use both principles, demand and quality. No authorial position is taken.

G. E. Evans, however, in the second edition of his text *Developing Library and Information Center Collections* (1987), dismisses the criteria out of hand in a discussion of book selection meetings: "Personal experience with such meetings suggests that somewhere in the dim, dark past, a permanent general scale of literary values may have existed upon which each book could be weighed, but somewhere in the more recent, chaotic past the scale was misplaced" (88).

The word *chaotic* is indicative of the increased rate of change in our time, and it reminds us that one of the traits of a democratic frame of mind is an acceptance of change and a belief that it is just a part of life. Only a librarian raised in the tradition would see change as chaotic. Combining rapid change with the profession's gradual acceptance of the attitudes of scientific research, it is possible to see why the traditional criteria have been "misplaced."

Evans is easy-going about taking a position for or against the democratic stance and seems satisfied with a value-pluralistic philosophy. Summarizing Katz (1980), Evans, without comment, says: "The most widely practised position is that of the pluralist. When funds are more readily available, a more liberal philosophy dominates; when funding remains static, or worse, decreases, the liberal aspects of programming disappear and traditional services are emphasized" (102). The word *pluralist* as used here clearly does not mean anything like "democratic." It means librarians, in practise, take no position or any position. They are practical and base their decisions, not on a philosophy, but on whether or not they have money. This is an excellent example of a profession in transition–rudderless in a changing, chaotic sea, hanging on for dear life to old beliefs and new attitudes as the wind shifts and their little ship slips in and out of control.

REPRISE

Curious about the British view of these matters, and assuming, quite subjectively, that I would find a more traditional attitude, I turned to the fourth edition of David Spiller's text *Book Selection* (1986). It turned out to be a good example of the process of transition from traditional book selection principles to a more scientific approach. The first sentence of the preface is a case in point: "In the interests of continuity, the title of 'Book selection' has again been retained for this present edition. In many ways 'Book provision' would make a more appropriate title, indicating a broader approach to all the processes involved in making stock available in the library" (i). The focus on processes is a reflection of the guiding paradigm of our culture, systems theory–the interest in process and relations, how it is structured, and how to do it. Observing the aspects of the environment to grasp structures and connections is one of the characteristics of the democratic frame of mind. Concern for the substance of the book's content is rejected in favor of study of the process of collection building by needs surveys. In effect, the focus on "selection" is gone and Spiller retains the old title as an expedient way of providing market recognition. It is significant, in this context, to see that Evans changed his chapter heading "Selection of Books" in the original 1979 edition to "Selection Process" in the 1987 second edition.

Still, there are some vestiges of the quality approach left. Spiller (1986) tells us that "user surveys have shown that approximately 80% of fiction issues fall into the 'recreational' category. Few librarians would advocate the funding of recreational reading on this scale" (161). Not yet, anyway. But once those librarians are trained to respond to the results of research, when they have adopted the open-minded attitudes of science and democracy, they will provide recreational reading on that scale.

As do most writers on collection development, Spiller comments on "low culture" materials. Here he smells the odor of the swarm of beasts, and it is worrisome. Discussing interlibrary loan service, he writes: "It is true that some of the items requested at the 'lower level' of provision–out-of-print romances, comics, and so on–are refused, although in an effort to seduce more readers into their libraries some authorities are increasingly extending their services to include such publications" (10-11).

The "authorities," so aptly named, are easily classified with Che Guevara's "ideologically more advanced vanguard" and Lenin's "bourgeois intelligentsia," who are "the vehicle of science," which is the basis of "modern socialist consciousness" (quoted in Smith 1987, 217). These authorities are caught in the act of seduction, selecting "bait," their goal not to give service wanted but to teach what ought to be. I see here no open minds, just the pressures of the marketplace at work.

Spiller makes no comment. He has himself rejected the elitist principle of the Guevaran vanguard of "diffusion of a knowledge of good books." He writes: "Nor is it suggested that part of a librarian's work should be to influence readers' tastes towards a better kind of novel" (1986, 160). This was a change from his position in the first edition in 1971, although even then he was showing signs of doubt: "It may seem presumptuous to attempt any kind of active, advisory approach to the reader through book selection. This is fair comment if the reader's knowledge of books is wide enough to enable him to select from the resources available. If this is not so, then the librarian is obliged to offer assistance, through his own experience." Spiller then concluded: "There is no alternative to this approach if the profession is to have a spirit in addition to flesh and bones" (13).

Fifteen years later the missionary spirit has dissipated. In its place there seems to be nothing but a focus on processes – on the technical aspects of the system. That there could be another "spirit" to nerve the profession has not yet been recognized. The objectivity and openness of the scientific researcher examining the processes of the system have not yet bred the attitudes of democracy as a professional philosophy, but they are looming on the horizon.

AGAINST THE SCIENTIFIC METHOD

There are some who see the adoption of scientific attitudes and values as a negative force in librarianship. Recently John Berry (1988) challenged the American Library Association Planning Committee's assertion that "research on library practice should decide policy and principle" (4). Berry wants policy and principle to remain in the hands of the party ideologues.

Curtis Wright (1986) has been telling us for years that empirical science is the wrong way for librarianship to go. Because we have followed the advice of information science, we are now living with the results of the "scientizing of a humanistic idea-business that cannot be scientized" (743).

Wright has two main concerns. One is that the most pervasive view of librarianship today, by librarians, is that it is a business, bereft of those lofty goals to enrich and ennoble the lives of citizens. He is correct, if the evidence from collection development texts is representative. Our goal is to increase profits, counted as circulations. Wright (1979) sees research as "a means of coping with entrepreneurial problems" (72). He does not see it as a way to democratize the profession.

Wright's second concern is that scientific research, with its attitude of objectivism and impartiality, is not only an inappropriate method but a dangerous one for learning about human beings. This objection is expressed very sensitively in the following passage: "You cannot hover aloof and distant over the people whose subjective processes you are studying by refusing to experience the roles and functions they perform in the social order. The subjective processes that generate rational behaviour in a human being must be communicated to observers through intimate familiarity with the empirical lives of the people they observe" (1986, 750).

We need to heed such an admonition, for there is a very real danger in adopting a hard-science methodology insensitively. It is the hardening of the methodological categories that creates within us a "technological conscience." As Manfred Stanley (1978) describes it, we learn to translate everything into "quantitative-operational terms appropriate to the cybernetic notion of meaning as 'information'" (177-78). Meaning, in this way, is stripped of all its human, sensuous relationships. People are seen as Frants and Brush (1988) perceived them in a recent article in the *Journal of the American Society for Information Science*: "We shall consider a human being as a complex adaptive (cybernetic) system" (86). This shadow creature belongs to the world of Don Ihde's (1974) hermeneutic relationships, in which the system engineer manipulates the environment by watching the dials on a machine and never actually goes into the environment at all. The library collection manager in such a system would never see a book or a patron but would make decisions based on computerized circulation data matched to some electronic database listing titles tagged with rating devices (Neill 1982).

These are legitimate concerns, and we must be wary of falling into a rigidity of methodology that would be as authoritarian and tyrannical as any other ideology. The habits of mind of the democrat are needed to keep the habits of mind of the technocrat from gaining control.

The fact is, we do not have to choose hard-science methods or none. The debate about ways of studying humanity is not settled by choosing one method and rejecting another, but by choosing the best of all methods in the search for better ways with open and critical minds. There is no either/or situation here.

OUTREACH AND RESEARCH

It is interesting that in an area of library activity where the lives of the users needed to be understood in the way Wright intended, research played a dominant role. The outreach projects galvanized into existence out of the radical democratization of American society in the 1960s were geared to reporting mechanisms in order to get and maintain funding. Some, such as the High John project, were even called "experiments."

They were perceived then, and are now in most cases, as exceptions to normal service. They would be classed by Evans among those "liberal aspects of programming" to be abandoned in tough economic times.

As an aside, in the light of Wright's concern, it was soon discovered in these projects that people from the target communities, not librarians, had to be given jobs in the workplace to gain the trust of the members of those communities.

Much of the literature about work with the disadvantaged and ethnic groups is research literature. Unable to call on experience, the organizers had to rely on observations and reports. Brown's (1971) work included a chapter on "research and experiments." Hanna's (1978) report is a popularized version of a research project and includes the "scientific" apparatus. Lipsman's (1972) often-cited work is a formal research report undertaken at the request of the U.S. Office of Education.

In a veiled comment on the reporting skills of librarians, Lipsman appealed for better data collection. She noted that reports from the projects under study were "frequently subjective, narrative accounts of highlights of the previous year and optimistic hopes for the one ahead" (143). She then discussed simple methods for collecting data but added: "None of these various data collection techniques, however, can collect the kind of program impact information that would be furnished by a classical experimental design" (145).

This is where Curtis Wright's warning applies, but only as a caution to ensure that humanistic factors are considered. Lipsman was not a librarian but a program analyst for the Office of Planning and Evaluation Manpower Administration in the U.S. Department of Labor. In 1972 quantitative, empirical research by librarians and library school faculty was embryonic.

In Britain the same relationship existed. Wherever the processes of radical democratization took librarians into contact with the disadvantaged, research followed. Coleman's (1981) report was written while she was a research officer with the British Library Research and Development Department, which succeeded the Office for Scientific and Technical Information in 1974. She noted that librarians, by and large, were confused about the basic purpose of public libraries. In light of the present discussion of librarianship in the context of the traits and values of democracy, it is revealing to read Coleman's summation of the perceptions of librarians by the (disadvantaged) public: "They see librarians as book-stampers and local authority bureaucrats employed by a system whose principal, if not sole, function is to lend books . . . and are surprised to find librarians becoming involved in the community." She then categorized librarians as "unimaginative, unable to think independently or critically," and with a very narrow-minded view of their role. Librarians offered excuses for not crossing their self-defined professional boundaries as follows: "For not developing services to the disadvantaged – librarians are not social workers; in the area of education – librarians can take no part in formal education; in the area of community information – librarians are not qualified to give advice" (59-60). All of these negations keep the adjective "quality" attached to collections and not to service.

A companion to Coleman's more general report is Clough and Quarmby's (1978) major survey of the ethnic groups in the United Kingdom and public library provisions for them. Supporting Lipsman's complaint about the quality of the information available, Clough and Quarmby justified their methodology because a solution to the problem of providing adequate service to the whole community was only to be found as the result of fairly detailed research. They had seen that "a great deal that had been written in many parts of the world was of a descriptive or hortatory nature that gave very little indication of the size and nature of the problem" (5). The subjective, in other words, can be as biased in research as in book selection, and some method of distancing the observer from the observed is necessary – *pace* Curtis Wright. But once the size and nature of the problem is discovered, and action to solve it decided, it is necessary to engage the passions and the wisdom of the human relations artist.

CONCLUSION

The argument of the paper has been structured on a few major contentions. (1) The attitudes of the scientific mind – objectivity, openness, and criticism – are the same as the traits and characteristics of the democratic mind. (2) Professional librarians have not been and are not yet scientific or democratic in the attitudes they bring to the work they do. (3) The increase in the quantity and quality of research in the field of librarianship over the past quarter of a century has begun a process of attitudinal change from authoritarianism to a questioning of authoritarianism. (4) This process is at an early stage and has left librarians confused about their role and the place of the library in the community. They are especially wary of the enigmatic emblem of private industry competition being waved in front of them by anonymous figures and loose-jawed futurologists. (5) Evidence of this transition period can be found in the texts on collection development.

The conclusion seems to be, therefore, that we must give up the emphasis on building collections based on the criteria of literary values and open the door to materials more attractive to the information skills and personal interests of the ill-educated and those members of our communities with orientations opposed to the social and political establishment. The wealth of women's literature in the field of health care is a good example.

Curley and Broderick's fears about the daily racing form and the sensational press need not concern us. These materials are justified because they serve the needs of citizens and taxpayers.

But to say that the emphasis on the traditional criteria must be loosened does not mean that they can be ignored. Not at all. After all, one can assume, unless Curley and Broderick are right about the results of letting in the swarm of beasts, that the middle class will still be with us and must get the service it wants. We must also remember that reading has benefits unique to its medium. *What* is read might not be as important as the act of reading itself (Neill 1985).

Outreach must be taken for granted as *normal* service, not as an exception to the norm. Librarians must be educated to think critically and scientifically. They must be taught that their purpose is to get beyond general library patrons to targeted and defined communities within communities. They must be nerved by a radical democratization of the old professional philosophy of service to all.

Appendix

Literary Values (based on Haines 1950)

In the form of questions, these criteria are applied with qualifications and not in every case. (1) Is the style appropriate comprehensible (crude, dignified)? (2) Do the characters come to life as individual human beings? Is there consistency and vitality in character creation? (3) Is there excellence of expression indicative of the writer's craftsmanship? (4) Is the structure sound, rambling, elaborate, well-knit? (5) Is there a degree of unity in form and expression? (6) Is there a valid interpretation of the phase of life? (7) Is the spirit or atmosphere appropriate (delicate, satirical, somber, passionate, or miasmic)? (8) Does it contain enough truth, beauty, pleasure, or active good to make it worthwhile? (9) Does it leave any kind of fine or wholesome feeling in the mind of the reader? (10) Do other criteria apply: local setting, timeliness, popular appeal?

Truth Values (mainly from Gardner 1981)

Depending on the work, the following factors must be considered: (1) authoritativeness (sources), (2) factual accuracy, (3) significance of subject, (4) sincerity of the author's purpose, (5) responsibility of the author's opinions, (6) impartiality (unbiased), (7) recency, (8) organization and arrangement, (9) comprehensiveness (scope), (10) style.

Note that some or all of these facets would be part of any definition of the word *good* in the expression "good books" as used, for example, in the Jewett quote.

Note

An earlier version of this paper was savaged by my Philosophy of Library and Information Science class (Spring 1988), resulting in a complete turnaround in my argument. They have my appreciation.

References

Barbu, Zevedei. *Democracy and Dictatorship: Their Psychology and Patterns of Life*. London: Routledge & Kegan Paul, 1956.

Beniger, James R. *The Control Revolution: Technological and Economic Origins of the Information Society*. Cambridge, Mass.: Harvard University Press, 1986.

Berry John. "Practice and Principle: The Fee Example." *Library Journal* 113, no. 2 (February 1, 1988): 4.

Bloom, Allan. *The Closing of the American Mind*. New York: Simon and Schuster, 1987.

Bobbio, Norberto. *The Future of Democracy: A Defence of the Rules of the Game*. Trans. Roger Griffin. Edited and with an introduction by Richard Bellamy. Minneapolis: University of Minnesota Press, 1987.

Broadus, Robert M. *Selecting Materials for Libraries*. 2d ed. New York: H. W. Wilson, 1981.

Brown, Eleanor Frances. *Library Service to the Disadvantaged*. Metuchen, N.J.: Scarecrow Press, 1971.

Carter, Mary Duncan, Wallace John Bonk, and Rose Mary Magrill. *Building Library Collections*. 4th ed. Metuchen, N.J.: Scarecrow Press, 1974.

Clough, Eric, and Jacqueline Quarmby. *A Public Library Service for Ethnic Minorities in Great Britain*. London: Library Association, 1978.

Coleman, Patricia M. *Whose Problem? The Public Library and the Disadvantaged*. London: Association of Assistant Librarians, 1981.

Curley, Arthur, and Dorothy Broderick. *Building Library Collections*. 6th ed. Metuchen, N.J.: Scarecrow Press, 1985.

Ditzion, Sidney. *Arsenals of Democracy*. Chicago: American Library Association, 1947.

Emery, Olga Beatty, and Mihalyi Csikszentmihalyi. "An Epistemological Approach to Psychiatry: On the Psychology/Psychopathology of Knowledge." *Journal of Mind and Behavior* 2, no. 4 (Winter 1981): 375-96.

Evans, G. Edward. *Developing Library and Information Center Collections*. 2d ed. Littleton, Colo.: Libraries Unlimited, 1987 (first edition 1979).

Frants, Valery I., and Craig B. Brush. "The Need for Information and Some Aspects of Information Retrieval Systems Construction." *Journal of the American Society for Information Science* 39, no. 2 (March 1988): 86-91.

Gardner, Richard K. *Library Collections: Their Origins, Selection, and Development*. New York: McGraw-Hill, 1981.

Giuliano, Vincent E. "A Manifesto for Librarians." *Library Journal* 104, no. 16 (September 15, 1979): 1837-42.

Grotzinger, Laurel. "Characteristics of Research Courses in Masters Level Curricula." *Journal of Education for Librarianship* 17, no. 2 (Fall 1976): 85-97.

Guignon, Charles B. *Heidegger and the Problem of Knowledge*. Indianapolis, Ind.: Hackett Publishing Co., 1983.

Haines, Helen E. *Living with Books*. 2d ed. New York: Columbia University Press, 1950 (first edition 1935).

Haney, Roger, Michael H. Harris, and Leonard Tipton. "The Impact of Reading on Human Behavior: The Implications of Communications Research." In *Advances in Librarianship* 6, 139-216. New York: Academic Press, 1976.

Hanna, Patricia Brennan. *People Make It Happen: The Possibilities of Outreach in Every Phase of Public Library Service*. Metuchen, N.J.: Scarecrow Press, 1978.

Harris, Michael H. "Portrait in Paradox: Commitment and Ambivalence in American Librarianship." *Libri* 26, no. 41 (December 1976): 281-301.

_____. "State, Class, and Cultural Reproduction: Toward a Theory of Library Service in the United States." In *Advances in Librarianship* 14, 211-52. New York: Academic Press, 1986.

Heilprin, Lawrence. "The Library Community at a Technological and Philosophical Crossroads: Necessary and Sufficient Conditions for Survival." *Journal of the American Society for Information Science* 31, no. 6 (November 1980): 389-95.

Heim, Kathleen, M. "The Changing Faculty Mandate." *Library Trends* 34, no. 4 (Spring 1986): 581-606.

Houser, Lloyd, and Alvin M. Schrader. *The Search for a Scientific Profession: Library Science Education in the United States and Canada*. Metuchen, N.J.: Scarecrow Press, 1978.

Ihde, Don. "The Experience of Technology: Human-Machine Relations." *Cultural Hermeneutics* 2, no. 3 (Spring 1979): 267-79.

Karetzky, Stephen. *Reading Research and Librarianship: A History and Analysis*. Westport, Conn.: Greenwood Press, 1982, 60-78.

Katz, William A. *Collection Development: The Selection of Materials for Libraries*. New York: Holt, Rinehart & Winston, 1980.

Kilgour, Frederick G. "EIDOS and the Transformation of Libraries." *Library Journal* 112, no. 16 (October 1, 1987): 46-49.

Lipsman, Claire K. *The Disadvantaged and Library Effectiveness*. Chicago: American Library Association, 1972.

Lynch, Mary Jo. "Research and Librarianship: An Uneasy Connection." *Library Trends* 32, no. 4 (Spring 1984): 367-83.

Mann, Peter. *From Author to Reader: A Social Study of Books*. London: Routledge & Kegan Paul, 1982.

Mason, Ellsworth. Introduction. *Library Trends* 28, no. 3 (Winter 1980): 341-43.

Metzger, Philip A. "An Overview of the History of Library Science Teaching Materials." *Library Trends* 34, no. 3 (Winter 1986): 469-88.

Nauratil, Marcia J. *Public Libraries and Nontraditional Clienteles*. Westport, Conn.: Greenwood Press, 1985.

Neill, S. D. "Andrew Carnegie: Kind Master." *Focus on Ontario Libraries* 12, no. 5 (November/December 1986): 17-22.

_____. "Books and Reading and a Singleness of Purpose." *Canadian Library Journal* 42, no. 2 (April 1985): 57-62.

_____. "The Likely Impact of New Technology on Libraries." *Canadian Library Journal* 39, no. 5 (October 1982): 305-7.

Nisbet, Robert. *History of the Idea of Progress*. New York: Basic Books, 1980.

Pankake, Marcia. "From Book Selection to Collection Management: Continuity and Advance in an Unending Work." In *Advances in Librarianship* 13, 185-210. Orlando: Academic Press, 1984,

Radway, Janice A. *Reading the Romance: Women, Patriarchy, and Popular Literature*. Chapel Hill: University of North Carolina Press, 1984.

Smith, Tony. *Thinking Like a Communist*. New York: W. W. Norton & Co., 1987.

Spiller, David. *Book Selection*. London: Clive Bingley, 1971.

Spiller, David. *Book Selection*. 4th ed. London: Clive Bingley, 1986.

Stanley, Manfred. *The Technological Conscience*. New York: Free Press, 1978.

Tague, Jean. "The Role of Research in Information and Library Education." In *Education of Library and Information Science Professionals*, ed. Richard K. Gardner, 121-34. Littleton, Colo.: Libraries Unlimited, 1987.

____, and Jill Austin. "From Librarian to Information Scientist: Educational Directions for a Changing Profession." *Canadian Journal of Information Science* 2 (1986): 24-40.

Whitehead, Alfred North. *Adventures of Ideas*. New York: Macmillan Co., 1933.

Wright, H. Curtis. "The Symbol and Its Referent: An Issue for Library Education." *Library Trends* 34, no. 4 (Spring 1986): 729-76.

____. "The Wrong Way to Go." *Journal of the American Society for Information Science* 30, no. 2 (March 1979): 67-76.

Looking Back at the Twentieth Century: Implications of Our Format Choices on Libraries and the Preservation of Information

RHODA K. CHANNING

Today's librarians are faced with the need to make frequent, important, and difficult decisions about the formats in which information is acquired. In this paper, I would like to accomplish several objectives: first, to describe the options we face in decision-making; second, to look at the criteria we use in making our choices; third, to address the implications of those choices for us and those who follow; and last, to try to suggest an approach for our profession to take to fulfill what we think of as our traditional and archival responsibilities.

In some cases librarians might like to have more format options. A public librarian may know that a large-type edition or an audiotape of a particular title, of primary interest to an older clientele, would be more useful than the book that is available. For many in the academic sector, the other shoe has still to drop; that is, the revolution long expected in electronic publishing has not yet materialized. Most of the books and journals we buy are available only in print, and then not for very long! In the area of reference tools, however, there has been enormous change and a wide range of formats are being offered. The ERIC database, essential to the study of education and related fields, is one example of a resource that can be acquired in several formats: two sets of printed indices, plus a printed thesaurus of descriptors; magnetic tape that can be mounted on the campus mainframe computer with access by anyone who has an account; several compact discs for use with a microcomputer and disk drive; or not acquired at all but accessed either through an end-user or intermediated online search. Similar options exist for databases in business and economics, chemistry, medicine, psychology, and sociology, as well as for dissertations and government documents. The markets for reference tools utilizing electronic media in music, art, and other areas of the humanities have been slower to develop, but momentum is increasing as the technology continues to improve and make converts. In Australia there is a product now on the market called the "Smart Book," with a "reader unit" and a tiny ROM pack in a compressed format so that the whole is about the size of a book, with six buttons to perform searching, indexing, calculation, forwarding, and so on, and a liquid crystal display screen. The first title made available, according to Blake (1988), was the Bible, followed for some reason by the Commerce Clearing House *Master Tax Guide*. A recent *Newsweek* article on hypermedia (Rogers 1988) indicated that publishers are rushing to produce interactive, multimedia packages that will be of great interest in the instructional marketplace. I will not take the time to review all the varieties of media currently on the market; we know that the dust has not yet settled on the formats provided by vendors, and the future will only add to the proliferation.

Not only in the acquisition but also in the preservation of information do we have vastly expanded options: we may conserve the artifact, that is, the book or manuscript; we can pay for a facsimile reproduction or photocopy in-house on acid-free paper; we can use microfilm produced according to a variety of standards, or perhaps resort to optical disk technology like that used in the Library of Congress Pilot Project, which has been the subject of so many articles (Parker 1985; Price 1985).

Let us look at how we make our choices. Most librarians ask questions relating to costs and convenience. The cost of duplicating formats for the same tool is a consideration. Can we afford to keep ERIC in paper and also get the CD ROM? We look at the service implications of relying on CD ROM or magnetic tape, the ease of use, and the amount of support they require. We look at the way the products differ in different formats and attempt to select the one that adds the most value. Political factors related to the library's place in the college may be considerations in decision-making. If the library does not take an important, even a leadership role, other providers of electronic information will appear, most often the computer center. Many librarians feel that a library cannot and should not be the sole gatekeeper of information, but that the library is the best place for promoting the use of information resources to the largest number.

Several factors have acted as deterrents to the adoption of the newer media. Among these deterrents are fears regarding the obsolescence of particular formats, lack of equipment, the need for greatly increased funding for hardware and software, and physical plant limitations. Older buildings can be difficult to renovate or rewire for the electronic library. Space for workstations is at a premium everywhere, but near service points it is perhaps most difficult to convert general-purpose seating to dedicated workstation space. Many library automation ventures receive start-up assistance from grants. Some librarians look at the grant opportunities for funding the new resources and are dissuaded from pursuing them by the knowledge that public relations will suffer if the exciting new services and databases are cancelled when the soft money runs out. In a way, it is fair to say there is no turning back. Infotrak, which we added on an experimental basis a few years ago, got mixed reviews from the reference staff, but public acceptance was overwhelming. It would have been a serious error to cancel it, at least without substituting something better and equally easy to use. Last, in slowing adoption of new media, we must recognize some uncertainty about the labor implications of the shift to an electronic information center. Does the staff have the sophistication to handle questions from remote users about information on magnetic tape? Is there someone always available to unjam printers and replace ribbons and ink cartridges? Will the time it takes to train users of CD ROM in search strategies be too great to give without degradation of other reference services? If librarians are not asking some of these questions, they should be.

As we turn to the implications of our format choices, some of the decision criteria will again be discussed, but the first implication I want to address focuses very sharply on what I will call the integrity of the database. At the 1988 American Library Association meeting in New Orleans, I heard Robert Hayes, dean emeritus of the UCLA Library School, address this issue, not once, but twice! One illustration suggested by his remarks (Hayes 1988) makes his point very well. Envision a professor in the library school doing research in some aspect of cataloging practice. He cites a record in OCLC that shows some peculiarity and publishes an article. He is roundly attacked by a reviewer who has checked his sources and failed to find that OCLC record. What happened? A flawed record was updated and disappeared forever. Let's hope he had a printout! This is a trivial example, to be sure, but what of the electronic journal or reference book? What will prevent revisions from appearing, blurring the picture of the evolution of knowledge as we see it in distinct print editions? What about censorship? The ease of tampering with electronic information could prove tempting in many repressive societies. It takes no effort to make global changes in a document on a word processor, or to excise a paragraph. Publishers could customize a book: one version for a liberal school district, another for a conservative one.

There are also implications to be drawn from the origins of many databases in the for-profit sector. Many of the new and improved databases are produced by and for profit-making agencies. Why should that matter? One reason is that history is not as interesting to many commercial enterprises as more current information is. If we want to know about airline service to Buffalo, New York, we can dial up the Dow-Jones service or call our travel agent and get excellent information about flights offered now and in the near future. But if we are doing research on the effects of the deregulation of the airlines on traffic to minor airports, we must use other sources because they do not store historical data in such databases. They were not designed for historians.

There are other implications of the commercial origins of databases. Many of the contracts or licensing agreements require us to limit use, in violation of our library's mission and general policy. The preferential pricing arrangements we often enjoy with vendors like Lexis, Westlaw, and Standard and Poor have clear restrictions on those eligible to use their services. Vendors are not yet prepared for the tendency of our profession to share information. They are now increasingly confused by the networking movement, which permits multiple users to access the same disk simultaneously. What will happen as we expand our networks over consortia? Will they arrive at pricing strategies that allow us to realize economies of sharing resources, and give them a fair return? We have to face the fact that the relatively small size of the library market puts it at a disadvantage. Customers who pay have say over the content and direction of online products.

In turning to the implications for preservation of choosing the new media, I am defining preservation very broadly: having the information we can access now available to users in the twenty-first century. Some of the implications are clear, others very cloudy. I offer you a list of issues:

- Magnetic media are inherently unstable, and therefore tape backups are of limited help. Tape libraries require specialized maintenance that is labor-intensive and generally unavailable. Detecting problems can be difficult, and resolving them with suppliers is even harder if much time has elapsed.

- Some of the software we use in connection with CD ROM will develop bugs, degrading over time just as the software we use in our microcomputers does.

- Projects such as the Library of Congress undertaking to convert two million pages to optical disk are certainly very exciting and hold out promise of incredibly fast information retrieval of the best value-added kind. But what do we really know about the life of this new medium? What environmental threats, weaknesses, and special problems accompany it? Time will tell, but as attention is given to this technological solution to the decay of paper, there is a real danger of both ignoring more traditional means of preservation and assuming that what is selected by the Library of Congress or another project site to be committed to disk is what your library wishes to preserve.

- We know a lot more about the life of paper and paper chemistry than about any other medium. We can guess that unless we take steps to preserve the low-use but important titles for our collections, they will not be reformatted and will be lost to those twenty-first-century scholars who may be as intrigued to find these titles mentioned in a catalog somewhere as we are to find a scrap of the Dead Sea Scrolls.

- In 1987 an article by Margaret Cribbs appeared in *Online*, with the title "The Invisible Drip – How Data Seeps away in Various Ways." This article stressed the consequences of improper storage and handling. We must be sure that our staff is trained in handling library materials and that our storage conditions maximize the normal life of the new media. In very few libraries, even those with air conditioning, are we able to maintain the optimal environment for printed materials. We have too much light, too much dust, and too many fluctuations in both temperature and humidity. Lots of effort will be required to establish and monitor conditions in our libraries in areas for nonprint media.

- Did you know that film, tape, and photographs could be attacked by fungi? I learned about it only recently. This "microbiodegradation," as the authors (Czerwinska and Kowalik) of a 1979 article term it, is caused by improper storage, but can be prevented by disinfection of the storage area.

- The uncertainties regarding the formats that will endure, and the length of time in which they will be marketed and supported, make us all gamblers as we invest in this or that format. Are there libraries still purchasing phonograph records? 8mm or 16mm film? We have dealt with the dilemma of VHS versus Beta, half-inch versus three-quarter-inch videocassette formats. If our choice is wrong, we risk committing scarce resources to hardware that will sit unused because of an inadequate universe of products in that format.

- Obsolescence of equipment is inevitable, whether our format choice is good or bad. Upgraded equipment may not be compatible with the software we acquired early on but will be needed for newer products. We do not need to ask whether service and replacement parts will be available in 1998 for the disk drive bought today. We know that this disk drive will be upgraded or replaced or obsolete before then. The budget implications of these short-term investments deserve careful analysis.

- There is another situation with ominous implications for preservation. When we do not buy but instead lease a product, with an agreement that we will send back this month's or year's tape or disk when we receive the new one, we assume a risk. If the price increases become too much to absorb and we cancel, we must return everything. If at the same time we have already cancelled any existing paper equivalent, there will be gaps in our collections that may be difficult to fill. This return provision is no different from the practices of some print publishers, but there may be more print alternatives, or more room for negotiation.

- It is worth our while to examine for a moment the structure of the publishing industry. According to a publisher who spoke at the American Library Association July 1988 preconference, "Collection Development in an Electronic Age," publishers reach their break-even on paper sales. Other media spin-offs from the paper are essentially gravy. As libraries move toward cost containment and cancel the paper versions of the Wilson Indexes, for example, we alter the profit margins of the Wilson Company, which then must increase the cost of CD ROM and online products, which leads to our cutbacks in those media, and so on. Publishers may be forced to withdraw products from the market because of competition, inadequate return on investment, or undercapitalization. Businesses fail for lots of reasons, or are purchased by other companies. The result is not only lack of support – and it is important to remember, electronic products need more support than printed books – but difficulties in using and maintaining these electronic products. Common examples of problems users report are dirty or missing data on magnetic tapes and changes in format without documentation. When the vendor fails, we may be unable to fill the information gap with other media.

- A subtle problem requiring in-depth attention from collections staff relates to the different content in different formats of essentially similar databases. One may cover different years, or include abstracts. We must know what our trade-offs are, or risk losing something of value.

- In a recent article on copyright in a journal published by reproductive rights organizations, I read a statement that stayed with me, although I neglected to note the author's name. He said something like, "Librarians don't like torsos," by which he meant that librarians like to have complete runs of serials on their shelves. If we opt to cancel print subscriptions, we will indeed be left with only parts of our indexing

452

and abstracting services. We may find ourselves uncomfortable with this state of affairs. Our users will also have the inconvenience of using two media, possibly in different locations.

- One implication of the choice of electronic formats is a need for the creation and organization of technical documentation. Now and for future users, we must be able to see the specifics of our system and network software and hardware, what is compatible with it, how it is assembled, and how, if at all, it has been customized for our installation. Can this Wilson product, or UMI product, be used with or connected to my SilverPlatter network? Does the contract require that a product be installed on a stand-alone workstation? Technical documentation has a life of its own. The Inter-University Consortium for Political and Social Research sends with each data file a multipage description of the files and size of files on each tape, plus a partial data dump and a codebook. Documentation can fill a large office very quickly. It is essential to have it, and if we make the choice to provide these formats, someone on the staff must be assigned responsibility for documentation.

In thinking about what our current enthusiasms portend for the future, we soon see even broader issues than preservation.

- Shifts in collecting patterns mean physical changes, from general stack shelving to secure, special-purpose storage. Although it is to be hoped and expected that as we complete more linkages between systems we can approach one-stop shopping, so that the user of electronic information finds whatever is needed in the "box"–that is, the terminal and monitor, using menus or commands–that scenario will not come to pass immediately. At first there will be a good deal more labor involved in retrieval, service, and training. There will be rationing and inconvenience for the user.

- Last among the implications I would suggest to you are the social implications. Technology is deepening the division between the information-rich and the information-deprived. Government data made available only in machine-readable form are inaccessible to many users. The school library that can offer Boolean searching, printing of citations and abstracts, and free, full-text database searching is turning out a differently prepared individual than one in which the student is limited to linear searching in printed sources and is made to spend large amounts of time copying citations and running through microfilm.

At last I have come to the part of my presentation where I propose solutions to all the problems I have outlined, ways to keep the faith with the traditions of our profession and those scholars seeking knowledge in the next century. Actually, I prefer to propose approaches rather than solutions because what we are lacking is a process for making the transition and safeguarding what we have at the same time. There are a few essential keys to success: cooperation, networking, participation, and communication, and they are by no means discrete. In addition, certain stakeholders are especially important to the success of the transition.

The staff in each institution must be educated about the costs and benefits of the choices being made in the library, especially as they will bear many of the costs in terms of new and additional work and continuing education. Training in each new system and its maintenance, and in the care and documentation of software, may be developed in a large library or in state, regional, or local organizations to ensure the inclusion of librarians from small libraries.

Continue or initiate communication with your users so that they feel at once a part of and in some control over information resources. Every satisfied user is an advocate for the library. Every dissatisfied user is a source of information and an opportunity to improve. Observation and dialogue can provide clues leading to improvements in software and instruction.

Cooperate with the technical people outside the library, and with the university administration, to work towards the highest level of support for information technologies. Use their expertise in the handling and storage of electronic data, and share with them what you learn in your professional reading on related subjects. Keep them informed of your needs and your plans, and look for ways to support them in theirs. Seek a role on any committee dealing with campuswide technological issues so that the library perspective is not forgotten.

Cooperate with other institutions in formal ways – consortia, regional compacts, and the like – to establish central storage facilities where the paper torsos can be combined to regenerate complete sets of low-use materials. The concept of a national library of record may be unrealistic, but regional facilities like the Center for Research Libraries (Illinois) could be very helpful. Participate in joint microfilming projects that seem appropriate to your clientele and your collections. Funding is available for some projects.

Become active in your local network to share resources, especially high-tech, high-cost resources. There is no need for any library to be information-deprived if we each recognize our sphere of responsibility. The small public library may not be able to compete in terms of collections, but the telephone and the computer should make it possible for these libraries to get the information they need to the patron from a database or a designated reference center.

Participate in professional organizations, especially in standards committees and committees that interact with the next set of shareholders, vendors, and publishers. Cooperation and communication are vital here to establish goodwill and to convince the bottom-line people that the library marketplace, although small, can make a positive contribution to the development of better products through our expertise as information providers and our feedback. Publishers want to stay in business and meet their customers' needs. So do vendors. We must convince them that our needs are met by high-quality products with minimal overlap, and with minimal restrictions on use. We must convince them that keeping titles available for printing on demand is to their advantage. We must convince them to talk to one another, not only in person but in their systems, so that we can choose products freely. We must encourage them to adopt standards in everything, from the quality of microfiche to the protocols in online searching, and we must do so in ways that clearly delineate the advantages to them in market growth and heightened prestige.

In the remainder of this century, we will be learning, talking, worrying, and trying to develop a global information superstructure, that will be as seamless as possible. Technology will help shape this superstructure, but it is for us to determine its values, to ensure that service to users remains our highest priority. Librarians have shown themselves to be capable of managing enormous changes. Let us keep heart as we prepare for equally eventful decades to come.

References

Blake, K. (1988). "The Electronic Book." *Library Hi Tech* 6, no. 1: 7-11.

Cribbs, M. A. (1987). "The Invisible Drip . . . How Data Seeps away in Various Ways." *Online* 11, no. 2 (March): 15-16, 26-28.

Czerwinska, E., and Kowalik, R. (1979). "Microbiodegradation of Audiovisual Collections." *Restaurator* 3, nos. 1-2: 63-80.

Hayes, R. (1988). "Managing Scholarly Information: Implications and Strategies." Paper presented at the American Library Association, Resources and Technical Services Division preconference on Collection Development in the Electronic Age, New Orleans, Louisiana, July 8.

Parker, E. B. (1985). "The Library of Congress Nonprint Optical Disk Pilot Program." *Information Technology and Libraries* 4, no. 4 (December): 289-99.

Price, J. W. (1985). "Optical Disks and Demand Printing Research at the Library of Congress." *Information Services and Use* 5, no. 1 (February): 3-20.

Rogers, M. (1988). "Here Comes Hypermedia." *Newsweek* (October 3): 44-45.

Beyond Access:
Implications of the Information Age
for the Public Library

JOHN C. BLEGEN

Current thinking about the future often produces this assertion: information is now a commodity, rendered scarce by certain government policies.[1] The thesis is that we have entered a phase that goes beyond industrial production to the production of information. Some thinkers, particularly those writing in library literature, refer to a study by Marc Porat that indicated a sharp rise in the percentage of the work force composed of "knowledge workers." Tom Ballard, never loath to explode a myth, points out that almost no one has actually *read* Porat, and this includes Ballard himself.[2] The study, it seems (I have not read it either), is nine volumes long. Ballard's skimming and his judicious use of glosses, however, tell him that Porat has included some questionable categories of workers in the information column, blurring the distinction between "service" workers and true "information" workers. The rise of the information age, for Ballard at least, has been exaggerated.

There is other evidence that something has changed in the way society processes and digests information, and the very bulk of Porat's specious study is not a bad example. As a public library practitioner, I will leave it to others to decide whether *post* is the proper prefix for *industrial*, and whether *information* and *economy* can stand close together without (theoretically) stinking, but I must affirm that information looms large in the concerns of our contemporaries. This is a simple observation. And it has not always been true; it is something new.

Our century has seen a link forged between economic success and access to information, to intellectual resources, to knowledge. This happens on many levels, from the acquisition of a skill ("know-how") to the benefits of

457

education. Indeed, the rise of the importance of information coincides with the rise of the public library. The public library is born, it is true, in a *political* surge. The founding fathers supported libraries because the democratic demon had been set loose: we had better have an informed public. An informed, enlightened, and astute public – and, we should all agree, a public more or less broad, depending on the founding father in question – but not necessarily a wealthy public.

As the nineteenth century drew to a close and thousands of immigrants arrived eager to survive and succeed, the connection between information and success became explicit. The public library, and particularly the urban public library, began to enjoy high use and high prestige.

With this change in role and rise in prestige, the public library developed two major service components beyond the maintenance of collections of books. The reader's advisory service was the staff support element of recreational or "spontaneous" reading. The library staff member was to provide answers to the eager patron wanting something good to read. There was a seriousness about the advisory function – it was clear that the more one read the more one developed an economically valuable skill – but it was also clear that the patron's activity was to take place during disposable, leisure time. The second component of library service was clearly allied with the economic function. Reference service was the librarian's acknowledgement that what we are now calling the "artifact" (the book) was a mere container of information, and that there were many containers. The reference librarian provided an answer to any question, using the resources that the library had been able to accumulate. Almost unnoticed in the proper practice of reference service was a principle that we will revisit later: the reference librarian always cited the source of the information.

Supporting these two public service staff activities – reader's advisory and reference – were the background efforts that were often thought (by the public) to be the librarian's principal tasks: cataloging, filing, and shelving. Collection development, perhaps the most important underpinning for excellent reader's advisory and reference services, was very much a part of the librarian's life, but it was largely invisible to the public. Somehow the stuff was just there. (I am still amused by the reactions of nonlibrarians who come to work in a library – financial officers, facilities managers, personnel specialists – when they discover that a major portion of the library's function is to buy rather than to preserve.)

So the public library stood as an economic boon, the people's university (the only free one besides the old CCNY), with its reader's advisory and reference service arms, the major source of an increasingly valuable economic and intellectual commodity. At the beginning of the process, we see young Henry Mencken, who began "an almost daily harrying of the virgins at the delivery desk" for more information about the fabulous world he was discovering.[3] And in the midst of the progression, in a strange echo, we find Richard Wright fighting for access to the library's resources to find out what a white man like Mencken could have said to make other white men so mad at him.[4]

To read the annual reports of the major public libraries during the 1920s, 1930s, and 1940s is to see the functions of a vital information resource, much supported by public use and accustomed to the importance of its role. Budget problems are there, to be sure, and staffing is never sufficient. But there is a confidence that begins to weaken in the 1950s, and to disappear in the 1960s. By the 1970s, the large urban public libraries that lead the public library profession are without any question the suburban systems.

I have taken the time for this capsule history because we have a very paradoxical situation facing us. At a time when we were in the midst of the *industrial* society, information *was* a key commodity for a major part of the population of this country. And the public library was a key provider (if not *the* key provider), building the basis of good feeling that now supports those suburban libraries. Now that we have moved to the so-called postindustrial society, however – or the information society, in which the economy (if we listen even to people other than the verbose and apparently unreadable Marc Porat, people like Peter Drucker) is information-based[5] – that old stalwart version of the library, the large urban library, has become identified with "culture" (always a pejorative in a city budget process) rather than with education or information. There are, of course, some obvious reasons: changes in the demographic composition of cities, failure of most urban school systems, reductions in budgets crippling the purchasing power of city libraries and therefore virtually curtailing proper collection development, and failure (often because of lack of funding, but sometimes because of lack of vision) to take advantage of new technology and to respond to new forms of information. And all of these are, to some degree, true. But there has been a shift in the way information is used by society, and that shift seems to inform the general structure of what has happened to large urban libraries. I will attempt to discuss that shift in a moment.

I should not leave this point, however, without adding that the function and prestige of the successful suburban libraries are qualitatively different now from what they were for those urban libraries forty years ago (when most of the suburban systems did not exist). Briefly, the successful suburban systems have built upon the provision of popular materials, profiting from the demographic changes that brought about their birth. Having done that, however, they are now in a position to take advantage of many technological changes that will permit them to play a central role in the new information climate. Once dependent on the nearby urban library for "serious" information, the suburban (and even the rural) system can now possess many of those resources on microform or CD ROM, and those that it cannot possess are only a modem-equipped phone call away.

The impact of technology on public libraries has been well documented in a variety of places, but I need to touch on several aspects of this impact in order to get to my central point. Technology has increased access to information in public libraries to an astounding degree. In Maryland, for example, holdings from over ninety libraries of all types can be browsed through or thoroughly searched by any Maryland citizen who walks through the door of a public library anywhere in the state. While this is still done in many locations by using microfiche, in many libraries the citizen searches a CD ROM database (which, as a bonus, includes the union list of periodicals). Another automated network permits that citizen to request and receive a desired item found in that catalog, no matter where that item is. Elsewhere, the technology permits availability (in the trade, "item-level") information, whether a book is in or out, and, if out, when it should be back. So access to the traditional has been geometrically increased. Online databases have been used by public libraries since the mid-seventies, but that use for some time was limited to the large systems that could afford to pay high, up-front subscription costs. No longer. Virtually every medium-sized and large public library now does online searching, and many do it (or at least some of it) at no extra cost to the patron. Public libraries are clearly connected to the new information sources. Some are beginning to provide access to nonbibliographic databases and gateways for end-user searching, bulletin boards for home or office computer commuters, and an increasing number of databases for walk-in users at CD ROM workstations.

What the urban public library has lost – its central position in the information supply system – is being reclaimed by the suburban systems as they dip into new technology. Those older urban systems, now following rather than leading, are beginning to rebound (several large budget increases have occurred recently), jumping, as they become able, on the technology bandwagon.

It would appear, then, that everything is fine, that we have suffered only a slight setback brought on by all of those factors listed a moment ago (demographics, cuts in funding, inflation, etc.). But it is my belief that something else has changed, something in the basic structure of information, and the structure of how we think about it, that must be taken into account as we approach the next century. If I have taken so much time with history in a conference aimed at the twenty-first century, it is, after all, to approach that century with a useful historical perspective. This change, this shift, is the real subject of this presentation. I shall attempt to define it (having finally finished with stating the context) and to draw some principles for future public libraries from it.

Information is, we are told, a commodity today. Companies are, or will increasingly be, in Peter Drucker's phrase, information-based. A corporation must be able to marshal vital information about markets, populations, trends, world events, and scientific breakthroughs. Information can even be illegal, contraband, a security risk, an actionable offense, or a reason to go to prison if one uses the "insider" variety to manipulate the stock market. Most of this has always been true, and it may be said that we are simply dealing with a question of degree. That is, the technological possibility of instant, worldwide access to information and the equally dazzling possibility of instantaneous, worldwide *production* of information have simply increased the amount of this commodity. The technology, we might say, is driving the proliferation of information. This seems plausible when we consider that some of this information is done *automatically*, without human intervention, that computers are responding to each other and creating *new* data. This seems to be causing both consternation and temptation on Wall Street, provoking feelings that it must be stopped; at the same time, visions of where it could lead, both apocalyptic and utopian, are legion.

Regardless of what may or may not be the realities of the world economy, there has been, I believe, a qualitative change in the way we view data, information, and knowledge, not just a quantitative one. One way of saying this is that information has become more *important* for all of us than ever before. And this is probably what Peter Drucker is talking about when he refers to an "information-based organization": information is now just as important as various raw materials or personnel. Drucker is also very clear in his definition: "Information is data endowed with relevance and purpose. Converting data into information thus requires knowledge. And knowledge, by definition, is specialized."[6]

I will come back to this remarkable formula because it will help to define what the public librarian of the future ought to be doing. For now, it seems simply to echo Gregory Bateson's phrase, one that guides much of the thought about information today: "Information consists of differences that make a difference."[7] If we consider the economic dimension of information, we can point out some aspects that are very perplexing. Stewart Brand, in his book on MIT's Media Lab, quotes Jay Ogilvy, a strategic adviser to the London Stock Exchange, in these terms:

> What gets me is how utterly inappropriate our basic economic categories are. We need to recast the concept of property, for one thing, because in Marx's terms property is by definition *alienable:* that is, unlike your elbow, which is you and not yours, property must be transferable to another (*alia* equals other). I sell you the cow. You got the cow. I don't have the cow anymore. I sell you the information. You got the information. I still have the information. That's the anomaly. Another anomaly: intrinsic in information is the "difference that makes a difference" – *to a receiver.* So the condition of

of the receiver is an important part of whether a given signal is or is not information. Is it news or isn't it news? Well, that depends on the receiver and the receiver's ability to understand it. That's not true of a ton of steel. It's not true of a ton of wheat. A third anomaly is the notion of depreciation, the very notion of inventory–information doesn't depreciate the way physical things do.[8]

In simple terms, if information is moving into the place in our lives that property (commodities) once occupied, we are probably going to try to push it around among ourselves in the same way that we have pushed commodities around; but it is *peculiar,* and it is not going to respond as expected. Put slightly differently, we might say that we used to have an accepted way of treating data, information, and knowledge (to follow Drucker); we, or many of us, have abandoned that way. We have shifted our way of conceptualizing the problem.

The shift has been noticed recently by thinkers as different as Theodore Roszak and Allan Bloom. The "old" structure is hierarchical, immanent, residing in the Platonic notion of the forms. There is an authority that becomes the subject of commentary, glosses, accounts. The seeker of information used to be the seeker of knowledge and, prior to that, the seeker of truth. This structure appears in its most naive form in the college term paper: one must examine many sources, being sure to cite each one fully, and the truth (or the comprehensive treatment, or the basic problem, or a new framing of the question) will appear. The facts receive their importance from the source, their value is referential. The authority, the source, the citation is the foundation of all reference work, the skeleton supporting any librarian's response to a question.

Allan Bloom sees in this appeal to authority a process of learning, almost a rite of passage. In the development of a thesis, of a set of conclusions, one learns at the foot of the ancients, one builds upon the works of those who have gone before us.[9] Theodore Roszak, while politically quite the opposite of the authoritarian Bloom, sees the same structure, but he sees it as a wealth, a richness of context surrounding knowledge. The many connections surrounding an idea, what Nietzsche would call a genealogy, are what Roszak sees the mind following in creative thought. And these connections are what differentiate human creative thought from artificial intelligence and other modes of thought modeled on the structure of computers.[10] Without getting involved in that particular debate, I am suggesting that Roszak's conception of the structure of knowledge is a product of the same intellectual climate as the hierarchical structure seen by Bloom. Something–both writers sense this–has happened, or is in the process of happening, to the way we think about information.

The shift, I believe, is the disappearance, devaluation, and, perhaps, dissimulation of the authority, and what results is that the hierarchy of information, the vertical structure of knowledge, flattens. Technology, while having a hand in the speed and reach of the shift, is certainly not the cause and may even be the salvation, *pace* Theodore Roszak. Technology, however, is certainly not entirely innocent.

Technology, in increasing the degree of access, as we have seen, has created certain expectations. David H. Lewis, in a recent article called "Inventing the Electronic University," both cites and expresses some of these expectations:

> Students may expect the library to be as powerful and easy to use as electric teaching tools. Unfortunately, libraries are rarely easy to use. If analysis with new computer tools becomes easier and more productive than library research, students can be expected to use the new tools rather than the library. If libraries do not improve their services so that they remain an essential teaching tool, they risk becoming irrelevant to the teaching process.[11]

And his own expectations appear in statements like this one:

> As the process of scholarly communication becomes more completely electronic, efficiencies will come into play and library service both inside and outside the library should improve. To take a mundane example, when books and articles are online, there is little reason to require students to wait in lines at reserve desks, or even come to the library, to read them. Librarians will be able to create and provide information resources that reach beyond their walls.[12]

Technology has also brought down some of the boundaries existing in the information production process. (In the university we would call this the scholarly process, but the fundamental distinctions are the same wherever information is produced.) Lewis predicts that the scholarly process will become "seamless,"[13] a continuum in which the distinctions between producer, fabricator, publisher, and consumer of information become blurred, since all in the chain use the same machines and have access to the same pool of information. In this blurring of distinctions we again see the shift from the old information *ethos* to the new. Such a blurring carries with it some forbidding implications, expressed well by Gordon Neavill:

> The malleability of information that is one of the major advantages of computer-based electronic systems has as its corollary the potential transience of information. Nothing inherent in the technology of computer-based electronic systems ensures that information in the system will survive. ... When information is freed from the confines of a physical container it is rendered vulnerable. It can be altered or revised without any indication that

a change has been made. It can be purged from the system altogether. Information without a physical container cannot survive on its own.[14]

While I do not share Neavill's faith in the physical container, the point is well taken. It becomes a more crucial point when one reflects that media that have been taken as even more trustworthy than print are also now subject to the "malleability" that digital translation allows. Stewart Brand considers this threat while reporting a conversation with Kevin Kelly:

> We've been spoiled by a hundred years of reliable photography as a place to put faith, but that century was an anomaly. Before then, and after now, we have to trust in other ways. What the magazines who routinely use creative retouching machines say is "Trust us." [Brand continues:] You can't trust the medium, you can only trust the source, the people. It's the same with text, after all. The only way my words are evidence is if I don't lie, even though it's so, so easy to do.[15]

What Brand has in mind here is the so-called digital *faux*, the use of a photographic image that is stored in digital form for a kind of retouching that is absolutely undetectable, seamless. This capability for intellectual fraud (or at least, uncertainty and danger) resides in the very nature of digital storage. If we talk of information literacies, in this context, we must raise Brand's problem of trust, the problem of authority and reliability.

Perhaps the information society is that place where appeals to authority are either missing or hidden, where the informational unit no longer carries any family name. Separated from the old structure expressed by the likes of Bloom and Roszak, information begins to look very much like property, a true commodity: it can be packaged, mass-produced, advertised, marketed, distributed, marked down, inflated, remaindered, exchanged. But our discussion has shown that this is merely an appearance, albeit a pervasive and extremely attractive one.

That the public library must provide access to this "material" is clear, but we can now see that the mere provision of access is not simple. Others have dealt with the economic forces that are in the process of disenfranchising those without the means to pay for the commodity. But when the commodity appears innocent, isolated, and self-contained when it is not, the information professionals must have some kind of strategy to deal with the dangers of their trade. We must find ways in which the public library can provide real access, critical access, by connecting the commodity to its hidden context and antecedents.

What I am calling for here is something that might be named "critical librarianship." The mission of the critical librarian is to bring a specialized knowledge of the information universe to bear on the mass of data that society produces and, to follow Drucker's formula, to use that specialized knowledge to turn the data into useful, relevant information. This will appear to economists immediately as a process that adds value. Good reference librarians have been doing it for years, rather mechanically it is true, by citing the source of a piece of information. The critical librarian will add whatever ancillary information is necessary to place the answer to a query in the proper context.

David Lewis has seen that there is a serious problem ahead for librarians in the "flattening" of the information hierarchy, as we have been discussing it, a quality control problem the likes of which we have never seen:

> The loss of the publication hurdle, which occurs when everyone becomes a desktop publisher, will lead to an enormous increase in low-quality materials, and the already challenging intellectual task of selecting items for inclusion in library collections will become even more difficult.[16]

Beyond the problems of collection development, which will also be rendered more complex by the proliferation of formats and by the loss of the physical package, is the problem of communicating with the library's public. The current conventional wisdom in public libraries is that bibliographic instruction is the responsibility of academe and that public libraries should simply deliver the goods. I have felt for some time that this is an oversimplification of the barriers that a public library customer faces when approaching the library, and I have long felt that we should do more to empower the customer to unlock the resource that we maintain. (In fairness, I must point out that several public libraries are making serious efforts to solve this problem.) But the critical librarian will have to develop ways of communicating the context of information to the future customer, and these methods should also have the objective of educating the customer, making the customer aware of the provenance of data. "Be careful with that," we must say, "if you don't know where it's been." There is an echo of this level of concern in what one of Jerry Pournelle and Larry Niven's characters in *Lucifer's Hammer* thought about technology itself:

> "Damnedest thing," he said. "Whole nation depends on technology. Stop the wheels for two days and you'd have riots. No place is more than two meals from a revolution. Think of Los Angeles or New York with no electricity. Or a longer view, fertilizer plants stop. Or a longer view yet, no new technology for ten years. What happens to our standard of living? . . . Yet the damn fools won't pay ten minutes' attention a day to science and technology. How many people know what they're doing? Where do these carpets come from? The clothes you're wearing? What do carburetors do? Where do sesame seeds come from? Do *you* know? Does one voter out of thirty? They won't spend ten minutes a day thinking about the technology that keeps them alive."[17]

The point is that the information-poor certainly need access to information, but their need does not stop there. Beyond access, the public library must provide the information specialists of the future – specialists who will demystify, connect, and explicate the desired information while implementing programs that will foster true information literacy – with the ability to determine what is important in the sea of data and to see the connections underlying the seemingly innocent facts.

Notes

1. Virgil Blake and Thomas Surprenant, "An Information Policy for the Information Age," *Wilson Library Bulletin*, May 1988, 44.

2. Thomas Ballard, "The Information Age and the Public Library," *Wilson Library Bulletin*, June 1988, 74.

3. Henry L. Mencken, *Happy Days* (New York: Alfred A. Knopf, 1940; reprint, 1964), 174.

4. Richard Wright, *Black Boy* (New York: New American Library, 1964), 267-71.

5. Peter F. Drucker, "The Coming of the New Organization," *Harvard Business Review*, January-February 1988, 45-53.

6. Ibid., 46.

7. Gregory Bateson, *Mind and Nature: A Necessary Unity* (New York: Bantam, 1980), 110.

8. Stewart Brand, *The Media Lab* (New York: Viking, 1987), 248.

9. Allan Bloom, *The Closing of the American Mind* (New York: Simon and Schuster, 1987). The position that Bloom writes *from* is most evident in his more pointed attacks on the American way of thought. See particularly "Books," 62-67, and "Music," 68-81.

10. Theodore Roszak, *The Cult of Information* (New York: Pantheon, 1986). See especially ch. 5, "Of Ideas and Data," 87-107.

11. David W. Lewis, "Inventing the Electronic University," in *College and Research Libraries*, July 1988, 293.

12. Ibid.

13. Ibid.

14. Gordon B. Neavill, "Electronic Publishing, Libraries, and Survival of Information," *Library Resources and Technical Services*, January-March 1984, 77.

15. Brand, *Media Lab,* 221-22.

16. Lewis, "Electronic University," 297.

17. Larry Niven and Jerry Pournelle, "Dr. Charles Sharps," in *Lucifer's Hammer* (New York: Fawcett Crest, 1978), 51.

Impacts, Implications, and Possible Future Scenarios for Public Libraries as a Result of Online Database Searching in Reference Departments

JANICE HELEN MCCUE

What does the future hold for the public libraries in the twenty-first century? Let's make the question more specific! What impact will online database searching have on the reference departments of the twenty-first-century public libraries, and what will be the implications? There are no easy answers to these questions. Let's look at what has been taking place in the reference departments of public libraries for some clues.

To accomplish this, I would like to present to you some of the results of my research concerning online searching in public libraries. This research was prompted by the fact that the public libraries are undergoing significant changes brought about by the advent of online searching, and there is a new concern with evaluating the effectiveness of online search services, as well as the factors that influence the achievement of high-quality results. Little research had been done on these topics, and a body of expertise needed to be developed to identify and investigate differences in the results achieved. Part of the research traces just what happens when an individual requests an online database search.

The research was conducted in two stages. The first stage involved testing and comparing the quality of online search results. The second stage included the analysis and evaluation of the results, as well as follow-up interviews with the online searchers and their supervisors to document the factors that influence the quality of the search.

From June 25, 1984, to October 24 of the same year, I presented a request for an online database search to twenty-one public libraries. These libraries were located in sixteen states from across the continental United

States. The request was in the form of a multifaceted question, and each searcher was asked to conduct the search on two different databases. The online searchers had no knowledge that they were being tested, but they would become aware of this technique in the follow-up interviews that I employed in the second stage of the research. This method of data collection, known as "unobtrusive measurement," has been judged to be an accepted technique as long as the names of the participating institutions and individuals are not disclosed.

The multifaceted question was carefully selected so that subject specialization would not be a factor. The question that was presented was sufficiently serious in nature and yet timely enough to be discussed in current, fairly popular journals, magazines, and newspapers. The question that finally evolved was, "How have the unprofitable loans to the United States energy sector and to the Third World countries affected the major banks of the United States?"

To maintain uniformity in presenting the question, I personally visited each library and submitted a typewritten, detailed online search request. The instructions specified that (1) the databases ABI/INFORM and National Newspaper Index were to be used in the search, (2) thirty minutes were to be spent conducting the search, (3) only citations and descriptors would be retrieved, (4) the years 1979 to 1984 would be searched, and (5) the search was to be left intact, including the search strategy. Keywords were included in the instructions as a means of providing some input because I would not be present for the actual running of the search; I wanted to avoid any contamination of the results. It was stressed to each searcher that these keywords were merely suggestions, and that the final selection of words and terms employed in the search strategy rested with the searcher.

The most important and often the most troublesome aspect of an online search is the search strategy. In order to have a test that could measure the performance of the libraries, it was necessary that this part of the procedure be placed entirely in the hands of the searcher. An underlying hypothesis of the study is that the quality of search results is greatly dependent upon the individual who is doing the searching.

To keep the selection process of participating libraries as even as possible, several criteria were established. One criterion was that the sample be drawn from those libraries serving an urban population. At the time this study was started, online reference had approximately a fourteen-year history in public librarianship, and for the most part it had been major public libraries that had been conducting online searching for a considerable period of time.

In a few cases, urban libraries could not be selected because they did not offer online searching, but in each case a nearby, affluent suburban library served as a suitable substitute because it offered online searching to the same population as the urban libraries. It is important to mention that, of those libraries identified as potential candidates for the study, many had to be excluded because they were very specific about restricting the use of online searching to those patrons who had a valid library card from their particular geographic location. And in some other cases, libraries were excluded because their policy of not charging would only allow for what they explained would be – and the following are their words – "a quick and dirty search."

Another criterion was that the libraries under investigation have access to the same databases arbitrarily picked for this experiment. This presented no problem because most public libraries subscribe to the vendor Dialog, which supplies access to the two databases chosen for this investigation.

To make certain that the simulated patron-online searcher encounter occurred during a representative time period, I telephoned each sample library to obtain an appointment. Although eleven of the contacted libraries stated that they did not require an appointment, most searchers revealed that they encouraged appointments because it enabled a time slot to be set aside for a presearch interview. Same-day delivery of the printouts was requested at each library, and thirteen of the libraries were able to accommodate this request. Of the remaining libraries, six provided service within one to five days, and two mailed the online printouts to a forwarding address. The reasons given for the delays were scheduling patterns, shortage of staff, or malfunctioning database equipment.

An important aspect of the online technology is that it provides a printout from the computer terminal. The printout creates an opportunity to evaluate the quality of a search in a way that was not previously possible. By examination of computer printouts, one can tell a great deal about how searches were conducted, such as terms used, time spent searching, and skill in searching techniques. The printouts also display the vendor charges.

Stage two of the research included three phases of analysis. The first phase was a performance analysis by an outside team of database search experts from leading financial institutions. The second phase involved my analysis of the printouts as scored by the panelists. The third phase was a statistical analysis of the raw data derived from the scoring process and the follow-up interviews.

In the first phase, the expert panelists evaluated search results using a point system of scoring. The focus of the evaluation was the skill of the twenty-one online searchers in retrieving citations that would provide information for the single multifaceted question, and in using two different databases. The comparison of performance scores showed that there was a wide difference in the quality of searching from library to library.

The panelists' experience in the scoring phase led them to confirm that the quality searches appeared to be those that had been thoroughly thought out and were well prepared before the searcher went online at the terminal.

According to the panelists, a prepared searcher has alternative strategies ready to compensate for any inadequacies in the initial strategy.

After scoring the forty-two searches, the panelists observed that, no matter what search strategy was used, many citations of the same quality were retrieved. At times, as many as fourteen libraries retrieved the same excellent citation. The panelists also indicated that, no matter how detailed the search strategy was, it still retrieved unwanted citations along with those that were relevant.

The panelists further revealed the influence of the individual searcher when they affirmed that, if index terms were not entered correctly via such techniques as nesting, stacking, adjacency, and truncation, quality citations would not be retrieved. The consensus was that terms must be mixed and matched correctly if they are to be effective. The panelists were also in agreement that, although the limitation of index terms to the descriptor field could be effective in specifically narrowing the search, this technique should be used with caution. The reason for this was that adding too many restrictions could lead to becoming overly specific, resulting in too few relevant citations.

An assessment of the online database searches scored by the panelists led them to conclude that the best online searches were attained by those searchers who retrieved the largest number of citations. The panelists enlarged upon this finding by stating that, to obtain quality citations, there has to be sufficient volume for the selection process; such volume can be achieved by the use of a broad search strategy that can be narrowed as the search progresses. Interestingly, the major finding of the statistical analysis revealed that a strong relationship exists between the quality of the search and the number of citations retrieved. However, this finding does not mean that quantity is the only variable that affects quality. What the research did reveal is that from the collected data the only factor that significantly affected quality was the variable quantity.

Included in stage two of the study was my analysis of the wide range of performance scores. The question that was uppermost in my mind as I was analyzing the scores was what factor or factors caused such a wide range of performance scores. The first relationship to be considered was the cost factor.

From an examination of the performance scores I observed that, of the five lowest scoring results, three sets of scores were the result of searches executed at libraries that did not charge a fee for the requested search. A closer look at these three libraries might prove fruitful.

For example, at the first library the online searcher read and accepted the request but did not tell me that the library's policy limited the search to eight minutes' free search time. I was told only that the library did not charge a fee for an online database search. When I returned the next day to pick up

470

the printouts, the online searcher revealed the library's policy. As a direct result of the eight-minute free search time policy, the searcher retrieved only two quality citations.

When I presented the search request at the second noncharging library, the only information given pertaining to the cost was the explanation that the library did not charge a fee for an online database search request. However, when I returned for the printouts of the search results, the searcher stated that the free search for a patron was restricted to the library's policy of a fixed dollar amount. In other words, the library would only absorb the vendor's charges for a database search that were kept under twenty-five dollars.

At the third noncharging library, a similar scenario took place. During the course of the investigation, it was made clear that the library policies were upheld despite the nature of an individual's search request. My request for a thirty-minute search at the terminal could not be honored, and it was apparent that results were limited by the library's policy of restricting all free searches to either a fixed dollar amount or a fixed amount of search time. For example, there was no time for the online searcher to use an alternative strategy in the event that the final results contained either too few citations or too many citations that might not be relevant.

From this small sampling of public libraries that offer online searching without charging a fee, my conclusion is that the greatest drawback appears to be that the no-fee policy restricts the patron's request, limits the online searcher's connect time at the terminal, and thus hampers the search results.

The data pertaining to the SEARCH SAVE command showed that seven of the twenty-one libraries used this technique. The SEARCH SAVE command stores a search strategy and allows this stored strategy to be recalled for use at another time in different databases. The use of the SEARCH SAVE command was equally dispersed among the low, medium, and high range of performing scores. Thus, no relationship was observed. However, one interesting observation occurred in the low performing range. The identical strategy without any modifications was used to search both databases. Although the SEARCH SAVE command is viewed as a time-saving technique, the search results might reflect a poor performance score because the saved search terms were inappropriate for use in the second database. Additional study is needed to determine if the SEARCH SAVE command is employed by some searchers who do not want to spend the time or effort in developing a new search strategy. This type of use might be associated with searchers who demonstrate a lack of interest.

The information obtained from the scoring of the general techniques revealed that very few typographical mistakes, misspelled words, or incorrect procedures occurred. The scoring for this segment had a basis of 100. The lowest score for a tested library was 93, and the average range of the remaining scores was between 97 and 98. Seven of the top performing libraries were rated 100 in this category. This seems to indicate that the majority of the searchers kept their mistakes to a minimum, and thus valuable connect time was not wasted correcting errors.

Up to this point, the major focus of the discussion has been on the performance evaluation of the printouts. In order to interpret the results more fully, I interviewed the twenty-one online searchers and the twenty-one online reference supervisors. These follow-up interviews enabled me to explore possible relationships that exist between the performance score and the information supplied by the interviewee. Because of the unobtrusive nature of the study, I must say that I gulped and swallowed several times before telephoning each supervisor and each searcher to inform them of the study. Quite frankly, I had serious concerns about their reactions when they were told the manner in which the searches were conducted. However, none of the participants raised any objections, and all agreed to participate in the follow-up interviews. This response rate of 100 percent suggests that the participants support research efforts in the profession and are willing to contribute information that might add to the knowledge of online searching in public libraries.

The follow-up interviews with the online reference supervisors sought information concerning the relationships that might exist between the quality of the searcher's performance and administrative practices. All the supervisors agreed that many factors contribute to the success of an online search. Statistical analysis showed that three factors had a slight influence over the quality of the results achieved.

The first factor that tended to have a slight influence over the outcome was the library's policy regarding fees. The supervisors associated with libraries that subscribed to a no-charge policy seemed to suggest that the impact of these policies hampered the searching practices of the online searcher. Research is clearly needed to determine the effects of this policy on performance, since this statistical finding was also a finding of my analysis that I discussed earlier.

An analysis of the libraries that regularly charged a fee for database searching revealed a variety of charging patterns. Some of the information, such as surcharges and rush fees for same-day service, confirmed my research findings regarding fee policies. A breakdown of the collected information revealed the following:

1. At one library the fee is charged only for connect time, and in some instances the searcher lowers the charge because of typographical mistakes or improper search strategy.

2. A second library reported a $15 surcharge added to the actual connect cost incurred (e.g., print charges and communication

charges). The supervisor noted that the surcharge attempts to cover the cost of preparation and follow-up. Normally, if the searcher spends more than one hour this cost is not passed along to the patron. Exceptions to this rule include the many requests to check the Dun and Bradstreet file, for which there is a $5 flat-rate charge, regardless of whether or not it is successful. The supervisor emphasized that these particular searches cost the library more than $5.

3. A third library revealed that its fee was the vendor's charge plus 15 percent. The 15 percent was used for supplies, and the supervisor mentioned that the library neither made nor lost money with this arrangement.

4. A fourth library revealed that the fee policy included the actual cost of the search, a $10 surcharge, plus a $10 rush fee for same-day service.

5. A fifth library stated that a 50 percent discount to college students was part of the publicized charging policy. What was not publicized was the aspect of the policy that granted discounts to struggling businesses–particularly those in the start-up stages. Naturally, this was a difficult area to define and was always left to the online searcher's discretion in conjunction with a predetermined set of library guidelines.

6. The fee policy at a sixth library stressed that, if a search took more than ten minutes and needed interpretation on the part of the online searcher, a fee would be charged.

In discussing the variety of fee structures, it was interesting to find that one supervisor did not foresee problems with fees because the library did not anticipate conducting a heavy volume of searches in the future. It was perceived that the demand just would not exist. In fact, the prevailing viewpoint at this particular library was that, as people become more involved with personal computers, they will probably do their own searching.

The consensus of the twenty-one interviewed supervisors was that public librarianship is facing some very critical years ahead, and that the subject of fees for online searching may be one of the prime factors in deciding its future course.

The findings relating to the second factor showed that, when the same staff member conducted both the presearch interview and the online search, the performance scores tended to be higher. The input associated with the presearch interview aspect was considered by the majority of the interviewed supervisors to be one of the most influential factors affecting the search outcome.

In discussing the priority that was placed on the importance of having the search conducted by the same professional librarian who conducts the presearch interview, the following comments were obtained from three of the interviewed supervisors: (1) a presearch interview is very specialized, since the searcher needs to know exactly what the patron is looking for–even if that means going back and doing a second presearch interview; (2) this format is a key ingredient in successful searching; and (3) there is the possibility that segments might be lost in the communication process when more than two librarians are involved in the different stages of the searching process.

The supervisors who subscribed to the theory that any librarian could conduct the presearch online database interview made these comments: (1) In one instance, online search assignments were rotated daily so that, for example, on Monday one searcher would conduct the presearch interview–which must be set up by an appointment–and on Tuesday another searcher would conduct the actual search. (2) It was not generally feasible for the same person to conduct the search because the scheduling pattern was so irregular. (3) Many times various staff members worked nights and weekends, so the policy was that any staff member at the desk accepted the online database search request. If a problem occurred in relationship to what the patron really expected from the search, a telephone call to the requester was made by the actual online searcher.

The third factor that gave evidence of a slight relationship to the quality of a search performance seemed to suggest that libraries that provided a private area for searching produced better search results. Some supervisors reported that conducting a search within this type of a setting reduces distractions, promotes the searcher's concentration, and might be responsible for more cost-effective searches.

A breakdown of the twenty-one libraries shows that the twelve libraries that provided a separate area for searching were in the top range of the performance scores. One of the supervisors reported that clear windows were installed in the separate computer area so that users would be attracted to the database search service. Several other supervisors set aside a small, private area with sufficient space for the patron, the online searcher, and terminal equipment.

The seven libraries that reported integrating the terminal within the same reference area were among the libraries with the lowest scores. The remaining two libraries that described a different arrangement were in between the top and the low scores. Their arrangement was as follows: one supervisor reported that she had a microcomputer that she carried back and forth between the reference desk and office; the other supervisor stated that the online database searching was conducted in a busy, noisy area that was not open to the patrons but was filled with library personnel engaged in such activities as book repair and cataloging.

Although not statistically significant, the supervisors discussed additional impacts as a direct result of online search service. One of the projected impacts is the strong possibility that it might lead to the cancellation of subscriptions to printed indexes. The high cost of these indexes could justify the library administrator's decision to balance the budget by subscription cancellations. The fact that these indexes could be accessed via the database would be the rationale. Much has been written on this subject. The major concern is that this type of decision-making could result in an information-deprived segment of the population, given fee-based database searching.

In response to my question, "What qualifications are expected of online searchers?" the following information was obtained. The majority of supervisors showed a strong interest in training all reference librarians to conduct online searching. They felt that almost all reference librarians could become excellent online searchers, particularly if they were open-minded about database searching, willing to experiment with something new, and persistent and flexible.

Experience has shown several of the supervisors that many searchers who are technically proficient do not necessarily produce quality results. Knowing all the keys to use and the buttons to push is not the simple answer to the question, "What makes a good searcher?" The ability to prepare a good search strategy, supervisors say, includes imagination in the use of synonyms and skill in the use of a variety of approaches.

Additional comments by the supervisors demonstrated that subject expertise would not be a prerequisite in a library that did not have subject departmentalization. What would be needed is a generalist, the type of person who reads *Time*, *Newsweek*, and whatever magazine, journal, daily newspaper, or other printed format is necessary to stay abreast of current happenings. This is the kind of individual who is at least aware of what is going on and has the ability to place the question in the correct field.

During my follow-up interviews with the online searchers, I learned that their characteristics as measured by education, online training, and previous work experience were all similar in nature. However, it was noted by the online supervisors and the online searchers, and later confirmed by statistical analysis, that the more time the searchers spend per month conducting searches, the higher the number of excellent hits they obtained–giving support to the quantity finding. It seems logical that if a sufficient number of searches are performed monthly, the searcher will be able to maintain a certain level of skill. Three other statistically slight relationships emerged as components in successful searching, namely, (1) recency of degree, (2) currency of backup material, and (3) time spent at the terminal conducting a search. These relationships can be applied only to the twenty-one tested libraries. Aside from these variables, the responses show that online searching is sensitive to many factors. An alteration in one factor may influence the quality of the search outcome.

The factor of the online searcher's impact on search results is receiving a considerable amount of attention in today's library literature. The uppermost question is what traits account for the differences among the searchers' performances. Each searcher's behavior is unique in the performance of a search. It is very difficult to predict whether a given searcher will perform well or will not perform well. The problem is associated with the fact that there are indefinable qualities in a searcher's characteristics. For example, how would a researcher measure a searcher's enthusiasm, or perceptiveness, in conducting an online search?

Additional information contributed by the searchers showed that online searching has increased interlibrary loan requests and collection usage. There is also a concern that database searching will put a strain on the library's budget.

In terms of user evaluation of the online search results, I found that only one of the twenty-one online searchers requested a user evaluation form to be completed to determine satisfaction with the search results. Interestingly, it was the top-scoring searcher who requested this procedure. The merit of investigating the role of this type of evaluation of the quality of the search results is another area of potential research interest. The questions that need answering are: (1) Can user satisfaction measurement provide the necessary feedback to assess performance activities? (2) Will a systematic record of evaluation each time a requester uses the online search services enable management to identify areas of weakness?

The future of online searching in any particular library rests in large part on the attitudes of the people providing the service; that includes the library director, the head reference supervisor, and the online searcher. The major factor that surfaced during my research was the impact of individual personalities upon the success of the online search service.

This era is a fascinating one in which to observe the way information technology interacts with society. Online searching in public libraries is a powerful metaphor of our time. It demonstrates the paradox of modern technology in that it has the tendency to create new problems while solving old ones. The public libraries investigated in my study are playing a major role in the use of online technology. They are not playing a wait-and-see game. And it is precisely this process that sometimes results in actually creating the outcome.

Note

For more complete information on this topic, see Janice Helen McCue, *Online Searching in Public Libraries* (Metuchen, N.J.: Scarecrow Press, 1988).

School Library Media Center
Networking for the Year 2000

JULIE TALLMAN

The word *networking* has been given many definitions, one of the best coming from the National Commission on Libraries and Information Science (NCLIS) 1978 Task Force on the Role of the School Library Media Program in the National Program. Networking is the "formal arrangement whereby materials, information and services provided by a variety of types of libraries and/or other organizations are made available to all potential users" (National Commission on Libraries and Science 1978, 6). NCLIS had the idea that each student would have equal opportunity to the part of the total information resource that would satisfy that student's needs for educational, working, and recreational information.

Most of the literature on networking, unless specifically related to schools, tends to forget the contributions school media centers can make to networks. However, many multitype networks being established today do include schools, which indicates an increase in the realization that school library media centers have resources that infrequently overlap with other library resources. Schools, after all, are the "unseen majority" of libraries; approximately two-thirds of the over 100,000 libraries in this country are in the schools.

Certain concepts about networks are applicable for any type of library. Big regional networks have problems overcoming the long arm of OCLC. Consequently, vendors of small systems that can be connected through telecommunications have an increasingly bright future. State agencies sponsoring systems, such as Access Pennsylvania, lend themselves to more natural and feasible networking, even for the smallest school. Contracts and copyrights are proving to be problems with OCLC, a costly and difficult agency when there is a question about who owns what records. Some libraries choose not to join OCLC, or a regional representative, because of costs and rights to materials. Alternatives are there for the large libraries, but the little outfit still is struggling alone.

According to Barbara Evans Markuson (1980, 6), "We need ... to identify conditions that would make networks irrelevant or unfeasible and thus reversible." She identifies five scenarios that would cause network problems: catastrophes, economic crises, energy crises, new technology, and major changes in libraries themselves (Markuson 1980, 14). All of these would affect the networks in various ways. Catastrophes speak for themselves. Economic crises have the wherewithal to so severely curtail library funding that funding for networking would surely be cut. An energy crisis like the crisis in the 1970s could cause a repeat of networks such as OCLC having to install diesel-powered generators as backups. The fourth crisis would be a technological change that would make our present networking technologies nonfunctioning. We need to plan for technology's smooth integration. Lastly, we need to think futuristically about what libraries will be like in twenty years. Will we have libraries as we know them, or will user patterns and access change so dramatically that our institutions will be superfluous to the information chain? Whatever the probabilities of any of the above occurring, we must do some planning.

The United States has a decentralized and locally controlled library system that lends itself to independence and diversity. The hierarchy involved is by type of library, that is, academic, public, special, and school. Traditionally, networking for U.S. libraries has meant a jointly developed system among one or several types of libraries–but not all–for faster and more complete information access. Such networks have developed from local initiatives in a cooperative effort (Markuson 1980, 14). The danger in such local efforts exists when the most affluent libraries band together but the have-nots stay have-nots, increasingly isolated. The already noticeable inequities of access are accentuated.

Building on that problem is the problem of school library media centers and networks. Depending on the definition, networks are a relatively recent phenomenon. The large networks have not been designed for the small library and the average user (Stevens, 40). When Norman Meise first conceptualized networking in 1966 (Stevens, 45), he probably was not thinking about the tens of thousands of school libraries, but more about the largest academic libraries, and possibly, the largest public libraries. Actually, in a sense, networking has been happening since the American Library Association was first established in 1876, with all the cooperative schemes that it developed. Because librarians operate on the premise that programs must fill immediate needs, they have always been searching for cooperation. But it was not until OCLC that American libraries realized that formal "networks were a practical way of offering library services on a cooperative basis" (Stevens, 34).

School library media centers have been trying to establish cooperative efforts for a long time. Many school library media specialists are isolated and unaware of resources outside of what can be offered from their own collections. The critical issues become what kind of networking services and access are wanted. Many specialists are still unaware of networking benefits. Perhaps what has been offered on national and regional scales has not been useful, or, just as important, perhaps the participation of school libraries has not been welcomed.

Richard Sorensen takes an aggressive stance on the role of school library media centers in networking. He states that school media programs must actively participate in all stages of development, operation, and governance. School programs need to meet the direct information needs of their clientele, which can be quite different from the needs of other libraries' clients. Networking is vital to meeting those needs, and school library media programs have much to offer other libraries (Sorensen 1980, 309). In some situations, the only libraries available are those in the local schools, which need to serve the general public as well as students. Most people worry about the overlap between schools and other libraries. But schools have many unique resources that the rest of the library population could find useful, such as specialized materials and equipment. Schools deserve our attention as the training ground for tomorrow's efficient and productive users of information.

What is preventing the more active participation of schools in networking? Sorensen talks about five factors. The first is the psychological fear of public, academic, and special librarians that schools will drain their resources and not give anything back. School library media specialists also fear loss of autonomy, time factors, cost factors, and change itself (Sorensen 1980, 314) – nothing very different from other libraries, except that school budgets can be smaller.

School library media specialists have political and legal factors to overcome, such as boundaries, territories, and other people's jurisdictions. Sometimes city councils do not get along with school boards, or with other school districts and their city councils; sometimes the school district covers several boundaries between squabbling cities. Traditionally, school budgets have not allowed for interlibrary loan expenditures or other related transactions. Some school libraries still do not have the most basic of all communications hardware: the telephone. Finally, planning, which is so important in networking, is inhibited by geographical barriers such as boundaries and distance, by great differences in collections, by the authority of the individuals involved, or by the exclusion of the libraries the network should be serving.

According to Carol Doll (1983), networking has not been a priority for schools. School media specialists have been concentrating on building collections which Doll says is important because every school should have a good basic collection (1983, 196-97). On the other hand, her study indicates that school specialists are not opposed to networking (194). She found that school media collections do not overwhelmingly overlap (195); the average overlap is approximately 30 percent, and the school-public overlap approximately 50 percent (196). Reversing the examination reveals that about 30 percent of the titles found in the public library are found in the school collection, a difference due to the larger size of the public library (197).

Since students show a strong inclination to extend their independent research for term papers beyond the school resources (Mancall and Drott 1980, 99, 103), the 70 percent more titles in the public library can make a significant difference to them. The equipment and audiovisual resources from the school can also make a significant difference to the public library patrons. Perceived and actual access to resources is the most important factor associated with the use of libraries (Mancoll and Drott 1980, 102). If networking brings the resources to the students, in a form perceived to be accessible, information use will increase. Some use depends on the specificity of teacher assignments and the accessibility of media center staff.

How can the school library media center afford to collect or have the space to store all the materials that schools need to support the curriculum and reading needs of the students? Many schools have space problems and have to choose which resources they can retain and which they have to discard, particularly periodicals and periodical indexes. Curriculum changes are frequent occurrences in schools: new programs are instituted, old ones are changed or dropped, new teaching staff who approach the subject matter differently are added, and new administrative directives on the goals of the school are written. Some states have been using cooperative agreements to solve these problems, particularly New York State.

New York State established school participation in multitype networking with pilot projects funded by the *Laws of 1978*. From 1979 to 1984 the state funded twelve pilot school library systems to demonstrate the feasibility of resource sharing and connections between school library media centers. Now the entire state has the systems installed, and forty-eight school library systems operate within BOCES (Bureau of Cooperative Educational Services) or big city school district boundaries. The charges given to the School Library System mandate development of computerized union catalogs, interlibrary loan and delivery systems, and sharing the services of a professional and clerk who would support colleagues in the field with service, communication, and problem solving. Each system also has to belong to a liaison group representing public library systems and reference and research library resources systems for its area. Each system develops and updates a "member plan of service," which holds them to certain responsibilities toward the system and serves as an evaluation tool for determining how well the system and its members are working together successfully.

In her dissertation work, Barbara Immroth (1980, 148) found that effective leadership is vital to making the network successful. The School Library System is trying to provide the leadership through the personnel funded in each system office. The implications for successful multitype networking for New York State school libraries are threefold. First, collection management is improved. Second, students have fuller access to resources in the area. Third, the network provides hitherto unavailable opportunities for decision-making interaction with peers in other school districts or buildings (Fisher 1986, 148). Information is exploding at librarians more and more each day. To manage such an explosion, media specialists must develop strategies for sharing with each other their current awareness of information and how it is being disseminated. Otherwise, media specialists rob their clients of true access.

Participating libraries also share in cooperative collection development, which means splitting up specialties among the system partners so that each library has its separate responsibilities and all libraries know where materials can be located. This allows concentration on important curriculum areas, as well as a stronger core collection, without draining the budget through scatter-buying. Very few libraries have sufficient budget to purchase all the needs for the curriculum, even for some of the assignments. Help from system colleagues for the duration of the assignment is a welcome relief. Nothing is more frustrating than telling a youngster that the librarian cannot help in time to get the assignment finished.

Where then is this type of networking headed for the 1990s and the year 2000? Will it still be viable? Right now, the systems are providing union catalogs, interlibrary loan and delivery coordination, support in problem solving, cooperative collection development leadership, telephones and modems for each library, CD ROM technology, databases, and access to virtually any library in the country. The future is limited only by the available funding, which is very tight. Ten years from now, school library systems might evolve into LANs or extended LANs (local area networks).

LANs are one of the important concepts from the 1980s. They are providing the answer, both technologically and philosophically, to the networking of the future. No longer will we be so concerned about the unmatchability of all the various technologies we are using, such as IBM PCs or MacIntoshes. We will also have fast and reliable networking capabilities with multiple remote locations.

Libraries cannot be as self-sufficient as in the past. It is not fair to our clients or to ourselves to maintain that posture. If we try, we cheat the client of a multitude of information sources, and we cheat the client of an awareness of information use in the twenty-first century, where they will be spending the majority of their working lives. We also cheat ourselves out of the effectiveness, efficiency, and creativity produced through access to information when the need demands it. Marlyn Kemper (1987, xvi) says the "creative use of such computer networks as LANs makes the volume of knowledge growing exponentially manageable." Kemper provides a succinct description of its benefits:

> The LAN has emerged as a viable tool for coping with the mix of requirements for sharing equipment, providing access to common databases, and improving electronic communications. Within the library environment, the LAN can be utilized to support a variety of applications, including circulation control, word processing, cataloging OPAC display, acquisitions, electronic mail, and file transfer. (1987, xvii)

The LAN is a viable alternative to present methods for communicating between workstations, distributing data, and distributing mail. LANs can be set up within libraries, within school buildings, and within regions. Basically, there are three configurations available for LANs. One is the tree, which is a straight line cable with attached branches for each workstation. Another configuration is in a star shape, with all the workstations interconnected on the points of a star, and the third is in the form of a circle, with each workstation at a place on the circle. Each has its own advantage. Other advantages of LANs are better support, reliability, faster response time, and internetworking capabilities (Kemper 1987, 4). Workstations, mainframes, minicomputers, microcomputers, terminals, CAD/CAM equipment, and other systems can all be connected to LANs. Picture a school building with a microcomputer in each classroom connected directly to all the other microcomputers in the building, including the library. The students can call up the library to access databases and other information resources immediately, when it is most valuable for them – when learning actually takes place. Meanwhile, the library media center is connected on an extended LAN to other schools and libraries in the region so that databases are shared, resources are tapped, and information is accessible back in the classroom for the students. It is all accomplished through reliable, dedicated technology. Basically, the LANs are making available at each locale service performed at another locale. Through the use of LANs, librarians are responding to the increasing trend to produce and disseminate information electronically.

LANs are sophisticated telecommunications devices, capable of electronic transmission of data, voice, and video information from site to site. The devices include all software, procedures, and hardware involved in the transmission. They are the futuristic and present mergers of computers and communications. They have already been implemented in hospitals, libraries and information centers, homes, businesses, and universities. As Kemper states: "Within the library setting, computer networks such as LANs are created to reduce the costs of labor intensive operations, streamline support services, and maximize performance thereby allowing users to exchange information in a heterogeneous environment without concern for the vendor equipment or technologies involved" (1987, 28). LANs are part of the second phase of the computer revolution: the linking together of the micros we already have, thereby giving us team computing.

Key networking issues are library cooperation, linking local systems to databases, and network behavior and governance. The School Library System in New York State has a tremendous headstart on making a firm foundation for viable LANs in each region. The future might hold such an extended LAN, especially since some resources in the state are already involved in developing LANs. Schools have to think about their library media centers as evolving into environments with the objects of rapid information transfer to students and clients, storage and retrieval of data, and shared technical service operations that support the existence of the media center. A LAN type of network will encourage and allow the media center to offer itself as a total information resource.

Bibliography

Articles

Angier, Jennifer J. "Local Area Networks (LAN) in the Special Library: Part 1—A Planning Model." *Online* 10 (November 1986): 19-28.

Angus, Beatrice E. "Why a School Library System? The Perspective of a New Coordinator." *Bookmark* (Spring 1986): 139-42.

Ballard, Tom. "Public Library Networking: Neat, Plausible, Wrong." *Library Journal* 107 (April 1, 1982): 679-83.

Berglund, Patricia. "School Library Technology." *Wilson Library Bulletin* (June 1986): 56-57.

Bohl, Janet. "'We Thought We Could . . .': A Comparison of Pilot and Permanent School Library Systems." *Bookmark* (Spring 1986): 152-58.

Brown, Dale W., and Nancy A. Newman. "Regional Networking and Collection Management in School Library Media Centers." In *Collection Management for School Library Media Centers*, ed. Brenda H. White, 147-53. New York: Haworth Press, 1986.

Doll, Carol A. "School and Public Library Collection Overlap and the Implications for Networking." *School Library Media Quarterly* 11 (Spring 1983): 196-97.

Fisher, Phyllis. "Extending the Carpet: School Libraries, Access, and the Information Implosion." *Bookmark* (Spring 1986): 148-51.

Hicks, Doris A., and John Shaloiko. "Rochester (NY) Area Resources Exchange: An Intersystem Pilot Project." *Catholic Library World* (February 1981): 291-96.

Hoehl, Susan B., and Jennifer J. Angier. "Local Area Networks (LAN) in the Special Library: Part 2–Implementation." *Online* 10 (November 1986): 29-36.

LaPier, Cynthia B., and Christopher L. Spezialetti. "The School Librarian: A New Image." *Saanys Journal* (Summer 1987): 15-17.

Mancall Jacqueline C., and M. Carl Drott. "Tomorrow's Scholars: Patterns of Facilities Use." *School Library Journal* 26 (March 1980): 99-103.

Markuson, Barbara Evans. "Revolution and Evolution: Critical Issues in Library Network Development." In *Networks for Networkers*, eds. Barbara Evans Markuson and Blanche Woolls, 3-28. New York: Neal-Schuman, 1980.

Meise, Norman R. *Conceptual Design of an Automated National Library System*. Metuchen, N.J.: Scarecrow Press, 1969.

"Network Advisory Committee Meets to Identify Key Issues in Networking." *Library of Congress Information Bulletin* 44 (August 5, 1985): 214-15.

"Network Advisory Committee Meets: Networking–A Changing Concept." *Library of Congress Information Bulletin* 45 (October 13, 1986): 345-47.

Palmer, Judith B., Jeanne Domville, and Laura Shelly. "Northern Area Network: School and Public Library Cooperative Collection Management." In *Collection Management for School Library Media Centers*, ed. Brenda H. White, 155-70. New York: Haworth Press, 1986.

Saley, Al. "The Effects of Small Budgets on the Principles of Development of Collections for Small School Library Media Centers." In *Collection Management for School Library Media Centers*, ed. Brenda H. White, 79-82. New York: Haworth Press, 1986.

Sorensen, Richard. "The Role of School Media Programs in Library Networks." In *Networks for Networkers*, eds. Barbara Evans Markuson and Blanche Woolls, 309-19. New York: Neal-Schuman, 1980.

Stevens, Norman D. "An Historical Perspective on the Concept of Networks: Some Preliminary Considerations." In *Networks for Networkers*, eds. Barbara Evans Markuson and Blanche Woolls. New York: Neal-Schuman, 1980.

University of the State of New York, State Education Department, and New York State Library. "New York State's School Library Systems." (1987).

Woolls, Blanche. "SLJ/Make Your Point." *School Library Journal* (April 1986): 44.

_____. "Warp, Woof, and Loom: Networks, Users, and Information Systems." In *Networks for Networkers*, eds. Barbara Evans Markuson and Blanche Woolls, 267-90. New York: Neal-Schuman, 1980.

Books

Bridges, Stephen P. M. *Low-Cost Local Area Networks*. New York: Sigma Press, 1986.

Kemper, Marlyn. *Networking: Choosing a LAN Path to Interconnection*. Metuchen, N.J.: Scarecrow Press, 1987.

Markuson, Barbara Evans, and Blanche Woolls, eds. *Networks for Networkers: Critical Issues in Cooperative Library Development*. New York: Neal-Schuman, 1980.

Martin, S. K. *Library Networks, 1986-87: Libraries in Partnership*. White Plains, N.Y.: Knowledge Industry Publications, 1986.

National Commission on Libraries and Science, Task Force on the Role of the School Library Media Program in the National Program. *The Role of the School Library Media Program in Networking*. Washington, D.C.: Government Printing Office, 1978.

White, Brenda H., ed. *Collection Management for School Library Media Centers*. New York: Haworth Press, 1986.

Dissertations

Immroth, Barbara Froling. "The Role of the School Library Media Program in a Multitype Library Network." Unpublished Ph.D. diss., University of Pittsburgh, 1980.

Weeks, Ann Carlson. "A Study of the Attitudes of New York State School Library Media Specialists Concerning Library Networking and Technology." Unpublished Ph.D. diss., University of Pittsburgh, 1982.

OPACs: Context for the Development of Cataloging and Classification Theory

FLORENCE E. DEHART AND KAREN MATTHEWS

Robin, a machine-stored memory of a human being in Pohl's *The Annals of the Heechee*, considers himself more kingly than any king where information is concerned. Although Frederick the Great, for example, had a faculty of all the experts he could afford to feed, Robin has every authority on every subject at his fingertips without having to feed them. They are all subsumed into his one all-purpose data-retrieval program, "Albert Einstein," programmed by his wife Essie, a programming specialist, who provides Robin with information about a group Robin regards as "the Foe."[1] Catalogers now find themselves faced with groups of reference librarians, bibliographic database specialists, and computer experts who may at times seem like Robin's "Foe."

The reason is that catalogers' principal role in managing library catalogs could be on the verge of replacement by shared arrangements. Rowland Brown, currently president of OCLC, explains, for example, that "reference librarians will become increasingly active participants in the OCLC membership in ways as diverse as those librarians involved in cataloging, interlibrary loan, acquisitions and serials."[2] Reference librarians and others, along with catalogers, will contribute, then, in a major way to OPAC (online public access catalog) functioning. This paper examines how the dynamics of OPAC environments, in which the contributions of cataloging will interact with other components in providing user service, could enhance development of the theoretical base of cataloging and classification.

THE NEED FOR THEORY DEVELOPMENT IN CATALOGING

Recent calls in the cataloging literature for research have implications for theory development. First, several definitions are necessary, as well as a brief establishment of the relation of research to theory development. "Cataloging," according to Wynar's definition, is "the process of describing an item in the collection, conducting subject analysis, and assigning a classification number." "Descriptive cataloging" is "the phase of the cataloging process concerned with the identification and description of library material, the recording of this information in the form of a catalog entry, and the choice of name and title access points for the resultant bibliographic record." "Subject cataloging" is "the assignment of classification numbers and subject headings to the items of a library collection."[3] "Cataloging" is used from this point on to mean both cataloging and classification.

The relationship between research and theory is explained by Grover and Glazier: "The purpose of research is to test and to generate theory. Research must first describe relationships among phenomena; it must in turn explain those relationships. This explanation of relationships constitutes a theory."[4] Theoretical development in descriptive cataloging could benefit from further research. According to Fidel and Crandall, the experience of the cataloging community in code design should be employed to create a theoretical framework of rules for database design.[5]

Theoretical development relative to Library of Congress (LC) subject headings could benefit from further research on the problem of adopting thesaural codes, according to Dykstra. Her proposals, and a possibly ensuing debate over the appropriateness of applying standards for thesaurus construction to the Library of Congress subject headings list, could stimulate development of a theoretical framework that would not only, in her words, "ensure a shift in LCSH from an unruly to a rule-based system [but also] put librarians concerned with subject access in an excellent position to contribute to the design of fully automated retrieval systems and thus carry us over into the next century as important players in this field."[6]

Research on the application of the Dewey decimal classification (DDC) to online catalogs also has potential for theory development. According to Cochrane and Markey, the results of the DDC Online Project have "the potential to impact on the design philosophy of library classification schedule- and index-making, the future of patron use of library classification, and the design of online catalogs' subject searching capabilities."[7] Chan's identification of the need to study how the DDC, the LC classification, and LC subject headings might "act as complements, each filling lacunae in the other" within an OPAC, has implications for theoretical development concerning forms of subject analysis.[8]

COMPUTERIZED RETRIEVAL POTENTIALS AND CATALOGING

Cataloging will now be examined in relation to the computerized retrieval potentials afforded by automation. "In recent years," according to Sellberg, "the central importance of the cataloger's art was reaffirmed with the development of online catalogs."[9] This is because traditional cataloging records can be accessed in OPACs through the retrieval mechanisms associated with reference bibliographic databases such as ERIC (Educational Resources Information Center).

Cataloging records can be coded for automated manipulation using Boolean operators for searching on controlled and uncontrolled terms, or parts of terms, in all indexed fields in various combinations. For example, a search strategy recommended by Holley is to "to combine the two subject based parts of the record, the subject headings and the classification number."[10] Results could be printed out according to a format of the user's choice, ranging from a brief citation to a full MARC (machine-readable cataloging) record.

Searches could also take place on parts, or facets, of classification numbers. Wajenberg supplies an example based on the DDC: "If a student of comparative literature wished a comprehensive listing of works about symbolism in poetry, the system could search not only the class number 809.1915 (the number for general and comparative studies of symbolism in poetry), but also every occurrence of 1009 from Table 3, followed by 15 from DDC Table 3-A. That would retrieve works on symbolism in French poetry, American poetry, etc., wherever those tables had been applied."[11] Items could be accessed under more than one classification number and classification scheme, as in the Carnegie-Mellon BROWSE System, designed almost a decade ago.[12]

OPACS: DEFINITIONS, OBJECTIVES, ENVIRONMENTS

OPAC Definitions

The potential contributions of cataloging will now be placed within the interactive framework of OPAC environments. There is no such thing as a generic, or standard, OPAC. Further, as Hildreth points out, the open-ended nature of OPAC interactive information retrieval systems with regard to access points, functions, files, and links to other catalogs and information resources makes precise definition impossible.[13] However, we take Hildreth's conception of the online catalog as an online library as our definition of an OPAC as we look toward the twenty-first century. From this point of view, an OPAC might be defined as "an intelligent gateway to diverse, integrated information resources for both the information specialist and the library patron or end user; a gateway accessible not only in libraries, but at places of work, study, leisure, and the home."[14] OPACs may vary widely in philosophies, capabilities, and characteristics, depending on user service objectives.

OPAC Objectives

According to Braddock, the future belongs to the sharp-eyed realists who determine where the technology *should* go to meet users' unmet demands, rather than to the wide-eyed visionaries who speculate on where the technology can go.[15] Or, as Adams points out, we can allow technology "to shape the future role of libraries or we can pattern it to serve the chosen values of the profession."[16] Formulation of general OPAC objectives must be patterned on the goals and objectives of the parent institution, where applicable, and of the library or information center that the OPAC serves. Social roles of the agency, including archival, cultural, educational, recreational, informational, and research, determine the library's goals and objectives, and consequently, an OPAC's environment.

OPAC objectives must accommodate two overlapping paradigms: the bibliographic control paradigm and the information transfer paradigm. According to the bibliographic control paradigm, the world's knowledge is recorded, stored, and organized so that it may be passed from one generation to the next. Although some may find the word *control* objectionable, as used here the word is intended to mean the fostering of the usage of materials through management of information leading to access. According to the information transfer paradigm, on the other hand, librarians create and tailor services to fulfill identified user needs that they have assessed and attempt to determine reasons for nonuse so that appropriate services might be rendered. It should be emphasized that libraries do not face an "either-or" choice between the bibliographic control and information transfer paradigms, but rather, must encompass both.

OPACs could inspire librarians and information specialists to rethink institutional and information agency objectives. We can appreciate Robin's feelings, who, although he had all the world's data available to him, wonders how much more he can learn without being wise.[17] According to Kochen, wisdom, "in one sense the ultimate purpose of our intellect and the scientific enterprise, and therefore of central concern to information disciplines, means bringing knowledge and understanding to bear on shaping our world for human ends by human means."[18]

Does a particular library aim to help users acquire knowledge and wisdom? Or simply information? Should those who design OPACs attempt to motivate people to unearth hidden biases or act on the greenhouse effect, ocean pollution, the homeless population, or nuclear crisis in a world that resembles at times the gigantic enterprise of destruction painted by Bernanos in his novel, *Monsieur Ouine*?[19] Does a particular information agency subscribe to Yovit's definition of the value of information being how much it changes the *effectiveness* of a decision-maker?[20] Or to Rosenberg's criteria, according to which "the quantity and quality of knowledge possessed by an individual or a computer can be judged by the variety of situations in which the individual or program obtains successful results?"[21] Perhaps subject analysis would be viewed in a different light under these objectives.

Is a library's objective to fulfill educational goals, including that of OPAC literacy, perhaps defined as the ability to access OPACs in pursuit of information, knowledge, and wisdom? Before people can attain OPAC literacy to any appreciable degree, they must have attained literacy. Although worthwhile, an objective of full OPAC literacy for all persons may be difficult to achieve, for Work reminds us that "the goal of conquering illiteracy–even in America's privileged society–has only been partially met."[22]

Is equal access to information an objective? Borgman hopes that we will not build "systems for which access is inequitable." Her comments were prompted by the results of her study involving students who had taken an equal number of math, science, and computing courses. Engineering and science majors outperformed the social science and humanities majors."[23] Another aspect of access, according to Dykstra, is that "intellectual freedom and the right to know, increasingly illusive, are directly affected by the sophistication of our capability to make the contents of our library collections accessible."[24]

Those information agencies frequented by researchers could have as an objective to build into an OPAC's organization opportunities for browsing and serendipitous experiences. Databases themselves might serve as research tools to build knowledge in subject fields. For example, Salvaggio comments on the research potential of the online *MLA Bibliography*: "By the way it relates and narrows terms and classifies 'approaches,' the new subject guide to the *MLA Bibliography* tells what literary critics have been writing about–and a good deal about their profession itself."[25] Perhaps traditional cataloging tools and subject representation policies could be designed in a way to reflect and provide information on the structure of an area of study, record its historical trends and developments, and discover relationships between works never dreamed of by their authors.

A library's objectives might include fulfillment of the recreational function. Paulson warns that "literature differs radically from the sort of communicative act likely to predominate in an information society, for what we regard as most significant in the experience of literary reading cannot be translated into machine language."[26] Nonetheless, fiction readers might benefit, for example, from catalogers' adoption and use of the categories established by Pejtersen for analyzing fiction.[27]

The library or information center goals and objectives that have been established for fulfilling determined social roles must be translated into specific OPAC objectives for user service. The totality of components of an OPAC's design for serving users constitutes that OPAC's environment.

OPAC Environments

It is an understatement that the OPAC environment of the twenty-first century will be complex. The OPAC coordinator's major task will be to heed Waters's warning about reference expert systems, which may also apply to OPAC development: "My concern is that this process may produce thousands of building blocks of different sizes and shapes–but never a cathedral of learning."[28] A more accurate, if less poetic, term for "cathedral" might be "web of learning."

According to Rice, "the online environment is just beginning to realize the concept of global bibliographic access via the local terminal."[29] Microcomputer database management systems could enable an individual to interface with online catalogs and to exchange messages with library staff and other patrons. Telefacsimile copies of desired material could be obtained. In turn, online catalogs could be linked to other files of material in electronic form, including other libraries' catalogs and files created by publishers and booksellers.

Various types of systems could be incorporated into a single OPAC, such as bibliographic information retrieval systems, knowledge-based expert or question-answering systems, and database management systems. A variety of databases serving different purposes could be mounted as well. For example, the structure of the new OCLC system, according to Brown, will permit the mounting of databases such as the eighteenth-century short-title catalog for reference services, but, it could also be used for copy cataloging.[30] Some databases may be difficult to organize because they will be subject to ongoing evolution. Searches that have been saved for subsequent recall by other interested patrons constitute still another component of OPAC environments.

"Pseudobibliographic" online records that serve purposes other than bibliographic cataloging, such as those including pathfinders, could be accommodated by the MARC format, as suggested by Jarvis and Dow.[31] Location information, including maps of the library and circulation, processing, and binding information, could be provided. A corollary function could be served by computerized retrieval from shelves of physical items not available in machine form.

Figure 1: Walkthroughs

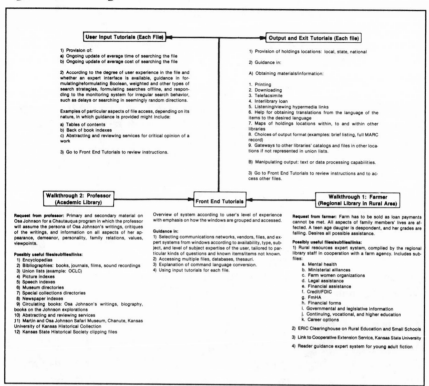

Included among the capabilities and gateway features for searching an OPAC might be guides to the user for specifying search parameters; Boolean operations, including nesting, set building, and automatic reformulation of queries; proximity operations; field specification; front-end index term searching, without field specification but with an output report of field locations; number of titles associated with each match; truncation; automatic word stemming; spelling correction; fuzzy matching; displays of co-indexed terms for browsing; and document ranking. In full-text searching, Tenopir notes, the capability of searching for words in the same sentence and of weighting by number of times search words occur in a document are desirable features.[32]

The connecting element of OPAC environmental components could be provided by hypertext and hypermedia formats. A hypertext system, as Smith explains, allows users "to *link* information together, thereby creating trails through associated materials."[33] In this manner, other files, such as reviewing services, could serve as reference or supplementary files to the initial file, such as a full-text monograph accessed by a user. Our catalogs will then be, in the words of DeBuse, "an integral part of civilization's store of knowledge, not something standing outside of it and pointing from a distance."[34]

Hypermedia, defined as follows by Smith, could turn the OPAC into a megamedia unit: "*Hypermedia* is similar to hypertext, but instead of linking just text, users can link to other media, such as graphics, video, spreadsheets, animations and voice."[35] The application of hypertext and hypermedia to OPACs must be tempered by Fox's concern that the implementation philosophy be based on human factors. Otherwise, users may feel lost in a system that may be overly rich in capability to the detriment of being able to trace steps back through a procedure as desired.[36]

Walkthroughs

Although it is not surprising that reference questions and procedures for culling answers from multiple sources can involve complexity, OPAC environments will become even more complex as OPACs succeed in translating user thought processes into action. The "walkthroughs" below (see also Figure 1) allow two queries to be traced through a hypothesized OPAC environment to provide a visual dimension of the complexity inherent in OPAC searching.

Walkthrough 1: Farmer

"Walkthrough 1: Farmer" is hypothesized to include provision of full-text material compiled by a library staff of a regional library. It was inspired by the *Rural Resource Manual* of the Central Kansas Library System and reflects input from Michael Haddock, formerly a farmer and now a reference librarian at the Sterling Evans Library, Texas A&M University. The phenomenon of library-prepared additions to OPACs will likely appear with increasing frequency, according to Dowlin.[37] In this walkthrough, a user approach may include accessing cataloged fiction to select desired young adult novels.

Walkthrough 2: Professor

"Walkthrough 2: Professor," designed with the assistance of Barbara Robins, a reference librarian at the William Allen White Library, Emporia State University, pictures a hypothesized interactive, multilinear procedure for providing a professor with the information needed to prepare her part in a Chautauqua (popular adult education) program. The professor can access cataloged reference and circulating books, as well as subject headings from other thesauri, not necessarily assigned according to uniform indexing policies. These include thesauri used in three off-campus agencies.

Unique Contributions of Cataloging to the OPCA Environment

Although no typical or standardized OPAC environment may be projected, possibly unique contributions of cataloging in the context of other OPAC components may evolve from the various settings. For example, three studies in which we have been engaged[38] suggest that coextensive LC headings could assume the function of supplying the necessary context for searching in conjunction with indexed terminology from tables of contents, abstracts, and reviews that may be meaningless or ambiguous without that context.[39] Simply adding greater quantities of LC headings on a haphazard basis may not be cost-effective in user service. Type of material, including subject and publication date, must be considered.

Bishop's admonition that librarians should understand the issues of bibliographic control and be able "to relate a library's catalog to regional, national and international bibliographic databases"[40] may be central to the primary role of cataloging in OPAC functioning. Increasingly sophisticated demands will be made on the bibliographic function in support of the information transfer function in OPAC settings.

Possible emphasis on subject areas could evolve to help counteract a circumstance surrounding general-purpose systems, as described by Wormell: looking at the environment of current IR (information retrieval) systems, the indexer "knows very little about the heterogeneous group of potential users and their various information needs."[41] LC subject headings could eventually merge with specialized thesauri such as those for medicine, art, and architecture, and those under consideration in the fields of history, music, astronomy, and religion.[42]

The physics section of the DDC scheme might be redesigned to resemble more closely the Physics and Astronomy Classification Scheme, under which various journals classify their papers. Readers are aided, according to the publishers of the scheme, "by the common hierarchy present in all of them."[43] The necessity to create, implement, and evaluate devices for managing and accessing multiple databases and thesauri,[44] as well as to switch between macro- and microlevel databases, will arise. The contributions of cataloging, unique or shared, to OPAC search functions could be redefined in evolutionary fashion. Whether Charles Cutter would recognize the outcome is an interesting speculation.

Nonetheless, present contributions of library cataloging must not be overlooked in the newer environments. For example, cataloging must still contribute to bibliographic control by identifying, describing, and locating holdings from local to universal levels, and by enabling users to access this information through authority control of author, title, and subject listings. According to Dwyer, these control aspects could even unleash serendipity: "It may seem ironic, but the rigidity of authority control enhances serendipity and, in an age when our limited, hierarchical models of organization are becoming anachronisms, serendipity and intuition provide new avenues to knowledge."[45]

Another major goal must continue to be striving to make bibliographic control as free as possible from inadequacies, inaccuracies, and misleading entries. As Sellberg comments, "The need to follow form and content standards in nationally shared databases makes it imperative that even part-time or occasional catalogers know a great deal. Incompetent and nonstandard cataloging by improperly trained catalogers diminishes the cost-effectiveness of shared bibliographic utilities."[46]

METHODOLOGICAL DIRECTIONS FOR THEORY BUILDING IN CATALOGING

Research on the effectiveness of cataloging for user service in OPACs would necessarily be performed in the context of other OPAC functions and operations. A paraphrase of a statement by Miksa confirms that view: The direction that offers the most hope for the future relative to cataloging is no less than a thorough reexamination of the fundamental role of the OPAC in how knowledge is best organized and made available.[47]

The data to be analyzed in research studies on OPAC user services will obviously be complex in nature. The analysis of complex data lends itself especially well to qualitative methodology under what Lincoln and Guba refer to as the naturalistic paradigm.[48] This is not to rule out quantitative methodology under the traditional positivistic paradigm when appropriate to the nature of the data. Following is a discussion of the relation of research on OPAC effectiveness to five aspects of research as viewed under the naturalistic paradigm.[49]

The first aspect pertains to the difficulty of constructing and controlling variables according to the positivistic mode in research on complex systems, such as OPACs. Soergel's identification of variables that could affect information transfer, and thus OPAC transactions, is illustrative. Those variables are source, receiver, source-receiver relationship, substance of the transaction, medium used, quality of results, and cost-benefit aspects.[50]

The second aspect involves researcher and participant interaction, including feed-forward provided through computer-monitored data. The systemic epistemology introduced by Bateson calls for "an assessment of theorizing and researching of communication processes by recognizing that research, itself, is an interactive process subject to the same assumptions applied to other interactive systems."[51] This recognition is less likely to be addressed under the positivistic paradigm.

The third relates to generalization. Cronbach's statement that, "when we give proper weight to local conditions, any generalization is a working hypothesis, not a conclusion," might characterize research on OPACs, considering the likely variety in individual OPAC "personalities."[52] Current interest in tailoring responses to the same request according to individual user profiles is also a factor that may lessen emphasis on generalization.[53] One wonders whether Kehoe's confidence in information retrieval theory being able to help assure generalization, associated with the positivistic paradigm, will be upheld: "Lacking enough in-depth information about how experts search, basing a system on information retrieval theory may be the only means to avoid an *ad hoc* system, one which is not generalizable to a broad range of searching situations or for a variety of users."[54]

The fourth aspect pertains to cause and effect. Bates uses terms such as "uncertainty," "variety," "complexity," and "indeterminacy" to describe recommended design principles for subject access in OPACs.[55] These characteristics are hardly conducive to the establishment of cause and effect, a goal under the positivistic paradigm. The difficulty of controlling a large number of variables, as mentioned above, also figures in the problem, as pointed out by Radecki.[56] These variables may interact simultaneously to produce the observed results.

The fifth aspect relates to values. Recognition of the values held by users and those assisting them is necessary when conducting research on OPAC effectiveness. Measurement of socio-emotional content needs to be addressed. Defined by Rice and Love as "interactions that show solidarity, tension relief, agreement, antagonism, tension, and disagreement," this content might well be part of OPAC interactions involving human viewpoints expressed in language.[57] Research under the positivistic paradigm, however, aims to be free from the influence of values.

This section on research might aptly be concluded by a paraphrase of Ford's statement that traditionally central areas of library education curricula–cataloging, classifying, indexing, techniques, and the like–must decrease in *relative* importance vis-à-vis the need to develop analytical, critical, and evaluative skills to be used in understanding, applying, and carrying out research.[58] We suggest instead that these traditionally central areas of library education, central to effective user service, emphasize the development of analytical, critical, and evaluative skills to be used in understanding, applying, and carrying out cooperative research projects that cross traditional library departmental boundaries.

CONCLUSION

The development of cataloging theory under the naturalistic paradigm to support unique but compatible roles for cataloging in fulfilling OPAC objectives of the twenty-first century is essential. This development stands an almost certain chance of materializing within the context of dynamic, interactive OPAC environments in which searchers must depend on the symphonic interplay of component contributions to user access.

Catalogers may well share an experience similar to one that befalls Robin. As it turns out, other forces gain access to the OPACs, and at one point, a voice, which seems old and familiar, makes clear that those who may be regarded as "the Foe" do not wish to make OPACs go back to traditional card catalogs. Rather, they want to build better OPACs. Furthermore, just as Albert predicts to Robin a successful dialogue with "the Foe," so does the voice predict success to catalogers.[59] Whose voice is it? Undoubtedly, it is that of Callimachus, the poet and scholar, as well as cataloger of the Royal Library at Alexandria, whose breadth of experience spans that of the reference librarian, the bibliographic database specialist, and the computer expert. Callimachus adds, smiling, that these others are his children, too.[60]

Notes

1. Frederick Pohl, *The Annals of the Heechee* (New York: Ballantine Books, 1987), 170.

2. Rowland C. W. Brown, "Reference and OCLC," *OCLC Newsletter*, no. 168 (May/June 1987): 3.

3. Bohdan S. Wyner, *Introduction to Cataloging and Classification*, 7th ed. by Arlene Taylor (Littleton, Colo.: Libraries Unlimited, 1985): 603.

4. Robert Grover and Jack Glazier, "Implications for Application of Qualitative Methods to Library and Information Science Research," *Library and Information Science Research* 7, no. 3 (July -September 1985): 249-50.

5. Raya Fidel and Michael Crandall, "The AACR2 as a Design Schema for Bibliographic Databases," *Library Quarterly* 58, no. 2 (April 1988): 123-24, 140.

6. Mary Dykstra, "LC Subject Headings Disguised as a Thesaurus," *Library Journal* 113, no. 4 (March 1, 1988): 46.

7. Pauline Cochrane and Karen Markey, "Preparing for the Use of Classification in Online Cataloging Systems and in Online Catalogs," *Information Technology and Libraries* 4, no. 2 (June 1985): 109.

8. Lois Mai Chan, "Library of Congress Classification as an Online Retrieval Tool: Potentials and Limitations," *Information Technology and Libraries* 5, no. 3 (September 1986): 191.

9. Roxanne Sellberg, "The Teaching of Cataloging in U.S. Library Schools," *Library Resources & Technical Services* 32, no. 1 (January 1988): 30.

10. Robert P. Holley, "Subject Cataloging in the U.S.A.," *International Cataloguing* 14, no. 4 (October/December 1985): 44.

11. Arnold Wajenberg, "MARC Coding of DDC for Subject Retrieval," *Information Technology and Libraries* 2, no. 3 (September 1983): 251.

12. M. S. Fox and A. J. Palay, "The BROWSE System: An Introduction," in *Information Choices and Policies, Proceedings of the ASIS Annual Meeting, 1979, Volume 16*, 42d Annual Meeting, Minneapolis, Minnesota, October 14-18, 1979, ed. Roy D. Tally and Ronald R. Deultgen (White Plains, N.Y.: Knowledge Industry Publications), 185.

13. Charles Hildreth, "Online Public Access Catalogs," in *Annual Review of Information Science and Technology*, vol. 20 (White Plains, N.Y.: Knowledge Industry Publications, 1985), 246.

14. Ibid.

15. An address by Braddock, a Citibank/Citicorp's group executive, referred to by Gabriel D. Ofiesh, "The Seamless Carpet of Knowledge and Learning," in *CD-ROM: The New Papyrus: The Current and Future State of the Art*, ed. Steve Lambert and Suzanne Ropiequet (Redmond, Wash.: Microsoft Press, 1986), 301.

16. Judith A. Adams, "The Computer Catalog: A Democratic or Authoritarian Technology?" *Library Journal* 113, no. 2 (February 1, 1988): 31.

17. Pohl, *Annals*, 336.

18. Manfred Kochen, "Library Science and Information Science: Broad or Narrow?" In *The Study of Information: Interdisciplinary Messages*, eds. Fritz Machlup and Una Mansfield (New York: Wiley, 1983), 375.

19. Georges Bernanos, *Oeuvres Romanesques* (Paris: Bibliothèque de la Pléiade, 1961), 1858.

20. M. C. Yovits et al., "External Documentation and Its Quantitative Relationship to the Internal Information State of a Decision Maker: The Information Profile," *Journal of the American Society for Information Science* 38, no. 6 (November 1987): 407.

21. Jerry M. Rosenberg, *Dictionary of Artificial Intelligence and Robotics* (New York: Wiley, 1986), 99-100.

22. Williams Work, "Communication Education for the Twenty-First Century," *Communications Quarterly* 30, no. 4 (fall 1982): 265.

23. Christine L. Borgman, "The User's Mental Model of an Information Retrieval System: An Experiment on a Prototype Online Catalog," *International Journal of Man-Machine Studies* 24, no. 1 (January 1986): 61.

24. Dykstra, "LC Subject Headings," 46.

25. Ruth Salvaggio, "Interpreting the *MLA Bibliography*," *Scholarly Publishing* 14, no. 4 (July 1983): 363-68

26. William Paulson, *The Noise of Culture: Literary Texts in a World of Information* (Ithaca, N.Y.: Cornell University Press, 1988), 180.

27. A. M. Pejtersen, "Design of a Computer-Aided User-System Dialogue Based on an Analysis of Users' Search Behaviour," *Social Science Information Studies* 4, nos. 2 and 3 (April/July 1984): 178.

28. Samuel T. Waters, "Answerman, the Expert Information Specialist: An Expert System for Retrieval of Information from Library Reference Books," *Information Technology and Libraries* 5, no. 3 (September 1986): 211.

29. James Rice, "Serendipity and Holism: The Beauty of OPACs," *Library Journal* 113, no. 2 (February 15, 1988): 141.

30. Brown, "Reference and OCLC," 3.

31. William E. Jarvis and Victoria E. Dow, "Integrating Subject Pathfinders into a GEAC ILS: A MARC-Formatted Record Approach," Information Technology and Libraries 5, no. 3 (September 1986): 214.

32. Carol Tenopir, "Evaluating Online Systems," *Library Journal* 113, no. 10 (June 1, 1988): 87.

33. Karen E. Smith, "Hypertext–Linking to the Future," *Online* 12, no. 2 (March 1988): 32.

34. Raymond DeBuse, "So That's a Book . . . Advancing Technology and the Library," *Information Technology and Libraries* 7, no. 1 (March 1988): 17.

35. Smith, "Hypertext," 33.

36. Telephone conversation August 17, 1988 with Dr. M. S. Fox, Carnegie-Mellon University, who originated the BROWSE system with Dr. A. J. Palay, Carnegie-Mellon University.

37. Kenneth Dowlin, Presentation at the School of Library and Information Management, Emporia State University, April 16, 1988.

38. Florence E. DeHart and Karen Matthews, "Subject Analytics and Tables of Contents in Essay Collections," *Technical Services Quarterly* 6, no. 3/4 (1989); Florence E. DeHart and Richard Reitsma, "Subject Searching and Tables of Contents in Single-Work Titles," accepted by *Technical Services Quarterly* 7, no. 1 (1989); and Florence E. DeHart and Karen Matthews, "Subject Enhancements and OPACs: Planning Ahead," Presented at Kansas Library Association, College and University Libraries Section, October 7, 1988.

39. DeHart and Reitsma, "Subject Searching."

40. David F. Bishop, "Foreword: Education and Training for Catalogers and Classifiers," *Cataloging & Classification Quarterly* 7, no. 4 (Summer 1987): xii.

41. I. Wormell, "Cognitive Aspects in Natural Language and Free-Text Searching," *Social Science Information Studies* 4, nos. 2 and 3 (April/July 1984): 134.

42. Toni Petersen, "Multiple Authorities in Library Systems," in *Authority Control Symposium,* Papers presented during the 14th Annual ARLIS/NA Conference, New York, N.Y., February 10, 1986, ed. Karen Muller (Tucson, Ariz: The Society, 1987), 25. (Occasional Papers no. 6.)

43. *Physics and Astronomy Classification Scheme, 1988* (New York: American Institute of Physics, 1988).

44. Carol A. Mandel, *Multiple Thesauri in Online Bibliographic Systems: A Report Prepared for Library of Congress Processing Services* (Washington, D.C.: Cataloging Distribution Service, Library of Congress, 1987).

45. James R. Dwyer, "The Road to Access and the Road to Entropy," *Library Journal* 112, no. 14 (September 1, 1987): 134.

46. Sellberg, "The Teaching of Cataloging," 36.

47. Francis Miksa, "The 19th Dewey: A Review Article," *Library Quarterly* 50, no. 4 (October 1980): 489.

48. Yvonna S. Lincoln and Egon G. Guba, *Naturalistic Inquiry* (Beverly Hills, Calif.: Sage Publications, 1985), 37.

49. Ibid.

50. Dagobert Soergel, *Organizing Information: Principle of Data Base and Retrieval Systems* (Orlando, Fla.: Academic Press, 1985), 38.

51. Bateson's work is referred to by Sheila McNamee, "Accepting Research as Social Intervention: Implications of a Systemic Epistemology," *Communication Quarterly* 36, no. 1 (Winter 1988): 50.

52. Lee J. Cronbach, "Beyond the Two Disciplines of Scientific Psychology," *American Psychology* 30, no. 2 (February 1975): 124-25.

53. Viswanath Subramanian, Gautam Biswas, and James C. Bexdek, "Document Retrieval Using a Fuzzy Knowledge-Based System," *Optical Engineering* 25, no. 3 (March 1986): 454.

54. Cynthia A. Kehoe, "Interfaces and Expert Systems for Online Retrieval," *Online Review* 9, no. 6 (December 1985): 501.

55. Marcia J. Bates, "Subject Access in Online Catalogs: A Design Model," *Journal of the American Society for Information Science* 37, no. 6 (November 1986): 358.

56. Tadeusz Radecki, "Incorporation of Relevance Feedback into Boolean Retrieval Systems," in *Research and Development in Information Retrieval: Proceedings,* Berlin, Masy 18-20, 1982, ed. Gerard Salton and Hans-Jochen Schneider (Berlin: Stringer-Verlag, 1983), 135.

57. Ronald E. Rice and Gail Love, "Electronic Emotion: Socioemotional Content in a Computer-Mediated Communication Network," *Communication Research* 14, no. 1 (February 1987): 93.

58. Nigel Ford, "Psychological Determinants of Information Needs: A Small-Scale Study of Higher Education Students," *Journal of Librarianship* 18, no. 1 (January 1986): 59.

59. Pohl, *Annals of Heechee,* 336-37.

60. Pohl, *Annals of Heechee,* 341.

Librarians and Archivists: Coming Together

BRADFORD KOPLOWITZ

Libraries and archives coexist with one another. This was ably illustrated in the 1976 book, *Archive-Library Relations*, in which Robert L. Clark, Jr. wrote, "The past tended to emphasize the differences, but now an established yet changing archival profession and a library profession with many generalists have created an atmosphere of cooperation and concentration on points of commonality."[1] Over a decade later, has the relationship between librarians and archivists changed, and is there a pattern to the change?

Librarians and archivists face common problems in trying to achieve a balance between confidentiality and public access, and between budgetary restraints and collection building. Two problem areas in particular, description and conservation, have led to increased cooperation and resource sharing between the allied professions of librarian and archivist. Although the principle of provenance remains the basis for the classification and arrangement of archives, more and more archives are employing a new mode of description, the archival and manuscripts control format (AMC). Through the application of this standardized, library-type format, archivists are able to link their holdings for the first time in computerized databases. Thus, library method and practice is helping to break down the insularity of archival institutions.

A second problem area, materials conservation, traditionally of primary concern for archivists, has only just commanded such attention from librarians. This is understandable because of the uniqueness and cost of archives and manuscripts vis-à-vis the multiplicity and relative cheapness of publications. In the case of description, archivists have out of necessity adapted to the ways and means of librarians. Conversely, librarians have begun to place the same emphasis on conservation as have archivists.

Librarians and archivists are beginning to think about description and conservation on similar lines. Besides being a necessitated response to exigency, there is a more direct explanation for this concurrence. Formerly, archivists generally came to their discipline from departments of history with either a masters degree or a doctoral degree. However, analysis of recent surveys of the archival profession shows that a majority of present-day archivists have received their formal education in library studies, and that this trend is increasing. Through a commonness born of interdisciplinary approaches and cooperation, librarians and archivists are indeed coming together.

DESCRIPTION

The great experiment in early archival automation was the selective permutation index, or SPINDEX. In 1966, SPINDEX I was initiated in the Library of Congress to provide content information using the technique of key-word-in-context.[2] In the late sixties, SPINDEX II, with its eleven programs and three modules, provided greater flexibility in merging, updating, and modifying data. A decade later, with the addition of electronic photocomposition and dual-level indexing, the application of SPINDEX III resulted in the *Directory of Archives and Manuscript Repositories in the United States*, which represents the first stage in the development of a national archival database.[3]

Ironically, SPINDEX, which was designed to be adaptable for use at each successive hierarchical level of description, had severe limitations as a batch processing system without database searching capability. Thus, SPINDEX produced standardized printed guides at the repository level but lacked the interactive, updatable characteristics of an online system. It is obvious that SPINDEX was largely an attempt by archivists to venture into that "brave new world" of automation on their own. In part, this resulted from the unique requirements for the description and arrangement of archives and manuscripts, as well as from continued frustrations over the Anglo-American Cataloging Rules (AACR). AACR2, which, like its predecessor, lacks a capacity for hierarchical searching, separates description from arrangement by failing to relate catalog information to other finding aids such as inventories.[4]

As the eighties approached, the question remained of how best to achieve a synergy of the computer and archives. In 1977 the Society of American Archivists (SAA) established the National Information Systems Task Force (NISTF), which four years later worked with a task force from the Research Libraries Group (RLG) to develop a new computer communications format and functional requirements for archival support in the Research Libraries Information Network (RLIN). The AMC format, which was approved by the American Library Association (ALA) committee that advises the Library of Congress on machine-readable cataloging formats,[5] was explicitly designed to describe single items as well as collections with application to any type of material organized according to archival principles and methods. Thus, the new format would accommodate the hierarchical needs of archival description. The other prerequisite for any shared access system was the creation of an inputting standard.

The RLG standard for use of the AMC format specifies cataloging rules, form of personal and corporate names and subject headings, and required fixed fields and variable fields.[6] The standard for descriptive cataloging is Steven L. Hensen's *Archives, Personal Papers, and Manuscripts: A Cataloging Manual for Archival Repositories, Historical Societies, and Manuscript Libraries*, with AACR2 to establish the form of personal and corporate names, and the *Library of Congress Subject Headings* or the *National Library of Medicine Subject Headings* for topical subject headings.

A survey conducted in 1986 of entries on RLIN showed a lack of uniformity in topical index terms and authority control, especially on the local level.[7] Specifically, Steven L. Hensen has identified problems with the use of pseudonyms; the use of names without birth and death dates to distinguish among individuals; and the simplified rules for corporate bodies that do not permit hierarchical entries, a necessary component in describing an organization's structure.[8] These findings are disturbing and call attention to a need for a concentrated program to police data entered on RLIN.

In an even more telling critique of the application of the AMC format on RLIN, Richard C. Berner states:

> The bibliographic record is still just an impressionistic scope and content note tied to no particular finding aid. All that the RLIN project has done is to add administrative control data to this note.

> If used only at this accession level of control, RLIN is but an automated NUCMC [National Union Catalog of Manuscript Collections]: an accession announcements system that operates separately from the in-house finding aids system. Few repositories can afford such an elaborate reporting system; economy dictates that any national reporting system be but the summary tip of the local systems. This means that the system should be able to accommodate data shown to the folder or item level.[9]

The first point concerning the bibliographic record ignores field 351, which provides for the delineation of series arrangement, thereby creating a direct linkage to the functional structure of a repository's internal finding aids. For small collections without series divisions, the scope and content note, field 520, is an appropriate place to enter file folder or item-level information. Furthermore, the accusation that RLIN is nothing more than an "automated NUCMC" does not accord with such system attributes as online updatability, accessibility, expandability, and standardization, which is what AMC format is all about. It is no doubt costly to participate in such a system, but if archives are to integrate their collections with other types of materials in library catalogs, improve local and networkwide subject access to holdings, and introduce automation into the archival environment, then they must make the necessary commitment to share information through bibliographic utilities.[10]

In March 1987, the SAA surveyed archival repositories in the United States and Canada concerning their automation activities. Of the 1,400 repositories to receive a survey form, 261 completed the questionnaire. As regards the AMC format, seventy repositories reported current utilization, sixty-four planned implementation within five years, and thirty-seven had no plans for conversion at all.[11] This data evidence a strong trend towards acceptance by archivists of the AMC format. In their use of standardized, bibliographic description, archivists have adopted a library practice that was unthinkable only a few years ago. Katherine Morton observes that "archivists, manuscript curators, and librarians are now talking in tags, sharing information, and generating various bibliographical and administrative products."[12] The mind-set of the solitary archivist who creates in-house finding aids as unique as the materials he preserves is giving way to that of the information specialist who prepares a shared catalog in a standardized language accessible through a direct online network such as RLIN or OCLC to repositories everywhere.

CONSERVATION

It is the very nature of archives, their uniqueness, that causes archivists to consider their conservation. This consideration is apparent in the long-standing concern of archivists in the areas of security, environmental control, preservation treatment, and storage. Such awareness has not always been the case with librarians, since most library materials are less dear in terms of cost and rarity. While the library specialist such as the special collections librarian may have been aware of preservation needs, it is only recently that the library community, in general, has begun to view conservation as a management problem requiring solution. One obvious reason for this growing concern is that the deleterious effects wrought by the paper manufacturing processes begun in the late nineteenth century are only now being felt.

The activities of libraries and librarians in confronting this "quiet crisis" are rather remarkable. In 1976 a planning conference for a national preservation program called for the establishment of a national preservation office in the Library of Congress.[13] Two years later, the Institute on the Development and Administration of Programs for the Preservation of Library Materials at Columbia University developed into both the educational program for conservation administration at Columbia University's School of Library Service and a library journal with preservation as its focus, the *Conservation Administration News*.[14]

Librarians in the West promulgated their own conservation agenda beginning in 1979 with a colloquium held at the University of Oklahoma.[15] The following year, the Western States Materials Conservation Project, which was sponsored by the Western Council of State Libraries and the National Historical Publications and Records Commission, produced the following results: (1) a conservation needs assessment study of libraries and archives, and (2) the Western Conservation Congress, established with the goals of providing an information clearinghouse, conservation services, and a network of laboratories in the West.[16]

When the ALA preservation committee was expanded in 1980 to become the Preservation of Library Materials Section within the Resources and Technical Services Division (RTSD), conservation had achieved a symbolic level of equality with the cataloging and classification, reproduction of library materials, resources, and serials sections.[17] Three years later, the RTSD and the Library of Congress cosponsored a conference that examined model library preservation programs and their funding priorities.[18]

In 1986 the conservation issue attained world stature with the International Conference on Preservation of Library Materials held in Vienna, which brought together more than 120 directors of national libraries.[19] Andrew Broom has noted an increasing cooperation on the conservation issue between the International Council on Archives and the International Federation of Library Associations and Institutions.[20] At its 111th membership meeting held in 1987, the Association of Research Libraries presented the program,"Preservation: A Research Library Priority for the 1990s" which focused on the development of both locally and nationally coordinated efforts in the United States and Canada.[21] William Welsh remarks, "The last decade has brought a dramatic improvement in the level of awareness about the preservation problem, in the variety and quality of the methods and techniques for combatting it and in cooperative mechanisms for pooling resources to do the job."[22] The conservation activities of libraries and librarians since 1976 demonstrate that the long-held axiom of archivists to "think preservation" has in fact become part of the librarian's ethos.

EDUCATION

Why do librarians and archivists exhibit a growing receptivity to the methodology and practices of each other's discipline? One possible explanation comes from analysis of surveys of the archival profession. The educational data gathered for the SAA's first membership directory in 1956 failed to differentiate between the M.A. and M.L.S. degrees.[23] A decade later, Philip P. Mason's salary survey analyzed job classifications by function rather than by educational background.[24]

For the first time, the comprehensive survey of SAA membership in 1970 provided a breakdown by formal education,[25] and similar surveys conducted in 1979 and 1982 also accumulated such statistics.[26] Table 1 shows the composite distribution of the archival profession by formal education and clearly demonstrates that the percentage of archivists with a graduate degree in library science is increasing rapidly.

This trend is also validated by the comprehensive survey in 1980 of college and university archivists, which reported the level of education at 15 percent with a Ph.D., 35 percent with an M.L.S., 29 percent with another advanced degree, and 21 percent with a B.A. or B.S. Surveyors Nicholas Burckel and Frank Cook state, "The greatest number of staff across all categories have the Master of Library Science degree, followed by those having some other advanced degree, most often a Master of Arts degree in history."[27] By contrast, 47.7 percent of the respondents to the 1970 survey listed an undergraduate history major, and 63.8 percent listed a graduate history major. It should be noted that the 1985 census of archival institutions did not collect data on the formal educational background of archivists.

In recent years, educators have engaged in a lively debate concerning the proper schooling and training of archivists. Nancy E. Peace and Nancy Fisher Chudacoff maintain that that education should result in the M.L.S. degree "because archivists and librarians share the same goal of information control and dissemination, [and] are therefore members of the same profession and should receive the same type of professional education."[28] Moreover, Canadian archivist W. I. Smith contends that with similar functions and an increasing emphasis on information rather than on the medium of record, archivists and librarians should receive "a combined professional education . . . in the same professional schools."[29] On the other hand, Richard C. Berner holds that to train archivists in librarianship "is to ignore the past history of failure that has resulted from assigning a central position to cataloging."[30]

No matter which side one takes, the membership surveys show that more and more archivists are coming into their profession after receiving their formal educational training in a library course of study. Thus, the meeting of minds of librarians and archivists as evidenced in their shared concerns and approaches to problems of description and conservation is reflective of a shared formal education.

CONCLUSION

Archive-Library Relations pointed out that common problems and shared concerns were leading to increased communication, cooperation, and resource sharing between librarians and archivists. This trend has continued and even strengthened, with an interdisciplinary approach being applied to problems of description and conservation.

Technology is playing a major role in this dynamic. Margaret Child has speculated on what she terms a "fall[ing] together" of libraries and archives when methodological distinctions between the control of archival documentation and printed matter cease to have meaning, since both may exist on the same medium, such as a videodisk.[31] Library automation networks such as OCLC and RLIN require standardized bibliographic description and an educational background in computer formatting, as well as librarianship. To benefit from these systems, archivists have had to conform.

Preservation problems for libraries, as well as archives, are massive in nature. It is not the treatment of individual volumes but rather of entire holdings that has forced regional and national responses such as the production of mass deacidification technology and digital storage of information on optical disk. These technologies and the problems they are designed to remedy are so large and costly that they, in turn, require cooperative approaches.

In a paper presented at the Conference of the Ohio Academy of Sciences in April 1983, Joel Wurl argued that despite their coexistence and shared concerns over public relations and legal issues, libraries and archives lack mutual awareness and a common methodology.[32] In an article entitled "Integration or Separation," William Joyce took a more balanced approach by contrasting divisive factors such as traditions and conventions in the handling and processing of collections, patterns of training and experience, and research interests, with uniting pressures such as changing patterns of patron research use, technological change, administrative reality, and the growing use of the concept of "intrinsic value" in determining conservation priorities for both published and unpublished materials.[33]

Differences will always exist between the methodologies employed by librarians and archivists. Whereas librarians catalog distinct items, archivists view records as being part of "a collective unity in which documents derive meaning from their context . . . and are arranged by their functional origins, not identified by their cultural purpose."[34] Berner calls the principle of provenance an "inferential information system" that not only reveals the inherent meaning of records but also reaffirms the identity of the archivist.[35]

The separate identities of librarian and archivist are not incompatible with mutual understanding and awareness. This is very important, since generally archivists work side by side with librarians, constituting a single community. It truly is one community! For not only are librarians and archivists addressing common problems and concerns in such areas as description and conservation through interdisciplinary approaches to sharing information and resources, but they are also beginning to think alike.

Table 1

Survey	Ph.D.	M.A. and M.L.S.	M.A. or M.S.	M.L.S	B.A. or B.S.	Other
1970	16.6%		35.5%	12.1%	21.9%	8.5%
1979	19.3%	14.7%	29.2%	17.8%	14.8%	3.8%
1982	16.4%	16.0%	28.9%	20.2%	13.2%	5.0%

Source: Evans and Warner, "American Archivists and Their Society: A Composite View"; Deutrich and DeWhitt, "Survey of the Archival Profession – 1979;" Bearman, "1982 Survey of the Archival Profession."

Notes

1. Robert L. Clark, Jr., ed., *Archive-Library Relations* (New York: R. R. Bowker Co., 1976), xii.

2. Richard C. Berner, *Archival Theory and Practice in the United States: A Historical Analysis* (Seattle: University of Washington Press, 1983), 87.

3. Nancy A. Sahli, "Interpretation and Application of the AMC Format," *American Archivist* 49 (Winter 1986): 11.

4. Berner, *Archival Theory and Practice,* 83.

5. Richard H. Lytle, "An Analysis of the Work of the National Information Systems Task Force," *American Archivist* 47 (Fall 1984): 363.

6. Research Libraries Group, *RLG Standard for Use of the AMC Format* (Stanford, Calif.: Research Libraries Group, 1985), 1-4.

7. Avra Michelson, "Description and Reference in the Age of Automation," *American Archivist* 50 (Spring 1987): 195.

8. *Library of Congress Information Bulletin* 45 (November 10, 1986): 373.

9. Richard C. Berner, "Archival Management and Librarianship: An Exploration of Prospects for Their Integration," *Advances in Librarianship* 14 (1986): 280.

10. Michelson, "Description and Reference," 193.

11. Lisa B. Weber, "Automation Survey Results," *SAA Newsletter* (November 1987): 5.

12. *Library of Congress Information Bulletin* 45 (November 10, 1986): 373.

13. Library of Congress, *Proceedings of the Planning Conference for a National Preservation Program Held at the Library of Congress in Washington, D.C., on December 16 and 17, 1976.* (Washington, D.C., 1981).

14. *Final Narrative Report of the Institute on the Development and Administration of Programs for the Preservation of Library Materials* (Washington, D.C.: National Endowment for the Humanities, 1978).

15. *Oklahoma Librarian,* vol. 30, no. 4 October 1979.

16. Howard P. Lowell and Karen Day, *Western States Materials Conservation Project: Final Report* (Denver, Colo.: Western Council of State Libraries, December 1980).

17. Susan Garretson Swartzburg, ed. *Conservation in the Library* (Westport, Conn.: Greenwood Press, 1983) 6.

18. Jan Merrill-Oldham and Merrily Smith, eds., *The Library Preservation Program; Models, Priorities, Possibilities: Proceedings of a Conference, April 29, 1983, Washington, D.C.* (Chicago: American Library Association, 1985).

19. "International Conference on Preservation of Library Materials, Vienna, 7-10 April 1986," *IFLA Journal* 12 (1986): 240-42..

20. Andrew Broom, "The ICA Committee on Conservation and Restoration," *IFLA Journal* 12 (1986): 316.

21. *ARL Newsletter* 137: 6.

22. William Welsh, "Internal Cooperation in Preservation of Library Materials," *Collection Management* 9 (Summer/Fall 1987): 131.

23. Ernst Posner, "What, Then, Is the American Archivist, This New Man?" *American Archivist* 20 (January 1957): 5.

24. Philip P. Mason, "Economic Status of the Archival Profession," *American Archivist* 30 (January 1967): 108.

25. Frank B. Evans and Robert M. Warner, "American Archivists and Their Society: A Composite View," *American Archivist* 34 (April 1971): 157-72 (Table 7).

26. Mabel Deutrich and Ben DeWhitt, "Survey of the Archival Profession – 1979," *American Archivist* 43 (Fall 1980): 533; David Bearman, "1982 Survey of the Archival Profession," Society of American Archivists' Archives, University of Wisconsin, University Archives, Madison, Wisconsin.

27. Nicholas Burckel and J. Frank Cook, "A Profile of College and University Archives in the United States," *American Archivist* 45 (Fall 1982): 417.

28. Nancy E. Peace and Nancy Fisher Chudacoff, "Archivists and Librarians: A Common Mission, a Common Education," *American Archivist* 42 (October 1979): 458.

29. Ian Ross, "Library-Archive Relations: The Question of Education," *Canadian Library Journal* 37 (February 1980): 43.

30. Richard Berner, "Archival Education and Training in the United States, 1937 to Present," *Journal of Education for Librarianship* 22 (Summer/Fall 1981): 17.

31. Margaret S. Child, "Reflections on Cooperation among Professions," *American Archivist* 46 (Summer 1983): 291.

32. Joel Wurl, "Libraries and Archives: Critical Distinctions, Mutual Concerns, and the Need for Increased Cooperation," *ERIC* LI ED 250 011 (April 1983).

33. William Joyce, "Rare Books, Manuscripts, and Other Special Collections," *College and Research Libraries* 45 (November 1984): 444.

34. Ibid., 443.

35. Berner, "Archival Management and Librarianship," 257.

Contributors

HERBERT K. ACHLEITNER currently holds the rank of associate professor at the School of Library and Information Management at Emporia State University. He has held faculty posts at other institutions, including the University of Southern California and the Universidade de las Americas in Pueblo, Mexico. Besides his master's degree in librarianship from the University of Denver, he has an M.A. (Northern Illinois University) and Ph.D. (University of Colorado) in the field of history. He has published a variety of articles, chapters in books, papers, and reports. One of his research ventures included the editing of a volume entitled *Intellectual Foundations for Information Professionals* (distributed by Columbia University Press, 1987). Information needs analysis and planning, the sociology of information, and the theory of information transfer are his three areas of special competence and interest.

STEVEN E. ALFORD is an associate professor of humanities at Nova University, located in Fort Lauderdale, Florida. He earned his M.A. and Ph.D. in comparative literature from the University of North Carolina at Chapel Hill, and from 1982 to 1985 he was enrolled in graduate courses in computer education at Nova University. He is a member of two scholastic honor societies, Phi Beta Kappa and Phi Kappa Phi. For the period 1980-81, Dr. Alford received a Fulbright student fellowship to study at the Albert Ludwigs Universität in Freiburg, West Germany. His publications include articles in the *Carolina Quarterly* and *Issues in Higher Education*, as well as a book, *Irony and the Logic of the Romantic Imagination* (Peter Lang Publishers, 1984).

MICHAEL S. AMEIGH is an instructor in the Department of Mass Communication at St. Bonaventure University. He received a B.A. in economics and business administration from State University College at

Fredonia, New York, and an M.S. in public communication from Syracuse University. Mr. Ameigh is currently completing a doctoral program in telecommunications at the S. I. Newhouse School of Communication at Syracuse. He has authored a number of conference papers and other scholarly publications, such as eleven articles on artificial earth satellites published in April 1989 by Salem Press in *Magill's Survey of Space Science.* His articles include "Intelsat, the International Communication Consortium," "Radio Astronomy Satellites," "Soviet Early Warning Satellites," "Domestic Communications Satellites," "Eastern Block Satellites," and "Synchronous Meteorological Satellites."

JAMES V. BIUNDO is the director of university relations at Southeast Missouri State University. He has made a number of formal presentations to civic, professional, business, and industry organizations, including the International Association of Business Communicators, the Council for the Advancement and Support of Education, the Society of Educators and Scholars, and the World Future Society. He has written a book on expository writing, *In the Beginning: The Written Process* (McCutchan Publishing Company, 1975), as well as numerous articles on language, communications, and marketing.

VIRGIL L. P. BLAKE, an assistant professor at the Queens College Graduate School of Library and Information Studies, received his doctorate in library science from Rutgers University. He also holds an M.L.S. degree from S.U.N.Y. (Albany), a certificate in education from Fitchburg State College, and an A.B. in history from Clark University. His areas of research and teaching speciality include public librarianship, school library media centers, materials selection, cataloging and classification, and media services. He has authored a number of reviews and articles appearing in journals such as *Library Research, Evaluation Review, Public Libraries, Library Journal, The Bottom Line, Collection Management, Collection Building, Wilson Library Bulletin,* and *Urban Academic Librarian.*

JOHN C. BLEGEN is the executive librarian at the Glenview Public Library in Illinois. Prior to this position, he was the assistant director of the Enoch Pratt Free Library in Baltimore, Maryland. He earned his M.S.L.S. from the Catholic University of America and a doctorate in French literature from Johns Hopkins University. During the years 1968-73, Dr. Blegen was an instructor and later an assistant professor of French at the State University of New York at Binghamton.

SANDRA BRAMAN, an assistant professor at the School of Communication, Information, and Library Studies at Rutgers University, received her Ph.D.

from the University of Minnesota School of Journalism and Mass Communication in 1988. The title of her dissertation was "Information Policy and the United States Supreme Court." Dr. Braman is currently engaged in a multiyear research program aimed at analyzing various information policy-making arenas in terms of operational definitions, value hierarchies, and modes of argument. Among the articles she has published are "Public Expectations Versus Media Codes of Ethics" in *Journalism Quarterly*, and "The 'Facts' of El Salvador According to Objective and New Journalism" in the *Journal of Communication Inquiry*.

BARRY AUSTIN CENTINI is presently associated with the Army Continuing Education System (ACES) located in Washington, D.C. His work includes an analysis of ACES automation needs, a written plan to meet those needs, and developing evaluation methodology. Previously, he held various posts at Nova University and Emory University. Dr. Centini earned a B.S. in sociology from Franklin and Marshall College, an M.S. in geological engineering from the University of North Carolina at Chapel Hill, and an M.S. from Nova University.

RHODA K. CHANNING received her B.A. in English from Brooklyn College, her M.S.L.S. from Columbia University, and her M.B.A from Brooklyn College. She is the assistant university librarian for information resources and collection preservation of the O'Neill Library at Boston College. She is a member of various professional organizations, including the Association of College and Research Libraries, the Library and Information Technology Association, and the American Library Association. Ms. Channing has also served as an on-site visitor for the ALA's Committee on Accreditation. She has authored articles and presented a number of formal papers. Some of her areas of interest include collection development and managing technological change.

JERE W. CLARK is a professor and the chairperson of the Department of Economics and Finance and coordinator of the Center for Interdisciplinary Creativity, at Southern Connecticut State University (SCSU). His Ph.D. is in quantitative economics from the University of Virginia (1953). He is best known as an original general systems modeler and "whole brain futurist."

JUANITA STONE CLARK is a free-lance artist and served for several years as director of research for the SCSU Center for Interdisciplinary Creativity. She completed most of the course work leading toward her M.F.A degree at the University of Georgia (1948). In addition to papers in nine referenced books, Jere and Juanita Clark have jointly published twelve articles in *Business Journal, Business Quarterly, Educational Technology Futurics,*

General Systems Bulletin, International Associations, Journal of Creative Behavior, Southern Economic Journal, and *Technology Tomorrow.*

ANTHONY DEBONS is L. J. Buchan Distinguished Professor of the Department of Computer Information Systems at Robert Morris College and professor emeritus of the School of Library and Information Science at the University of Pittsburgh. He has served as visiting professor emeritus at the School of Librarianship of the University of Puerto Rico and at the Department of Information Engineering of Jilin University of Technology (Changchun, People's Republic of China). His Ph.D. and M.A. degrees in experimental psychology are from Columbia University, and his B.A. in psychology and sociology is from Brooklyn College. Dr. Debons has written extensively in the field of information science. He has authored numerous monographs, book chapters, conference papers, journal articles, research grant reports, and consultant reports and has made formal presentations before professional organizations both in the United States and abroad. His most recently published book is *Information Science: An Integrated View* (G.K. Hall, 1988), which he coauthored with Esther Horne and Scott Cronenweth. His areas of speciality include analysis of information systems, information counseling, information theory and practice, human factors (display, vision), and research methods.

FLORENCE E. DEHART has M.L.S. and Ph.D. degrees in library service from Rutgers University and an M.A. degree in French literature from Seton Hall University. She has worked in the cataloging and reference areas of academic and special libraries and has taught at the University of Wisconsin-Milwaukee and the University of Western Ontario. She is presently a professor in the School of Library and Information Management, Emporia State University, where she teaches courses and publishes in the area of the organization of information.

JEFFERSON NICHOLLS EASTMOND, JR. is an associate professor of the Department of Instructional Technology at Utah State University. He graduated from the University of Utah with a B.A. in economics and a Ph.D. in educational psychology. He also attended Ohio University, where he achieved the M.Ed. in elementary education. Dr. Eastmond has authored numerous articles and reviews that have appeared in a wide range of prominent journals, papers published in conference proceedings, and consultant reports for a variety of agencies and institutions. He is a member of the American Educational Research Association, the Association for Educational Communications and Technology, and the American Evaluation Association. He presently teaches courses in college teaching, research, and evaluation in instructional media.

JOSEPH S. FULDA has authored numerous articles and reviews appearing in law and science journals and newspapers. He was educated at the City College of New York and received his graduate degrees from New York University and Columbia University. He is currently research assistant professor of biomathematical sciences at the Mount Sinai School of Medicine in New York City.

MARY F. HABAN is a professor of library science at James Madison University. She received her Ph.D. from the University of Pittsburgh, her M.S.C.S.E. from the University of Evansville, her M.L.S. from the Carnegie Institute of Technology, and her A.B. from the College of Mount Joseph. Her professional experiences are varied and include staff and administrative positions in public, school, and academic settings, as well as teaching in the areas of library science, computer science, and school library media services (first at Duquesne University and later at James Madison University).

MARTHA LARSEN HALE, dean and associate professor of the School of Library and Information Management at Emporia State University, received a bachelor's degree in history from the University of New Hampshire, an M.L.S. from Syracuse University, and a Ph.D. in public administration from the University of Southern California. She is an active participant in a number of professional organizations, including the American Society for Public Administration, the Association of Library and Information Science Educators, the Public Library Association, and the American Library Association. Her research interests are varied. She has authored a broad spectrum of publications, including formal papers, consultant reports, books, contributed chapters, and articles appearing in journals such as *Public Libraries, Community Analysis,* and *College and Research Libraries.*

JAMES S. HEALEY is the director of the Division of Library and Information Science at San Jose State University. He holds a B.A. in English (Stonehill College), an M.S. in library science (Simmons College), and a doctor of library science degree (Columbia University). Dr. Healey has published numerous items, including book chapters, papers, and a monograph entitled *John E. Fogarty: Political Leadership for Library Development.* His articles have appeared in journals such as *Journal of Technical Services, Public Libraries, Journal of Education for Librarianship, Journal of the American Society of Information Science,* and *College and Research Libraries.* He has also been active in a number of professional organizations, including the American Library Association, the Special Libraries Association, the California Library Association, and the Association of Library and Information Science Educators.

Contributors

ROBERT JACOBSON is a principal consultant with the California State Assembly Utilities and Commerce Committee. The committee, chaired by Assemblywoman Gwen Moore (D-Los Angeles), oversees the PUC's regulation of all utilities, including telecommunications firms, as part of its broader jurisdiction over telecommunications and information policy. In his spare time, Dr. Jacobson studies the "information environment," that intangible space sustained by the media of communication in which ideas and perceptions are formed. His doctoral thesis, *An Open Approach to Information Policymaking* (Ablex, 1989), explored how the common experience of the information environment could be harnessed to enable laypersons to participate in policy decision-making. Before joining the assembly in 1981, Dr. Jacobson was a Fulbright research scholar studying telecommunications policy in Scandinavia. He has a Ph.D. in planning from the University of California at Los Angeles and master's degrees in communication management and television production from the University of Southern California and UCLA, respectively.

PIERRETTE KIM JAMISON is an artist and graduate student completing a Ph.D. in instructional systems technology and curriculum at Indiana University. She received a B.S. in physical education, health, and recreation and an M.S. in instructional systems technology from the same institution. A major research topic of interest is censorship and investigating its impact on educational practices and materials. Ms. Jamison is currently a computer graphic artist and consulting designer at Bibliogem Inc., a software development company.

EARL C. JOSEPH is the president of Anticipatory Sciences Incorporated (ASI) and for the past thirty years has been a consulting futurist. At ASI and previously at the Sperry Corporation, his professional activities incorporated futures consulting, forecasting, assessment, issues scanning, and research efforts in fifty ongoing investigative topical areas, including futures relative to library management, technology, economy, politics, society, and education. Dr. Joseph has participated in a number of studies and panels for the U.S. government's Office of Technology Assessment and other groups on library futures. He is on the teaching staff of five colleges and universities where he teaches about the future. Dr. Joseph is also the president of the Minnesota Futurists (a chapter of the World Future Society) and editor of its publications *Futurics* and *Future Trends*.

MARLYN KEMPER is associate professor of information sciences at Nova University's Center for Computer and Information Science. Her M.A. in anthropology is from the Temple University. She also earned an Sc.D. in information science from Nova University and a master's in library science

520

from the University of South Florida. Her publications include a monograph entitled *Networking: Choosing a LAN Path to Interconnection* and various articles. Dr. Kemper is listed in *Marquis' Who's Who in America, Marquis' Who's Who in the World,* and *Marquis' Who's Who in the South and Southwest.*

HARRY MAYANJA KIBIRIGE received a Ph.D. in library and information science from Pittsburgh University, an M.S.L.S. from the University of Wales (UK), an A.L.A. from Liverpool Polytechnic (UK), and a bachelor's degree from the University of East Africa (Uganda). His current post is assistant professor at the Queen's College Graduate School of Library and Information Studies. Dr. Kibirige has also held positions as senior programmer/analyst at the University of Pittsburgh libraries, dean of the East African School of Library and Information Science, and director of libraries at Uganda Technical College. He has published two monographs, *The Information Dilemma: A Critical Analysis of Information Pricing and the Fees Controversy* (Greenwood Press, 1983) and *Local Area Networks in Information Management* (Greenwood Press, 1989). Professor Kibirige has also authored a number of articles appearing in *Reference Quarterly, International Library Review, UNESCO Bulletin for Libraries,* and *Libri* and has prepared contributions to compilations such as the *ALA Encyclopedia of Library and Information Services* (Robert Wedgeworth, editor) and *World Librarianship* (Richard Krzys and Litten Gaston, editors).

BRADFORD KOPLOWITZ is the assistant curator of Western history collections at the University of Oklahoma. Prior to this position he served as the head of the state archives division of the Oklahoma Department of Libraries. After earning a bachelor's degree in history and a master's degree in American history from the University of Missouri, he received a master's degree in library science from the University of Oklahoma. He has published both articles and papers and belongs to numerous professional organizations, including the Society of American Archivists, the Organization of American Historians, and the Association of College and Research Libraries.

BARBARA H. KWASNIK is an assistant professor in the School of Information Studies at Syracuse University. She was previously an adjunct lecturer and research assistant at Rutgers University, School of Communication, Information, and Library Science, where she did her doctoral work. Before beginning her doctoral studies, she was a practicing librarian at Dutchess County Community College, Poughkeepsie, New York, where she was head of technical services. Her other academic degrees include a bachelor's and an M.L.S. from Queens College (CUNY) and an M.A. in English literature from the State University of New York at

Binghamton. Professor Kwasnik teaches in the areas of organization of information, theory of classification, and information use in everyday life. Her current research interests are developing methodologies for studying information-related behavior. In particular, she is examining personal classification behavior, especially as it is affected by a person's problem situation and purpose. The title of her dissertation is "The Influence of Context on Classificatory Behavior." A second area of interest is in the cognitive processes of browsing and the structure of classificatory systems, particularly the nature of unspecified term relationships.

JANICE HELEN MCCUE, the director of Tristate Data Consultants, Inc., received a doctorate of library science degree from Columbia University, a master's of library science degree from Pratt Institute, and a B.A. degree in English literature from St. John's University. Her areas of expertise are desktop publishing, online searching, computerized indexing, and data research consulting. Dr. McCue has authored a monograph, *Online Searching in Public Libraries: A Comparative Study Performance* (Scarecrow Press, 1988).

HILARY MCLELLAN is an assistant professor of educational technology within the Division of Teacher Education at Kansas State University in Manhattan, Kansas. Dr. McLellan has served as a researcher on several projects involving the design and implementation of technological innovations in education at both the National Center on Effective Secondary Schools, University of Wisconsin-Madison, and Kansas State University. She served as the director of a software development project funded by the National Cancer Institute and as a codirector of several research projects involving educational applications of microcomputer and CD ROM technologies. Currently, she serves as an associate editor of the *School Science and Mathematics Journal.* Dr. McLellan received a B.A. in humanities in 1972 from the University of California-Riverside, an M.S. in environmental science in 1976 from Miami University of Ohio, and a Ph.D. in educational technology in 1987 from the University of Wisconsin-Madison. She has taught graduate courses on instructional design, interactive system design, computers in education, instructional television, and videodisk.

LINDA MAIN has a Ph.D. from the University of Illinois-Urbana-Champaign, an M.A. from the University of Dublin, Trinity College (Ireland), and an M.Lib. from the University of Wales, Aberystwyth (UK). She is currently assistant professor in the Division of Library and Information Science, San Jose State University, teaching microcomputer applications, automated library systems, and database management. She has held positions at the University of Illinois-Urbana-Champaign and the University of Dublin, Trinity College.

KAREN MATTHEWS has an M.L.S. degree from Rutgers University and a sixth-year diploma in library-information studies from Southern Connecticut State University. She has held the position of serials librarian at the Providence (Rhode Island) Public Library and recently has been cataloger and online searcher at the William Allen White Library, Emporia State University. She also publishes in the area of the organization of information.

MARIANO MAURA-SARDO received an M.L.S. from the Graduate School of Librarianship at the University of Puerto Rico and an M.S. in information science from the University of Pittsburgh's School of Library and Information Science, where he is currently a doctoral student. The title of his dissertation is "Convertibility of the OCLC Online Union Catalog Subject Heading to Non-English- Language Subject Heading."

GERALD P. MILLER, a doctoral student in information studies, received an A.M.L.S. from the University of Michigan, where he is currently enrolled, an M.Div. in theology from St. John's Seminary, and a B.A. in history from Sacred Heart Seminary. His dissertation is entitled "The Effect of Managerial Bias on Information Source Selection." He has published articles in journals such as *Library Hi-Tech News* and *Serials Review.* Mr. Miller is a member of the Academy of Management, the Institute of Management Science, the International Interactive Communication Society, and the Association of Library and Information Science Educators.

S. D. NEILL, one of the founding faculty members of the School of Library and Information Science at the University of Western Ontario in 1967, has published widely on many aspects of librarianship and information science. His main teaching areas are reference work, storytelling for children, and the philosophy of the profession. He came to academia after sixteen years as a practicing librarian in school and public libraries. He has also served on a number of library boards. His present research is an extensive critique of the work of Marshall McLuhan. A range of other research interests are also represented in recently published articles such as: "The Dilemma of the Subjective in Information Organization and Retrieval," *Journal of Documentation* (1987); "Can There Be Theory of Reference?" *Reference Librarian* (1987); and "Censorship: A Clash of Values," *Canadian Library Journal* (1988).

DONALD E. PHILLIPS is an associate professor of communication in the Center for Media and Communication Studies, Washburn University,

Topeka, Kansas. His previous teaching positions have been at Northern Kentucky University and Valdosta State College. He is the author of three books in communication: *Student Protests, 1960-1969: An Analysis of the Issues and Speeches,* published in 1980 (now in a second printing) and *Student Protest, 1960-1970: An Analysis of the Issues and Speeches,* (revised edition with a comprehensive bibliography), published in 1985, both by the University Press of America, and *Karl Barth's Philosophy of Communication* (volume two in the series, "Philosophische Texte and Studien"), published in 1981 by Georg Olms Verlag. Professor Phillips is a lifetime member of Delta Tau Kappa, the international social science honor society, and a member of the Philosophy of Communication Interest Group of the International Communication Association, the Speech Communication Association, and other regional, national, and international scholarly organizations.

JOHN FREDERICK REYNOLDS, an assistant professor in the English Department of Old Domimion University, earned his Ph.D. (rhetoric/composition) from the University of Oklahoma and his M.A. (English), his M.A. (speech communication), and his bachelor's degree with a double major in English and speech communication from Midwestern University. He has taught both on the undergraduate and graduate levels. Professor Reynolds has made numerous formal presentations at professional meetings and has published articles appearing in a variety of journals, including *Portfolio, Journal of the Radix Teachers Association,* and *Rhetoric Society Quarterly.* Among his research and teaching interests are rhetoric and composition, word processing literacy, modern rhetorical theory, experimental composition research, British literature to 1700, and modern world literature.

JOHN VINSON RICHARDSON, JR. is an associate professor and associate dean at the Graduate School of Library and Information Science, University of California at Los Angeles. He received his Ph.D. in library science from Indiana University and his M.L.S. from Vanderbilt University, Peabody College. His bachelor's degree, with a sociology major and philosophy minor, is from Ohio State University. Dr. Richardson has a lengthy publication record that includes monographs, book reviews, articles, notes, newsletter and opinion pieces, book chapters, and consultant reports. A few representative monograph titles are: *The Spirit of Inquiry: The Graduate Library School at Chicago, 1921-1951* (American Library Association, 1982), *Government Information: Education and Research 1928-1986* (Greenwood Press, 1987), and *Microcomputer Software for Performing Statistical Analysis: A Handbook Supporting Library Decision-Making,* with Peter Hernon (Ablex, 1988). He has chaired numerous committees in various professional organizations, served on the editorial advisory board of *Index to Current*

Urban Documents, and assisted as a manuscript referee for publications such as *Government Publications Review, Library and Information Science Research,* and *Library Resources and Technical Services.*

LEENA SIITONEN, an assistant professor at the Graduate School of Library and Information Studies, University of Rhode Island, received her doctorate and master's degrees in library science from the University of Pittsburgh. She also earned a B.A. degree in Finnish language and literature from the University of Turku and a diploma in librarianship from the Institute for Social Studies, Tampere, Finland. Professor Siitonen has published on a variety of topics, including microcomputers in the public library context, online searching, and CD ROM technology. She is also very active in the international library community: she travels extensively and makes formal presentations in locales such as the People's Republic of China, Australia, Thailand, and Brazil.

JENNIFER SHADDOCK is a doctoral student in the English Department of Rutgers University. She earned an M.A. from the University of Colorado and a B.A. from Colorado College, both degrees in the field of English literature. Ms. Shaddock has taught a broad spectrum of courses in speciality areas such as the nineteenth-century British novel, prose and poetry, women writers and feminist theory, film, and English composition. She has published articles in *Praxis* and *Mid-Hudson Language Studies.* Her memberships in professional organizations include the Modern Language Association, the Northeastern Modern Language Association, and Victorian Studies Association.

DONALD L. SHIREY received an M.Ed. and a Ph.D. in educational research from the University of Pittsburgh. He is currently the associate chair and associate professor of the Department of Information Science, University of Pittsburgh. His research and teaching interests include the foundations of information science, research methods, statistical analysis of data, and institutional research and planning. He has held memberships in a number of professional organizations, including the Research Institute of Information Science and Engineering, the American Statistical Association, and the American Society for Information Science. Dr. Shirey has written articles published in a variety of journals, and his contributions to books include "Statistical Methods and Analysis," "Factor Analysis," and "Critical Incidence Technique" (for the *Encyclopedia of Library and Information Science*).

KAREN PATRICIA SMITH, an assistant professor at the Queens College Graduate School of Library and Information Studies, received her Ed.D. in curriculum and teaching and her M.A. in the teaching of English from Teachers College, Columbia University. She also holds an M.S. in elementary education and a B.A. in music history from Lehman College of the City University of New York. Prior to her current position, she served as principal and director of integration/human relations in Yonkers, New York. Dr. Smith has published articles in *Children's Literature Association Quarterly, School Library Journal,* and *Top of the News.* Her many teaching and research interests are reflected in her work in a variety of professional organizations, including the American Library Association, the Association of Supervision and Curriculum Development, the Children's Literature Association, the Folklore Society, and the International Reading Association.

SHEILA SMITH-HOBSON, currently writing a dissertation to complete the requirements for the Ed.D. degree, earned her B.A. in English journalism from Mundelein College, her M.A. in mass communications from New York University, and her M.Ed. in communication from Teachers College, Columbia University, where she is also completing her doctorate. Since 1972 she has been a full-time lecturer at Lehman College of the City University of New York in the Department of Academic Skills/SEEK program. Her areas of specialty include television writing and production, as well as multicultural, intercultural, and nonverbal communication. Ms. Smith-Hobson has been an active author for over twenty years, with contributions to magazines, newspapers, and books. She has also served as editor for the African American Educator Series produced by ECA Associates. Her memberships in professional organizations include the International Visual Literacy Association, the International Communications Association, the African Literature Association, and the International Organizations for Journalists.

JULIE TALLMAN, a doctoral student at the School of Library and Information Science, University of Pittsburgh, has specialized in the youth services, behavior, and books and printing concentration areas. Her proposed dissertation topic deals with the academic experiences of international doctoral students in United States library and information schools. Ms. Tallman's previous work experience includes twelve years in school media centers and university libraries. She has also published in the school, history, and archive areas. Ms. Tallman has a master's degree in history from the State University College of Arts and Science at Plattsburgh, New York, a master's in library science from McGill University, Montreal, and a sixth-year certificate of advanced studies in Educational Media from the University of Maine at Orono, Maine.

RAYMOND G. TAYLOR, JR. is a professor and the department head of educational leadership and program evaluation at North Carolina State University. He has an Ed.D. in statistics counseling from the University of Pennsylvania, a B.D. in theology and history from the Episcopal Theological

School, and a B.S. in mathematics from Bucknell University. His postdoctoral education also includes an M.P.A. from Pennsylvania State University and an M.B.A. from the University of Southern Maine. Dr. Taylor's list of publications numbers well over one hundred items and includes monographs, chapters in books, articles published in professional journals, and papers appearing in conference proceedings. Dr. Taylor has also made numerous presentations before international, national, regional, and state bodies, such as the American Educational Research Association, the American Psychological Association, the National School Boards Association, the American Association of School Administrators, and the International Conference on Technology and Education held in Edinburgh, Scotland. He has also served as a consultant on special projects for the U.S. Office of Education, the Pennsylvania Department of Education, the Maine State Department of Educational and Cultural Services, the North Carolina State Department of Public Instruction, and other state and organizational entities.

ANNE F. THOMPSON is the director of the Graduate School of Librarianship at the University of Puerto Rico. She holds a doctorate in library science from Florida State University. The research topic for her dissertation is a music bibliography of Puerto Rico in the nineteenth and twentieth centuries.

RENEE TJOUMAS, after finishing her master's degree in English at the University of Georgia, received a master's degree in library science from the University of Michigan and her Ph.D. in library science from the University of Pittsburgh. With a Fulbright grant, she studied in Brazil, writing her doctoral dissertation on university libraries within the information structure of a developing region. After earning her doctorate, she taught at the Library School at the Catholic University of America and is now an assistant professor at Queen's College in New York. She has published articles in periodicals such as *Public Libraries* and *Collection Management* and has authored chapters of several books. She has been active in planning reference workshops and is currently exploring a number of public service and outreach programs associated with combating illiteracy.

FAITH VAN TOLL, the director of Wayne State University's Shiffman Medical Library, received her B.A. in history from St. Mary's College (South Bend, Indiana) and her M.S.L.S. from Wayne State University. She is an active member of a number of professional organizations, including the Medical Library Association, the Association of Academic Health Sciences Library Directors, and the Michigan Health Sciences Library Association. Ms. Toll has also served as a consultant for the National Library of Medicine.

BILL H. WASHBURN, the director of the Office of Information Technology and an associate professor of computer information systems at Colorado State University, received his Ph.D. in education and his M.S. in philosophy from Stanford University. The title of his dissertation is "Standards of Excellence: An Investigation of Criteria Used to Judge Academic Excellence in a Research University." Among his many areas of expertise are LAN consulting, mainframe and minicomputer services, and facilities management, as well as microcomputer and hardware/software consulting. Dr. Washburn works extensively on behalf of the university with the Colorado Commission on Higher Education, the state-sponsored Colorado Advanced Technology Institute, and the Colorado Telecommunications Association.

CHAR WHITAKER has an M.L.S and an M.A. from San Jose State University. She is currently a librarian at San Jose Public Library, working in children's services, media, and reference. She is an adjunct faculty member in the Division of Library and Information Science, San Jose State University (teaching microcomputer applications) and at Foothill Community College (teaching audiovisual equipment). She was formerly head of the English Department at the Yucca Valley High School, Yucca, California.